AF819581

UPSC Mains

250+ Q&A for

INDIAN ECONOMY

General Studies III

AMIT MANGTANI

arihant
SUCCESS AND NOTHING LESS

arihant
SUCCESS AND NOTHING LESS

ARIHANT PUBLICATIONS (INDIA) LIMITED

Administrative & Production Offices

Regd. Office
'Ramchhaya' 4577/15, Agarwal Road, Darya Ganj, New Delhi -110002
Tele: 011- 47630600, 43518550

Head Office
Kalindi, TP Nagar, Meerut (UP) - 250002
Tel: 0121-7156203, 7156204

Sales & Support Offices
Agra, Ahmedabad, Bengaluru, Bareilly, Chennai, Delhi, Guwahati, Hyderabad, Jaipur, Jhansi, Kolkata, Lucknow, Nagpur & Pune.

PRICE ₹375.00

PO No : TXT-XX-XXXXXXX-X-XX

Published by Arihant Publications (India) Ltd.

For further information about the books published by Arihant, log on to www.arihantbooks.com or e-mail at info@arihantbooks.com

Follow us on

PREFACE

It gives an immense pleasure in presenting to you the book **'250+ Q&A of Indian Economy'** which is the first of its kind in the field of Civil Service Preparation. Indian Economy for Mains is one crucial subject and has more than 50% weightage in General Studies Paper-III along with some overlapping in GS Mains Paper-I and GS Paper-II.

Inspite of its importance, there is hardly any organised content of Indian Economy and even lack of content on some topics for the Mains preparation. Not only that, this one subject requires good enrichment for the students to score high marks. Moreover, students often face problems in writing Most Effective Answer for the questions of **GS Paper-III** which translates into low score.

The aim of this book is to provide students a **One Stop Solution** for the preparation of Indian Economy in the most-unique manner of Mains Questions and Answers format.

Salient Features of the Book

1. Each unit is directly mapped with the syllabus of Indian Economy which makes it easy for the students to understand the topics and reading only **relevant information to the exam** syllabus.
2. **Comprehensive analysis** of each unit through the topic-wise coverage of syllabus by referring to vast array of documents such as previous 5 years Economic Survey, last 3 year's budget documents, NITI Aayog various reports on important issues, RBI reports, etc.
3. Questions under each unit are made on both the static and current topics and are highly analytical keeping in mind the latest trends of **UPSC exam**.
4. **Incorporation of PYQs** chapter-wise so that students get an idea about the repeated themes being asked in the economy questions and can gauge the pattern of questions being asked in the exam.
5. **Detailed Answers** are provided based on Toppers answer writing style format. Most importantly, all possible information about the related topic is given and not just restricted to limited information given in various different sources.
6. Answers are provided with the latest data, facts, government schemes and other best practices which can be used by the students to get a higher edge of marks over others.
7. **Practice questions** along with each unit, so that students can practice additional questions on various topics.

Overall, this book is not just a compilation of **Mains Questions** and **Answers** but the unique features make the book transcend the boundary from Mains Q&A to a full-fledged book of Indian Economy for Mains.

Students can connect with me on my Telegram channel t.me/freeiasprep where I post all relevant information (MCQs, Mains Q&A, Current events and Handwritten Notes) of Indian Economy. In case of any feedback, you can send a mail to amitmangtani.faculty@gmail.com.

Amit Mangtani
Founder, MentorsHut
Economics Faculty, Sunya IAS

CONTENTS

SYLLABUS

General Studies-III: Economic Development

- Indian Economy and issues relating to planning, mobilization, of resources, growth, development and employment.
- Inclusive growth and issues arising from it.
- Government Budgeting.
- Major crops-cropping patterns in various parts of the country, - different types of irrigation and irrigation systems storage, transport and marketing of agricultural produce and issues and related constraints; e-technology in the aid of farmers.
- Issues related to direct and indirect farm subsidies and minimum support prices; Public Distribution System- objectives, functioning, limitations, revamping; issues of buffer stocks and food security; Technology missions; economics of animal-rearing.
- Food processing and related industries in India- scope' and significance, location, upstream and downstream requirements, supply chain management.
- Land reforms in India.
- Effects of liberalization on the economy, changes in industrial policy and their effects on industrial growth.
- Infrastructure: Energy, Ports, Roads, Airports, Railways etc.
- Investment models.

UNIT 1

Indian Economy and Issues Relating to Planning, Mobilisation of Resources, Growth, Development and Employment

Concepts of GDP (Limitation of GDP)

Q.1 'The use of Gross Domestic Product as a measure of public well-being results from the idea that economic growth is always synonymous with enhanced quality of life.' In this context, discuss the limitations of GDP as a measure of welfare. What are the possible alternate approaches to measure welfare? (250 Words, 15 Marks)

Ans. **Introduction** Gross Domestic Production (GDP) is the final value of goods and services which is produced within the geographical boundaries of a country during a specified period of time. GDP estimates are released quarterly and annually by the National Statistical Office.

Higher GDP growth rates are generally associated (although not necessarily) with increased **employment opportunities,** improved living standards and higher per capita income, thus it is synonymous with enhanced quality of life. But this presumption of economic growth always synonymous with enhanced quality of life is not correct.

Importance of GDP as an indicator

- **Per Capita as Proxy** GDP growth rates reflect growth of per capita income which is used by economists to gauge quality of life in a country.
- **Indicator of the Health of an Economy** GDP is important because it gives information about the size of the economy and how an economy is performing. In broad terms, an increase in real GDP is interpreted as a sign that the economy is doing well.
- **Linked with Employment generation** When real GDP is growing strongly, employment is likely to be increasing as companies hire more workers for their factories and thus, people will have more money in their pockets.
- **Comparison of Economic Performance of various countries across the World** GDP at Purchasing Power Parity (PPP) terms is used to compare economic well-being of two countries. Usually, GDP of developing countries in PPP terms tends to be much higher than in real terms.

Limitations of GDP as a measure of welfare

It is vital to understand that GDP is not intrinsically harmful or incorrect, but it **measures only partial economic activities.** Using it as an indicator of overall well-being is ambiguous and dangerous. A list of the major problems of GDP as a proxy to sustainable societal development includes:

- **Does not capture inequalities in the country** GDP only focuses on the per capita income (i.e., GDP divided by total population) but does not focus on the distribution of income to different sections of society. Thus, GDP does not capture any type of inequality in the society – Income inequality, Gender inequality or Caste inequality.
  - **Alternate Approach** Gender Inequality Index, Inclusive Development Index, etc.
- **Environmental costs** The production of goods and services can have negative environmental impacts, such as pollution and climate change. However, these costs are not included in GDP. This means that GDP can overstate the true welfare of a country.
  - **For example,** GDP takes a positive count of the cars we produce but does not account for the emissions they generate; it includes the value of building new cities but does not discount for the vital forests they replace.
  - **Alternate Approach** Green GDP
- **Leisure time**: People value leisure time, but it is not included in GDP. This is because leisure time is not spent producing goods or services. However, leisure time can contribute to people's well-being.
  - **Alternate Approach** 'Net Economic Welfare (NEW)' popularized by Paul Samuelson.
- **Does not capture non-monetary transactions** Many important activities, such as raising children, volunteering, and caring for the elderly, are not included in GDP. This is because these activities are not sold in markets. However, these activities can contribute to people's well-being.
- **Ignores informal economy** GDP calculations often struggle to accurately measure economic activity in the informal sector, which can be significant in many developing countries. This exclusion may lead to an underestimation of the true economic output and employment generated by these informal activities.
- **Human development** GDP doesn't measure the factors which leads to human development like education, health etc. which severely impacts quality of life being lived by people.
  - **Alternate Approach** Human Development Index (HDI)
- It counts every expenditure as positive and does not discriminate welfare-enhancing activity from welfare-reducing activity.

The list makes clear that GDP not only falls short in evaluating critical aspects of quality of life, but it also triggers and fosters activities that are contrary to long-term societal well-being.

Possible Alternative Approaches to Measure Welfare

- **Human Development Index** It was created by economist Mahbub ulHaq (Pakistan), followed by economist Amartya Sen in 1990 and is published by the United Nations Development Programme. It is a composite index that measures average achievement in human development taking into account three critical dimensions: Health, Education and Standard of Living. Thus, it captures welfare from a broader perspective.
- **Green GDP** It is an indicator of economic growth with environmental factors taken into consideration along with the standard GDP of a country. It factors biodiversity losses and costs attributed to climate change.

  Recently, the **United Nations Statistical Commission** adopted the SEEA Ecosystem Accounting (SEEA EA) i.e., Green GDP.
- **Gross National Happiness Index** The Gross National Happiness Index takes a holistic and psychology-based approach to measuring **social welfare**. It was developed in Bhutan and builds on four pillars: Governance, Socio-economic development, Cultural preservation and Environmental conservation.
- **Social Progress Index** The Social Progress Index provides an extensive framework that is based on three key dimensions Basic human needs, Foundations of well-being and Opportunity.

Conclusion

Although there is value in using GDP as one economic indicator, it is clear that it does not provide a full and reliable appraisal of a country's economic health for the present or the future and certainly does not address quality of life, happiness, wellness and other crucial societal parameters. It should be complemented with other indices of welfare too.

New GDP Series

Q.2 Explain the difference between computing methodology of India's Gross Domestic Product (GDP) before the year 2015 and after the year 2015.(150 Words, 10 Marks) **UPSC Mains PYQ 2021**

Ans. **Introduction** Gross Domestic Product (GDP) is the final value of goods and services which is produced within the geographical boundaries of a country during a specified period of time. GDP estimates are released quarterly and annually by the National Statistical Office.

In 2015, a new series was launched to compute GDP by modernising the methodology and including new data sources in accordance with UN standards titled as 'System of National Accounts, 2008'.

Rationale (Importance) Behind Adopting New GDP Series

- **Capture Structural Changes in an Economy** Change of base year is a common occurrence and is done to take into consideration the changing times, the outlook of the economy and keeping in mind the composition of the economy.
  - This ensure that macroeconomic indicators remain relevant and reflect the structural changes more realistically.
- **Improving Credibility of Data** Complete review of the existing database and methodology employed in the estimation of various macroeconomic aggregates.
  - There has been an improved coverage of the financial corporations, local bodies and autonomous institutions which will have an impact on the estimates of Gross Value Added (GVA).
- To implement the recommendations of the **UN System of National Accounts (SNA), 2008** regarding international guidelines on the compilation of national account for the **purpose of global standardisation and comparability.**

Difference in Computing Methodology

The 2011-12 series of National Accounts Statistics incorporates changes in data sources, expansion in the coverage of activities and improvements in procedures that are aligned to the latest recommendations of UN System of National Accounts 2008.

Criteria	Pre-2015 GDP Calculation	Post-2015 GDP Calculation
Base Year	2004-05	2011-12
Official GDP	GDP at factor cost at constant prices	GDP at constant market prices
Sector-wise Estimates	Earlier GDP at factor cost and thus concerned with only cost of production.	Valuing industry-wise estimates as Gross Value Added (GVA) at basic prices.
Agriculture Data	Confined to value addition in farm produce.	Goes beyond farm produce and includes the livestock data.
Estimation of Manufacturing Activity	IIP and Annual Survey of Industries (ASI) data was used which comprises over two lakhs factories.	Firms annual accounts with Ministry of Corporate Affairs (MCA-21) was used which covers five lakhs companies.
Financial Sector	Limited to few mutual funds and NBFCs as compiled by RBI.	Expanded the coverage by including stock brokers, stock exchanges, asset management companies, mutual funds and pension funds, as well as the regulatory bodies, SEBI, PFRDA and IRDA.
Calculation of Labour Income	It provided equal weightage to all the labour income.	It uses a concept called effective labour input where all labour is not treated equal.
Local Coverage	Limited coverage	Improved coverage of economic activities of local bodies.

Conclusion

The new method is statistically more robust since it estimates more indicators such as consumption, employment and the performance of enterprises and incorporates factors that are more responsive to current changes

Potential Output

Q.3 Define potential GDP and its determinants. What are the factors that have been inhibiting India from realising its potential GDP? (150 Words, 10 Marks) **UPSC Mains PYQ 2020**

Ans. Potential GDP Potential GDP is the highest market value of goods and services that can be produced in an economy over a period of time with efficient utilisation of the available resources and without getting any inflationary pressures. Unlike normal GDP that estimates during current duration, potential GDP seeks to find the highest value that can be obtained.

Determinants of Potential GDP

Economic Factors

- **Labour Force** A larger and more skilled labour force can increase the productive capacity of an economy while a declining labour force can limit the economy's potential for growth.
- **Capital Formation** Creation of more capital goods like heavy machineries, factories, infrastructure, production of more electricity, etc, results into better realisation of potential GDP.
- **Natural Resources** The availability of natural resources, such as land and minerals, can also contribute to the productive capacity of an economy.
- **Investments and Savings** The major source of funding investment is domestic savings. The gross domestic savings rate has fallen from around 34% of GDP in 2011-12 to 31.4% in March 2020-21.
- **Human Resources** India has 62.5% of its population in the age group of 15-59 years which is ever increasing and will be at the peak around 2036 when it will reach approximately 65%. This can lead to higher economic growth provided there is investment in health, education, skill development and other essential services.
- **Efficient Utilisation of Resources** The higher the ICOR, the less efficient we are in the use of capital. As we look at the Indian performance in the last five years, there is a decline in the investment rate and a rise in ICOR; both of which can only lead to a lower realisation of potential GDP.
- **Technological Progress** Technological advancements can increase the potential for growth and productivity by improving the efficiency of production processes, increasing the quality of goods and services and reducing the cost of production.
- **Government Policies** Government policies, such as tax and regulatory policies, can also impact the economy's potential for growth. Policies that support investment and innovation can increase the potential for growth, while policies that stifle investment and innovation can limit the potential for growth.

Non-Economic Factors

- **Social Institutions** Caste system as a system of inequality that burdens the Indian economy with inefficiencies in the allocation of labour and other critical resources, reducing the full development of human capital in society.
  - At the same time, certain institutions can lead to social capital which results in much higher output of the country.
- **Political Stability** Economic growth and political stability are deeply interconnected. The uncertainty associated with an unstable political environment may reduce investment and the pace of economic development. Examples: Pakistan, Sri Lanka in the recent times.
- **Governance** Adoption of good governance principles will reduce regulatory cholesterol, red-tapism, corruption and move towards a citizen-friendly administration which can attract higher investment in the country.
  - Corruption has a direct impact on the economy by reducing investment, slowing down economic activity, and distorting market competition.

Factors Inhibiting Potential GDP

- **Infrastructural Bottlenecks** Logistics cost in India is USD 293 billion amounting to 14% of GDP while it is 8.14% of GDP in USA, according to Economic Survey 2020-21.
- **Slow Implementation of Labour Reforms** Rigidity in labour laws continued to affect foreign as well as domestic investments in India. e.g., The new labour codes do not provide flexibility to fix work hours beyond eight hours a day.
- **Excessive Public Sector Role** The government remains an active participant in several entities including banks, airlines and infrastructure firms. It controls 70% of the banking industry.
- **High NPAs of Banks** It constrained the availability of loans/investments in the economy.
- **Skilling and Reaping Demographic Dividend** Insufficient training capacity, low industry interface and lack of entrepreneurial skills. According to India Skills Report 2021, due to lack of professional skill sets, only 45.9% of graduates are found employable, a decline from 46.21% in 2020.
- **Income Stagnation** According to the Centre for Monitoring of Indian Economy (CMIE), the monthly jobless rate rose to 23.52% in April, 2021. Also, the rural income has recorded zero or negative growth due to agricultural crisis. This has impacted the demand aspects in India.
- **Slow Pace of Infrastructure Development** India is still at the position where China was 20 years ago in terms of infrastructure development. The plans are ambitious, but the problem is in resources i.e. infrastructure funding.
- **Funding Issues** NITI Aayog has estimated that USD 4.5 trillion will be needed by 2030 to fund infrastructure. Banks do not have enough long-term liabilities to match such loans.
- **Lack of investments** An investment of ₹ 100 lakh crore will require supply of investment from all possible sources which is difficult especially due to COVID-19 slowdown.
- **Protectionism, Trade Wars, COVID-19** Affected the international trade which may negatively hamper our export led growth model and results into less realisation of potential GDP
- **Poor Education and Health Outcomes** India have relatively low levels of education and health outcomes compared to other countries at similar levels of development, which can limit the productive capacity of the labour force.
- **Regulatory Environment** India's complex and bureaucratic regulatory environment has been a major constraint to the country's economic growth. This includes regulations that limit foreign investment, slow the process of starting a business and restrict the flow of goods and services across borders.

Steps to be Taken to Realise Potential GDP

- **Mobilise Domestic Saving and Raise Fixed Investment Rates** Assuming other factors remain same to achieve a goal of 85 trillion economy, we need 39% domestic saving rate and 41.2% of investment rate.
- **Job Creation** Unshackling MSMEs could help to achieve greater profits, job creation and enhanced profits.
- **Support from Financial Sector in the Form of More Credit** This would require higher capitals available with the banks.
- **Increasing the Export Competitiveness** PLI schemes in sectors of pharma, electronics and other sectors are steps in right direction.
- **Skill Development** Mapping skill requirements for a demand driven skill development ecosystem through intensive surveys. Allocating more resources at the disposal to district skill committees.
- **Effective Resource Utilisation** Monetization unlocks the resources of the under-utilised assets and bring cash flow into the economy, thereby stimulates growth in the economy.
- **Capital Formation** Access to credit for critical sectors and promotion of activities of NBFCs, MSMEs etc.
- **Addressing Sector Specific Stress**
  - Agriculture – Investments in food processing and value addition, farm equipments etc.
  - Manufacturing – Increased focus on labour intensive industries and thereby promoting inclusive growth.
  - Banks- Helps in reducing NPAs of the banks by recapitalisation.

Conclusion

Comparing potential GDP to real GDP-that is, potential output to actual output can give insight into how the economy is performing in comparison to its potential. An economy that is underutilising its resources is said to be operating below its potential and government must undertake various reform measures to achieve the potential output.

Private Investment and USD 5 Trillion Economy

Q.4 Among several factors for India's growth, private investment is the key driver to become a USD 5 trillion economy. Do you agree with this view? Justify your opinion. Also, highlight the steps taken by the government to address the fall in private investments. (250 Words, 15 Marks)

Ans. Introduction India is currently ranked as the world's **fifth largest economy in terms of nominal GDP with GDP of USD 3.5 trillion and world's third largest when the GDP is compared on the basis of Purchasing Power Parity (PPP).**

Chief Economic Advisor while presenting to Economic Survey 2022-23 observed that India has the potential to grow at 6.5 to 7% and will become 5 trillion economy by 2025-26 and 7 trillion by 2030.

Importance of Private Investment

As per the Economic Survey 2022-23, more than 50% of the aggregate demand is met by consumption and investment contributes around 30% to the GDP. It is recommended that a sustained high growth can be achieved by 'virtuous cycle' of investments, savings, exports supported by a favourable demographicphase. In this Investment, especially private investment, is the 'key driver' to sustain this high growth.

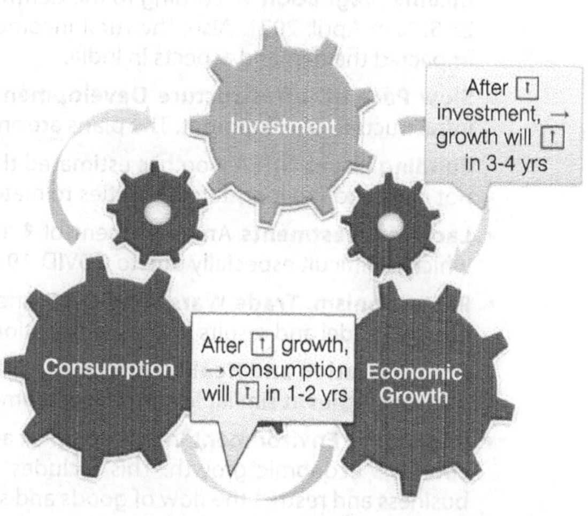

- **Key Driver** Investment, especially private investment, is the 'key driver' that drives demand, creates capacity, increases labour productivity, introduces new technology, allows creative destruction and generates jobs.
- **Infrastructure** Private investment into building a robust physical and social infrastructure is key to putting India in a highgrowth trajectory. Private sector participation in the infrastructure space is crucial as funding cannot depend on public investment alone.
  - **For Example** National Infrastructure Pipeline which aims to invest ₹ 111 lakh crore in various socio-economic economic infrastructure projects, involves the mobilisation of private sector resources.
- **Reduces Logistics Cost** Government aims to reduce logistics cost from 14% of GDP to 8-9% of GDP under the recently launched National Logistics Policy, 2022. This in turn requires huge investment in infrastructure and private investment can play a significant role.
- **Boost Exports which increases your Aggregate Demand** Capital investment enhances total factor productivity, which in turn enhances export performance. Therefore, investment becomes crucial to enhancing export performance.
- **Job Creation** When examined across the entire value chain, capital investment fosters job creation as the production of capital goods, research and development and supply chains generate jobs.
- **International Experience** In the long run, countries with higher private investment experience higher rates of growth. The Chinese experience illustrates how a country with the highest investment rates also created the most jobs.

Reasons for Low Private Investment

Despite its significance, **India's Gross Capital Formation (investment rate) has fallen about 10.4 percentage points from a high of 40 per cent of GDP in 2010-11 to about 29.6 per cent in 2021-22.** This is due to abrupt stalling of infrastructure projects, increased global uncertainties, continued stress in India's domestic financial system, uncertain tax regime, arbitrary laws etc.

- **There are multiple reasons for the decline in investments** Supply chain problems, land acquisition problems, lack of environmental and other clearances, lack of promoter interests, tough labour laws and other regulatory burdens among others.
- The biggest reason remains **lack of funds**, as a Centre for Monitoring of Indian Economy reports. The main source of funds, bank credit, has not been very reliable in the recent few years. Credit offtake by key sectors in the economy has been declining.

- In short, banks are unwilling to lend, and the monetary policy transmission mechanism is not working in India. The main reason for declining credit growth is the twin balance sheet problem – the situation where both banks and private firms have stressed balance sheets.
- Nearly 17 per cent of the entire bank loans in India are stressed, a significant share of which may not be repaid, which explains the reluctance of banks to lend. Nearly 40 per cent of debt is owned by overleveraged corporates who are unable to make interest payments.

- **Slowdown of private investment in infrastructure projects** For instance, private "under implementation" infrastructure projects (expressed in 2021 rupees) peaked in 2011/12 at about ₹ 36 trillion and now stand at ₹ 10 trillion.
- Another problem with **large government borrowing** is that it does not leave any room for private borrowing and investment.
  - Of the three sectors of the economy – government, business, and households – it is only the last that has a positive savings rate. The household sector financial savings is about 7 per cent of GDP, the combined fiscal deficit of the states and union government is well above that figure. PSU borrowings require about 1.5 per cent of GDP in addition to government's borrowings. This leaves no room for private sector borrowing, which explains the lack of funds and low investment rates.

Steps taken by the Government to raise Private Investment

The **government has taken the following steps in recent times** to boost private investment:

- **Launch of flagship schemes** such as Aatmanirbhar Bharat, Production Linked Incentive (PLI) Scheme, etc are expected to attract Foreign Direct Investment (FDI) in India.
- **Improvement in Ease of Doing Business** to attract private investment. In this context, steps have been taken to ease trading across borders by enabling post-clearance audits, integrate trade stakeholders in a single electronic platform, upgrade port infrastructures, and enhance electronic submission of documents etc.
- **National Investment and Infrastructure Fund** has been created with a capital of approximately Rs.400 billion to provide investment opportunities to commercially viable projects. This will be a solution in the short-term with regard to sluggishness of private investments.
- **Reduction in tax rates:** The government has **cut down the corporate tax rate** to 22% from 30%. It also **lowered the tax rate for new manufacturing companies** to 15% to attract new foreign direct investments.
- **Labour Reforms** To improve ease of compliance and ensure uniformity in labour laws, the government has consolidated 29 **central labour laws** into four codes namely-Wages; Industrial Relations; Social Security; and Occupational Safety, Health and Working Conditions.
- PPP is being encouraged through the **New Education Policy 2020 as well as National Health Policy.** Several investment models such as HAM, BOT, EBC, etc. have been brought in the infrastructure sector.
- **Increased liberalisation of FDI regime** in diverse sectors such as defence, pharmaceuticals, retail, aviation etc. has been done. Effort to divest government holdings in state-owned corporations is another encouraging sign.

Conclusion

Continuing the creation of an ecosystem for private investment, especially in the new economy, is therefore critical to enable the virtuous cycle of investment, demand, exports, growth and jobs. Speedy labour and land reforms, a predictable and stable taxation regime, facility for renegotiating PPP projects, speedier implementation of **National Infrastructure Pipeline** should be undertaken to build confidence among investors so as to attract private investments.

Nature of Indian Economy (Recovery of Indian Economy)

Q.5 Has Indian economy recovered from the pandemic-induced contraction? Justify your opinion. Discuss the future outlook of Indian economy by highlighting various growth drivers and downside risks.
(250 Words, 15 Marks)

Ans. **Introduction** India's economy has been significantly impacted by the COVID-19 pandemic, resulting in a contraction in GDP in 2020. According to the Ministry of Statistics and Programme Implementation (MoSPI), India's Gross Domestic Product (GDP) contracted by 6.6% in the financial year 2020-21 (April 2020 to March 2021) due to the impact of the COVID-19 pandemic.

However, the Indian economy has seen a broad-based recovery which can be seen in growth rate in FY 2021-22 AND FY 2022-23. This has been possible because of fiscal and monetary stimulus measures undertaken by the Government and RBI respectively.

India's Economic recovery from the pandemic-induced contraction

- **GDP growth** The growth in real GDP during 2022-23 is estimated at 7.0 per cent and 9.1 per cent in 2021-22 which shows that Indian economy has recovered from the shock of pandemic.
- **Rebound of private consumption** The rebound in consumption was engineered by the near-universal vaccination coverage (more than 2 billion doses, world's 2nd largest vaccination drive) overseen by the government that brought people back to the streets to spend on contact-based services, such as restaurants, hotels, shopping malls, and cinemas, among others.
- **Release of 'Pent-up demand'** was reflected in the housing market too as demand for housing loans picked up. Consequently, housing inventories have declined, prices are firming up, and construction of new dwellings is picking up pace and this has stimulated innumerable backward and forward linkages that the construction sector is known to carry.
- **Rise in Exports** Merchandise exports have registered highest ever annual exports of USD 447.46 billion with 6.03% growth during FY 2022-23 surpassing the previous year (FY 2021-22) record exports of USD 422.00 billion.
- **Service Sector** The service sector, which is a significant contributor to India's GDP, has also shown signs of recovery. According to Economic Survey 2022-23, the service sector in India grew at 8.4% in FY22 compared to a contraction of 7.8% in the previous financial year.
- **Agriculture sector** The agriculture sector, which was relatively less impacted by the pandemic, has continued to grow. According to the Ministry of Agriculture and Farmers' Welfare, the sector grew at a rate of 3.6% in 2020-21.
- **Unemployment rate** The unemployment rate in India, which increased significantly during the pandemic, has been gradually declining. According to the Centre for Monitoring Indian Economy, the unemployment rate was 6.5% in April 2021, down from a peak of 23.5% in April 2020.
- RBI's most recent survey of consumer confidence released in December 2022 pointed to improving sentiment with respect to current and prospective employment and income conditions.

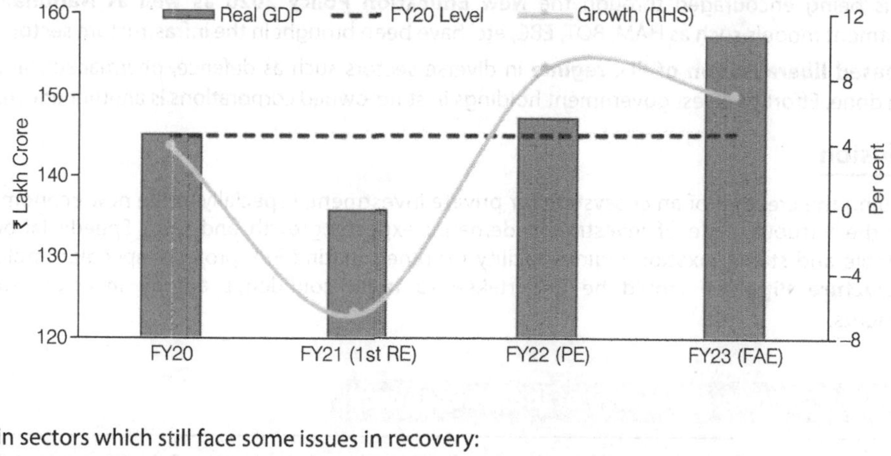

However, certain sectors which still face some issues in recovery:

- **Faltering Manufacturing Growth Rate** India's economic growth decelerated to 4.4% in the October-December quarter of FY23 mainly due to a contraction in the manufacturing sector. The manufacturing sector's output, as per the gross value added in the third quarter of this fiscal, contracted by 1.1% compared to a growth of 1.3% in the year-ago period.

- **MSME Sector** Small business faced closure and drop in production, thus their revival is still a continuing process.
- **Sectoral Revival** Certain sectors are still in the of process recovery and demand has not reached pre pandemic level like aviation etc.
- **K-Shaped Recovery** Issues of demand and effect of pandemic has resulted into K-shaped recovery in Indian economy.

Growth Drivers of Indian Economy

Economic Survey 2022-23 projects a baseline GDP growth of 6.5% in real terms in FY24. The projection is broadly comparable to the estimates provided by multilateral agencies such as the World Bank, the IMF and the ADB and by RBI, domestically. This optimistic growth forecasts stem from a number of positives:

- **Rebound of Private Consumption** The uptick in private consumption has also given a boost to production activity resulting in an increase in capacity utilisation across sectors.
- **Focus on Capital Expenditure** The central government continued its focus on capital expenditure for 2023-24 to aid economic recovery at a time private investment are yet to show clear signs of revival. The government capital expenditure for FY24 is pegged at ₹ 10 lakh crore, forming about 3.3% of the GDP.
- A sustained increase in private capex is also imminent with the **strengthening of the balance sheets of the Corporates** and the consequent increase in credit financing it has been able to generate.
  - As per the data on non-financial debt from the bank for International Settlements, in the course of the last decade, Indian non-financial private sector debt and non-financial corporate debt as a share of GDP declined by nearly thirty percentage points.
- **Well-capitalised Public Sector banks (PSBs)** The Gross Non-Performing Assets (GNPA) ratio of SCBs has fallen to a seven-year low of 5.0, while the Capital-to-Risk Weighted Assets Ratio (CRAR) remains healthy at 16.0 and well above the regulatory requirement of 11.5. The health of NBFCs has continued to improve as well.
- **High Credit Growth Especially MSMEs** Bank credit grew by 15% year-on-year in the fiscal ended March 2023 due to higher demand for funds as economic activity picked up. The credit growth to the Micro, Small and Medium Enterprises (MSMEs) sector has been remarkably high, over 30.6% , on average during January-November 2022, supported by the extended Emergency Credit Linked Guarantee Scheme (ECLGS) of the Union Government.
- **Strong Domestic Demand** India has a large and growing consumer market, which is expected to support demand for goods and services and drive economic growth.
- **Government Reforms** The government has announced several reform measures in recent years, such as the Goods and Services Tax (GST), the Insolvency and Bankruptcy Code (IBC), PLI scheme which are expected to support long-term growth.
- **Digital Transformation** India's digital transformation is expected to support growth in the technology and services sectors, particularly in areas such as e-commerce, fintech.
- **Infrastructure Investments** The government has announced several infrastructure investments, such as the National Infrastructure Pipeline (NIP) and the PM GATI-SHAKTI, which are expected to create employment opportunities and support economic growth.
- **Attracting Foreign Investment** India has been taking steps to improve its investment climate, such as by easing foreign investment restrictions and improving the ease of doing business, which is expected to attract foreign investment and support growth.

Downside Risks to Indian Economy

- **Inflation Rate** Inflation is a big worry for India because of the high global commodity prices and depreciation of rupee. It is for this reason that the RBI is following tight monetary policy since the last 12 months which has an impact on India's growth prospects.
- **Falling Global Demand** Global economy have been hit with three major shocks – COVID-19 pandemic, Russia-Ukraine conflict and increased interest rates by US Fed along with slowdown in China impact global demand and thus hampering the export growth of India.
- **Widening Current Account Deficit (CAD)** High commodity prices of fuel, fertilisers, metals and others is worsening India's CAD problem.

- **Depreciating Rupee** This is leading to imported inflation which in turn will lead to increase in interest rates by the RBI, thus hampering India's growth prospects.
- **Rising Interest Rate Scenario** It imposes several kinds of challenges like flight of foreign capital, decline in profitability of banks etc. thus creating uncertainty in economy.
- **High Fiscal Deficit** Fiscal deficit estimate for 2023-24 is at 5.9% of GDP.
- **Debt Levels** The pandemic has also led to a significant increase in private and public debt levels, which may impede long-term growth prospects. India's public debt as a percentage of GDP was 89.3% in 2020, as per data from the International Monetary Fund (IMF).
- **External Factors** External factors such as global economic conditions and geopolitical tensions may also pose challenges for the Indian economy in the post-pandemic period. e.g., Russia-Ukraine crises
- **Unemployment Issue** What makes India's unemployment even more worrisome is the fact that this is happening even when the labour force participation rate which maps the proportion of people who look for a job has been falling.

Future Outlook

Dwelling on the Outlook for 2023-24, the Economic Survey 2022-23 observed that India's recovery from the pandemic was relatively quick and growth in the upcoming year will be supported by solid domestic demand and a pickup in capital investment. It observed that aided by healthy financials, incipient signs of a new private sector capital formation cycle are visible and more importantly, compensating for the private sector's caution in capital expenditure, the government raised capital expenditure substantially.

India's Consumption-Led Economic Model

Q.6 What are the factors that contributed to India's consumption-led model? Is this model sustainable in nature? Give your opinion with proper arguments. (150 Words, 10 Marks)

Ans. **Introduction** India having reached the landmark of becoming the fifth largest economy in the world and is on the march to reach the $5 trillion milestone by FY26. While there are several drivers to the growth the core strength lies within India is its population (of 1.4 billion) and its demographics. Economic Survey 2022-23 observed that India's economy is mainly driven by domestic consumption as it constitutes around 57% of the GDP of the country.

Factors Contributing to India's Consumption-led Model

Consumption led growth relies on higher consumer spending to raise aggregate demand which will give a boost to production activity resulting in an increase in capacity utilisation across sectors and consequently to faster economic growth. The Indian growth story has largely been consumption-driven over the last three decades since economic liberalisation because of the various factors:

- **High Young Population** India became the world's most populated country with population crossing more than 1.4 billion population and 62.5% of its population is in the age group of 15-59 years which have high aspirations.
- **Rapid Increase in Disposable Income** GDP per capita increased by almost 6 times in the last 30 years which resulted into higher disposable income thus, fuelling India's consumption-led growth.
- **Increased Consumerism** LPG reforms led to increased consumerism in the country which refers to the belief that a person's well-being and happiness depend fundamentally on obtaining consumer goods and material possessions. This promotes excessive materialism which can be witnessed in higher smartphone sales, increased e-commerce orders, rapid growth rate of automobile and aviation sector.
- **Government Intervention** Government intervention via subsidies, seventh Central Pay Commission, One Rank One Pension, etc., have fuelled the India's economic growth in the past and can continue to do so in the future.
- The rise of 'networks' have driven steady consumption growth as India experienced an unprecedented rise in telecom, financial and road networks. This drove a rise in awareness as well as demand for a host of consumer goods, including mobile phones, cars, two-wheelers and houses.

- **Post-pandemic Factors**
  - **Near-universal Vaccination Coverage** More than 2 billion doses that led to rebound in consumer sentiments and spend on various contact-based services such as tourism, hospitality, cinemas, restaurants and others.
  - **Release of 'Pent-up' Demand** There has been rapid increase in consumer demand after the pandemic period which can be seen in the higher demand for personal and housing loans.
- **Developed Countries Experience** US in 1960s had a population demographics similar to India today and its share of consumption was also similar to India today around 60%. The per capita income of US in 1960 was USD 3000 versus India's per capita at USD 2277 in 2021. However, in the growth from USD 560 billion economy to USD25 trillion, the share of consumption has moved to more than two-thirds (at 68% as of 2022).

Challenges in the Sustainability of Consumption-led Model

- **Tightening of Monetary Policy** RBI is continuously increasing interest rates to contain inflation but it has its negative impact on the consumer demand. This is witnessed in the decline of IIP for both consumer durables and non-durables. This could also lead to high cost of government borrowing which impairs the ability of government to finance the consumption requirements.
- **High Fiscal Deficit** High government consumption expenditure can lead to higher fiscal deficit and consequently higher public debt and the government has limited bandwidth in fiscal deficit. (BE2023-24 projects FD to be at 5.9% of the GDP and public debt of CG is around 60% of the GDP).
- **Current Account Deficit (CAD)** Consumption-led demand could result in an increase in imports (in response to higher demand) and thus adds to already high CAD.
- **Higher Inflation** Demand pressures from rising incomes, in the absence of an adequate supply response, could lead to higher inflation in certain sectors such as real estate witnessed during 2008-2014.
- **Slackening of Future Growth** High private and government spending limits the ability to spend on capacity creation and rising debt burdens will crowd out the private investment in an economy. This will impact the spending on infrastructure which plays a multiplier effect on Indian economy.
- **Skewed Towards Food and Non-discretionary Items** India's consumption basket is heavily skewed towards food having a 30-32% share and the next largest share taken by transport (15-17%).
- **High Unemployment** It is a serious challenge as it affects the disposable income of the person and thus leads to decrease in demand.

Measures to be Taken by the Government

- **Raise purchasing power of the masses** through government interventions.
- **Tackle the unemployment crisis** Action will be needed on multiple fronts including investments in human capital, the revival of the productive sectors and programmes to stimulate small entrepreneurship.
- **Investment led growth** could be the alternative for increasing employment rate and thus raising Purchasing Power Parity.
- **Export led growth** can solve the problem of fiscal debt or current account deficit.

Conclusion

With a 1.4 billion population, India will remain a consumption driven economy and the share of consumption within GDP may even rise as witnessed in the US case. But the mix of consumption may also warrant a change as the shift in mix to higher value products will be the driver of value growth.

India's Structural Transformation

Q.7 How India's structural transformation is unique compared to that of other developed countries? Also, examine the reasons of such structural transformation. (150 Words, 10 Marks)

Ans. **Introduction** The contribution made by the different sectors of the economy, namely the agricultural sector, the industrial sector and the service sector in the GDP of the country makes up the **structural composition of the economy.** In some countries, growth in agriculture contributes more to the GDP growth, while in some countries the growth in the service sector contributes more to GDP growth.

Occupational structure of an economy shows how much percentage of the total workforce is employed in different sectors viz., agriculture (primary), industry (secondary) and services (tertiary).

General Structural Transformation

As a country develops, it undergoes 'structural change'. Usually, with development, the share of agriculture declines and the share of industry become dominant. At higher levels of development, the service sector contributes more to the GDP than the other two sectors. So, in general it follows the below trend as experienced by many developed countries such as US, UK etc or by developing countries like China etc.

Agriculture (Primary Sector) → Industry (Secondary Sector) → Service (Tertiary Sector)

Such transformation also involve the transfer of labour from farming to sectors – particularly manufacturing and modern services – where productivity, value-addition and average incomes are higher.

India's Unique Structural Transformation

- India shifted **directly from Agriculture to Services by passing the industrial sector**. The difference is while most developed countries entered the phase of predominance of services in their economies after going through a phase of industrialization and spurt in manufacturing sector, India's industry failed to show similar growth and it arrived into service sector dominance straight away.
- As per PLFS 2021-22, agriculture still employ around 46% of the working force inspite of its contribution to only 16% of the GVA. Thus, India witnessed a **slow change in occupational structure from agriculture to services sector**.

Indian economy when it embarked on the development process after Independence in 1950, with about 60 % of GDP accounted for by agriculture, industry contributing about 13 % and services about 27 %. Similar comparisons hold in respect of the share of labour force in different sectors: agriculture accounted for about 75 %, industry for about 11 percent and services accounted for 16 % of total employment in 1950, in India.

The share of agriculture in GDP in India has declined from around 60 % in 1950-51 to 36.38 % in 1983 and further declined to 14 % in 2010 11. That of industry increased from 13 to 24 percent and reaches to 28 % and of services from 28 to 40 and further rises to 58 %. With respect to the labour force, agriculture currently employs around 46% of the working force, 29% is employed in the service sector and remaining 25% is employed in the industrial sector.

Reasons for India's Unique Structural Transformation

There are various factors that led to India's unique structural transformation and it can be broadly divided into two categories:

Slowdown of Secondary Sector (Industrial Sector)	Growth of Tertiary Sector (Service Sector)
License Raj The purpose of the licensing system was to establish government control over industrial development and provided it a desired direction according to the government's socialist agenda. This prevented the growth of industrial sector.	**Skilled Labour Force** India has a large and well-educated labour force, which was well-suited for the service. The service sector, particularly the IT and business process outsourcing (BPO) sectors, has been able to take advantage of this skilled labour force.
Lack of Investment in Infrastructure India has a poor infrastructure, which makes it difficult for industries to operate effectively. **High Cost of Doing Business** India has a high cost of doing business, which includes high taxes, bureaucratic red tape and high energy costs.	**Impact of Globalisation** Globalisation has resulted in the demand of many services such as banking, telecommunication, tourism, financial service and thus service sector in India showed the rapid growth. The service sector was able to take advantage of this liberalization, particularly in the areas of IT and BPO.

Slowdown of Secondary Sector (Industrial Sector)	Growth of Tertiary Sector (Service Sector)
High Logistics Cost Logistics cost in India amounts to 14% of GDP while it is 8.14% of GDP in USA, according to Economic Survey 2022-23. Lack of **Access to Credit** Indian industries often have difficulty accessing credit, which makes it difficult for them to invest in new technologies and expand their operations.	**Low Capital Requirement** The service sector requires relatively low capital investment compared to the industry sector. This has made it easier for entrepreneurs to set up service-based businesses, leading to a growth in the service sector.
Protectionism Protectionism has created a closed market, which has prevented foreign companies from competing with domestic companies, resulting in a lack of innovation and productivity. **Low Adoption of Technology** It prevented the industries to reduce its cost of production and thus, could not compete with the big MNCs. Many industries got shut down after 1991 reforms.	**Government Policies** The Indian Government has implemented several policies to support the growth of the service sector, including tax breaks, subsidies and investment in infrastructure.
Low Labour Productivity India has low labour productivity compared to other developing countries, which has led to a decline in the growth rate of the industrial sector. This was also due to prevalence of rigid labour laws.	

Conclusion

A strong industrial base can generate more employment opportunities, increase productivity and create a more diversified economy. It also allows for the country to be less dependent on exports and more self-sufficient. Therefore, government has undertaken various measures in the recent years such as Make in India, Atmanirbhar Bharat scheme, Production Linked Incentive (PLI) schemes in 14 sectors, liberalisation of foreign direct investment policy, ease of doing business and many other reform measures.

Growth vs Development (India's Progress towards SDGs)

Q.8 With reference to the Sustainable Development, critically analyse India's progress towards the achievement of Sustainable Development Goals (SDGs). (150 Words, 10 Marks)

Ans. **Introduction** UN have adopted Sustainable Development Goals (SDGs) as a universal call to action to end poverty, protect the planet and ensure that by 2030 all people enjoy peace and prosperity. There are 17 SDGs and 169 targets that are integrated - they recognise that action in one area will affect outcomes in others and that development must balance social, economic and environmental sustainability.

About Sustainable Development The concept of sustainable Development was emphasised by the United Nations Conference on Environment and Development (UNCED), which defined it as: **'Development that meets the need of the present generation without compromising the ability of the future generation to meet their own needs'.**

India's Progress towards Sustainable Development Goals (SDGs)

The following narrative encapsulates India's progress across the SDGs:

- **Sashakt Bharat-Sabal Bharat (Empowered and Resilient India)** India has successfully lifted more than 415 million people out of multidimensional poverty between 2005-06 to 2019-21 through economic growth and empowerment. Enhanced access to nutrition, child health, education, sanitation, drinking water, electricity and housing, has led to reduced inequalities especially among people in vulnerable situations.
- **Swachh Bharat - Swasth Bharat (Clean and Healthy India)** Through a nationwide initiative triggered by the Clean India Campaign and the National Nutrition Mission, India achieved 100% rural sanitation and sharp reduction in stunting and child and maternal mortality rates. Universal health coverage has been institutionalised through Ayushmaan Bharat, the world's largest health protection scheme which provides an annual cover of USD 7,000 to 100 million families, covering nearly 500 million individuals.
- **Samagra Bharat-Saksham Bharat (Inclusive and Entrepreneurial India)** Social inclusion is pursued through universalizing access to nutrition, health, education, social protection and developing capabilities for entrepreneurship and employment. Financial inclusion through Jan Dhan-Aadhaar-Mobile (JAM) trinity – near universal access to bank accounts aided by the Jan Dhan Yojana (National Financial Inclusion Scheme); Aadhaar card (National unique identity number) for over 90% of the population and expansive access to mobile phones, has propelled new avenues of credit, insurance and Direct Benefit Transfers (DBT) to the poor, including to over 200 million women, thereby accelerating their economic empowerment.
  - The Mahatma Gandhi National Rural Employment Guarantee Act (MNREGA) is being used to give unskilled workers jobs and raise their standard of living.
- **Satat Bharat–Sanatan Bharat (Sustainable India)** India's climate action strategies call for clean and efficient energy systems, disaster resilient infrastructure and planned eco-restoration. Acting on its nationally-determined contributions, India has electrified 100% of its villages, reduced 38 million tonnes of CO_2 emissions annually through energy efficient appliances, provided clean cooking fuel to 80 million poor households and set a target to install 450GW of renewable energy and restore 26 million hectares of degraded land by 2030. Globally, India stands third in renewable power, fourth in wind power and fifth in solar power. India launched the Coalition for Disaster Resilient Infrastructure and the International Solar Alliance to leverage global partnerships for climate action and disaster resilience.
- **Sampanna Bharat-Samriddh Bharat (Prosperous and Vibrant India)** India is one of the fastest growing emerging market economies with a young population and burgeoning innovation and business ecosystem. With a GDP of more than USD 3 trillion in present times and world's fifth largest economy, India strives to become a USD 5 trillion economy by 2025 and pursue an inclusive and sustainable growth trajectory by stimulating manufacturing, building infrastructure, spurring investments and fostering technological innovation.

- **NITI Aayog "SDG India Index"** It is the world's first government-led sub-national measure of SDG development. It was launched in 2018 and has been developed to capture the progress of all States and Union Territories (UTs) in their journey towards achieving the SDGs. This index is based on the idea of cooperative and competitive federalism, which says that action needs to be taken at all levels.

While, multiple initiatives were taken to achieve SDGs in India, Lancet Report published in 2023 highlighted the status of India's SDG performance:

- At the all-India level, the one SDG indicator that has already been achieved is related to adolescent pregnancy in the age group of 10–14 years.
- India is also On-Target to meet 13 out of the 33 indicators, including Internet use, women having a bank account, full vaccination (card), improved sanitation, multidimensional poverty and many others.
- India is not on-target for 19 of the 33 SDGs indicators (Sustainable Development Goals) of the United Nations, which is more than 50% of the indicators. The critical off-target indicators include access to basic services, wasting and overweight children, anaemia, child marriage, partner violence, tobacco use and modern contraceptives.

Progress Indicators	SDGs
Good	Health; Water; Sustainable energy; Reduce inequality; Inclusive cities; Sustainable consumption; Inclusive societies
Moderate	Poverty; Education; Sustainable economy; Sustainable industrialisation; Urgent action on climate change; Strengthen global partnerships
Poor	Hunger; Gender equality
Stable	Conserve sea and marine resources; Protect the environment

Challenges in the Achievement of SDGs

Structural Challenges

- **Imbalance in Economic Development** This has altered the ecological balance which threatens sustainable development.
- **Rapid Urbanisation** This has led to increasing demand-supply gaps in housing, infrastructure, employment and other economic opportunities and services.
- **Regional Variance** There is great imbalance in poverty levels between states and between urban and rural areas. e.g., Chhattisgarh has around 40% population below the poverty line while it is 1% in the Andaman and Nicobar Islands.

Implementation Challenges

- **Financing SDGs** SDG targets like zero hunger, poverty, etc requires significant investments to eliminate them. Being home to one-third of the world's 1.2 billion extremely poor, the Indian Government alone cannot fund these SDG targets.
- **Systemic Weaknesses** Delays in fund flow at the local level along with inadequacy of human resources, training and capacity of line departments, Panchayati Raj Institutions and Municipal Corporations entails poor planning and weaken the implementation and monitoring of SDGs.

- **Lack of Access to Resources** Inequalities continue to exist in women's access to and ownership of land and other assets.
  - In rural India, while 75% of rural women workers are engaged in agriculture, women's operational landholding is only 13.96%. The absence of land ownership limits their access to inputs, such as, seeds, fertilisers, credit, as well as agricultural extension services
- **Lack of Awareness and Poor Participation by Marginalised Communities** (SCs, STs, OBCs and minorities) in planning and implementation of SDGs at the local level.

Monitoring Challenges

- **Defining Indicators** There is a lack of clear definition, reliable and standardised data and inconsistent use of terminology in selecting appropriate indicators. In order to ensure effective implementation of the SDGs, the important definition of indicators like quality education, safe drinking water, poverty, hunger etc. needs to be revised.
- **Monitoring outcomes** Due to the lack of preparation of development indicators, irregular data reporting on outcomes and lack of capacity of data preparation at state, district and block levels.
- **Measuring Progress** Non-availability of data in respect to sub-national levels, periodicity issues, lack of innovation-oriented research and incomplete coverage of administrative data have made accurate measuring progress of SDGs difficult.

Measures to be taken for Achieving SDGs by 2030

- **Localizing SDGs** It involves the process of understanding, adapting, planning, implementing and monitoring the SDGs from national to local levels by relevant institutions.
  - Local and Regional Governments (LRGs) must prepare to implement and monitor the SDGs in their communities by mobilising local resources, building capacities for effective and responsive leadership, promote ownership and participating in development cooperation and peer to peer learning.
- **Education, Employment and Human Resource Development** There is a need to refashion education and skill development so that the existing, emerging and future labour force has the capability and requisite opportunities to engage in appropriately gainful employment. It is necessary to invest in and enhance quality and accessibility of health care, especially for the economically weaker sections and people in vulnerable situations.
- **Identifying and Prioritising Districts**: On critical indicators of health and social determinants of health, there is a need for a greater degree of precision in identifying and prioritising districts for intervention. Meeting these goals will require prioritising and targeting specific areas within India.
- **Promoting Women's Entrepreneurship** As the economy gets increasingly digitised and women's access to technology improves, women increasingly find a level playing field and welcome the ambience for innovation. This situation calls for gender-responsive and inclusive procurement both in public and private sector. Initiatives like the Atal Innovation Mission and Women's Entrepreneurship Platform of NITI Aayog, aim to create an ecosystem of innovation, research and entrepreneurship across the country to engage young girls and women.
- **Infrastructure** There is need to invest in new, resilient infrastructure or retrofit existing infrastructure to make it more sustainable. Proper infrastructure is needed for equitable access and delivery of services such as power supplies, healthcare services and sewerage networks that are essential for sustainable development.
- **Enhance Funding** Estimating the cost to achieve the SDGs and developing and implementing the tools to attract SDG-related finance and investments are key requirements for the timely achievement of the ambitious targets under the SDG framework. Enhancing the financial resources to have better unit cost of services and adequate payment to staffs and their trainings, who are engaged with social and economic sectors should be given top priority for better implementation of SDGs.
- **Focus on 3As (Awareness, Action and Accountability)** To improve the accuracy of the indicator measurement and avoid double counting, a single clustered indicator is needed to accelerate the progress towards the SDGs by embracing a '3As' approach –
  - **Raising Awareness** The right tools and information can play a critical role in the implementation and monitoring of the SDGs.
  - **Taking Action** As millions of people are becoming aware of the goals, more and more are taking action across the globe.
  - **Holding Decision Makers** Accountable by collecting, analysing and sharing data to monitor progress, and by bringing stakeholder's perspectives on the SDGs to decision makers to promote accountability.

Conclusion

If India succeeds in attaining the SDGs, it would mean a larger section of the world has achieved it. Therefore, it is imperative for India to develop effective methods for implementing, monitoring and measuring the progress of SDGs.

Economic Growth vs Human Development

Q.9 Despite consistent experience of high growth, India still goes with the lowest indicators of human development. Examine the issues that make balanced and inclusive development elusive.
(150 Words, 10 Marks) **UPSC Mains PYQ 2019**

Ans. **Introduction** India has grown rapidly since 1991 with an average economic growth in the last 30 years of around 7 percent and currently India's economy is more than USD 3 trillion economy and the fifth largest economy in nominal terms. But this growth has not resulted in a corresponding increase in its Human Development Index (HDI). According to the Human Development Report of 2021-22, India ranks 132 out of 191 countries declined by First rank from the previous year. India is ranked worst among the BRICS economies and below than most of its neighbours such as Sri Lanka (79), Bangladesh (129), etc.

Issues that make balanced and inclusive development elusive

- **Jobless Growth** Since India's growth is led by services (which is not a labor-intensive sector), it has been considered as jobless growth as the employment growth has declined for the same level of economic growth. Thus, growth has only affected a very small section of India. Employment elasticity has fallen from close to unity in the 70s to 0.4 in the 90s to less than 0.1 in the present times.
- **Uneven Growth** The growth has been uneven across sectors and locations. For instance, agriculture has been lagging behind and in countries such as India and China, some regions have advanced faster than others. Policies are also relatively ignored the agriculture sector.
- **Poverty** A significant portion of the population is still living below the poverty line, lacking access to basic necessities such as food, water, and healthcare. As per Global Multi-dimensional Poverty Index, more than 16% of India's population is still multi-dimensionally poor in 2019-21.
- **Casteism** A major weakness is that the growth is not perceived as being adequately inclusive for many groups, especially Scheduled Castes (SCs), Scheduled Tribes (STs) and weaker section. Development will not be inclusive if some groups are discriminated against, overtly or covertly.
- **Unequal Distribution of Wealth** Oxfam Inequality Report, 2023 observes that the richest 1% in India now own more than 40% of the country's total wealth, while the bottom half of the population together share just 3% of wealth. The total number of billionaires in India increased from 102 in 2020 to 166 in 2022. This results in an uneven distribution of wealth across the various sections of the society and it marks the prevalence of high inequality in the Indian socio-economic paradigm which led to non-inclusive growth and low human development.
- **Low Public Investment on Social Infrastructure** On comparison with similarly placed emerging economies, India spends way too low in the education and health sector. India spends 3% of GDP on education and 2% of GDP on health.
- **Education Status** Access, quality and learning outcomes all are far lower than what anyone would have desired. Dropouts are only one outcome of bad quality. Poor learning outcomes, low employability of graduates, low productivity and consequent low wages constitute another set of outcomes. All these outcomes are reflected in the Annual Status of Education Report (ASER) which concluded that the quality of education is far from satisfactory. Even Economic Survey highlighted this via the concept of 'Learning Poverty'.
- **Health Challenges** India is grappling with numerous health issues such as malnutrition, poor hygiene and inadequate healthcare infrastructure. Even after many government schemes, both the infant mortality rate and the maternal mortality rate remains high.
- **Malnutrition** There is a high prevalence of malnutrition in Indian children, reflected in a high percentage of child stunting, wasting and underweight.

- As much as 50% of malnutrition is caused, not by a lack of food or poor diets, but due to poor water, poor sanitation facilities and unhygienic practices.

- **Corruption** Corruption is a widespread problem in India, affecting the distribution of resources and opportunities, leading to a lack of trust in the government and institutions.

Futuristic Measures

- **Higher Public Investment in Social Infrastructure** The government needs to increase public expenditure on health and education as envisaged by National Health Policy 2017 (2.5% of GDP) and New Education Policy 2020 (6% of GDP).
- **Employment Generation** The government should also focus on promoting labour-intensive sectors such as gems and jewellery, textiles and garments and leather goods. e.g., Recent PLI schemes and Atmanirbhar Bharat is a step in the right direction.
- **Boost Formalisation of Labour** For a higher standard of living, it should ensure that work is quantitatively and qualitatively enhanced in the country. The country's efforts in terms of employment guarantee schemes have been lauded for its role in reducing unemployment.
  - India needs to reform its rigid labour market governed by obsolete laws, address problems of child labour and forced labour and bring about wage equality. Recent codification of labour laws into 4 codes is a step in the right direction.
- **Improved Health Outcomes** Promotion of Primary Health Centre under Ayushman Bharat, which focuses on preventive healthcare is a step in the right direction.
- **Boost Learning Outcomes** Indian Government must also focus on improving quality and access in education. Education has a major role in promoting inclusive economic development. It can particularly help reduce the share of informal employment going forward and promote social inclusion.
- **Promote skill Development** Skill framework in India needs to integrate with industries, so as to increase the employability of the Indian labour force.
- **Curb Digital Divide** The government should make efforts to curb digital divide, as it creates and reproduces socio-economic backwardness.
- **Strengthening Agriculture** Policy makers and government officials need to work on agriculture productivity, in order to be more inclusive.
- **Energy Efficiency** Efforts are needed to increase energy and resource efficiency, notably through lower fossil fuel subsidies and accelerate the adoption of clean technologies.

Conclusion

Though the government has initiated many schemes for enhancing human capital i.e., Skill India, Digital India, Startup India, Ayushman Bharat. However, the results are not yet promising. India needs to address the various parameters of human development separately and simultaneously.

Green Accounting Measures

Q.10 'Green Growth' is not just the mere announcement of environment-related initiatives but it involves a comprehensive assessment of the environmental and social impacts of production pattern in an economy. Examine the statement in the context of various measures undertaken by the government for greening India's GDP. (250 Words, 15 Marks)

Ans. **Introduction** The concept of green growth recognises that economic growth and environmental sustainability are not mutually exclusive and that policies and investments that promote both can create long-term benefits for society. **Budget 2023** made Green Growth as one of the seven priorities of the government (**Saptarishi Programme**). **The UN defines** greening GDP as 'the process of integrating environmental considerations into the measurement of economic activity.'

Steps Taken for Green Growth in India

- **Panchamrit Commitment**
  - India will reach its **non-fossil energy capacity to 500 GW by 2030.**
  - **Decarbonisation of economy** India will meet 50% of its energy requirements from renewable energy by 2030.
  - India will reduce the total projected carbon **emissions by one billion tonnes** from now onwards till 2030.
  - By 2030, India will reduce the **carbon intensity of its economy by less than 45%.**
  - **Net-zero carbon emissions** India will achieve the target of **Net Zero by the year 2070**. These Panchamrit will be an unprecedented contribution of India to climate action.
- **Addressing both Demand and Supply Side Measures:** It addresses both demand side and supply side issues. Supply side is taken care by renewable energy while demand side is taken care by initiatives of increasing energy efficiency in buildings, industries and transportation. These include the **Energy Efficiency Building Code; Perform, Achieve and Trade (PAT) scheme.**
- **Promoting Environmental Conscious Life Style LIFE...L, I, F, E,** i.e., Lifestyle For Environment Today promotes a mass movement of Environmental Conscious Life Style. What is needed today is Mindful and Deliberate Utilisation, instead of Mindless and Destructive Consumption.
- **Reducing Pollution** The Indian Government has launched a number of initiatives to reduce pollution, including the **National Clean Air Programme (NCAP)** and the National Mission for Clean Ganga (NMCG).
- **Conserving Natural Resources** The Indian Government has launched a number of initiatives to conserve natural resources, including the National Forest Policy, the National Water Policy, and the National Biodiversity Strategy and Action Plan.
- **Supporting sustainable agriculture** The Indian government has launched a number of initiatives to support sustainable agriculture, including the **PM PRANAM (Promotion of Alternate Nutrients for Agriculture Management Yojana).**

Reasons for Environmental Accounting

- **Comprehensive Assessment of the Production of Goods and Services** It intends to capture the intimate interplay between various components of the natural environment and the economy.
  - **Ecosystem services,** also known as the 'GDP of the poor', are the services provided by the environment and enjoyed by the human community free of cost; these services are **absent in the Traditional System of National Accounts (SNA)** of a country. It is increasingly being recognised that SNA must be re-designed into a more holistic indicator that will factor in not only the value of non-marketed ecosystem services, but also the impact of human endeavours in the form of environmental externalities. Such improvements to the traditional SNA is known as Natural Resource Accounting or Green Accounting.
- **Capture the Negative Externalities of Economic Growth** In traditional accounting of agricultural GDP, output is measured in monetary terms, leaving out externalities such as the depletion of forests and groundwater resources.
  - Policies such as agricultural subsidies have often increased the affordability of chemicals and high-yield variety seeds, which are prime examples of technologies that can lead to land deterioration.
  - These inefficient methods cause detrimental effects including falling water tables, surface water pollution and rising salinity — yet, such ecological losses are left out in current accounting methodologies.
  - The declining quality of freshwater in India can be mostly attributed to the mismanagement of industrial waste
- **Create more Awareness about the Environmental Conservation** Since these ecosystem services are provided at no monetary cost, the importance of conservation is grossly underrated, especially in the developing world. The interlinkage and interdependence between humans and the environment can be better understood by gaining clarity on the valuation of natural capital stocks and corresponding ecosystem flow services.
- **Transition Towards Green Economy** The transition from a 'brown economy' to a 'green economy' is mostly hindered by the problem of capital misallocation. Environment accounting measures optimises the capital allocation.

- **Mandate of Sustainable Development Goals (SDGs)** Goals 13, 14 and 15 of the United Nations Sustainable Development Goals (SDGs) 2015 suggest linkages to the need of Green Accounting in the context of combating climate change, conservation of marine resources, and protection of terrestrial ecosystem, respectively. **Goal 15.9 mentions the integration of biodiversity values and ecosystem services into local and national accounts**, development planning and poverty reduction measures.
- **Aid to Policy Formulation** Sound database can help policy makers to understand the potential impact of their decisions

Steps Taken for Assessment for Green GDP

India has taken the following measures for greening India's GDP are as follows :

- **NCAVES** (National Capital Accounting with Valuation of Ecosystem Services) is an initiative aimed at integrating the valuation of ecosystem services into the national accounting framework.
  - The NCAVES Project, funded by the European Union, has been jointly implemented by the United Nations Statistics Division (UNSD), the United Nations Environment Programme (UNEP) and the Secretariat of the Convention of Biological Diversity (CBD). India is one of the five countries taking part in this project.
  - Natural Capital Accounting is an umbrella term covering efforts to make use of an accounting framework to provide a systematic way to measure and report on stocks and flows of natural capital.
  - **Valuation of Ecosystem Services** NCAVES seeks to assess and assign economic values to the various ecosystem services provided by India's natural resources, such as forests, wetlands, rivers, and biodiversity. This helps in recognising the contributions of ecosystems to the economy and informing policy decisions.
  - **Integration into National Accounts:** The project aims to incorporate the values of ecosystem services into the national accounts, ensuring that they are accounted for in the country's economic indicators and planning processes. This integration provides policymakers with a comprehensive understanding of the importance of natural resources in economic development.
- **Compilation of the Environment Accounts** as per the UN System of Environmental-Economic Accounting (UN-SEEA) framework and release environmental accounts in its publication 'EnviStats India' on an annual basis from 2018.
- Another tool under the NCAVES project is the **development of the India-EVL Tool** which is essentially a look-up tool giving the values of various ecosystem services in the different states of the country.
- **Green GDP** Reserve Bank of India (RBI) has published a paper in October 2022, where researchers have estimated India's green GDP to be somewhere between ` 165.9 trillion to 167.7 trillion for 2019. The calculation of Green GDP is done in the following manner:

Green GDP = GDP – (Carbon dioxide damage + particulate emission damage) – (Opportunity cost of energy depletion + mineral depletion + Net forest depletion) + Expenditure on environmental protection.

- **Gross Environment Product** Uttarakhand Government initiated valuation of its natural resources in the form of Gross Environment Product (GEP) which accounts for the economic value of the ecosystem in providing products and services and it is one of the components of Green GDP.
- **TEEB India** is a national-level initiative that seeks to integrate the values of biodiversity and ecosystem services into decision-making processes. It was launched in 2018 by the Ministry of Environment, Forest and Climate Change (MoEFCC) in collaboration with the United Nations Development Programme (UNDP).
- **Environmental Impact Assessment (EIA)** EIA started in 2006 evaluates the potential environmental impacts of proposed projects, policies, or activities before they are implemented. EIA is designed to identify and assess the potential effects of these projects on the environment, including natural resources, ecosystems and human well-being.
- **National Biodiversity Action Plan (NBAP)** 2008 mentions as one of its core targets, the 'valuation of goods and services provided by biodiversity and use of economic instruments in decision making process.'

Challenges Associated with Estimation of Green GDP

- **Data Availability and Quality** Obtaining comprehensive and consistent data can be challenging, particularly in developing countries where data collection and reporting systems may be weak.
- **Methodological Complexity** Methodological challenges arise in valuing natural resources, assessing environmental damages and determining appropriate weights and measures.

– The current Environment Impact Assessment scenario in India has often been cast with doubts due to inadequate methodologies and the qualitative nature of estimation.

- **Lack of Standardisation** There is no globally standardised approach to estimating Green GDP. Different countries and organisations may adopt varying methodologies and indicators, making it difficult to compare and aggregate results across regions or globally.
- **Limited Monetary Valuation** Valuing natural resources and ecosystem services in monetary terms is challenging. Assigning accurate economic values to environmental goods and services, such as clean air, biodiversity and scenic beauty, is subjective and often controversial.
- **Information Asymmetry** The objective of such valuation is mainly to create environmental markets to ensure the appreciation of ecosystem services and move towards a cleaner environment. The reason why such markets fail is the lack of information and knowledge and the non-participation of various stakeholders. This information asymmetry causes the divergence between market prices and the value of environmental resources, causing the disorganisation of environmental market.
- **Integration with GDP Calculation** Integrating environmental factors into the conventional GDP framework is a complex task. It requires harmonising environmental and economic data, accounting for trade-offs between economic growth and environmental sustainability and ensuring compatibility with national accounting systems.
- **Irregularity in the Release of Green GDP data by the RBI.**

Conclusion

United Nations (UN) has been a strong advocate for greening GDP. In 2012, the UN released a report called **'Towards a Green Economy: Pathways to Sustainable Development and Poverty Eradication.'** The report argued that 'greening GDP' is essential for achieving sustainable development and poverty eradication. In 2016, the UN released a set of **guidelines for greening GDP**.

Although this form of accounting is impeded by problems such as inefficient computation methodologies as well as lack of data and of political will, it is imperative to reach a comprehensive indicator of a nation's performance to outline alternative sustainable development frameworks.

Planning in Indian Economy (Overall Appraisal of Economic Reforms)

Q.11 Do you agree with the view that the mixed results of economic reforms in the last three decades can be attributed to the reforms being half-baked and incomplete? Discuss. (250 Words, 15 Marks)

Ans. **Introduction** In return for the USA 7 billion loan to manage the 1991 Balance of Payment (BoP) crisis, IMF expected India to liberalise and open up the economy by removing restrictions on the private sector, reducing the role of the government in many areas and removing trade restrictions between India and other countries.

Thereafter, India announced the New Economic Policy (NEP), 1991 with wide ranging structural reforms introducing liberalisation, privatisation and globalisation. It was aimed to liberalise the economy, promote growth, attract foreign investment and improve the overall business environment which have catapulted Indian economy to become fifth largest economy in the world.

Economic Reforms Adopted and Their Positive Impact

Annual Growth of GDP

1950-80	3.5%
1980-92	5.5%
1992-2003	6.0%
2003-15	8.0%

- **LPG Reforms Resulted into Faster Economic Growth** The country has experienced significant improvements in its GDP growth rate, with average annual growth rates exceeding 7% in the past two decades. Thus, it was able to surpass the so-called Hindu rate of growth, which stagnated at 3.5% until the 1980s. Liberalisation of economy has kindled animal spirits leading to building of a competitive domestic industry.
- **Faster Decline in Poverty Levels** In the post-reform period, poverty declined faster in the 2000s than in the 1990s. Poverty declined by 1.36 percentage points per annum after 1991, compared to that of 0.44 percentage points per annum prior to 1991.

- **Trade Liberalisation** Economic reforms have focused on liberalising trade policies, reducing tariff barriers and promoting international trade. As a result, India's trade volumes have increased significantly and the country has become more integrated into the global economy. India's imports in FY23 rose 16.5 % to USD 714 billion as against USD 613 billion in FY22 while exports saw a rise of 6% to USD 447 billion in FY23, up from $442 billion in FY22.
- **Foreign Direct Investment (FDI)** Economic reforms opened up several sectors to foreign investment and relaxed regulations on FDI. This resulted in increased inflows of foreign capital into various sectors of the Indian economy, leading to technological advancement, job creation and overall economic development.
  - FDI has consistently increased from USD 62 billion in 2014-15 to around USD 84 billion in 2021-22, which is the highest ever FDI inflows into India.
- **Industrial Development** Liberalisation measures have boosted industrial development in India. The dismantling of industrial licensing, de-reservation of industrial sector and the reduction of bureaucratic hurdles have facilitated the establishment of new industries and encouraged existing ones to expand.
  - e.g., As of April 2022, India's auto industry is worth of more than USD 100 billion and contributes 8% of the country's total export and accounts for 7.1% of India's GDP.
- **Disinvestment of Public Sector** Government stakes in Public Sector Enterprises were reduced to enhance their efficiency and competitiveness.
- **Financial Sector Reforms** The financial sector in India has undergone significant reforms, including the deregulation of interest rates, the establishment of new private banks and the introduction of capital market reforms. These measures have led to the development of a more robust and efficient financial system, increased access to credit and improved financial inclusion.
- **Technological Advancements** The liberalisation policies have attracted foreign technology and expertise, facilitating knowledge transfer and technological advancements in various sectors.
  - **Example** The Indian IT industry has been generating substantial revenue. In the fiscal year 2020-2021, the industry's revenue was estimated to be around USD 194 billion, according to the National Association of Software and Service Companies (NASSCOM).
- **Improved Business Environment** Economic reforms have aimed to improve the ease of doing business in India by simplifying regulations, reducing bureaucracy and promoting transparency.
  - **Example** Initiatives such as the implementation of the Goods and Services Tax (GST) have streamlined taxation, while digitisation efforts have simplified administrative processes.

Incomplete Reforms

The reforms undertaken in 1991 leave much to be desired as can be seen below:

- India is still only at the bottom of the lower middle-income category.
- The share of the manufacturing sector in GDP remained stagnant at around 16%. It was 16.41% in 1989-90 and is 16.2% in 2015-16 and 17.4% in 2020.
- The disparities between the rich and the poor and between infrastructurally backward and more developed states have increased.
- Economic reforms have accelerated growth but failed to generate adequate employment. For example, the rural unemployment rate, after declining to 5.61% in 1993-94, rose to 7.21% in 1999-2000.
- The agriculture, urban informal sector and forest dependent communities did not see adequate reforms.

While India has undertaken significant economic reforms over the years, there are several areas where further reforms are still needed. Some reforms that have not yet been fully implemented in India include:

- **Labour Reforms** India's labour laws are often criticised for being rigid and restrictive, which can discourage employment generation and hinder the growth of businesses, especially small and medium-sized enterprises. Although multiple labour laws are codified into 4 labour codes, it has not been implemented in the country.
- **Land Acquisition Reforms** Land acquisition for industrial and infrastructure development has been a contentious issue in India. The current land acquisition laws are perceived as complex and time-consuming, leading to delays and increasing project costs.

- **Inadequate Infrastructure** India has not been able to invest adequately in infrastructure which could help in industrialisation of economy specially in railways. Lack of infrastructure remains the biggest impediment in growth of the manufacturing sector in India.
- **Financial Sector Reforms** Strengthening the banking system, improving access to credit and enhancing transparency and accountability in the financial sector are crucial for sustainable economic growth.
  - According to the World Bank, India's domestic credit to the private sector at 55% of GDP in 2020 is remarkably below the world average (148%) and lowest among its Asian peers — China (182%), South Korea (165%) and Vietnam (148%).
  - Priority Sector Lending (PSL) requirements arguably divert funds from productive sectors.
  - Government crowds out funds and makes the financial market fragile, which negatively impacts the growth of the corporate bond market in India.
- **Tax Reforms** The Indian tax system is complex, with multiple layers of taxes and numerous exemptions. Simplifying and rationalising the tax structure, reducing tax rates and minimising tax disputes can improve ease of doing business, promote investment, and boost economic growth.
- **Agricultural Reforms** Agriculture sector has remain untouched from liberal reforms which has restricted the flow of private investment required to increase productivity, reduce wastage and build a resilient supply chain. There is a need for further reforms to address issues related to agricultural productivity, market access, price volatility and farmer income.
- **Health and Education Reforms** India's health and education system faces several challenges, including quality gaps, skill mismatches and inadequate access to quality education, especially in rural areas.
- **Governance Reforms** There is also an issue of corruption in the bureaucracy and the police-judicial system. Public-sector corporations remain large, wasteful, and unreformed.

Way Forward

- **Ease of Doing Business** Improvements in the ease of doing business are essential to attract investments, promote entrepreneurship and encourage business growth. Simplifying regulations, reducing bureaucratic red tape and streamlining administrative processes can create a more favourable environment for businesses to thrive.
- **Tax Reforms** Continued tax reforms, including simplification of the tax structure, reduction of tax rates and minimising exemptions, can enhance business competitiveness and stimulate investment.
- **Labour Reforms** Rationalising labour regulations, promoting labour market flexibility and implementing fair and transparent labour practices can attract investments, stimulate job creation and enhance productivity.
- **Infrastructure Development** Significant investments in infrastructure are needed to support economic growth. Public-private partnerships and streamlined approval processes can help accelerate infrastructure projects.
- **Financial Sector Reforms** Strengthening the financial sector is crucial for sustained economic growth. Credit to Gap ratio need to be improved to fuel a rapid economic growth.
- **Agricultural Reforms** Comprehensive reforms in the agricultural sector are necessary to boost rural incomes, improve productivity, and enhance food security. Measures such as land reforms, contract farming, market reforms, irrigation development, and technological advancements can drive agricultural growth and rural prosperity.
- **Education and Skill Development** Investing in education and skill development is crucial to nurture a skilled workforce that can contribute to economic growth.
- **Governance and Anti-Corruption Measures** Strengthening governance, promoting transparency and implementing effective anti-corruption measures are essential for fostering investor confidence and ensuring a level playing field for businesses.
- **Environmental Sustainability** Incorporating sustainability principles into economic growth is vital for long-term development. Reforms should prioritise environmental protection, promote clean and renewable energy, encourage sustainable industrial practices and foster responsible resource management.

Conclusion

The economic reforms of 1991 have run its course and there is a need to introduce Economic Reforms 2.0 focusing on development of infrastructure and agriculture. India needs to de-nationalise banks and introduce complete rupee convertibility. In addition to it, further reforms related to land, labour, direct tax and financial sector are required.

It is crucial to ensure that the reforms are inclusive, equitable and mindful of social and environmental considerations to achieve sustainable and inclusive double-digit growth in India.

Change in the Nature of Planning

Q.12 Do you think that Indian development planning is a transition from centralised planning to indicative planning and subsequently to market-based development? Explain. (150 Words, 10 Marks)

Ans. **Introduction** India adopted a centralised planning approach after gaining Independence in 1947. The objective was to achieve rapid economic development through a planned and controlled economy but LPG reforms 1991 demanded a change in planning. Indicative planning started from eight Five Year Plan which involves setting broad development goals and providing guidelines while allowing more flexibility and market forces to play a role in resource allocation.

Centralised Planning in India

Planning Commission was constituted in 1950 with an aim to oversee the country's economic and social development, chiefly through the formulation of five year plans. The main objective of economic planning in India is to achieve balanced and sustainable economic growth that benefits all sections of society.

India adopted a centralised planning at the time of independence via the Planning Commission because of the following reasons

- **Adoption of Keynesian Ideas** After the Global Depression of 1929, it was realised that state (public sector) play an important role in economic growth which requires a planned approach to government resources. Such ideas were increasingly being adopted by various countries across the world.
- **Erstwhile Soviet Union became an Economic Superpower** Soviet Union was the one who adopted planned approach to economic and social development and it became an economic superpower and not affected by the Global Depression of 1929 unlike the Western countries.
- **Low Private Resources in India at the Time of Independence** and thus, Bombay Plan 1944 (group of various industrialists) emphasised upon planned approach to economic development.
- **Underdeveloped Indian Economy** The economy was faced with the problems of mass poverty, ignorance and diseases which were aggravated by the unequal distribution of resources between groups and regions.
- **Pre-Independence Continuity** A planned approach to development was started when National Planning Committee was constituted in 1938 under the chairmanship of Jawahar Lal Nehru.

Features of Centralised Planning in India

- **Five-Year Plans** India's planning process began with the introduction of the First Five Year Plan in 1951. These plans were formulated by the Planning Commission, which was responsible for setting development goals and allocating resources across sectors.
- **Interventionist State** The state influenced much of the economic activities of the private sector through various instruments like license and allocation of critical inputs, including foreign exchange under its control. This phase came to be known as license-permit-quota raj.
- **State Control and Public Sector Dominance** Centralised planning involved a significant degree of state control over key sectors of the economy. The government played a crucial role in resource allocation, investment decisions and ownership of key industries, leading to the establishment of public sector enterprises.

- **Industrial Policy Resolution, 1956** clearly stated that 'the state would assume predominance and direct responsibility for setting up new industrial undertakings and for developing transport facilities.'

- **Nationalisation of Key Industries** Coal mining and exploration, extraction, refining and distribution of crude oil, not within the exclusive public sector, were nationalised for spurring growth. Many textiles mills were nationalised to protect labour. Banks were nationalised in many phases in 1956, 1969 and 1980 to make available credit to priority sector and to expand branches in unserved areas.
- **Private Sector to play a Complementary Role** While centralised planning emphasised state control and public sector dominance, it also recognised the importance of private enterprise. Example Industrial Policy Resolution, 1956 classified the industries into three schedules under which Schedule A industries are reserved for the public sector while Schedule C industries are open to private sector.
- **Prioritisation of Key Sectors** Centralised planning focused on the development of key sectors such as agriculture, industry, infrastructure and social welfare. The plans aimed to address poverty, unemployment and regional disparities through targeted interventions in these sectors. e.g., Second Five year plan adopted Mahalanobis model to emphasis upon heavy industrialization.
- **Import Substitution** The Mahalanobis model aimed to reduce dependence on imports by promoting domestic production. It advocated for import substitution policies, encouraging the domestic production of goods that were previously imported.
- **Top-Down Approach** Centralised planning model followed a top-down approach in which decisions were taken at top and implemented at lower level. For states, the Planning Commissions would approve the state plans for expenditure.

Transition Towards Indicative Planning

India underwent LPG Reforms in 1991 and as the economy opened up for private sector, the role of government in economy needed to be more as a partner with private sector instead of controller of private sector. The economic planning was now to be based on competition instead of controls.

For the Planning Commission to be relevant in the post-reform era, it adopted indicative planning which is more flexible than centralised model of planning.

Features of Indicative Planning

- **Guidelines and Targets** Eighth Five Year Plan (1992-97) adopted the practice of Indicative Planning which sets broad guidelines, goals and targets for economic development. Instead of detailed, rigid plans, it provides a framework within which economic activities can be pursued.
- **From Resource Allocation to Social Sector** Instead of resource allocation or investment planning primarily through public sector investment unmindful of its productivity, the planning was now to be oriented to more towards development of social infrastructure, where market will fail in bringing balance between societal need and private supply.
  - Planning will continue to play an important role in the areas like environment and forest, rare minerals, land and water, where market fail to play an allocative role.
- **Private Sector Participation** Indicative planning encourages private sector participation and entrepreneurship. It recognises the importance of private enterprise in driving economic growth, innovation and job creation. Industrial Policy Resolution, 1991 emphasised upon de-reservation and de-regulation of various sectors.
- **From 'One-Size Fit All' Approach to Flexibility and Adaptability** Indicative Planning allows for flexibility and adaptability to changing circumstances and market dynamics. It recognises that economic conditions and priorities can evolve over time and plans need to be responsive to these changes.
- **From State-led to Market Mechanisms** Indicative Planning acknowledges the role of market forces in resource allocation. It allows market mechanisms, such as supply and demand, competition and price signals, to influence the allocation of resources and the functioning of the economy.
- **From Centralised to Decentralised Planning** Indicative planning often adopts a bottom-up approach, involving local governments, communities, and stakeholders in the planning process. It recognises the importance of local knowledge, preferences and needs in shaping development strategies.
  - **Example** 73rd and 74th Constitutional Amendment leads to Bottom-Up approach by creating District Planning Committees (DPCs).

- **Strategic Sectoral Planning** While indicative planning provides flexibility, it also identifies strategic sectors or priority areas for focused attention. These sectors may include infrastructure development, education, healthcare or sustainable development, where targeted interventions and investments are required.

Market Based Development

Replacement of Planning Commission with NITI Aayog has pushed market-based development in India. NITI Aayog, the policy think tank of the Government of India, has played a crucial role in promoting market-based development and economic reforms.

- **Shift from Centralised Planning** NITI Aayog was established in 2015 to replace the Planning Commission and usher in a new era of policy formulation. It signifies a shift from a centralised planning approach to a more market-oriented and decentralised approach. **Example** Aspirational Districts Programme which aims to improve the quality of life in 115 districts.
- **Cooperative and Competitive Federalism** NITI Aayog promotes cooperative federalism, giving more decision-making power to the states and encouraging competition among them to attract investment, improve governance and implement reforms. **Example** School Education Quality Index, State Health Index, Composite Water Management Index.
- **Advocacy for Economic Reforms** NITI Aayog has been a vocal advocate for economic reforms to enhance market efficiency and attract investment. It has actively recommended and supported policy initiatives such as the Goods and Services Tax (GST), bankruptcy code, labour reforms, ease of doing business measures and sector-specific reforms in areas like agriculture, healthcare, and education.
- **Public-Private Partnership (PPP)** NITI Aayog has emphasised the importance of public-private partnership in driving economic growth and development. It has advocated for increased private sector participation in infrastructure projects, social sectors and technology-driven initiatives.
- **Ease of Doing Business** Government is more committed to promote ease of doing business for attracting private and foreign investments in India rather than controlling the private sector.

Conclusion

The nature of planning in India has gone through various phases according to the demands of an economy in last 75 years from a centralised state-controlled process to a market-based method in which demand and supply play central role in the allocation of resources.

Critical Appraisal of NITI Aayog

Q.13 How the setting up of NITI Aayog has changed the planning perspective in India? Discuss the achievements and challenges of NITI Aayog since its origin. (250 Words, 15 Marks)

Ans. **Introduction** The setting up of NITI Aayog in 2015 replaced the Planning Commission, which was established in 1950. NITI Aayog is a think tank that provides strategic and technical advice to the government on policy matters. It is different from its predecessor in many perspectives from a centralised top-down approach to decentralised bottom-up approach with an aim to realise the idea of Minimum government and maximum governance.

Niti Aayog Has Shifted Planning Perspective in Many Ways

- **Shift from Centralized Planning** NITI Aayog has shifted the focus from centralized planning to decentralised planning. The institution promotes co-operative federalism and encourages states to take ownership of their development.
  - **Example** Aspirational Districts Programme which aims to improve the quality of life in 115 districts.
- **More Involvement of States** NITI Aayog involves State Governments in the planning process by creating a platform for dialogue between the Centre and the States. This has led to a more collaborative and cooperative approach to development planning.
  - **Example** School Education Quality Index, State Health Index, Composite Water Management Index.

- **Emphasis on Evidence-based Policy** NITI Aayog has a data-driven approach to policy making, which involves the use of evidence-based research and analysis. This helps to ensure that policy decisions are based on accurate information.
  - **Example** Digital India initiative.
- **No 'One-size Fits All' Approach** India is a diversified country and its states are in various phases of economic development along with their own strengths and weaknesses and in this context, a 'one size fits all' approach to economic planning is obsolete.
- **Focus on Innovation and Entrepreneurship** NITI Aayog promotes innovation and entrepreneurship as a means to achieve economic growth and development. It has launched several initiatives, such as the Atal Innovation Mission, to support startups and entrepreneurs.
- **Convergence than Silos** The work of NITI Aayog also includes cutting across the silos within the government, for example, still, the maximum number of malnourished children in the world are in India. **POSHAAN ABHIYAAN by NITI Aayog** is best place to achieve this convergence and push the agenda forward.
- **Promoting Economic Reforms** NITI Aayog has been actively involved in bringing reforms in the economy like agricultural sector in India. It has advocated for the implementation of various reforms, such as the model Agricultural Land Leasing Act and the Pradhan Mantri Fasal Bima Yojana, to improve the productivity and income of farmers.
- **Greater Emphasis on Social Sectors** NITI Aayog has placed a greater emphasis on social sectors such as health, education and social security. Example SDG index
- **Shift Towards Outcome-based Monitoring** NITI Aayog has shifted the focus of monitoring and evaluation from inputs and outputs to outcomes. This helps to ensure that policies and programmes are achieving their intended objectives.
  - **Example** Output-outcome monitoring framework.
- **Emphasis on Sustainable Development** NITI Aayog has placed a greater emphasis on sustainable development and environmental conservation.
  - **Example** E-Mobility, Atal Bhujal Yojana.
- **Encouraging Private Sector and Civil Society Participation** NITI Aayog has encouraged greater private sector participation in development planning through initiatives such as the Public-Private Partnership (PPP) model. This helps to leverage private sector resources and expertise for public good.
  - **Example** NGO DARPAN

Achievements of NITI Aayog

- **Co-operative and Competitive Federalism** Number of steps have been taken by NITI Aayog to **foster cooperative federalism through structured support initiatives** and engagement with the States/UTs on a continuous basis. These include meetings between the Prime Minister/Cabinet Ministers and all Chief Ministers; subgroups of Chief Ministers on subjects of national importance; sharing of best practices; policy support and capacity development of State/UT functionaries; launching of the Aspirational Districts Programme for development of backward districts.
  - It **encourages healthy competition among states** through transparent rankings, in various sectors, along with a hand-holding approach. Some of the indices launched by NITI Aayog are School Education Quality Index, State Health Index, Composite Water Management Index, Sustainable Development Goals Index, India Innovation Index and Export Competitiveness Index.
- **Adoption of Holistic and Long-term Planning** NITI Aayog has developed a comprehensive Vision Document, Strategy, and Action Agenda for India's development. The documents provide a roadmap for achieving the long-term vision and goals of the country and involve the identification of key challenges, opportunities, and specific policy interventions to address them.
- **Policy Formulation** NITI Aayog has played a crucial role in the formulation of various policies and initiatives in India. It has been instrumental in the formulation of the National Health Policy, the National Nutrition Mission, and the Atal Innovation Mission among others.
- **Digital Transformation** NITI Aayog has been at the forefront of India's digital transformation, spearheading initiatives such as the National Health Stack, National Strategy for Artificial Intelligence and Digital India. These initiatives are aimed at leveraging technology to improve service delivery, enhance transparency and promote innovation.

- **Balanced Regional Development** The programme has achieved significant success in improving development outcomes in these districts, with several districts recording improvements in areas such as health, education and agriculture. For instance, in 10 indicators of health, 73 Aspirational Districts have surpassed the state averages.
- **Ease of Doing Business** NITI Aayog has been instrumental in improving India's ranking on the Ease of Doing Business index. Through its close collaboration with State Governments, NITI Aayog has implemented several reforms aimed at simplifying regulatory processes and improving the ease of doing business in India.
- **Sustainable Development Goals** NITI Aayog has been actively involved in implementing the United Nations' Sustainable Development Goals (SDGs) in India. It has developed a comprehensive SDG Index for India, which tracks progress across 16 SDGs. NITI Aayog has also launched several initiatives. Example: E-Amrit for e-vehicle
- **Agricultural Reforms** NITI through its Model land leasing law, Agricultural Marketing and Farmer Friendly Reforms Index is working to transform agriculture in India.

Challenges Before NITI Aayog

- **Coordination with States** One of the biggest challenges faced by NITI Aayog is ensuring effective coordination with State Governments. While the think tank has made significant progress in promoting cooperative federalism, there is still a need to improve the level of engagement with State Governments to ensure that policies are implemented effectively.
- **Limited Financial Resources** NITI Aayog has limited financial resources at its disposal, which can limit its ability to implement its plans and initiatives. This is especially challenging in a country like India, where there are several competing demands for resources.
- **Data Availability** NITI Aayog's policy recommendations are heavily reliant on data and there have been challenges in accessing timely and reliable data. This has impacted the think tank's ability to make evidence-based policy recommendations in certain areas.
- **Implementation of Policies** Another challenge faced by NITI Aayog is the effective implementation of policies. While the think tank has played a key role in formulating policies, the implementation of these policies often falls under the purview of other government departments, which can result in delays and suboptimal outcomes.
- **Balancing Interests** NITI Aayog often needs to balance the interests of various stakeholders, such as State Governments, industry bodies and civil society organisations. This can result in competing priorities and trade-offs, which can be difficult to manage.
- **Capacity Building** NITI Aayog needs to build capacity within its own organisation as well as in other government departments to effectively implement policies.
- **Lack of Monitoring Power** NITI Aayog does not have any monitoring power over ministries and thus, effective implementation of policies and programmes becomes difficult.

Conclusion

NITI Aayog has made significant achievements in promoting cooperative federalism, policy formulation and ease of doing business in India. However, it also faces several challenges, such as limited financial resources, unequal development and limited participation of civil society. Addressing these challenges will be crucial for NITI Aayog to achieve its goals and promote sustainable development in India.

Mobilisation of Resources (Sources and Challenges of Resource Mobilisation)

Q.14 Along with highlighting the various sources of financial resource mobilisation, critically examine the challenges in mobilisation of resources in the current global environment. (150 Words, 10 Marks)

Ans. **Introduction** Resource mobilisation is a strategic process aimed at identifying and acquiring the necessary resources crucial for the development, implementation and sustained progress towards a national mission. In practical terms, resource mobilisation involves establishing and strengthening relationships with resource providers and enhancing skills, knowledge and capacity to effectively utilise these resources.

Sources of Financial Resource Mobilisation

- **Tax Revenues** Taxation is a primary source of revenue for governments. However, challenges such as tax evasion, aggressive tax planning and the existence of informal sectors hinder effective mobilisation of resources. In India, **the highest tax-to-GDP ratio stood at around 11.7% in 2021-22,** indicating a need for huge improvement. Most importantly, only 5% of the Indians pay tax.
- **Foreign Direct Investment (FDI)** FDI plays a crucial role in resource mobilisation by attracting foreign capital, technology and expertise. Challenges in this area include global economic uncertainties, policy instability, and competition from other countries.
- **Domestic Savings** Mobilising resources from domestic savings is essential for investment and economic growth. However, challenges such as low savings rates, financial illiteracy and lack of formal banking access in rural areas limit the potential for domestic resource mobilization. In India, **the gross savings rate was around 30% of GDP in 2021-22.**
- **Banks** They are the prime financial institutional source of resource mobilisation accepting deposits from the public and creates credit.
- **Angel Investors** Invests in small startups or entrepreneurs as a onetime investment to help the business propel or an ongoing injection of money to support and carry the company through its difficult early stages.
- **Innovation Funding** It is a SEBI registered venture capital fund focusing on Information and Communication Technologies and Life Sciences that invests in innovation led, early-stage Indian firms. Example India Innovation Fund.
- **Capital Markets** Raising capital through stock markets and bond markets is an important source of financing for businesses. Challenges include market volatility, regulatory complexities, and limited access to capital markets for small and medium-sized enterprises. As of April 2021, there were 5,582 listed companies in India with a total market capitalisation of approximately USD3.1 trillion.
- **Development Aid** Foreign aid can play a crucial role in resource mobilisation for developing countries. However, challenges include changing priorities of donor countries, conditionalities attached to aid and the need for effective utilisation of aid funds. In 2019, India received around USD 4.2 billion in development aid.
- **Remittances** Remittances from overseas Indians contribute significantly to India's resource mobilisation. Challenges in this area include fluctuations in global employment opportunities, economic downturns in host countries and the high cost of remittance transactions. **India is the largest remittance recipient country in 2021-22.**
- **Public-Private Partnerships** (PPPs) Collaboration between the public and private sectors can mobilise resources for infrastructure development. Challenges include policy and regulatory frameworks, project selection and risk-sharing arrangements. In India, PPP projects have faced challenges related to land acquisition, clearances and contract enforcement.

Challenges in the Mobilisation of Resources

- **Tax Evasion and Aggressive Tax Planning** One of the significant challenges is the **evasion of taxes and aggressive tax planning,** which reduces the amount of revenue collected by governments. In India, the tax gap, representing the difference between potential tax revenue and actual tax collection, was estimated to be around 5.8% of GDP in 2019-2020.
- **Illicit Financial Flows from Developing Countries** Illicit financial flows involve resources that have been obtained, transferred or used illegally or illicitly and is indicative of deeper structural problems of political governance in these countries.
- **Informal Economy** The existence of a large informal economy poses challenges in resource mobilisation. In India, the **informal sector accounted for approximately 45% of the country's Gross Value Added (GVA) in 2019-2020.**
- **Low Savings Rates** Mobilising resources from domestic savings is crucial for investment and economic growth. However, India's gross national savings rate was around 30% of GDP in 2020-2021, which is relatively low compared to other countries.
- **Limited Access to Formal Financial Services** Financial inclusion remains a challenge, particularly in rural areas, where access to formal banking and financial services is limited. In India, as of March 2021, around 190 million individuals still did not have access to formal banking services.

- **Volatile Capital Flows** Fluctuations in global capital flows can impact resource mobilisation, particularly in emerging economies like India. In 2020, India witnessed a net outflow of portfolio investment worth USD 16.6 billion due to the global economic uncertainties caused by the COVID-19 pandemic.

Way Forward

- **Improving Tax Compliance** Strengthening tax administration, utilising technology and raising awareness can curb tax evasion. For instance, **India's introduction of Goods and Services Tax (GST) simplified tax compliance and broadened the tax base.**
- **Promoting Financial Inclusion** Expanding banking networks, encouraging digital payments and providing financial literacy programmes can enhance access to formal financial services. India's **Pradhan Mantri Jan Dhan Yojana (PMJDY)** aimed to provide banking access to the unbanked population.
- **Attracting Investment in Infrastructure** Creating an attractive investment climate, streamlining regulations and offering incentives can attract infrastructure investment. **India's National Infrastructure Pipeline aims to** attract private investment in sectors like energy, transportation and urban infrastructure.
- **Implementing Measures to Reduce Unemployment and Underemployment** Promoting entrepreneurship, supporting job creation in key sectors and targeted programmes for youth and women can reduce unemployment. Initiatives like Make in India and Startup India foster entrepreneurship and job creation in India.
- **Strengthening Public-Private Partnerships (PPPs)** Enhancing the framework for PPPs can mobilise resources for infrastructure projects. For example, the development of smart cities in India involves collaborations between the government and private entities, attracting investments in sectors like urban infrastructure and technology.
- **Encouraging Foreign Direct Investment (FDI)** Creating an investor-friendly environment, simplifying regulations and offering incentives can attract FDI. **India's Make in India campaign** aims to promote FDI in sectors like manufacturing, defense and electronics, boosting resource mobilisation and economic growth.

Conclusion

Addressing these challenges requires concerted efforts, policy reforms and targeted interventions. It involves improving tax compliance, promoting financial inclusion, enhancing skills training and education, attracting investment in infrastructure and implementing measures to reduce unemployment and underemployment.

Savings vs Economic Development

Q.15 "The virtuous cycle of growth and development can only sustain if the savings rate is high in the economy". Explain the statement while highlighting the importance of 'Household savings' for a developing country such as India. (150 Words, 10 Marks)

Ans. **Introduction** The rate of savings has been an important economic variable for economic development of, particularly, countries like India. The extent of domestic savings is the only ultimate source for capital formation, which is indispensable for rapid economic development in India. The excess of income over consumption expenditure is referred to as savings.

Economic Survey 2022-23 observed that India's **Gross Domestic Savings is 28.2% in 2020-21 and under that, household sector contributes the highest in domestic savings.**

Classification of Domestic Savings

Domestic savings accrue from three sectors, which are as follows

- **Government or Public Sector** Government savings come from surpluses of public enterprises and other public financial institutions.
- **Private Corporate Sector** Private corporate sector comprises all non-government financial/non-financial corporate enterprises, co-operative institutions and quasi-corporate bodies. Savings of the private sector is also known as undistributed profits which is a part of profit in operating surplus included in national income calculations.

- **Household Sector** The household sector is the largest contributor to domestic saving. It is important as it reflects how efficiently savings are converted into investment with the role of the financial sector's intermediation in the process. These sectors include the saving of: Households (families), non-profit institutions like college, hospitals, etc and non-corporate business units. The saving of the household sector is taken as the sum of its investments in various instruments of financial saving and in the form of physical assets.

Household savings can be divided into three parts:

- **Physical Assets** The physical assets include housing, machinery, furniture, fixtures and real estate.
- **Financial Assets** currency, bank deposits, shares and debentures, claims on government, mutual funds, national savings certificates, life insurance funds and provident and pension funds.
- **Unaccounted Savings of the Household Sector** The unaccounted savings of the household sector are always kept in the form of gold, silver and durable goods on which information is very scanty.

Importance of Savings (especially Household Savings) for Growth and Development

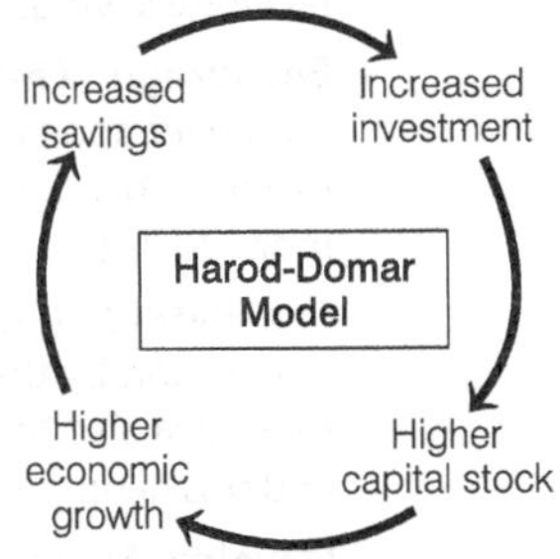

- **Investment and Capital Formation** A high savings rate provides a larger pool of funds available for investment. When individuals and businesses save a significant portion of their income, it allows financial institutions to channel those savings towards investment in productive activities such as infrastructure development, research and development and capital formation.
- **Investment and Productivity** Higher savings enable increased investment, which leads to improved productivity and economic growth. In India, private investment has a significant impact on GDP growth, accounting for around 70% of total investment
- **Reduced Dependence on External Borrowing** High savings rate reduces the need for external borrowing, enhancing economic stability.
- **Job Creation** Investment driven by savings leads to job creation, which is crucial for addressing unemployment and poverty.
- **Financing Social Development** High savings rate enables investment in human capital. India's expenditure on education as a percentage of GDP increased from 2.8% in 2010 to 3.2% in 2019, indicating investment in social development. This can help address social inequalities and improve the standard of living for marginalised sections of society.
- **Long-term Planning and Intergenerational Equity** High savings rates encourage long-term planning and investment in the future. Individuals and households with a culture of saving are more likely to allocate resources towards education, healthcare and retirement, ensuring intergenerational equity and a higher quality of life for future generations.
- **Financial Stability** A high savings rate enhances financial stability by providing a buffer against economic shocks and reducing reliance on external borrowing. Household savings in India amounted to 29.6% of GDP in 2020-2021 (Source: Reserve Bank of India).
- **Entrepreneurship and Startups** Savings enable individuals to accumulate capital for entrepreneurial ventures, promoting the growth of startups and fostering a culture of innovation. India is among the top countries globally in terms of the number of startups, with over 50,000 startups in 2020 (source: NASSCOM).
- **International Experience** It is observed that economies witnessing rapid economic growth such as China, India, Indonesia, Malaysia, Singapore, South Korea and Thailand are also characterised by high saving rates. Similarly, many countries in sub-Saharan Africa and Latin America typically save at a low rate and experience slow economic growth.
- **Foreign Direct Investment (FDI)** A high savings rate attracts foreign investors by signaling economic stability and providing domestic resources for investment. India has been one of the largest recipients of FDI, with cumulative inflows reaching USD 653 billion from April 2000 to December 2022

Measures to Boost Domestic Savings Rate Especially Household Saving

Boosting the domestic savings rate is crucial for economic development and investment within a country. Here are some measures that can help in increase the domestic savings rate especially household savings:

- **Tax Incentives** Provide tax incentives and benefits for saving and investment. Offer tax deductions or exemptions on certain savings instruments, such as retirement accounts, fixed deposits or specific investment schemes. These incentives can encourage individuals to save more by reducing their tax burden.
- **Pension and Retirement Schemes** Establish and promote robust pension and retirement schemes that provide individuals with a secure and attractive long-term savings option. **Example** Atal Pension Yojana.
- **Enhance Social Security Nets** Strengthen social security systems to provide a safety net for individuals, particularly in times of economic uncertainty or unforeseen events.
- **Promote Formal Financial Institutions** These institutions offer safe and regulated saving options, fostering trust and confidence among savers. Providing financial services to previously unbanked or underbanked populations can facilitate savings mobilisation.
- **Encourage Employer-Sponsored Savings Programmes** Encourage employers to establish and promote employer-sponsored savings programmes, such as provident funds or employee retirement schemes. These programmes can facilitate automatic deductions from salaries and employer contributions, making it easier for individuals to save regularly.
- The **PMRPY** (Pradhan Mantri Rojgar Protsahan Yojana) scheme aims to incentivise employers for employment generation by the government paying the full employers' EPS contribution of 12%, for the new employees, for the first three years of their employment and is proposed to be made applicable for unemployed persons that are semi-skilled and unskilled.
- **Develop Savings Culture and Behavioural Change** Promote a savings culture through awareness campaigns, education and public discourse. Behavioural interventions, such as setting savings targets, automatic transfers and nudges, can also encourage individuals to save consistently.
- **Strengthen Financial Inclusion** Enhance financial inclusion by improving access to financial services, especially in rural and underserved areas. Expand the reach of banking services, promote mobile banking, and develop innovative digital payment solutions to facilitate savings and financial transactions for the unbanked and underbanked population. Example: Pradhan Mantri Jan Dhan Yojana
- **Dealing with Tax Evasion** Plugging the loopholes for checking widespread tax evasion
- **Utilisation of excess capacity of these public sector undertakings** and also raising their efficiency;

Conclusion

By encouraging a high savings rate, India can sustain the virtuous cycle of growth and development, ensuring long-term economic prosperity and achieving its sustainable development goals.

Privatisation of Public Sector Banks (PSBs)

Q.16 The state-controlled section of India's banking sector continues to be a major problem for policy makers. Do you agree with this view? Discuss whether the privatisation of public sector banks is a solution to all the problems? (250 Words, 15 Marks)

Ans. Introduction Public Sector Banks (PSBs) are those banks where the government holds more than 50% ownership. As per RBI data, the share of Public Sector Banks (PSBs) in total credit by Scheduled Commercial Banks stood at 54.8% in March 2022 as compared to 65.8% five years ago and 74.2% 10 years ago. This indicates a significant but declining role of PSBs in Indian economy.

Budget 2021-22 announced the privatisation of two state-run banks and since then, privatisation of PSBs is thought of as a panacea for all the problems being faced by them.

Positive Contribution of PSBs

Public Sector Banks (PSBs) in India have made several positive contributions to the Indian economy. Here are some key areas where PSBs have played a significant role:

- **Financial Inclusion** PSBs have been instrumental in promoting financial inclusion by providing banking services to the unbanked and underbanked population by expanding their branch network to reach remote and rural areas. **Example:** Massive nationalisation undertaken in 1969 and 1980 changed the nature of banking to 'Mass banking' from 'Class banking'.
- **Infrastructure Development** PSBs have actively participated in financing infrastructure projects, including transportation, energy, and telecommunications. They have provided long-term loans and financial support for the development of critical infrastructure, contributing to economic growth and improving connectivity across the country. Example: Increased lending during the growth boom period of 2003-2008.
- **Credit to MSMEs** PSBs have been key providers of credit to Micro, Small, and Medium Enterprises (MSMEs). They offer specialized schemes and financial products tailored to the needs of MSMEs, supporting their growth and employment generation.
- **Implementing Government Programmes and Social Schemes** PSBs have played a vital role in implementing various government programmes and social schemes, such as Pradhan Mantri Jan Dhan Yojana (PMJDY), Pradhan Mantri Mudra Yojana (PMMY) and Atal Pension Yojana (APY). They have helped in providing banking services, loans and insurance coverage to millions of individuals under these schemes.
- **Stabilising the Banking System** PSBs have been the backbone of the Indian banking system, providing stability and resilience during times of economic volatility. Their widespread presence and government backing have instilled confidence in depositors and helped maintain financial stability.

Issues in Public Sector Banks (PSBs)

- **Non-performing Assets (NPAs)** The state-controlled banks in India have been struggling with a high level of NPAs for many years. The gross NPAs of public sector banks in India stood at around 5.53% in December 2022 (from the peak of 14.6% in March 2018) of their total loans. This has affected the profitability and lending capacity of these banks.
- **Capital Adequacy Ratio (CAR) Requirements** State-controlled banks in India also face challenges with much higher capital adequacy norms (RBI recommendation of 12%), which limits their ability to lend and expand their operations.
- **Inefficient Management** The state-controlled banks in India are known to have inefficient management practices. According to a report by the Reserve Bank of India, public sector banks in India have a higher cost-to-income ratio than private sector banks indicating poor management.
- **Lack of Autonomy** The state-controlled banks in India also face challenges with autonomy in decision making. Political interference and bureaucratic delays have been major issues. For instance, the merger of several public sector banks was delayed due to issues related to the allocation of board seats and the transfer of employees.
- **Huge Corruption** Corruption is also a major issue in the state-controlled banking sector. There have been several cases of fraud and mismanagement in public sector banks in India, such as the USD 2 billion fraud at Punjab National Bank in 2018.
- **High Competition from Private Sector Banks** The state-controlled banks in India also face challenges with competition from private sector banks and foreign banks. Private sector banks have been growing faster than public sector banks in terms of profitability and market share.
- **Slow Pace of Digitalisation** The state-controlled banks in India have been slow to adopt digitalisation, which has put them at a disadvantage compared to private sector banks. According to a report by KPMG, public sector banks in India lag behind in digital capabilities, with only a few banks offering advanced digital services.

- **Government Intervention** Government intervention in the state-controlled banking sector has been a double-edged sword. While government funding has helped public sector banks in times of crisis, it has also created moral hazard and led to lax lending practices. At present PSBs are under the dual control of the RBI and the Department of Financial Services of the Ministry of Finance. The RBI handles the governance side of the PSBs under the RBI Act, 1934.
- **Limited Regulatory Power of RBI over PSB's** The Standing Committee on finance noted that the RBI had stated that some powers available to the RBI under the Banking Regulation Act, 1949 are not available in the case of PSBs. These include: (i) removing and appointing Chairman and Managing Directors of banks, (ii) superseding the Board of Directors and (iii) granting licences.
- **Policy Paralysis** PSB officials fear of 3C's (CAG, CVC and CBI) unlike their private counterparts leading to policy paralysis.

Possible Impact from Privatization of Banks

Privatisation of Public Sector Banks (PSBs) can potentially bring several benefits to the banking sector and the overall economy. There are multiple reasons that why public sector banks should be privatised

- **Solution to Many of the Problems of Public Sector Banks** Privatisation can help in dealing with most of the issues of PSBs as highlighted above such as reducing NPAs, improving governance and management, removing bureaucratisation, no dual control of RBI and government and thus, no oversight by 3Cs and improved technology adoption for bringing down the costs.
- **Improved Efficiency and Performance** Privatisation can introduce market discipline and increase competition in the banking sector. Private banks are often driven by profit motives and have a greater focus on efficiency and performance.
- **Access to Capital and Technology** Private banks generally have greater access to capital markets, enabling them to raise funds more easily for expansion and investment. New investors, both domestic and foreign, who can infuse capital and technology into the banks, thereby enhancing their capabilities to adopt advanced banking technologies and innovative practices.
- **Enhanced Risk Management** Private banks are typically more proactive in managing risks due to their profit-oriented approach. Privatisation can, therefore, help mitigate the risks associated with non-performing assets (NPAs) through credit appraisal mechanisms, loan recovery processes and stricter lending criteria and improve overall asset quality.

Gross NPAs as a Proportion of Gross Advances : 2003-4 to 2020-21

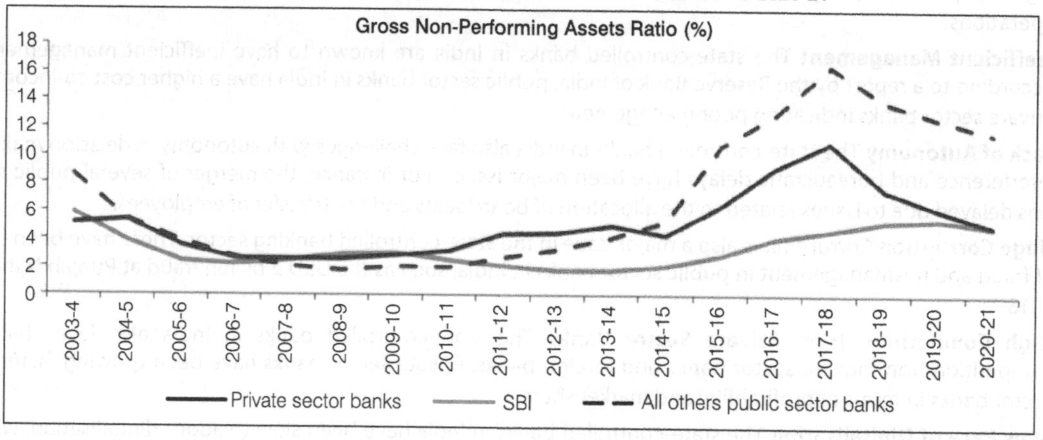

- **Fetches More Market Value** When the Economic Survey reviewed bank nationalisation in 2020, it was found that every rupee of taxpayer money invested in PSBs fetches a market value of just 71 paise. This is called the market to book ratio. In stark contrast, every rupee invested in new private sector banks fetches a market value of ` 3.70. In other words, private banks give more than five times more value than PSBs.
- **Innovation and Customer Focus** Private banks are more responsive to changing market dynamics and customer preferences, leading to the introduction of new products, services, and digital banking solutions.
- **More Branches and Thus More Jobs** It is observed that in the last 7-8 years, private sector banks have been able to open much more branches and consequently higher jobs in the banking sector.
- **Fiscal Impact** Privatisation can have positive fiscal implications for the government. The sale of government stakes in PSBs can generate revenue, helping in reducing fiscal deficits and allowing the government to redirect resources to other priority areas such as infrastructure, healthcare and education.

While privatisation can bring efficiency and innovation but it cannot be a panacea for all the problems faced in banking sector. There are various concerns against the privatisation of banks:

- As per the stated policy of the Reserve Bank of India, banks cannot be run by industrial houses. However, excluding the industrial houses, there are no entities that have the required financial capability to take over any of the government banks.
- Private banks have a long history of failures, as noted above (>1500 banks failed between 1935-1969). Recently, the RBI had to come to the rescue of Lakshmi Vilas Bank and YES Bank by pumping of capital by other entities to save these banks. Bank failures and lack of Government intervention will increase the risk in the banking system.
- Banks owned by the sovereign government provide more comfort level to depositors. Expansion of private sector in banking will reduce consumer confidence in the sector.
- Private banks operate with the sole aim of adding shareholder value. In contrast, the government banks also try to serve society and ensure implementation of all government programmes for the social sector. Privatisation might have a negative impact on financial inclusion, agriculture credit etc.
- Bank workers are opposed to privatisation. as they fear loss of jobs.

PJ Nayak Committee recommendations for Reforming PSB's

- **Governance Reforms** The committee recommended several governance reforms, such as separating the roles of Chairman and Managing Director/CEO in PSBs, strengthening the role of non-executive directors, enhancing the independence of boards, and improving transparency and accountability in board-level decision-making.
- **Performance Evaluation** The committee emphasised the need for a robust performance evaluation system for boards, directors and the management of banks. It recommended the implementation of a formal performance evaluation process to assess the effectiveness of board members and senior executives.
- **Risk Management** The committee stressed the importance of strengthening risk management practices in banks. It recommended the establishment of dedicated risk management committees at the board level and the appointment of qualified risk professionals to enhance the risk management framework of banks.
- **Technology and Digital Banking** The committee highlighted the significance of technology and digital banking in the banking sector. It recommended that banks adopt innovative technologies to improve operational efficiency, customer experience, and risk management.
- **Human Resources and Compensation** The committee suggested reforms in human resource policies and compensation structures to attract and retain high-quality talent in the banking sector. It recommended the introduction of performance-linked compensation and greater flexibility in recruitment and promotions.

Conclusion

The recommendations of the PJ Nayak Committee aimed to strengthen governance practices, enhance transparency and improving the overall efficiency of bank boards in India should be implemented in letter and spirit. These recommendations should be followed for subsequent reforms in the banking sector, including changes in corporate governance practices and the appointment of independent directors in PSBs.

India's NPA problem and Bad Bank

Q.17 Explain the rationale behind the creation of Bad bank in India. Also, examine the structure of bad bank in India along with associated challenges. (250 Words, 15 Marks)

Ans. **Introduction** Indian banking sector has faced significant challenge of Non-Performing Assets (NPA) (loans which have gone bad) especially public sector banks having gross NPA to 14.6% in March 2018. While number of initiatives were taken by the Government and RBI for the resolution of NPA problem, the most recent and significant one has been the creation of Bad Bank in India. This is in line with the Economic Survey 2016-17 recommendations of setting up a centralised Public Sector Asset Rehabilitation Agency (PARA) to deal with the Twin Balance Sheet problem (TBS).

What is a Bad Bank?

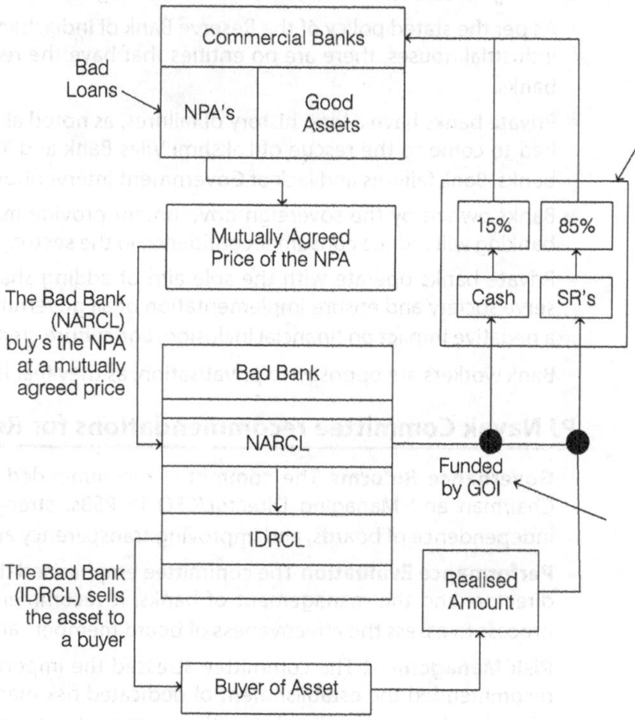

- The roots of a Bad Bank are in the SARFAESI Act, 2002. The Act provided banks and other financial institutions with a roadmap for the recovery of their bad loans. The Act also allowed the formation of Asset Reconstruction Companies (ARCs).
  - In 2002, India's first ARC was established called ARCIL. Henceforth, multiple private companies were registered with RBI as ARCs.
  - Banks were allowed to pass on their NPAs to ARCs. These ARCs in turn could approach the borrowers and manage the settlement of the outstanding loans.
- A bad bank is a specialised financial institution created to buy and hold Non-Performing Assets (NPAs) from other banks and financial institutions.
  - This way, the commercial banks will get rid of their bad loans (NPAs) thereby they can focus more on their core business and its growth.
  - The bad bank then works to recover the value of these NPAs through various means, such as asset reconstruction, debt restructuring or sale of assets.
- The primary objective of a bad bank is to help banks clean up their balance sheets by removing NPAs, thereby enabling them to focus on their core business of lending. This can also help to boost investor's confidence in the banking sector and support economic growth.

Structure of Bad Bank

- **Creation of National Asset Reconstruction Company Limited (NARCL)** It is a newly incorporated 'bad bank' set up by banks to aggregate and consolidate stressed assets for their subsequent resolution.
  - Public Sector Banks (PSBs) wil maintain 51% ownership in NARCL while rest will come from the private sector.
  - NARCL proposes to acquire stressed assets of about ₹ 2 lakh crore in phases within extant regulations of RBI.
  - It intends to acquire these through 15% cash and 85% in Security Receipts (SRs) and the contingency buffers offered by the government in the form of guarantee of ₹ 30,600 crore worth of Security Receipts (SR) issued by NARCL become important.
  - **Funding Sources** The funding for bad banks in India is expected to come from a combination of sources, including the government, banks and financial institutions, and private investors.

- **Operational Autonomy** Bad banks are expected to have operational autonomy in managing their assets and taking decisions related to resolution strategies. However, they will be subject to regulatory oversight to ensure transparency and accountability.

- **India Debt Resolution Company Ltd (IDRCL)** IDRCL is a service company/operational entity which will manage the asset and engage market professionals and turnaround experts.
  - Public Sector Banks (PSBs) and Public FIs will hold a maximum of 49% stake and the rest will be with private-sector lenders.
  - The NARCL will acquire assets by making an offer to the lead bank. Once NARCL's offer is accepted, then, IDRCL will be engaged for management and value addition.
  - The primary job of IDRCL is to handle the resolution process. They are responsible for conducting the auctions and selling the debt-linked assets for cash. The liquid cash so generated will then be used to clear the outstanding dues of the commercial banks.

Rationale behind the creation of a bad bank in India are as follows

- **Resolution of NPAs** The primary rationale behind the creation of a bad bank in India is to resolve the issue of high levels of Non-Performing Assets (NPAs) in the banking sector. As of March 2023, the gross NPA ratio of Indian banks stood at 5.5%, with public sector banks accounting for the majority of the NPAs.
- **Free Up Resources** Banks have to set aside a part of their operating revenue as part of provisioning requirements to cover up for the potential doubtful advances. A bad bank can take over the bad loans of the bank, thereby freeing up the bank from the provisioning requirements which means the unutilised money can be used for lending purposes.
- **Act as a Specialised Entity** A bad bank would be specialised in maximising the recovery out of a bad loan, as this would be its primary task. In contrast, banks are not in the business of recovery; therefore, their capability to resolve the loans is minimal.
- **Supporting Economic Growth** The bad bank will be capitalized by the government, which will enable it to purchase NPAs from banks at a discount. This will provide banks with the necessary capital to make new loans and support economic growth.
- **Address Risk Aversion Behaviour** It addresses a major bottleneck to India's growth over the last few years due to heightened risk aversion in the banking sector. This risk aversion was largely an outcome of piling up of non-performing assets in the system due to excessive lending between 2008 to 2012.
- **Professional Management** The bad bank will be managed by professionals with expertise in resolving NPAs. This will enable the efficient resolution of NPAs and maximise the value recovered.
- **Minimise Loss to the Banking system** The creation of a bad bank will help to minimize the loss to the banking system due to NPAs. It will enable banks to focus on their core business of lending and reduce the burden of NPAs on their balance sheets.
- **Boost Investor Confidence** The creation of a bad bank is expected to boost investor confidence in the Indian banking sector. It will provide a transparent mechanism for resolving NPAs and enhance the credibility of the banking sector.
- **International Best Practices** The creation of a bad bank is in line with international best practices. Countries such as the United States, Sweden and Spain have successfully implemented bad bank models to resolve their banking sector's NPA problems.
  - **Example** In 2012, Spain created the 'Sociedad de Gestión de Activos Procedentes de la Reestructuración Bancaria' (SAREB), also known as the Spanish Bad Bank. The Spanish Bad Bank model is often considered a successful example as it helped alleviate the burden of non-performing assets from the banking system, restored confidence in the financial sector and facilitated the recovery of the Spanish economy after the financial crisis.

Challenges for Bad Bank

- **Funding Constraints** The funding for bad banks is likely to come from the government, banks and financial institutions and private investors. However, raising funds may be a challenge due to concerns around the valuation of stressed assets and the risks involved in their resolution.
- **Asset Valuation** The valuation of stressed assets is a complex process and may be subject to dispute between the selling institutions and the bad bank. The bad bank may also face challenges in pricing the assets correctly to attract buyers. This can also lead to huge haircut for the banks. Also, banks have been cautious of taking big hair cuts because of the scrutiny from the 3 Cs (CBI, CVC and CAG).
- **Moral Hazard** The creation of a bad bank raises concerns about moral hazard. If the bad bank is seen as a bailout mechanism for troubled borrowers, it may discourage responsible lending practices and encourage future loan defaults.
- **Impact on Credit Culture** The establishment of bad banks may have unintended consequences on the credit culture in the country. It may encourage banks to take on excessive risk, knowing that they can transfer the stressed assets to a bad bank in the future.
- **Operational Efficiency** Bad banks may face challenges in managing and resolving a large volume of stressed assets efficiently. They may need to invest in technology and infrastructure to support their operations.
- **Legal and Regulatory Challenges** Bad banks may face legal and regulatory challenges in resolving stressed assets, especially those involving multiple lenders or complex structures. They may also face challenges in enforcing collateral or recovering dues from defaulting borrowers.
- **Asset Quality** Bad banks may need to deal with a large volume of stressed assets with varying degrees of quality. They may need to prioritise their resolution strategies based on the level of stress and the potential for recovery.
- **Fear of Unethical Practices** Since there would be pressure on the bad bank to perform, it is possible that the employees might turn towards unethical practices to boost recovery out of a bad loan. This has been a continuing
- **Not Addressing the Underlying Issue** Without governance reforms, the public sector banks (accounted for 86%, of the total NPAs) may go on doing business the way they have been doing in the past and may end up piling-up of bad debts again.
  - Also, the bad bank idea is like shifting loans from one government pocket (the public sector banks) to another (the bad bank).

Way Forward

Bad banks are only the firefighters. They are not going to prevent banks from generating more NPA. At present, the majority NPAs are also the result of oversight and corruption within the bank. Hence, banks must be held accountable for their NPAs. Also, regulatory oversight and proper risk management frameworks are essential to mitigate the risks associated with bad bank operations.

Insolvency and Bankruptcy Code, 2016

Q.18 Inordinate delays and deep haircuts have hampered the effectiveness of Insolvency and Bankruptcy Code (IBC), 2016. Examine and suggest measures to improve the performance of IBC. (250 Words, 15 Marks)

Ans. **Introduction** The bankruptcy proceedings in India were governed by multiple laws - Companies Act, SARFAESI Act, Sick Industrial Companies Act with courts and debt recovery tribunals all having a say in this process. This whole insolvency process used to take around 4.3 years to conclude in India and recovery amount was low of around 27%. To deal with twin balance sheet problem and exit problem in the banking sector, Economic Survey recommended the enactment of Insolvency and Bankruptcy Code. The code was introduced in 2016 to overhaul the corporate distress resolution regime in India and consolidate previously available laws to create a time-bound mechanism with a creditor-in-control model as opposed to the debtor-in-possession system.

Enactment of IBC has been a paradigm shift from the earlier loan recovery legislatures as in the earlier laws, borrowers were in control, in IBC it is the creditors who are in control over the recovery process.

About Insolvency and Bankruptcy Code (IBC)

- IBC was introduced in 2016 that aims to consolidate the laws relating to insolvency of companies and limited liability entities (including limited liability partnerships and other entities with limited liability), unlimited liability partnerships and individuals, presently contained in a number of legislations, into a single legislation.
- It covers all individuals, companies, Limited Liability Partnerships (LLPs) and partnership firms.
- A key innovation of the Insolvency and Bankruptcy Code is four pillars of institutional infrastructure.
- The first pillar of institutional infrastructure is a class of regulated persons, the 'Insolvency Professionals'. They would play a key role in the efficient working of the bankruptcy process. They would be regulated by 'Insolvency Professional Agencies'.
- The second pillar of institutional infrastructure is a new industry of `Information Utilities'. These would store facts about lenders and terms of lending in electronic databases. This would eliminate delays and disputes about facts when default does take place.
- The third pillar of institutional infrastructure is in adjudication. The NCLT will be the forum where firm insolvency will be heard and DRTs will be the forum where individual insolvencies will be heard. These institutions, along with their Appellate bodies, viz., NCLAT and DRATs will be adequately strengthened so as to achieve world class functioning of the bankruptcy process.
- The fourth pillar of institutional infrastructure is a regulator viz., 'The Insolvency and Bankruptcy Board of India'. This body will have regulatory over-sight over the Insolvency Professional, Insolvency Professional agencies and information utilities.

Impact of IBC

- **Behavioural Change**
  - It has initiated a cultural shift in the dynamics between lender and borrower, promoter and creditor.
  - It leads to responsible corporate behaviour by encouraging higher standards of corporate governance, including cash and financial discipline, to avoid consequences of insolvency.
  - The threat of promoters losing control of the company or protracted legal proceedings is forcing many corporate defaulters to pay off their debt even before the insolvency can be started.
- **Credit discipline** Ease of credit flow is necessary for attainment of Ease of doing business and economic growth. Under the IBC regime, ₹ 2.5 lakh crore has been brought back into the banking system as a result of resolution of insolvencies.
- **Increase in the resolution of stressed assets**
  - IBC which aims at the turnaround of the debtor while masimizing returns for the creditors with average recovery of nearly 43% under the IBC as against of 23% by early mechanisms.
  - A key objective of the IBC is to allow companies to be liquidated swiftly to maximise value if resolutions cannot be reached.
  - India improved its 'Resolving Insolvency' ranking from 137 in 2017 to 52 in 2020.
  - Out of the total admitted claims of ₹ 7.56 lakh crore under the IBC until December 2021, the recovery rate is 33.10% down from 35.89% at the end of September 2021. It is an improvement over the earlier mechanism.

Challenge-1 with IBC: Delay in the Resolution Process

While in 2018, when the timeline was 270 (180+90) days, most cases (from companies that owed less than ₹ 50 crore to those which owed more than ₹ 1000 crore) were completed in under 300 days. However, in FY22, it took 772 days to resolve cases involving companies that owed more than ₹ 1,000 crore.

Reason for Delays

- **Overburdened National Company Law Tribunal (NCLT)** Lack of adequate infrastructure, shortage of judicial members and inadequate technical capacity have resulted in delays in the disposal of cases.
  - For instance, of the 2,600 cases that were closed by December 2021, 55% ended in liquidation while only 16% were completed with proper resolution plans approved by the lender.
- **Lack of Qualified Insolvency Professionals** There is a shortage of qualified and experienced insolvency professionals who can effectively handle the resolution process.

- **Multiple Litigations** The IBC has witnessed numerous litigations, including challenges to the eligibility of resolution applicants and disputes related to the interpretation of the code.
- **Operational Challenges** Various operational challenges, such as incomplete or inadequate information provided by corporate debtors, difficulties in valuing complex assets and lack of cooperation from stakeholders can impede the smooth progress of the resolution process and result in delays.
- **Interplay with Other Laws** The resolution process under the IBC may be affected by other laws and regulations, such as environmental laws, labour laws and tax laws.

Challenge-2 with IBC: Deep Haircuts

One of the significant issues in the Insolvency and Bankruptcy Code (IBC) is the issue of haircut, which refers to the reduction in the value of outstanding debt that creditors may have to accept during the resolution process. The Parliamentary Standing Committee on Finance in 2021 noted an average haircut of 80% by the creditors in more than 70% of the cases in the 5 years of the IBC. As per The Hindu Data Team, almost 33 of 85 companies with more than ₹ 1,000 crore debt had been given haircuts above 90% by the lenders. **For example, the Videocon Group was given a haircut of 95.3% by the creditors.**

Reasons for Deep Haircuts

- **Distressed Financial Condition** Companies undergoing insolvency proceedings often have significant financial distress, with accumulated losses, high levels of debt and poor financial performance. As a result, the value of their assets may be insufficient to cover the outstanding debt, leading to deep haircuts.
- **Delay in Resolution Process** Legal and regulatory hurdles, including litigation and disputes, can delay the resolution process and impact the recovery value. Lengthy legal proceedings can erode the value of the assets and increase the likelihood of deep haircuts.
- **Lack of Competitive Bidding** The success of the resolution process depends on the participation of potential buyers and investors. In some cases, the lack of competitive bidding or limited interest from buyers can result in lower realisation from the sale of assets, leading to deeper haircuts.
- **Poor Asset Quality** The quality and marketability of assets held by the insolvent company can impact the recovery value. If the assets are non-performing or have limited demand in the market, the liquidation value may be significantly lower, necessitating larger haircuts.

Other Challenges in IBC

- There have been **more liquidations than resolutions.** As per the IBBI data of 3400 cases in the last six years, more than 50% of the cases ended in liquidation while only 14% cases found a proper resolution.
- **Digitisation of the IBC Ecosystem** The lack of digitisation has led to the insolvency process being stymied with long delays much beyond the statutory limits.

Measures to Improve IBC

- **Strengthening Infrastructure** Adequate infrastructure and resources should be allocated to the NCLT and the Insolvency and Bankruptcy Board of India (IBBI) to enhance their capacity to handle the increasing caseload efficiently.
- **Addressing Operational Challenges** Certain operational challenges have hampered the effectiveness of IBC. To overcome these challenges, the following steps can be taken:
- Streamline and simplify the processes involved in the resolution, liquidation and appeal stages.
- Develop a robust information management system to ensure seamless coordination and exchange of information among stakeholders.
- Enhance the quality and availability of professionals involved in the insolvency resolution process, such as resolution professionals, valuers and forensic auditors.
- **Capacity Building** Training and capacity-building programmss should be conducted to enhance the pool of qualified insolvency professionals which can alleviate some of the delays.
- **Fast-track Mechanisms** Introduction of fast-track mechanisms for smaller insolvency cases can help expedite the resolution process and reduce the burden on the NCLT.

- **Coordinated Approach** Cooperation and coordination among stakeholders, including lenders, resolution professionals, corporate debtors and regulatory authorities, are crucial to ensure the smooth progress of the resolution process.

Conclusion

IBC should be subjected to periodic review and amendments to address emerging challenges (such as introduction of Pre-packaged Insolvency Resolution Process (PIRP)/pre-packs) via IBC Amendment 2021) and incorporate feedback from stakeholders. This will ensure that the code remains relevant and effective in the long run.

Development Finance Institutions and NaBFID

Q.19 To what extent, Development Finance Institutions (DFIs) since Independence have achieved their objectives? How is 'National Bank for Financing Infrastructure and Development (NaBFID)' different from the earlier DFIs? (250 Words, 15 Marks)

Ans. Introduction With the enactment of National Bank for Financing Infrastructure and Development (NaBIFD) Act 2021, the focus now shifts from the need of a development financial institution for infrastructure development to making NaBFID structurally and operationally efficient and efficacious. This is important particularly in the background of experience of the DFIs like IFCI and IIIFCL which failed to deliver as expected.

National Bank for Financing Infrastructure and Development (NaBFID)

- **NBFID** NBFID is set up as a corporate body with authorised share capital of one lakh crore rupees. Shares of NBFID may be held by: (i) Central Government, (ii) multilateral institutions, (iii) sovereign wealth funds, (iv) pension funds, (v) insurers, (vi) financial institutions, (vii) banks and (viii) any other institution prescribed by the Central Government. Initially, the Central Government will own 100% shares of the institution which may subsequently be reduced up to 26%.
- **Functions of NBFID** NBFID have both financial as well as developmental objectives. Financial objectives will be to directly or indirectly lend, invest or attract investments for infrastructure projects located entirely or partly in India. Central Government will prescribe the sectors to be covered under the infrastructure domain. Developmental objectives include facilitating the development of the market for bonds, loans and derivatives for infrastructure financing.
- **Support from the Central Government** The Central Government will provide grants worth ` 5,000 crore to NBFID by the end of the first financial year. The government will also provide guarantee at a concessional rate of up to 0.1% for borrowing from multilateral institutions, sovereign wealth funds and other foreign funds.

Development Finance Institutions (DFIs)

The Development Finance Institutions (DFI) or Development Finance Companies (DFC) are organisations owned by the government or public institutions to provide funds for infrastructure and large-scale projects, where it often becomes unviable for large banks to lend.

Availability of medium to long-term funds for infrastructure projects has always experienced its fair share of difficulty due to primarily two reasons:

- Infrastructure projects are predominantly financed by banks. Shorter term resource (liability) base of banks, vis-à-vis long gestation period of projects (assets) makes an asset liability mismatch endemic in such bank finance.
- Corporate bond market is yet to attain vibrancy despite numerous initiatives.

DFI's Since Independence

- **IFCI** Industrial Finance Corporation of India was established in 1948 as a fully owned government enterprise. It is India's first Development Finance Institution.

- **ICICI** Industrial Credit and Investment Corporation of India Limited was established in the year 1955 by an initiative of the World Bank and was the first DFI in the private sector. ICICI Bank Limited was established in 1944 and in 2002; both were merged together making it the first universal bank of India.
- **IDBI** Industrial Development Bank of India was set up in 1964 under RBI and was granted autonomy in 1976. Back then it was responsible for ensuring adequate flow of credit to various sectors and was converted into a universal bank in 2003.

Critical Evaluation of DFIs

Positive Contribution	Challenges Faced by DFIs
Providing Long-Term Capital DFIs played a crucial role in providing long-term capital to industries like loans, equity investments to support the establishment and expansion of industries, including large-scale manufacturing, infrastructure projects and agriculture-related enterprises. **Risk Assessment and Management** They conducted thorough project appraisals, due diligence and risk analysis to evaluate the feasibility and profitability of industrial ventures, thereby promoting responsible lending practices.	**Funding Constraints** DFIs often rely on long-term funds for their lending activities. However, mobilising adequate long-term funds at competitive rates can be challenging. DFIs have faced difficulties in raising funds from the market, particularly during periods of economic uncertainty or when interest rates are high.
Sector-Specific Focus DFIs specialised in financing specific sectors such as agriculture, small-scale industries, housing and infrastructure. This sector-specific approach enabled targeted financial support to industries that were considered critical for India's economic growth and social development.	**Asset Quality and Non-Performing Assets (NPAs)** Like other financial institutions, DFIs face the risk of non-performing assets. High levels of NPAs can erode the profitability and financial stability of DFIs, limiting their ability to lend and support new projects.
Technical and Managerial Assistance DFIs not only provided financial support but also offered technical and managerial assistance to industries. They facilitated the transfer of technical know-how, expertise, and best practices to promote industrial efficiency, productivity and competitiveness. DFIs collaborated with international agencies and institutions to access global expertise and promote technological upgradation.	**Plagued with systemic issues** During the 1970-80s, DFI got discredited for mounting non-performing assets, allegedly caused by politically motivated lending and inadequate professionalism in assessing investment projects for economic, technical, and financial viability. **Example** IFCI in India and KFW in Germany were both created in 1948. Unfortunately, the irony is that KFW is currently running with an asset portfolio of something like US$ 26 billion whereas IFCI is reporting losses accumulated over time.
Catalysing Private Investment DFIs played a catalytic role in attracting private investment by providing a financial anchor for industrial projects. By participating as equity partners, offering guarantees and extending credit enhancements, DFIs encouraged private investors to join hands in industrial development, particularly in sectors with high capital requirements and longer gestation periods.	**Narsimhan Committee (1991)** recommended disbanding of the DFI and the existing DFI were converted into commercial banks. **Transition to Commercial Banks** With financial sector reforms and liberalisation in the 1990s, the role of DFIs diminished as commercial banks started offering long-term financing. DFIs like IDBI transformed into commercial banks, which impacted their focus and operations.
Development of Capital Markets DFIs played a crucial role in developing India's capital markets by acting as intermediaries between savers and investors. They mobilised funds from individual and institutional investors and channelled them into industrial projects, facilitating the growth of the financial sector and fostering investment opportunities.	**Governance and Efficiency** Some DFIs have faced governance challenges, including issues related to transparency, accountability and effective management practices.

Why National Bank for Financing Infrastructure and Development (NaBFID)?

- **Long-term Debt Financing Needs** A professionally managed Development Financial Institution is necessary to act as a provider, enabler and catalyst for infrastructure financing especially in the wake of Twin Balance Sheet problem which has affected public sector banks the worst.
- **National Infrastructure Pipeline aims to invest more than** ₹ 100 lakh crore on infrastructure projects and thereby, DFI can provide the much-needed finance.
- **High NPAs of Commercial Banks** The surge in NPAs in the banking sector and the need to augment financing of infrastructure for kick-starting the growth cycle have led to a renewed policy attention on setting up DFIs.
- **Reducing Stalled Infrastructure Projects** Stalled projects have high sunk cost to the economy. Out of 6835 projects identified in December 2019 under National Infrastructure Pipeline (NIP), only about 225 have been completed and the remaining face, among other things, funding issues.
- **High Economic Growth Rate** The COVID-19 pandemic has exacerbated inequality, the poverty gap, unemployment and the economy's slowing down. Thus, infrastructure building through DFIs can help in quick economic recovery.
- **Achieving the Target of USD 5 Trillion Economy** The government has envisaged attaining the target of becoming a USD 5 trillion economy by 2025. NITI Aayog has estimated that USD 4.5 trillion will be needed by 2030 to fund infrastructure. DFI is a step in the right direction towards this goal.
- **International Experience** DFIs in China, Brazil and Singapore has been successful in both domestic and international markets.

How is 'National Bank for Financing Infrastructure and Development (NaBFID)' different from the earlier DFIs?

National Bank for Financing Infrastructure and Development (NaBFID) is a new development finance institution (DFI) established in India. It was set up with an aim of providing long-term financing for infrastructure projects and promoting the development of the infrastructure sector in the country. While NaBFID shares some similarities with earlier DFIs, there are key differences that set it apart.

- **Mandate and Focus** NaBFID has a specific mandate to focus on financing infrastructure projects. Its primary objective is to provide long-term funds for infrastructure development across various sectors, such as energy, transportation, water supply and telecommunications.
  - In contrast, earlier DFIs had a broader mandate and were involved in financing a range of sectors beyond infrastructure.
- **Beyond Financing** The role of NaBFID goes beyond financing and extends to coordination with central and state governments, regulators, financial institutions, institutional investors and other stakeholders within and outside india to support infrastructure financing including domestic bonds and derivatives markets.
- **Ownership and Governance** NaBFID is owned by the Government of India and is expected to have a professional and autonomous governance structure. It will operate as a statutory body, governed by a board of directors comprising professionals from the finance and infrastructure sectors.
  - Earlier DFIs in India were either wholly owned by the government or had a significant government stake, but their governance structures varied.
- **Financial Resources** NaBFID has a planned capital base of ₹ 20,000 crore (approximately USD 2.7 billion), which will be infused by the government and institutional investors. It will also have the authority to raise additional funds from the market, both domestically and internationally.
  - Earlier DFIs relied primarily on government funding and loans from multilateral financial institutions.
- **Outside the purview of investigative agencies** NaBFID, as per the Act, will remain outside the purview of the 3Cs namely, CAG, CVC and CBI, for bonafide commercial decisions taken. For the first time, the law provides such an immunity to officers and employees of a bank/FI enabling faster decision-making and should help in bringing professionalism in the functioning of NaBFID.
- **Technology Integration** NaBFID intends to leverage technology in its operations, including the use of digital platforms for loan processing, monitoring and reporting. It aims to enhance transparency, efficiency and ease of doing business.
  - This emphasis on technology integration sets it apart from earlier DFIs that may have had limited technology infrastructure and digitisation capabilities.

Conclusion

The establishment of NaBFID reflects a focused approach to infrastructure financing and development, with an emphasis on professional governance, financial sustainability and technology integration. These aspects distinguish it from earlier DFIs in India and highlight the intention to address the evolving needs and challenges of the infrastructure sector in the country. Less the interference. more effective would NaBFID be. This also holds the key for government's plan to dilute its equity up to 26% over the years,in favour domestic and international investors.

Role of NBFCs in Indian Economy

Q.20 While bringing out the difference between NBFCs and banks, critically examine the role of Non-Banking Financial Companies (NBFCs) in the economic development of country. (150 Words, 10 Marks)

Ans. Introduction Non-Banking Finance Companies (NBFCs) form an integral part of the Indian financial system. They comprise a heterogeneous group of financial intermediaries and come under the regulatory purview of the Reserve Bank. They are gaining momentum in last few decades since 1990s. The banking sector is financing only 40% to the trading sector and rest is coming from the NBFC and private money lenders. At the same line 50% of the credit requirement of the manufacturing is provided by NBFCs.

About Non-Banking Finance Companies (NBFCs)

NBFC's are incorporated under Companies Act, 2013 and cater a wide range of financial services like the business of loans and advances, acquisition of stocks, bonds, securities, debentures or shares issued by the government or local authorities.

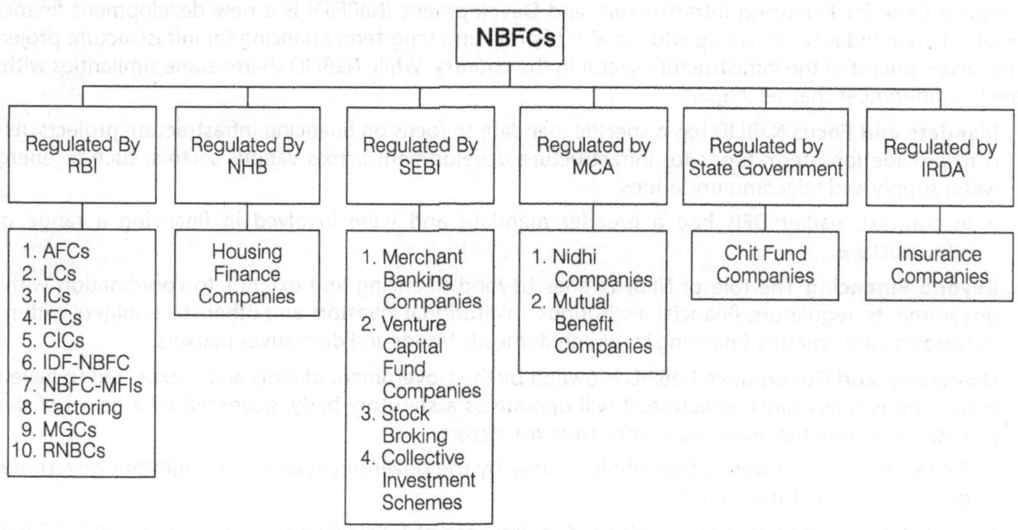

Difference Between NBFCs and Banks

Criteria	Banks	NBFCs
Establishment Act	Banking Regulation Act, 1949	Companies Act, 2013
Acceptance of Deposits	Both demand and time deposits permitted.	Demand deposits not allowed but time deposits allowed if the term of deposit is atleast one year.
Payment and Settlement System	Banks can issue cheques and form part of payment and settlement system.	NBFCs cannot take part in Payment and Settlement Systems i.e., it cannot issue cheques drawn on itself.

Criteria	Banks	NBFCs
Deposit Insurance Facility of DICGC	Available for the banks.	Not available for the NBFCs.
Foreign Investment	Upto 74% capital in banking companies may be acquired for foreign owners.	100% capital may be held by foreign owners subject of minimum capitalisation requirements under FDI.
Licensing Conditions	Licensing norms are tightly controlled and generally, it is perceived to be quite difficult to get a license for a bank.	It is comparatively much easier to get registration as an NBFC. Besides, there are NBFCs currently registered, many of which may be available for sale

Role of NBFCs in Economic Development

- **Inclusive Growth** NBFCs play an important role in promoting inclusive growth in the country, by catering to the diverse financial needs of bank-excluded customers. And very importantly, they also reach out to areas inaccessible to regular banking.
- **Promotes Financial Inclusion** NBFC-MFIs provide access to basic financial services such as loans; savings, money transfer services, micro-insurance etc to poor people and attempt to fill the void left between the mainstream commercial banks and money lenders.
- **Infrastructure Financing** NBFC's capitalize mega and large infrastructural projects which uplifts the economy at an extensive level. The long-term credit services with feasible interest rates ensure sustainable economic growth. Infrastructure Finance Companies and Infrastructure Debt Funds are NBFCs exclusively into financing the infrastructure sector.
- **Mobilisation of Resources** Non-banking financial companies help in rotation of resources, asset distribution and regulation of income to shape the economic development. They enable converting savings into investments and thus, helps in the mobilisation of funds/resources in the economy.
- **Factoring** NBFC-Factors are almost exclusively engaged in providing factoring service. This is perceived as complimentary to bank finance.
- **Boosting Capital Market** There are specialized NBFCs that are exclusively engaged in capital market investment i.e. trading in securities. These NBFCs therefore help in giving liquidity to the capital market. Further, NBFCs also lend to investors for investing in capital market.
- **Boost Employment** NBFCs help is attain the objective of macroeconomic policies of creating more jobs in the country by promoting small and medium scale enterprises and private industries through lending them loans.
  - The start-ups and small-sized businesses are dependent on funds offered by NBFCs.
- **Render Long-term Credit** NBFCs extend long-term credits to infrastructure, commerce and trade companies. The traditional banks expect timely, schedules and short-term repayment of loans that may not always suit the requirements of these industries.
- **Game-Changer in the Financial Sector** With quicker decision-making ability and prompt provision of services, NBFCs act as not just complements but also substitutes to banks.
- **Nurtures Standard of Living** NBFC also shapes up society by uplifting living standards. Such entities drive foreign endowments from various regions, countries and agencies to support economic development. Further, NBFC's participate in raising funds from the public and converting it into capital for industrial and several other sectors. An increase in emerging businesses raises the demand for manpower hence creates employment, which eventually raises the purchasing power of people and upgrades their living standards.

Challenges of NBFCs

- **Asset-Liability Mismatch:** NBFCs have been relying on raising short-term funds which were then lent as long-term loans. This leads to a situation of asset-liability mismatch. Several NBFCs are faced with a liquidity crunch (a time when cash resources are in short supply and demand is high), liabilities maturing and coming up for payment faster than loans in the same tenure.
- **Asset Quality Issues** A lot of these Non-Banking Financial Companies (NBFCs) are classified as housing finance companies. They lend money either to the developers or to the homebuyers. The end result is that the money lent out by these companies is heavily invested in the housing sector. The problem is that the Indian housing sector has gone bust. Stalwarts like Amrapali group, Supertech, Unitech, etc. have all gone bust. This creates a Four Balance Sheet Problem (Public Sector Banks, Corporates, NBFCs and Real Estate).
- **Defaults and Debts in the Sector** A major problem arose in the NBFC sector in September 2018 when there were large-scale defaults by some firms of the Infrastructure Leasing & Financial Services (IL&FS) group including subsidiaries and associate entities. The group incurred huge outstanding debt, estimated to be ₹ 91,000 crore, of which about ₹ 57,000 crore was from bank loans. This, in turn, adversely impacted the lending banks. Yet another major defaulter was Dewan Housing Finance, a non-banking housing finance company, which had an outstanding loan of close to ₹ 40,000 crore when the liquidity crisis erupted.
- **Misalignment in product Offerings with Customer Needs** Small NBFCs, in an effort to capture markets, have expanded into new geographic locations and diversified their product portfolio but are misaligned with consumer needs.
- **Lack of a Strong Regulator** Except for housing finance companies, it is also one of the challenges faced by NBFCs.

Conclusion

Over the years, NBFCs have played an important role in providing growth capital to various sectors of the economy. Concerted effort across stakeholders is required to prevent a financial contagion that can cut off the critical supply of capital to the grassroots of the nation.

Issues Relating to Employment (Formal vs Informal Sector)

Q.21 Do you think it is necessary to generate employment in the formal sector rather than in the informal sector? Give your opinion. Also, examine why the Indian economy is dominated by informal employment and identify the measures to be taken for greater formalisation of the economy. (250 Words, 15 Marks)

Ans. **Introduction** Economic Survey 2021-22 observed that close to 90% were in the informal nature of employment and it was observed that there are many different definitions of formal and informal sectors. The most common ones are: (a) whether a worker has a formal contract; (b) whether a worker is a regular/salaried worker (as opposed to self-employed or casual); (c) whether a firm is registered with any branch of the government; (d) whether the firm pays taxes and (e) whether a worker receives social security.

As per **National Commission for Enterprises in Unorganised Sector (NCEUS) classification**, "The unorganised sector consists of all unincorporated private enterprises owned by individuals or households engaged in the sale and production of goods and services operated on a proprietary or partnership basis and with less than ten total workers." Formal sectors represent all jobs with specific working hours and regular wages and the worker's job is assured. Conversely, informal or unorganized sectors are the ones where the employees or the workers do not have regular working hours and wages and are exempted from taxes.

Need for Generating Employment in the Formal Sector

Need arises because of the various advantages of generating employment in the formal sector and certain challenges associated with the informal sector. Those are given below:

- **Protection of Labour Rights** In the formal sector, labour laws, enable the workers to protect their rights in various ways. On the other hand, informal sector lacks security both legally and economically. Therefore, there is the greater exploitation of the workers who are outside the reach of the labor legislation.

- **No Fixed Working Hours** Long working hours beyond labour standards are common in India in the unorganised sector. In particular, there is no fixed working time in the agriculture sector because there are no laws which can act as a guideline for farm workers' working conditions.

- **Better Wages and Social Security Protection** The workers in the formal sector form trade unions bargains with employers for better wages and other social security measures. They earn more than those in the informal sector. Workers and enterprises in the informal sector do not get regular income; they do not have any protection or regulation from the government workers are dismissed without any compensation.
- **Skill Development of Employees** The employers in the formal sector are motivated to invest in the upgradation of skills of employees while the informal employment does not result into any upgradation of skills.
- **Improved Production of Goods/Service** Contract workers do not feel as much loyalty to the company as regular workers would, reducing employers' incentive to invest in their training. Indeed, there is evidence that hiring contract workers today hurts a firm's productivity tomorrow, precisely because contract workers do not accumulate "firm-specific human capital".
- **Reduced Gender Disparity** Women constitute the majority of informal participants, but they receive the least benefits and are characterized by lower paying, income volatility, and the lack of a robust social safety net.
- **Increased Tax Returns** Informal operations pose many challenges to the government, like the inability to raise tax revenue, collect data and regulate firms. Formalisation leads to more tax revenues with an increase in tax-to-GDP ratio. Formalisation provides a level-playing field for tax-compliant entities, expanding the tax base so that the burden falls more equitably on all the players rather than a select few.
  - There will reduction in the generation of black money.
  - With increased revenue, government can invest in education, health, skill development etc.
- **No Separate Statistics** There are no official statistics available representing the true state of the economy, which makes it difficult for the government to make policies regarding the informal sector in particular and the whole economy in general.
- **Reduction of Poverty** Unorganised sector workers had a much greater rate of poverty in the organised sector than their counterparts.
- **Prevention from the Impact of Disaster/External Crisis** Many natural disasters such as floods, drought, famine, earthquakes and so on have devastating effects on the informal sectors. This problem is exacerbated by the lack of social security. Example: Unequal impact of COVID-19 on Migrant workers and formal IT professionals.

Reasons for Informalisation in Economy

- **Predominance of service-sector led growth** because of India's unique structural transformation requires skilled labour that was available with a miniscule section of the population.
- **Absence of thrust on labour-intensive manufacturing** which can lead to creation of formal employment for millions looking to move away from agriculture.
- **Impact of globalisation** It is said that globalisation has led to the informalisation of the economy and reduced formal employment in the following ways:
  - **Decline in public employment:** The proportion of formally employed workers fall as governments cut their work force unless.
  - **Restrictive labour laws** which promote contract hiring in order to circumvent rigid hiring and firing provisions.
  - Market-mechanisms and competition led to closure of obsolete industries such as textile mills, reducing formal jobs. The newer industries were capital intensive rather than labour intensive, thus absorbing lesser workforce than what they laid to retrenchment of.
- **Advent of the Fourth Industrial Revolution and automation** poses even more dangers to present formal sector jobs since workers with current skills will be rendered obsolete unless they undergo skill reorientation.
- India, with increasing integration into global economy, also suffered during various global crises such as the Southeast Asian crisis, Gobal Financial Crisis in 2008 and the Eurozone crisis in 2011. This shelved corporate expansion plans and led to closure of several industries, reducing formal sector employment.

- **Government Policies** As per Economic Survey - Dwarfism (smaller firms, employing less than 100 workers) dominate the Indian economy, these never grow beyond their small size in order to get tax benefits and incentives, and hold back job creation and productivity.
- **Lack of skill development of employees** which hindered their participation in the formal sector.

Measures to be Taken for Formalising the Economy

Government has undertaken various measures in the recent past to formalise the economy such as implementation of Goods & Service Tax, digitalisation of economy, launch of E-Shram portal, codification of labour codes and many other schemes such as PM SVANidhi-Micro Credit Scheme for street vendors.

Other measures which can also be taken to boost the formalisation the economy are as follows

- **Generation of Formal Sector Jobs** Making labour markets, as well as social safety nets, more flexible, investing in human capital and prioritising a conducive legal and policy framework, will lead to the creation of enough formal employment opportunities.
- **Strengthening of MSMEs** Which employ 40% of informal workforce will contribute to economic recovery, job creation and economic formalisation.
- **Simplifying Registration Processes** There is a need to ease rules for informal business conduct that will bring informal enterprises and their workers into the fold of formality.
  - A Self-Help Group initiative that organises informal workers can contribute to the creation of self-reliance and address issues related to their working conditions.
  - Labour compliance could be improved by standardising and simplifying procedures across several acts.
- **Skilling the Labour** Unless the labour force is not skilled and educated, they will not be accommodated in the formal sector and the efforts to formalisation will result in unemployment.
- **Financial support:** Giving financial support to help small-scale industries stand on their own is a crucial step in bringing them to the organised sector. Schemes like MUDRA loans and Start-up India are helping the youth carve a niche in the organised sector.
- **Comprehensive Data of Informal Sector:** It is necessary to build a comprehensive statistical base on various dimensions of the informal economy as an integral part of the National Statistical System, enabling policy makers to make informed decisions.

Conclusion

Contract labour use has grown throughout the world over the last few decades that provides badly needed jobs for the poor, but it harms workers' protection, earning predictability and social benefits and India is no exception. To exploit its demographic dividend, India's economy needs to create enough 'good jobs' – jobs that are safe and pay well and encourage firms and workers to improve skills and productivity.

Status of Unemployment and Multiple Agencies

Q.22 While giving an account of the status of employment trends in Indian economy, critically examine the methods used by various agencies in estimating unemployment data. (150 Words, 10 Marks)

Ans. **Introduction** A sound policy framework requires the support of robust institutions that collect and transmit good data regularly. This is especially true with respect to employment data collection which is provided by multiple agencies but each source or method faces certain challenges.

Status of Employment Trends

While there are many surveys conducted by the government to estimate employment and unemployment indicators, the most preferred one in the recent times is Periodic Labour Force Survey (PLFS). The latest annual findings of PLFS is available for 2021-22 which observed the following employment trends:

- **Labour Force Participation Rate (LFPR)** The percentage of persons in the labour force (that is, working or seeking work or available for work) in the population increased from 54.9% in the previous year to 55.2% (LFPR for male is 77.2% and for female is 32.8%) during 2021-22.
- **Unemployment Rate** It shows that the unemployment rate at 4.1% in 2021-22, compared with 4.2% in 2020-21. The rural areas recorded an unemployment rate of 3.2% and urban areas recorded an unemployment rate of 6.3%.
- **Worker Population Ratio (WPR)** It increased from 52.6% of the previous year to 52.9%.
- **Decline in Salaried Workers** The percentage of salaried people has dropped from 21.2% in 2019-2020 to 19% in 2021, which means that 9.5 million people have left the salariat and become jobless or part of the informal sector.
- **Dominant share of employment in Agriculture** The sectoral composition of the workforce shows that 45.6% of the workers in India are engaged in agriculture & allied activities, 30.8% in services and 23.7% in industry.
- **Formal vs Informal Employment** Around 90% of the population is engaged in informal sector.

Analysis of Informal Employment

- **Income-wise Analysis** The data showed that 94.11% of the registered informal workers have a monthly income of ₹ 10,000 or below.
- **Social Category Analysis** 74.44 percent of registered workers are below the socially backward classes, including 45.32 percent OBC, 20.95 percent SC and 8.17 percent ST. The proportion of the General Category workers is 25.56 percent.
- **Age-wise analysis** 61.72 percent of the registered workers on the portal are of the age from 18 years to 40 years, while 22.12 percent are the aged from 40 years to 50 years.
- **Gender analysis** 52.81 percent of registered workers are female and 47.19 percent are male.
- **State-wise** analysis Top-5 states in terms of registrations are Uttar Pradesh, Bihar, West Bengal, Madhya Pradesh and Odisha.
- **Occupation wise** Agriculture is at the top with 52.11 percent of enrolments done by those related to the farm sector followed by domestic and household workers at 9.93 percent and construction workers at 9.13 percent.

Agencies and Sources to Track Unemployment Data

The following are the agencies involved in the collection of employment data and their sources for the data. These sources may be classified into three broad categories: household surveys, enterprise and industry surveys and data from government schemes as detailed below.

- **Household Surveys** These are the primary method of generating employment and unemployment data. Of the available options, it is the one that covers most comprehensively the entire labour force and thus provides the most valid statistical estimates of employment and unemployment for an entire economy. This is especially true in India, where a large section of the workforce is either self-employed or spread over a vast number of small, unorganised enterprises.
- The following are the employment statistics collected from household surveys, of which two are periodical official surveys while the third is collected During decennial Census from households.
  - **Employment-Unemployment Survey** conducted by the National Sample Survey Organisation (NSSO) replaced by **Periodic Labour Force Survey (PLFS)** from 2017-18 on an annual basis.
  - **Annual Labour Force Survey** conducted by the Ministry of Labour and
  - **Decennial Population Census** conducted by the Registrar General of India and Census Commissioner.
- **Enterprise Surveys**
  - **The Economic Census** The Economic Census covers the entire universe of non-agricultural establishments regardless of size or sector. As such, it extends to both industrial and services establishments.
  - **Annual Survey of Industries** The Annual Survey of Industries (ASI) uses the enterprises registered under the Factories Act, 1948 as its sample frame and covers industrial units with 10 or more workers, if using power, and units with 20 or more workers, if not using power.

- Unorganised Sector Surveys of Industries and Services Using the Economic Census as the sample frame, the NSSO has occasionally conducted surveys of unorganised industry and services.
- **Quarterly Employment Survey** The Labour Bureau conducts the Quarterly Enterprise Surveys (QES) to measure employment in eight broad sectors of industry and services including manufacturing, construction, trade, transport, education, health, hotels and restaurants and business process outsourcing.

- **Government Schemes** Administrative data and government schemes are also potential source for gathering data on job creation. The former includes data from the Employees' Provident Fund Organisation (EPFO), the Employees' State Insurance Corporation (ESIC), the National Pension Scheme (NPS) and other similar sources relating to large private organisations.

Deficiencies in the Existing Surveys

- The major limitation of the surveys (whether it is household surveys or enterprise surveys) is its low frequency and the time lag between data collection and availability of the results. Typically, data collection takes place once every five years. The survey results usually become available with a lag of more than a year. This delay makes the data less relevant as policy inputs.
- Census data is collected only once in ten years, the estimates are available after much time lag. So these estimates rarely form the basis of formulation of employment policies.
- Enterprise surveys do not adequately cover the self-employed and farm workers.
- Economic Census fails to capture the entire non-agricultural workforce as it covers only those with 10 or more workers and thus, its coverage is very limited.
- Annual Survey of Industries provides a wide range of employment-related indicators, such as number of employees, man days, product(s) manufactured, capital invested, value of plant and machinery, wages and salaries, PF contribution, workmen welfare expenses, etc., but has rarely been used to count the total number of workers in the economy.
- The Annual Survey of Industries has several gaps such as out-dated sample frame, limited coverage and time lag in collecting data.
- Further, available fields for drawing samples for such surveys often do not cover small, unorganised enterprises and, therefore, leave out workers employed by them.
- Sources in administrative datasets are even more partial in coverage than enterprise surveys. Also, individuals enrolled in them may be those already working but not previously enrolled, so duplication must be guarded against.
- Jobs generated in education and health sectors are particularly important from the viewpoint of job creation and they can provide valuable data. But this source is limited by its highly partial coverage.

Periodic Labour Force Survey (PLFS)

- Considering the importance of availability of labour force data at more frequent time intervals, National Statistical Office (NSO) launched Periodic Labour Force Survey (PLFS) in April 2017.
- It is India's first computer-based survey which has been constituted based on the recommendation of a committee headed by Amitabh Kundu.
- The objective of PLFS is primarily two-fold:
  - To estimate the key employment and unemployment indicators (viz. Worker Population Ratio, Labour Force Participation Rate, Unemployment Rate) in the short time interval of three months for the urban areas only in the 'Current Weekly Status' (CWS).
  - To estimate employment and unemployment indicators in both 'Usual Status' (ps+ss) and CWS in both rural and urban areas annually.

Conclusion

Periodic Labour Force Survey was started in 2017–18 to provide a rich source of data for examining labour and employment issues and for designing appropriate policies to address them.

Demographic Dividend and Employment Creation

Q.23 To capitalise on its demographic dividend, India must create well-paying, high productivity jobs. In view of this, discuss the challenges in creation of such jobs in India. What policy measures can help in addressing these challenges? (250 Words, 15 Marks)

Ans. Introduction According to Economic Survey 2018-19, India's demographic dividend will peak around 2041, when the share of working-age, i.e. 20-59 years, population is expected to hit 59%. Also, more than 54 % of our population is younger than 25 years in age.

About Demographic Dividend

Demographic dividend is a situation of having a relatively larger working-age population than non-working age population in a country. A fall in the dependency ratio and availability of surplus resources for investments results in economic growth. At a later stage of this demographic transition, when the working-age population starts maturing, the motivation to save increases. When these additional savings are channelled efficiently, it prolongs the economic growth leading to a second demographic dividend.

Asian economies such as Japan, South Korea and China were able to benefit from the rise in their working population by managing to engage their population in productive employment, which enabled sustained periods of high growth. Similarly, the creation of well-paying and high productivity employment opportunities for its bulging workforce will be crucial for India if it wants to escape falling into the 'middle-income trap'.

Challenges in the Creation of High Productivity Jobs

- **Jobless Growth** India experienced job growth of 3% per annum in the 70s at a time when India's economy grew at 33.5% per annum but over the last 3 decades India's economy grew at over 5-8% per annum but job growth has been close to 1% per annum Employment elasticity has fallen from close to unity in the 70s to 0.4 in the 90s to less than 0.1 today.
- **Impact of Automation** It is expected that automation will lead to displacement of labour and apart from loss of jobs, those workers may be displaced geographically to other places in search of alternate jobs causing emotional stress to them and their families.
  - Nearly 12 million Indian women could lose their jobs by 2030 owing to automation, according to a McKinsey Global Institute Report.
- **High Dependence on the Informal Sector** Around 90 % of the labour force (mostly unskilled and semi-skilled) is employed in the less productive and low paying informal sector.
- **Low Human Development Parameters** At rank 132 on the Human Development Index, 2021 and 107 on the Global Hunger Index, 2022 India lacks behind on crucial human development parameters. It has negatively affected the efficiency of the workforce and its potential to engage in high productivity employment opportunities.
- **Low Female Labour Force Participation** Periodic Labour Force Survey 2021-22 estimates that LFPR for female is 32.8%) during 2021-22.
- Lack of **Quality Education and Required Skill Sets** The troubling scenario of education and skills is evident from the data of Pratham survey of 2018, which shows that just half of the children in the 5th standard could read a text from the 2nd standard. According to another survey, at least 47% of graduates in India are not employable for any industry role.
- **Poor Skill Development** The 2015 Report on National Policy on Skill Development and Entrepreneurship estimated that only 4.7% of the total workforce in India had undergone formal skill training compared with 52% in the US, 80% in Japan and 96% in South Korea.
  - According to the India Skill Report, 2019, only 45.6% of the youth graduating from educational institutions are employable.
- **Stagnant Manufacturing Sector** Though the sector has multiplier effect over employment generation, it contributes just 16% of the GDP.
  - Domestic manufactures face high tariffs leading to higher raw material cost at home, emanating from the unfavourable inverted duty structure. E.g., Electronics sector.

Policy Measures in Addressing the Challenges

The government has taken many steps to create well-paying, high productive jobs, such as the codification of the labour laws, ease of exiting a business (Insolvency and Bankruptcy Code), increased investment in infrastructure, Pradhan Mantri Kaushal Vikas Yojana, Make in India initiative, Atmanirbhar Bharat, Start-up India and Stand-up India, Pradhan Mantri Mudra Yojana, etc. In this context, policy measures that require further attention are:

- **Rapid growth has to be central to any employment strategy** for the simple reason that a faster growing economy will generate more jobs.
- **Growth of stronger clusters and networks of small enterprises** MSMEs create more employment per unit of capital, and support inclusive growth. They need to be organised in effective clusters.
- **Promoting Labour Intensive Industries** There are a number of labour-intensive manufacturing sectors in India such as food processing, leather and footwear, wood manufacturers and furniture, textiles and apparel and garments. Special packages, individually designed for each industry are needed to create jobs.
- **Decentralisation of Industries** Decentralisation of Industrial activities is necessary so that people of every region get employment.
- **Development of the rural areas** will help mitigate the migration of the rural people to the urban areas thus decreasing the pressure on the urban area jobs.
- **Boosting exports** Economic Survey 2019-20 suggests of integrating 'Assemble in India' under 'Make in India' particularly in network products which is also labour intensive and will increase India's share in world exports.
- **Investment in human capital** There is an urgent need to increase investment in sectors such as education, health and nutrition. Quality education and need-based training and skill enhancement should be the focus of educational and employment programmes.
- **Development of skills** through a combination of apprenticeships and training institutes run by the private sector, with an eye to the demand for skills in the market, is critical. This becomes more important in the context of Fourth Industrial Revolution.
- **Growth of a 'life-long learning' system** The formal education system must be supplemented by affordable and accessible, 'just-in-time, needs aligned' learning modules.
- **Rapid use of technology as an enabler** Technology can enhance productivity through increased market access, real-time information, quick dispute resolution, and development of transparent mechanisms. This would help in job creation as well as formation of Brand India that can attract investment.

Conclusion

Silo approaches will not produce the rapid changes required in the Indian employment ecosystem. Systematic methods must be applied by governments at all levels for consultative multi-stakeholder policy formulation and implementation.

Labour-Intensive Job Creation

Q.24 India's challenge of jobs requires the attention towards labour-intensive sectors. Examine the statement while highlighting certain sectors that can be emphasised. (150 Words, 10 Marks)

Ans. India's Job Challenge Recently, former RBI Governor, Raghuram Rajan said that the country's economic growth is "insufficient for the kind of jobs" it needs.

India is facing a job challenge on three aspects:

- **Low Employment Generation**
  - The unemployment rate in India has been hovering around 7% or 8%, up from about 5% five years ago, according to the Centre for Monitoring Indian Economy. At the same time, the workforce shrank as millions of people dejected over weak job prospects pulled out, a situation that was exacerbated by COVID-19 lockdowns.
  - Unfortunately, the challenge of jobs is not reflected in official statistics on unemployment. According to Periodic Labour Force Survey, 2021-22, unemployment rate is 4.1% on usual status basis in 2021-22.

- **High Informal Jobs:** Around 90% of the population is engaged in informal sector. Thus, India faces the challenge of creating 'good jobs' **which are formal and productive and** have the potential for broader social transformation and can generate exports and growth.
- **Low Female Workforce Participation Rate** As per Periodic Labour Force Survey (PLFS) data 2020-21, India's female workforce participation rate is 24.2% which is among the lowest for emerging economies (China had 61% of its women in workforce while the US had 55%). Also, there are considerable variations behind FWPR in rural (27.1) and urban (17%) areas.

Sectors for Job Creation

There are **two groups of industries** that hold the greatest potential for export growth and job creation.

First, there exists a significant unexploited export potential in India's traditional unskilled labour-intensive industries such as textiles, clothing, footwear and toys.

- The GVCs in these industries are controlled by **'buyer driven' networks** wherein the lead firms that are based in developed countries concentrate in higher value added activities such as design, branding and marketing.
- Physical production is carried out through sub-contracting arrangements, by firms in developing countries. Examples include the production networks of Wal-Mart, Nike, Adidas etc.
  - **Labour-Intensive Jobs** The data picked up from Economic Survey 2016-17 shows that the apparel sector is the most labor-intensive, followed by footwear. Apparels are 80-fold more labour-intensive than autos and 240-fold more jobs than steel. Leather goods are 33-fold more labor-intensive than autos and 100-fold more jobs than steel.
  - **Jobs Especially for Women** Apparels and Leather sectors offer tremendous opportunities for creation of jobs, especially for women. The opportunity created for women implies that these sectors could be vehicles for social transformation. In Bangladesh, female education, total fertility rates and women's labour force participation moved positively due to the expansion of the apparel sector.

Second, India has huge potential to emerge as a major hub for final assembly in a range of products, referred to as 'network products'.

- The GVCs in these industries are controlled by leading MNEs such as Apple, Samsung, Sony etc. In general, these products are not produced from start to finish within a given country; instead, countries specialise in particular tasks or stages of the good's production sequence.
- Labour abundant countries, like China, specialise in low skilled labour-intensive stages of production such as assembly while the richer countries specialise in capital and skill-intensive stages such as R&D.

Job creation by "Assemble in India for the World"

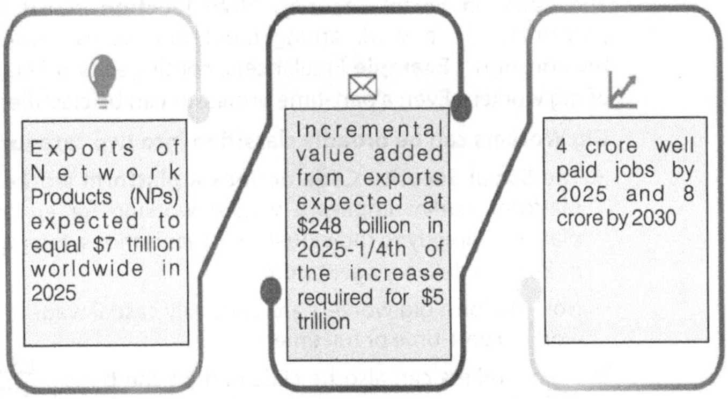

- **India is emerging as an assembly centre for telecom handsets.**

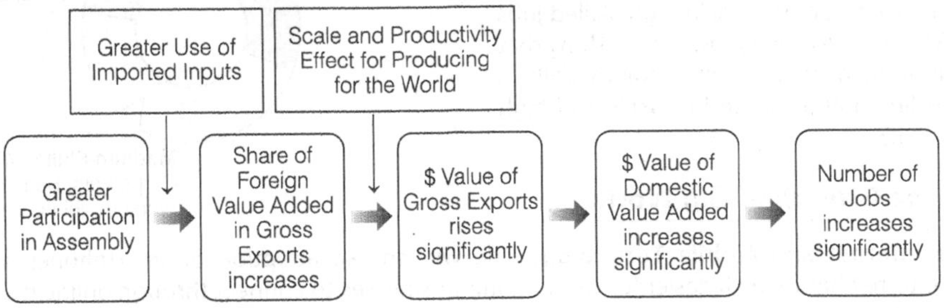

Conclusion

The most labour-intensive manufactures are food processing, leather and footwear, wood manufactures and furniture and apparel and garments. These product groups account for 50% of manufacturing employment in India (total manufacturing is 60 million of the total employment in India of 475 million in 2011-12). Unfortunately, however, it is the unorganised segment of these labour-intensive manufacturing firms that employ most workers, not the organised segment.

Gig Economy

Q.25 Along with highlighting the major drivers for the recent growth of gig workers, critically examine the challenges being faced by them. What measures should be taken by the government to address the challenges? (250 Words, 15 Marks)

Ans. **Introduction** According to recently released NITI Aayog report on Gig Economy, India's gig workforce is expected to expand to 2.35 crore by 2029-30. The report estimates that in 2020–21, 77 lakh (7.7 million) workers were engaged in the gig economy. An estimated 56% of new employment in India is being generated by the gig economy companies across both the blue-collar and white-collar workforce.

Gig Workers

- A gig economy is a free market system in which temporary positions are common and organisations contract with independent workers for short-term engagements.
- Gig workers have a non-standard work arrangement with their employers and share a non-traditional employer-employee relationship.
- Newly passed labour codes for the first time in India have defined gig and platform workers.
- The **Code on Social Security, 2020 [Section 2(35)] defines a gig worker** as 'a person who performs work or participates in a work arrangement and earns from such activities outside of traditional employer-employee relationships.' **Example** Freelancers, contingent workers, independent contractors, etc. can come under the umbrella of gig workers. Even a part-time professor can be classified as a gig worker.
- **Gig Workers can be broadly classified into two categories - platform and non-platform-based workers.**
  - The **Social Security Code defines a platform worker** as "a person engaged in or undertaking platform work". A platform worker implies a worker working for an organisation that provides specific services using an online platform directly to individuals or organisations. **Examples of platform workers** include Ola or Uber drivers, Swiggy or Zomato delivery agents, etc.
  - Non-platform gig workers are generally casual wage workers and own-account workers in the conventional sectors, working part-time or full time.
- The gig workers can also be classified on the basis of skills. These are high-skilled, medium-skilled and low-skilled workers. According to the NITI Aayog Report, at present, about 47% of the gig work is in medium-skilled jobs, about 22% in high-skilled jobs and about 31% in low-skilled jobs. Trends show that the concentration of workers in medium skills is gradually declining and that in low skills and high skills is increasing.

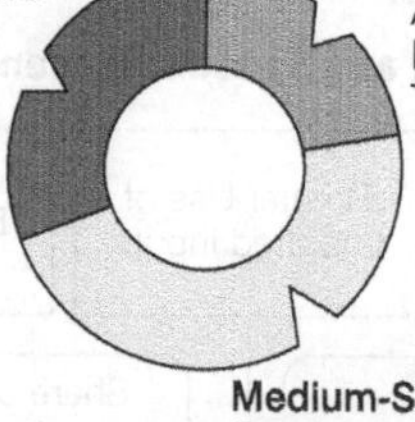

Drivers for the Growth of Gig Workers

- **Rise of the Internet and Mobile Technology** The widespread adoption of smartphones and the availability of high-speed internet has made it easier for workers and businesses to connect through online platforms, facilitating the growth of the gig economy.
- **Growth of E-commerce** The rapid growth of e-commerce in India has led to a significant increase in demand for delivery and logistics services, which has in turn led to the growth of the gig economy in these sectors.

- **Emergence of a Start-up Culture** The start-up ecosystem in India has been developing rapidly. For start-ups, hiring full-time employees leads to high fixed costs and therefore, contractual freelancers are hired for non-core activities. Start-ups are also looking at hiring skilled technology freelancers (on a per project basis) in areas such as engineering, product, data science and ML to bolster their tech platforms.
- **Economic Liberalisation** The Indian Government's economic liberalisation policies have led to increased competition and a more open market, which has encouraged the growth of the gig economy.
- **Increasing Demand for Flexible Work** The gig economy is particularly attractive for Indian workers who are looking for flexible work arrangements that allow them to balance their personal and professional lives.
- **Progressive Approach to Work by Millennials** The market is full of potential with the rise of globalisation and digital invasion. Work pressure and hectic schedules in private sectors have further changed the perception of millennials lately. Factors such as growth opportunities, a steady flow of jobs, a better work-life balance and flexibility encourage young talent to abandon corporate work culture freelancing.
- **Demographic Factors** The gig economy is also driven by the large and growing number of young, educated and ambitious Indians who are seeking to improve their livelihoods with side-income generation.

Challenges Faced by Gig Workers

- **Accessibility** Even though the gig economy is accessible to all those who are willing to engage in such employment, access to internet services and digital technology can be a restrictive factor. This has made the gig economy largely an urban phenomenon. This further exacerbates income inequality.
- **Job and Income Insecurity** Gig workers do not get benefit from labour regulations pertaining to wages, hours, working conditions and the right to collective bargaining. Example: Recent protest by the Blinkit workers. There are regular protests by the Ola and Uber workers.
- The contractual relationship between the platform owner and gig worker denies the latter access to many workplace entitlements.
- **Occupational Safety and Health Risks** Workers engaged in employment with the digital platforms, particularly, women workers in the app-based taxi and delivery sectors, face various occupational safety and health risks. This has been aggravated in the background of quick commerce culture (10 min delivery).
- **Skills Mismatch** Varying degrees of vertical and horizontal skills mismatch can be observed on online web-based platforms. According to International Labour Organisation (ILO) surveys, workers with higher educational achievements are not necessarily finding work commensurate with their skills.
- **Increasing stress** among the gig workers due to pressure from algorithmic management practices and performance evaluation on the basis of ratings.
- **Social Isolation** Gig workers may not have the same social connections and support systems as traditional employees, as they often work independently and may not have a physical workplace.
- **Lack of Data** There is a lack of data and research on the gig economy in India which makes it difficult for policy makers to understand its size, scope, and impact on the economy and workforce.

NITI Aayog Recommendations to Address the Challenges

- **Catalysing Platformization** A Platform India initiative, built on the pillars of accelerating platformisation by simplification and handholding, funding support and incentives, skill development, and social financial inclusion, like the immensely successful Startup India initiative, may be introduced.
- **Accelerating Access to Finance for Platform Workers** Access to institutional credit may be enhanced through financial products specifically designed for platform workers and those interested to set-up their own platforms. Venture capital funding, grants and loans from banks and other funding agencies should be provided to platform businesses of all sizes at the pre-revenue and early-revenue stages.
- **Skill Development for Platform Jobs** Platform-led models of skilling and job creation need to be promoted for the gig and platform sector. Platforms can collaborate with the Ministry of Skill Development and Entrepreneurship and the National Skill Development Corporation (NSDC) to nurture skilled workers and micro-entrepreneurship
- **Enhancing Social Inclusion in the New-age Digital Economy** Platform businesses can undertake partnerships with Civil Society Organisations (CSOs) to enable different sections of workers such as women workers and PwDs to take up employment opportunities in the platform sector through skill development, access to finance and assets.

- **Extending Social Security for Gig and Platform Workers in India** Platforms can offer paid leaves, and access to insurance along with pension and retirement benefits. Gig and platform firms may consider providing income support to workers. This will help in providing assured minimum earnings and social security from income loss in the wake of uncertainty or irregularity in work.
- **Recommendations for Future Estimations of Platform Workers** Undertake a separate enumeration exercise to estimate the size of the gig economy and identify the characteristic features of gig workers. During enumerations, collect information to identify gig workers. This could include questions on the nature of contract between worker and job creator, use of technology in work, etc.
- **RAISE Framework for Operationalising the Code on Social Security (CoSS), 2020** As Central and State Governments draw up rules and regulations under CoSS 2020, they could adopt the five-pronged RAISE approach to ensure realisation of full access to social security for all gig and platform workers:
  - Recognise the varied nature of platform work to design equitable schemes.
  - Allow augmentation of social security through innovative financing mechanisms.
  - Incorporate, while designing schemes, the specific interests of platforms, factoring the impact on job creation, platform businesses and workers. Support workers to subscribe to government schemes and welfare programmes through widespread awareness campaigns.
  - Ensure benefits are readily accessible to workers
- **Linking Women Empowerment with Gig Economy** There is a need to build the right physical and social infrastructure that supports the engagement of women in the gig workforce.

Social Security Code, 2020 Provisions for Workers

- The Code on Social Security, 2020, gives a legal identity to the term gig worker. The Code defines gig worker as a person who performs work or participates in a work arrangement and earns from such activities outside of traditional employer-employee relationship.
- Section 114 of the Code mentions that the Central Government may frame and notify suitable security schemes for the gig and platform workers. The matters covered in the Section 114 of the Code are; (a) Life and disability cover; (b) Accident Insurance; (c) Health and maternity benefits; (d) Old age protection; (e) Creche; (f) Any other benefit determined by the government.
- The Code recommends that schemes may be funded through a combination of contributions from Union and State governments, as well as gig platform aggregators.
- The National Social Security Board will have oversight of the welfare of gig economy workers and will include representatives of both aggregator companies and gig workers.
- The Code also mandates that the Union Government establish a Social Security Fund for gig economy workers.

Conclusion

Gig Economy has the potential to create jobs for India's large workforce, especially the low-skilled workers. The government must take appropriate steps to support the expansion of gig economy and platforms. At the same time, the interests of the gig workers must be protected to provide them with just work conditions as well as social security benefits. Achieving the balance will need some effort from all stakeholders.

Female Workforce Participation Rate (FWFPR)

Q.26 Female Workforce Participation Rate (FWPR) remains low in India despite economic development and rising education levels of women and girls. Discuss the reasons behind low female workforce participation rate in India. Suggest measures for improvement. (250 Words, 15 Marks)

Ans. **Introduction** As per Periodic Labour Force Survey (PLFS) data 2020-21, India's female workforce participation rate is 24.2% which is among the lowest for emerging economies (China had 61% of its women in workforce while the US had 55%.). Also, there are considerable variations behind FWPR in rural (27.1) and urban (17%) areas. According to a 2018 study by the ILO, more than 95% of India's working women are informal workers who work in labour-intensive, low-paying, highly precarious jobs/conditions and with no social protection.

Reasons behind low FWPR in India:

The decision of and ability for women to participate in the workforce is the outcome of various economic and social factors that interact in a complex fashion at both the household and macrolevel.

- **Lack of opportunities:** In recent times, rural distress has affected women the most as income-generating opportunities have disappeared. The problem of 'labour demand constraints' or the lack of suitable job opportunities is acute for women in rural India, with a fall in the availability of farm jobs and the lack of economic opportunities in non-farm employment.
- **Increased Mechanisation** Mechanisation of farm and non-farm activities has also reduced opportunities for work. Nearly 12 million Indian women could lose their jobs by 2030 owing to automation, according to a McKinsey Global Institute report.
- **Improving Women Literacy** With women aged above 15 increasingly enrolling for higher studies in colleges, their participation in workforce could have dropped.
- **Effect of Household Income** With increasing household incomes, especially over the last three decades, the need for a 'second income' reduced. This reduced women's participation especially in subsidiary activities 'secondary income' due to change in preferences. This effect is especially seen in urban women worforce.
- **Gender Discrimination:** For every woman, 98% of the inequality she faces would be caused by discrimination because of gender.
  - **Higher Education** Tertiary-level female enrollment rose from 2 percent in 1971 to only 30 percent in 2019 (World Bank data). As of 2018-19, only 2 percent of working-age women received formal vocational training, of which 47 percent did not join the labour force (NSSO, 2018-19).
  - **Skill Training** Consequently, women form only 17 percent of cloud computing, 20 percent of engineering, and 24 percent of data/artificial intelligence jobs (WEF, 2020).
  - **Wages** The World Economic Forum's gender gap report 2022, where India was ranked at 135th position out of 146 countries.
- **Gender Bias** Constraints in form of casteist and patriarchal notions of purity and pollution where women are prohibited from certain jobs, especially in the food processing, sericulture and garment industries has added to the low participation.
- **Familial Responsibilities** Unpaid care work continues to be a women's responsibility, with women spending on average five hours per day on domestic work. Women regularly sacrifice wages, career progression and education opportunities to meet family responsibilities, safety considerations and other restrictions.
  - This burden of unpaid work on women has been increasing disproportionately with a reduction in family sizes and distress migration of rural males.
- **COVID Effect** The COVID-19 pandemic has come as a shock, resulting in massive job losses for women, especially informal workers, and slower recovery of women-led micro businesses. It has also deepened gender digital divides, disrupted girls' schooling and placed millions of female health workers at risk.
- **Under Reporting** Finally, though most women in India work and contribute to the economy in one form or another, much of their work is not documented or accounted for in official statistics and thus women's work tends to be under-reported.
  - Economic Survey 2022-23 observed that for instance, clubbing productive work (collection of firewood, poultry farming) with domestic duties can in one sweep shift a significant proportion of women in the labour force into the out-of-labour-force category.
- **Other Factors** Lack of sanitation, sexual harassment at workplace, unsafe travelling, poor child-care facilities and care homes for the elderly etc. has prevented women from working in the industries.

Measures for Improvement

- **Providing Skill Training** Skill training of women in job roles aligned to the gig, platform and care sectors as well as other emerging sectors such as those covered under the Production-Linked Incentive Scheme needs to be encouraged.
  - Online skill training can also be beneficial to women who face constraints in physical mobility due to social norms, domestic responsibilities or concerns over safety.
  - Governments could introduce mandatory or incentives-based gender targets across skill training institutions.

- Enabling women to **acquire both physical assets** (through credit facilities, revolving funds, etc.) and **employable skills** is crucial for them to take up employment opportunities in new and emerging sectors.
- **Higher Public Investments** Greater investment in better health and care facilities would not only improve the well-being of India's people and hence their economic productivity, but will also lead to more employment opportunities for women.
  - **Example** National Education Policy (NEP), 2020 has set the goal to achieve 100% enrolment of girls in schools by 2035 and 50 % in higher education institutions.
  - Government has also started the practice of 'Gender Budgeting' since 2005-06.
- **Providing Child Care Services** This initiative will significantly support women in managing their care responsibilities, enabling them to devote sufficient time to paid employment.
  - The National Creche Scheme which lays out specific provisions for working women has suffered diminished government funding. Revitalising the provisions of the scheme and adding a network of public and workplace crèches can be hugely beneficial.
  - Child-care subsidies could be provided to free up mothers' time to enter the labour force which would have significant implications in increasing female employment.
- **Role of State Governments** State Governments may establish gender-based employment targets for urban public works.
- **Bridging Digital Divide** Firms and NGOs should come together to invest in bridging the digital gender divide, offering free mobile phones and laptops to girls from disadvantaged communities and offer long term training.
- **Equality Between Men and Women** The principle of equal remuneration for work of equal value that is protected by Indian law must be put to actual practice. Improved wage-transparency and gender-neutral job evaluation is required to achieve this end.

Conclusion

Women's labour force participation and access to decent work are important and necessary elements of an inclusive and sustainable development process. According to the IMF, raising women's participation in the labour force to the same level as men can boost India's GDP by 27%.

Policy makers in India should take a comprehensive approach to improve labour market outcomes for women through improving access to and relevance of education and training programmes, skills development, access to child care, maternity protection and provision of safe and accessible transport, along with the promotion of a pattern of growth that creates job opportunities.

Labour Codes and Impact

Q.27 To what extent, India's labour reforms will support the formalisation of India's labour market and improve its flexibility, with positive efficiency gains? Justify your opinion. (250 Words, 15 Marks)

Ans. Introduction The government in the recent past came up with four labour codes - Code on Wages 2019; Code on Social Security 2020; Occupational Safety, Health and Working Conditions Code (OSH&WC) 2020 and the Industrial Relations Code 2020 - to modernise the labour laws, protect the workers and for ease of doing business. The four codes subsume some 140 central and State labour laws and introduced new rules, regulations, concepts and definitions.

About Labour Codes

The Second National Commission on Labour (2002) (NCL) found existing legislation to be complex with archaic provisions and inconsistent definitions. To improve ease of compliance and ensure uniformity in labour laws, the NCL recommended the consolidation of Central labour laws.

- **Code on Wages, 2019** It combines multiple wage-related laws and introduces provisions for minimum wages, timely payment of wages and transparent wage calculation methods. The code provides a comprehensive framework for wages across industries and sectors.

- It universalises the provisions of minimum wages and timely payment of wages to all employees irrespective of the sector and wage ceiling and seeks to ensure 'Right to Sustenance' for every worker and intends to increase the legislative protection of minimum wage.

- **Industrial Relations Code, 2020** This code brings together provisions related to industrial relations, trade unions, and resolution of industrial disputes. It simplifies the process for forming trade unions and introduces mechanisms for dispute resolution.
- **Social Security Code, 2020** The Social Security Code amalgamates laws related to social security benefits, including provisions for old-age pension, health insurance and maternity benefits. It extends social security coverage to workers in the informal sector.
- **Occupational Safety, Health, and Working Conditions Code, 2020** This code consolidates laws related to occupational safety, health and working conditions. It sets standards for workplace safety, welfare facilities and employment conditions.

Impact of Labour Reforms

India's labour reforms have the potential to support the formalisation of the labour market and improve flexibility, leading to positive efficiency gains.

Formalisation of the Labour Market India's labour market has long suffered from a large informal sector, characterised by low wages, lack of social security and limited employment benefits. Labour reforms aimed at formalisation can address these challenges:

- **Simplified Labour Laws** Streamlining regulations can reduce multiplicity of definition and authority for business, reduce compliance burdens and thus, encouraging informal enterprises to transition into the formal sector.
  - The four codes subsume some 140 Central and state Saws (Labour is a concurrent subject in the Seventh Schedule) reducing the problem of 'regulatory cholestrol' which hampered the growth of formal sector jobs as observed by Economic Survey 2015-16.
- **Single Licensing Mechanism** The codes provide for a single licensing mechanism. It will give fillip to industries by ushering in substantive reform in the licensing mechanism. Currently, industries have to apply for their licence under different laws.
- **Universal Social Security** The reforms emphasise the expansion of social security coverage to all workers, including those in the informal sector. This can provide a safety net, increase workers' confidence, and incentivise formalisation.
  - It provides for universal social security for both organised and informal workers as well as gig and platform workers.
  - Provision has been made for creation of a Social Security Fund to fund schemes for extending benefits like death and accident insurance, maternity benefit and pension to cover 80% of the county's workforce who do not now come under any kind of social security cover.
  - A National Social Security Board will be set up for formulating suitable schemes for unorganized workers, gig workers and platform workers.
- **Skill Development and Training** Labour reforms also focus on enhancing skills and employability. By promoting training programms and upskilling initiatives, workers can acquire the necessary skills for formal sector employment, increasing their chances of formalisation.
  - Provision of Re-skilling Fund for skill development of workers. This assumes importance as old skills get redundant in the age of automation.
- Statutory provision has been made for the **first time to issue appointment letter to every employee of the establishment which leads to formalised contract of employment** that increases job security and enables a worker to claim statutory benefits such as minimum wages, social security etc .
- **Labor Market Reforms in Specific States** Apart from the Central reforms, some Indian states have implemented their own labour law reforms. For instance, states like Rajasthan, Madhya Pradesh and Uttar Pradesh have introduced amendments to labor laws to attract investments and promote ease of doing business.

Improved Flexibility

Flexibility in the labour market is essential for adapting to changing economic conditions, promoting job creation and fostering innovation. Labour reforms aim to enhance flexibility in the following ways:

- **Promotion of Big Enterprises** Under the Industrial Relations Code, 2020, the threshold for layoffs and retrenchment has been raised from 100 workers or more to 300 workers. Thus, establishments with less than 300 workers have flexibility in setting terms for hiring and firing.
- **Restrictions in Trade Unions** Trade unions that have a membership of at least 10% of the workers or 100 workers will be registered. Earlier, workers could go on strike by giving between two weeks and six weeks of notice. Henceforth, under the Industrial Relations Code, trade unions have to give 60 days' strike notice.
- **Fixed-Term Employment** The reforms introduced provisions for fixed-term employment contracts, allowing employers to hire workers for specific projects or seasonal work. This flexibility can encourage hiring and reduce the hesitation of employers to take on permanent employees.
- **Ease of Doing Business** Simplified labour laws and compliance procedures can reduce administrative burdens for businesses making it easier to start and operate formal enterprises. This can lead to more job opportunities and increased formal sector participation.
- **Labour Market Mobility** Reforms that facilitate labour market mobility by removing restrictive barriers can improve efficiency. For example, the reforms introduce provisions for inter-state and intra-state portability of social security benefits, enabling workers to move across regions more freely.
- **Gig Workers and Platform Workers** Recognising the growing gig economy, the reforms address the rights and welfare of gig workers and platform workers. The codes outline provisions for their social security coverage, working conditions and dispute resolution.

Potential Challenges from Labour Codes

- **Implementation by the States** As labour laws in India come in the Concurrent List of the Constitution, the Centre and the states must pass and notify these. The Centre has notified the rules, but the states have not.
  - Some states have approved one or two of the four new labour codes. The Maharashtra cabinet approved the Industrial Relations Code rules in March.
  - One of the disagreement states has is the uniform definition of wage in the Code of Wages. It has introduced a concept called floor wage that will be determined by the Centre. No State Government can fix a minimum wage lower than the floor wage. This removes the difference between the wages of male and female labour for the same work.
- There can be delay in the nation-wide roll out of labour reforms due to the **2024 General Elections.**
- **Opposition by the Trade Unions** There are various provisions in the labour codes such as notice of 60 days before going to strike, no mention of single scheme for unorganised worker, etc are being opposed by the trade unions.
- **No-Right Based Framework** The Code does not emphasise social security as a right, nor does it make reference to its provision as stipulated by the Constitution.
- **Monitoring and Enforcement** Adequate enforcement mechanisms and capacity building for regulatory authorities are necessary to ensure compliance and protect workers' rights.
- **Small Startups and Informal Sector Left-out From Social Security Coverage** There are no specific provisions for social security of employees in small startups, Micro, Small and Medium Enterprises or workers in small establishments having less than 300 workers. This would enable companies to introduce arbitrary service conditions for their workers.
- **Urban Centric** The codes fail to extend any form of social protection to the vast majority of informal sector workers which is predominant in rural areas including migrant workers, self-employed workers, home-based workers and other vulnerable groups.
- **Addressing Informality** Labor reforms should address the informal sector comprehensively, ensuring that workers in informal occupations are not left behind.
- **Issue of Invisible Labour** None of the new codes address the issue of invisible labour. Invisible labour has the most arduous job profile, with no weekends off, no working hours, no vacations, no recognition, onerous chores and are of course, unpaid.
  - Childcare, household work, looking after the elderly are some examples of unpaid work and constitute invisible labour.

Conclusion

The recent labour law reforms in India aim to strike a balance between worker protection and ease of doing business. The consolidation of labour laws, expansion of social security coverage and provisions for flexibility in employment contracts are significant steps toward modernising the labour market and improving worker welfare. However, effective implementation, monitoring and addressing the concerns of various stakeholders will be crucial to ensuring the desired outcomes of these reforms.

National Employment Policy (NEP)

Q.28 "India needs a National Employment Policy (NEP) that would encompass a set of multi-dimensional interventions covering a whole range of social and economic issues." Elaborate. (150 Words, 10 Marks)

Ans. **Introduction** India, despite achieving an impressive and steadily rising economic growth in recent years, still faces the twin challenge of creating adequate decent employment opportunities for young men and women joining the labour market every year (As per PLFS Report 2020-21, Unemployment rate is 4.2%) and facilitating the transition from informal to formal employment for those already in the labour market (around 90% of the workforce is employed in informal sector).

Underlying Principles of National Employment Policy (NEP)

There is need to create a National Employment Policy (NEP) that would encompass a set of multidimensional interventions covering a whole range of social and economic issues affecting many policy spheres and not just the areas of labour and employment. The policy would be a critical tool to contribute significantly to achieve the goals of the 2030 Agenda for Sustainable Development.

The underlying principles for the National Employment Policy may include enhancing human capital through skill development; creating sufficient number of decent quality jobs for all citizens in the formal and informal sectors to absorb those who are available and willing to work; strengthening social cohesion and equity in the labour market; coherence and convergence in various initiatives taken by the government; supporting the private sector to become the major investor in productive enterprises; supporting self-employed persons by strengthening their capabilities to improve their earnings; ensuring employees' basic rights and developing an education training and skill development system aligned with the changing requirements of the labour market.

Multi-dimensional Interventions in National Employment Policy (NEP)

- **Analysing and Improving Labour Market Data** Availability of detailed, reliable and comprehensive information on the labour market is critical to meet the employment challenge through well-targeted policies and programmes. At present, the dearth of statistical data on the labour market in India poses serious constraints to employment planning and promotion. The policy would lay stress on an effective Labour Market Information System (LMIS) for identifying skill shortages, training needs and available employment opportunities.
- **Synergy between Different Sectors of the Economy** Employment creation is not restricted to one sector or policy. It covers various sectors and is impacted by various polices. In India, employment promotion is identified as one of the important milestones of various programmes. The National Employment Policy will ensure coordination and coherence across policy initiatives and programmes in different sectors.
- It needs to focus on labour-intensive sectors such as apparel and textiles, leather and footwear and there exists a huge potential to emerge as a major hub for final assembly in a range of products, referred to as 'network products'.
- **Education and Skill Development** Skill-mismatch, formal skill training and re-training is seen as a significant issue for employability. The advent of automation, the growing importance of digital ecosystems and independent work are challenging labour markets around the world while also creating new and better opportunities. The National Employment Policy will ensure that the education, training and skill development system is aligned with the changing requirements of the labour market under Industry 4.0.
- **Improving Women's Participation in the Economy** With just 25.1% of women in the LFPR as per PLFS 2020-21, the numbers of women in the workforce remain strikingly low compared to other developing countries. No single policy intervention will address the full range of constraints they face.

The content of the NEP, in line with SDG 5 on Gender Equality, will focus on developing women's human capital and capabilities and investing in their ability to adapt to changing labour markets; providing support for their care responsibilities; establishing gender-sensitive labour market regulations; and enhancing their voice and capacity for collective action.

- **Employment and Income in Agriculture** Improving livelihood opportunities and income of those engaged in agriculture is extremely important and would have an impact on the effort to end poverty in all its forms (SDG 1) and for reducing inequality (SDG 10). The contents of the NEP would incorporate new and innovative ways to get over the problem of land fragmentation, make farmers a participant in higher value addition and skilling rural youth in new technologies that can be incorporated in agriculture and agro-based industries.
- **Micro and Small Enterprise and Entrepreneurship Development** The Micro, Small and Medium Enterprises (MSMEs) are the largest generator of employment. However, it is essential that they have access to training, incubator support to develop and execute their ideas and credit to finance their ventures. The contents of the NEP would include measures for creating awareness among these units to leverage the facilities offered to them by and the government and simplifying processes through which they can avail these facilities.
- **Targeted Programmes for Employment Generation** Targeted Programmes for employment generation, particularly those that take the form of an Employment Guarantee Scheme create a role for the government in the provision of employment to all those willing and able to work, should the labour market not offer such employment. The National Rural Employment Guarantee Scheme in India has already achieved a significant breakthrough in providing a certain level of employment security, particularly to informal workers and strengthening public works.
- **Employment Opportunities for the Vulnerable Sections** The issue of promoting employment opportunities for minorities, SC/ST, the differently abled and women within these categories, assumes greater importance given the relative disadvantages they may have experienced.
- **Employment and Labour Standards** Although the formal sector is largely protected by labour legislation and standards, it is important that policy initiatives are also focussed on improving incomes, working conditions, and promoting occupational health and safety for those engaged in the informal sector. The NEP would laydown strategies to incorporate the informal sector under the fold of labour legislation, social security and international standards.
- **Monitoring** The NEP would facilitate to establish an effective national coordinating and monitoring mechanism involving both state and civil society organisations to enhance employment promotion and creation.

Conclusion

While seeking to improve the overall enabling environment for accelerated economic growth and employment promotion, the formulation of a National Employment Policy would thus provide the roadmap for achieving sustainable economic growth while strengthening social cohesion and equity in the employment and livelihoods landscape.

Critical Analysis of MGNREGA

Q.29 What are the core objectives of the Mahatma Gandhi National Rural Employment Guarantee Scheme (MGNREGS)? Critically analyse its efficacy in dealing with the challenge of rural unemployment. (250 Words, 15 Marks)

Ans. **Introduction** MGNREGS was introduced through an Act of Parliament, Mahatma Gandhi National Rural Employment Guarantee Act, 2005, to enhance the livelihood security of people in rural areas by guaranteeing hundred days of wage employment in a financial year to a rural household whose adult members (at least 18 years of age) volunteer to do unskilled work.

- The Central Government bears the full cost of unskilled labour and 75% of the cost of material (the rest is borne by the states).
- It is a demand-driven, social security and labour law that aims to enforce the 'right to work'.
- Ministry of Rural Development (MRD), Government of India in association with State Governments, monitors the implementation of the scheme.
- Agriculture and allied activities constitute more than 65% of the works taken up under the programme.

Core Objectives of MGNREGA

- Providing not less than one hundred days of unskilled manual work as a guaranteed employment in a financial year to every household in rural areas as per demand, resulting in creation of productive assets of prescribed quality and durability.
- Strengthening the livelihood resource base of the poor.
- Strengthening of Panchayati Raj Institutions.

Achievement of MGNREGA

- MGNREGA has helped to **reduce rural poverty** to a greater extent, in turn, it has also been described as a 'stellar example of rural development' by World Development Report 2014.
- **Youngest Workers Rise** Share of the workforce in the 18-30 age bracket began moving up after the financial year 2017-18. The ratio of young workers among total MGNREGA workers has been rising to 9.1 % in 2018-19 and 10.06 % in 2019-20 from 7.73% in 2017-18.
- **Total Number of Individuals** For instance, 6.71 crores in 2014-15,7.21crore in 2015-16, 7.65 crores in 2016-17 and 7.76 crores in 2018-19.
- **Ensuring Livelihood for People in Rural Areas**
  - Large **Scale Participation of Women, Scheduled Castes and Scheduled Tribes (SCs/STs)** and other traditionally marginalised sections of society. SCs/STs account for 51% of the total person-days generated and women account for 47% of the total person-days generated.
  - Increasing the wage rate in rural areas and strengthening the rural economy through the creation of infrastructure assets.
- Facilitating sustainable development
- Strengthening PRIs by involving them in the planning and monitoring of the scheme.

Challenges

- **Large Number of Incomplete Works** There has been a delay in the completion of works under MGNREGA and inspection of projects has been irregular. Also, there is an issue of quality of work and asset creation under MGNREGA.
- **Fabrication of Job Cards** There are several issues related to the existence of fake job cards, the inclusion of fictitious names, missing entries and delays in making entries in job cards.
- **Low Wage Rates** Currently, MGNREGA wage rates of 17 states are less than the corresponding state minimum wages. The low wage rates have resulted in a lack of interest among workers in working for MGNREGA schemes, making way for contractors and middlemen to take control, locally.
- **Insufficient Budget Allocation** Almost every year, more than 80% of funds get exhausted within the first six months. Thus, the fund allocation is insufficient to ensure proper implementation on the ground.
- **Regular Payment Delays** Despite the order of the Supreme Court, no provision has yet been worked out for calculation of full wage delays and payment of compensation for the same.
- **Too Much Centralisation Weakening Local Governance** A real-time MIS-based implementation and a centralised payment system has further left the representatives of the Panchayati Raj Institutions with literally diminished its role in implementation, monitoring and grievance redress of MGNREGA schemes. It has hardly have any power to resolve issues or make payments.

Steps Need to be Taken

- **Regulation of Job Cards** Offences such as not recording employment related information in job cards and unlawful possession of job cards with elected PRI representatives and MGNREGA functionaries should be made punishable under the Act.
- **Participation of Women** Since the income of female workers typically raises the standard of living of their households to a greater extent than their male counterparts, the participation of women must be increased through raising awareness about MGNREGA.

- **Participation of People with Disabilities** Special works (projects) must be identified for people with disabilities and special job cards must be issued and personnel must be employed to ensure their participation.
- **Utilisation of Funds** Department of Rural Development should analyse reasons for poor utilisation of funds and take steps to improve the same. In addition, it should initiate action against officers found guilty of misappropriating funds under MGNREGA.
- **Context Specific Projects and Convergence** State Governments should be allowed to undertake works that are pertinent to their context. There should be more emphasis on skilled and semi-skilled work under MGNREGA.
- **Payment of Unemployment Allowance** Dated receipts for demanded work should be issued so that workers can claim unemployment allowance. Funds for unemployment allowance should be met by the central Government.
- **Regular Monitoring** National Level Monitors (NLMs) are deployed by the Ministry of Rural Development for regular and special monitoring of MGNREGA and to enquire into complaints regarding mis-utilisation of funds, etc. Frequency of monitoring by NLMs should increase and appropriate measures should be taken by states based on their recommendations.
- Additionally, social audits must mandatorily be held every six months.
- **Training of Functionaries** Training and capacity building of elected representatives and other functionaries of PRIs must be done regularly as it will facilitate their involvement in the implementation of MGNREGA.

Conclusion

Though the achievements of the programme in terms of its impact on rural demand, political participation, women's empowerment and improvement in rural infrastructure are hard to quantify, these have been crucial in sustaining the demand for the programme. MGNREGA has been a strong pillar on which the foundation of rural prosperity of the last decade has been based.

Automation vs Employment

Q.30 Critically analyse the impact of automation and new emerging technologies on employment and job creation. Outline the steps that India could take to prevent its adverse impact. (250 Words, 15 Marks)

Ans. **Introduction** ChatGPT, Google Bard and Microsoft Bing Chat are the Artificial Intelligence chatbots which have recently been in news. It raises the debate again about the impact of automation and other emerging technologies on the jobs.

Automation is an emerging trend which will have a perceptible impact on the way industry operates in the years to come. Advances in robotics, Artificial Intelligence (AI) and machine learning, autonomous transport, cloud computing and Internet of Things (IoTs) are ushering in a new age of automation, as machines match or outperform human performance in a range of work activities, including those which require cognitive capabilities.

According to ILO, 'Robotic automation is having the greatest impact, replacing low-skilled jobs and simple assembly tasks.' In the case of Japan and Thailand, the percentages of their activities being automated are 55.7 and 54.8 respectively and activities that can be automated across the world works out to over 40 %. **In the case of India, as much as 51.8 % of activities is amenable to automation.**

Impact on Employment and Job Creation

- **Job Augmentation** AI technologies can augment human capabilities by automating repetitive and mundane tasks, allowing workers to focus on more complex and higher-value activities.
- **New Job Roles** The adoption of AI often creates entirely new job roles and positions that didn't exist before. These roles include AI engineers, data scientists, AI trainers etc . The demand for these specialised skills is growing, resulting into job opportunities in emerging fields. Example: **New skills such as big data analytics, cloud and cyber-security services**, Internet-of-Things, among others as areas that would create job roles going ahead.
- **Industry Transformation** AI can revolutionise industries by enabling the development of innovative products, services and business models. This transformation can lead to the **creation of new businesses and startups, driving job creation in related sectors.**

- **Skill Development** The integration of AI technologies necessitates the development of new skills and expertise. This leads to increased demand for training programms, certification, and educational initiatives that focus on AI-related skills. (Learn, Unlearn and Re-learn)
- **Enhancing Productivity** AI can reshape existing job roles by automating repetitive tasks and enhancing focus on tasks that require creativity and problem-solving skills. This reshaping of job roles can lead to more productivity of human labour.
- **Entrepreneurship and Innovation** AI technologies can empower entrepreneurs and small businesses by providing access to advanced tools and resources. Startups leveraging AI can disrupt traditional industries, create new markets and stimulate job creation.
- **Safety of Workers** Worker safety is an important aspect of automating certain hazardous industrial operations. Automated systems keep workers away from endangered workplace, thus safeguarding them against the hazards of the factory environment.

Challenges (Negative Impacts) of Automation on the Labour force

- **Widespread Job Losses** AI technologies have the capability to automate repetitive and routine tasks, which can lead to job displacement for workers engaged in such tasks. According to the **World Bank (2016), in developing countries many more jobs are at risk: 69 % in India.** For Example, Entry level jobs in IT sector is facing serious risk of elimination with growing artificial technology.
- **Impact on Specific Industries** Some industries are more susceptible to job losses due to AI automation. For example, sectors such as automobile manufacturing, customer service, IT AND ITeS may experience significant disruptions as AI technologies are deployed.
- **Dislocation of Labour** Apart from loss of jobs, those workers may be displaced geographically having to relocate to other places in search of alternate jobs causing emotional stress to them and their families.
- **Higher Impact on Female Workforce** Automation threatens to impact women more than men as women form a large proportion of the workforce in retail, business processing outsourcing and textiles, clothing and footwear.
  - Nearly 12 million Indian women could lose their jobs by 2030 owing to automation, according to a McKinsey Global Institute report.
- **Skill Mismatch** AI implementation may require workers to possess new skills or upgrade their existing skills to adapt to changing job requirements.
- **Inequality and Job Polarisation** The adoption of AI technologies may widen the gap between high-skilled and low-skilled workers, contributing to income inequality. While AI may create new high-skilled job opportunities, low-skilled workers may face difficulties in finding suitable employment.

Steps that India could take to prevent its adverse impact are as follows

- **Comprehensive Adoption of AI** Government and private sector need to adopt AI in a comprehensive and holistic manner to reap its benefits and challenges.
- **National Strategy for Artificial Intelligence (AI)** In India it is a comprehensive plan developed by NITI Aayog to promote the development, adoption and responsible use of AI technologies across various sectors.
- **Reskilling and Upskilling Programmes** Implement comprehensive training programmes to reskill and upskill workers, enabling them to acquire the skills necessary to work alongside AI technologies. This includes promoting digital literacy, data analytics and other AI-related skills. Example: Microsoft, Nasscom's FutureSkills launched AI-skilling initiative in India.
  - **Budget 2023-24** launched Pradhan Mantri Kaushal Vikas Yojana 4.0 to impart skill training to the youth according to the needs of Fourth Industrial Revolution.
- **Focus on Soft Skills** Emphasise the development of soft skills, such as critical thinking, problem-solving, creativity, and adaptability. These skills are less likely to be automated and can complement AI technologies in the workplace.
- **Realigning Education System** The government and industry bodies have to coordinate with educational bodies and universities to bring about changes and expose students to cutting-edge technologies like robotics, artificial intelligence, machine learning, nano technology, etc. **Example: National Education Policy, 2020 is a step in this direction.**

- **Social Security Measures** It is important to develop social security measures for workers affected by AI-driven job displacement. This can include unemployment benefits, income support and healthcare provisions to ensure a smooth transition for affected individuals. Example: Robot Tax proposed by Bill Gates.
- **Support Entrepreneurship and Innovation** Encourage entrepreneurship and innovation by providing resources, funding and mentorship to individuals and startups working on AI-related solutions. This can create new job opportunities and drive economic growth.
  - **Example** Smart Mobility, including Transports and Logistics: Potential use cases in this domain include autonomous fleets for ride sharing, semi-autonomous features such as driver assist and predictive engine monitoring and maintenance.
- **Public-Private Partnerships** Foster collaboration between the government, private sector and civil society organisations to develop AI strategies and policies that prioritize job creation, worker protection and social impact.
- **Focus on Research and Development** Investments in AI research and development to advance state-of-the-art technologies, encourage innovation and support the growth of AI startups and entrepreneurship.
  - **Example** AIRAWAT (AI Research, Analytics and Knowledge Assimilation platform) will be a cloud platform which will support advancement of AI-based developments in image recognition, speech recognition, natural language processing for research and development.

Conclusion

It is important to note that while AI may lead to job displacement in certain sectors, it also has the potential to create new job opportunities in emerging fields. To mitigate the negative impacts, it is essential to invest in reskilling and upskilling programmes, provide support for affected workers, foster a culture of lifelong learning and promote a fair and inclusive transition to an AI-enabled economy.

Skill Development vs Employment

Q.31 'A large proportion of youth entering the labour market is not readily employable and need reskilling'. Why is it necessary to promote skill development? To what extent, various initiatives taken by the government have succeeded in achieving the objectives? (250 Words, 15 Marks)

Ans. Apart from the problem of creating jobs for the burgeoning young population, India faces the mammoth task of imparting skills to workers seeking jobs to make them 'employable' – i.e., suitable for the nature of work and the skills which the jobs demand, as will be evident from the following facts.

India's Demographic Profile

- India is witnessing a phase of demographic dividend as India has 62.5% of its population in the age group of 15-59 years which is ever increasing and will be at the peak of around 2036 when it will reach approximately 65%.
- According to Economic Survey 2018-19, India's demographic dividend will peak around 2041, when the share of working-age, i.e., 20-59 years, population is expected to hit 59%. Also, more than 54 % of our population is younger than 25 years in age.
- As per the Periodic Labour Force Survey (PLFS) 2020-21, India's labour Force Participation Rate (LFPR) is 41.6 % (57.5 % for males, 25.1 % for females).
  - The 2015 Report on National Policy on Skill Development and Entrepreneurship estimated that only 4.7% of the total workforce in India had undergone formal skill training compared with 52% in the US, 80% in Japan, and 96% in South Korea.
  - According to the India Skill Report, 2019, only 45.6% of the youth graduating from educational institutions are employable.

Need for Skill Development

- **Demographic Dividend** The 'demographic window' is only a span of few decades. The skilled youth is required to save demographic dividend from becoming demographic disaster.
- **Demand for Skilled Workforce** The Confederation of Indian Industry (CII) had projected Incremental Human Resource Requirements till 2022 at 201 million, making the total requirement of the skilled workforce by 2023 at 300 million.
- **Outsourcing of Skill** India could become the supplier of talent and skills if its workforce across age groups is equipped with employable skills that keep pace with the exponentially changing technological ecosystem.
  - Over the next two decades, the labour force in the industrialised world is expected to decline by 4%, while in India it will increase by nearly 20%.
- **Changing Nature of Work** Rising role of technology in the background of Fourth Industrial Revolution and emerging technologies such as Internet of Things (IoT), cloud computing, artificial intelligence, etc. is changing the nature of work and therefore making the old skills obsolete.
- **Huge Manufacturing Base** COVID-19 pandemic is bringing a transformation in global supply chain as it was heavily dependent on China's manufacturing industry. This offers an opportunity for India to become a leading supply chain hub but this requires a skilled manpower matching to the demands of industry.
- **Sectoral Mobilisation** Less number of people will be required to work in farming as productivity improves. This would result in sectoral mobilisation of workforce from agriculture to secondary and tertiary activities.
- **Better Employment** Skills are needed to those currently in colleges for them to be better employed and to shift the labour from informal sector to formal sector.

Initiatives taken for Skill Development

- **Establishment of Training Institutes** Over time, a fairly vast institutional system for training and skills has evolved. This includes 15,154 Industrial Training Institutes (ITIs) (including 11,892 private institutes); 36 Sector Skills Councils, 33 National Skills Training Institutes, and 2,188 training partners registered with National Skill Development Corporation (NSDC).
- Setting up of a full-fledged **Ministry of Skill Development and Entrepreneurship** in 2014 to coordinate all skill development efforts across the country and enhance employability through skill development.
- **National Skill Development Corporation (NSDC)** It is a Public Private Partnership in India, under the Ministry of Skill Development and Entrepreneurship with an objective to create training capacity in the country; fund vocational training initiatives and create a market ecosystem for skill development.
- **Pradhan Mantri Kaushal Vikas Yojana** The flagship Pradhan Mantri Kaushal Vikas Yojana (PMKVY) scheme was launched in 2015 to provide short-term training, skilling through ITIs and under the apprenticeship scheme. Also, the programme certifies the youth who are already good at a skill by evaluating them.
  - Since 2015, the government has trained over 13 million youth under this scheme.
- **FutureSkills Prime** It is a skilling ecosystem focused on emerging technologies, powered by a partnership between MeitY, NASSCOM and the IT industry. It seeks to propel India to become a global hub of talent in emerging technologies.
- **Skill India Digital Platform (Budget 2023-24)** The digital ecosystem for skilling will be further expanded with the launch of a unified Skill India Digital platform for enabling demand-based formal skilling, linking with employers including MSMEs and facilitating access to entrepreneurship schemes.
- **SANKALP and STRIVE** The SANKALP programme which focuses on the district-level skilling ecosystem and the STRIVE project which aims to improve the performance of ITIs are other significant skilling interventions.
- **Initiatives from Several Ministries** Nearly 40 skill development programmes are implemented by 20 central Ministries/Departments. The Ministry of Skill Development and Entrepreneurship contributes about 55% of the skilling achieved.
  - Initiatives by all ministries have resulted in nearly four crore people being trained through various traditional skills programmes since 2015.

- **Mandatory CSR Expenditure in Skilling** Since the implementation of mandatory CSR spending under the Companies Act, 2013, corporations in India have invested over ₹ 100,000 crores in diverse social projects.
  - Of these, about ₹ 6,877 crores were spent on skilling and livelihood enhancement projects. Maharashtra, Tamil Nadu, Odisha, Karnataka and Gujarat were the top five recipient states.
- **National Policy on Skill Development and Entrepreneurship, 2015** aims to empower individuals through improved skills, knowledge, qualifications, to provide access to decent employment and ensure India's competitiveness in the global market. The vision of the Policy is "to create an ecosystem of empowerment by skilling on a large scale at speed with high standards and to promote a culture of innovation based entrepreneurship which can generate wealth and employment so as to ensure sustainable livelihoods for all citizens in the country". The policy identified four thrust areas:
  - **Inhibiting Factors** It addresses key obstacles to skilling, including low aspirational value, lack of integration with formal education, lack of focus on outcomes, low quality of training infrastructure and trainers, etc.
  - **Demand and Supply Gap** The policy seeks to align supply and demand for skills by bridging existing skill ga.
  - ps, promoting industry engagement, operationalising a quality assurance framework, leverage technology and promoting greater opportunities for apprenticeship training.
  - **Equity** The policy targets skilling opportunities for socially/geographically marginalised and disadvantaged groups and especially women.
  - **Entrepreneurship** The policy seeks to educate and equip potential entrepreneurs, both within and outside the formal education system. It also seeks to connect entrepreneurs to mentors, incubators and credit markets, foster innovation and entrepreneurial culture, improve ease of doing business and promote a focus on social entrepreneurship.

Challenges faced in Skill Development

Skill development programme faces many challenges on account of rapid changes in technology, the massive numbers of persons to be trained, training institutions involved and the widely dispersed locations where the skilling takes place.

- **Lack of Basic Education** In the absence of basic level education, it would be difficult to upskill the younger population for higher-end jobs. A 2020 NSO survey revealed that one out of every eight students enrolled in a school or college drops out before completing education; 63% of these are at the school level. Less than 40% of students pursued higher secondary and/or higher education.
  - **Futuristic Measure–Reversing Dropouts Trend** Irrespective of rural or urban setting, the public school system must ensure that every child completes high school education and is pushed into appropriate skilling, training and vocational education in line with market demand.
  - Deploying new technology to put in place virtual classrooms together with Massive Open Online Courses (MOOCS) would further help yield a higher educated workforce.
- **Insufficient Training Facilities** According to a survey conducted by the NSSO, in India, there is a lack of training facilities in as many as 20 high-growth industries such as logistics, healthcare, construction, hospitality and automobiles.
  - India has roughly close to 5,500 public (ITIs) and private (ITC) institutes as against 500,000 similar institutes in China.
- **Lack of Awareness** Persons aspiring for training may not be aware of government-run skill development programmes. Certain surveys have shown that large numbers of youth were not aware of various training facilities being provided.
  - **Futuristic Steps** Disseminating information widely in both urban and rural areas about various skill development initiatives is required.
- **Changing Demands under Industry 4.0** The technology overhaul has resulted in the creation of new types of jobs that require special skill sets; the higher-end jobs which require more 'human' skills such as networking, creativity, problem-solving, etc.
  - **Futuristic Steps** General, professional and vocational education, both at school and higher levels, need to be overhauled to prepare students to become 'employable' on completion of education. This is especially relevant for polytechnics, ITII and engineering institutions which have to prepare students in emerging and cutting-edge technologies like robotics, artificial intelligence, machine learning, nano-technology, etc. for which there will be demand from industries in coming years.
- **Lack of Focus on Upskilling/Reskilling** it is the upskilling and re-skilling needs of the larger working population that have been largely unmet which have become important in the era of Fourth Industrial Revolution.

- **Futuristic Measure-Incorporate Upskilling in the Goals** There is more than enough evidence that upskilling the already employed workforce could lead to greater productivity in the economy, higher incomes for workers and higher profitability for firms.
- The PMKVY could equally prioritise upskilling initiatives in the PPP mode. Many countries such as the UK, Germany and Australia have proactive participation from industry players in their skilling efforts.

- **Shortage of Qualified Trainers and Assessors** There is huge shortage of qualified trainers in the VET system an even more acute shortage of qualified and competent assessors to assess trainees. A significant proportion of trainers have neither the requisite teaching skills nor the relevant industry experience.
- **Low industry Participation** Industries or firms may be reluctant to spend on in-house training or upskilling staff since those trained may quit jobs to join other firms seeking better prospects thus benefitting the latter firm and not the firm that incurred the training cost.
  - **Futuristic Measure - Involving Corporate Sector** Investing in skill development is a win-win solution for corporate India as well as the nation - according to a NASSCOM Report in 2021, investing in skill training programmes resulted in more than 600% return on outlays.
  - There should be close coordination between skill development agencies and industry to ensure that priority is given for imparting those skills which the industries need.
- **Low level of female participation in the labour force and on top of that there is under-representation of women in skill development programmes.**
  - **Futuristic Measure** Skilling initiatives need to be complemented by a wider push towards women's empowerment through gender sensitisation and creation of economic opportunities for women. Facilities like hostels for women trainees, flexible work models and preparing women for jobs more suited to them such as in 'gig economy' electronics and hardware industry, health and education sectors are especially relevant in this context.
- **Inadequate Monitoring and Evaluation (M&E)** Monitoring arrangements are inadequate, with little third-party monitoring of quality and outcomes. There is no formal and active feedback mechanism in place to capture 'learning experiences' of and 'outcomes' for the beneficiaries.

Conclusion

India being one of the youngest nations in the world with the average Indian being 29 years (the average Chinese is 37 years and Japanese, 48 years) has the potential to convert this pool of young population into human capital provided steadfast attention is given to skilling and education. This needs a coordinated effort from all stakeholders including government agencies Industries, educational and training institutes and students, trainees and job seekers.

Budget 2023-24 launched PMKVY 4.0 to provide the skills in line with Industry 4.0 requirements which includes Artificial Intelligence, soft skills, robotics, drone technology, 3D printing, the Internet of Things, Mechatronics, etc. It is to be implemented with industrial partnerships.

Check Your Preparation

1. "Creating an ecosystem for private investment is critical to enable the virtuous cycle of growth". In light of this statement, bring out the obstacles to achieve the target of becoming a $5 trillion Indian economy. What steps should be taken to revive private investment in the economy? (250 words, 15 marks)
2. Whether India realises its growth potential or gets stuck in a middle-income trap depends on both policy choice and institutional design. Explain. (150 words, 10 marks)
3. Do you think planning has a role in the context of market-based development of India? If yes, discuss the changes that have been brought by the NITI Aayog in India's planning. (150 words, 10 marks)
4. The enactment of Insolvency and Bankruptcy Code (IBC) has created a paradigm shift in the regulatory framework and processes governing corporate insolvency. In the light of this statement, critically examine the impact of IBC along with the future reforms required in this law. (250 words, 15 marks)
5. Indian labour and employment have been characterised by the persistent dominance of the unorganised sector. How the government does intend to tackle this? (150 words, 10 marks)

UNIT 2

Inclusive Growth and Issues Arising From It

Components of Inclusive Growth (Meaning of Inclusive Growth)

Q.1 Rather than focusing solely on quantity, inclusive growth concerns iteself with the quality of growth. Examine. Aslo, higlight the core components of 'Inclusive Growth'. (250 Word, 15 Marks)

Ans. **Introduction** India is ranked world's fifth largest economy in absolute number (USD 3.5 trillion economy) and ranked third in terms of PPP but looking at the various social indicators such as Human Development Index, Inclusive Development Index, Global Hunger Index, etc., India is not performing well. These facts emphasise that focus must be broadened from quantitative growth (GDP) to the qualitative aspect as well.

Concerns with the Economic Growth

- Growth of economies in the world is usually measured in quantitative terms using various indicators such as Gross Domestic Product (GDP), National Income and per capita income etc. However, focusing solely on quantitative growth has been criticied due to the following reasons:
- **Vicious Cycle of Exploitation** Short-term growth strategies aimed at maximising GDP growth has created a 'vicious cycle' - growth driven by the exploitation of human and natural capital.
- **Jobless Growth** India has witnessed jobless growth with high levels of unemployment. India witnessed a rapid GDP growth especially after LPG reforms but the employment elasticity has fallen from close to unity in the 70s to 0.4 in the 90s to less than 0.1 in the present times.
- **Poor Investments in Social Infrastructure** India also needs considerable improvement in several social indicators such as maternal health, education, etc., as it was still ranked 132 among 191 countries in the Human Development Index 2021-2022. India's ranking in Global Hunger Index stands at 107 in 2022 with almost all the neighbouring countries ahead of it.
- **Does not Capture Income Inequality** Lack of focus on distribution of growth creates inequality which poses a threat to economic expansion and social cohesion around the world. For instance, the Oxfam report highlights that since 2000, the poorest half of the world population has received just 1% of the total increase in global wealth, while the 50% increase has gone to the top 1% only.
- **Environmental Impact** Quantitative parameters do not capture the negative impact of economic growth on the environment which ultimately affects the living standards in the society. As per Amartya Sen, Development is about the freedom but living in the polluted air will not be considered development.

Concept of Inclusive Growth

In this context, the concept of inclusive growth holds prominence. OECD defines inclusive growth as the economic growth that is distributed fairly across society and creates opportunities for all. World Bank defines the IG as follows: 'Inclusive Growth refers both to the pace and pattern of growths, which are interlinked and must be addressed together' This expands the focus from quantitative growth (GDP) to the qualitative aspect as well. In broad sense, IG means the inclusion of all sections of society in the process of economic development and sharing of its benefit. While Indian Constitution always aimed for Inclusive Growth and various initiatives were taken since Independence, the concept of inclusive growth was first spelled out in Eleventh Five Year Plan and subsequently in Twelfth Five Year Plan.

Inclusive Growth Concerns with the Quality of Growth

India's Constitution from the Independence strives for the inclusive growth which can be seen from the socialistic principles of DPSPs such as Article 38 or Article 39. These provisions are aimed at minimising income inequalities, prevent concentration of wealth, a living standard for all, wage equality between men and women and many other provisions.

- **Long-Term Perspective** The inclusive growth approach takes a **longer-term perspective** and addresses the structural and fundamental problems in society and the economy.
- **Equal Society** When growth is 'inclusive' and 'pro-poor', the incomes of poor people grow faster than those of the population as a whole, i.e., inequality declines.
- **Boost Economy** It leads to a **wider distribution of wealth** which creates a demand in a country and hence leads to domestic demand-driven growth. It **creates a strength in the economy** to withstand shocks and growth becomes sustainable in the longer run.
- **Increase in the Living Standards** With better wealth distribution, the overall standard of living increases. For example, people move away from polluting sources of energy such as wood, cow dung etc and adopt more environment-friendly sources such as LPG which further improves environmental sustainability.
- **Realisation of Basic Human Rights** Each individual by virtue of being human have certain rights such as Right to Life, Right to Basic Health, Right to Education, etc. Focus on inclusive growth helps in the realisation of these rights.
- **Realisation of Constitutional Goals** Indian Constitution aimed for the egalitarian society, minimisation of income inequalities, equal pay for equal work, etc., which can be fulfilled by the focus on inclusive growth.

Core Components of Inclusive Growth

Inclusive growth is a multi-dimensional concept which includes several interrelated elements of inclusive growth as depicted in the given figure:

- **Economic Growth** India is among the fastest-growing major economies in the world. The target of becoming a USD 5 trillion economy by 2024-25 can allow India to reduce inequality, increase social expenditure and provide employment to all.
- **Equality of Opportunity** In terms of access to markets, resources and unbiased regulatory environment are the ends to mean of equality. In-equalities exist in various manners which are social inequalities, rural-urban divide, regional disparities, digital divide etc. To realire the Inclusive Growth in its ultimate form, equality is the most fundamental criteria.
- **Financial Inclusion** Financial inclusion is necessary for inclusive growth as it leads to the culture of saving, which initiates a virtuous cycle of economic development.
- **Social Development** It means the empowerment of all marginalised sections of the population like SC/ST/OBC/Minorities, women and transgender. Empowerment can be done by improving institutions of the social structure i.e., hospitals especially primary care in the rural areas, schools, universities, etc. Investment in social structures will not only boost growth (by fiscal stimulus) but will also create a healthy and capable generation to handle future work.

- **Skill Development** Harnessing the demographic dividend will depend upon the employability of the working age population, their health, education, vocational training and skills.
- **Technological Advancement** The world is moving towards an era of Industrial Revolution 4.0. These technological advancements have capabilities to either decrease or increase the inequality depending on the way these are being used. Several initiatives have been taken by the government, e.g., Digital India Mission, so that a digitally literate population can leverage technology for endless possibilities.
- **Good Governance** It is the mechanism for integrating inclusive growth, public administration and accountability towards envisaged outcome. For example, problems in poor health infrastructure may be an impediment to Inclusive Growth and can often be traced back to poor governance of the Ministry of Health and Family Welfare. Decentralisation of rural governance is critical for achieving Inclusive Growth.
- **Sustainable Development** Without adopting a sustainable practice in Inclusive Growth, the implementation of inclusive growth policies is bound to falter. Sustainability needs to be achieved at three levels – financial, social and environmental.

Conclusion

As detailed in the World Bank's Poverty and Shared Prosperity Report, the growth strategy should be geared towards creating opportunities for the least well-off people and preparing them for participating in their country's growth process and achieving sustainable development.

Social Infrastructure and Inclusive Growth

Q.2 Investment in social infrastructure is a key to engineer an inclusive and sustainable growth in India. Elaborate. (150 Words, 10 Marks)

Ans. **Introduction** Social infrastructure covers a range of foundational services and facilities that meet the social needs by building strong communities and contributes towards a good quality of life in areas such as health, education, recreation, skill development etc.

Social Infrastructure and Inclusive Growth in India

Investment in various components of social infrastructure lead to inclusive and sustainable growth in India in the following ways:

- **Education** Education encourages changes in knowledge, skills, values and attitudes to enable a more sustainable and just society for all. In order to ensure that every child between 6 to 14 years attains quality elementary education, the Right to Education Act was passed in 2009. Recently, New Education Policy 2020 was also passed to align the education system according to the needs of Fourth Industrial Revolution.
- **Health** As per the WHO, better health is central to human happiness and well-being. It also makes an important contribution to economic progress, as healthy people live longer, are more productive and save more. India moved a step towards Universal Health Care through initiatives such as Ayushman Bharat Pradhan Mantri Jan Arogya Yojana, National Health Mission, among others.
- **Skill Development** Skill development is one of the key strategies to realise the potential of India's demographic advantage and ensure upward mobility of workers through upskilling and re-skilling. Realising its importance, the government has introduced schemes such as **National Skill Development Mission, Deen Dayal Upadhyaya Grameen Kaushalya Yojana etc.**
- **Women's Empowerment** At present, India has approximately about 32% women in the workforce. The IMF estimates that equal participation of women in the workforce will increase India's GDP by 27%. Further, according to World's Resources Institute, women's inclusion in the labour force can also advance low-carbon, sustainable development. Schemes such as Mahila Shakti Kendra, NaiRoshi, Stand-Up India etc. are initiatives in this regard.
- **Environment** The government's goal of inclusive development and economic growth will remain unfulfilled if environmental sustainability is not addressed. Ensuring clean air and water and efficiency in resource use are central to equitable growth. Government's target of net zero carbon emissions by 2070 and meeting 50% energy needs from renewable sources are step in this direction.

- **Justice** To improve ease of living for the common man, especially the poor and marginalised, it is pertinent to have an efficient and credible criminal justice system. Further, Alternate Dispute Resolution Mechanisms such as Lok Adalats ensure inexpensive and efficient resolution of disputes.
- **Achievement of UN SDGs** 17 SDGs and 169 targets envisaged in the Agenda 2030, are closely interrelated with social infrastructure as observed by the Economic Survey.
- **Reaping Demographic Dividend** India has 62.5% of its population in the age group of 15-59 years which is ever increasing and will be at the peak around 2036 when it will reach approximately 65%. This will boost economic growth and leads to rapid industrialisation provided there is huge public investments in like education, skill development, health, housing and connectivity.
- **Provisions for Social Security** To further the cause of inclusive growth and provide comprehensive social security cover, the government enacted Unorganised Workers Social Security Act, 2008, which includes various schemes like Rashtriya Swasthya Bima Yojana, Janani Suraksha Yojana, National Family Benefit Scheme etc. Beside these, the Central Government launched three other schemes i.e., Atal Pension Yojana, Pradhan Mantri Jeevan Jyoti Bima Yojana, Pradhan Mantri Suraksha Bima Yojana, to specifically extend social security to the unorganised sector.

Conclusion

To reap the demographic dividend, proper investment in human capital is needed by focussing on education, skill development and healthcare facilities. If the increased workforce is not sufficiently skilled, educated and provided gainful employment, we would be facing demographic disaster instead.

Inter-generational and Intra-generational Issues of Inclusive Growth

Q.3 Explain intra-generational and inter-generational issues of equity from the perspective of inclusive growth and sustainable development. (150 Words, 10 Marks) **UPSC Mains PYQ 2020**

Ans. **Introduction** Inter-generational and intra-generational equity are two hands of the doctrine of sustainable equity. Sustainable equity aims to find a proper balance between inter-generational equity (between the present and future people) and intra-generational equity (between the rich and the poor of the present generation).

Intra-generational Equity

Intra-generational equity deals with the equity among the same generations as far as the utilisation of resources are concern. It includes fair utilisation of global resources among the human beings of the present generation issues of intra-generational equity from perspective of inclusive growth.

- **Rich and Poor Divide** While the rich have access to proper education and thus good employment opportunities, the poor lack access to education and lag behind in employment. According to World Inequality Report (2022), the top 10% holds 57% of the total national income, while the bottom 50% holds just 13% in 2021. Welfare schemes like subsidies, reservations, etc., are provided by the governments to help the vulnerable section of society.
- **Gender Inequalities** Gender inequalities deny the female population education, good food, respect and opportunity to obtain gainful employment, making development non inclusive. Male literacy rate is about 82% and Female literacy rate is 65.5% according to Census 2011 showing wide gender gap regarding literacy. This inequality exists in the wages and other forms of discrimination exist against women.
- **Digital Divide** COVID-19 has increased the digital divide among the population especially the marginalised sections. The Oxfam Inequality Report (2021) points out that only 15% rural households had an internet connection.
- **Rural and Urban Divide** The developmental gap between the rural and urban areas is quite significant in India. SECC for rural India reveals that in 75% households, the monthly income of the highest earning member is less than ₹ 5,000. And more than 80% rural people are without a salaried job.
- **Dependency on Developed Nations** Developing nations are dependent on foreign aid by the developed nations for funding their programmes of poverty alleviation and employment. **Example** Soft loans from international financial institutions like IMF and World Bank put conditions on recipient countries which may be detrimental to the goal of inclusive growth.
- **Transfer of Burden** Shifting of polluting industries to least developed countries creates unintended consequences.

- **Sea Level Rise** The sea level rise caused due to increased global warming activities of developed countries affects littoral countries adversely. **Example** Tuvalu, a remote South Pacific nation, is facing threats due to sea level rise caused by global warming activities of developed countries.
- **Regional Disparities** Regional disparities in development causes violent conflicts and law and order problems in the society. **Example** Insurgency in North-East and left wing extremism in Eastern India due to sustainable development deficit.
- **Inequitable Vaccine Access** The COVID-19 vaccines are patented by the market forces depriving their access for least developed countries.

Inter-generational Equity

It is the development of resources by one generation to enhance economic sustainability for the future generation. It signifies the rights and interests of the present and future generations regarding the resources of the Earth.

- **Resource Exploitation** The inter-generational equity has become crucial in the present times, due to the growing imbalance in the distribution of resources, ongoing degradation of environment and depletion of resources.
  - This imbalance is more profound between the Global North and the Global South.
- **Global Warming** Due to historic pollution of developed and industrialised nations, the developing countries are prone to increased disasters. Example Excessive use of HCFCs by global North led to ozone layer depletion, which negatively affected livelihoods of the poor and sustainable development strategies.
- **Mindless Deforestation** The need for rapid industrialisation leads to cutting of trees, thereby resulting into destruction of loss of habitat, biodiversity loss and deprivation of traditional rights.
- **Caste Suppression** Caste discrimination and violence has been continuing over centuries in India. According to NCRB data, 2020, crimes committed against Scheduled Castes (SCs) showed an increase of 9.4% over 2019.
- **Literacy Rate** The higher literacy rate among the current generation makes higher paying service sector jobs easily available to them while older generations are mostly employed in low paying jobs.
- **Lack of Technological Transfer** Developed countries unwilling to help developing countries in climate change mitigation, which is a result of their ruthless pursuit to economic growth at the cost of the environment.
- **Digital Illiteracy** The COVID-19 pandemic had highlighted the stark digital divide that exists between the people of present generation and older generations. This digital literacy helped the present generation work from home and continue earning while the older generation found it difficult.

Conclusion

In a developing country like India, intra-generational and inter-generational equity are more important as resources are required for ensuring the development of all, including the future generation to distribute the fruits of rapid economic growth.

India's Progress towards Inclusive Growth (Strategy of Inclusive Growth)

Q.4 It is argued that the strategy of inclusive growth is intended to meet the objectives of inclusiveness and sustainability together. Comment on this statement. (250 Words, 15 Marks) **UPSC Mains 2019**

Ans. **Introduction** Inclusive growth refers to the economic growth that is distributed fairly across society and creates opportunities for all. It refers to 'broad-based', 'shared', and 'pro-poor growth'.

Strategy for Inclusive Growth

Inclusive growth can be achieved through a multi-pronged approach which involves the measures to be undertaken mainly under 4 major pillars – Faster economic growth generating employment opportunities, investment in social infrastructure to ensure equality of opportunity and providing social safety nets to the extreme poor population supported with strong institutions and good governance.

Inclusiveness

- **Regional Development Strategy** Inclusive growth ensures that the development is balanced and sustainable. It supports the marginalised social groups and territories thus promoting inclusiveness and sustainability.
  - **Example** Establishment of the PSU's in the backward regions.
- **Skill Development** Skill development increases the employability of the disadvantaged sections of the population promoting inclusiveness.
  - **Example** Pradhan Mantri Kaushal Vikas Yojana, SANKALP initiatives etc.

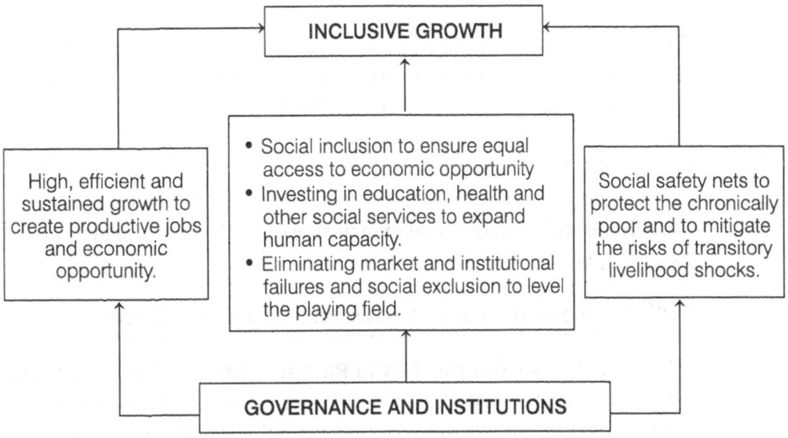

- **New Generation Inequalities** The inclusive growth addresses new generation inequalities arising with divergence in enhanced capabilities. **Example** The proportion of the adult population with tertiary education is growing more than six times faster in high human development countries than in low human development countries.
- **Access to Infrastructure** Inclusive growth strategy ensures access of people to basic infrastructure and services such as health and education. **Example** Setting up of IIT in North Karnataka region.
- **Productive Employment** Inclusive growth focuses on productive employment rather than income redistribution as a means of increasing incomes for excluded groups.
- **Longer-term Perspective** The Inclusive growth approach takes a longer-term perspective, where it is important to recognise the time lag between reforms and outcomes.
- **Poverty Alleviation** The inclusive growth strategy includes the poor and weaker sections as well as lagging regions as partners and beneficiaries of economic growth.

Sustainability

- **Reduction of Wastage** The strategy of inclusive growth increases the resource efficiency and promotes the circular economy.
- **Regional Development Strategy** Inclusive growth ensures that the development is balanced and sustainable. It supports the marginalised social groups and territories thus promoting inclusiveness and sustainability. Example Establishment of the PSU's in the backward regions.
- **Sustainable Development** It leads to less resource depletion thereby protecting the flora and fauna.
- **Inclusion of Future Generation's Needs** The strategy incorporates the needs of future generation into the planning aspects and thus leads to the sustainable development.
- **Economic Sustainability** Inclusive growth creates strength in the economy to withstand shocks and growth becomes sustainable in the longer run. **Example** In India, more than half of the population is dependent on agricultural activities.
- **Environment Sustainability** With better wealth distribution people move away from polluting sources of energy and adopt more environment-friendly sources. **Example** Increased shift from wood, cow dung towards LPG and renewable sources of energy promoting circular economy.

Conclusion

Indian Government along with the State Governments and Local Governments should continue to focus on eradicating poverty and achieving sustainable development in order to improve the lives of India's people. Through innovative partnerships with an international organisation, civil societies and private companies, inclusive and equitable growth can be targeted.

Critical Analysis of India's Progress towards Inclusive Growth

Q.5 Has India experienced the process of 'Inclusive Growth' since the Independence? Give your opinion. Also, highlight the various government policies pursued in this direction. What, in your opinion, can be done to expedite the process? (250 Words, 15 Marks)

Ans. Introduction Inclusive growth means the inclusion of all sections of society in the process of economic development and sharing of its benefit. While Indian Constitution always aimed for inclusive growth and various initiatives were taken since Independence, the goal of inclusive growth was explicitly spelled out in Eleventh Five Year Plan and subsequently in Twelfth Five Year Plan.

India's Growth Process towards Inclusive Growth

- **Moving Away from the 'Hindu Rate of Growth'** From an annual average growth rate of 3.5% during 1950 to 1980, the growth rate of the Indian economy accelerated to around 6.0% in the 1980s and 1990s. The era of the 2000s saw an impressive growth of around 8.8% propelled by the structural reforms of the 90s which slowed down to around 7.5% during the second decade.
- **Expansion in Per Capita Income** Since 1947, India has achieved tremendous progress in raising growth, income levels and standards of living. The average Indian citizen earned an income of just around ₹ 7,513 during 1950-51 which increased to ₹ 86,647 and ₹ 1,72,000 in 2014-15 and 2022-23 respectively illustrating achievement in this regard.
- **Reduction in Poverty Levels** The overall poverty ratio declined from 45.3% in 1993-94 to 37.2% in 2004-05 and to 21.9% in 2011-12 as per Tendulkar Committee estimation. Around 415 million people in India climbed out of poverty between 2005-06 and 2019-21, with the incidence of poverty falling from 55% to just over 16% over this period, according to the Global Multi-dimensional Poverty Index 2022.
- **Boom in the Various Sectors of Economy (i.e. Agriculture, Industry and Services)** Agriculture sector continues to be an important sector in the Indian economy and generates livelihood for more than half the population. Industrial sector also witnessed a higher growth and attracted private sector participation as well as foreign investment. In services, new sectors such as Information Technology and telecommunications have transformed the landscape, creating new opportunities such as e-commerce and startups. India's IT skills are renowned the world over.
- **Social Development Indicators** India has also come a long way in terms of improving its human development indicators. Literacy rates have increased significantly, from 18.3% during 1950s to 52% during 1990s to 73% during 2011. This has been accompanied by major improvements in other socio-economic indicators such as increase in the gross enrollment ratios in primary education.

Challenges/Obstacles in Achieving the Goal of Inclusive Growth

- **Slowing of Economic Growth** Indian economy in the recent times have seen various economic shocks such as COVID-19 and adoption of structural reforms such as Demonetisation and which has posed a challenge to the fast economic growth.
- **Stagnant Private Investment to Around 29% of GDP** in the last few years has affected the pace of economic growth.
- **Jobless Growth** Growth has been largely jobless in India especially after LPG Reforms 1991 and the employment growth has declined for the same level of economic growth. India witnessed a rapid GDP growth especially after LPG reforms but the employment elasticity has fallen from close to unity in the 70s to 0.4 in the 90s to less than 0.1 in the present times.
- **Informalisation of Labour** This jobless growth in recent years has been accompanied by growth in casualisation. Of around 61 million jobs created in India over 22 years post-liberalisation of the economy in 1991, 92% were informal jobs, according to an analysis of National Sample Survey Office data for 2011-12.

- **Rigidity in the Labour Laws** Various labour laws such as Industrial Disputes Act, 1951, Trade Unions Act, 1926, Contract Labour (Regulation and Abolition) Act, 1970, etc., have discriminated against formal employment and leading to a decline in the productivity of an economy. Thus, there is increased cost of production for the companies and thus losing trade competitiveness during the time of globalisation.
- **Imabalanced Growth Across Various Sectors of Economy** Growth has been uneven across sectors and locations along with low productivity in agriculture. For instance, agriculture which is supporting the livelihood of 50% of the population has been lagging behind and growth rate is less than 4% every year and some regions have advanced faster than others.
- **Financial Exclusion** Lack of timely and adequate credit has hampered the potential output of an economy.
- **Fiscal Constraints** Fiscal policies play a very important role in achieving inclusive growth but low economic recovery post Corona-pandemic has put the burden on the resources of the state and meeting fiscal deficit targets has resulted in the reduction of expenditure on welfare schemes.
- **High Poverty Levels** As per Global MPI Report 2022, India still has the largest number of poor people worldwide at 22.8 crore and 16.4% of the population is multi-dimensionally poor in 2019-21.
- **Poor Living Standards**
  - The reasons for low ranking in living standards include high debt-to-GDP ratio translating into low government spending, thus slowing down the pace of economic reforms and exacerbating income inequality.
  - Even the educational enrollment rates are relatively low across all levels, leading to notable differences in performance and living standards among students coming from different socio-economic backgrounds.
  - Additionally, low labour force participation coupled with large informal economy restricts the social mobility of workers, thus exposing them to vulnerable employment situations, ultimately lowering their living standards.
- **Widening of Various Forms of Inequalities in India** - income, rural vs urban, regional based, gender based and many more.
- **Environmental Sustainability** Despite its initiatives on the global scale for combating environmental problems, India faces problems related to environmental sustainability including increasing air and water pollution especially in metropolitan and industrial cities, degradation of forest and agricultural land, loss of biodiversity, loss of ecosystem resilience, rapid depletion of resources due to industrialisation etc.
- **Protection of Future Generation from Further Indebtedness** Issues like high debt-to-GDP ratio, income inequality, increasing external debt, , prevailing corruption, tax evasion, etc., can led to increased indebtedness and economic problems for future generation.
- **Digital divide** in the recent times is posing an increasing challenge to the inclusive growth.
- **Administrative issues** like leakages, mistargeting of resources, corruption, low capacity building, etc., have impacted the implementation of welfare schemes.

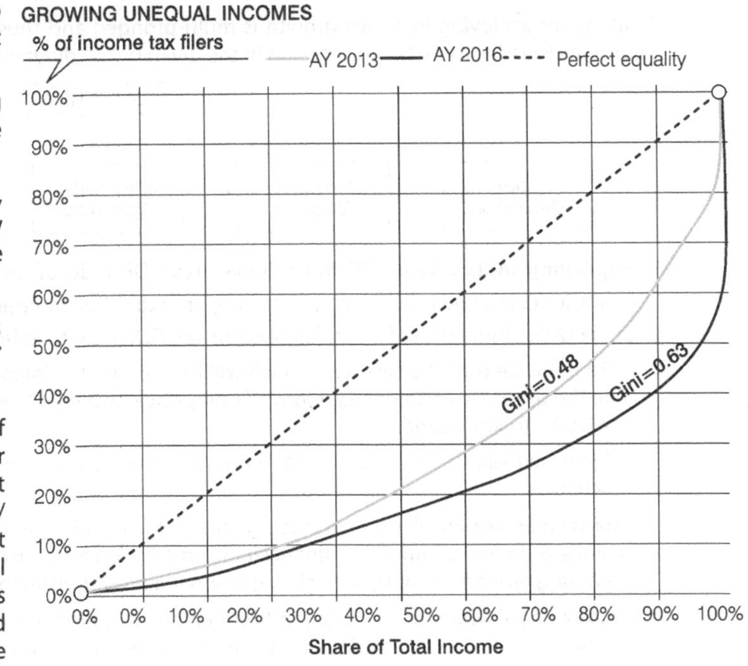

Government Interventions towards Inclusive Growth

Achieving inclusive growth has been one of the main priorities of the government. For promoting inclusive growth, the government is implementing various programmes/ schemes for creating better employment opportunities, strengthening social infrastructure and providing basic amenities like water, electricity, roads, sanitation and housing for covering all sections of the population.

Some of the measures that were launched for achieving Inclusive Growth;

The government is aggressively focusing on the strategy of inclusive growth in its various programme and policies.

- **Financial Inclusion** The combination of **Aadhaar, PMJDY and a surge in mobile communication** has reshaped the way citizens access government services. The government has also launched many flagship schemes to promote financial inclusion and provide financial security to empower the poor and unbanked in the country. These include the Pradhan Mantri Mudra Yojana, Stand-Up India Scheme, Pradhan Mantri Jeevan Jyoti Bima Yojana, Pradhan Mantri Suraksha Bima Yojana and Atal Pension Yojana.
- **Women and Inclusion** India have said that gender equality and emancipation of rural women is a key driver of inclusive growth in the country, with discourse on women's empowerment progressing from viewing women as recipients of welfare benefits to engaging them as active agents of change. Some of the schemes that were launched include Pradhan Mantri Matru Vandana Yojana (PMKVY), Pradhan Mantri Ujjwala Yojana .
- **Poverty and Inclusive Growth** Interventionist policies that redistribute resources or entitlements have an important impact on the extent of equity in incomes that is achieved. Improvements in literacy and education reduce inequality of income. Progressive income tax systems, including recurrent property taxes, high taxes on luxury expenditure of the affluent, capital gains taxes would enable better income distribution by reducing incomes of the rich and enabling policy interventions that enhance the entitlements of the poor.
- **Skill Development and Inclusive Growth** Harnessing the demographic dividend will depend upon the employability of the working age population, their health, education, vocational training and skills. The Indian Government has undertaken numerous initiatives for skill development such Pradhan Mantri Kaushal Vikas Yojana (PMKVY) Rozgar Mela, Pradhan Mantri Kaushal Kendras (PMKK) Capacity Building Scheme.
- **Education and Inclusive Growth** Higher Education is a powerful tool of increasing access to highly skilled and high paid jobs and by providing this employment it helps in achieving inclusive growth. Thus access of Quality Education at all levels of society is needed to achieve goal of inclusive growth. Some of the schemes launched in this direction are Sarva Shiksha Abhiyaan Scheme for Higher Education Youth in Apprenticeship and Skills etc.
- **Health and Inclusive Growth** Health is of vital importance to achieve inclusive growth. Some of the schemes launched include Mission Indradhanush, Ayushman Bharat–PM Jan Arogya Yojana, Pradhan Mantri Swasthya Suraksha Yojana (PMSSY).

Towards an Inclusive Growth

Strategy for achieving inclusive growth is multi-pronged and thus requires interventions in a majority of sectors of the economy. Broadly, it can be understood in the given below diagram:

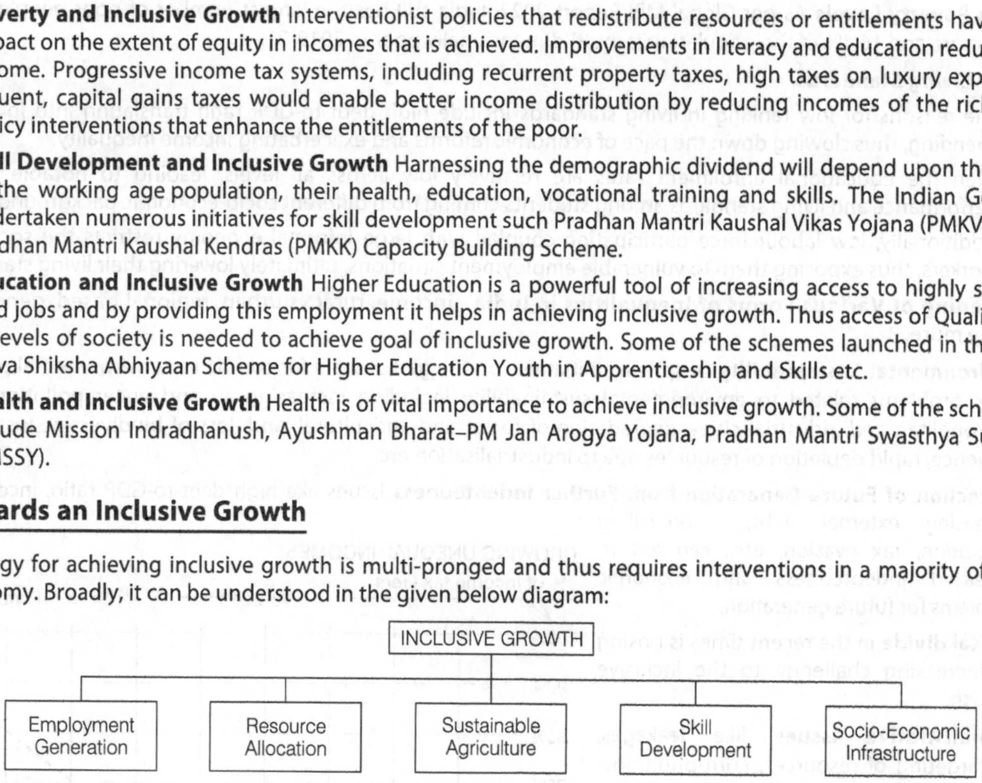

- **Improving India's Tax-GDP Ratio** India's tax-GDP ratio of around 11% is much lesser than the average of OECD countries (35%) and is low even when compared to other emerging economies like Brazil (34%), South Africa (27%) and China (22%). India should aim to increase its tax-GDP ratio to at least 22 per cent of GDP for 2 major reasons:
  - To enhance public investment which will have multiplier impact on an economy and more importantly, it will crowd in the private investment. Economic Survey once observed that private investment is a key driver for India to achieve a USD 5 trillion economy.
  - Increased Tax-GDP ratio can help in the redistribution of resources through increased allocation on various welfare schemes.
- **Financial Sector** Problems in accessing finance are a major impediment in the performance of small and medium size businesses in India. Improving financial intermediation and ensuring broader access to financial services is critical for equalising growth. In short, financial inclusion is a pre-requisite for the achievement of inclusive growth.
- **Labour Regulations** Better designed regulations can attract more labour-intensive investment and improve the job prospects for India's unemployed and those trapped in poor quality jobs and the 80 million new entrants who are expected to join the workforce over the next decade.

- **Sustainable Agriculture** Raising agricultural productivity requires a return to investments in agricultural technology and infrastructure. Getting the rural economy moving will also require facilitating rural non-farm entrepreneurship.
- **Employment Generation** With an emphasis on labour-intensive manufacturing sector. The employability of labour needs to be enhanced by improving health, education and skilling outcomes and a massive expansion of the apprenticeship scheme. This will also help in reaping the Demographic Dividend enjoyed by our economy.
- **Attention to Lagging States** Lagging states create an attractive investment climate by reforming cumbersome regulatory procedures, improving rural connectivity, establishing law and order, creating a stable platform for natural resource investment that balances business interests with social concerns and providing rural finance.
- **Socio-Economic Infrastructure** Growth to be inclusive needs to develop economic infrastructure so that all sections of the society will have access to safe drinking water, electricity, housing, toilet, transport and financial inclusion.
- **Using Globalisation** Trade openness, FDI policies, import-export policies can be attuned to facilitate linkages between demand and supply for goods and services which specifically target small and medium scale enterprises.

Conclusion

Inclusive growth is a sine qua non for the sustenance of Indian democracy. Rising inequality and relative deprivation experienced by the vulnerable sections of the society could undermine the foundations of democracy as witnessed in few monarchies of Arab nations during the Arab Spring which was fuelled by similar concerns.

Financial Inclusion: Meaning and Linkage with SDGs

Q.6 United Nations Sustainable Development Goals (SDG) 2030 view financial inclusion as a key enabler for achieving sustainable development. Also, what benefits it bring to various stakeholders of the society? (150 Words, 10 Marks)

Ans. **Introduction** Financial inclusion has been defined as "the process of ensuring access to financial services, timely and adequate credit for vulnerable groups such as weaker sections and low-income groups at an affordable cost".

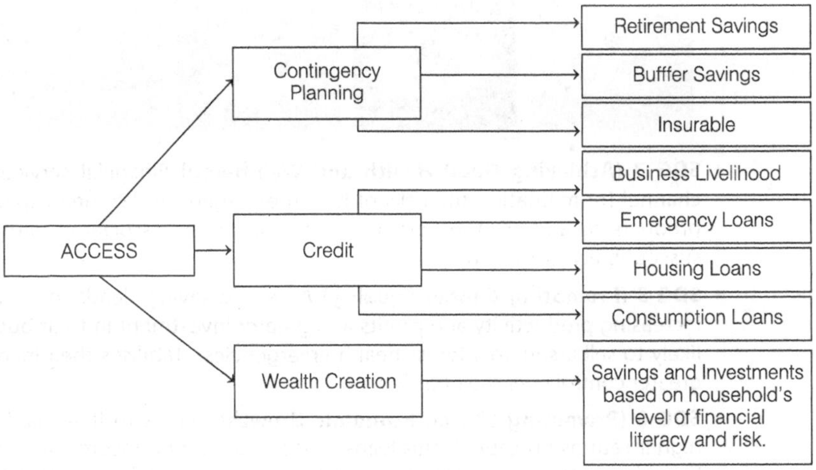

According to the World Bank, financial inclusion means that individuals and businesses have access to affordable financial products and services that meet their needs. Accessibility, affordability and availability of financial services are 3 pillars of financial inclusion. It is a method of offering banking and financial solutions and services to every individual in the society without any form of discrimination.

Financial Inclusion and Sustainable Development Goals (SDGs)

Financial inclusion is increasingly considered as a key driver of economic growth and poverty alleviation. Accessibility to formal finance like banking services can promote job creation, reduce vulnerability to economic shocks and increase investments in human capital. Importance of financial inclusion is visible from the fact that seven of the seventeen UN SDG Goals consider financial inclusion as a key enabler for achieving sustainable development.

- **SDG1 (Eliminating Extreme Poverty)** Financial services such as savings can have direct and indirect impacts on poverty. For example, giving individuals access to savings instruments can increase a country's net savings which can lead to an increase in productive investment and consumption.
  - Savings allow families to increase their capacity to absorb financial shocks, smooth consumption, accumulate assets, and invest in human capital such as health and education. Such investments help people climb out of poverty and ultimately can lead to higher growth.
  - Indian Government effort to open banks in rural areas helped cut rural poverty by up to 17 percentage points as per the report.
- **SDG 2 (Reducing Hunger and Promoting Food Security)** A lack of access to credit and insurance prevents farmers from making investments that could increase crop yields and strengthen food security. Access to agricultural insurance can embolden farmers to make more and riskier investments, which can lead to increased earnings.

- **SDG 3 (Achieving Good Health and Well-being)** Financial services like medical insurance can provide a formal channel for mitigating the risks of health emergencies. Women especially have a high demand for health insurance products to address the common health concerns associated with pregnancy and child birth, including greater susceptibility to infection.
- **SDG 5 (Promoting Gender Equality)** Access to savings leads to positive economic outcomes for women, including increasing productivity and profits and greater investment in their businesses. Having savings also makes women less likely to sell assets to address health emergencies, stabilises their incomes in times of economic shocks and provides greater control over their funds.
- **SDG 8 (Promoting Shared Economic Growth)** Access to financial institutions and products allows people to gain higher returns on capital. This leads to increase in their income and consequently affects economic growth. Effective financial systems can mobilise savings to finance productive economic ventures and improve the probability of successful innovations.
- **SDG 9 (Promoting Innovation and Sustainable Industrialisation)** Access to financial services, particularly credit, is likely to allow more businesses to be started and allow existing firms to expand their services by enabling greater investment in inventory, labour and other means of production. An increase in the number of MSMEs allows economies to create job opportunities for business owners and their employees. A study in India showed that increased access to credit enables the wealthiest 5% to 10% of entrepreneurs to increase profits substantially.
- **SDG 10 and SDG 16 (Towards Equitable and Peaceful Societies)** People with access to financial services are better positioned to succeed economically and build a decent life, ultimately making it easier to reduce inequality (SDG 10) and promote peace (SDG 16). By providing a foundation for equitable growth and improving the lives of the poor, financial inclusion helps reduce inequality and the likelihood of social turmoil.
- **SDG 17** on strengthening the means of implementation. There is an implicit role for greater financial inclusion through greater savings mobilisation for investment and consumption that can spur growth.

Benefits of Financial Inclusion to Various Stakeholders of Economy

- **Boost GDP** Financial inclusion can support overall economic growth and the achievement of broader development goals. Digital finance alone could benefit billions of people by spurring inclusive growth that adds USD 3.7 trillion to the GDP of emerging economies within a decade, according to a report by the McKinsey Global Institute.
- **Stable Economy** Financial inclusion creating more stable financial systems and economies, mobilising domestic resources through national savings and helping to boost government revenue.
- **Digitising Payments** For health, education or other social safety nets – yields big benefits for individuals, in addition to improving efficiency for governments and aid agencies by reducing transaction costs and leakage. In India, digitising government transfers cut bribe demands for receiving the payment by 47% and boosted beneficiaries' payments by excluding middlemen who skimmed funds.

Benefits to the Banks	• Attracting low cost deposits to reduce the dependence on bulk deposits from corporates. Opportunity for the banks to cross sell various products. • Access to Business Opportunity.
Benefits to the Users	• Access to insurance resulting in a cushion against unplanned expenses. • Receiving social security transfers.
Benefits to Technology Providers	• Wider markets for smart cards. • Opportunity of new business.
Benefits to the Government	• Reduction in the cost of subsidies. • Reduction in inefficiency from the system. • Raising of resources through various investment options.
Benefits to the Economy	• Bringing the additional savings into the formal financial channel. • Faster and Inclusive Economic Growth • Development of Agriculture and other sectors.

Conclusion

Financial inclusion is important for any economy. The availability of banking facilities and strong bank branch network are the major facilitators of developmental activities. The problem of financial exclusion needs to be tackled if we want our country to grow in an equitable and sustainable manner.

Financial Inclusion in India: Status and Challenges

Q.7 Mere opening of bank accounts will not transform into financial inclusion in India. Examine. With a number of issues continuing to be a roadblock, a large section of India's rural population is still 'financially excluded'. Discuss. (250 Words, 15 Marks)

Ans. **Introduction** Financial inclusion has been defined as 'the process of ensuring access to financial services, timely and adequate credit for vulnerable groups such as weaker sections and low-income groups at an affordable cost'.

The main concept of financial inclusion is to ensure availability of financial services in the most accessible and affordable manner. It is more than just opening of bank accounts and comprises of the following financial services:

- bank accounts for savings and transactional purposes,
- low-cost credit for productive, personal and other purposes,
- financial advisory services,
- Insurance facilities (life and non-life) etc.

Pradhan Mantri Jan Dhan Yojana (PMJDY) is the National Mission for Financial Inclusion. It goes beyond the opening of bank accounts and aims to provide a comprehensive financial inclusion. It ensures access to financial services, namely, Banking/ Savings and Deposit Accounts, Remittance, Credit, Insurance, Pension in an affordable manner.

Extent of Financial Exclusion in India

- India still has the second-largest unbanked population in the world and according to a recent report by the Reserve Bank of India, on a scale of 100, India's annual Financial Inclusion Index in 2022 stood at 56.4.
- **Non-operative/Dormant Accounts** Around 20% of the accounts are inoperative and 8.2 % of PMJDY accounts are zero balance accounts. The dormancy in PMJDY accounts currently can be attributed to factors such as lack of information on operational procedures, product features and account duplication.
- As per Global Findex Report, 2017, over 190 million Indian adults still do not have a bank account.
- **Duplicate Accounts** According to a survey by Microsave, 31% of Jan Dhan Accounts were duplicate accounts. Duplicate implies that the Jan Dhan account holder had a second bank account in his name.
- **No Increase in Formal Credit** Share of small borrowers in total credit has been declining since 2014. Small agricultural credit has stagnated since 2014. Small personal loans (for home, vehicle, durable goods etc) declined in the same period. The credit-deposit ratio has more or less stagnated in rural areas and has deteriorated slightly from 58.2% in 2014 to 57.7% in 2016 for semi-urban populations.
- Today, Indian women stand at the forefront as the country witnessed a sharp fall in gender gap in terms of bank accounts. This gender gap was 6% in 2017, a decline from 20% in 2014.
- Digital channels are able to provide most of the banking services; they are unable to popularise loan products through digital platform due to lack of digital literacy.

Reasons for Rural Financial Exclusion

- **Socio-economic Factors** Financial exclusion is related to the social conditions of low income households, who are not able to access the available financial products and services. Various constraints such as low income, low savings and generally low levels of awareness hinders financial inclusion in the rural areas.
- **Supply Side Impediments** These include geographical factors such as distance from the bank coupled with remoteness and less population in rural areas reduces the financial inclusion.
- **Poor Rural Infrastructure** Dismal rural infrastructure like poor transportation, electricity, telecommunication and internet services etc. creates operational hurdles.
- **Perception of Obligation** The financial institutions are reluctant to serve small value and unprofitable customers with irregular income. Banks perceive inclusion as an obligation rather than a business opportunity. This discourages banks from providing financial services to low income individuals.
- **Trust** The local money lenders or small financial companies enjoy trust and are able to attract business, whereas formalised financial institutions remain unattractive.
- **Lack of Documents** Another factor preventing them from accessing formal financial institutions are the requirement of various document proof. The poor generally lack documents such as Aadhaar card, income certificate, birth certificate, address proof etc.
- **Financial Illiteracy** Lack of financial literacy is the major hurdle. The rural population as a result, relies mostly on the informal sector for availing finance at high rates which lead to the vicious circle of poverty and debt repayment.
- **Operational Issues** Frequent loan waivers driven by political agenda aggravate bankers' woes, cumbersome documentation procedures etc.
- **Social and Cultural Constraints** Promotion of financial products like insurance, digital payments is challenging in rural areas.

Conclusion

Though significant progress has been made in rural finance through SHGs, public sector banks, cooperatives and RRBs, more policy and technological innovations such as improving financial literacy, doorstep delivery, facilitating growth of online and paperless banking, etc., are need of the hour to address financial exclusion of rural population.

Financial Inclusion Approaches in India

Q.8 Highlight the various approaches/measures taken by the government and RBI for promoting financial inclusion in India. (150 Words, 10 Marks)

Ans. Introduction In a diverse country like India, financial inclusion is a critical part of the development process. Since independence, the combined efforts of successive governments, regulatory institutions and the civil society have helped in increasing the financial-inclusion net in the country.

There have been various approaches adopted to improve financial inclusion in India:

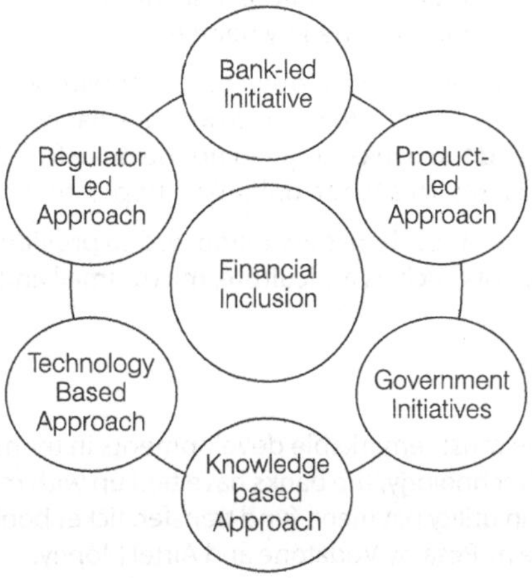

Product Based Approach

Reserve Bank of India has been proactive, liberal and supportive while making policies so as to enable financial institutions to come up with innovative products for enabling a common man to get the benefit of the financial inclusion plan. Some products developed for fulfilment of this approach are:

No- Frills Account (NFAs)	This concept was introduced by RBI in November 2005 to provide access to basic baking services by financially excluded peoples. Under this approach banks open accounts with zero balance or very minimum balance requirement for the under-privileged. In 2012, the banks under RBI guidelines came-up with a better version of the no-frill accounts where they would open Basic Savings Bank Deposit Accounts (BSBDAs) for all individuals with the facility of debit card, cheque book, internet banking, overdraft limits at minimal charges. However, the number of transactions could be restricted so as to prevent misuse of such accounts.
Kisan Credit Cards (KCCs)	Under this scheme banks issue smart cards to the farmers for providing timely and adequate credit support from single window banking system for their farming needs.

Bank Led Approach

- **Self Help Group - Bank Led Initiative (SLBP)** The SBLP or Self Help Group – Bank Linkage Programme has been the major institutional based innovation in India for enabling access and covering the gap of reaching financially excluded population of the country in the last two decades. In this model, the banks involve themselves with a group of local people with the idea of enabling them to pool up their savings. The same is deposited with the bank against which the bank also provides a certain amount of credit facility.
- **Business Facilitators (BFs)/Business Correspondents (BCs)** The BC/BF model is a model which based on Information and Communication Technology (ICT). In this model, the intermediaries or BC/BFs are technologically empowered by the banks to provide the last mile delivery of financial products and services.

Regulatory Approach

Simplified KYC Norms	• Under current KYC norms, a customer has to provide number of documents for opening an account as per RBI guidelines. However, the people living in rural areas face problem in fulfilling these norms. To enable banks to tap in this huge opportunity of rural banking in unbanked areas and to meet the objective of financial inclusion, RBI has relaxed a number of norms for accounts opened by people .
Bank Branch Authorisation	• RBI has permitted banks to open branches without taking authorisation, thus deviating from its normal norms, in tier 3 to 6 city, towns or villages. This would enable the government, regulator and the banks to speed up the drive for financial inclusion and this make available the financial services to the unbanked population of the country.
Priority Sector Lending	• Introduced in 1969, banks are mandated to provide 40% of the adjusted bank credit to the priority sectors such as agriculture; micro, small and business enterprises; etc.

Technology Based Approach

Mobile Banking	• One of the most remarkable developments in terms of innovation in order to harness the full power of technology, the banks have tied up with mobile operators to provide financial services like bill and utility payment, fund transfer, ticket booking, shopping etc. Some examples of this model are m-Pesa by Vodafone and Airtel Money.
Kiosk / ATM Based Banking	• In some states, the State Government has taken initiatives for providing kiosk based model for access to financial services. Also banks have used the technology to enable their ATMs to virtually act like a 24x7 branches.
Branchless Banking	• Some of the leading banks have come up with this concept where there would be an online system with chat facility assisting the person to make use of various electronic machines for depositing and withdrawing cash and cheques.

Knowledge Based Approach

Financial education, financial inclusion and financial stability are three elements of an integral strategy to empower people to make effective use of the financial services network. While financial inclusion works from supply side, financial education feeds the demand side by promoting awareness among the people regarding the needs and benefits of financial services offered by banks and other institutions. These two strategies together promote greater financial stability.

- RBI had issued guidelines on the Financial Literacy Centres (FLC) in June 2012 for setting up FLCs. It was advised that the rural branches of scheduled commercial banks should increase efforts through conduct of outdoor Financial Literacy Camps atleast once a month.

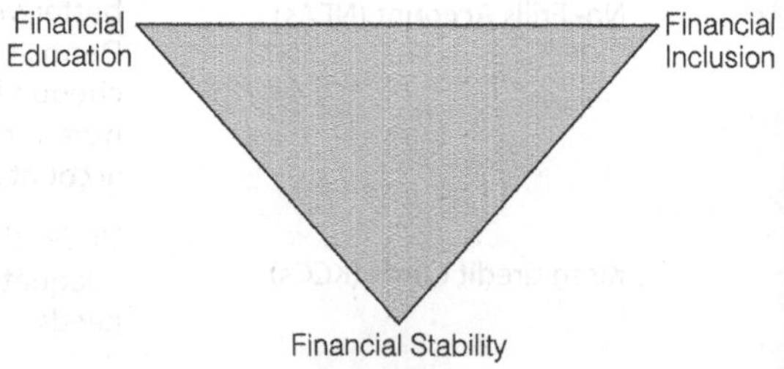

The Financial Tripod

- The Centre for Financial Literacy (CFL) project has been conceptualised by the RBI in 2017 as an innovative and participatory approach to financial literacy at the Block level involving select banks and Non-Governmental Organisations (NGOs). Initially set up in 100 blocks on a pilot basis, the project is now being scaled up across the country to every block in a phased manner by March 2024.
- Pocket Money is a flagship programme of Securities and Exchange Board of India (SEBI) and National Institute of Securities Markets (NISM's) flagship programme aimed at increasing financial literacy among school students.

Important Government Initiatives

Nationalisation of Banks	Considered as the first step towards financial inclusion which changed the nature of banking from 'class banking' to 'mass banking'.
Overdraft Facility	Basic savings bank accounts with overdraft facility of ₹10,000 to every eligible adult.
Pradhan Mantri Jan Dhan Yojana	**Financial Literacy Programme** Promoting savings, use of ATMs, Getting ready for credit, availing insurance and pensions, using basic mobile phones for banking.
Insurance and Pension Schemes	Government has launched many insurance and pension schemes. This includes Atal Pension Yojana, Pradhan Mantri Suraksha Bima Yojana and Jan Suraksha Yojana.
Pradhan Mantri Mudra Yojana	Pradhan Mantri Mudra Yojana provides formal access of financial facilities to non-corporate small business sector. The basic objective of the scheme is to promote and ensure bank finance to the unfunded segment of the Indian economy.
Digital Initiatives	Initiatives like Digital India, payments banks and small finance banks have helped to improve the reach of formal financial services to economically disadvantaged sections. This will help to provide financial services to both the unbanked and the underbanked population, especially in rural/remote regions.

Conclusion

The government is committed to its target of increasing the inclusion of every household in the financial system so that the masses can get all the legitimate benefits arising out of the growth of the country and in turn, the funds mobilised from the people not earlier in the formal channel could also be brought in the formal channel thereby giving the economy of the country an extra thrust to lead the path of growth.

Financial Inclusion and Gender Inequality

Q.9 Discuss the importance of financial inclusion in bridging gender inequalities. Examine the relevant inclusive measures initiated by the Government of India and their effectiveness in bringing women under the institutional finance fold. (250 Words, 15 Marks)

Ans. **Introduction** Since 2014, according to data from the Ministry of Finance, over 460 million bank accounts have been opened; 56% are owned by women. This implies remarkable FI that has significantly reduced the gender gap, from 17% in 2011 to 6% in 2017.

As per the data from Ministry of Finance, nearly 20% of women in India remain without access to a bank account. Among those who do have a bank account, there are gaps in use of such accounts and they also continue to lack access to savings and credit.

Importance of Financial Inclusion Measures for Women

- **Building Financial Resilience** Women are decision-makers for spending and savings in most low-income households. They are thus more committed and disciplined savers than men. Thus, it is economically viable for banks to target women, while contributing to such social good. This can help in dealing with various shocks like COVID-19 pandemic.
- **Increasing Social Capital** Women's engagement with financial institutions and their ability to access participation in work and credit from such institutions can increase their social capital. Thus, empowering 230 million women Jan Dhan customers financially leads to the potential upliftment of 920 million lives, at an average family of four. This results in direct improvements in outcomes of health, education and employment.

- **Critical For Women's Empowerment and Poverty Reduction** Providing low-income women with effective and affordable financial tools to save and borrow money, make and receive payments and manage risk is critical to both women's empowerment and poverty reduction.
  - In turn, such progress helps achieve the collective goals of eradicating poverty, promoting inclusive growth and reducing inequality.
- **Fulfilment of Sustainable Development Goals** Helps in the economic empowerment of women which is one of the targets under SDG 5 – Gender Equality.

Government Measures towards Financial Inclusion

India has been successful in bringing women under formal credit system according to Findex 2017 estimates, 77% of Indian women now own a bank account against respective 43% and 26% in 2014 and 2011 owing to the following measures.

- **Self-Help Group System,** where commercial banks open accounts for groups with 15-20 members, usually low-income women, using their pooled savings. The banks then use the funds to issue loans to the members. This model helps in bringing more women under sustainable development in a cost effective manner within a short span of time.
- **The Bank Sakhis Programme** by the National Rural Livelihoods Mission trains SHG members to work as BCs in rural districts.
- **Pradhan Mantri Jan Dhan Yojana (PMJDY) Programme** is a government initiative to provide access to financial services to all Indians.
- The effective implementation of Aadhaar-based eKYC collection and authentication lowered barriers of entry to the formal financial system. It has allowed the Jan Dhan-Aadhaar-Mobile (JAM) trinity to lay the foundation to bring 230 million unserved and underserved women into the formal financial services ecosystem.
- The PM Mudra Yojana targets the financial inclusion of women by providing collateral-free loans up to ₹ 1 million for small and micro enterprises.
- **Direct Benefits Transfer (DBT)** Since its inception in 2013, the Indian Government has cumulatively transferred 16.8 trillion to beneficiaries through DBT. This has led to the FI of women, as they constitute a good number of beneficiaries under the schemes.

Status of Financial Inclusion among Women

- According to a recently released report by Women's World Banking, most women only access their PMJDY accounts to withdraw the benefit transfers that they receive in them from the various government initiatives that they are eligible for and most of them do not use these accounts for savings, to build a credit history or avail of any financial products such as insurance and loans.
- **Bank Account** The percentage of women who have a bank or savings account that they themselves use has increased from 53% in NFHS-4 (2015-16) to 79% in NFHS-5 (2019-21).
- **Access to Credit** As per NFHS-5 (2019-21), women's access to credit remains low, even as awareness about micro-credit programmes has increased. Only 11% have ever taken a microcredit loan. Women's use of microcredit programmes is higher in rural areas (12%) than in the urban regions (9%).
- **Digital Gender Divide** The digital gender divide remains pervasive, both in terms of access and literacy - 53.9% of women have a mobile phone that they themselves use; 71% of women who have a mobile phone can read text messages. Only 22.5% of women with mobile phones use them for financial transactions.
- **Inactivity in the Account** According to the Global Findex Survey 2021, of the women-owned bank accounts in India, more than 32% are inactive. The gender gap in account inactivity is highest in the country at 12 percentage points. Of the women who have a bank account, less than one-fifth save formally with the bank; for many, usage is limited to withdrawal for emergencies, withdrawing salary or availing government benefits
- **Interest Rates** Interest rates paid by female household heads are on average higher than their male counterparts. The gender differential reduces with per capita income improvements, showing poverty accentuates gender divisions.

Gender Based Barriers to Financial Inclusion

Demand Side Barriers	Supply Side Barriers	Legal and Regulatory Barriers
Lack of bargaining power within the household	Inappropriate product offerings.	Account opening requirements that disadvantage women.
Concentration in lower paying economic activities.	Lack of gender specific policies and practices for product design and marketing.	Barriers to obtaining formal identification.
Competing demands on women's time related to unpaid domestic work.	Inappropriate distribution channels.	Legal barriers to owning and inheriting property and other collateral.
Lack of assets for collateral.	Inaccessibility: Most financial services are beyond the reach of most women, particularly in the rural hinterland.	Lack of gender inclusive credit reporting systems.
Lack of formal identification	Dearth of targeted financial education and awareness campaigns tailored to women's specific needs and challenges.	
Reduced mobility or financial decision making power due to time constraints or social norms (patriarchal culture).	Rural women not exposed to the benefits of digital payments.	
Lower rates of cell phone ownership among women needed to access many digital products.		

Way Forward

- **Promote the Use of Digital Payments Among Women** This will reduce physical and financial risks for women associated with travelling to the bank branch. Thereby, reducing the time and effort required to manage their finances. Further, they offer a level of privacy, confidentiality and a sense of control over women's financial information.
- **Gender-Disaggregated Data** Financial service providers need to deploy strategies that focus on the Jan Dhan women segment by using sex-disaggregated data. For instance, target and communicate with women and design products and processes to be women-centric.
  - At a policy-level, collecting and analysing gender-disaggregated data is vital for the creation of products and services for low-income women.
- **In-design Changes** The design tweaks that take into account the specific needs and preferences of women can enhance their access to financial products, as well as the impact of those products on women's ability to make investments and smooth consumption in the face of income shocks.
  - Financial Products which allow women greater degrees of control and privacy surrounding their incomes and spending decisions appear to be particularly promising.
- **Promote Women's Access to, and Literacy in Digital Tools** An underlying factor that restricts women's use of formal financial services is the lack of capability to conduct transactions.
- **Nurture the Ecosystem of Business Correspondents in rural Areas** To ensure women have digital and financial capabilities, India should nurture the ecosystem of business correspondents in rural areas. The correspondents should offer a broader range of services than just plain banking. Such as overdrafts for emergencies, micro-insurance, micro-pension and other similar products. The BC model circumvents the challenges women face with mobility and literacy.
- **Deepen Convergence With Self-Help Groups** SHGs can also be tapped to run financial literacy centres for women. Livelihood and skill-development programmes by SHGs can be integrated with other initiatives in digital financial inclusion.

Conclusion

While awareness in the financial literacy has a key role to play, simultaneously strengthening infrastructure and removing gender disparity by empowering more women at the forefront will have a strong role in making the progress and paving the way forward for better and stronger implementation, of 'Banking- financial services', for all.

Digital Financial inclusion: Modern Approach

Q.10 Identify the factors that have facilitated digital financial inclusion in India. Mention the steps that have been taken by the government in this regard. What are the challenges that remain going forward? (250 Words, 15 Marks)

Ans. **Introduction** Digital financial inclusion means the deployment of a range of digital financial services at an affordable cost to reach financially excluded and underserved population. It requires a robust communication infrastructure for retail agents, along with digital transaction platforms and electronic devices such as mobile phones and payment cards.

Factors that have Facilitated Digital Financial Inclusion in India

- **Limitations of Traditional Banking Systems** Conventional banking models are proving to be uneconomical for low ticket size of transactions, deposits, loans, etc. in rural and remote regions.
- **Mobile Phone Penetration and Cheap Internet** It has offered an innovative low-cost channel to extend the reach of banking and payment services.
- **Direct Benefit Transfers and Government-to-Citizen Payments** Around 433 schemes under 56 ministries are being channelized through DBT e.g. MGNREGA payments, fuel and fertiliser subsidies, insurances and pension schemes, etc.
- **Fintech Revolution** It is led by a host of players, including commercial banks, telecommunication firms, payment banks, small finance banks and financial technology companies.

Other than the factors mentioned above, government policies have played a crucial role in facilitating digital financial inclusion. Steps taken by the government in this regard are:

- **Jan Dhan-Aadhar-Mobile Trinity** Government has provided a Jan Dhan bank account to nearly 381 million people. It has also developed Aadhar enabled payment systems and mobile based applications for transaction purposes. RuPay debit cards have also been issued under PMJDY for ATM withdrawals and Point of Sale payments.
- **Unified Payment Interface** Launched by the National Payment Council of India, it allows users to easily make payments directly from their bank accounts using only a Virtual Payment Address (VPA) linked to the recipient's bank account and phone number.
- **Digital India** To provide internet access to rural areas, National Optical Fibre Network has been launched. It also includes universal access to mobile connectivity, development of mobile based applications and banking and insurance mission mode projects. To increase fintech literacy programmes such as DigiShala and Digital Jagriti have been started.
- **National Strategy for Financial Inclusion (2019-2024)** It focuses upon strengthening the ecosystem for digital financial services in all tier II to tier VI cities by March 2022.
- **RBI Initiatives** In August 2019, RBI introduced Regulatory Sandbox (RS) to foster responsible innovation in financial services.

Digital Financial Inclusion Initiatives

The evolution of DFS in India since 2014 can be broadly broken up into three phases of growth.

- The first phase, from early 2014 to around August 2016 was characterised by steady growth of around 2% per month in transaction volumes on the major digital platforms.

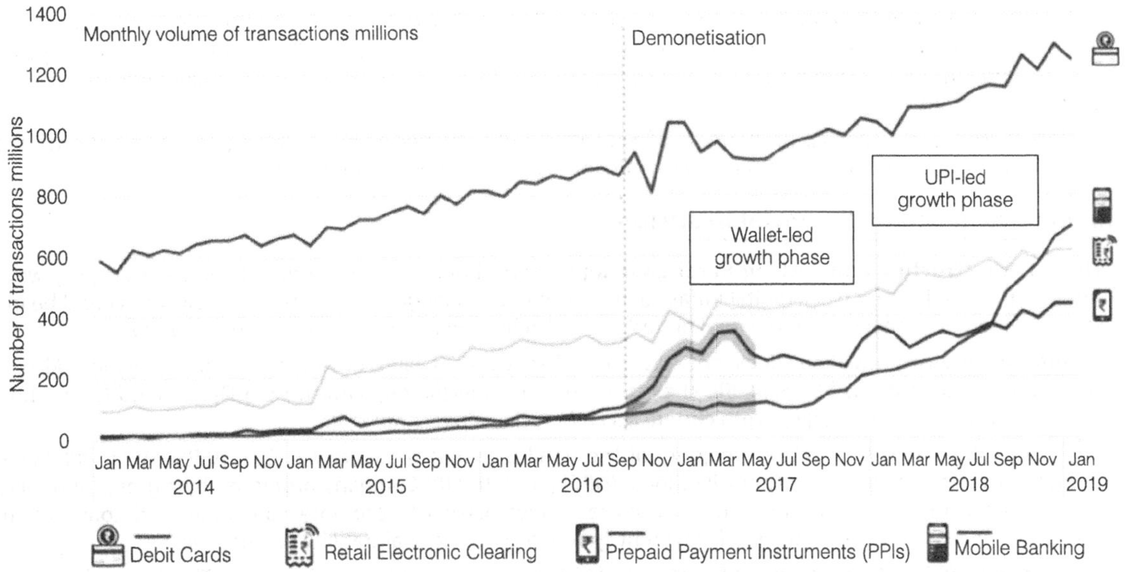

- Then, in the last few months of 2016, transactions through pre-paid instruments (PPIs – mostly digital wallets like Paytm and Mobikwik) began to grow rapidly – the volume of PPI transactions trebled between September 2016 and January 2017. This second phase was driven primarily by demonetisation.
- This growth tailed off however and the third phase was driven not by pre-paid instruments but by the introduction of Unified Payments Interface (UPI), NPCI's interoperable digital payments platform that grew from barely any transactions in mid-2017 to overtake PPIs and debit cards as the primary vehicle for digital transactions.

There are various initiatives that have been taken in this regard as follows

- **Jan Dhan-Aadhaar-Mobile (JAM) Trinity** The combination of Aadhaar, Pradhan Mantri Jan-Dhan Yojana (PMJDY) and a surge in mobile communication has reshaped the way citizens access government services.
- **DBT Transfers and Government to Person (G2P) Payments** PMJDY has been closely linked with the growth of the government's Direct Benefit Transfer (DBT) mission.
- **Expansion of Financial Services in Rural and Semi-Urban Areas** Reserve Bank of India (RBI) and National Bank for Agriculture and Rural Development (NABARD) have taken initiatives to promote financial inclusion in rural areas. These include:
  - Opening of bank branches in remote areas,
  - Issuing Kisan Credit Cards (KCC),
  - Linkage of Self-Help Groups (SHGs) with banks,
  - Increasing the number of Automated Teller Machines (ATMs),
  - Business correspondents model of Banking Payment Infrastructure Development Fund (PIDF) scheme, etc.
- **Promotion of Secure Digital Payments** With the strengthening of the Unified Payments Interface (UPI) by National Payments Corporation of India (NPCI), digital payments have been made secure, compared to the past.
  - The Aadhaar-Enabled Payment System (AEPS) enables an Aadhaar Enabled Bank Account (AEBA) to be used at any place and at any time, using micro ATMs.
  - The payment system has been made more accessible due to offline transaction-enabling platforms, like Unstructured Supplementary Service Data (USSD), which makes it possible to use mobile banking services without internet, even on a basic mobile handset.
- **Fintech Companies have been at the Forefront of the Growth in Digital Payments in India** These include payment companies that facilitate P2P and retail payments through mobile wallets or UPI, such as Paytm, PhonePe, PayU, MobiKwik and FreeCharge, as well as technology companies like Pine Labs and Mswipe who provide hardware and POS devices for digital payments.

- **Enhancing Financial Literacy** The Reserve Bank of India has undertaken a project titled 'Project Financial Literacy." The Objective of the project is to disseminate information regarding the Central Bank and general banking concepts to various target groups, including, school and college going children, women, rural and urban poor, defence personnel and senior citizens.
  - Pocket Money is a flagship programme of Securities and Exchange Board of India (SEBI) and National Institute of Securities Market (NISM) aimed at increasing financial literacy among school students.

Challenges in Digital Financial Inclusion

- **Digital Infrastructure and Lacking Rural Coverage** Smart phone numbers in rural India are low along with weaker internet penetration and weak digital infrastructure. The key challenge that needs to be resolved would be improving tele and internet connectivity in the rural hinterland and achieving connectivity across the country.
- **Regulatory Framework** India does not have a unified code of laws governing fintech activities. Also, multiple regulatory bodies such as RBI, SEBI, IRDAI exist. There is no specific regulator for Big Data, Cloud Computing AI and Distributed Ledger Technology (crypto currencies and blockchain technology).
- **Payment Infrastructure** Currently, majority of the retail payment products viz., CTS, AEPS,NACH, UPI, IMPS etc are operated by National Payments Council of India (NPCI), a Section(8) Company promoted by a group of public, private and foreign banks. There is a need to have more market players to promote innovation and competition and to minimise concentration risk in the retail payment system from a financial stability perspective.
- **Data Protection and Cyber security** The Indian data protection regime needs a revamp. The Personal Data Protection Bill and the National Cyber Security Strategy 2020 is still in pipeline.
- **Systemic Risk in the Digital Payment Ecosystem** Digital payment transactions undertaken through UPIs are concentrated among few non-banking players Example Google Pay, PhonePe, Paytm.
- **Trust and Security in Digital Commerce** The surge in digital transactions has increased the risk for possible security breaches, both for consumers and businesses.
- **Literacy and Understanding** Digital finance providers moving into lower income markets will continue to face challenges around literacy (financial, digital and general) and the ability to comprehend the concepts and practical implications of using digital finance products.

Conclusion

Steps like developing the regulatory framework for digital finance, ensuring digital consumer protection, promoting digital financial literacy, supporting local level innovation such as use of feature phones and bridging digital and analogue financial lives of the rural consumers through Cash-In and Cash-Out (CICO)etc. can promote digital financial inclusion and has the potential to reduce poverty and aid in faster achievement of other sustainable development goals.

Assessment of Pradhan Mantri Jan Dhan Yojana (PMJDY)

Q.11 'Financial Inclusion is an enabler for Inclusive Growth.' In this context, do you agree with the view that Pradhan Mantri Jan Dhan Yojana (PMJDY) led interventions produced both transformational as well as directional change? Critically comment. (250 Words, 15 Marks)

Ans. Introduction Pradhan Mantri Jan Dhan Yojana (PMJDY), launched in August 2014, is the national mission on financial inclusion. The objective of PMJDY is to ensure access to various financial services, such as availability of basic savings bank account, access to need-based credit, remittance facility, insurance and pension to the otherwise excluded sections, i.e., weaker sections and low-income groups. There were three basic tenets of the scheme:

- **Banking the Unbanked** Opening of Basic Savings Bank Deposit (BSBD) account with minimal paperwork, relaxed KYC,-KYC, account opening in camp mode, zero balance & zero charges.
- **Securing the Unsecured** Issuance of Indigenous Debit cards for cash withdrawals and payments at merchant locations, with free accident insurance coverage of ₹ 2 lakhs.
- **Funding the Unfunded** Other financial products like micro-insurance, overdraft for consumption, micro-pension and micro-credit.

Financial Inclusion as an enabler of Inclusive Growth

- **Includes Everyone** Financial inclusion provides banking services for everyone entering into the economic sphere which helps to promote inclusive growth. **Example** Jan Dhan Bank accounts is a very significant step which provided bank accounts to all which further help in their inclusion in formal economy.
- **Culture of Savings** Financial inclusion is necessary for inclusive growth as it leads to the culture of saving, which initiates a virtuous cycle of economic development.
- **A Means of Growth** Financial inclusion stands just not as tool for economic growth but also as a means of individual growth. Ex: Women having bank accounts enables them to enter into the formal financial sphere.
- **Increases Formal Economy** Financial inclusion promotes formal economy by regularising the banking habits. **Example** Jan Dhan Bank helped government to filter out the ghost beneficiaries of direct benefit transfer.
- **Inclusion of Under Privileged** The hitherto undeveloped and the weaker sections of the society receives inclusion into the formal economy. **Example** Today, India has Aadhaar linked bank accounts, which helped in providing the benefits of a banking services to various underprivileged sections of nation economy.

PMJDY produced both Transformational and Directional Change in Indian Economy

- **Banking the Unbanked** This pillar of Jan Dhan Yojana pertains to opening of Basic Savings Bank Deposit (BSBD) account with minimal paperwork, relaxed KYC, e-KYC, account opening in camp mode, zero balance and zero charges. Aadhar contributed to **account ownership in about 80% of adults (from 35% in 2011)**.
  - The bank accounts were once seen as to have minimum balance, but under PMJDY there can be zero balance accounts.
- **Social Empowerment** Rural PMJDY accounts stand at 67%. Women PMJDY accounts stand at 55.2%. Thus, giving the rural poor and women an opportunity to enhance their standard of living.
- **Priority to Women** The overdraft facility of the PMJDY which is available to only one account per household is preferably to the lady of the house.
- **Increase in Bank Deposits** Deposits have increased 7.60 times with an increase in accounts by 2.58 times between August 2015 and August 2022. The average deposit per account is ₹ 3,761.
- **Securing the Unsecured** It pertains to issuance of indigenous debit cards for cash withdrawals and payments at merchant locations, with free accident insurance coverage of ₹ 2 lakh. With more than 13 crore beneficiaries enrolling for the low-cost accident insurance cover and close to 5.5 crore for the life cover.
- **Funding the Unfunded** Funding the Unfunded pertains to other financial products like micro-insurance, overdraft for consumption, micro-pension and micro-credit.
- **Formalisation of Financial System** It provides an avenue for the poor to bring their savings into the formal financial system, an avenue to remit money to their families in villages besides taking them out of the clutches of the usurious money lenders.
- **Infusion of Technology** Traditional Indian economy has been transforming as digital economy with the infusion of technology and Jan Dhan Yojana has a big role in this.
  - The Yojana has helped in opening the bank accounts in rural areas through Banking Correspondents just because of technology infusion.
- **Identifying Beneficiaries** Beneficiaries identification and provision of transfers has become easier, there is a reduction of ghost beneficiaries too.
  - **Example** PMJDY accounts grown three-fold from 14 crores in 2015 to 46 crores in 2022.
- **Reduction of Leakages in Welfare Schemes** The scheme has managed to bring much needed financial discipline among the financially excluded and the middlemen have been cut to a large extent by enabling direct credit to the accounts of the various Direct Benefit Transfer (DBT) schemes. Global Findex Report 2021 observed that transitioning from cash to biometric smart cards has reduced leakage by 47% in pension payments.
- **Foundation Stone for People-centric Economic Initiatives** PMJDY has been the foundation stone for people-centric economic initiatives. Whether it is direct benefit transfers, COVID-19-related financial assistance, PM-KISAN, increased wages under MGNREGA, life and health insurance cover, the first step of all these initiatives is to provide every adult with a bank account, which is possible because of PMJDY.

- **Remittance Services** Jan Dhan Yojana served as an avenue to remit money to migrant's families in villages.
- **Enhancing Financial Literacy** The PMJDY further promotes financial literacy through usage of debit cards and their usage.
  - **Example** RuPay debit card must be used for every 45 days, which indicates promoting the usage of bank accounts continuously.

Challenges of PMJDY

However, financial inclusion is not just about opening bank accounts, but also about using these accounts and providing access to formal credit.

- **Non-operative/Dormant Accounts** Around 20% of the accounts are inoperative and 8.2% of PMJDY accounts are zero balance accounts. The dormancy in PMJDY accounts currently can be attributed to factors such as lack of information on operational procedures, product features and account duplication.
- **Duplicate Accounts** According to a survey by Microsave, 31% of Jan Dhan Accounts were duplicate accounts. Duplicate implies that the Jan Dhan account holder had a second bank account in his name.
- **Less Emphasis on Financial Literacy** A major limitation of the PMJDY has been the weak mechanism to impart financial literacy among the poor masses.
- **No Increase in Formal Credit** Share of small borrowers in total credit has been declining since 2014. Small agricultural credit has stagnated since 2014. Small personal loans (for home, vehicle, durable goods etc) declined in the same period. The credit-deposit ratio has more or less stagnated in rural areas and has deteriorated slightly from 58.2% in 2014 to 57.7% in 2016 for semi-urban populations.
- **Continued Presence of Moneylenders** Dependence on informal credit has not decreased. According to Household Survey on Indian's Citizen Environment and Consumer Economy, 2016, two out of three people of the poorest section of the society take credit from informal sources. Most of these people fail to repay loan in time and get into debt trap.
- **PSU Banks Not Benefiting** Compared to private sector banks, PSU banks are not performing so well. 64% of private sector accounts have zero balance as against 71% accounts in PSU banks.

Conclusion

To address the above identified challenges and consolidate the gains made so far, the government decided to make the Pradhan Mantri Jan Dhan Yojana (PMJDY) an open-ended scheme (meaning that it will continue indefinitely). There has been a shift in focus from 'every household' to 'every adult', with added emphasis on usage of accounts by enhancing Direct Benefit Transfer (DBT) flows through these accounts, promoting digital payments through the use of RuPay cards, etc

Microfinance (Microfinance and Financial Inclusion)

Q.12 While highlighting the significance of microfinance for Indian economy, critically examine the effectiveness of microcredit that has come under question in recent times due to multiple reasons. (150 Words, 10 Marks)

Ans. **Introduction** Microfinance is defined as financial services such as savings account, insurance funds and credit provided to poor and low income clients so as to help them increase their income, thereby improving their standard of living. The basic feature of the microcredit is that these are the loans given without security.

The core idea of micro-credit is that a small loan will provide access to the larger economy to people who typically live outside the scope of the institutions on which the mainstream economy rests. The concept of microfinance has been highlighted since 1970s with an aim to uplift the poor section of the society and to enhance economic growth. It is being promoted in India by agencies like NABARD via Microfinance Institutions (MFIs), formation of Self-Help Groups (SHGs) among others.

Microcredit is delivered through a variety of institutional channels including Scheduled Commercial Banks (through Business Correspondents), Regional Rural Banks (RRBs), Cooperative Banks, Non-Banking Financial Companies (NBFCs) and Microfinance Institutions (MFIs).

Channels of Micro-finance in Indian Economy

There are two channels through which microfinance is being operated in India:

- **SHG-Bank Linkage Programme (SBLP)** In the year 1992, NABARD initiated this channel. This model incites women to unite together to form a group of 10-15 members where all the women belonging to financial backward classes contributes by giving their individual savings to the group at regular intervals. Thereafter, loans are provided to the members of the group by their contributions. Self-Help Groups (SHGS) also at later stage provide loans for income generating activities. It has been observed that once these self-help groups reach to the level of stability, they function almost independently with minimal support from NABARD, SIDBI and Non-Governmental Organisations.
- **Growth of Microfinance Institutions (MFIs)** These are financial institutions that provide loans and other financial services to poor sections of the society. Usually, they operate in rural areas and among low income urban people by extending small loans. These companies are regulated as NBFC-MFIs under the Non-Banking Financial Company Micro Finance Institutions (Reserve Bank) Directions, 2011 of the Reserve Bank of India (RBI).

Importance of Microfinance for Indian Economy

- **Access of Formal Financial System to Low Income People** Access to formal banking channels are low due to the lack of resources and nature of formal credit institutions. Consequently, in India, microfinance institutions and Self-Help Groups are leading to other traditional banking channels as they are catering the need of credit to poor people.
- **Cheaper Interest rate than Informal Lending** A major benefit is the accessibility to loans at a relatively cheaper rate compared to the informal moneylenders, coupled with reduction in economic vulnerability. The SHG-linked programmes have also been successful in mobilising voluntary savings from poor households.
- **Prompting Entrepreneurship or Employment Generation** The utmost significance of microfinance in India is that it dispenses the access to the capital to small entrepreneurs or marginal farmers which helps in the generation of self-employment or entrepreneurial activities.
- **Poverty Alleviation Measure** It act as an anti-poverty vaccine for the people living in rural areas. It aims at assisting communities of the economically excluded to achieve greater level of asset creation and income security at the household and community level. Thus, bringing many people out of the poverty trap.
- **Promotion of Gender Equality** The concept of microfinance focuses on women also by granting them loans. It act as a tool for the empowerment of poor women as women are becoming independent, they are able to contribute directly to the well beings of their families and are able to confront all the gender inequalities. The major targets of microfinance are the poor rural and urban households and women too.
  - According to NABARD, the SHG-Bank Linkage Programme, covers 14.2 crore families through 119 lakh SHGs (87% of which are women) as of 31st March, 2022.

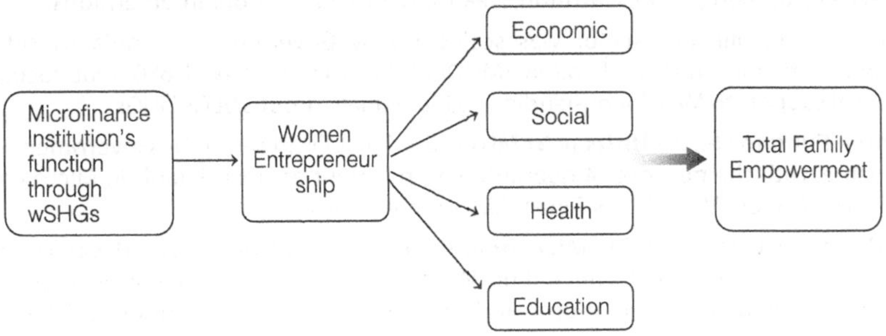

- **Rehabilitation** Microfinance is able to provide access to finance in naxal areas as well. It has thus helped in rehabilitation of the conflict-affected people.
- **Rural Development** Microfinance boosts economic activities in the rural area and thus aids in rural development. It helps create livelihood opportunities as well.

Effectiveness of Micro-Credit Institutions

Recent studies have shown that the impact of micro-credit has been very limited. Various reasons can be attributed to this such as:

- **High NPAs in Post-Pandemic Period** The overall NPA of the sector shot up from 4% as at end-March 2020 to 14% in September 2022 as per RBI's Financial Stability Report, 2022.
- **Rigid Repayment Schedules** Many microcredit programmes require that repayment starts almost immediately and then follows a strict weekly schedule. This makes it difficult for borrowers to use the money they receive for productive investments that may take time to be realised.
- **High Interest Rates** MFIs are private institutions and do not get any subsidised credit for their lending activities. Thus, they tend to charge higher interest rate. **Example** Andhra crisis in 2010 including many cases of exploitation of loanees.
- **Information Asymmetry** Many micro-credit borrowers have little or no formal credit history, meaning lenders have been unable to screen out unproductive borrowers. This curtails further lending to needy borrowers.
- **Inability to Generate Funds** MFIs face difficulty to raise sufficient funds as they are generally not 'for-profit'. This restricts their access to funds from private equity investors or other market-based avenues of funding.
- **Heavy Dependence on Banks** MFIs are dependent on borrowing from banks. For most MFI's funding sources are restricted to private banks. Funds available from these banks are typically for short term, generally 2 years. Moreover, Banks tend to disburse loans at the end of financial year to meet the targets. This can create issues for MFIs if there is delay in repayment of loans by borrowers.
- **Limited Purposes of Fund Utilisation** Even as microfinance plays an important role in helping poor families start businesses, pay off expensive loans, withstand health shocks; none of these is likely to prove significant in terms of reducing national poverty numbers.
- **Provision of Funds** Most micro-credit institutions raise funds from expensive sources like banks and NBFCs. This raises the interest charged on these loans making them unaffordable for the majority of the target population.
- **Regional Imbalances** There is unequal geographical growth of MFIs and SHGs in India. About 60% of the total SHG credit linkages in the country are concentrated in the Southern states. In poorer regions like in Jharkhand, Bihar etc where the proportion of the poor is higher, the coverage is comparatively lower. This could be attributed to lack of State Government support, NGO concentration and public awareness.

Measures Taken for Micro-Finance Sector

- **DAY-NRLM works on four components,** *viz.*, Institutional Building and Capacity Building (IBCB), Financial Inclusion via SHG-Bank Linkage Programme (SBLM), Farm Livelihood and Non-farm Livelihood and Convergence for Social Inclusion, Social Development, Food, Nutrition, Health, WASH and Gender interventions.
- **MUDRA** Support to Microfinance sector was scaled up by Government of India by setting up the Micro Units Development and Refinance Agency Limited (MUDRA) in 2015. It is an NBFC that focuses on micro-enterprises, extending financial support to MFIs for on-lending to individuals/groups/JLGs/SHGs.
- **Credit Guarantee Fund for Micro Units (CGFMU)** is the Trust Fund set up by Government of India and managed by NCGTC as a Trustee, with the purpose of guaranteeing payment against default in Micro Loans extended to eligible borrowers by Banks/ NBFCs/ MFIs/ Other Financial Intermediaries.
- **RBI has issued Master Directions for Microfinance loans for all Commercial Banks** (including SFBs, LABs and RRBs), PUCBs, StCBs, DCCBs and NBFCs (including MFI and HFC). The directive has brought all the institutions dealing with microfinance lending on one platform and as a result, these institutions will be regulated uniformly. The

directive will bring transparency in operations to enable customers to make an informed choice regarding their credit need and encourage healthy competition among lending institutions. **Microfinance loans are now collateral-free loans for households having annual income up to INR 3 lakh.**

Way forward

- The current financial inclusion activities by the MFIs need to move **beyond providing basic training facilities to creating ownership-linked initiatives.**
- **Expand Product Range** A diversified menu of micro loan products linked to sustainable income generation activities via micro enterprises or a creation of community-based pooled enterprise could possibly make it more attractive and compatible with the requirements of women. In addition, linking such developmental initiatives to an institution to nurture, monitor and handhold those activities in the formative stages is crucial for sustainability.
- **Interest Rate Transparency** MFIs are employing different patterns of charging interest rates and a few are also levying additional charges. MFIs should transparently inform the borrowers regarding the interest rate charged on the loans.
- **Encourage Microfinance Penetration** Encouraging MFIs for opening new branches in areas of low Microfinance penetration by providing financial assistance will increase the outreach of the Microfinance. This will increase rural penetration of Microfinance.
- **Use of Technology** MFIs should use new technologies, IT tools and applications to reduce operational costs.
- **Different Sources for Raising Funds** In the absence of sufficient finances, the reach of MFIs becomes limited. MFIs should look for other sources for funding their loan portfolio e.g., by converting to for-profit company (NBFC).
- There is a need to consider adopting **more flexible operating models, providing skills training and offering services such as portability of accounts** to provide greater access for a longer duration of time. Further, community information (friends, family, colleagues, and local leaders) should be used to identify productive entrepreneurs and assess credit risk.

Conclusion

The Microfinance sector has played an important role in ensuring inclusive and balanced development. Yet the benefits of Microfinance have been limited to some regions. Moreover, the sector faces issue of rising bad loans along with several operational challenges for the MFIs. There is a need for comprehensive regulation of the sector to make it more inclusive and sustainable.

Self-Help Group Bank Linkage Programme (SBLP) and Financial Inclusion

Q.13 The Self-Help Group (SHG) Bank Linkage Programme (SBLP), which is India's own innovation, has proved to be one of the most effective poverty alleviation and women empowerment programmes. Elucidate.
(200 Words, 12.5 Marks) **UPSC Mains 2015**

Ans. **Introduction** A committee constituted under the chairmanship of Dr. C. Rangarajan to prepare a comprehensive report on 'Financial Inclusion in the Country' identified weak community network as one of the significant reasons for financial exclusion.

- Thus, SBLP programme was started at the initiative of NABARD in 1992 to link the unorganised sector with the formal banking sector and has now become one of the largest micro-finance programmes in the world.
- The SHGs which follow 'Panchsutras' viz. conduct of regular group meetings, regular savings within the group, internal lending based on the demand of members, timely repayment of loan and maintenance of proper books of accounts are considered to be of good quality and over years have proved themselves to be good customers of banks.

About Self-Help Group Bank Linkage Programme

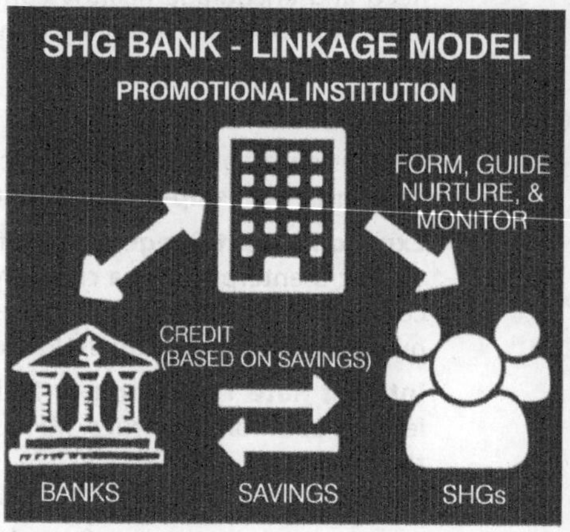

- Under this programme, banks were allowed to open savings accounts for Self-Help Groups (SHGs).
- SHGs are registered/unregistered entities which usually has a membership of 15 to 20 members from very low income families, usually women. They mobilize savings from members and uses the pooled funds to give loans to the needy members.
- Under this programme, banks provide loans to the SHGs against group guarantee and the quantum of loan could be several times the deposits placed by such SHGs with the banks.
- Banks should consider entire credit requirements of SHG members, namely, (a) income generation activities, (b) social needs like housing, education, marriage, etc and (c) debt swapping.
- The recovery rates of loans are good and banks have found that the transaction cost of reaching the poor through SHGs is considerably lower rather than direct lending by the bank.
- Based on the NABARD report on 'Status of Microfinance in India 2021-22', SBLP touches 14.2 crore households through 119 lakh SHGs.

SBLP has been an Effective Tool of Poverty Alleviation and Women Empowerment

- **Poverty Alleviation** The poverty alleviation intervention of the SHG is in the form of undertaking economic programmes to provide employment, giving micro finance services to the poor so that they can get themselves acquainted with skills and occupational diversification. This new initiative was taken up by Swarna Jayanti Gram Swarozgar Yojana, implemented in 1999 which is today known as Deendayal Antayodaya – National Rural Livelohood Mission (DAY-NRLM), to organize the poor into Self-Help groups.
- **Financial Inclusion** Priority Sector Lending norms and assurance of returns incentivise banks to lend to SHGs. The SHG-Bank linkage programme pioneered by NABARD has made access to credit easier and reduced the dependence on traditional money lenders and other non-institutional sources.
- **Asset Creation** The formation of SHGs has benefited its members by increasing their assets, incomes and employment opportunities and there has been a significant shift in the use of the loans from personal consumption to their being used for income generating purposes.
- **Breaking the Vicious Cycle of Inter-Generational Poverty Transfer** In addition, members have been able to increase savings and accumulate capital and in doing so, are now more financially stable. This has helped people in moving out of the vicious circle of poverty and unemployment.
  - **Example** Podupu Lakshmi Scheme implemented in the state of Andhra Pradesh has used development Self-Help Groups (SHGs) extensively as a primary tool of poverty alleviation and empowerment. Similarly, Jeevika Project of Bihar, Mahalir Thittam in Tamil Nadu, Kudumbashree in Kerala and TRIPTI/Mission Shakti projects in Odisha.
- **Training and Capacity Building** Cumulatively, as on 31st March, 2022, 4.7 lakh SHG members have been trained under MEDPs (Micro Enterprise Development Programmes) and 1.20 lakh SHGs given end-to end training under Livelihood Enterprise Development Programmes (LEDPs) to equip them for setting up their own enterprises.
- **Alternate Source of Employment** It eases dependency on agriculture by providing support in setting up micro-enterprises, e.g., personalised business ventures like tailoring, grocery and tool repair shops.
- **Changes in Consumption Pattern** It has enabled the participating households to spend more on education, food and health than non-client households.
- **Impact on Housing and Health** The financial inclusion attained through SHGs has led to reduced child mortality, improved maternal health and the ability of the poor to combat disease through better nutrition, housing and health – especially among women and children.
- **Voice to Marginalised Section** Most of the beneficiaries of government schemes have been from weaker and marginalised communities and hence their participation through SHGs ensures social justice.

Women Empowerment

- **Economic Empowerment** Women in rural areas are now able to create independent sources of income by working in multiple sectors as Business Correspondents (BC), Bank Sakhis, Kisan Sakhis and Pashu Sakhis and creating their own independent business.
  - It has played a major role in dealing with the issue of 'Feminisation of Poverty' by ensuring the women empowerment across social, economic, political and psychological spheres.
- **Political Empowerment** SHGs empowers women and inculcates leadership skill among them. Empowered women participate more actively in Gram Sabha and elections.
- **Social Empowerment** There is evidence in this country as well as elsewhere that formation of Self-Help Groups has a multiplier effect in improving women's status in society as well as in the family leading to improvement in their socio-economic condition and also enhances their self-esteem.

Challenges of Self-Help Groups

SHGs are important tools of micro financing. Over the years SHGs have achieved tremendous progress in bringing about social and economic upliftment in the life of its members. However, despite the spread and success of SHGs, they suffer from various drawbacks:

- **Lacks Up-Gradation of Skills** Most SHGs are not making use of new technological innovations and skills. This is because there is limited awareness with regards to new technologies and they do not have the necessary skills to make use of the same. Furthermore, there is a lack of effective mechanisms.
- **Weak Financial Management** It is also found out that in certain units the return from the business is not properly invested further in the units and the funds diverted for other personal and domestic purposes like marriage, construction of house etc.
- **Inadequate Training Facilities** The training facilities given to the members of SHGs in the specific areas of product selection, quality of products, production techniques, managerial ability, packing, other technical knowledge are not adequate to compete with that of strong units.
- **Lack of Stability and Unity especially among Women SHGs** In the case of SHGs dominated by women, it is found that there is no stability of the units as many married women are not in a position to associate with the group due to the shift of their place of residence. Moreover, there is no unity among women members owing to personal reasons.
- **Inadequate Financial Assistance** It is found that in most of the SHGs, the financial assistance provided to them by the agencies concerned is not adequate to meet their actual requirements. The financial authorities are not giving adequate subsidies to meet even the labour cost requirements.
- **Regional Disparities** In percentage share of SHGs savings linked during 2021-22, the Southern region registered the highest share at 36% followed by the Eastern region (27.4%) and Western region (11.4%).
- **Poor Progress in Improvements in Income** Though there has been social empowerment of the poor, the economic gain to bring about a qualitative change in their life has not been satisfactory. Many of the activities undertaken by the SHGs are still based on primitive skills related mostly to primary sector enterprises. With poor value addition per worker and prevalence of subsistence level wages, such activities often do not lead to any substantial increase in the income of group members.
- Only a **minority of the Self-Help** Groups are able to raise themselves from a level of micro-finance to that of micro-entrepreneurship. The critical constraining factor is that SHG members face a lot of problems in marketing of their produce besides low level of skills.
- It has been observed that among SHGs, in case there is withdrawal of promoting institutions, there is a tendency for a slip in performance.

Way Forward and Government Measures

- The Government should play the role of a facilitator and promoter, create a supportive environment for the growth and development of the SHG movement.
- **Expanding SHG Movement to credit deficient areas of the Country** such as Madhya Pradesh, Rajasthan, States of the North-East.
- **Rapid expansion of financial infrastructure** (including that of NABARD) and by adopting extensive IT enabled communication and capacity building measures in these states.
- **Extension of Self-Help Groups to Urban/Peri-Urban Areas** Efforts should be made to increase income generation abilities of the urban poor as there has been a rapid rise in urbanisation and many people remain financially excluded.
- **Positive Attitude** Government functionaries should treat the poor and marginalised as viable and responsible customers and as possible entrepreneurs.
- **Monitoring** Need to establish a separate SHG monitoring cell in every state. The cell should have direct links with district and block level monitoring system. The cell should collect both quantitative and qualitative information.
- **Need Based Approach** Commercial Banks and NABARD in collaboration with the State Government need to continuously innovate and design new financial products for these groups.
- With a view to improve the information base and introduce data-based monitoring at the SHG level, there exists a need to draw up a time bound programme for upgrading quality of book keeping and introducing an MIS which provides timely and accurate record of transactions.

Conclusion

Over the last three decades, the SBLP has proven to be a great medium for social and economic empowerment for rural women. Today, these Self-Help Groups are seen as more than just a conduit for credit – they also act as a delivery mechanism for various other services ranging from entrepreneurial training, livelihood promotion activity and community development programmes.

Poverty: Concept, Estimation and Measures Taken(Types of Poverty)

Q.14 Distinguish between absolute measure and relative measure of poverty in India. What kind of measure is used in estimating poverty in India? Briefly highlight the parameters used by the government to determine the extent of poverty in India. (250 Words, 15 Marks)

Ans. **Introduction** Poverty can be defined as the state in which an individual or household is not able to fulfil the minimum consumption needs. It is not always about money, but it also entails access to basic facilities such as proper hygiene, sanitation, food, shelter, drinking water, health, education, transport, whose deprivation as a whole is considered poverty in the present times. As per the Tendulkar Committee, 21.9% of people in India live below the poverty line in 2011-12. Eradication of poverty is an important objective of economic policy. Therefore, measurement of poverty has to be sound as it has significant policy implications.

Types of Measurement: Absolute Poverty vs Relative Poverty

- **Absolute Measure of Poverty** The absolute measure of poverty refers to the determination of poverty based on a fixed threshold or poverty line. It establishes a minimum income or consumption level necessary to meet basic needs such as food, clothing, shelter, education and healthcare. The poverty line is set based on the cost of a basket of essential goods and services (known as 'Poverty Line Basket'). When the income of the household is below the poverty line, then the person or family is regarded as poor.
- **Relative Measure of Poverty** The relative measure of poverty acknowledges that poverty is a relative concept, influenced by the overall economic condition and distribution of resources within a society. It reflects the idea that individuals or households may be considered poor if their income or resources are significantly lower compared to the rest of society, even if they meet basic needs. The relative measure of poverty highlights income inequalities and social disparities within a given context.

Parameters	Absolute Measure of Poverty	Relative Measure of Poverty
Definition	Absolute poverty is a state in which a person or family is highly deprived of the basic needs making their livelihood difficult.	Relative poverty is a condition when a person or family is unable to reach the minimum average living standard in the society.
Calculation	Determines the minimum income/ consumption required to meet basic needs.	Identifies individuals/households falling below a certain percentage of the median or average income/ consumption.
Purpose	Assessing the number of people living below the poverty line and monitoring changes over time.	Analyzing income inequality trends, comparing poverty levels across region/countries and evaluating the impact of economic growth and policies on income distribution.
Poverty Line	Fixed poverty line calculated based on the cost of a basket of essentials goods and services.	Percentage of median or average income/consumption, often set at a certain threshold.
Income inequality	Does not consider income inequality within the society.	Consider income inequality and the distribution of resource within the society
Policy Implication	Helps in targeting resources and interventions to alleviate absolute poverty	Highlights disparities and the need for redistributive policies to address relative poverty

Poverty Estimation in India along with the Parameters Taken into Consideration

- Poverty line estimation in India has been based on the consumption expenditure and not on the income levels due to difficulties in assessing incomes of self-employed people, daily wage labourers, etc, large fluctuations in income due to seasonal factors, additional side incomes as well as data collection difficulties in largely rural and informal economy of India.
- Consumption is measured in terms of a collection of goods and services known as reference Poverty Line Baskets (PLB).
- These PLB were determined separately for urban and rural areas and based on a per-day calorie intake of 2400 (rural) and 2100 (urban), each containing items such as food, clothing, fuel, rent, conveyance and entertainment, among others.
- **Parameters Taken into Consideration** Various committees since Independence emphasised upon different parameters.
  - **Alagh Committee** and then by **Lakdawala Committee** defined the poverty line as the per capita consumption expenditure level to meet average per capita daily calorie requirements (calorie-based requirements) of 2400 kcal per capita per day in rural areas and 2100 kcal per capita per day in urban areas.
  - The Tendulkar Committee recommended shifting from calorie consumption-based poverty estimation to a uniform poverty line basket accounting for private expenditure on health and education. It is based on its calculations on the consumption of the items like cereal, pulses, milk, edible oil, non-vegetarian items, vegetables, fresh fruits, dry fruits, sugar, salt and spices, other food, intoxicants, fuel, clothing, footwear, education, medical (non-institutional and institutional), entertainment, personal and toilet goods.
  - Even **Rangarajan Committee** recommended both food components and non-food components such as education, clothing, conveyance, house rent, etc should be taken into consideration.
  - **Socio-Economic Caste Census (SECC)** measures the multi-dimensional poverty with respect to 7 deprivations such as Households with Kutchha house, No adult member in working age, Household headed by female and no working age male member, Household with handicapped members and no able bodied adult, Household with no literate over 25 years, Landless households engaged in manual labour and SC/ST households.

The official poverty line is the national average expenditure per person incurred to obtain the goods in the PLB. Since 1973-74, prices for goods in the PLB have been periodically adjusted over time and across states to deduce the official poverty line.

Issues in the Poverty Estimation

- While absolute poverty measurement provides a standardised and straightforward approach to assessing poverty levels, there are several issues associated with this method. Some of the key issues include:
- **Lack of Contextual Consideration** Absolute poverty measures often rely on a fixed poverty line or income threshold that is applied uniformly across different regions or countries. This approach fails to account for variations in the cost of living, purchasing power, and specific socio-economic conditions in different areas.
- **Inadequate Assessment of Basic Needs and thus does not Capture Multi-dimensional Aspect of Poverty** Absolute poverty measures typically focus on income or consumption expenditure as indicators of poverty, assuming that meeting a specific income threshold automatically ensures access to basic needs. However, this approach may overlook other critical dimensions of poverty, such as healthcare, education, sanitation and social protection, which are essential for a decent standard of living. Absolute poverty measures may not adequately capture non-monetary aspects of deprivation.
- **Failure to Capture Income Inequalities** Absolute poverty measures do not take into account income inequalities within a society. They do not consider the distribution of income and the relative position of individuals or households within the income distribution.

Conclusion

To address the limitations in poverty estimation, NITI Aayog launched National MPI on lines of Global MPI. Also, SECC which captures multi-dimensionality of poverty is increasingly used in the welfare schemes such as Ujjwala Yojana.

These two measures, the official poverty line based on consumption expenditure and multidimensional poverty indices, together contribute to a more comprehensive understanding of poverty in India, incorporating both monetary and non-monetary aspects of deprivation.

Estimation of Poverty

Q.15 Though there have been several different estimates of poverty in India, all indicate reduction in poverty levels over time. Do you agree? Critically examine with reference to urban and rural poverty indicators. (200 Words, 12.5 Marks) **UPSC Mains 2015**

Ans. **Introduction** Government has adopted a three-pronged strategy since Independence to deal with poverty alleviation – Growth-oriented approach, Directly targeted alleviation programmes and Basic needs approach. This has been successful in reducing poverty levels from more than 60% since Independence over time.

Need for Poverty Line Estimation

Task Force on Poverty under Vice-Chairman Prof. Arvind Panagariya setup in 2015 stated that poverty line have 3 main uses :

- **Identification of Poor** Due to limited resources with the government, it is important to identify the extreme poor which needs to be targeted first so that extreme poverty can be eliminated. This helps in the optimal allocation of resources.
- **Allocation of Expenditure on Expenditure Programmes** Poverty estimates in the form of poverty line are used to formulate poor-centric poverty elimination plans.
- **Tracking Poverty Over Time and Across Regions** Poverty estimates are not just important for academic purposes but are also crucial to track the impact and success of various government policies, especially social welfare schemes that are intended to eliminate poverty.
- **Constitutional Requirement** Poverty estimation paves the way for poverty elimination, that in turn prepares the ground for a just and equitable society. SDG 1 also aims for the eradication of extreme poverty.

Poverty line estimation in India has been based on the consumption expenditure and not on the income levels due to difficulties in assessing incomes of self-employed people, daily wage laborers etc, large fluctuations in income due to seasonal factors, additional side incomes as well as data collection difficulties in largely rural and informal economy of India.

Committees to Estimate Poverty Levels

Various committees and working groups have been constituted since Independence to come up the most appropriate poverty line estimation.

- **VM Dandekar and N Rath (1971)** It made the first systematic assessment of poverty in India, based on National Sample Survey (NSS) data.
- **Alagh Committee (1979)** Official poverty counts began for the first time in India based on the approach of this Task Force. It constructed a poverty line for rural and urban areas on the basis of nutritional requirements and related consumption expenditure. These lines were based on the assumption of different Poverty Line Baskets (PLBs) for rural and urban consumption.
- **Lakdawala (1993)** It did not redefine the poverty line and retained the separate rural and urban poverty lines recommended by the Alagh Committee at the national level based on minimum nutritional requirements which was 2400 calories per day for rural areas and 2100 calories per day for urban areas.
- **The Tendulkar Committee (2009)**
  - It recommended a shift away from basing the poverty lines from calorie norms used in all poverty estimations since 1979 and towards target nutritional outcomes instead.
  - Instead of two separate PLBs for rural and urban poverty lines, it recommended a uniform all-India urban PLB across rural and urban India.
  - It recommended using Mixed Reference Period (MRP) based estimates, as opposed to Uniform Reference Period (URP) based estimates used in earlier methods for estimating poverty.
  - It recommended incorporation of private expenditure on health and education while estimating poverty
  - The national poverty line for 2011-12 was estimated at ₹ 816 per capita per month for rural areas and ₹ 1,000 per capita per month for urban areas.
- **Rangarajan Committee (2014)**
  - It reverted to the practice of having separate all-India rural and urban poverty line baskets and deriving state-level rural and urban estimates from these.
  - It recommended separate consumption baskets for rural and urban areas which include food items that ensure recommended calorie, protein and fat intake and non-food items like clothing, education, health, housing and transport.
  - This committee raised the daily per capita expenditure to ₹ 47 for urban and ₹ 32 for rural from ₹ 32 and ₹ 26 respectively at 2011-12 prices.
  - Monthly per capita consumption expenditure of ₹ 972 in rural areas and ₹ 1407 in urban areas is recommended as the poverty line at the all India level.

Reduction in Poverty Levels over time with respect to Rural & Urban Poverty

- Based on the estimation of Tendulkar Committee, there has been a decline in the poverty level from 45.3% in 1993-94 to 21.9% in 2011-12.
- Rural poverty witnessed a significant decline in poverty from 50.1% in 1993-94 to 25.7% in 2011-12 while urban poverty declined from 31.8% to 13.7% in the same period.

Year	Lakdawala			Tendulkar			Rangarajan		
	R	U	T	R	U	T	R	U	T
1993-94	37.3	32.4	36.0	50.1	31.8	45.3	–	–	–
2004-05	28.3	25.7	27.5	41.8	25.7	37.2	–	–	–
2009-10	–	–	–	33.8	20.9	29.8	39.6	35.1	38.2
2011-12	–	–	–	25.7	13.7	21.9	30.9	26.4	29.5

- **As per Global MPI Report 2022,** the incidence of poverty fell from 36.6% in 2015-2016 to 21.2% in 2019-2021 in rural areas and from 9.0% to 5.5% in urban areas.
- According to the update by World Bank on Indian poverty using the new poverty line of USD2.15 per day, 10% of Indians were poor in 2019, down from 22.5% in 2011. Rural India had more poor than the urban: 11.9 per cent in rural areas and 6.4 per cent in urban areas.
  - Extreme poverty is 12.3 percentage points lower in 2019 than in 2011, with greater poverty reductions in rural areas.

Conclusion

Poverty lines have to be recalibrated depending on changes in income, consumption patterns and prices, as India is now a middle-income country, with an estimated per capita income of around USD9,000 in Purchasing Power Parity as per World Economic Outlook Dataset.

Dynamic Issues of Poverty and Inequality (Critical Analysis of Poverty Alleviation Measures)

Q.16 The recent UNDP Global Multidimensional Report, 2022 finds that India has significantly reduced the number of 'multidimensional poor'. In light of the sharp decline in the number of poor people, critically analyse the changes in the poverty alleviation policies of the Indian Government in the post-LPG era. (250 Words, 15 Marks)

Ans. **Introduction** Around 415 million people in India climbed out of poverty between 2005-06 and 2019-21, with the incidence of poverty falling from 55% to just over 16% over this period, according to the **Global Multi-dimensional Poverty Index** 2022.

Approach to Poverty Alleviation by the Government since Independence

Government has adopted a three-pronged strategy since Independence before LPG to deal with poverty alleviation - Growth-oriented approach, Directly targeted alleviation programmes and Basic needs approach as discussed in the earlier question. It has been successful in reducing poverty levels from more than 60% since Independence over time.

- **The first one is growth-oriented approach (Trickle-Down Approach)** It is based on the expectation that the effects of economic growth — rapid increase in gross domestic product and per capita income — would spread to all sections of society and will trickle down to the poor sections also. This was the major focus of planning in the 1950s and early 1960s. It was felt that rapid industrial development (Nehru-Mahalanobis Strategy of Import Substitution Industrialisation) and transformation of agriculture through green revolution in select regions would benefit the underdeveloped regions and the more backward sections of the community.
- **The second approach emphasises upon directly targeted poverty alleviation programmes** Which has been initiated from the Third Five Year Plan (1961-66) and progressively enlarged since then. It aims to increase the income and employment for the poor through the creation of additional assets and by means of work generation. Expanding self-employment programmes and wage employment programmes are being considered as the major ways of addressing poverty. Examples of wage-based and self-employment programmes are Rural Employment Generation Programme (REGP), Prime Minister's Rozgar Yojana (PMRY), Swarna Jayanti Shahari Rozgar Yojana (SJSRY), National Rural Employment Guarantee Programme, MGNREGA, etc.
- **The third approach to addressing poverty is to provide minimum basic amenities to the people** India was among the pioneers in the world to envisage that through public expenditure on social consumption needs - provision of food grains at subsidised rates, education, health, water supply and sanitation - people's living standard could be improved. Programmes under this approach are expected to supplement the consumption of the poor, create employment opportunities and bring about improvements in health and education. Example: PDS System, Antayodaya Anna Yojana, Integrated Child Development Services (ICDS), Mid-Day Meal Scheme, Ujjwala Yojana, Sarva Shikhsa Abhiyaan, etc.

Change in the Poverty Alleviation Measures in the Post-LPG Era

While the earlier poverty alleviation measures have resulted in the reduction of poverty levels, there have been faster reduction in poverty in the post-LPG era. Poverty declined by 1.36 percentage points per annum after 1991, compared to that of 0.44 percentage points per annum prior to 1991. In the post-reform period, poverty declined faster in the 2000s than in the 1990s. Also, India lifted as many as 415 million people out of multi-dimensional poverty between 2005-06 and 2019-21. This has been due to the various changes in the policies adopted in the post-LPG Era.

- **Shift from Welfare to Rights-Based Approach**
  - MGNREGA generated over 279 crore person-days of employment, benefiting more than 12 crore households since its inception (Ministry of Rural Development).
  - The Right to Education Act (RTE) ensured free and compulsory education for children aged 6-14 years, benefiting over 22 crore children (Ministry of Education).
- **Emphasis on Skill Development and Entrepreneurship** Government initiated several programmes to enhance vocational training and promote self-employment. Skill India Mission, Startup India and Standup India are examples of initiatives launched to provide skill training, encourage entrepreneurship and facilitate access to finance for aspiring entrepreneurs.
- **Shift towards Inclusive Growth** In the post-LPG era, there has been a shift towards inclusive growth as a means to alleviate poverty. The government recognised the need to ensure that the benefits of economic growth reach the marginalized and vulnerable sections of society.
- **Targeted Programmes and Identification of Beneficiaries** The Antyodaya Anna Yojana (AAY) identified the poorest households and provided them with heavily subsidised food grains, benefitting over 2.5 crore families (Ministry of Consumer Affairs).
- **Focus on Human Development and not just Growth**
  - The **National Health Mission (NHM)** improved access to healthcare services, resulting in the decline of Maternal Mortality Rate (MMR) from 301 in 2001-03 to 97 in 2023 (Ministry of Health and Family Welfare).
  - The **Sarva Shiksha Abhiyan (SSA)** achieved significant progress in achieving universal elementary education, with the Gross Enrollment Ratio in primary education reaching 97.4% in 2022 (Ministry of Education).
- **Financial Inclusion and Social Security** Pradhan Mantri Jan Dhan Yojana (PMJDY) facilitated financial inclusion, with over 43.04 crore bank accounts opened and deposits worth more than ₹ 1.46 lakh crore (Ministry of Finance).
- **Asset Creation and Employment Generation** Pradhan Mantri Awas Yojana (PMAY) aimed to provide affordable housing to all by 2022, with over 1.12 crore houses sanctioned and 77 lakh houses completed (Ministry of Housing and Urban Affairs).
- **Use of Technology and Direct Benefit Transfer (DBT)** Direct Benefit Transfer (DBT) resulted in the transfer of ₹ 17.82 lakh crore across various schemes, benefitting over 64 crore beneficiaries and eliminating middlemen (Ministry of Finance). The use of technology-driven platforms like JAM applications improved the efficiency and transparency of welfare programmes.
- **Public-Private Partnerships (PPPs)** Public-Private Partnerships were encouraged in sectors like healthcare, education and skill development to enhance service delivery and leverage private sector expertise. Initiatives like the National Skill Development Mission engaged private sector players and provided skill training to over 4 crore individuals (Ministry of Skill Development and Entrepreneurship).
- **Decentralisation and Community Participation** Panchayati Raj institutions were strengthened to enable local governance and decision-making, empowering communities to participate in poverty alleviation initiatives (Ministry of Panchayati Raj). Gram Sabhas and Village Development Committees were involved in the planning and implementation of programs like MGNREGA and PMGSY.
- **Monitoring and Evaluation** Robust monitoring and evaluation mechanisms were established to assess the impact of poverty alleviation programmes. Regular evaluations, such as the Social Audit under MGNREGA, helped in identifying gaps and improving implementation.

Issues and Challenges in Poverty Alleviation Programmes

- **Multi-dimensional** It is multi-dimensional menace which needs convergence and synergy from all level of institutions which is generally lacking.
- **Targeting and Identification** Many poverty alleviation programs rely on income thresholds or socio-economic indicators to identify beneficiaries. However, these criteria can be subjective and prone to errors, leading to inclusion and exclusion errors.
- **Implementation and Last-Mile Delivery Challenges** Challenges such as corruption, bureaucratic inefficiencies, lack of capacity and accountability, and inadequate infrastructure can hamper the smooth delivery of benefits and services to the intended beneficiaries. Leakage at different levels has led to diversion of resources meant for deprived ones.
- **Sustainable Livelihoods** Poverty alleviation programmes often focus on providing immediate relief or income support. However, sustainable poverty reduction requires a focus on building livelihoods and empowering individuals to become self-reliant. This includes providing access to education, skills training, healthcare and productive assets, as well as facilitating market linkages and entrepreneurship opportunities. This kind of support has not been adequately provided to poor people
- **Social and Cultural Factors** Poverty is not solely an economic issue but is influenced by social and cultural factors. Deep-rooted social inequalities, gender discrimination, caste-based hierarchies and cultural barriers can impede poverty reduction efforts.
- **Persistent Regional Disparities** Regional disparities continue to pose a challenge in poverty reduction, with certain states and regions experiencing higher poverty rates compared to others. States like Bihar, Uttar Pradesh, and Jharkhand still face significant challenges in reducing poverty rates (official poverty estimates).
- **Informal Sector Employment** The informal sector, which employs a significant portion of the population, often lacks job security, social protection and adequate wages. Providing sustainable livelihood opportunities and improving conditions in the informal sector remain a challenge.
- **Inclusive Growth and Marginalised Communities** Ensuring inclusive growth and addressing the specific needs of marginalised communities, such as Scheduled Castes, Scheduled Tribes, and Minorities, remains a challenge. These communities often face social exclusion, discrimination, and limited access to resources and opportunities.
- **Climate Change and Vulnerability** Climate change impacts, such as extreme weather events, natural disasters and agricultural challenges, disproportionately affect the poor and vulnerable communities. Building resilience and implementing climate change adaptation strategies are crucial to mitigate the adverse effects on poverty alleviation efforts.
- **Digital Divide** Modern digital divides also add up to the issues. World Development Report 2017 highlights India's lagging in encashing Digital Dividend resulting Digital Divide. Thus, poor are not able to reap the benefits of digital technologies.

NITI Aayog Strategy to Combat Poverty

The strategy for combating poverty must rest on two legs: sustained rapid growth that is also employment intensive and making anti-poverty programmes effective.

- **Employment-intensive Sustained Rapid Growth** Sustained rapid growth works through two channels: first, by creating jobs that pay steadily rising real wages, it directly dents poverty and, second, it leads to growth in government revenues which in turn allow the expansion of social expenditures at faster pace.
  - India needs acceleration in the growth of organised labour-intensive sectors such as apparel, footwear, food processing, electronic and electrical appliances, other light manufactures, construction and retail trade.
  - Creation of a handful of Coastal Economic Zones (CEZs) that can provide the focal point for the location of employment-intensive industries allowing them to exploit the economies of scale and agglomeration.
- **Making Anti-poverty Programmes More Effective** Making anti-poverty programmes such as the Public Distribution System (PDS), Mid-day Meal Scheme, MGNREGA and Housing for All more effective represents the second leg of the strategy to eliminate abject poverty.
  - **Example** MGNREGA can be made more effective by allowing it to impart skills. This would also pave the way for many workers to exit the program. Use of DBT transfers in various subsidy schemes.

Conclusion

The changes in the poverty alleviation strategy after the LPG reform aimed to address the multi-dimensional aspects of poverty, enhance inclusivity and promote sustainable development. The focus shifted towards rights-based approach, targeted interventions and empowerment, with an emphasis on human development, asset creation and social security

Continued efforts and collaboration between the government, civil society organisations, and international partners are essential to overcome these challenges and achieve sustainable poverty reduction in India.

Feminisation of Poverty

Q.17 The link between gender and poverty is oversimplified and suffers from statistical "invisibility". Examine the above statement in the context of 'Feminization of poverty' and enumerate the measures taken by the government to address gender-specific poverty. (250 Words, 15 Marks)

Ans. **Introduction** Diana Pearce in 1976 coined a term for this "Feminisation of Poverty", following the observation of women in America. 'Feminisation of Poverty' refers to a phenomenon in which women are disproportionately represented among the world's poor and highlights the trend that women are more likely to experience poverty as compared to men. As per Global Multi-dimensional Poverty Report, 2022 India is the only country in South Asia in which poverty is significantly more prevalent among female-headed households than among male-headed households. About 19.7 per cent of people living in female-headed households live in poverty compared with 15.9% in male-headed households.

Problem of Statistical Invisibility of Women Activities

- **Non-recognition of Household Activities** Women are subjected to 'dual burdens' of household work and work performed for income-generating activities. Household work is unpaid and unrecognised and is classified as 'unproductive work' and no equation calculates its direct or indirect value to the economic system.
  - According to Census 2011, the 'non-working' population was around 728.9 million. Of these, 159.9 million individuals who stated that 'household work' was their main activity were women.
- **Policy Invisibility** Economists have argued that non-valuation or under-valuation of women's productive input into the economy weakens women's position and creates defective policies. Unless women's non-market work is monetised and added to the GDP, miscalculations would continue to occur.
- The range of women's varied skilled non-paid work directly contributes to the economy. By shouldering all these responsibilities, women make all other forms of labour possible. However, women are ignored from economic and GDP prospective.
- **Time-Poverty** Women face time deficiency for meeting their personal requirements and it is termed as 'time poverty' in a simpler way and is often linked to the 'crises of care'. Oxfam's India Inequality Report 2020 highlighted that societal norms in rural areas do not allow women to ask men to share the burden of housework.

Reasons for Feminisation of Poverty Linkage between Women and Poverty

It is of vital importance that we conceptualize poverty as multidimensional with many contributing factors taking into account the following.

- **Gender Differences and Earning Prospects** Gender differences in earnings play an important part in women's poverty, but other factors such as gender disparities in land and property ownership, gender divisions of labour, gender differences in power and decision-making are often ignored.
  - **Gender Wage Gap** Persistent gender wage gaps result in lower incomes for women. According to the World Economic Forum's Global Gender Gap Report 2021, the global gender pay gap stands at 16.0%, In countries like India, the gender pay gap is around 20-30% as per wage index.
  - **Limited Access to Education** Gender disparities in education hinder women's economic prospects. In India, the gender gap in literacy remains significant, with a female literacy rate of around 70% compared to a male literacy rate of around 84%.

- **Limited Access to Resources** Women face barriers in accessing productive resources like land, credit, and technology. In many regions, women own less land than men, limiting their income-generating potential. In India, women own only about 12.7% of agricultural land, as per the Agricultural Census 2015-16.
- **Discrimination in Employment** Women often face discrimination in hiring, promotion and job opportunities.

- **Unpaid Labour** Women are prone to be particularly exposed to time poverty as a result of multiple labour burdens, many of which are unpaid or underpaid and which impact heavily on their scope to exit poverty through engaging in activities with higher returns.
  - Women bear a disproportionate burden of unpaid care work, including household chores and childcare. This limits their time and opportunities for income-generating activities. In India, women spend nearly six hours per day on unpaid care work, which is about ten times more than men.
- **Lack of Social Protection** Insufficient social protection measures leave women vulnerable to economic shocks and poverty. In many countries, women are less likely to have access to social safety nets, such as unemployment benefits, pensions, and healthcare coverage, which further exacerbates their economic insecurity.
- **Conflict and Displacement** The United Nations High Commissioner for Refugees (UNHCR) estimates that over half of the world's refugees and Internally Displaced Persons (IDPs) are women and girls. They face heightened risks of violence, exploitation, and loss of livelihoods. In conflict-affected areas, women often lack access to essential services, including education and healthcare, exacerbating their vulnerability to poverty.
- **Cultural and Social Norms** Deep-rooted gender norms and stereotypes can reinforce women's economic disadvantage. Traditional gender roles that assign women primarily to caregiving and domestic responsibilities can limit their opportunities for education employment, and economic independence.

Government Measures to Address Feminisation of Poverty

The Government of India has implemented various measures and programs to address the issue of feminisation of poverty and promote gender equality. Here are important initiatives:

- **Beti Bachao Beti Padhao** This programme aims to address gender-biased sex selection, promote the education of girls and improve the status of women in society.
- **Mahila E-Haat** It is an online platform that provides a direct market link to women entrepreneurs, enabling them to showcase and sell their products and services.
- **Pradhan Mantri Mudra Yojana** This scheme facilitates access to credit for women-owned micro and small enterprises, encouraging women's entrepreneurship and economic empowerment.
- **Sukanya Samriddhi Yojana** It is a savings scheme that promotes the welfare and financial security of the girl child, encouraging parents to save for their education and other future needs.
- **National Rural Livelihood Mission (NRLM)** This programme aims to empower rural women by promoting Self-Help Groups (SHGs) and providing them with access to credit, skills training and livelihood opportunities.
- **Mahatma Gandhi National Rural Employment Guarantee Act (MGNREGA)** This flagship programme guarantees 100 days of employment per year to rural households, prioritising women's participation and ensuring gender-sensitive implementation.
- **Pradhan Mantri Ujjwala Yojana** This scheme aims to provide clean cooking fuel to women from below poverty line households, reducing their exposure to harmful smoke and improving their health and well-being.
- **National Nutrition Mission (Poshan Abhiyaan)** It focuses on addressing malnutrition among women and children through targeted interventions, including the provision of nutritious food, healthcare and behaviour change communication.
- **Swachh Bharat Mission (Clean India Campaign)** This programme emphasises the construction of toilets, particularly for women, promoting sanitation and hygiene and ensuring their safety and dignity.
- **Women Helpline Scheme** It establishes a nationwide helpline number (181) to provide emergency assistance and support to women in distress, addressing issues such as violence, harassment and discrimination.

Conclusion

Feminisation of Poverty can be eradicated by practising equity, presenting resources for the women, practising gender equality in term of pay which has the main impact on what kind of life a woman is living. International Monetary Fund (IMF) estimates that India could increase its GDP by nearly 27% by achieving more equitable participation of women in the workforce.

Interventions from governments include the enactment of laws that would remove barriers to women entering the workforce, mandating protection of women at the workplace and legislating quotas for women in political office and on company boards. The private sector should also lower the barriers to women moving into positions of responsibility, providing for family leave and leadership training and sponsorship of women.

Rural Poverty vs Urban Poverty

Q.18 Bring out the differences between Rural poverty and Urban poverty. Also, discuss the reasons behind the shift in trends in poverty from rural to urban areas. (150 Words, 10 Marks)

Ans. Introduction Poverty is a state or condition which is characterised by a situation in which a person or community lacks the financial resources and essentials for a minimum standard of living. India has witnessed tremendous growth over the last two year which have resulted in the decline of poverty from 45% to 22% between 1994 and 2012 based on Tendulkar Committee estimation. However, a considerable proportion of the Indian population still continues to remain below the poverty line. As more and more people migrate to the cities in search of better economic opportunities, the locus of poverty in India is shifting to cities as well.

Rural Poverty vs Urban Poverty

Criteria	Rural Poverty	Urban Poverty
Causes	Stagnation in agriculture, fragmented landholdings, lack of diversified economic activities, disguised unemployment, caste system, ineffective implementation of rural development programmes and lack of institutional support	Urban areas invite migration leading to overpopulation vis-à-vis the available resources for exploitation leading to the development of slums, lower wages to informal labour, higher rate of inflation, etc.
Composition	Landless agricultural labourers, sharecroppers, craftsmen.	Casual labour in informal sector, hawkers, daily wage earners, etc.
Environmental Surroundings	Shabby nature of houses, lack of access to basic amenities – large travelling distances, open defecation in fields, etc.	Slum areas, houseless households, access to basic amenities but is irregular and of poor quality.
Skill Level	Largely unskilled – labour intensive	Semi-skilled; Less labour intensive.
Feeling of Relative Deprivation	Low and consequent lesser crime rate but high cases of suicide	High and therefore higher crime rates. Example – Mumbai has one of the world's largest slums and thus high feeling of relative deprivation resulted in many gangsters originated from Mumbai.

The given table below indicates the variation of rural and urban poverty over the following years based on the estimation of various committees:

Year	Lakdawala			Tendulkar			Rangarajan		
	R	U	T	R	U	T	R	U	T
1993-94	37.3	32.4	36.0	50.1	31.8	45.3	–	–	–
2004-05	28.3	25.7	27.5	41.8	25.7	37.2	–	–	–
2009-10	–	–	–	33.8	20.9	29.8	39.6	35.1	38.2
2011-12	–	–	–	25.7	13.7	21.9	30.9	26.4	29.5

Shift in Trends from Rural Poverty to Urban Poverty

Urban areas becoming a focus of poverty which can be seen from the following facts:

- **Urban Poverty in India is over 25%,** some 81 million people live in urban areas on incomes that are below the poverty line. Although rural poverty remains higher than urban poverty, the gap is closing, i.e. focus of poverty is shifting to urban areas. By 2030, urbanisation in India is projected to reach 50 percent.

  Today, one in every six of India's urban households live in slums, a number forecast to rise exponentially over the coming years.
- **Migration towards Urban Centres** has increased, indicating that economic reforms have not been effective in creating jobs in small and medium towns as well as rural areas. Poverty was higher among rural to urban migrants, while the most successful migrants are those who move from one urban area to another.

  Moreover, there is **No standard definition of slums** and the massive lack of research provides no account of the lives of the urban poor.
- **Slum Dwellers Lack Access to Basic Services** Most slum dwellers do not have access to clean water, sanitation and health care facilities. They face a constant threat of eviction, removal, confiscation of goods and have virtually no social security cover. Some 54% of urban slums do not have toilets; public facilities are unusable due to a lack of maintenance.

There are various reasons behind this increasing urbanisation of poverty

- **Push-Pull Factors** In India, the causes of urban poverty can be linked to the lack of infrastructure in rural areas (push factor), forcing inhabitants of these regions to seek out work in India's mega-cities (pull factor). The urban poor is largely the overflow of the rural poor who migrate to urban areas in search of alternative employment and livelihood.
- **Lack of Skills** Most of the poor are not able to participate in the emerging employment opportunities in different sectors of the urban economy as they do not have the necessary knowledge and skills to do so.
- **Indebtedness** Unemployment or underemployment and the casual and intermittent nature of work in urban areas lead to indebtedness, that in turn, reinforces poverty.
- **Informalisation of Labour** Jobless growth witnessed after LPG Reforms led to increased informalisation of labour which created irregular income among the urban workers.
- **Increasing Gig Economy** Recent boost to gig economy while generated employment opportunities have also posed challenges for the gig workers such as no fixed employment terms, uncertain income according to the whims and fancies of employer and many more. **Example** Recent BlinkIt gig worker protest against the reduction in fee per delivery.
- **Inflation** A steep rise in the price of food grains and other essential goods further intensifies the hardship and deprivation of lower-income groups.
- **Unequal Distribution** The unequal distribution of income and assets has also led to the persistence of poverty in urban India.
- **Unsatisfactory Growth** The overall growth of agriculture and industry have not been impressive. The gap between poor and rich has actually widened.
- **Asymmetrical Development** The Green Revolution exacerbated the disparities regionally and between large and small farmers. There was unwillingness and inability to redistribute land. The benefits of economic growth have largely not trickled down to the poor.

Conclusion

India needs a systemic policy to deal with haphazard and unplanned rural-urban migration with participative planning at its heart. The government needs to strengthen the health, education and physical infrastructure to enhance the capabilities of individuals residing in urban areas, thereby addressing the root cause of urban poverty.

Universal Basic Income as Tool of Poverty & Inequality

Q.19 Explain the concept of 'Universal Basic Income' and examine if it is better than the present subsidies and other income support-schemes in India. Compare the relative merits and demerits of these schemes from India's point of view. (250 Words, 15 Marks)

Ans. **Introduction** India made a remarkable progress in bringing down poverty from about 70% at Independence to about 22% in 2011-12 (based on Tendulkar Committee estimation), poverty alleviation is still one of the greatest challenges to Indian Economy and even SDG Goal 1 requires the countries to eliminate extreme poverty. As per Global MPI Report 2022, India has the largest number of poor people worldwide at 22.8 crore and 16.4% of the population is multi-dimensionally poor in 2019-21. To alleviate the poverty, government have adopted various poverty alleviation programmes since Independence and now this recent emergence of 'Universal Basic Income (UBI)' is gaining attention in India after the recommendation of Economic Survey 2016-17.

The Economic Advisory Council (EAC) to the Prime Minister released a report on inequality prepared by the Institute for Competitiveness which supported the provision of Universal Basic Income as an elementary safety net.

Concept of Universal Basic Income

The concept of UBI implies that the state or a public institution grants unconditionally a 'basic guaranteed sum of money' on regular basis to every citizen in a country, including children, irrespective of their economic status or occupation. This will be in addition to any other source of income or earnings of the citizens. It is a social security measure, the primary objective being to combat poverty, assist those who are unemployed and enable every citizen to meet the basic needs and maintain a decent, minimum standard of life. It is premised on the idea that a just society needs to guarantee to each individual a minimum income which they can count on and which provides the necessary material foundation for a life with access to basic goods and a life of dignity.

Poverty Alleviation via Subsidy and other Income-Support Schemes

Subsidies have been the mainstay of Indian state to deal with poverty since Independence.

In India, there are non-merit subsidies like those for food under the Public Distribution System (PDS), fertilisers, cooking gas, kerosene, etc. which are 'targeted' towards specific groups of population and 'merit' subsidies for education, primary healthcare, nutrition, forestry, ecology, environment, rural development programmes, village and small industries, etc. where the benefits are reaped by the society as a whole.

The Indian Government operates multiple income support schemes, each targeting specific groups or addressing particular needs. These schemes include the Mahatma Gandhi National Rural Employment Guarantee Act (MGNREGA), the Pradhan Mantri Kisan Samman Nidhi (PM-KISAN), the Pradhan Mantri Jan Dhan Yojana (PMJDY) and various social welfare programs. It has been successful to reduce the Indian poverty to a certain extent in the following ways

- **Affordability and Access** Subsidies can make essential goods and services more affordable and accessible for low-income individuals and vulnerable populations. **Example** Food Subsidy, Agricultural subsidies for various inputs.
- **Promotion of Social Infrastructure** Subsidies can help in the strengthening of social infrastructure such as Education via RTE Act, 20119 & National Education Policy, 2020; Health via National Health Mission; Skill Development via various skill development programmes.
- **Social Welfare** Subsidies can contribute to social welfare by addressing inequality and reducing the gap between different sections of society. **Example** Food subsidy under PM Garib Kalyan Yojana
- **Market Corrective Measures** Subsidies can be employed as market corrective measures to address market failures or negative externalities. They can offset the costs associated with certain public goods or services, encourage desired behaviours and correct market imbalances.
- **Safety Net** Subsidies and income support act as a safety net for individuals and households during times of economic distress, such as unemployment, disability or natural disasters. **Example** Pension schemes such as Atal Pension Yojana and Insurance scheme such as PM Jeevan Jyoti Yojana or PM Jeevan Bima Yojana.

Rationale Behind the Idea of UBI

- **Issues with the Existing Subsidy Schemes**
  - **Huge Fiscal Burden** Subsidies and income support schemes impose a significant fiscal burden on the government. Economic Survey 2016-17 highlighted that there are around 960 government schemes which cost government of around 5% of the GDP.
  - **Leakages and Inefficiencies** There is a risk of leakages and inefficiencies in the delivery of subsidies and income support. These schemes may suffer from corruption, mismanagement and ineffective targeting, leading to benefits not reaching the intended beneficiaries. **Example**, subsidies for cooking gas and kerosene and in electricity and water tariffs are enjoyed more by the affluent sections that use these facilities relatively more than the poor.

- **Dependency and Disincentives** Long-term dependence on subsidies and income support can create a sense of dependency among beneficiaries, discouraging self-reliance and self-motivation.
- **Distortion of Markets** Subsidies, particularly in sectors like agriculture, can distort market dynamics by artificially influencing prices, production decisions and resource allocation. This can lead to inefficiencies and market distortions, affecting the overall economy.
- **Impact on Environment** Power and fertiliser subsidy is leading to water stress and environmental pollution. **Example** Declining groundwater table in Punjab.

- **Social Justice** A Universal Basic Income promotes many of the basic values of a society which respects all individuals as free and equal. It promotes liberty because it is anti-paternalistic, opens up the possibility of flexibility in labour markets.
- **Fastest Way of Reducing Poverty** Universal Basic Income may simply be the fastest way of reducing poverty in the Indian context, a relatively low level of assured regular income to every individual could serve as a prop and enhance family's welfare. Unlike the present system of subsidies, UBI may empower families at the bottom rung of the ladder and help them to become more self-reliant and take economic decisions relevant to their lives.
- **Administrative Efficiency** A UBI will reduce the burden of financing a plethora of separate government schemes and administrative burden of implementation. The UBI, by design, should effectively tackle issues related to misallocation and leakage because transfers are directed straight to the beneficiaries' bank accounts. Finally, given the fewer avenues for leakages, monitoring a UBI would be easier than many other schemes.
- **Employment** UBI is an acknowledgement of the government's duty to guarantee a minimum living standard (Article 43 of Indian Constitution) is even more urgent in an era of Industry 4.0 as automation with increasingly efficient computer systems, robotics and artificial intelligence is causing loss of jobs in various countries. Moreover, UBI could also open up new possibilities for labour market. They allow for more non-exploitative bargaining since individuals will no longer be forced to accept any working conditions, just so that they can subsist.
- **Insurance Against Shocks** Poor households often face multiple shocks such as bad health, job loss or aggregate shocks such as crop loss, water borne diseases, loss of property and natural disasters. **Example Recent COVID-19 impact** on migration. The UBI income floor will provide a safety net against health, income and other shocks.
- **Freedom of Choice** A UBI treats beneficiaries as agents and entrusts citizens with the responsibility of using welfare spending as they see best which may not be the case with in-kind transfers.
- **Improvement in Financial Inclusion** Payment transfers will encourage greater usage of bank accounts, leading to higher profits for Banking Correspondents (BC) and an endogenous improvement in financial inclusion. Credit increased income will release the constraints on access to credit for those with low-income levels.
- **Women Empowerment** In 2011, a pilot study of Universal Basic Income was conducted in 8 villages of Madhya Pradesh for 18 months. Reviewing the UBI trial in India (2013-2014), SEWA Bharat and UNICEF concluded that "women's empowerment was one of the more important outcomes of this experiment,". Women receiving UBI participated more in household decision making and benefitted from improved access to food, healthcare and education.
- **Global Experience** Among the developed economies, where economic growth had stagnated, most cash transfers schemes have broadly adhered to the principles of UBI.
  - Canada, provided USD1,400 per month to those who lost income due to the COVID-19 pandemic.
  - The United States offered its citizens cheques of USD 1,200 for individuals or USD 2,400 for those who were married.
  - South Korea issued cash transfers of USD 820 for its citizens and Japan announced cash transfers of USD 931 per person.

Challenges in the Implementation of UBI

- **Fiscal Sustainability** If UBI is universal, which means all citizens, regardless of their financial capacity, are by default beneficiaries will widen the existing rich-poor gap in India. Adopting a universal approach in India would result in higher government expenditure as it will have to ensure that no citizens are excluded. Once introduced, it may become difficult for the government to wind up a UBI in case of failure.
- **Conspicuous Spending** UBI is not tied to the recipients' behaviour, and they are free to spend the money as they wish. Households with lack of awareness about fiscal management may spend on wasteful activities. There is no guarantee that the given cash will be spent on productive activities, health and education, etc. It may be spent on tobacco, alcohol, drugs and other luxury goods etc.

- **Reduction in Labour Force** A minimum guaranteed income might make people lazy and opt out of the labour market.
- **Increase the Rate of Inflation** Replacing things like food programmes with UBI might expose the population to more market risks and inflation. Price fluctuation will affect the purchasing power of the consumers.
- **Lack of Connectivity Channel Between Government and Beneficiary** In India, the poorest live in mostly remote areas and lack recourse to banking and often mobile phones is a major concern.
  - Economic Survey also points to JAM (Jan Dhan, Aadhaar and Mobile) system as a prerequisite for a successful UBI implementation.
- **Gender Disparity induced by Cash** Gender factors may influence the control and sharing of UBI within a household, with men exercising control over spending of the assured basic income, especially in the lower rungs of society who need it the most. This does not happen with other in-kind transfer schemes like PDS, LPG, etc.
- **Federal Challenge** Centre-State negotiations on cost sharing for the programme could delay its implementation. Since Indian states are at different levels of development, maintaining a uniform financial transfer will be challenging.

Conclusion

It would be more prudent to take a middle road towards quasi-universal basic income. The government should retain existing in-kind programs that deliver necessities and enhance one's quality of life, such as food security, healthcare, sanitation and education. Once it demonstrates, over time, that it has built a stable system for income transfers, it could revisit the policies towards UBI.

State of Inequality in India

Q.20 While recent Oxfam India's report highlights only wealth inequality in India, COVID-19 pandemic exposed the multiple inequalities. Elaborate. Also, comment upon the reasons for increasing inequality in India along with various measures. (250 Words, 15 Marks)

Ans. **Introduction** Recently released Oxfam India's report on inequality in India finds that just 5% of Indians own more than 60% of the country's wealth, while the bottom 50% of the population possess only 3% of the wealth. Beyond economic inequalities, COVID-19 pandemic exposed the other social inequalities also.

Multiple Forms of Inequalities exposed by Covid-19 Pandemic

Given the slow progress of inclusive policies, pandemic only exposed the already relevant economic and social inequalities in the country.

- **Income Inequalities** Oxfam India's report, "Survival of the Richest: The India Story", says that between 2012 and 2021, 40 % of the wealth created in India has gone to just 1% of the population and only a mere 3% of the wealth has gone to the bottom 50%, adding that the total number of billionaires in India increased from 102 in 2020 to 166 billionaires in 2022.
  - Following the pandemic in 2019, the bottom 50% of the population have continued to see their wealth chipped away. By 2020, their income share was estimated to have fallen to only 13 per cent of the national income and have less than 3% of the wealth.
- **Extreme Hunger** COVID-19 has struck at a time when hunger or undernourishment keeps rising. The number of hungry Indians increased to 350 million in 2022 from 190 million in 2018. The widespread hunger is resulting in 65% of the deaths among children under the age of 5 in 2022. India's ranking in Global Hunger Index 2022 declined to 107 out of 121 countries.
- **Financial Exclusion** Bank savings are there for 62% upper caste households whereas this is 49% for SC households. Hence, ability to invest in technology is lower for SC households.
- **Education Inequalities** A literature suggests that a total of 320 million learners in India have been adversely affected by the COVID-19 pandemic and have transitioned to e-learning. With huge regional and household disparities in access to the internet and technology, this transition has not been possible for all students and educators. The rapid shift to e-learning prompted by the pandemic has resurfaced long-standing issues of inequality and a digital divide in India that must be addressed by future economic, education and digitalisation policies.

- **Formal vs Informal Labour** The pandemic and lockdown have affected 1.4m migrant workers and others working in the unorganised sector (90% of India's population is engaged in disorganised work). The migrant workers have either moved back home along with their children or are unable to send remittances home this season.
- **Gender Inequalities** In most Indian households, responsibilities like cooking, cleaning and washing have always predominantly burdened women and girls. Employment is one of the strongest predictors of women's empowerment and India has one of the lowest female employment rates in the world, on a par with Saudi Arabia. The COVID-19 pandemic, and the measures taken to tackle it, are making matters worse. Physical distancing measures, school closures and overburdened health systems have meant increased demand on women and girls to provide around the clock care for children, the sick and the elderly. The absence of household help has forced women into house hold work.
- **Caste Inequalities** India has a long history of social distancing engraved in the caste system with purity and pollution practices regarding sharing of food, water and strict rules of marriage, and forbiddance of inter-caste and inter-religious marriages to maintain the purity of blood and lineage. Hence, a term like social distancing invokes discriminatory practices and perceptions of who is considered to be a potential carrier of the contagion.
  - The assessment by National Campaign on Dalit Human Rights finds that lack of awareness and poor coverage of the scheme severely curtailed the capacity of the marginalised to afford medical assistance during the pandemic.
- **Urban Poor** While tech workers and other white-collar professionals enjoy a 'win-all' with health, income and employment, there are large swathes within the informal workforce who would be facing inequalities in health, income and employment. Health-income-employment triple insecurity faced by the urban poor has grown exponentially as they live in densely-populated urban neighbourhood where diseases spread much faster, generating further income losses and job uncertainties.

Reasons for Increasing Inequality in India

- **Agricultural Wages** Stagnation in agricultural wages owing to stagnating yields, crop failures, post-harvest damages and climate risks have impacted income levels of nearly 50% of the population that draws sustenance from agriculture. Real agricultural wages have grown at nearly 2.5% in 1990's while Public sector salaries grew at 5% during the same time.
- **Skewed Growth** A considerable share of economic growth was cornered by the service sector that employed nearly a third of the population. On the contrary, agriculture grew at less than 3% in the last few decades.
- **Regional Disparity** Incomes remain subdued in relatively backward states of Rajasthan, Bihar, Chhattisgarh etc. which have lagged behind in GSDP growth owing to Infrastructure deficit and Governance deficit. Hill states and border areas too show the slow pace of economic growth due to geographical and security challenges.
- **Failure of Trickle Down Effect** Employment grew merely by 0.5% per annum from 2004-05 to 2011-12 - the period that saw the highest growth of GDP by 8.5% per annum.
- **Informalisation of Economy** As per ILO data 81% of total employment is informal in nature. The contractual labourers remain outside of the ambit of labour laws and are bereft of social security and fair wages.
- **Capital-led growth** Growing economic inequalities are also due to over-reliance on capital and finance as the drivers of growth and neglect of labour. Trade and Financial globalisation processes have weakened the bargaining position of relatively immobile labour as opposed to fully mobile capital, resulting in widespread unemployment and exploitation of workforce.
- **The Gender Dimension** India is ranked 132 out of 187 countries on the Gender Inequality Index (GII). Female LFPR in India stands at round 32% based on recent PLFS survey and there also is a considerable gender wage gap which contributes to the income inequality in the country.
- **Inefficient Redistribution** With only 6 out of 100 Individuals paying taxes (only 5% Indians pay taxes) and tax to GDP ratio being 11% (Economic Survey), India is not efficient at redistribution of wealth. The income gap between rich and poor also worsens due to prevalence tax evasion, black money. Failure to tax rich people and corporations fairly exacerbates inequality as governments then resort to taxing the rest of society more. Heavy reliance on consumption taxes like GST increases inequality and is regressive in nature because poor people pay a larger share of their incomes.

- **Low Investment in Public Health** India's investments in public health are among the lowest in the world, and most cities lack any kind of public primary health services.
- **State Withdrawal** In order to improve their fiscal performance and keep public debt obligations under permissible limits, states reduced welfare expenditures and withdrew crucial support in health and education, leaving the domain open to the private sector. This further exacerbated inequality.

Measures Needed to Contain Inequality

- **Improving the State of Agriculture** This is essential as half of the population relies on agriculture for their sustenance. The need is to reduce the cost of Inputs - by investing in irrigation technologies, preventing fertiliser overuse etc., to ensure remunerative prices for farmers - through MSP reforms, eliminating middle men by promoting platforms like e-Rashtriya Kisan Agri Mandi etc. and to promote research to improve farm productivity.
- **Employment-oriented Growth** Promoting labour intensive industries such as leather and apparel, as suggested by NITI Aayog can be instrumental in raising incomes of the bottom 50%.
- **Tax Efficiency** India needs to improve tax to GDP ratio and bring it on par with emerging economies (23%). This can be done by lowering income tax threshold, preventing tax evasion and generation of black money, simplifying tax procedures to improve compliance and campaigning to inculcate a habit of tax paying.
- **State to be the Dominant Provider of Merit Goods** Health, nutrition, education - Public sector spending in these sectors needs to increase to around 6% of GDP which currently stands at around 2%. Increased social spending has been shown to reduce inequality by 20% across OECD countries.
- **Preventing Deprivation** Enforcing laws against eviction and exploitation such as LARR, Forest rights act can also avoid impoverishment of people while also ensuring income security through land and forest resources.

  There is significant evidence that higher wages and stronger labour rights - especially for women workers who tend to work in the lowest paid and most insecure jobs - are key to reducing inequality.

Conclusion

Inequality slows economic growth, undermines the fight against poverty and increases social tensions. World Bank predicts that unless governments tackle inequality then the goal of eradicating extreme poverty by 2030 will not be met.

Check Your Preparation

1. What is Inclusive Growth? Identifying its important features, discuss why it is an important objective of India's growth plans. (150 words, 10 marks)
2. Assess the reasons for bringing the unbanked population to the institutional finance fold. Also, highlight certain financial inclusion measures adopted since Independence. (150 words, 10 marks)
3. How does Self Help Groups (SHGs) aid in strengthening the functional capacity of the poor in employment and income generating activities? Critically evaluate the problems faced by women SHGs in availing the benefits offered by microfinance model. (250 words, 15 marks)
4. The various anti-poverty programmes have not achieved the desired socio-economic progress in India. In this context, critically analyse the major poverty programmes since Independence with special reference to MGNREGA. (250 words, 15 marks)

UNIT 3

Government Budgeting

Nature of Government Budgeting (Objectives of Fiscal Policy)

Q.1 Fiscal policy of India has two objectives, namely improving the growth performance of the economy and ensuring social justice to the people. Elaborate. Are these two objectives contradictory in nature? Give your opinion. (150 Words, 10 Marks)

Ans. **Introduction** Fiscal policy refers to the use of government spending, taxation and borrowing to influence the overall state of the economy. It is one of the key tools available to the government to manage economic activity, stabilise the economy and achieve certain macroeconomic objectives. The idea is to find a balance between tax rates and public spending, depending on the circumstances in the economy. Inflationary pressures in the economy warrant a 'contractionary fiscal policy' which involves increasing taxes, decreasing public spending or both. Whereas, recessionary pressures in the economy warrant an 'expansionary fiscal policy' which involves decreasing taxes, increasing public spending or both.

Fiscal Policy and Growth Performance

Fiscal policy plays a crucial role in promoting economic growth by influencing aggregate demand, investment and overall economic activity. The measures undertaken to achieve this objective include:

- **Infrastructure Development** The government allocates funds for the development of infrastructure such as roads, bridges, ports, and power plants. This boosts investment, enhances productivity and facilitates economic growth.
  - **Example** ₹ 10 lakh crore capital investment in BE 2023-24 a steep increase of 33% for third year in a row, to enhance growth potential and job creation, crowd-in private investments and provide a cushion against global headwinds.
- **Stimulating Private Investment** Fiscal policy provides incentives and support to encourage private investment in various sectors. This can be achieved through tax incentives, subsidies and other measures that reduce the cost of investment and promote business expansion.
  - **Example** In the Union Budget 2021-22, an outlay of ₹ 1.97 lakh crores for the Production-Linked Incentive (PLI) schemes for 13 key sectors, to create national manufacturing champions and generate employment opportunities for the country's youth.
- **Promoting Consumption** Increase in income tax exemption in Budget 2023-24 will lead to more disposable income with the households and therefore increase the consumption. This will directly result into higher economic growth.
- **Research and Development (R&D)** The government allocates resources for research and development activities to foster innovation, technological advancement and productivity growth. This promotes economic competitiveness and enhances long-term growth prospects.

- **Promoting Small and Medium Enterprises (SMEs)** Fiscal measures, such as tax exemptions and credit facilities, are implemented to support the growth of SMEs. These enterprises play a crucial role in job creation, fostering entrepreneurship and driving economic growth.
  - **Example** Under **Emergency Credit Line Guarantee Scheme (ECLGS)** 100% credit guarantee is extended to the lending institutions for loans extended by them under the scheme to eligible borrowers. As on 30.11.2022, guarantees amounting to ₹ 3.58 lakh crore have been issued under ECLGS, benefiting 1.19 crore borrowers.
- **Boost Exports** Recent Foreign Trade Policy 2023 has been launched to promote exports and facilitate ease of doing business for exporters. This has a direct bearing on economic growth and social justice.

Fiscal Policy and Social Justice

Fiscal policy also aims to ensure social justice by reducing income and wealth inequalities, addressing poverty and providing equal opportunities to all citizens. The measures undertaken to achieve this objective include:

- **Progressive Taxation** Progressive tax policies are implemented to ensure that individuals with higher incomes contribute proportionately more to public finances. This redistributes wealth and helps in reducing income inequality.
  - **Example** Income Tax in India
- **Subsidies and Welfare Programmes** The government provides subsidies and implements social welfare programmes to support vulnerable sections. These programmes aim to alleviate poverty, improve access to basic amenities and ensure social inclusion.
  - According to the Budget document, the government has pegged total subsidies on food, fertilisers and fuel at ₹ 5.22-lakh crore in its revised estimate (RE) for FY23.
- **Education and Healthcare** Fiscal policy allocates resources for the provision of quality education and healthcare services. Investments in education and healthcare infrastructure, along with subsidies and scholarships, aim to enhance human capital, improve social well-being and promote equal opportunities.
  - Finance Minister announced that 157 new nursing colleges will be established in co-location with the existing 157 medical colleges established since 2014.
- **Rural Development** Fiscal measures are directed towards rural development, agricultural support and employment generation in rural areas. This helps in reducing rural-urban disparities, improving agricultural productivity and ensuring equitable growth.
- **Financial Inclusion** Fiscal policies are designed to promote financial inclusion by expanding access to banking services, microfinance and affordable credit for marginalised sections of society. This facilitates economic empowerment and reduces income disparities.

Is improving the growth performance of the economy and ensuring social justice contradictory?

While the objectives of improving growth and ensuring social justice may have different focus areas, they are not as such contradictory.

- Inclusive growth and equitable distribution of resources can foster sustainable economic development.
- A thriving economy with reduced inequalities can generate more opportunities for all segments of society, leading to social progress and stability.
- Economic growth can have positive spill-over effects on social welfare. It generates tax revenues that can be used to fund social programms, infrastructure development and public services.
- It also provides opportunities for skill development, education and entrepreneurship, contributing to social mobility and improved quality of life. Thus, sustained economic growth can lay the foundation for social welfare.

However, it is important to note that challenges may arise in balancing these objectives

- For example, funding social welfare programmes and addressing social justice concerns may require significant fiscal resources, which can impact fiscal stability and economic growth if not managed prudently.
- Rapid economic growth without adequate attention to social welfare can lead to unequal distribution of wealth, exclusion and social unrest.
- On the other hand, excessive focus on social welfare without supporting economic growth can strain public finances, hinder investment and entrepreneurship and limit resources available for long-term sustainable development.

Conclusion

Therefore, striking a balance and adopting sound fiscal management practices is crucial to achieve both objectives effectively. When implemented in a coordinated manner, they can contribute to sustainable and inclusive development, benefiting the economy and society as a whole.

Zero-Based Budgeting

Q.2 'Zero-Based Budgeting (ZBB) is a budgeting process that allocates funding based on programme efficiency and necessity rather than budget history.' In this context, how ZBB is different from the traditional budgeting? Has this budgeting practice been ever implemented in India? (150 Words, 10 Marks)

Ans. **Introduction** Zero-Based Budgeting (ZBB) departs from traditional budgeting by requiring each programme to be justified from scratch, regardless of past budgets. It focuses on efficiency and necessity, assessing expenses based on their value and alignment with organisational goals. ZBB enables a disciplined and strategic allocation of resources, eliminating inefficiencies and ensuring funding is prioritized for high-value programmes.

Difference between ZBB and Traditional Budgeting

Criteria	Traditional Budgeting	Zero-Based Budgeting (ZBB)
Budgeting Approach	Uses previous year's budget as base	Starts from a 'zero base'
Funding Allocation	Based on historical budget figures	Based on programme efficiency and necessity
Budget Justification	Often relies on incremental changes	Requires justification for all expenses
Resources Allocation	May not align with the current priorities	Prioritises resources based on value and goals.
Decision-making Process	Often relies on the historical data	Involves a thorough analysis of costs and benefits
Accountability	May lack transparency in spending	Promotes fiscal responsibility and accountability

Benefits of ZBB

- Zero based budgeting examines all existing and new programmes and activities. This exercise helps in identifying inefficient or obsolete functions within the area of responsibility. In this way resources are allocated from low priority programmes to high priority programmes.
- This system facilitates identification of duplication of efforts among organisational units. Such inefficient activities are eliminated and some other activities are merged.
- All expenditures, under this system are critically reviewed and justified and all operational activities are evaluated in greater detail in terms of their cost effectiveness and cost-benefits. This requires managers to find alternative ways of performing their activities which may result in more efficient procedures.
- ZBB provides for quick budget adjustments during the year. If revenue falls short in this process, it offers the capability to quickly and rationally modify goals and expectations to correspond to a realistic and affordable plan of operations.

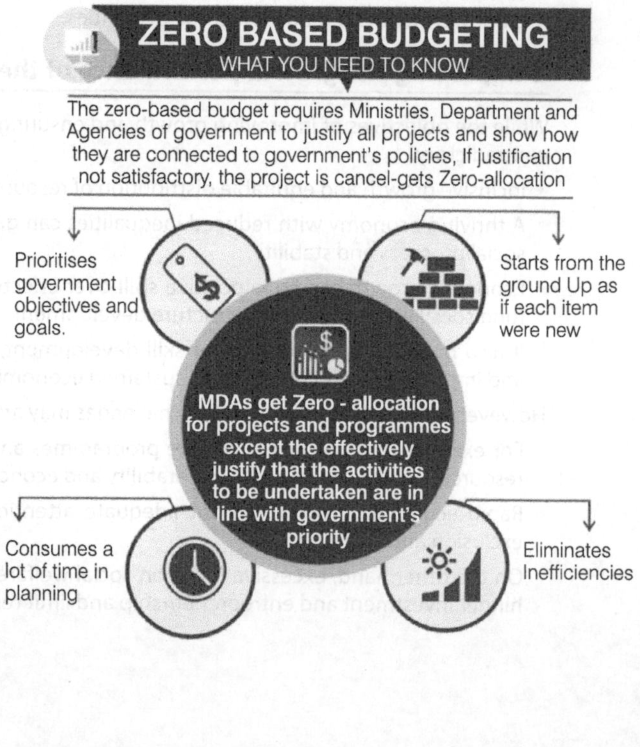

- ZBB ensures greater participation of personnel in formulation and ranking processes. This helps in promoting level of job satisfaction and thus resulting in better control and operational efficiency in the organisation.
- Zero Base budgeting is a flexible tool that can be applied on a selective basis. It does not have to be applied throughout the entire organisation or even in all the service departments.

Implementation of ZBB

Zero-Based Budgeting (ZBB) has been implemented in India in certain context. While not extensively adopted across all sectors, there have been instances of ZBB being implemented at various levels of government and in specific organisations.

- In India, zero-based budgeting was adopted by the Department of Science and Technology in 1983.
- In 1986, the Indian Government implemented zero-based budgeting as a system for determining expenditure budget. The government made it mandatory for all Ministries to review their programmes and activities and prepare their expenditure estimations based on the zero-based budgeting concept.
- Additionally, some State Governments in India have experimented with ZBB to enhance budgeting practices. For instance, the Government of Rajasthan initiated a pilot project to implement ZBB in its budgeting process. The objective was to allocate resources based on programme priorities and evaluate the effectiveness of existing programmes.

While the implementation of ZBB in India has not been widespread, these examples demonstrate that there have been efforts to introduce this budgeting practice to improve resource allocation, enhance efficiency and prioritise programme effectiveness.

Challenges Associated in the Implementation of ZBB

- **Mindset Shift** Overcoming resistance to new budgeting practices and promoting stakeholder buy-in through awareness and engagement.
- **Resource Intensive** Allocating resources for data collection, analysis and skilled personnel to facilitate the ZBB process.
- **Political Pressures** Establishing an independent evaluation process to mitigate biases and prioritise programme effectiveness.
- **Data Availability** Strengthening data collection mechanisms and investing in information systems to ensure accurate and reliable data.
- **Implementation at Scale** Phased implementation, starting with pilot projects, to learn and refine before scaling up.
- **Lack of Expertise** Providing an explanation for every line item and every cost is a problematic task and requires training for the managers.

Way Forward

- **Leadership Commitment** Strong top-level support to drive necessary changes and overcome resistance.
- **Capacity Building** Training officials in ZBB methodologies and techniques.
- **Gradual Implementation** Phased approach for learning, refining and modifying processes.
- **Stakeholder Engagement** Encouraging dialogue, soliciting feedback and fostering collaboration.
- **Monitoring and Evaluation** Robust mechanisms to assess impact and identify areas for improvement.

By addressing these challenges and adopting a strategic and phased approach, India can overcome obstacles and effectively implement ZBB to improve resource allocation, enhance efficiency and promote transparency in budgeting processes.

Outcome-based Budgeting

Q.3 It is imperative that the present system of budgeting in India should make a transition towards Outcome Budgeting for effective Public Finance Management in India. Critically examine the statement along with the challenges it brings for the policymakers. (250 Words, 15 Marks)

Ans. **Outcome Budgeting** Outcome budgeting is an approach to public finance management that focuses on measuring and evaluating the outcomes and impacts of government programmes and policies, rather than just tracking inputs and outputs.

It ensures that public funds are allocated and utilised efficiently and effectively, leading to better service delivery, informed decision-making, resource optimisation, and enhanced accountability in public finance management.

It was first introduced in India in 2005-06 as a revised version of the Performance Budget, wherein certain ministries of the government were required to produce an outcome budget.

Why India Should Adopt Outcome Budgeting

- **Results-Oriented Approach** Outcome Budgeting shifts the focus from expenditure to results. It emphasises the achievement of specific outcomes and the impact of government programmes on citizens lives.
  - Instead of measuring the number of schools built (output), Outcome Budgeting would assess the improvement in literacy rates or student performance (outcomes) resulting from educational investments.
- **Transparency and Accountability** Outcome Budgeting promotes accountability by holding government departments responsible for achieving the desired outcomes.
  - It requires setting clear targets and regularly monitoring progress.
  - By making the outcomes and performance of programmes transparent, it enables citizens and stakeholders to hold the government accountable.
  - For example, if the outcome target for reducing infant mortality is not achieved, it becomes evident where corrective actions are needed.
- **Resource Optimisation** Outcome Budgeting enables better resource allocation and optimisation. By assessing the effectiveness of various programmes, it allows policymakers to allocate resources to those programmes that have a higher likelihood of achieving desired outcomes.
- **Decision-making and Prioritisation** Outcome Budgeting helps in informed decision-making and prioritisation of government spending. By evaluating the outcomes and impacts of programs, policymakers can make more evidence-based choices and prioritise funding for initiatives that yield the best results.
- **Performance Evaluation and Learning** Outcome Budgeting facilitates continuous performance evaluation and learning. It enables the identification of successful strategies and practices that can be replicated or scaled up across different programmes and sectors.
- **Citizen-centric Approach** Outcome Budgeting aligns government programs with citizen's needs and aspirations. By focusing on outcomes that directly impact people's lives, it ensures that public funds are utilised for programs that address their priorities.

Challenges it Brings for Policymakers

- **Outcome Measurement and Attribution** Defining and measuring outcomes can be complex, particularly in a country as diverse as India. Linking specific outcomes to government interventions and policies requires rigorous data collection, monitoring, and evaluation mechanisms. It may be challenging to accurately attribute outcomes to specific government initiatives due to the presence of various contributing factors.
  - Scrutiny of the Outcome Budgets for the years 2013-14 to 2016-17 by the CAG revealed inconsistency in depicting scheme-wise achievements (outcomes) against targets already set in previous years. Audit noted that the Outcome Budget 2013-14 indicated unquantifiable targets like improvement of roads, bridges, drains, construction of market complexes, flyovers etc but achievements or outcomes were not included in the Outcome Budget of the following year i.e., 2014-15.
  - Thus, many Outcome Budgets produced by ministries are in effect are 'outlay budgets'.
- **Data Availability and Quality** India faces challenges in terms of data availability, completeness and accuracy, particularly at the grassroots level. Policymakers must address these data gaps to ensure effective implementation and evaluation of outcomes.
- **Institutional Capacity and Coordination** Outcome Budgeting requires a robust institutional framework and coordination among various government departments and agencies. Strengthening the capacity of government officials involved in outcome budgeting is vital for its successful implementation.
  - The internal audit system in the ministries is weak in terms of professional expertise and inadequate manpower. Thus, there is lack of independent, objective opinion to add value and improve the operation of schemes.
- **Political Pressures and Short-Termism** Outcome Budgeting requires a long-term perspective and may face resistance from political pressures focused on short-term results.

- **Behavioural and Cultural Shift** Implementing outcome budgeting requires a significant shift in the mindset and culture of the bureaucracy. It necessitates a focus on results, evidence-based decision-making and learning from failures. Changing the prevailing culture of inputs and process-based budgeting to outcome-oriented budgeting may take time and effort.
- **Citizen Engagement and Transparency** Outcome Budgeting can benefit from active citizen participation and transparency to ensure accountability and improve public trust. Policymakers need to engage citizens, civil society organisations, and other stakeholders in the budgeting process and make outcome data accessible to the public.
- **Resource Constraints** Shifting to outcome budgeting may require increased resources for data collection, evaluation and monitoring systems. Policymakers must carefully allocate adequate resources to build the necessary infrastructure and capacity for effective outcome budgeting.

Conclusion

The Delhi Government's Outcome Budget for 2017-18 shifts the bar for transparency and accountability in public spending to a new level. To successfully transition towards Outcome Budgeting, India needs to develop a robust framework that includes defining clear outcome indicators, setting realistic targets, establishing monitoring and evaluation mechanisms, enhancing data collection and analysis capacities and promoting a culture of evidence-based decision-making.

Gender Budgeting

Q.4 There is a need for revisiting India's approach to gender responsive budgeting. Analyse in the context of limitations faced in the implementation of gender budgeting in India. (250 Words, 15 Marks)

Ans. **Introduction** The Budget Year 2005-06 was very significant for women in the country, as for the first time the 'Gender Responsive Budgeting' (GRB) was adopted. The GRB is a method of planning, programming and budgeting that helps advance gender equality and women's rights.

About Gender Budgeting

- Gender Budgeting is a powerful tool for achieving gender mainstreaming so as to ensure that benefits of development reach women as much as men. It is not an accounting exercise but an ongoing process of keeping a gender perspective in policy/programme formulation, its implementation and review.
- GB entails dissection of the Government budgets to establish its gender differential impacts and to ensure that gender commitments are translated in to budgetary commitments.
- The rationale for gender budgeting arises from recognition of the fact that national budgets impact men and women differently through the pattern of resource allocation. Women, constitute 48% of India's population, but they lag behind men on many social indicators like health, education, economic opportunities, etc. Hence, they warrant special attention due to their vulnerability and lack of access to resources.

Evolution of Gender Budgeting in India

- Since 2005-06, the Expenditure Division of the Ministry of Finance has been issuing a note on Gender Budgeting as a part of the Budget Circular every year. This GB Statement comprises two parts- Part A and Part B.
  - Part A reflects Women Specific Schemes, i.e., those which have 100% allocation for women.
  - Part B reflects Pro Women Schemes, i.e., those where at least 30% of the allocation is for women.
- According to an IMF study, there are over 16 Indian states that have adopted gender-based budgeting, which is a good achievement. There are gender budgeting cells formed under 56 government ministries/departments to identify gender-related goals and the approach to achieve them.

Utility of Gender Budgeting

- It allows gender specific grant allocations in various schemes. **Example**, schemes like Start-up India and Stand-up India allocations must be specifically earmarked for women entrepreneurs.
- Provisions especially to attract women in the mainstream economy and targeting the section of women that hesitates to participate actively by leveraging benefits.

- Using technology to make women the financial head of family to increase her say in the matters that concern expenses and therefore empower them. The DBT in the Ujjwala scheme is step in right direction.
- Institutionalising GB at State Government level must be done to increase the share and commitment on state subjects.
- **Economic Upgradation of Women** Having a history of marginalisation of women in India, women centric schemes need to be brought to promote the welfare of women.
- **Women Entrepreneurship** With special provisions earmarked for the entrepreneurship of women in the budget, there will be a gender parity in working culture, as women find it more comfortable to work in places run and managed by women.
- **Gender Sensitive Plans** Gender responsive budgets policies can contribute to achieving the objectives of gender equality, human development and economic efficiency.

Challenges

- **Insufficient Allocation** Not only has the magnitude of the gender budget as a proportion of total expenditure of the Union Budget decreased, the budgetary allocations for promoting gender equality and women's empowerment have also shown a decline.

Gender Budget as % of Total Expenditure, 2005-06 to 2022

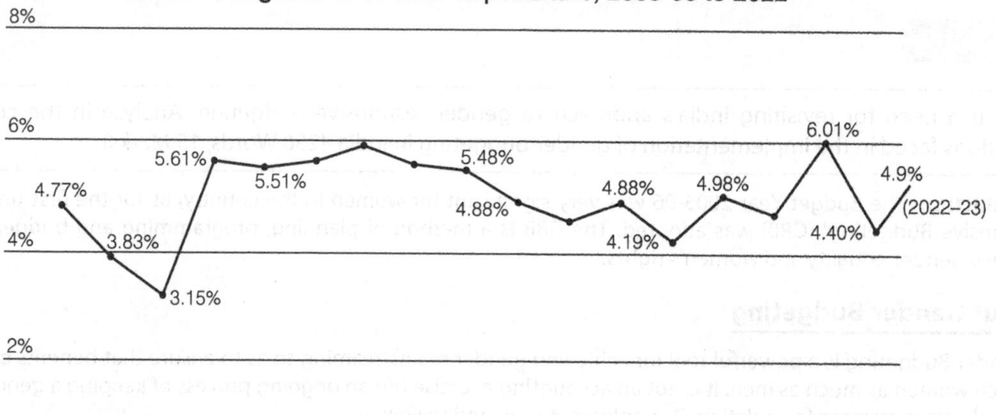

- **Un-utilisation of Gender Budget** Further, the budgets allocated are often not utilised and the same gets spent on other projects. Women empowerment is not a priority in most state budgets either. For example, the budget for implementation of the Protection of Women from Domestic Violence Act, 2005 is low across all states in India.
  - There are only a few 'big budget' women exclusive schemes of the Ministry of Women and Child Development (MWCD) like the Nirbhaya Fund and the Beti Bachao Beti Padhao campaign.
- **Concentrated in a Few Sectors** Over the last decade, four Ministries–Rural Development, Education, Health and Women & Child Development have received between 85-90% of the Gender Budget expenditure. This limits adoption of a more holistic approach.
- Lack of political will and resources for implementing gender budgeting effectively.
- Lack of data and information on the gender impacts of government policies and programmes.
- **Lack of Impact Assessment** Though it is mandatory to release the Gender Budget Statement (GBS), there are no accountability mechanisms mandating impact assessment of allocations for women beneficiaries. Further, lack of data hampers policy making as well as impedes impact study for analysis of outcomes.
- **Inconsistent State-specific Approach** About 16 States in India currently undertake gender budgeting, however, the quality of statements produced and allocation undertaken vary significantly among states, owing to inadequate training of government officials.

- Lack of dedicated human resources to implement the interventions identified by the GBCs.
- **Monitoring remains one of the weakest links in the GRB work** with no designated mechanism for monitoring it at the national level.
  - There is an immediate need to conduct an assessment of gender-specific parameters and set goals accordingly. For example, it is important to understand time-bound goals for parameters such as female school enrolment, gender-based violence, health, labour force participation.
- **Very little information is available in the public domain** as regards the assumptions made by various ministries in the reviews of their expenditure profiles from a gender perspective.

Way Forward

- **Increase Allocations for Women Focussed Programmes** Despite an ambitious road map and MWCD's commitment to GRB at the national level, the Central Government's gender budget has never been more 1% of India's GDP. There is a pressing need to prioritise women's safety, education, health and workforce participation; which necessitates a significant increase in allocations.
- **Improve Targeting** Funds needs to be targeted towards priority sectors which suffer from the deepest gender inequalities. These sectors should be determined by rigorous research to ensure that targeted spending creates a virtuous cycle, and has a multiplier effort on women's living standards.
- **Create a Ranking for State Level Gender Budgets** Akin to the ease of doing business ranking, states should be ranked on the quality of gender budgets, impact analyses and gender audits of these allocations. Capacity building and technical support should be provided to State-level Gender Budget Cells by MWCD for this exercise.
- **An authority should be created for gender auditing** to conduct an annual impact assessment of budgetary allocations for all schemes, thus bringing accountability to the process.
- There is also a **critical need for capacity building** across government, corporates, public sector undertakings, NGOs and all involved agencies.
- A **national-level reporting** platform should be created under the ministry of statistics and programme implementation, which will collect the disaggregated data by sex for understanding the impact and outcome of the gender budgeting initiative.

Issues in the Budgetary Process

Q.5 While the budgetary reforms undertaken by the Central government in recent years have led to better management of government expenditure, there are still some issues in the budgetary process that still need redressal. Discuss. (250 Words, 15 Marks)

Ans. Introduction Budgeting refers to the process of planning, allocating and controlling financial resources by the government for a specific period. Its purpose is to determine the government's revenue sources and allocate funds to various sectors and programmes. It enables effective resource utilisation, supports economic growth and ensures accountability in the allocation and management of public funds.

Major Budgetary Reforms by the Government

- **Improved Fiscal Transparency and Realistic Revenue Assumptions in the Budget** The Union Government sought to improve transparency in fiscal accounts and statements by bringing below-the-line expenditures above it.
  - The government's Extra-Budgetary borrowings were brought down from ₹ 1.48 lakh crore in FY20 and ₹ 1.21 lakh crore in FY21 to ₹ 750 crore in FY22 (RE).
  - In the budget for FY23, there were no estimates for Extra Budgetary Resources.
  - Apart from cleaner fiscal accounting, last year's budget-based revenue projections on realistic assumptions, so there was a buffer for the government amid global uncertainties.
- **Discontinuation of Plan-Non Plan Classification** Plan and Non-Plan classifications of Government Expenditure were discontinued in Budget FY18. The reform put greater emphasis on Revenue and Capital classification of Government Expenditure.

- The Economic Survey noted that there was a conception built over the years that Plan expenditures were good while non-plan ones were not, which resulted in skewed budget allocations.

- **Merger of Railway Budget with the Main Budget** In FY18, the railway budget was merged with the Union Budget for a holistic view of the government's financial position. The initiative looked to facilitate multi-modal transport planning between railways, highways, and inland waterways. PM Gati Shakti scheme has reportedly strengthened this in subsequent years.
  - It also helped to enhance resources for both the Railways and the Union Government.
  - The merger exempts Railways from paying dividends to Government Revenues, while the survey claims the Finance Ministry gets more breathing room for resource allocation in the mid-year review.
  - It also allowed the Ministry of Finance to ensure there is a coherent emphasis on Capex across sectors in recent times.
- **Shifting the Date of the Budget to 1st February** From Budget FY18, the date of the Budget was moved to 1st February. Advancing it by a month paved the way to complete the Budget cycle before the start of next financial year and thus no need for the passage of vote on accounts. Ministries can also now plan better and execute schemes from the start of the financial year.
- **Use of Technology** The government has leveraged technology to enhance the efficiency and transparency of budgetary processes. This includes the implementation of online platforms for budget preparation, execution and monitoring.
  - The Public Financial Management System (PFMS) facilitates the direct transfer of funds from the Central Government to various implementing agencies, promoting transparency and reducing delays.
- **Emphasis on Outcome-oriented Spending** The reforms have emphasized the importance of outcome-oriented spending, focusing on achieving measurable outcomes and impacts rather than just allocating funds. This encourages accountability and ensures that public resources are utilised effectively.
  - The Atal Mission for Rejuvenation and Urban Transformation (AMRUT) is an example of outcome-oriented spending, where the Central Government provides funds to states based on their performance in achieving predetermined urban development outcomes.
- **Rationalisation of Subsidies** The government has taken steps to rationalise subsidies by targeting them to the intended beneficiaries and reducing leakages. This helps in better targeting of resources and avoiding wastage.

Issues in the Budgetary Process and Reform Measures

The Estimates Committee of Parliament (Chairman Mr. Girish Bhalchandra Bapat) report on the subject 'Recent Budgetary Reforms for Better Management of Government Expenditure' suggested further recommendations:

- **State-wise allocation** The funds allocated to different states do not reflect in this document. The Committee noted that people are interested in knowing the amount of money allocated to different states by the Central Government.
  - The committee recommended the Central Government to incorporate the state-wise allocation details in the Union Budget documents to bring transparency in transfer of funds to states.
- **Unspent Balances of States in Bank Accounts** The Committee observed that the grants transferred by the Central Government to states remain in state treasuries till they are transferred to implementing agencies. It noted that some State Governments deposit the unspent balance remaining from schemes/ grants in banks, which earn them a substantial amount of interest.
  - The committee recommended the Central Government to identify the interest earned by various states from such unspent balances in banks and frame guidelines (if none exist) for utilisation of the funds earned by them.
- **Underspending** The Committee observed that DEA conducts mid-year review of the expenditure by all Ministries and revises their expenditure ceiling for the year based on the progress of expenditure till date and their capacity to spend in the remaining year. It noted that despite advancement of the budget cycle, savings (i.e., underspending or under-utilisation of allocation) occurred in 99 departments in 2017-18, 97 in 2018-19, and 100 in 2019-20.
  - The Committee recommended that the objectives of advancement of the budget cycle in this front needs to be reviewed so that this trend is discontinued and funds available with the government in the union budget are optimally and fully utilized.
- **Monitoring the Implementation of Schemes** The Committee observed that the Secretary of a Ministry/ Department, being its Chief Accounting Authority, is responsible for monitoring the implementation of its projects/ schemes. However, the Committee noted that the Secretary, DEA, being an overall controller of the central government's accounting, is also equally responsible for monitoring the implementation of the projects/ schemes of various Ministries/Departments.

- The Committee recommended that a system may be evolved by DEA to track the progress of Ministries/ Departments on implementation of projects/ schemes, so that habitual defaulters who have not updated the progress can be identified while allocating the budget.

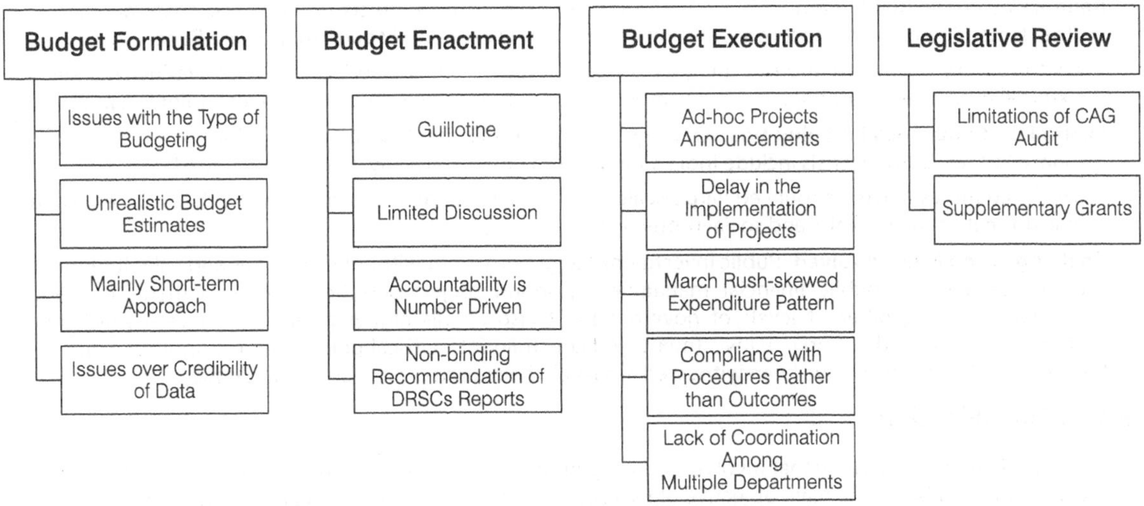

Other Measures Required

- **Subsidy Reforms** While subsidy rationalisation has been undertaken, there is a need for further reforms to ensure subsidies are better targeted to intended beneficiaries. Leakage and inefficiencies in subsidy delivery systems still exist, hindering optimal resource allocation and effective social welfare.
- **Participation and Accountability** Increasing public participation and ensuring accountability in the budgetary process remain crucial areas of focus. Involving citizens, civil society organisations, and other stakeholders in budget planning and monitoring can enhance transparency, inclusivity, and effectiveness.
- **Long-term Planning** There is a need for more robust long-term planning in the budgetary process. Aligning budget allocations with long-term goals and priorities can help address structural issues and promote sustainable development.
- **Adoption of Zero-based Budgeting**

Conclusion

Addressing these issues requires sustained efforts and continuous improvement in the budgetary process. Strengthening transparency, improving resource allocation, enhancing expenditure tracking, reforming subsidies, promoting participation, and emphasising long-term planning are essential steps toward further enhancing the management of government expenditure in India.

Fiscal Consolidation vs Public Investment

Q.6 In the background of increasing government debt post COVID-19 pandemic, which strategy should be adopted by the government to bring down public debt: Public Investment-led growth or Fiscal Consolidation? Justify your opinion with proper arguments. (250 Words, 15 Marks)

Ans. **Introduction** The COVID-19 pandemic has been a major shock to the global economy, causing widespread disruptions and hardships. To mitigate its effects, governments around the world have implemented unprecedented fiscal stimulus measures, such as income support, health spending, and infrastructure investment.

- However, these measures have also resulted in a sharp increase in public debt levels, which have reached historic highs in many countries. India's debt-to-GDP ratio rose to 87.8% in FY21. In FY22, it is estimated to decline modestly to 87.4%, with high nominal growth playing a role in bringing it down. This poses a serious challenge for fiscal sustainability and macroeconomic stability.

Public Investment-led Growth

Public investment-led growth is a strategy that involves increasing public spending on infrastructure, health, education, and other productive sectors to stimulate economic activity, create jobs, and enhance human capital and social welfare.

- **Benefits of Public Investment** Public investment can have positive effects on both aggregate demand and supply. On the demand side, it can boost consumption and private investment through multiplier effects.
  - On the supply side, it can improve the quality and quantity of public goods and services, reduce market failures and externalities, enhance productivity and competitiveness, and foster innovation and technological progress.
- **Examples of Countries Pursuing this Strategy** Some countries that have adopted public investment-led growth as a response to the COVID-19 crisis include India, China, South Korea, Germany, France, and Canada.
  - These countries have announced large-scale public investment plans in areas such as green energy, digital transformation, health care, and social protection.
- **Challenges and Risks Involved** Public investment-led growth is not without challenges and risks. It requires adequate fiscal space, efficient public financial management, sound project selection and implementation, and effective coordination among different levels of government. It also entails higher public debt levels, which may increase borrowing costs, crowd out private investment, and constrain future fiscal policy options. Another major challenges is the higher inflation which have been witnessed across all the countries post-Covid pandemic.

Fiscal Consolidation

Fiscal consolidation is a strategy that involves reducing public debt and deficit through spending cuts, revenue increases, or a combination of both. The main objective of fiscal consolidation is to restore fiscal sustainability and credibility, lower borrowing costs, and create fiscal buffers for future shocks.

- **Benefits of Reducing Public Debt and Deficit** Reducing public debt and deficit can have positive effects on both macroeconomic stability and growth.
- **On the Stability Side**, it can reduce the risk of sovereign debt crises, lower interest rates and inflation expectations, and improve investor confidence.
- **On the Growth Side**, it can enhance intergenerational equity, free up resources for productive uses, and facilitate structural reforms.
- **Examples of Countries Pursuing this Strategy** Some countries that have pursued fiscal consolidation in the aftermath of the global financial crisis include Greece, Ireland, Portugal, Spain, and the UK. These countries implemented austerity measures to reduce their fiscal imbalances and regain market access.
- **Challenges and Risks Involved** Fiscal consolidation is not without challenges and risks. It requires strong political commitment, social consensus, and institutional capacity. It also entails short-term output and employment losses, which may be exacerbated by negative feedback loops between fiscal contraction and economic activity. Moreover, it may have adverse effects on income distribution, social cohesion, and public service delivery.

Comparison and Evaluation of both strategies

- **Factors leading to the Choice of Strategy** The choice between public investment-led growth and fiscal consolidation depends on several factors, such as the initial level of public debt and deficit, the availability of fiscal space, the quality of public investment management, the structure of public spending and revenue, the state of the economy, the external environment, and the social preferences.
- **Role of Public Investment in Both Strategies** Public investment can play a role in both strategies. In public investment-led growth, it is the main driver of economic recovery. In fiscal consolidation, it can be protected or even increased within a broader framework of expenditure rationalisation and revenue mobilisation.
- **Significance of Growth for Both Strategies** Growth is crucial for both strategies. In public investment-led growth, it is the ultimate goal of public spending. In fiscal consolidation, it is a precondition for debt reduction. Therefore, both strategies need to be accompanied by complementary policies that support growth potential.
- **Evaluation of which Strategy is More Suitable** The evaluation of which strategy is more suitable depends on one's normative views and empirical assessments. However, based on the available evidence and arguments, I believe that public investment-led growth is more desirable than fiscal consolidation for the following reasons:
  - Public investment-led growth can generate higher short-term and long-term growth rates than fiscal consolidation by stimulating aggregate demand and enhancing aggregate supply.

– Public investment-led growth can create more jobs and reduce poverty than fiscal consolidation by expanding employment opportunities and improving living standards.

- Public investment-led growth can be financed in a sustainable manner by taking advantage of low interest rates mobilising domestic resources strengthening international cooperation.

Conclusion

Public debt reduction is a key challenge for many countries in the post-pandemic era. Public investment-led growth and fiscal consolidation are two alternative strategies to achieve this goal. However, public investment-led growth has more advantages than fiscal consolidation in terms of stimulating growth, creating jobs, reducing poverty, and addressing structural challenges. Therefore, public investment-led growth is a more desirable strategy, provided that it is financed in a sustainable way.

Critical Analysis of FRBM Act, 2003

Q.7 While enlisting the reasons behind the introduction of Fiscal Responsibility and Budget Management (FRBM) Act, 2003, critically examine the effectiveness of FRBM Act in reducing fiscal deficit. What reforms must be brought in the FRBM Act to make it more relevant in the background of current global and domestic challenges? (250 Words, 15 Marks)

Ans. Introduction The Fiscal Responsibility and Budget Management (FRBM) Act, 2003 envisions provisions for fiscal discipline on government spending. It aims to bring inter-generational equity in fiscal management and long-term macro-economic stability. It prescribes limit on fiscal deficit of 3% of GDP for Central and State Governments.

Reason for the Introduction of FRBM Act, 2003

The FRBM Act was enacted in 2003 as rising government borrowing and the resultant government debts have seriously eroded the financial health of the government. High revenue deficit due to higher expenditure on subsidies, salaries, defence etc compelled the government to make big borrowing from early 1990s onwards. With inadequate revenues, government resorted to high level of borrowing. The borrowing again produced high interest payments. In this way, interest payments became the largest expenditure item of the government. To arrest this financial weakness in its budget, the government has taken some serious deficit cut targets by introducing a law in the form of the FRBM.

Assessment of FRBM

- There was an improvement in the fiscal performance of both Centre and States because of the implementation of the FRBM Act.

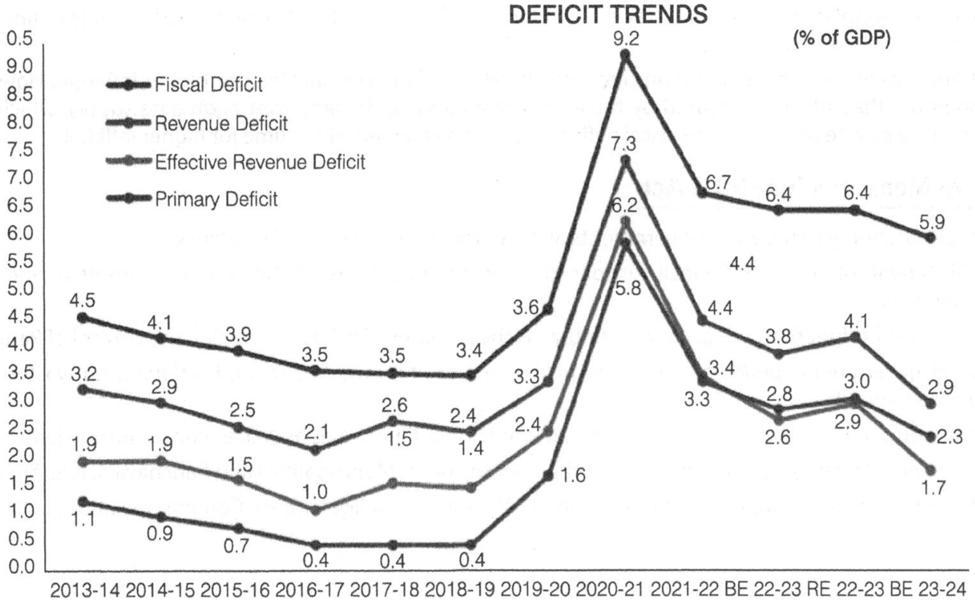

- States achieved the targets much ahead of the prescribed timeline. The Central Government was also on the right path of achieving this objective in the right time.
- However, due to the global financial crisis, this was suspended and consequently, the fiscal consolidation as mandated in the FRBM Act was put on hold in 2007-08. The crisis period called for increased level of expenditure by the government to boost demand in the economy. As a result of fiscal stimulus, the government has moved away from the path of fiscal consolidation.
- FRBM Act got amended in 2012 titled as FRBM 2.0 which brought new targets of fiscal deficit and aimed for elimination of effective revenue deficit. Post this, government moved to the path of fiscal consolidation till 2018-19.
- With the COVID-19 pandemic impact on the economy and to undertake higher expenditure to give a boost to the economy, government announced 20 Lakh crore stimulus package which led to higher fiscal deficit much above than the targets.
- While FRBM Act has maintained some kind of financial discipline, there were two major instances – 2008-09 and 2020-21 where governments moved away from the path of fiscal consolidation because of boosting higher economic growth.

Issues in FRBM Act

- The FRBM Act was totally undemocratic in its approach as it denied freedom to future governments in respect of fiscal management. Its aim was to bind future governments to a pre-specified fiscal policy framework which was in a way an anti-democratic measure.
- **Curb Spending Ability** It has been held that in order to meet its revenue deficit targets the government has to cut down on social sector expenditures on important segments like health and education. It led to low levels of capital expenditure.
- **Off Budget Borrowings** Since these are not accounted within the FD, it disrupts the entire purpose of the Act.
- It leads to neglect of equity as well as economic growth. Under the FRBM Act, 2003 the dice is heavily loaded against investments in not only human resources development, but also infrastructure. This is because of the view that the infrastructure investments on account of their large externalities do not directly contribute to the government revenue.
- **The FRBM Act did not address the problem of financing public expenditure in a serious manner** In the 1990s the tax-GDP ratio declined significantly. Hence, the need to raise this ratio should have received top priority under the legislation. But this did not happen. There was no target under the legislation for the tax-GDP ratio. Actually the FRBM Act could have provided for raising tax-GDP ratio by making improvements in tax administration and collections and effective measures to rein in tax evasion.
- **No Independent Agency** for giving fiscal forecasts and monitoring of fiscal targets
- **Flawed Assumptions** It makes a flawed assumption that lower fiscal deficits lead to higher and more sustained growth. This is not always true.
  - It also makes a flawed assumption that large fiscal deficits necessarily lead to higher inflation. However, economists point out that inflation is caused by the excess of aggregate demand over aggregate supply, which may come from public or private sectors. Hence, fiscal deficit must not be blamed all the time for higher inflation.

Reform Measures for FRBM Act

- Provide autonomy to the State Governments, with a proven record of fiscal prudency.
- Establishment of a Fiscal Council, as per the recommendations of NK Singh Committee and various finance commissions.
- Optimise off-budget borrowings to a minimum, as these routes of funds are outside the control of Parliament.
- Prudent government spendings, targeting productive capital investments and rationalising wasteful subsidies is an ideal way forward.
- Give impetus to the stalled projects to boost up employment, revenues as well as consumption demand.
- Devise innovative ways for raising capital at the level of states, Municipalities and Panchayats. e.g., Municipal bonds etc.
- Better coordination between agencies with financial implications like Finance Commission and GST Council.

Conclusion

Despite all its shortcomings, FRBM Act rightly emphasised upon the value of prudent fiscal management. There were amendments in the Act earlier and now the FRBM Review committee has made some welcome changes. This should be followed by both the Central Government and State Governments in the right spirit as the Act provides for a welcome fiscal discipline and greater transparency in fiscal operations.

Fiscal Council

Q.8 Constituting a Fiscal Council in India is crucial to ensure fiscal credibility in the aftermath of Covid pandemic. In this context, examine the possible functions of the council and the related concerns. (150 Words, 10 Marks)

Ans. Introduction Fiscal councils are independent public institutions aimed at strengthening commitment to sustainable public finances through public assessments of fiscal plans and provision of macroeconomic and budgetary forecasts.

Fiscal Council is crucial to ensure fiscal credibility in times of geopolitical uncertainties

- **Mismatched Budgets** Historically, interim budgets in India have consistently overestimated revenue growth and underestimated expenditure growth. The Finance Ministry's overall record in forecasting projections has been consistently poor under successive Finance Ministers in regular budgets too.
- **Provide More Accurate Forecasts** Fiscal Council does Budgetary forecasts to evaluate the realism of the budget estimates, and monitor progress and conformity to fiscal rules. This is unlike the institutions like CAG which does post-facto analysis.
- **Fiscal Council will Enhance the Effectiveness of the FRBM Process** The FRBM process as it exists now has several shortcomings. For example, failure to achieve the fiscal targets, lack of credibility on budgets due to shifting goal posts, creative accounting, creating new concepts such as effective revenue deficit, off-budget financing of expenditures etc.
  - **Case studies by the IMF and OECD** has confirmed that independent fiscal institutions effectively complements fiscal rules in monitoring their effective implementation and have contributed to improved fiscal performances.
- **Harmonized Statistics** Fiscal Council provides for co-ordination with all levels of government to provide harmonised fiscal statistics across government levels.
- **More Transparency** An unbiased report to Parliament helps to raise the level of debate and brings in greater transparency in regard to public money.
  - **More Accountability** Fiscal Councils in most countries are able to discipline lawmakers through 'comply or explain' obligations which entail governments to at least explain why they diverge from the Fiscal Council's views and thus brings more accountability.
- **Raising Public Awareness** Scientific estimates of the cost of programmes and assessment of forecasts could help in raising public awareness about their fiscal implications and make people understand the nature of budgetary constraint.
- **Commission Recommendations** 15th Finance Commission and NK Singh Committee recommended the creation of fiscal council as an essential part of 21st century fiscal architecture. 15th finance commission stated that the absence of an independent fiscal institution to assess and evaluate the fiscal plan as well as performance and forecasts published by the governments has further diminished the capacity to monitor compliance.
- **International Experience** 50+ developed and emerging market economies have found it necessary to have such an institution. For example, Congressional Budget Office in the US, Office of Budget Responsibility in the UK, Parliamentary Budget Office in Australia.

Possible Functions of the Fiscal Council

- **One**, providing multi-year macro-economic and fiscal forecasts.
- **Two**, evaluating fiscal performances vis-à-vis targets across all levels of government.
- **Three**, assessing the appropriateness and consistency of fiscal targets in the states.
- **Four**, undertake an independent assessment of long-term fiscal sustainability.
- **Five**, assessing fiscal policy statements by governments under fiscal responsibility legislations.

- **Six**, advising on the conditions for using escape clauses under fiscal responsibility legislations.
- **Seven**, policy costing of new measures with significant fiscal implications.
- **Eight**, providing analytical support to the Finance Commissions and publishing all their reports and underlying methodologies. FRBM mechanism hasn't delivered.

Concerns of the Fiscal Council

- **Dilute Finance Ministry Authority** Fiscal Council forces the Finance Ministry to use someone else's estimates will dilute accountability.
- **Executive Control** This leads to executive control of elected government, preventing government from moulding fiscal rules depending on situation and need.
- **Rigid Rules** Fiscal Council provides for rigid rules for fiscal prudence.

Conclusion

Fiscal council will help in improving comprehensiveness, transparency and accountability of budgetary data and reduce raise in debt which will jeopardise medium – growth prospects.

Off Budget Borrowings

Q.9 An increasing trend towards off-budget financing not only impairs the fiscal consolidation process but also goes against the financial accountability of the government. Do you agree? Substantiate.
(150 Words, 10 Marks)

Ans. **Introduction** Off-budget borrowings are loans that are taken not by the Centre directly, but by another public institution which borrows on the directions of the Central Government. Such borrowings are used to fulfil the government's expenditure needs.

But since the liability of the loan is not formally on the Centre, the loan is not included in the national fiscal deficit. This helps keep the country's fiscal deficit within acceptable limits.

Increasing Trend

- By end-FY21, the Centre had off-budgetary liabilities close to ₹ 6.7 trillion.
- The outstanding off-Budget liabilities of the Centre include about ₹ 49,000 crore for the Pradhan Mantri Awas Yojana - Rural, ₹ 20,164 crore for various irrigation projects, ₹ 12,300 crore for Swachh Bharat Mission Grameen, etc.
- The remaining off-Budget liabilities of ₹ 1.7 trillion are proving challenging to eliminate due to bondholders' reluctance to forego high-yield bonds.
- Comptroller and Auditor-General report of 2019 pointed out that this route of financing puts major sources of funds outside the control of Parliament. Such off-budget financing is not part of the calculation of the fiscal indicators despite fiscal implications.
  – Five Southern states – Telangana, Andhra Pradesh, Kerala, Tamil Nadu and Karnataka – accounted for ₹ 2.34 lakh crore, around 93% of the total off-Budget liabilities of eleven major states.

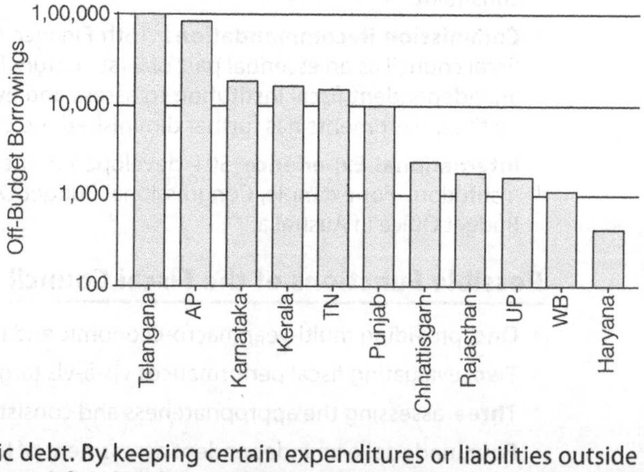

Issues with Off-Budget Financing

Impairs Fiscal Consolidation

Off-budget financing can impede the fiscal consolidation process, which aims to reduce fiscal deficit and stabilise public debt. By keeping certain expenditures or liabilities outside the budget, the government may artificially lower the reported fiscal deficit, making it challenging to achieve fiscal targets and sustain fiscal discipline.

- **Masks the True Picture of Fiscal Health** Since these borrowings remain in the books of state-owned companies like SPVs, FCI, etc., the figure for fiscal deficit seems underestimated.
- **Debt Burden** It also hides the actual debt burden of the government which puts the interest burden on the future generations. The cost is borne by the government in future, thereby creating future liability.
- **Create Doubt over Fiscal Consolidation** Though India is on a path of fiscal consolidation with the fiscal deficit reduced to 3.4% in FY 2018-19, investors often doubt over these figures due to unreported off-budget financing.
- **Crowding out Private Investment** With the use of off-budget sources of financing, the government crowds out investment by the private sector as there is already scarce liquidity in the market.
- **Fear of Inflation** Higher borrowing by government-owned entities will lead to an increase in the cost of borrowing, which may increase inflation in the economy.
- **Impairs Monetary Transmission** Increasing interest rates due to higher borrowing by the government would also hamper the monetary transmission of repo rate.

Goes against Financial Accountability

The Comptroller and Auditor General (CAG) of India and the 15th Finance Commission had red-flagged the off-Budget funding of welfare schemes through public sector entities and had urged the Centre to come clean on these.

CAG had earlier suggested a policy framework for off-budget financing that should include disclosures to Parliament about the amount, rationale and objective of such funding.

- **No Parliamentary Oversight** Since these expenditures are made outside budget, it is outside the scope of the budget discussion.
- **Lack of Scrutiny by Standing Committee** Departmentally related Parliamentary Standing Committee, which scrutinises demand for grants cannot keep government accountable for off- budget financing.
- **Against Constitutional provisions** Since no money can be appropriated without the authority of Parliament out of Consolidated Fund of India (Article 266), interest payment on off-budget financing goes against it.
- **No Consensus on the Use of Funds** Since no discussion precedes the recourse to these financing, the use of funds is at the pure will of the government.
- **Following Law only in Word not in Spirit** FRBM act requires central and state governments to keep fiscal deficit within a sustainable level but off budget borrowing does not follow the spirit of FRBM Act.
- **Diversion of Funds** Diverting funds from priority sectors such as health, education and infrastructure development to finance other government programs and subsidies.

Major steps of Government towards Fiscal Consolidation

- **Reduced Subsidies** The government has reduced the amount of money allocated for food, fertiliser and petroleum subsidies.
  - The food subsidy in 2022-23 (RE) was ₹ 2,87,194 crore. In 2023-24, it has been reduced to ₹ 1,97,350 crore.
  - Fertiliser subsidy in 2022-23 was ₹ 2,25,220 crore (RE); it has been reduced to ₹ 1,75,100 crore for FY24.
  - The petroleum subsidy in 2022-23 was ₹ 9,171 crore (RE); it has declined to ₹ 2,257 crore in 2023-24 (Budget estimate/BE).
  - The decrease in subsidies compared to the previous year is not as sharp, but it is still a positive step towards reaching a fiscal deficit target of 4.5% by 2025-26.
- **Capital Expenditure** In the Budget for 2023-24, capital spending is planned to rise to 3.3% of GDP and the government has provided an interest-free loan of ₹ 1.3 lakh crore for 50 years to states to boost growth.
- **Debt Management** The majority of the fiscal deficit is financed through internal market borrowings, with a small portion coming from securities against savings, provident funds and external debt.
  - In the 2023 Union Budget, India's external debt is only 1% of the total fiscal deficit, which is estimated at ₹ 22,118 crore.
  - The states are free to maintain a fiscal deficit of 3.5% of their Gross State Domestic Product (GSDP) with 0.5% tied to power sector reforms.

Conclusion

CAG has suggested that the government should put in place a policy framework for off-budget financing which should specify the rationale and objective of off-budget financing, quantum of off- budget financing and sources of fund, among others. Also, the government should consider disclosing the details of off-budget borrowings through disclosure statements in Budget as well as in accounts. Also, the government should establish an independent Fiscal Council to bring credibility to fiscal statistics and to ensure that FRBM targets are levied in letter and spirit.

Issues Related to Taxation (Tax-GDP Ratio)

Q.10 A very small fraction of the adult population files tax returns and an even smaller portion pays taxes. In the light of this observation, critically evaluate the reasons for low tax-GDP ratio in India. What reform measures should be taken by the government to address this tax gap? (250 Words, 15 Marks)

Ans. Introduction Tax-to-GDP ratio represents the size of a country's tax kitty relative to its GDP. It is a representation of the size of the government's tax revenue expressed as a percentage of the GDP.

While the ratio determines the extent to which the government is able to finance its expenditure from tax collections, it is also an indicator of tax compliance. Developed countries have a higher contribution of tax to their GDP.

India's tax-GDP ratio has remained around 11% since many years which is lesser than the desirable target of 23% (this is the average of emerging economies) and much lower than OECD average of 34%.

Reasons for India's low Tax-to-GDP Ratio

- **Low Tax Base**
  - **Income Tax** In India, the exemption threshold of income tax has been consistently raised, much rapidly than underlying income growth. This implies that relatively well-off people are subsidized at the cost of services which could be provided to poor with the forgone money. **Example** Budget 2023-24 raised the exemption limit of income tax from ₹ 2.5 Lakh to Rs. 3 Lakh.
  - Moreover, a complex system of exemptions, tax cuts, preferential tax rates, deferral of tax liabilities etc has led to large tax collection expenditure and a significant amount of revenue foregone.
  - The Finance Ministry had revealed that the number of people who filed income tax returns stood at 6.8 crore in 2020-21. This means that only 4.8% of the total population filed IT returns in 2021. Of these, only 1.69 crore paid tax since 65% of the taxpayers earned less than ₹ 5 lakh. So effectively, only 1.2% of the population pays income tax as of now.
- **Structural Issues** Several structural factors have impinged upon India's tax revenue performance such as:
  - **High Cash, Informal Economy** India is an informal economy (50% of GDP) with high cash in circulation (14.6% of GDP), which is difficult to track. Untraced transactions through illegal channels such as Hawala, lead to generation of black money and tax evasion.
  - **Agriculture Income is not taxed** A dominant portion of India's workforce is employed in agriculture and agricultural income is exempt under income tax. This results in a narrow tax base, which is heavily reliant on other sectors of the economy.
  - **Low Participation of Women in the Workforce** According to the World Bank report released in June 2022, Indian women's labour force participation has been steadily declining since 2005 and is at a low of 19% in 2021.
  - **Public Distrust** Poor public services, poor governance, inefficiencies, corruption, etc have created distrust in government. Studies in behavioural economics suggest that lower trust levels result in dishonesty, which explains the low willingness to pay taxes in India.
  - **Corruption** Officials authorised with tax collection, often collude with tax evaders. They demand expensive gifts, lands, cash, etc., to aid tax evasion. Lack of accountability, procedural loopholes and mild punishment can be cited as reasons for such corruption.
  - **Black money which** is generated from illegitimate sources is completely out of the tax system.
- **Weak Tax Administration** is considered a key barrier to effective and fair tax collection in the country.
  - Lack of technical expertise and lack of resources has reduced administrative capacity especially at state and local levels. Economic Survey, 2020 has highlighted that local bodies are not collecting property taxes adequately.

- **Lingering of Contentious, Adversarial Tax Issues** India has one of highest number of disputes between tax administration and taxpayers, with lowest proportion of recovery of tax arrears. Example The Vodafone tax dispute involving ₹ 20K crore lingering since 2008.
- **Loop-holes in Double Tax Avoidance Treaties** Provisions for tax exemptions from short term capital gains are often misused by companies to re-route their investments from such countries (called round tripping of funds). Similarly, issues related to tax-evasion, double non-taxation and transfer pricing need to be fixed.

Measures to Improve Tax-to-GDP ratio

- **Refining Tax Structure** A simplified tax structure with optimum number of taxes, optimum tax rates, low concessions etc., will help in reducing tax avoidance and evasion. **Akhilesh Ranjan Committee** tasked to draft a new direct tax law recommended 25% corporate tax rate, restructuring of income-tax slabs, incentives for startups and a shorter and simpler direct tax law.
  - Various committees, to consolidate the direct taxes, were constituted by the government like Raja Chelliah Committee (early 1990s), Vijay Kelkar Committee (2002) and Easwar Panel.
- **Reducing Tax Litigation** Tendency of tax officials to initiate an action without the necessary justification or assessment is reflected from low success rate of appeals (30%). Protracted tax litigation in India has not only put a burden on Indian judiciary but has also cost the government exchequer.
  - Reduction in tax terrorism is needed through clarity in taxation framework in the country and by reducing the discretionary powers of the tax department.
- **Formalisation and Digitisation of Economy** Formalising the economy by bringing these businesses and workers under the tax net can increase the tax base. This can be achieved by providing incentives for businesses to register themselves and comply with tax laws, and by simplifying tax laws to make compliance easier.
- **Bringing Agricultural Income into the Tax Net** Currently, agricultural income is exempt from income tax in India. However, many wealthy farmers earn a significant income from agriculture, but they do not pay taxes. Bringing agricultural income into the tax net can increase the tax base. This can be achieved by setting a minimum threshold for agricultural income to be taxed and by incentivising farmers to report their income.
- **Fast Tracking of Disputes** Fast tracking of tax disputes, reducing discretion of taxman and creating a predictable dispute resolution mechanism.
- **Tax Treatment of Cross Border Transactions** Arbind Modi Panel on Income Tax Reforms recommended that an income shall be deemed to be derived from a source in India, if the payment has been made from India, for any goods/services consumed or towards interest, dividend, bonus or any other return on capital.
- **Better Sync With Global Economy** Since India is much more integrated with the world globally in terms of business linkages and capital account convertibility, the differential treatment of foreign and domestic companies in the country should be gradually phased out.
- **Need of Technology infusion in the tax administration** to improve efficiency of tax collection.
  - Tax administration should be improved through use of technologies like AI and Big data analytics for analysing databases. This would help in tracking tax evasion, economic activities and identifying opportunities for expanding tax-net.
- **E-assessment** New Income Tax Act should provide a complete legal framework for the introduction of e-assessment based which will be paperless and faceless. It will enhance efficiency, effectiveness and accountability and eliminate all opportunities for rent seeking behaviour.
  - In faceless assessment, tax-payer doesn't have to appear before the assessing officer neither will he know who is assessing his/her return. Information will be sought from the assessee via email and there will be no physical movement of the document. Budget 2019-20 has initiated 'faceless assessment' on the pilot basis.

Conclusion

Development needs of the country require greater resource mobilisation. Recently, government has taken various steps to improve tax compliance including Aadhaar – PAN linkage, project Insight, e-way bills, project Saksham etc. More steps are needed especially in restoring trust among public.

GST and its impact on Indian Economy

Q.11 Enumerate the indirect taxes which have been subsumed under the Goods and Services Tax (GST) in India. Also, comment on the revenue implications of the GST introduced in India since July 2017.
(150 Words, 10 Marks) **UPSC PYQ Mains 2019**

Ans. Introduction The Goods and Services Tax (GST) is a value-added tax levied on most goods and services sold for domestic consumption. It is India's biggest indirect tax reform and was introduced in India from 1st July, 2017.

Following are the Salient Features of GST

- **Applicable On Supply Side** GST is applicable on 'supply' of goods or services as against the old concept on the manufacture of goods or on sale of goods or on provision of services.
- **Destination based Taxation** GST is based on the principle of destination-based consumption taxation as against the present principle of origin-based taxation.
- **Dual GST** It is a dual GST with the Centre and the States simultaneously levying tax on a common base. GST to be levied by the Centre is called Central GST (CGST) and that to be levied by the States is called State GST (SGST). Import of goods or services would be treated as inter-state supplies and would be subject to Integrated Goods & Services Tax (IGST) in addition to the applicable customs duties.
- **GST Rates to be Mutually Decided** CGST, SGST and IGST are levied at rates to be mutually agreed upon by the Centre and the States. The rates are notified on the recommendation of the GST Council.
- **Article 279A - GST Council** to be formed by the President to administer and govern GST. Its chairman is Union Finance Minister of India with ministers nominated by the State Governments as its members.
- **Multiple Rates** Initially GST was levied at four rates viz. 5%, 12%, 16% and 28%. The Schedule or list of items that would fall under these multiple slabs are worked out by the GST Council.
- **GST Exemptions** The GST would apply to all goods other than alcoholic liquor for human consumption and five petroleum products, viz. petroleum crude, motor spirit (petrol), high speed diesel, natural gas and aviation turbine fuel.

Taxes Subsumed under GST

- **At the Central level, the following taxes have been subsumed in the GST** Central Excise Duty, Additional Excise Duty, Service Tax, Countervailing Duty, Special Additional Duty of Customs and cess as far as they relate to supply of goods and services
- **At the State level, the following taxes have been subsumed in the GST** State Value Added Tax/Sales Tax, Entertainment Tax (other than the tax levied by the local bodies), Central Sales Tax (levied by the Centre and collected by the States), Octroi and Entry tax, Purchase Tax, Luxury tax and Taxes on lottery, betting and gambling.

Revenue Implications of the GST

- **Higher Revenue Mobilisation** GST revenues have shown reasonably high buoyancy with collections of over ₹ 1 lakh crore in the last 10 months and touching a record of ₹ 1.87 lakh crore in April 2023.
- **Increase in Tax Base** GST implementation has increased the indirect taxpayer base by more than 50%. Registration under the old indirect tax regime was 6.4 million. Registration of businesses increased to 11.2 million under the GST regime. Apart from that, the GST regime also brought a cash-driven informal economy into the tax net.
- **Higher Revenue Efficiency** Mandating the issue of e-invoicing for all businesses above ₹ 100 crore has enabled better invoice matching and detection of fake invoices that were used to claim the input tax credit. This has helped to improve tax compliance and has also enabled better enforcement.
- It helped the country in **transitioning to an automated indirect tax ecosystem.** From electronic compliances, generation of e-invoices to tracking movement of goods through e-waybill - everything is now online.
- **Formalisation of the Economy** The GST Composition scheme simplifies compliance and brings large number of small manufacturers under tax net whose taxable business turnover is upto ₹ 1.5 crore leading to the process of formalisation of the economy.
- **Tax to GDP Ratio** India's Tax-to- GDP ratio stands at around 11% in FY20 from 8.7% in the year 2000-01.

- **Tax to Final Consumption Expenditure** Some other analysis show that the tax-to-final consumption expenditure also grew from 10.3% in the year before GST (2015-16) to 11.9% in 2019-20.
- **GDP growth** According to Finance ministry, India's GDP might increase as much as 2% because of GST.
- **Tax compliance** Three years after the introduction of the Goods and Services Tax (GST), the number of registered taxpayers has increased from 1.08 crore to 1.23 crore. The number of returns filed has increased steeply and there is a significant presence of 'formal' entities.

Challenges in the GST system

- **Refund Delay Issues** The government has taken many steps to smoothen the process of export refunds, automatic processing of refunds has always been an area of major concern under GST.
- **Lack of Dispute Redressal Mechanism** There is no statutory mechanism under the GST regime that could ensure uniformity in the rulings passed by the Authorities.
- **Constant Amendments** Over the last few years, the GST law has seen many amendments which have often confused the taxpayer and as well the tax administrators which created misunderstandings and misconceptions.
- **Adaption and Technical Issues** Small and medium businesses are still grappling to adapt to the tech-enabled regime. The fundamental principles on which the GST law was built viz. seamless flow of input credits and ease of compliance has been impaired by IT glitches.
- **Complex Penalties** Many businesses are genuinely not able to monitor their vendor behaviour and feel that they should not be penalised for the tax compliance deficiencies of their vendors once they have paid the GST amounts to their vendors.
- **Other Concerns** Further, the 15th Finance Commission, in its report, has also highlighted several areas of concern in the GST regime relating to: multiplicity of tax rates, shortfall in GST collections vis-à-vis the forecast, high volatility in GST collections, inconsistency in filing of returns, dependence of states on the compensation from Centre.

Conclusion

Streamlining of anti-profiteering measures and simplification of compliance procedures also needs to be revisited to ensure that the cost efficiency and reduction in prices envisaged under GST law finally reach the common man. To overcome the issues of dispute related to GST and increase efficiency in tax administration, there is a need for a robust dispute redressal mechanism.

Black Money Problems

Q.12 Pandora leaks, Swiss leaks, Panama leaks and many more such leaks have highlighted the problem of black money generation in India which causes much disruption to the Indian economy. In this context, critically evaluate the factors behind the generation of black money and outline the measures to be taken to solve this menace. (250 Words, 15 Marks)

Ans. Introduction Generation of black money and it's stashing abroad in tax havens and offshore financial centres have dominated discussions and debate in public fora during the last years. Supreme Court of India and the public at large have unequivocally expressed concern on the issue, particularly after some reports suggested estimates of such unaccounted wealth being held abroad. Funds parked by Indian individuals and firms in Swiss banks jumped to 2.55 billion Swiss francs (over ₹ 20,700 crore) in 2020.

Factors behind the Generation of Black Money in India

- **Tax Evasion** Tax evasion is a significant contributor to black money generation in India.
  - According to a study conducted by the National Institute of Public Finance and Policy (NIPFP), tax evasion accounts for approximately 20% to 30% of India's GDP, resulting in a substantial amount of unaccounted wealth.
- **Corruption** Corruption plays a major role in the generation of black money. The Transparency International's Corruption Perceptions Index ranks India relatively low, indicating the prevalence of corruption in various sectors. The corrupt practices, such as bribery and embezzlement, result in the accumulation of unaccounted funds.

- **Parallel Economy** The presence of a parallel economy, where economic activities are conducted outside the purview of legal regulations, contributes to black money generation.
  - According to a report by the National Council of Applied Economic Research (NCAER), the site of the parallel economy in India was estimated to be around 45% of GDP in 2017-2018.
- **Cash-based Transactions** Cash-based transactions, particularly in sectors such as real estate and small businesses, facilitate the generation of black money.
  - According to a report by the Reserve Bank of India (RBI), currency in circulation in India increased from around 8% of GDP in 2000 to approximately 12% of GDP in 2020, indicating a significant reliance on cash transactions.
- **Illicit Activities** Illegal activities, such as smuggling, drug trafficking and illicit trade, contribute to the generation of black money.
  - The Narcotics Control Bureau reported that the value of seized narcotics increased from INR 3,678 crore in 2018 to INR 9,538 crore in 2019, indicating the scale of illicit activities in the country.
- **Hawala Transactions** Hawala transactions, an informal and unregulated system of money transfer, also contribute to black money generation.
  - According to the Financial Intelligence Unit, India, cases related to hawala transactions increased from 4,307 in 2018-2019 to 4,617 in 2019-2020, highlighting the continued prevalence of this illegal practice.
- **Real Estate Sector** The real estate sector in India is known for its involvement in black money transactions.
  - According to a study by Knight Frank India, around 30% of the total value of real estate transactions in major Indian cities is conducted through unaccounted cash, contributing to the generation of black money.
- **Offshore Accounts and Tax Havens** The use of offshore accounts and tax havens is another factor behind black money generation.
  - The Panama Papers leak revealed the involvement of Indian individuals and entities in offshore tax evasion schemes, highlighting the scale of the issue.

Measures that can be Taken to Address the Menace of Black Money in India

- **Strengthening Tax Administration** Enhancing tax administration and enforcement measures is crucial to curb tax evasion and promote voluntary compliance.
  - The government can invest in technology-driven solutions like the implementation of the Goods and Services Tax (GST) system, which aims to simplify and streamline tax collection processes, reduce tax evasion and increase transparency.
- **Promoting Digital Economy** Encouraging the adoption of digital payment systems and reducing dependence on cash transactions can help combat the generation of black money.
  - The government's initiative, such as Digital India, aims to promote digital transactions and financial inclusion, making it easier to track and monitor financial activities.
- **Implementing Stricter Anti-Corruption Measures** Strengthening anti-corruption laws and ensuring their effective implementation is vital.
  - The government has enacted legislation such as the Prevention of Corruption Act and established institutions like the Central Vigilance Commission (CVC) and the Central Bureau of Investigation (CBI) to investigate and prosecute corrupt practices.
- **Increasing Transparency in Real Estate** The real estate sector is known for its involvement in black money transactions.
  - The government's Real Estate (Regulation and Development) Act (RERA) aims to bring transparency and accountability to the sector by ensuring the registration of real estate projects, protecting the interests of buyers and curbing unaccounted cash transactions.
- **Strengthening Financial Intelligence Units** Enhancing the capabilities of financial intelligence units can help track and investigate suspicious financial transactions associated with black money.
  - The government has established the Financial Intelligence Unit-India (FIU-IND) to gather and analyse financial intelligence and share it with law enforcement agencies for further action.

- **International Cooperation** Collaborating with international organisations and other countries to exchange information, track illicit financial flows and recover assets held abroad is crucial in combating cross-border black money generation.
  - Initiatives like the Global Minimum Tax (GMT) facilitate proposal to impose a minimum rate of taxation on corporate income in most countries of the world by international agreement.
- **Promoting Whistleblower Protection** Encouraging individuals to report cases of black money generation through robust whistleblower protection mechanisms is essential.
  - The Whistleblower Protection Act provides safeguards to individuals who disclose information about corruption, fraud or any illegal activities, encouraging transparency and accountability.

Conclusion

It's important to note that these measures require a comprehensive and coordinated approach involving legislative changes, enforcement, awareness campaigns and international cooperation. Continuous evaluation, strengthening of institutions, and effective implementation of these measures are crucial in addressing this menace and promoting transparency and accountability in the Indian economy.

Global Minimum Corporate Tax Deal

Q.13 In the background of international agreement on 'Global Minimum Corporate Tax (GMCT)', examine the reasons and associated challenges for the adoption of such taxation system. How is the adoption of GMCT going to affect Indian economy? (250 Words, 15 Marks)

Ans. **Introduction** The Global Minimum Corporate Tax rate, or Simply Global Minimum Tax (abbreviated GMCT or GMCTR), is a minimum rate of tax on corporate income internationally agreed upon and accepted by individual jurisdictions. The aim is to reduce tax competition between countries and discourage multinational corporations (MNC) from profit shifting to achieve tax avoidance.

The need for a Global Minimum Corporate tax (GMCT) has been discussed and stressed upon from 2019 when OECD initiated it. In 2021, 136 nations agreed to the GMCT proposal by the OECD which features a 15% corporate minimum tax. Later, the G20 summit approved this proposal.

Pillar One	Pillar Two
Will cover top 100 global companies	Minimum global tax of 15% and subject to tax rules
Re-allocation of an additional share of profit to the market jurisdictions	The effective tax rate should be at least 15% else additional taxes would be owed in a company's home jurisdiction
'Amount A' Would apply to firms with over ∈20 billion in revenues and a profit marigin above 10%	
A portion of their profits would be taxed in jurisdictions where they have sales	
Between 20-30% of profits above a 10% margin may be taxed	
Review of ∈20 billion threshold to ∈10 billion after 7 tears	
India and other developin countries were pitching for a threshold of ∈1billion	
9 countries do not sign the deal proposal including Ireland, Estonia and Hungary	

Reasons for its Adoption

- **Preventing Base Erosion and Profit Shifting (BEPS)** Base erosion and profit shifting refer to the practices used by multinational corporations to shift their profits to low-tax jurisdictions, thereby reducing their overall tax liability.

- A global minimum tax helps to combat BEPS by ensuring that all countries have a minimum level of taxation, reducing the incentive for profit shifting.
- According to a report by Fair Tax Mark, between 2010 and 2019, multinational companies in the digital space across all offshore setups paid USD155 billion less than what the actual tax would have required them to pay.

- **Ensuring Fairness and Level Playing Field** A global minimum tax aims to create a level playing field for businesses by preventing unfair tax competition among countries. It seeks to address the issue of tax havens and jurisdictions that offer extremely low or zero tax rates to attract businesses.
  - It would ensure the imposition of a realistic and uniform corporate tax throughout the world. Over the past decades, many countries have attracted investment merely by lowering corporate tax rates. This, in turn, has pushed other countries to lower their rates as well.
- **Revenue Generation and Budgetary Stability** Accepting a global minimum tax can help countries generate additional tax revenue. This can be particularly beneficial for countries that have struggled with tax base erosion and faced challenges in collecting sufficient tax revenue from multinational corporations.
  - Countries lose out an estimated USD100 billion per year in tax revenue due to the absence of GMCT.
- **Improved Regulatory Regime** It would induce the countries to compete on other factors like better regulatory regimes, ease of doing business, access to global talent, etc. This healthy competition would create a sustainable business environment in them.
- **Encouraging Global Co-operation rather than Global Competition** Accepting a global minimum tax demonstrates a commitment to global cooperation and coordination in addressing tax challenges. It encourages countries to work together to establish common tax standards and avoid harmful tax practices.
- **Addressing Public Perception and Fairness Concerns** The acceptance of a global minimum tax can help address public concerns about tax fairness. It can enhance public trust in the tax system by ensuring that multinational corporations pay their fair share of taxes, reducing the perception of tax avoidance or evasion.

Associated Challenges of GMCT

Implementing a global minimum tax can face several challenges. Here are some of the key challenges:

- **International Cooperation and Consensus** Achieving international cooperation and consensus among a large number of countries with diverse interests and priorities can be a significant challenge.
- **Tax Competition and Jurisdictional Sovereignty** Countries that have benefited from offering low-tax regimes may be resistant to accepting a global minimum tax. They may argue that it infringes on their jurisdictional sovereignty and their ability to attract foreign investment through tax incentives.
  - For the effectiveness of GMCT, it should be adopted uniformly by all nations.
- **Complexity and Implementation Challenges** Implementing a global minimum tax requires complex changes to domestic tax laws and international tax frameworks. It may require significant administrative and operational adjustments, including capacity building and coordination among tax authorities.
- **Monitoring and Enforcement** Ensuring compliance with a global minimum tax can be challenging. It requires effective information exchange, cooperation among tax authorities and mechanisms to address potential tax evasion or avoidance.
- **Economic Impacts and Competitiveness** There may be concerns that implementing a global minimum tax could have adverse economic impacts, particularly on countries that have relied on low-tax regimes to attract investment. Balancing the goals of tax fairness and economic growth can be a challenge.
- **Mitigating Unintended Consequences** It is important to assess the impacts on investment flows, economic growth and cross-border trade. Measures should be in place to mitigate any negative consequences and ensure a smooth transition to the new tax framework.
- **Disruption of Supply Chains** Due to lack of clear agreement on the concept of the destination-based taxation many fear that there may be a disruption in the supply chain.

Effects on the Indian Economy

- **Forgone Revenue** India had already taken measures like equalisation levy and the latest digital services tax to minimise tax evasion by foreign corporates. The enactment of GMCT requires India to take down these policies and switch to the proposed two-pillar international norms. This would mean forgoing revenue of ₹ 4,000 crore which it earns through equalisation levy.

- **Revenue Gain** The operation of minimum rate would create a new pocket of revenue arising from the equalisation of taxes of corporates shifting profits to tax havens. Tax Justice Network estimates India to gain about **4 USD billion** annually under the new norms.
- **A Dip in Foreign Direct Investment** As the existing corporate tax in India is above the proposed global minimum of 15% there is a chance of a dip in foreign direct investment.
- **Leveling the Playing Field** A global minimum tax can promote a level playing field for businesses in India. It can help reduce the advantage enjoyed by multinational corporations that engage in aggressive tax planning and take advantage of tax havens or low-tax jurisdictions.
- **Potential Challenges for Tax Competition** India has used tax incentives and competitive tax rates to attract Foreign Direct Investment (FDI) and promote economic growth. A global minimum tax could limit India's flexibility to offer tax incentives as a means to attract investment.
- **Compliance and Administration** Implementing a global minimum tax requires robust compliance and administration mechanisms. India would need to strengthen its tax administration capabilities to effectively enforce the minimum tax rules and ensure compliance by multinational corporations.

Conclusion

Thus, Global minimum corporate tax is a significant step to address the base problem of tax evasion and a race to low taxes between countries. However, the detailed provision should be such that it balances the aspirations of both the developing and developed world.

Disinvestment and Asset Monetisation (Disinvestment Policy)

Q.14 Trace the evolution of disinvestment policy in India since Independence to the recent adoption of policy on strategic disinvestment. Also, comment upon the impact of disinvestment on the performance of Indian PSUs who have undergone disinvestment. (250 Words, 15 Marks)

Ans. Introduction Disinvestment is defined as the action of a government aimed at selling or liquidating its shareholding in a public sector enterprise in order to get the government out of the business of production and increase its presence and performance in the provision of public goods and basic public services such as infrastructure, education, health, etc.

Evolution of Disinvestment Policy in India

- For the first four decades after Independence, India pursued a path of development in which the public sector was expected to be the engine of growth.
- The liberalisation reforms undertaken in 1991 ushered in an increased demand for privatisation/disinvestment of PSUs.
- **1991** Sale of Minority Stake in Bundles Through auction
  - Till 1999-2000: Separate sale for each company in the following years
  - In August 1996, the Disinvestment Commission, chaired by GV Ramakrishna was set up to advise, supervise, monitor and publicize gradual disinvestment of Indian PSUs. However, the Disinvestment Commission ceased to exist in May 2004.
- **1999-2000 - Adoption of Strategic Sale** Sale of substantial portion of government shareholding in identified Central PSEs (CPSEs) up to 50 per cent or more, along with transfer of management control.
  - The Department of Disinvestment was set up as a separate department in December, 1999 and was later renamed as Ministry of Disinvestment in September, 2001. From 27th May, 2004, the Department of Disinvestment was brought under the Ministry of Finance.
- **2004-05** It was decided that the government may "dilute its equity and raise resources to meet the social needs of the people", a distinct departure from strategic sales.
  - National Investment Fund (NIF) was constituted in November, 2005, into which the proceeds from disinvestment of Central Public Sector Enterprises were to be channelised.

- **Strategic Sales have got a Renewed Push After 2014**
  - During 2016-17 to 2018-19, on average, strategic sales accounted for around 28.2% of total proceeds from disinvestment.
  - The Department of Disinvestment has been renamed as Department of Investment and Public Asset Management (DIPAM) from 14th April, 2016 which has been made the nodal department for the strategic stake sale in the Public Sector Undertakings (PSUs).
- **In Union Budget 2021-22** Government has approved a policy of strategic disinvestment of public sector enterprises that will provide a clear roadmap for disinvestment in all non-strategic and strategic sectors.
  - The policy, promised as part of the Atma Nirbhar Bharat package, states the government will exit all businesses in non-strategic sectors, with only a 'bare minimum' presence in four broad sectors.
  - Atomic energy, Space and Defence; Transport and Telecom; Power, Petroleum, coal and other minerals, and Banking and financial services.

Objective and Merits of Disinvestment

- **Reduce the Burden on the Government** Disinvestment of loss-making PSU's, would help the government to invest in profit-making PSU's which will minimise the burden on the government.
- **Smooth Decision** In the private sector, the decision-making process is quick and decisions are linked with the competitive market changes.
- **Better Governance** The disinvestment process would bring in better corporate governance, exposure to competitive corporate responsibility, improvement in the work environment, etc.
- **Better Participation** The market participation in the capital of PSUs through stock exchanges would enable the market to discover the latent worth of PSUs.
- **Better Revival Opportunities** The loss-making PSUs can be successfully revived by asking the strategic partner to infuse fresh capital and exercising excellent management control over sick PSUs.

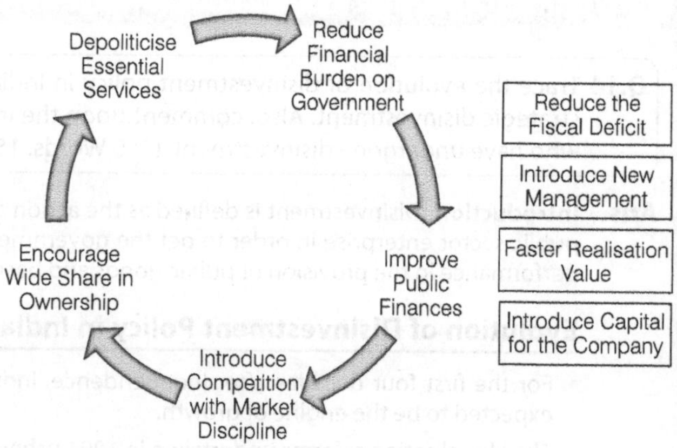

Impact of Disinvestment on the Performance of Indian PSUs (Economic Survey Observations)

- Disinvestment has a very strong positive effect on labour productivity and overall efficiency of PSUs.
- Privatisation improves capital allocation and economic efficiency.
- In the post-privatization period, firms show significantly higher profitability, higher efficiency, generally higher investment levels, higher output, higher dividends and lower leverage.
  - **Example** Hindustan Zinc's has seen a hundred-fold increase in its profits on the back of a six-fold expansion in capacities, since its takeover by Vedanta in 2002.
- Both the levels and growth rates of profitability, labour productivity and investment spending improve significantly following partial privatisation.
- **Increased Customer Satisfaction** comes in form of reduction in tariffs, increased data usage etc. in the telecommunication sector; increased penetration of banking services in the rural areas, and reduced airfares comparable to high-end consumers in the railways.

While disinvestment targets have become aggressive, actual receipts have fallen short of the targets.

- **Widening Gap of Estimates and Revenue Mobilization** Since 2010, barring two years (2017-18 and 2018-19), the central government's actual receipts from disinvestment have consistently fallen short of the budget estimate.

- **Time Taking Process** The Standing Committee on Finance has noted that the disinvestment process usually takes a long time with some entities even undergoing a fourth iteration.
  - **Example** In as many as 21 cases, cleared by the Union Cabinet since 2015-16, the central government is yet to conclude strategic disinvestment transactions.
- **Poor Participation** In the last six financial years, all the transactions where the government sold more than 51% of its shareholding in CPSEs, along with transfer of management control, have involved another CPSE picking up the government's stake.
- **Delay in Processing** Several strategic disinvestment transactions have been in the pipeline for a long time.
  - **Example** Sale of Bharat Petroleum Corporation Limited, approved in November 2019, is yet to be concluded.

Conclusion

Aggressive disinvestment, preferably through the route of strategic sale, should be utilised to bring in higher profitability, promote efficiency, increase competitiveness and to promote professionalism in management in CPSEs. This would, in turn, unlock capital for use elsewhere, especially in public infrastructure like roads, power transmission lines, sewage systems, irrigation systems, railways and urban infrastructure.

Strategic Disinvestment

Q.15 What do you understand by 'Strategic Disinvestment'? Examine the reasons behind the increased strategic sale of PSUs by the government. Also, explain why the disinvestment targets have not been met in the past? (250 Words, 15 Marks)

Ans. **Introduction** Government has approved a policy of strategic disinvestment of public sector enterprises in 2021-22 that will provide a clear roadmap for disinvestment in all non-strategic and strategic sectors. A number of transactions namely BPCL, Air India, Shipping Corporation of India, Container Corporation of India, IDBI Bank, BEML, Pawan Hans, Neelachal Ispat Nigam limited among others are proposed to be completed in FY 2021-22.

Strategic disinvestment would imply the sale of a substantial portion of the Government shareholding of a central public sector enterprises (CPSE) of up to 50%, or such higher percentage as the competent authority may determine, along with transfer of management control. In the Union Budget 2023-24, the government has set a disinvestment target of Rs. 51,000 crore which is the lowest in 7 years and 21% less than the budget estimate for the current year.

Rationale behind Strategic Sale

- **Role of Government** Strategic disinvestment is guided by the basic economic principle that Government should discontinue its engagement in manufacturing/ producing goods and services in sectors where competitive markets have come of age. Such entities would most likely perform better in the private hands due to various factors e.g. technology up-gradation and efficient management practices; and would thus create wealth and add to the economic growth of the country.
- **Source of income** Disinvestment proceeds have been a source of additional income. This is especially important at a time when private investment is falling and government is unable to meet its fiscal deficit targets.
- **Better Management** Many Government units often suffer from poor management and aggressive trade unionism and have become umpire-less playfields for political parties. It often leads to halting of PSUs projects thereby hampering the efficiency in long run.
  - **Economic potential of such entities** may be better discovered in the hands of the strategic investors due to various factors e.g. infusion of capital, technology upgradation, better accountability and efficient management practices etc.
  - **The financial performance of many PSUs** has improved drastically in many cases. E.g. Hindustan Zinc saw its net profits shoot up from Rs 67 cr at the time of its sale in FY03 to Rs 9,698 cr in FY19.
- **Transferring of public debt** Disinvestment allows the transferring of the Indian government's enormous public debt of its PSUs to the Indian private sector.

- **Impact of Privatisation** Economic Survey 2019-20 based on a comparative analysis of the before-after performance of 11 CPSEs that had undergone strategic disinvestment from 1999-2000 to 2003-04 observed that net worth, net profit, return on assets (ROA), return on equity (ROE), gross revenue, net profit margin, sales growth and gross profit per employee of the privatized CPSEs, on an average, have improved significantly in the post-privatization period compared to the peer firms.
- **Maximisation of the Potential of CPSEs** Disinvestment (through the strategic sale) of CPSEs unlocks their potential of these enterprises to create wealth evinced by the improved performance after privatization. This would have a multiplier effect on other sectors of the economy.

Unable to meet Disinvestment Targets

Government has always set ambitious targets for the disinvestment (₹ 1.75 Lakh Crore for 2021-22) but has been able to meet its disinvestment target only twice in the last eight years due to various reasons:

- **Weak market conditions** put the government on the back-foot for conducting share sale.

Target Disinvestment and Actual Disinvestment (2013-2023)

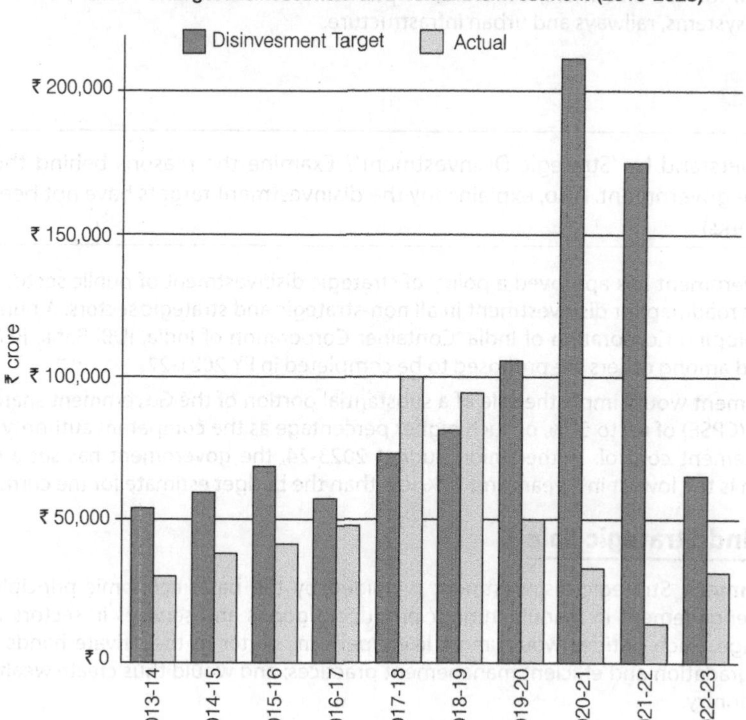

- Loss making units don't attract investment so easily.
- Most firms are not clear with their legal land rights.
- The Strategic sale in many firms was called off due to a lack of bidders and lapses in the bidding process. Eg. BPCL and Central electronics.
- Over the years the policy of divestment has increasingly become a tool to raise resources to cover the fiscal deficit with little focus on market discipline or strategic objective.
- **Labour Union Protest** It may lead to retrenchment of workers who will be deprived of the means of their livelihood. Private sector governed by the profit motive has a tendency to use capital intensive techniques which will worsen unemployment problem in India.

- **Strategic and National Security concerns** Strategic Disinvestment of Oil PSUs is seen by some experts as a threat to National Security since Oil is a strategic natural resource and possible ownership in the foreign hand is not consistent with our strategic goals.
- **Disinvestment in India has progressed at a snail's pace,** considering the rapid strides in privatisation that developing countries in East and South East Asia, Latin America, Central and Eastern Europe have made by transfer of ownership of productive assets to private investors, especially in the area of basic infrastructure (power, telecommunications, oil and minerals) and financial services.
- **Learning from the Privatisation Model of Singapore (Temasek Holdings Ltd)** The Government can transfer its stake in the listed CPSEs to a separate corporate entity. This entity would be managed by an independent board and would be mandated to divest the Government stake in these CPSEs over a period of time. This will lend professionalism and autonomy to the disinvestment programme which, in turn, would improve the economic performance of the CPSEs.

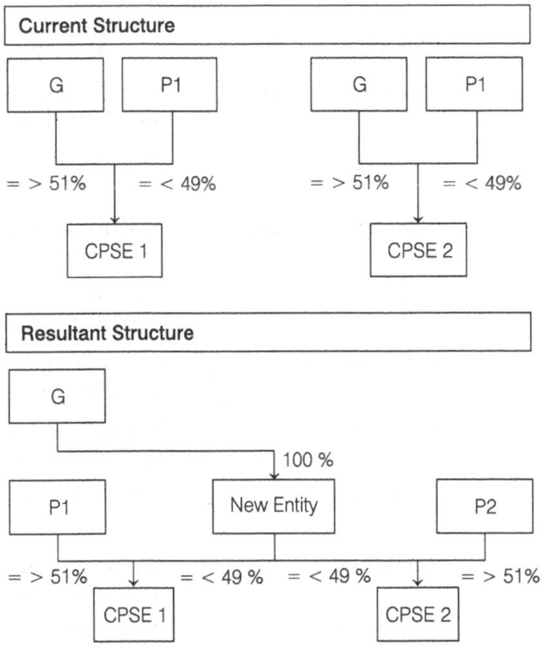

Conclusion

- The process of disinvestment undertaken by the government has enabled it to overcome various challenges however, the government will need to ensure confidence in the sale processes, a semblance of fair valuations, give officers some cover from potential post-transaction witch-hunts by auditors and investigating agencies.

Asset Monetisation

Q.16 How is 'Asset Monetisation' different from the 'Strategic Disinvestment'? In the background of National Monetisation Pipeline (NMP), what learnings must be drawn from the past disinvestment experiences so that NMP can successfully achieve its objectives? (250 Words, 15 marks)

Ans. **Introduction** 'Asset Monetization' and 'Strategic Disinvestment' are two different concepts related to the management and utilisation of government-owned assets.

- **Strategic Disinvestment** It is the sale of a significant amount of the government's stock in a Central Public Sector Company (CPSE) of 50% or a higher percentage as determined by the competent body, as well as managerial control transfer. The objective of strategic disinvestment is to promote efficiency, enhance competitiveness, attract private investment, and reduce the burden on the government's finances.
- **Asset Monetisation** It is based on the philosophy of creation through monetisation which is aimed at **tapping private sector investment for new infrastructure creation**. This is necessary for creating employment opportunities, thereby enabling high economic growth and seamlessly integrating the rural and semi-urban areas for overall public welfare.

About National Monetisation Pipeline

- Union Budget 2021-22 has identified monetisation of operating public infrastructure assets as a key means for sustainable infrastructure financing. Towards this, the Budget provided for preparation of a 'National Monetisation Pipeline (NMP)' of potential brownfield infrastructure assets.
- NMP estimates aggregate monetisation potential of ₹ 6.0 lakh crores through core assets of the Central Government, over a four-year period, from FY 2022 to FY 2025.
- The programme is envisaged to be supported through necessary policy and regulatory interventions by the government in order to ensure an efficient and effective process of asset monetisation. These will include streamlining operational modalities, encouraging investor participation and facilitating commercial efficiency, among others. Real time monitoring will be undertaken through the asset monetisation dashboard.

Difference between Strategic Disinvestment and Asset Monetisation

Criteria	Strategic Disinvestment	Asset Monetization
Ownership of Assets	Transfer of ownership of public sector assets to private entities	Retaining ownership of public sector assets while leasing them out
Objective	Reducing the government's stake in public sector undertakings	Unlocking value from underutilised or non-core government assets
Nature of Transaction	Sale of equity shares to private investors	Leasing or renting out government assets for a specified period
Control	Transfer of management control along with ownership	Retaining management control while leasing out assets
Revenue Generation	One-time inflow of funds from the sale of shares	Periodic inflow of revenue through leasing or rental agreements
Risk Mitigation	Transferring risks associated with the asset to the private sector	Retaining risks associated with the asset while generating revenue
Asset Utilisation	Involves selling of assets	Maximizing utilisation of underutilised or non-core assets
Sector Focus	Can be applied to a wide range of sectors and industries	Primarily focuses on sectors with potential for monetisation
Stakeholder Participation	Private investors become stakeholders in the disinvested company	Private entities become lessees or renters of the government assets
Employment Impact	Potential impact on employees of the disinvested company	Minimal impact on employment as assets are leased, not sold

India's Disinvestment Policy Provides Valuable Lessons for the Successful Implementation of the National Monetisation Policy

- **Transparent Process** Ensuring a transparent and well-defined process for asset valuation, selection and transaction execution is crucial.
  - **Example** Disinvestment of Hindustan Zinc Limited in 2002 faced criticism for undervaluing the asset and favoring the buyer, resulting in a loss for the government.
- **Investor Communication** Effective communication with investors on asset quality, revenue potential, and future growth prospects is vital to attract and retain their interest.
  - **Example** The Initial Public Offering (IPO) of Air India in 2018 had to be postponed due to investor concerns about the company's huge debt burden and its impact on profitability.
- **Sector Prioritisation** Prioritising sectors with high revenue potential and demand for infrastructure development is necessary for successful monetisation. Focus should be on sectors that are attractive to investors and have the potential for sustainable growth.
- **Policy Stability** Frequent policy changes or reversals can create uncertainty and deter potential investors.
  - **Example** The frequent policy changes in the telecom sector, such as the cancellation of 2G licenses in 2012 and the subsequent auctions, led to instability and impacted investor sentiment.
- **Institutional Framework** Establishing dedicated institutions and mechanisms for asset management, valuation, and transaction execution can streamline the disinvestment process and enhance efficiency.
  - **Example** Creation of the National Investment and Infrastructure Fund (NIIF) in 2015 has facilitated infrastructure investments by attracting long-term funds from domestic and international investors.
- **Employee Welfare** Taking care of the welfare and concerns of employees affected by disinvestment is important to avoid labour unrest and negative public perception.
  - **Example** The recent concerns raised by employees of Air India post disinvestment has brought out shortcomings of the disinvestment policy.

- **Post-Transaction Monitoring** Implementing robust monitoring mechanisms to ensure compliance with agreed-upon terms, utilisation of funds and performance of the privatised assets is essential for long-term success.
- **Investor Due Diligence** Conducting thorough due diligence on potential investors to ensure their credibility, financial strength, and ability to contribute to asset growth is critical. The disinvestment of Satyam Computer Services Limited faced challenges due to the fraudulent practices of the acquirer, highlighting the importance of diligent scrutiny.

Conclusion

The end objective of this initiative is to enable 'Infrastructure Creation through Monetisation' wherein the public and private sector collaborate, each excelling in their core areas of competence, so as to deliver socio-economic growth and quality of life to the country's citizens.

Fiscal Federalism and Finance Commission (Finance Commission Devolution Criteria)

Q.17 The criteria of devolution of funds from the Union to the States has undergone changes in the 15th Finance Commission compared with the 14th Finance Commission. Examine its implications. (150 Words, 10 Marks)

Ans. **Introduction** The Constitution under Article 280 provides for Finance Commissions every five years as a mechanism for sharing of taxes and revenues vertically between the Centre and States and local bodies and horizontally among all states, based on levels of development, demographic outcomes, prosperity and regional needs. The 15th Finance Commission (FC) has been constituted with the above objective for the period of 2021-26.

Devolution of Funds

- **Vertical Devolution** The share of states in Centre's taxes is recommended to be decreased from 42% during 2015-20 period to 41% for 2020-21. The 1% decrease is to provide for newly formed union territories Jammu and Kashmir and Ladakh.
- This has been a minor change that does not create a significant impact but States are simply entitled to them without having to fulfill criteria set by the Centre. This creates more room for fiscal autonomy for states.
- **Horizontal Devolution** There is a change in the criteria adopted by the 15th FC to determine the share of each state in the central taxes. Earlier there were 5 criteria each of which had a different weightage. The 15th FC adopted 6 criteria in 3 broad categories: need-based, equity-based and performance-based.

Revenue-sharing formulas in the 14th and 15th Finance Commissions

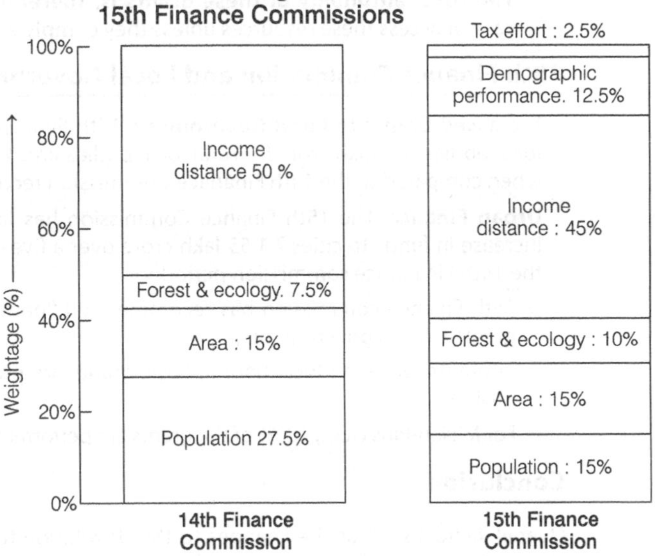

Criteria	14th FC 2015-20	15th 2020-21
Income Distance	50.0	45.0
Area	15.0	15.0
Population (1971)	17.5	–
Population (2011)*	10.0	15.0
Demographics Performance	–	12.5
Forest Cover	7.5	–
Forest and Ecology	–	10.0
Tax and fiscal efforts*	–	2.5
Total	**100**	**100**

Implications of the Change in Criteria

- **Use of the 2011 Population Metric** The 14th Finance Commission had, in its report, mentioned that the use of the 1971 Census data was "unfair" as it failed to capture new demographic changes in states. Thus, Finance Commission made the criteria to use the 2011 population data.
- **State's Reaction** The Southern states claimed that with this provision their successful policy implementation, including that of family planning campaigns, was effectively being penalised. Even though the Commission accepted the TOR and used the 2011 population statistic, they introduced 'demographic performance' as a parameter, which is basically a proxy for population control.
- **Tax Effort** Tax Effort was previously used by the 11th and 12th Finance Commissions. The 15th Finance Commission computed the Tax Effort by multiplying the 2011 population with the Own Tax Revenue (OTR) to GSDP (Gross State Domestic Product) ratio, unlike the previous commissions where they used only the OTR-GSDP ratio as a criterion to compute the share between states.
  - The change had an effect on the aggregate tax devolution to individual states. The inter-state tax shares have increased for some states while it has decreased for others.
- **Grants-in-Aid and Transfers** 15th Finance Commission has recommended an increase in conditional transfers. These are 'tied' funds. States are eligible to them only upon fulfilling certain criteria. All conditional grants are meant to 'nudge' states towards best practices in public finance management, with a view towards fiscal prudence.
  - While the share of conditional grants was equivalent to only 17% of the total Finance Commission transfers under the 14th Finance Commission period, it has now increased to nearly 57% of approved transfers under the 15th Finance Commission.
  - **The fiscal autonomy of these grants is, therefore, comparatively limited to untied funds** States themselves cannot access these resources unless they comply with the mandate determined by the Centre.

15th Finance Commission and Local Government

- **Increased Grants to Local Government** 15th Finance Commission have recommended grants of ₹ 4,36361 crore to local bodies (2.4 lakh crore for rural local bodies and 1.2 lakh crore for urban local bodies) which is an increase of 52% when compared to the 14th Finanace Commission recommendation.
- **Urban Finance** The 15th Finance Commission has taken bold, imaginative and far- sighted measures. Substantive increase in funds to cities ₹ 1.55 lakh crore over a five-year period from 2021-2026, a 78% increase over grants during the 14th Finanance commission period.
  - 15th Finance commission has recommended "performance-based grants" for incubation of new cities and health grants to local governments.
  - In grants for urban local bodies, basic grants are proposed only for cities/towns having a population of less than a million.
  - For Million-Plus cities, 100% of the grants are performance-linked through the Million-Plus Cities Challenge Fund (MCF).

Conclusion

Overall, factors such as the changes to the devolution formula, the higher proportion of conditional grants, the higher share of cesses and surcharges and the conservative limit set on state borrowings have potentially deepened the constraints on state finances which could strain fiscal relations between the Union Government and the States.

Fiscal Federalism and 15th Finance Commission

Q.18 In the background of recent instances hampering fiscal federalism in India, examine the role of Finance Commission in maintaining fiscal federalism in India. Discuss in the context of 15th FC recommendations. (250 Words, 15 Marks)

Ans. Fiscal Federalism Fiscal federalism in India refers to the division of fiscal powers and responsibilities between the Central and State Governments. The Finance Commission (FC) formed under Article 280 plays a crucial role in maintaining fiscal federalism by recommending the distribution of financial resources between the two tiers of government. Fiscal federalism was the economic counterpart of political federalism as distribution of resources was also essential alongside decentralisation of powers for achieving economic growth. But recent instances suggest otherwise.

Implication of the centralisation of fiscal measures

The division of powers in 7th Schedule have given more taxation powers to the Centre while the major expenditure responsibilities lie with the State Governments. This has the following implications:

- **Declining Ability of the State to Finance its Expenditure from their own Revenue** It has declined from 69% in 1955-56 to less than 38% in 2019-20. The expenditure of the States has been shooting up but their revenues did not.
  - State still spends 60% of the expenditure in the country - 85% in education and 82% in health.
- **Limited Avenues for Raising Tax Revenues** States cannot raise tax revenue because of curtailed indirect tax rights — subsumed in GST, except for petroleum products, electricity and alcohol — the revenue has been stagnant at 6% of GDP in the past decade.
- **Rising Inequality in India** The World Inequality Report estimates "that the ratio of private wealth to national income increased from 290% in 1980 to 555% in 2020. The poorest half of the population has less than 6% of the wealth while the top 10% nearly grab two-third of it"
- **Low tax-GDP Ratio** It has been one of the lowest in the world of around 11% of which is well below the average ratio of emerging market economies and OECD countries about 21% and 34%, respectively.
- **Curb in the Autonomy of States** By turning states into mere implementing agencies of the Union's schemes, their autonomy has been curbed. It also undermines the electorally mandated democratic politics of states.
- **Depletion of State's Resources** The diversion of a state's own funds to centrally sponsored schemes, thereby depleting resources for its own schemes, violates a constitutional provision. It only impedes states from charting their own autonomous path of development.

Inadequate financial powers with states lead to the following:

- **Vertical Fiscal Imbalance** State's capacity to augment its revenue is estimated to be just 37.5% (average).
- **Horizontal Fiscal Imbalance** Inequality in Fiscal health of states e.g., Bihar can generate revenue for just 37.6% of their expenditure while Haryana can do so for 82.6%.
- **Imbalances after Liberalisation** Market-based reform generated more inequality due to unequal capacity among states for infrastructure development.

Envisaged Role of Finance Commission and recent Instances of Hampering Fiscal Federalism

The 15th FC, constituted for the period 2021-2026, was tasked with addressing various challenges, including the impact of the Goods and Services Tax (GST) on state revenues, the need to promote sustainable development and the requirements of both the Central and State Governments.

- **Allocation of Financial Resources** Finance Commissions recommend the percentage of central taxes to be shared with the states, known as vertical devolution. The 15th Finance Commission recommended the share of states in the divisible pool from 42% (recommended by the 14th FC) to 41% (1% to Jammu Kashmir and Ladakh UTs now), considering the center's increased fiscal requirements.
- **Non-divisive Cess and Surcharges** Even the increased share of devolution, mooted by the Fourteenth Finance Commission, from 32% to 42%, was subverted by raising non-divisive cess and surcharges that go directly into the Union kitty.
  - This non-divisive pool in the Centre's gross tax revenues shot up to 15.7% in 2020 from 9.43% in 2012 shrinking the divisible pool of resources for transfers to states.
- **Horizontal Devolution** The 15th FC introduced several new parameters, including demographic performance, forest cover and tax effort, to better reflect the needs and performance of states. These factors aim to address regional disparities and attempts to ensure a fair and equitable distribution of resources.
- **Bridging Regional Disparities** Finance Commissions take into account regional disparities and imbalances in their recommendations. They use criteria like per capita income, population and geographical factors to ensure a more equitable distribution of resources.
- **Grants and Incentives** The 15th FC recognised the need for funds to local governments for basic services and created the Urban Local Bodies (ULB) grant. It also introduced the Sector Specific Grants, which aim to address specific development gaps and promote areas like healthcare, education, and disaster management.
  - Sector-specific grants of ₹ 1.3 lakh crore will be given to states for sectors like health, education, judiciary etc.
  - Grants to local bodies will be ₹ 4.36 lakh crore (i) Rs 2.4 lakh crore for rural local bodies, (ii) ₹ 1. 2 lakh crore for urban local bodies, and (iii) ₹ 70,051 crore for health grants through local governments.

- **Improving the State Finances** It suggests measures to improve the finances of states to supplement the resources of panchayats and municipalities.
- **Issue of Differential Interest** States are forced to pay differential interest — about 10% against 7% — by the Union for market borrowings.
  - The Centre has been setting the limits on the market borrowings of States under Article 293 of the Constitution. This goes against their autonomy.
- **Addressing Special Circumstances** Finance Commissions take into account special circumstances, such as the impact of GST implementation or natural calamities, in their recommendations. They can provide specific grants or incentives to address these challenges and support the fiscal needs of states during such periods.
- **Introduction of GST** States have lost the autonomy to decide the tax rates of subjects that fall within the State List. The inability of states to fix tax rates to match their development requirements implies greater dependence on the centre for funds.
- **Fiscal Consolidation** The 15th FC emphasised fiscal consolidation by setting performance-based incentives for states. States were encouraged to improve their fiscal management, enhance revenue generation and adhere to debt sustainability limits. These measures promote fiscal discipline and encourage states to adopt responsible fiscal practices.
  - The Commission suggested that the centre bring down fiscal deficit to 4% of GDP by 2025-26. For states, it recommended the fiscal deficit limit (as % of GSDP) of: (i) 4% in 2021-22, (ii) 3.5% in 2022-23, and (iii) 3% during 2023-26.

Other Recommendations for Ensuring Fiscal Federalism

- **Financial Rationalisation of CSS and Central outlays** in consultation with the State Government.
- **Issue of Centrally Sponsored Schemes** There are 131 centrally sponsored schemes, with a few dozen of them accounting for 90% of the allocation, and states required to share a part of the cost.
  - They spend about 25% to 40% as matching grants at the expense of their priorities.
  - These schemes, driven by the one-size-fits-all approach, are given precedence over state schemes.
- GST Council and the Finance Commission working need to be coordinated to optimize revenue targets
- Giving Permanent status to Finance Commission
- **Relook at the 7th schedule** Re-examination of entries of List I and List III as per changes in the polity, technology, and aspirations of society.
- **Effective devolution of funds to local bodies** through measures like more taxation powers, reforming the functioning of state finance commissions.

Conclusion

Finance Commission plays a vital role in maintaining fiscal federalism in India by recommending the distribution of financial resources between the center and states. The 15th FC's recommendations attempted to address various challenges and promote a balanced fiscal framework. However, ongoing issues like GST implementation and the fiscal burden arising from the pandemic require continuous assessment and recalibration of the FC's recommendations to uphold fiscal federalism effectively.

Check Your Preparation

1. What is gender budgeting? Give an account of the issues due to which gender budgeting has not been a fruitful exercise in India. Also, suggest measures required to address these issues. (150 words, 10 marks)
2. Examine the system of inter-governmental transfers from the Centre to the States in resolving vertical and horizontal fiscal imbalances with special reference to 15th Finance Commission. (150 words, 10 marks)
3. Parliamentary scrutiny over public finance is an important aspect of governmental accountability. In this context, discuss the role, importance and challenges in establishing a Parliamentary Budget Office (PBO) for effective oversight of budgetary process. (150 words, 10 marks)

UNIT 4

Issues Related to Agriculture: Major Crops-Cropping Patterns in Various Parts of the Country; Different Types of Irrigation and Irrigation Systems; Storage, Transport and Marketing of Agricultural Produce and Issues and Related Constraints; E-technology in the Aid of Farmers

Overview of Indian Agriculture (Types of Agriculture Revolution)

Q.1 Explain various types of revolutions that took place in Agriculture after Independence in India. How these revolutions have helped in poverty alleviation and food security in India? (150 Words, 10 Marks)

UPSC Mains PYQ 2017

Ans. **Introduction** India is primarily an agricultural economy and majority of people are still dependent on agriculture for their livelihood. As per 2018, agriculture employed 50% of the Indian work force and contributed 17–18% to country's GDP. After independence, development of agriculture has been assured by various revolutions supported by government.

Various Types of Revolution

- **Green Revolution** It was initiated in early 1960s to achieve food security in the country. Under this, new inputs like High Yielding Variety (HYV) seeds, fertilisers, pesticides etc were used to increase the production and productivity of agriculture sector. It resulted in a record grain output of 131 million tons in 1978-79 which established India as one of the largest food grain producers in the world.
- **White Revolution** Operation Flood (1970), an initiative of National Dairy Development Board has led to revolution in milk production in India. The world's largest dairy development programme transformed India from a milk deficient nation to world's largest milk producer. This has introduced in the new breeding technologies, high quality fodder, vaccination, veterinary facilities improved. The milk production in India increased from a level of 17 MT in 1950- 51 to about 187.7 MT in 2018-19. Presently, India ranks first in milk production, accounting for 20% of the total production in the world.
- **Blue Revolution** This revolution focused on management of fisheries sector and has led to phenomenal increase in both fish production and productivity from aquaculture and fisheries resources of the inland and marine fisheries. According to the Ministry of Fisheries, Animal Husbandry and Dairying, fish production increased from 7.52 lakh tonnes in years 1950–5 1 to 125.90 lakh tonnes in years 2018–19.

- **Other Revolutions** Other revolutions are also significant that includes Yellow Revolution (oil seed production), Golden Fibre Revolution (jute), Golden Revolution (horticulture), Silver Fibre Revolution (cotton) and Red revolution (meat production).

Impact of Revolutions on Poverty Alleviation and Food Security

Poverty Alleviation

- **Increase in Rural Income** Operation Flood has increased rural income by creating a national milk grid linking producers directly with urban consumers in over thousand towns and cities. It reduced middlemen and ensured that producers get major profit share.
- **Exports** The revolutions in meat, jute facilitated exports to global markets which have helped producers to get the remunerative prices thereby reducing the poverty levels.
- **Employment Opportunities** The pink revolution has created an additional employment opportunity in animal husbandry. It also gave scope for development of food processing industry which has huge potential in creating non-farm jobs.
- **Women Empowerment** These revolutions also provided income and employment to women leading to women empowerment helping millions to come out of poverty.
- **Reduced Vulnerability** The revolutions in agriculture reduced the incidence of famine and crop loss which pushes people into poverty.
- **Strengthening of Market Linkages** Due to revolution in agriculture sector, linkage in agriculture and industry has increased due to which production of grain has increased, thereby improved the rural income.
- **Diversification of Income** The revolutions in various areas such as meat, egg, fish production has helped the farmers diversify their income sources, helping them in periods of distress and poverty cycle.
- **Surplus Production** The revolutions have increased the production which took poor from subsistence-based agriculture to surplus farming thus improving the income levels.

Food Security

- **Increased Production** Green Revolution by providing impetus to production of rice, wheat through adoption of HYV seeds and better fertilisers helped in achieving the food security in the nation. It helped India come out of PL-480 agreements, through which India imports food grains from USA.
- **Availability and Affordability** The agriculture revolutions increased the availability of food grains like rice, wheat and also production in large quantities made them accessible to all the sections of the society.
- **Tackling Hidden Hunger** The Blue Revolution and availability of sea food also increased the nutritional levels among the people through increased protein in-take.
- **Nutritional security** The rise in milk production enhanced the per capita availability of milk to 337gms/day, leading to nutritional security of large masses.

Conclusion

To further carry on the momentum of these programmes and assure food security in long run, there is an urgent need for an 'Evergreen Revolution' that should focus on all-round development of the agriculture sector. Recently, government started Evergreen Revolution that focuses on all aspects of agriculture pertaining to various products, also called as Rainbow Revolution.

Impact of Green Revolution

Q.2 'While Green Revolution has transformed the image of India from a 'begging bowl' to a 'bread basket', it made Indian agriculture, in a way, a victim of its own success. This raises the need for Evergreen Revolution.' Analyse the statement. (250 Words, 15 Marks)

Ans. **Introduction** Green Revolution came at the time when India was not self-sufficient in ensuring food security. While GR resulted in food security but it has also created certain challenges for the Indian agriculture sector because of which Prime Minister recently called for 'Evergreen Revolution'.

About Green Revolution

- The Green Revolution technology came in a package of **HYV seeds**–irrigation–fertilisers. All these are needed together in correct proportions as both inadequacy and excessive use of water were harmful to these seeds. Availability of assured and controlled irrigation and use of chemical fertilisers thus became the two critical factors in raising the productivity of HYV seeds.
- Therefore, GR technology was more suited to the areas that had adequate irrigation facilities as well as proper water irrigation/drainage system. While on the one hand the HYV seeds required high doses of chemical fertilisers for their growth, the use of fertilisers in turn generated weeds, requiring the application of weedicides.
- One of the key features of HYV seeds is that they had shorter period of maturity which gave opportunity to farmers to grow more number of crops in a year. Thus, the GR technology helped increase cropping intensity. Higher level of productivity and cropping intensity under the GR technology made it a land-saving technology.
- GR technology helped in attracting more investment in manufacturing of farm machines, irrigation pumps, etc and also to set up banking and marketing infrastructure facilities in small towns and rural areas.

Transformation from Begging Bowl to Bread Basket

- **Status since Independence** The growth in food grain production (less than 2%) has been lower than population growth at the time of Independence. India produced 50.82 million tonnes of food-grains in 1950-51 which increased to only 70 mT in 1965-66. But after the Green Revolution, it increased to 130 Million tonnes in 1978 and today in 2022-23, India recorded the highest ever food-grain production of 323 million tonnes.
- **From Importer to Exporter** To meet the food shortage and to stabilise prices, India was forced to increasingly imports food from the US under the PL – 480 scheme started in 1956. Nearly 3 million tonnes of food grains were imported under this scheme in the very first year and the volume of imports kept rising thereafter reaching more than 4.5 million tonnes in 1963. Today, India is amongst top 10 wheat exporters and played a crucial role during Russia-Ukraine war.
- **Leading Producer of Food Grains** India is the world's largest producer of cereals in the world which shows our evolution of becoming a bread basket.

Indian Agriculture Become Victim of Green Revolution and the Need for Evergreen Revolution

- **Cereal-centric Agriculture** They have largely displaced more nutritious pulses and other cereals such as millets in consumption and led to the cereal-centric cultivation. Other crops such as pulses and oilseeds were left out of the ambit of the revolution. Major commercial crops like cotton, jute, tea and sugarcane were also left almost untouched by the Green Revolution.
- **Extinction of Indigenous Varieties of Crops** India lost about 1 lakh indigenous rice types during the Green Revolution. Indigenous rice, millets, lentils, etc were less grown after the Green Revolution. Hybrid crops, which grew faster, yielded more. Wheat, soybeans and rice are grown in greater quantities.
- **Food Consumption Pattern** The Food and Agriculture Organisation (FAO) found that millets production decreased and rice production increased from 1961 to 2017, making rice the country's staple food. The Green Revolution increases calorie intake but not diet diversity and nutritional security. Recently, government is pushing the cultivation of millets (Shree Anna) as reflected in Budget 2023-24.
- **Malnutrition** More than five decades after India launched the Green Revolution, it has not only failed to eliminate hunger but also malnutrition is at its high **Example** 49% women are anaemic, 35% kids are stunted.
- **Regional Disparities** The areas of extreme climate (precipitation and temperature) where controlled irrigation is not available the new seeds are not performing satisfactorily and thus, created inter-regional imbalance. It has hardly touched the Eastern region, including Assam, Bihar, West Bengal and Orissa and arid and semi-arid areas of Western and Southern India.
- **Agricultural Indebtedness** Agriculture become input-intensive which increased the cost of production and thus whem prices are unremunerative, it increased farmer distress and indebtedness.

- **Environmental Implications**
  - **Declining Ground Water Table** Currently, many parts of India are experiencing water stress due to irrigated agriculture. The crops introduced during the Green Revolution such as rice were water-intensive crops. **Example** Punjab.
  - **Impact on Soil Health and Crop Production** There has been soil erosion, declining soil fertility and salinisation of soil. Recently published Desertification and Land Degradation Atlas by ISRO shows almost 30% area as degraded. This directly impacts the crop production.
  - **Pests and Pesticide** Green Revolution has led to the increase in India's pesticide residue, despite its minimal pesticide usage. This pollutes water and soil. A pest imbalance causes pest attacks, another big issue.
  - **Health Hazards** The large-scale use of chemical fertilisers and pesticides such as Phosphamidon, Methomyl, Phorate, Triazophos and Monocrotophos resulted in resulted in a number of critical health illnesses including cancer, renal failure, stillborn babies and birth defects.
  - **Air Pollution** Air pollution introduced due to the burning of agricultural waste is a big issue these days.

Conclusion

The improvements brought out by the Green Revolution came at the cost of adverse environmental effects in areas subjected to intensive farming. However, where population pressure is high, there is no option except to produce more food. Hence, the need for the Evergreen Revolution was called out by Dr. MS Swaminathan, the Father of the Green Revolution in India.

Under the Evergreen Revolution, it is envisaged that productivity must increase, but in ways which are environmentally safe, economically viable and socially sustainable. The evergreen revolution involves the integration of ecological principles in technology development and dissemination.

Productivity Challenge

Q.3 'Despite high levels of production, agricultural yield in India is lower than other large producing countries.' In this context, identify the factors for low agricultural yield and suggest measures that can be taken to improve the productivity in India. (250 Words, 15 Marks)

Ans. Introduction Indian agriculture sector is the backbone of its rural economy as well as essential for its food security programme. India recorded the highest ever food-grain production of 323 million tonnes in 2022-23 and is among the top producers of several crops such as wheat, rice, pulses, sugarcane and cotton. It is the highest producer of milk and second highest producer of fruits and vegetables. Despite this, India's rice yield as reported in 2016, was 2191 kg/hectare vis-a-vis the global average of 3026 kg/hectare, while the yield of wheat was 2750 kg/hectare as against the world average yield of 3289 kg/hectare.

Although India ranks third in the production of rice, its yield is lower than Brazil, China and the United States. The same trend is observed for pulses, where it is the second highest producer.

Factors for Low Agricultural Yield

- **Fragmentation of Land Holdings** The average size of holdings in India is very low (1.08 hectares) because of which small, scientific cultivation techniques cannot be adopted and thus makes agriculture economical.
- **Small Size of Holdings** Also, small and marginal farmers constitute more than 86% of the total operational landholdings which prevents capitalist farming and thus promotes subsistence type of agriculture.
  - Marginal and small land holdings face number of issues, such as problems with using mechanisation and irrigation techniques. Also, it prevents them from accessing formal credit.
- **Inadequate Irrigation Facilities** Indian agriculture is mostly dependent on rainfall (only 48% irrigation coverage) and very few farmers avail the facility of artificial irrigation. Though over the time, more area was brought under irrigation, still there is a great scope for improving the irrigation facilities.
- **Inadequate Farm Credit** Farm Credit has been inadequate and costly despite the efforts of the government and the RBI to extend farm credit through formal channels. As per RBI Report 2019, only 40% of small and marginal farmers can access formal credit which affects their ability to purchase inputs.

- **Poor Land Record Management** also affects the access to formal credit.
- **Overcrowding in Agriculture** Disguised unemployment and low marginal productivity is an issue as too many people (around 45% of the workforce) are directly dependent on farming.
- **Fertilisers** Unscientific and imbalanced use of fertilisers and poor focus on organic agriculture leading to more input cost and even poor productivity. There has been a decline in soil health and thus affects the agricultural productivity.
- **Uneven Access to Modern Technology in Different Parts of the Country** Very few farmers are quick in following modern technology exposed to them which further hinders the increase in farm productivity.
- **Seeds** Low seed replacement rates, low quality seeds and poor RandD in seed varieties leading to poor crop productivity.
- **Pest Issues** In India the crop losses due to insect pests accounts for 15.7%
- **Climate Change** Leading to vulnerabilities like unusual floods and droughts, untimely rainfall etc. Example In March 2021, major part of wheat crop in Madhya Pradesh was destroyed due to untimely rainfall.
- **Unscientific Farming Practices** Example–Growing crops without proper soil testing, over- irrigation and excessive use of fertilisers etc.
- **Poor Financial Health of Farmers** This constraint them from using machines like pesticides sprayers, fencing to protect crops from animals etc.

Government Measures for Improving Agricultural Productivity

- **National Mission for Sustainable Agriculture (NMSA)** It is aimed at promoting sustainable agriculture by climate change adaptation measures, boosting agriculture productivity especially in Rainfed areas focusing on integrated farming, soil health management and synergising resource conservation.
- **National Mission on Agricultural Extension and Technology** The mission aims to disseminate information and knowledge to the farming community in local language/ dialect regarding agricultural schemes.
- **Kisan Credit Card (KCC) Scheme** Under this scheme, farmers are given short-term loans to purchase equipment and for their other expenses as well.
- **PM Krishi Sinchai Yojana** With the motto of 'Har Khet Ko Paani', PMKSY focuses on creating sources for assured irrigation and also creating protective irrigation by harnessing rainwater at micro level through 'Jal Sanchay' and 'Jal Sinchai'.
- **Soil Health Card Scheme** It gives information to farmers on nutrient status of their soil along with recommendations on appropriate dosage of nutrients to be applied for improving soil health and its fertility.
- **Sub Mission on Agricultural Mechanisation** It seeks to increase the reach of farm mechanisation to small and marginal farmers and to the regions where availability of farm power is low.
- **PM Fasal Bima Yojana** This scheme provides insurance coverage to farmers in case of destruction of crops so that farmers are encouraged to use high quality agricultural inputs.
- **Paramparagat Krishi Vikas Yojana (PKVY)** PKVY is an initiative to promote organic farming in the country. According to the scheme, farmers will be encouraged to form groups or clusters and take to organic farming methods over large areas in the country.

Measures to be Taken for Improving Agricultural Productivity

- **Irrigation Facilities** Canals, tubewells should be constructed to provide better irrigation facilities for the security of crops. Extensive flood control measures should be adopted to prevent the devastation caused by floods. Also, promotion of micro-irrigation facilities is also needed.
- **Institutional Credit** To save the farmers from the clutches of moneylenders, adequate credit facilities should be made available at reasonable cheap rates in rural areas. The land mortgage banks and co-operative credit societies should be strengthened to provide loans to the cultivators.
- **Supply of Quality Input** The farmer in the country should be supplied with quality inputs at proper times and at controlled prices.
- **Consolidation of Holdings** In various states, consolidation of holdings is not satisfactory. Therefore, efforts should be made towards completing the consolidation work in the specific period of time. Big areas of land which are lying waste, can be reclaimed and made fit for cultivation.

- **Development of Cottage and Small-scale Industries** In rural areas, more emphasis should be made to set up cottage and small-scale industries. This will raise the income of the peasants and keep them busy during the off season.
- **Land Reforms** It is also suggested that efforts should be made to plug the loopholes in the existing land legislations so that the surplus land may be distributed among the small and marginal farmers.

Conclusion

Agriculture is the biggest contributor in terms of employment to the country (about 48% of population). Efforts must be made to enhance the agricultural productivity and market efficiency to deal with agricultural crisis and for food security of the nation.

Cropping Pattern (Factors affecting Cropping Pattern)

Q.4 'Cropping pattern is a dynamic notion as it changes over space and time. The cropping pattern of a region is directly influenced by the geo-climatic, socio-cultural, economic, historical and political factors.' Substantiate the statement with relevant examples. (150 Words, 10 Marks)

Ans. **Introduction** Cropping pattern refers to the proportion of area under different crops at a particular period of time in a unit area. In other words, it is a yearly sequence and spatial arrangement of sowing and fallow on a given area.

It is a dynamic concept as the pattern changes depending on the place, circumstances and many other factors. It experiences significant changes from time to time because of the influence of physical, cultural, technological and economic factors. Sometimes a total replacement occurs. The changes due to differences in irrigation facilities are mainly happening from traditional crops to the HYV crops and from cereals to commercial and cash crops.

Factors Affecting Cropping Pattern of a Region

- **Geo-climatic Factors** It includes factors like nature of soil, climate, rainfall etc. In areas having sufficient rainfall and suitable conditions for water logging like in West Bengal, the most appropriate crop is rice. Jowar and Bajra are grown in rain-deficit areas such as Rajasthan and Gujarat. The fertile well-drained soil of Indo-Gangetic Plains is suitable for growing wheat. The black soil in Deccan and Malwa Plateau supports Cotton cultivation.
- **Socio-cultural Factors** It includes religion, customs, traditions etc. For example, Sikh farming community discards the cultivation of tobacco in Punjab despite profitability and favourable environmental conditions suitable for tobacco cultivation. Food habits also play a role – East and South India prefers rice as staple food while it is wheat in North India.
- **Economic Factors** Profitability is the most important factor in determining the cropping pattern of the country. Prices of agricultural commodities, income of farmers, availability of agricultural inputs and marketing facilities, nature of land tenure, availability of finance etc also determine cropping pattern. Price incentives like MSP/FRP for crops like sugarcane and wheat induces the farmers to shift over to that crop. Similarly, poor farmers with small land holdings prefer to grow cereals and other food-grains rather than opting for cash crops.
- Farmers have changed their crop patterns to reap the benefits of economic expansion due to which they are intensively moving towards the cultivation of cash crops from traditional crops.

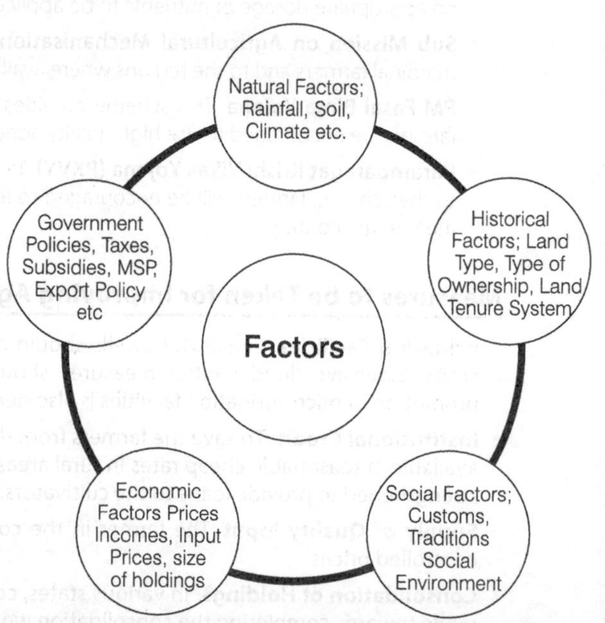

- **Infrastructural Factors** Irrigation has helped in the cultivation of rice in the areas which is not naturally suitable for its cultivation. Example: Punjab and Haryana gets less amount of rainfall but still able to cultivate rice. Also, good road infrastructure and cold storage facilities have boosted the production of horticulture crops. Where ever water is available, not only can a different crop be grown but even double or triple cropping will be possible.

- **Government Policies** Subsidies such as MSP play a very important role in the cropping pattern. There has been a shift from pulses to wheat-rice cropping pattern in certain areas.
- **Historical Factors** Crops such as tea, coffee, tobacco and cashew nuts were brought to India by British and Portuguese. British were responsible for construction of extensive canal networks in Punjab, Narmada valley and Andhra Pradesh. It supported agricultural reforms and influenced cropping pattern of these regions.
- **Political Factors** India's commitment to food security has given the boost to food grains production across the country. In socialist countries, even the combination of crops and their precise rotation is dictated by the government. **Example** Green Revolution was dictated by the need of ensuring food security.
- **Behavioural Factors** It is the farmer who evaluates the expected returns from a particular crop and chooses to cultivate it. These expected returns are more perceptual than actual even though pulses can give much higher returns to farmers, but a non-existence open procurement system drives them towards cultivation of cereal crops.

Conclusion

The cropping patterns determine the level of agricultural production. This reflects the agricultural economy of any region. The cropping patterns are beneficial in improving the fertility of the soil, thereby, increasing the yield of the crops. It ensures crop protection and availability of nutrients to the crops.

Rice-Wheat Cropping Pattern

Q.5 What are the major factors responsible for making rice-wheat system a success? Inspite of this success, how has this system become bane in India? (250 Words, 15 Marks) **UPSC Mains PYQ 2022**

Ans. **Introduction** The Rice-wheat cropping system is India's most widely adopted cropping system practiced on an estimated area of around 11 million hectares. This system is prevalent in Indo-Gangetic plains (IGP) and is predominant in Uttar Pradesh, Punjab, Haryana, Bihar, West Bengal, Madhya Pradesh etc. The pattern in itself is so robust that three-fourth of the country's annual domestic need for wheat and rice is fulfilled by a handful of states in the region.

Factors for Rice-Wheat System

- **Ideal Geographical Conditions** Cultivation of rice requires a good amount of water. Fortunately, in India, especially northern India, a good amount of water is available through annual monsoonal rainfall. Similarly, cultivation of wheat requires cool, moist weather, followed by dry, warm weather with optimum temperature range of 20-25 degree Celsius. Fortunately, this condition is available in Northern India during November to February every year.
- **Green Revolution in India** With the introduction of improved high yielding, input responsive, short duration rice and wheat varieties, the rice-wheat pattern became feasible and saw both crops grown in the same year. In this pattern, rice is grown during the summer months followed by wheat in the winter months. It is now found as a major system throughout the Indo-Gangetic Plains (IGP) . Both crops are grown in one calendar year.
- **MSP Policies** Procurement of marketed surplus of paddy (rice) and wheat at Minimum Support Price (MSP) completely insulated farmers against any price or market risks. Also, as per the government policy, the increase in MSPs of these two crops every year is comparatively more than the increase in the cost of production. So, farmers producing these crops generally have an increase in their profits year by year.
- **Technological Penetration** Increased availability of machines, irrigation technology led to increased cropping area and more productivity.
- **Food Preferences** Rice and wheat are core food preferences in India. So, farmers with low land-holding/subsistence farming produce rice and wheat for own consumption.

Issues Associated with this Cropping Pattern

- **Ecological Effects** Policy of free power for pumping out groundwater for irrigation led to the depletion of groundwater resources. Punjab and Haryana are already notified as over exploited zones of ground water.

- Declining water tables not only raise production costs due to higher energy requirements for pumping water from greater depths but such rapid rates of decline spark serious questions about the long-term sustainability of rice-wheat system itself in these areas.
- Similarly, air pollution due to crop residue burning in states like Uttar Pradesh, Punjab and Haryana during the months of November-December.
- **Loss of biodiversity** due to excessive use of hybrid seeds and fertilisers.

- **Overuse of Chemical fertilisers And Pesticides** The use of chemical fertilisers and pesticides has increased in order to maintain high crop yields, leading to soil degradation and poor underground water quality. Application of this poor-quality water to the agricultural and dairy sector leads to emergence of several severe diseases in animals and decreased the grain quality which ultimately affect the human health.
- **Pest and Disease Outbreaks** The monoculture nature of the rice-wheat system makes it susceptible to pest and disease outbreaks, which can lead to crop failures and reduced yields.
- **Lack of Crop Rotation** Crop rotation helps to maintain soil structure and nutrient levels and to prevent soil borne pests. Continuous plantation of wheat and rice on the same land has degraded the soil structure and nutrition levels in soil. Cereal crops like sorghum, maize and millet are more nutritious than wheat and rice and so should be given equal importance in the cropping system.
- **Income and Productivity** Rise in labour charges and exposure to global markets led to fall in incomes of farmers cultivating rice and wheat. The productivity is also very less compared to international standards around one/second of China and one/third of Africa.
- **Fiscal Challenge** In India, the per capita intake of rice and wheat is declining and consumers' preference is shifting towards other foods. However, rice and wheat procurement in the country has more than doubled after 2006-07. This is putting pressure on the higher subsidy bill of the government which is already in stressed situation.
- **Wastage of Food Grains** Open-ended procurement of rice and wheat has also exceeded the storage capacity of government and thus resulting in unscientific storage. This has led to wastage of food grains which was even observed by the Supreme Court.
- **Entrepreneurial Skills of Farmers** Procurement of almost the entire market arrivals of rice and wheat at MSP for more than 50 years has affected the entrepreneurial skills of farmers to sell their produce in a competitive market where prices are determined by demand and supply and competition.
- **Greenhouse Gas Emissions (GHGs)** Rice-wheat cropping system is known for plenty of methane generation and its contribution to global warming.

Conclusion

The traditional Green Revolution States would need to shed 'business as usual' approach and embrace an innovative development strategy in agriculture and non-agriculture to secure and improve the future of farming and rural youth. An Inclusive Ever Green revolution is needed with core pillar of sustainable development.

Crop Diversification

Q.6 'Crop diversification has the sound capacity for achieving the goal of nutritional security, income growth, food security, employment generation and sustainable agriculture development.' Justify the above statement along with the measures taken by the government to promote crop diversification. (250 Words, 15 Marks)

Ans. **Introduction** Crop diversification refers to the practice of cultivating a variety of crops instead of relying on a single crop. This can be done in various forms such as the addition of new crop(s) as intercrop and/or predecessor or successor crops, changing numbers of the crop (multi-cropping), modified cropping system and adopting a new, integrated cropping pattern with changing agronomical practices.

The traditional pattern of agriculture in India has wider crop diversity and is more stable and pro-nature. In the Garhwal Himalayan region of India, Barahnaja is a crop diversification system for cultivating 12 crops in a year. 'Barah anaaj' literally means '12 foodgrains' and is the traditional heritage of the area.

Type of Diversification	Nature of Diversification	Potential Benefit
Improved structural diversity	Makes crops within the field more structurally diverse	Pest suppression
Genetic diversification in monoculture	Cultivation of mixture of varieties of same species in a monoculture	Disease suppression, Increased production stability
Diversify field with fodder grasses	Growing fodder grasses alongside of food/pulse/oilseed/vegetable etc.	Pest suppression, opportunity to livestock farming
Crop rotations	Temporal divesity through crop rotations (Sequential cropping)	Disease suppression, Increased production stability
Polyculture	Spatial and temporal diversity of crops (Growing two or more crop species within the field)	Insect, pest disease suppression, climate change buffering and increased production
Agroforestry	Growing crops and trees together (Spatial and temporal diversity)	Pest suppression and climate change buffering
Mixed landscapes	Development of larger-scale diversified landscapes through mixture crops and cropping system with multiple ecosystems	Pest suppression and climate change buffering
Micro-watershed based diversification	Integration of crop with other farming components for year round income and employment generation, besides sustaining soil and environmental health	Insect, pest and disease suppression, climate change buffering and increased production, employment and income

Crop Diversification Helps in Achieving the Following Goals

- **Nutritional Security** Crop diversification enhances the availability of a diverse range of crops, leading to improved nutrition for the population.
  - Different crops have varying nutritional profiles and by cultivating a variety of crops, it becomes easier to address nutritional deficiencies and ensure a balanced diet for individuals.
  - Green Revolution resulted into cereal-centric cultivation of agriculture which ensured food security but lacks nutritional security. There has been a decline in the cultivation of pulses which affected its production and consequently inflation is very often seen in pulses.
- **Income Growth** Diversifying crops allows farmers to tap into multiple markets and diversify their income sources.
  - By growing a range of crops, farmers can take advantage of price fluctuations, market demand and value-added opportunities.
  - This reduces their dependency on a single crop and provides them with a more stable and sustainable income.
  - It can enable farmers to gain access to national and international markets with new products, food and medicinal plants.
  - Green Revolution has made the agriculture input-intensive which resulted in increased costs of production and thus affected the profitability of farmers.
- **Food Security** Crop diversification strengthens food security by reducing the risks associated with mono-cropping.
  - In case of a crop failure or pest outbreak affecting one crop, other crops can compensate for the losses and maintain overall food production.
  - This reduces vulnerability to food shortages and improves the resilience of the agricultural system.
- **Employment Generation** Diversifying crops creates employment opportunities along the entire value chain.
  - Different crops require different cultivation, harvesting and processing techniques, leading to increased demand for labour.
  - This generates employment in rural areas, reduces seasonal unemployment and contributes to rural development.
- **Sustainable Agricultural Development** Crop diversification plays a crucial role in sustainable agriculture. It promotes biodiversity, reduced soil erosion, enhances soil fertility and minimises the risk of pest and disease outbreaks because mono-cropping patterns have more chances to be attacked by the same types of insects and pests, which in turn are controlled by pumping the insecticides and pesticides.

- By adopting diverse cropping systems, farmers can reduce the use of chemical inputs, enhance ecosystem services and maintain the long-term productivity of the land.
- Adoption of crop diversification helps in the conservation of natural resources like the introduction of legumes in the rice-wheat cropping system, which has the ability to fix atmospheric nitrogen to help sustain soil fertility.
- Green Revolution has led to environmental consequences such as salinisation of soil, declining water table, etc. which has affected the agricultural productivity and puts a burden on the natural resources. Thus, crop diversification is promoted for sustainable agriculture practices.

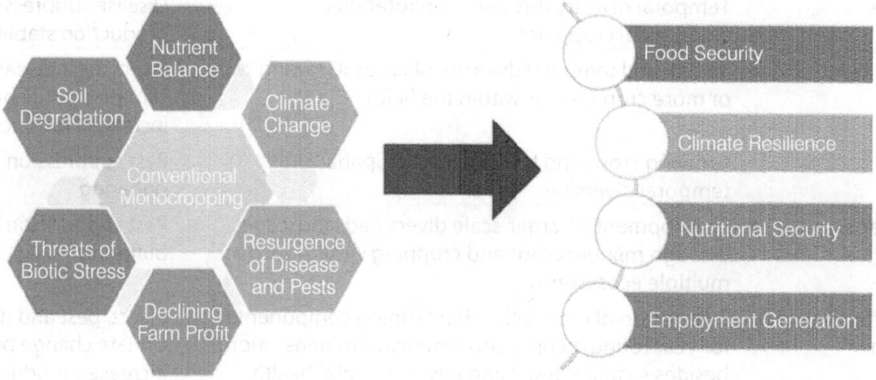

Challenges in Crop Diversification

- **Dependence on Monsoon** Around 55% of India's cultivable land is rain-fed with heavy dependence on monsoon. Hence, some crops may not be able to survive in the prevailing environmental conditions.
- **Fragmented Land Holding** It makes it difficult to use efficient modern technology on large scale, raises the cost of land boundary management, land disputes etc.
- **Shift from Food Crops to Commercial Crops** This especially includes cotton in the Deccan belt and Sugarcane in the Green revolution belt and Krishna-Godavari basin.
- **Inadequate Infrastructure** Poor basic infrastructure like rural roads, power, transport, communication, etc are major impediments for diversification.
- **Lack of Knowledge and Training** Indian farmers are inadequately trained. Further, there is persistent and large-scale illiteracy amongst farmers.
- **Over-use of Resources like Land and Water Resources** Crop diversification might amplify resource consumption, thereby creating a negative impact on the environment and sustainability of agriculture. For instance, Animal agriculture is the second-largest contributor to human-made Greenhouse Gas (GHG) emissions after fossil fuels.

Measures Taken by the Government to Promote Crop Diversification

- **National Mission on Oilseeds and Oil Palm (NMOOP)** This mission aims to increase the production of oilseeds and oil palm, encouraging farmers to cultivate these crops instead of traditional cereals. It provides financial support, subsidies and technical assistance to farmers to adopt oilseed and oil palm cultivation.
- **National Food Security Mission (NFSM)** The NFSM focuses on increasing the production of pulses, oilseeds and coarse cereals to meet the country's growing demand for food. It promotes the adoption of improved technologies, seeds and practices to diversify cropping patterns and enhance productivity.
- **Rashtriya Krishi Vikas Yojana (RKVY)** The RKVY supports State Governments in implementing various agricultural development programs, including crop diversification. It provides financial assistance for promoting the cultivation of alternative crops, setting up processing units and supporting market linkages.
- **Pradhan Mantri Krishi Sinchayee Yojana (PMKSY)** This scheme aims to improve water use efficiency in agriculture and promote the adoption of water-saving technologies. By ensuring adequate irrigation facilities, farmers are encouraged to diversify their crops and cultivate water-intensive crops in a sustainable manner.

- **Market Intervention Schemes** The government introduces various market intervention schemes to provide price support and procurement mechanisms for alternative crops. This helps to stabilise prices, ensure fair returns to farmers and incentivise the cultivation of diversified crops.

Conclusion

Crop diversification is recognised as one of the most environmentally feasible, cost-effective and reasonable approaches to reduce uncertainty in agriculture, particularly in the face of climate change. Crop diversification helps in minimising the alleviating second generations problem such as soil degradation, soil salinity, insect-pest and disease insurgence, environmental pollution, decline in farm profit, nutrient imbalance, climate change etc. Crop diversification promotes farm resilience or the ability of an agroecosystem to return to its former productive state after being perturbed, by increasing geographical and temporal biodiversity.

Land Productivity to Water Productivity

Q.7 The cropping pattern in India is highly skewed towards crops that are water-intensive. In this context, examine the need to shift the focus from 'land productivity' to 'irrigation water productivity'. (150 Words, 10 Marks)

Ans. **Introduction** Water productivity is a measure of water use efficiency in agriculture measured on basis of total water input and total crop output. Land productivity tells us about crop produced from unit area of agricultural land. Green Revolution focused on increasing production and land productivity while water was treated as surplus unlimited resource.

India's cropping pattern highlights the rampant cultivation of water intensive crops such as sugarcane production in Maharashtra, paddy in North-West India, which are amongst the water stressed regions of India. Along with this, India is the largest exporter of rice which is commonly observed as export of virtual water by the Economic Survey.

Reasons Behind this Trend of Water-intensive Crops Cultivation

- **Government's Incentive Structure** The government's policies for various inputs including subsidies on water, power and fertiliser has promoted farmers to cultivate crops, which are highly water intensive such as paddy and sugarcane. Rice and sugarcane crops together consume more than 60% of water available for irrigation.
- **Minimum Support Prices (MSPs)** Though MSPs are currently announced for 23 crops, the most effective price support is for sugarcane, wheat and rice.
- **Demand for Water Intensive Crops** Rice is one of the most important staple food crop in India. Similarly, there is large industrial demand for crops like cotton, which push the farmers to grow them as they bring larger profits.
- **Increased Water Demand by Crops** The new artificially modified HYV seeds have been giving higher crop yields, but they require more water than natural seeds.
- **Agri-export Basket** India's agri-export basket consists mainly of those items which are water-intensive such as rice, coffee, tea and therefore putting more pressure on the water resources.
- **Lack of Sensitisation** There is a lack of awareness among farmers about the strain on natural resources due to water-intensive crops. Mostly, the same cropping pattern keeps continuing over the next generation of farmers.

Need to Shift From 'Land Productivity' to 'Water Productivity'

Irrigation Water Productivity (IWP), defined as the yield produced per unit of irrigation water use, has become an important criteria which takes into account both agricultural production and water use efficiency. Increasing the value of IWP would not only alleviate the pressure of limited water resources but also ensure the food security.

Economic Survey 2018-19 suggests a transition from land productivity to irrigation water productivity, which emphasizes on more crops per drop, improving total nutrition per drop and total food crops per drop. The need for such a shift is due to the following factors:

- **Water Crisis** India has only 4% of world's water resources while accounting for 18% of world's population. This causes a stark gap in the demand-supply of water resources, leading to already water-stressed situation. In addition to this, growing water intensive crops has led to severe water scarcity across various regions like Vidarbha. As per the NITI Aayog, around 600 million Indians are facing high-to extreme water stress and the situation is set to worsen as water requirements increase.

- **Skewed Balance of Input and Output** India's agricultural sector accounts for 87% of groundwater extraction (as per Ministry of Jal Shakti) for irrigation purposes, but contributes only 15% to the country's GDP.
- **High Land Productivity but Low Water Productivity** States such as Tamil Nadu, Karnataka, Maharashtra and Andhra Pradesh, which have high land productivity, tend to have very low irrigation water productivity, reflecting inefficient use of water and the need to re-calibrate cropping pattern.
- **Nutrition and Food Security** To increase irrigation water productivity, there is need to focus on cultivation of less water intensive crops like millets, bajra etc. India could reduce the amount of water it uses for irrigation by a third and simultaneously address its persistent malnutrition problem, if it replaces its rice crop with more nutritious and less thirsty cereals
- **Climate Change** Climate change has increased the frequency of drought in the country. In the coming times, India is going to face water scarcity hence there is a need to focus on improving water productivity.
- **Soil Productivity** After decades of success of the Green Revolution, states like Punjab and Haryana are facing the challenge of soil salinity which has lowered the productivity of soil in the states. Degrading soil productivity is also affecting the sustainability of farming.
- **Spill-over Effects of Agricultural Water-stress is** seen in the form of agricultural pauperism, furthering into dearth of food, hunger, malnourishment, agri-inflation as well as increasing social division and lower ranks in indices such as HDI.

Futuristic Measures

In order to bring this shift, governments need to focus on crop diversification, sustainable practices like Zero Budget Natural Farming (ZBNF), nudging farmers to use micro-irrigation techniques such as drip irrigation and micro-sprinklers. The focus should be on growing crops, which are climatically suitable for any region. In Eastern India, water intensive crops can be grown while in semi- arid regions of India like Central India, Rajasthan etc the focus should be on cultivation of less water intensive crops like millets and bajra etc.

Use of traditional methods for water conservation (e.g., Johad) would improve alongside modern methods as fog catchers, grey water usage, water recycling, etc. ICT can optimise optimal water use can be in the form of Precision Agriculture, etc.

The Economic Survey suggests use of optimal fertiliser dose based on soil health status, promotion of neem coated urea, promotion of micro nutrients, promotion of organic fertilisers and promotion of water soluble fertilisers. Organic and natural farming techniques including Zero Budget Natural Farming (ZBNF) can improve both water use efficiency and soil fertility.

Conclusion

Therefore, devising policies such as 'Per Drop More Crop' to incentivise farmers to adopt efficient ways of water use should become a national priority to avert the looming water crisis and towards meeting SDGs. In addition to these measures, a combination of resource efficient methods; dynamic cropping patterns; climate change responsive farming and intensive use of technology should form the backbone of farming in India.

Fertiliser Sector (Distortions in the Fertiliser Sector)

Q.8 Multiple distortions exist in the fertiliser sector that leads to various adverse outcomes and hurting the farmers. Examine. To what extent, recently launched 'One Nation, One Fertiliser' scheme will correct these distortions in the fertiliser sector? Critically comment. (250 Words, 15 Marks)

Ans. **Introduction** Fertilisers are substances that provide one or more of the chemicals required for plant growth. There are 3 basic fertilisers in India - Urea, DAP and Muriate of Potash (MOP) which improves the productivity of crops. fertilisers can be both organic and inorganic. India is the second largest consumer of urea fertilisers after China. India also ranks second in the production of nitrogenous fertilisers and third in phosphatic fertilisers.

Distortions in Fertiliser Sector

However, fertiliser sector in India has been plagued by multiple distortions, leading to adverse outcomes and causing hardships for farmers. Some of these distortions include:

- **Subsidy Inefficiencies** The existing system of fertiliser subsidies in India has been prone to leakages, diversion and black market activities. Subsidies intended to benefit farmers often do not reach them effectively, resulting in a loss of financial resources and inadequate support for the targeted beneficiaries.
- **Imbalanced Nutrient Use** Farmers, driven by cost considerations, tend to use more nitrogen-based fertilisers (Urea is relatively cheaper than other fertilisers because urea is kept out of NBS regime and thus, there is still a maximum retail price on urea) while neglecting other essential nutrients which affects the nutrient balance in the soil.
  - Indian farmers are effectively applying just urea and DAP — both high-analysis fertilisers containing 46 per cent N and P respectively.
  - The effects of these – the current NPK ratio is about 13:5:1 (In Punjab, it has been found to be 34:8:1), as against the ideal 4:2:1 – would ultimately show up in crop yields.
  - Plants, like humans, will respond poorly to fertilisers if only one or two nutrients are given in excess.
- **End used Based Subsidies** Urea is subsidized only for agriculture which creates an incentive to divert subsidised urea to industrial purposes and smuggling across the border. Subsidies like this violate the One Product-One Price principle (Products should be priced similarly to discourage diversion of subsidised goods from eligible to ineligible consumers).
- **Fiscal Pressure on the Government** Fertiliser subsidy has more than doubled in a short period of 5-6 years. For 2023-24, the Union Budget has estimated fertiliser subsidy at ₹ 1,75,100 crores (from ₹ 66,468 crores in 2017-18). The subsidy increased at higher level due to the recent upsurge in the prices of energy, the international prices of urea and other fertilisers and India's dependence on imports.
- **Price Distortions** Fertiliser prices in India are regulated by the government, which often leads to inconsistencies and artificial pricing.
  - The fixed prices may not reflect the actual costs of production, resulting in market inefficiencies and inadequate incentives for manufacturers to invest in research and development.
  - Subsidies haven't been able to fix industrial crisis and India is still importing urea.
- **Impact on Soil** Excessive usage of fertiliser cause soil salinity leading to lower growth potential. Example: 30% of soils have found increasing trend of salinisation.
- **Lack of Quality Control** The quality of fertilisers available to farmers is often questionable, with instances of spurious or adulterated products. The absence of stringent quality control measures leads to ineffective fertilisation, lower yields and financial losses for farmers.

Overall, according to Economic Survey 2016, the fertiliser sector is highly regulated, which causes a major distortion in the sector. The subsidy which is intended to help small farmers benefits a small proportion of them. 24% of the subsidy is spent on inefficient urea producers. Of the remaining, 41% is diverted to non-agricultural uses and abroad and of the remaining, 24% is consumed by large farmers.

'One Nation, One Fertiliser' Scheme

Union Ministry of Chemicals and fertilisers announced the implementation of the 'One Nation One Fertiliser' scheme under which a single brand and logo for fertilisers will have to be used by all manufacturers under the Centre's fertiliser subsidy scheme newly renamed as a Prime Minister's scheme - 'Pradhan Mantri Bhartiya Janurvarak Pariyojna' (PMBJP).

- The single brand name for UREA, DAP, MOP and NPK etc would be BHARAT UREA, BHARAT DAP, BHARAT MOP and BHARAT NPK etc respectively for all fertiliser Companies, State Trading Entities (STEs) and fertiliser Marketing Entities (FMEs).
- Also, a logo indicating the Fertiliser subsidy scheme namely Pradhan Mantri Bhartiya Janurvarak Pariyojna will be used on said fertiliser bags.
- Under the scheme, companies are allowed to display their name, brand, logo and other relevant product information only on one-third space of their bags.
- On the remaining two-thirds space, the 'Bharat' brand and Pradhan Mantri Bharatiya Jan Urvarak Pariyojana logo will have to be shown.

The recently launched 'One Nation, One Fertiliser' scheme aims to address some of these distortions in the fertiliser sector.

- **Direct Benefit Transfer (DBT)** The scheme intends to create a unified national market for fertilisers by introducing a single point payment system, ensuring a Direct Benefit Transfer (DBT) to farmers and promoting the use of neem-coated urea.
  - The introduction of Direct Benefit Transfers (DBT) under the scheme can help address subsidy inefficiencies by reducing leakages and ensuring that the subsidy reaches the intended beneficiaries directly.
- **Reduction of Transport Subsidies** Besides paying subsidies to companies for the cost of production, the government also pays manufacturers freight subsidies or the cost of ferrying their products to the end-user. So, another argument for the launch of single-brand fertilisers is to reduce transport subsidies, estimated to be over ₹ 6,000 crore per year.
- There would be no need for Indian Farmers fertiliser Cooperative (IFFCO) to move fertilisers across states because of the single brand, thus reining in the fertiliser subsidy expenditure.
- **Nutrient Management** The 'One Nation, One Fertiliser' scheme does not explicitly address the issue of imbalanced nutrient use.
  - **Encouraging farmers to adopt integrated nutrient management** practices and promoting the use of organic and bio-fertilisers alongside chemical fertilisers would be essential to tackle the problem of soil degradation and promote sustainable agriculture.
- **Price Regulation** While the scheme aims to establish a national market, it does not address the issue of price distortions caused by government regulations.
  - Unless there are efforts to streamline pricing mechanisms and ensure fair pricing based on market dynamics, the problem of artificial pricing may persist.
- **Quality Control** The scheme's emphasis on promoting neem-coated urea can contribute to addressing the issue of spurious and adulterated fertilisers to some extent.
  - However, stringent quality control measures robust monitoring and strict enforcement of standards would be crucial to ensure the availability of quality fertilisers throughout the country.

However, there are some concerns associated with 'One Nation, One Fertiliser' scheme

- Companies that manufacture fertiliser will be discouraged from engaging in marketing and brand-building initiatives. Therefore, they risk losing their long-standing reputation and the farmers' faith in their goods.
- Fertiliser businesses frequently engage in extension efforts, such as field-level demonstrations, crop surveys, etc., to provide effective strategies for applying nutrients and to connect with farmers. However, all of these operations will now come to an end.
- Currently, the corporation is held responsible if a bag or batch of fertiliser does not adhere to the necessary criteria. However, that might now be entirely transferred to the government.
- **Regulation** A government brand will add another layer of regulation to the fertiliser manufacturing sector where almost every aspect- from product pricing to cost structure to geographical distribution and sale- is controlled by the government.

Conclusion

In conclusion, while the 'One Nation, One Fertiliser' scheme holds promise in addressing some distortions in the fertiliser sector, its effectiveness in correcting these distortions will depend on the implementation, monitoring and complementary measures taken to address broader issues such as imbalanced nutrient use, pricing mechanisms and quality control.

A comprehensive and critical approach is required to ensure that the scheme brings about meaningful improvements and benefits for farmers in the fertiliser sector.

PM-PRANAM and Alternative Fertilisers

Q.9 There is a need to promote alternative policies in the fertiliser sector in India to enhance the productivity of agriculture, provide an alternative to chemical fertilisers and balance the fiscal impact of fertiliser subsidy. Discuss the statement in the context of PM-PRANAM scheme announced in Union Budget 2023-24. (250 Words, 15 Marks)

Ans. **Introduction** The fertiliser sector in India plays a vital role in supporting agricultural productivity and food security. With a growing population and increasing demand for food, the sector has witnessed significant growth. According to the Indian Agricultural Statistics Research Institute (IASRI), the consumption of chemical fertilisers in India increased from 13.6 Million Metric tonnes (MMT) in 2000-01 to 31.1 MMT in 2019-20, reflecting its importance in ensuring sustainable and efficient agricultural practices for the nation's development.

Key Issues Associated with Fertilisers Sector

- **Excessive Reliance on Chemical fertilisers** India has a significant dependence on chemical fertilisers, with a limited focus on organic and natural inputs.
- **Lack of Availability and Affordability of Organic fertilisers** The availability and affordability of organic fertilisers are limited, hindering their adoption by farmers. According to the Ministry of Agriculture and Farmers Welfare, the production of organic fertilisers was around 7.7 lakh metric tons in 2019-20, which is relatively low compared to the demand.
- **Subsidy Burden on the Government** The subsidy on chemical fertilisers places a significant fiscal burden on the government. fertiliser subsidy has more than doubled in a short period of 5-6 years. For 2023-24, the Union Budget has estimated fertiliser subsidy at ₹ 1,75,100 crores (from ₹ 66,468 crores in 2017-18). The subsidy increased at higher level due to the recent upsurge in the prices of energy, the international prices of urea and other fertilisers and India's dependence on imports.

Fertiliser prices skyrocketed last year after sanctions against Belarus, a major producer.

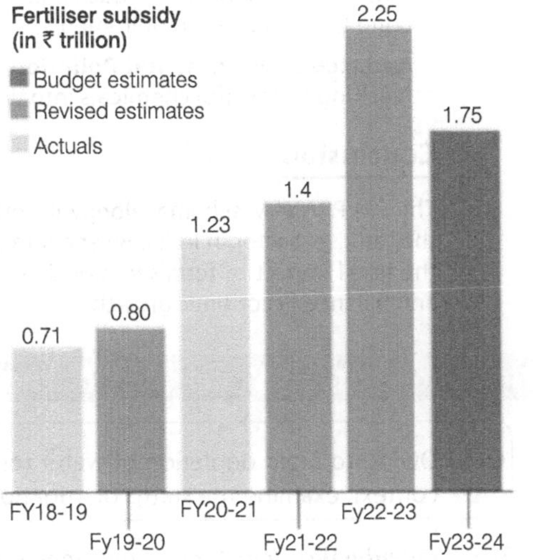

- **Environmental Pollution** The excessive use of chemical fertilisers contributes to environmental pollution, particularly water pollution. The Central Pollution Control Board (CPCB) reported that excessive nitrate levels, mainly from agricultural sources, were found in 14% of India's groundwater monitoring stations.
- **Soil Degradation and Nutrient Imbalance** The continuous use of chemical fertilisers without proper soil nutrient management has led to soil degradation and nutrient imbalances. As per the Indian Council of Agricultural Research (ICAR), about 17.9 million hectares of Indian soils suffer from nutrient deficiencies, which negatively impact crop productivity.
- **Inefficient Distribution and Logistics** The distribution and logistics system for fertilisers in India face challenges, leading to delays and inadequate availability, particularly in remote areas. This can impact timely and efficient access to fertilisers for farmers.
- **Limited Research and Development** Research and development in the fertiliser sector, particularly in organic and natural inputs, is relatively limited compared to chemical fertilisers. There is a need for increased investment in R & D to develop innovative and sustainable solutions for soil health and crop nutrition.

PM Programme for Restoration, Awareness, Nourishment and Amelioration of Mother Earth (PM-PRANAM) Scheme

Budget 2023-24 launched PM-PRANAM scheme which aims to reduce the usage of chemical fertilisers by encouraging the use of alternative fertilisers or bio-fertilisers. It will incentivise States and Union Territories to promote alternative fertilisers and balanced use of chemical fertilisers which will consequently bring down the subsidy burden.

- **Enhanced Agricultural Productivity** The PM-PRANAM scheme aims to promote organic farming and increase the availability of organic fertilisers, bio-fertilisers and other natural inputs. By providing support and incentives for organic farming, the scheme can contribute to sustainable and high-yield agricultural practices.
- **Alternatives to Chemical fertilisers**: The PM-PRANAM scheme encourages and promotes soil fertility, reduces environmental impacts and provides a healthier option for farmers and consumers. Encouraging the use of bio-fertilisers, compost and organic manures as alternatives to chemical fertilisers can reduce environmental pollution
- **Reduced Fiscal Burden of Fertiliser Subsidy** Promoting organic farming and natural inputs through the PM-PRANAM scheme can help in balancing the fiscal burden of fertiliser subsidies, as organic and natural inputs generally require less financial support.
- **Improved Soil Health** Alternative policies focus on improving soil health through practices like nutrient recycling, crop rotation, cover cropping and organic amendments, resulting in long-term benefits for agriculture. The PM-PRANAM scheme can also address the issue of nutrient recycling and waste management in agriculture.
- **Increased Nutrient Efficiency** Alternative inputs such as bio-fertilisers, organic manures and microbial consortia enhance nutrient availability and improve nutrient use efficiency, leading to optimised crop growth and yield.
- **Research and Development** The PM-PRANAM scheme can support research and development efforts in the field of organic farming and natural inputs. This includes developing new and improved organic fertilisers, exploring innovative farming techniques and lead to the development of customised solutions, tailored to specific agro-climatic conditions and crop requirements.
- **Reduced Environmental Pollution** Alternative policies promote sustainable agricultural practices that reduce the leaching of harmful chemicals into water bodies, minimising water pollution and preserving ecological balance.

Conclusion

The PM-PRANAM scheme, alongwith other policy interventions, can play a vital role in promoting alternative policies in the fertiliser sector in India. By encouraging organic farming, providing alternatives to chemical fertilisers and addressing the fiscal impact of fertiliser subsidies, the scheme can contribute to sustainable agriculture, environmental protection and balanced economic growth.

Irrigation Systems (Water-Use Efficiency)

Q.10 Owing to rapid depletion of water resources, there is an urgent need to increase water use efficiency. In this context, examine the status of irrigation in India along with the various issues. (150 Words, 10 Marks)

Ans. **Introduction** India's per capita annual water availability has declined from 5,177 cubic metre (cm) in 1951 to 1,508 cubic metre (cm) by 2014 and is likely to reduce further to 1,465 cm and 1,235 cm by 2025 and 2050, respectively. More than a third of the country's population already lives in water-stressed areas. The 2018 drinking water crisis in Shimla is a grim reminder of the country's water woes. In India, about 80% of the current water use is drawn by agriculture. At present, irrigated area accounts for nearly 48% of the 140 million hectares (mha) of agricultural land in India and the rest is rainfed.

Water use efficiency indicates the ratio between effective water use and actual water withdrawal. It is to used describe how effectively water is delivered to crops and to indicate the amount of water wasted at plot, farm, command or system level.

Challenges Faced by the Irrigation Sector

- **Delay in the Completion of Projects** The biggest problem in our major and medium irrigation sectors right from the First Five Year Plan has been the tendency to start more and more new projects resulting in proliferation of projects. There is also delay in utilisation of potentials already present. In most of the projects, there have been delay in construction of field channels and water courses, land levelling and land shaping.
- **Time and Cost overruns** This have resulted from the delay in the completion of the irrigation projects.
- **Incomplete Projects** Around 557 irrigation projects have not been completed due to issues such as lack of synchronisation between project components, delayed tendering and contract management, issues in land acquisition, etc.
- **Regional disparities in Irrigation Development** The Ninth Five Year Plan Document estimated that the water resource development in North Eastern region through major, medium and minor schemes is only at the level of 28.6 per cent whereas in the Northern region it has reached about 95.3%. This indicates a wide regional variation in the development of irrigation facilities.

- **Underutilisation of Irrigation Potential** Inadequate budget provision for operation and maintenance of the irrigation system is significantly responsible for underutilisation followed by non-completion of distributaries, minors, field channels and on-farm development.
- **Inter-state Water Disputes** Irrigation is a state subject in India. Development of water resource is, therefore, being planned by states individually taking into account their own needs and requirement. However, all major rivers are inter-state in character. As a result, difference with regard to storage, priorities and use of water arise between different states. Narrow regional outlook brings inter-state rivalries over distribution of water supply.
- **Heavy Dependence on Ground Water** According to the Fifth Minor Irrigation Census, the groundwater level (providing 70% of India's irrigation needs and 80% of its domestic water supplies) in India has declined by 61% between 2007 and 2017.
- **Dependence on Flood Irrigation and Subsidies** Heavy dependence on flood irrigation and use of sink tube wells as components of green revolution along with heavy subsidies to farmers has led to overexploitation of groundwater and widespread environmental damage.
- **Decline in Water Table** There has been a steady decline in water table in the recent period in several parts of the country, especially in the Western dry region, on account over exploitation of ground water and insufficient recharge from rain-water.
- **Expensive Micro Irrigation** Most of the adopters are wealthier farmers and poor farmers cannot afford it.
  - International Development Enterprises (IDE), an NGO is actively working in Maharashtra and Gujarat innovate low-cost micro irrigation systems and create awareness among poor farmers.

Futuristic Measures

As per the National Commission for Integrated Water Resources, the irrigation sector will consume about 79% of the available water resources by 2050. This calls for focused attention to promote improved water management practices in irrigation projects.

The following measures could be taken to solve the challenges faced by the irrigation sector in India:

- **Adoption of micro-irrigation systems** As per the Ashok Dalwai Committee, micro irrigation delivers water savings of up to 40% over conventional flood irrigation. In this context, the Task Force on Micro Irrigation, 2004 estimated a potential of 69.5 million hectare under micro irrigation.
- **Focus on command area development (CAD) approach** The CAD was launched in 1974-75 (now part of Pradhan Mantri Krishi Sinchayee Yojana) to improve the utilization of created irrigation potential and optimize agriculture production and productivity. Adoption of command area approach leads to water saving, soil health management and prevents water logging. CAD is crucial to realise the government's vision of 'per drop more crop'.
- **Adoption of sustainable cropping patterns** Cropping patterns in states should be adopted based on agro-climatic zones. Improper cropping patterns affect both crop productivity and irrigation efficiency.
- **Impetus of agricultural extension services** Mass awareness through Krishi Vigyan Kendras and Melas is crucial to bring about real change on ground in terms of adoption of micro irrigation practices and change in cropping pattern.

Conclusion

To reduce the consumption of water and maximise agricultural productivity in the country, the government has taken various initiatives such as the National Water Policy (NWP) 2012, National Water Mission, PMKSY, setting up a dedicated 'Micro Irrigation Fund' with NABARD, etc. Ensuring their proper implementation remains the key.

Agricultural Policies vs Irrigation Productivity

Q.11 Technological solutions to increase irrigation productivity in India cannot make much headway unless pricing policies of agricultural inputs are put on the right track and farmers are incentivized for saving water. Elucidate. (250 Words, 15 Marks)

Ans. **Introduction** Irrigation productivity is defined as the amount or value of agricultural production obtained by using unit volume or value of water. India has low irrigation productivity due to unsustainable practices like flooding or canal and pumping groundwater resources. Technological solutions to increase water productivity like Drip irrigation, Micro-irrigation, etc, have had limited success in achieving 'Per Drop More Crop', due to skewed pricing policies of inputs like water, fertiliser, power, etc.

Technological Solutions to Increase Irrigation Productivity in India

- **Drip Irrigation** Drip irrigation pilots for paddy in the Karnal district of Haryana showed while it takes 3,065 litres of water to produce 1 kg of paddy grain under the traditional flood irrigation but under drip irrigation, it can be reduced to just 842 litres. It delivers water and nutrients directly to the plant's roots zone, in the right amounts, at the right time, so each plant gets exactly what it needs, when it needs it, to grow optimally.
- **Sprinkler Irrigation** In this method water is sprayed into the air and irrigation is done through spray heads so that it breaks up into small water drops which fall to the ground. In India, the area irrigated by the sprinkler system is less than 2.5 % of the total area under irrigation. It can save 25-30% of water compared to traditional flood irrigation.
- **Direct Seeding of Rice (DSR)** In DSR, the pre-germinated seeds are directly drilled into the field by a tractor-powered machine and there is no need for nursery preparation or transplantation involved in this method. It leads to increased water efficiency and less labour required.
- **System of Rice Intensification (SRI)** It is a farming methodology aimed at increasing the yield of rice produced in farming. It is a low-water, labor-intensive method that uses younger seedlings singly spaced and typically hand weeded with special tools.
- **Micro-irrigation** It is the slow application of water above or below the soil by surface drip, subsurface drip, bubbler and micro-sprinkler systems, thereby increasing the yield and productivity of crops.
  - Due to recurring droughts in the years 2012, 2015 and 2016, micro-irrigation has become a policy priority in India in form of Per Drop More Crop component of PMKSY.

Agricultural Policies Posing Challenge to Irrigation Productivity

- **Free or Highly Subsidised Power** dis-incentivises farmers from investing in water-conserving methods particularly in the country's North-West, the site of the erstwhile Green Revolution. It leads to over-extraction of groundwater and traditional flooding of fields.
  - This results in loss of around 60% of the water applied – in the form of surface runoff, percolation and bare soil evaporation that does not contribute to any increases in yield.
- **Economies of scale and operations don't allow farmers to adopt new irrigation methods** India has a very small average landholding size (1.08 hectares acres as per Agri Census, 2015-16) and that too is scattered over different places in small parcels.
  - This is making individual ownership of irrigation machinery economically unviable. Thus, there is a need for high government support.
- **Credit procedure for irrigation mechanisation is very cumbersome** The rate of interest is higher for such loans in comparison to crop loans.
- **Limitations of Subsidy** Irrigation mechanisation requires substantial investment. Subsidies by State or Central Government are available based on the budget allocation and not on farmer's requirement basis.
- **High cost of Installation of Modern Irrigation Techniques** doesn't allow farmers to invest in it. Modern irrigation methods like Micro-sprinklers require subsidies to the extent of 40-90% of its cost, however, the current subsidy regime is skewed in favour of Urea, power, MSP subsidy.
- **Subsidy under PM Fasal Bima Yojana doesn't cover insurance of Farm machinery,** thereby increasing the cost of maintenance for farmers and making its use unsustainable.
- **Skewed Cropping Pattern** High incentives for MSP and FRP as well as subsidised power have led to cropping of rice and sugarcane even in the water-scarce region of Marathwada, Western Rajasthan, etc. This doesn't allow incentives for farmers to diversify their crop to less water consuming more profitable horticulture products using drip irrigation.
  - As per a NABARD-ICRIER study on Water Productivity Mapping, rice and sugarcane alone consume almost 60 % of India's irrigation water.
  - There is a need to realign cropping patterns based on per unit of applied irrigation water productivity.
- **Imbalanced Use of Fertilisers due to Subsidy Regime** While the ideal NPK ratio is 4:2:1, the present ratio in Punjab and Haryana is 25:5:1. This skewed pricing doesn't incentivise farmers to minimise their consumption of urea using techniques like fertigation (dissolving fertiliser in drip irrigation).
  - The resultant imbalance in fertiliser use is polluting ground and surface water, affecting crop yield, leading to deterioration in soil health and is adversely impacting the environment.

- **Low-income Level of Farmers** 86% of farmers in India are small and marginal and earn on an average ₹ 6,426 per month as per the 2016 NSSO report. This hinders the huge investment needed for the mechanisation of irrigation.
- **Low Awareness** Farmers are not aware of new irrigation methods of using them and the budget for extension services is very limited.

Futuristic Measures

- **Agriculture expert Ashok Gulati** has recommended Switch from the highly subsidised price policy of water/power (and even fertilisers) to direct income support on a per hectare basis and investment policies that help with newer technologies and innovations. Water and power need to be priced as per their economic value or at least to recover a significant part of their costs to ensure sustainable agriculture.
- **A direct Cash Transfer to Farmers for Irrigation Machinery Subsidy** Experts suggest a gradual transition towards direct cash transfer of subsidy, instead of routing it through companies.
- **Recommendations of Committee on Doubling Farmers' Income headed by Ashok Dalwai** RandD should aim at developing and designing scale-neutral irrigation and other machinery. Further, machinery that can suit different terrain of geography deserves priority attention.
- **Awareness among farmers through the use of KVK and Kisan Mitra** for maintenance and operation of these new irrigation techniques
- **Small irrigation machinery/implements (individually operated)** need to be promoted keeping in view the versatility of various crops, cropping patterns and agriculture operations.
- **Need innovation in custom hiring service** or a rental model by the institutionalisation of high-cost irrigation machinery to reduce the cost of operation.
- The **use of FPOs should be supported** to include modern systems like drones, sensor-based applications, family drip irrigation (Israel water technique)

Micro-irrigation and Pradhan Mantri Krishi Sinchayee Yojana

Q.12 Promotion of micro-irrigation in India serves two major objectives-tackle the growing water crisis and improving agricultural productivity, but its penetration in India remains sub-optimal. Critically examine. Also, examine the performance of Pradhan Mantri Krishi Sinchayee Yojana (PMKSY) in this regard. (250 Words, 15 Marks)

Ans. **Introduction** India has only 4% of world's water resources while accounting for 18% of world's population. This causes a stark gap in the demand-supply of water resources, leading to already water-stressed situation. In addition to this, as per the NITI Aayog, around 600 million Indians are facing high-to extreme water stress and the situation is set to worsen as water requirements increase. According to the most recent Central Groundwater Board data, as many as 256 of 700 districts in India have reported 'critical' or 'over-exploited' groundwater levels.

As per Ministry of Jal Shakti, 87% of groundwater is used to meet the requirements of irrigation in agriculture and thus, adoption of micro-irrigation is envisaged to deal with the growing water crisis. Micro-irrigation (MI) refers to the techniques such as drip irrigation, sprinkler, rain-gun, porous pipe system etc where water is supplied directly to the crops and is considered an innovative water saving technology.

Micro-irrigation to Tackle Growing Water Crisis and Improving Agricultural Productivity

- **Water Use Efficiency** It has higher Water Use Efficiency (75-90%) as compared to the traditional flood irrigation methods (35-40%).
  - It helps in significant reduction of water loss due to runoff, evaporation etc. It further aids soil health management and prevents water logging.
  - This is significant for India where agriculture is largely rain-fed and faces vagaries of aberrant monsoons, soil degradation, nutrient deficiencies and declining groundwater table.
- **Energy Efficiency** It can effectively save power due to less water use and thereby reduction in energy requirements for pumping groundwater. Hence, this ensures energy consumption saving up to 30.5%.

- **Fertiliser Use Efficiency** Proper mixing of fertilisers and water, control of optimum dosage and direct application of fertilisers to the root zone result in the saving in fertiliser consumption up to 28.5%. This is significant for India where food and fertiliser gets highest subsidy allocation and non-judicious application of fertiliser is reducing soil fertility in many regions.
- **Increase in Productivity** It increases the crop yield (quantity and quality). Increasing population and water scarcity demands increased productivity in the long run. An increase in productivity would also support doubling farmers' income. For instance, the average productivity of fruits and vegetables has increased about 42.3% and 52.8%, respectively mainly because of crop spacing, judicious use of water and other inputs etc.
- **Irrigation Cost Saving** It will reduce the overall cost of irrigation in long-term due to decrease in labour requirement for irrigation, land-levelling, weeding and fertiliser application. Irrigation cost saving is up to 31.9%.
- **New Crop Introduction** An improved water scenario helps in addition to new crops or promotes inter-cropping. Moreover, the reduction in spacing between the plants helps in accommodating more numbers of plants.
- **Infrastructure Development** Infrastructure of MI systems can be created in months unlike other systems where it takes years to develop infrastructure such as dams, canals, etc.
- **Less Labour Requirement** With low growth of unwanted plants (weed), micro-irrigation needs less labour requirement and thus reduction in input cost.
- **Dryland Farming** It will facilitate cultivation in dryland areas, thus correcting agricultural production disparity between various regions of the country.

In order to promote micro-irrigation, the government has taken various steps in India. They are as follows:

- Early adoption of **National Mission on Micro Irrigation Programme**, which is now being implemented as 'Per Drop more **Crop' component under Pradhan Mantri Krishi Sinchayee Yojana**. Under it, financial assistance is available for farmers for adoption of micro irrigation system.
- A dedicated micro irrigation fund with NABARD under PMKSY has been set up.
- Partnership with countries such as Israel with the objective of sharing best practices and technical knowledge.
- Further, various steps have been taken by government for promotion of micro-irrigation include such as training and awareness programmes, organisation of workshops, seminars and interactive meetings, publicity creation through exhibitions, fairs and Kisan Melas and short duration films.

Following Challenges Exist in its Widespread Adoption

A study by FICCI and Irrigation of India reveals that only 7.73 million hectares of land were covered under micro-irrigation, compared to a potential of 69.5 million hectares. Six states- Rajasthan, Maharashtra andhra Pradesh, Karnataka, Gujarat and Haryana account for over 82% of India's micro-irrigation coverage. Thus, penetration of micro-irrigation is highly skewed and far below potential especially in a country like India which is a water-stressed economy.

There exists various challenges in the adoption of micro-irrigation techniques:

- **High Initial Cost** The cost of initial setup is too high which is not feasible for over 86% Indian farmers who are small and marginal.
- **Energy Crisis** Power outages, voltage fluctuations and unscheduled interruptions exist across rural and urban India which is a major deterrent in the adoption of irrigation systems.
- **Policy Concerns**
  - Delays in subsidy disbursement largely because of approving installation of equipment when funds for subsidy aren't yet available.
  - GST rate on drip irrigation systems exists at 12%.
  - Widespread private investment is missing.
- **Failure of the State Governments** for the ineffective implementation of the scheme and underutilisation of funds.
- **Technical Support** There is lack in support for maintenance (for example, rodent attack on piping, pore-clogging) and operation.
- **Declining Landholdings and Farm Income** Another impediment to the adoption of micro-irrigation is even more alarming because the data on India's operational landholdings shows that the average size of landholdings have halved since the 1960s. The declining size of landholdings impacts farm incomes and farm income is closely associated with the capability of the farmer to adopt expensive micro-irrigation systems.

Critical Analysis of PMKSY in Promoting Micro-irrigation

- **Financial Support** PMKSY provides financial assistance and subsidies to farmers for installing micro-irrigation systems. This support helps alleviate the financial burden associated with the initial investment and encourages farmers to adopt these water-saving techniques.
  - Up to 55% is available for small and marginal farmers and 45% for other farmers for adoption of micro-irrigation systems.
- **Awareness and Capacity Building** Information Communication Technology (ICT) interventions through the National e-Governance Plan in Agriculture (NeGP-A) to be made use of in the fields of water use efficiency and precision irrigation technologies. These efforts are crucial in bridging the knowledge gap and increasing awareness among farmers.
- **Focus on Water-use Efficiency** PMKSY recognises the importance of water-use efficiency in agriculture and highlights micro-irrigation as a key tool to achieve it. By promoting the adoption of micro-irrigation systems, the PMKSY aims to reduce water wastage, improve water-use efficiency and address water stress in agriculture.

However, there are certain areas, which requires further attention

- **Implementation and Monitoring** While the PMKSY provides financial support for micro-irrigation, the effective implementation and monitoring of the scheme at the ground level remain crucial. It is important to ensure that the benefits reach the intended beneficiaries and that the funds are utilised appropriately.
- **Integrated Approach** The PMKSY should adopt an integrated approach that combines micro-irrigation with other water management practices. This includes promoting watershed development, rainwater harvesting and efficient water distribution systems to ensure comprehensive and sustainable water management in agriculture.
- **Maintenance and Sustainability** Adequate attention should be given to the maintenance and sustainability of micro-irrigation systems. Farmers need support in terms of maintenance training, availability of spare parts and troubleshooting assistance to ensure the long-term viability and effectiveness of the systems.
- **Monitoring of Outcomes** It is crucial to monitor the outcomes of micro-irrigation adoption under the PMKSY. This includes assessing the impact on water savings, crop productivity and farmer income.

  Regular evaluation and feedback mechanisms can help identify any shortcomings and guide improvements in the implementation of the scheme.

Conclusion

While the PMKSY has taken positive steps in promoting micro-irrigation adoption, there are areas that require further attention to ensure the scheme's success. By focusing on effective implementation, reaching out to small farmers, adopting an integrated approach, addressing maintenance and sustainability concerns and monitoring outcomes, the PMKSY can enhance its impact in promoting micro-irrigation and efficient water use in agriculture.

Agriculture Credit and Insurance

Q.13 Availability and access to adequate, timely and low cost credit from institutional sources is of great importance to the farmers. Elaborate. Also, explain the mechanisms and agencies for agricultural credit in India. (250 Words, 15 Marks)

Ans. **Introduction** The need for agriculture credit is important when it moves from traditional agriculture to modern agriculture. The capacity of farmers to save and invest is very low. The farmers, therefore, need credit to increase productivity and efficiency in agriculture. This need is increasing over the years with the rise in the use of fertilisers, mechanization and overall increased costs of production.

Credit to agriculture, which was just about 20% of the sectoral GDP in the 1990s, grew to 51% in 2018. In the last five years, the increase was about 10% as per RBI's internal working group on agricultural credit. Economic Survey states that only 40.90% of small and marginal farmers could be covered by banks despite priority sector lending thus hindering the development of agriculture as around 86% of the farmers belong to small and marginal farmers who contribute more than 60% of the total food production.

Additional Facts

- **Institutional vs Non-Institutional Sources** The average loan taken by agricultural households indicated that 72% of the credit requirement was met through institutional sources and 28% from non-institutional sources.
- **Scheduled commercial banks contributed the major share (78 – 80 per cent) in agricultural and allied credit** The share of all co-operative banks/institutions (i.e. StCBs, DCCBs and PACS put together) constituted 15-16 per cent. RRBs contributed the remaining 5 per cent of the agricultural credit.
- **Crop loan accounts for more than 90 per cent of the total agricultural credit** though its contribution to total output is approx. 60 per cent which means that the allied sector gets only 10 per cent of total credit while contributing the remaining 40 per cent of the total output. The proportion of short-term crop loans to crop-related investment credit from 51:49 in the year 2000, drastically changed to 75:25 in 2018.

Importance of Farm Credit

- **Purchase of Inputs** Farmers need short-term finance to meet the cropping requirements like seeds, fertilisers, labour and other seasonal expenditure.
- **Improving Productivity** They also need long-term finance for land improvements, creation of irrigation facilities and purchase of farm machinery and equipment.
- **Small and Marginal farmers (86%)** dominate the Indian agriculture which generally don't have surplus to purchase the inputs or make any land improvements.
- **Adoption of New Technology** Credit encourages the farmers to adopt new technologies such as HYV seeds at the time of Green Revolution. This results in increasing productivity.
- **Shift Towards High-value Crops** Credit can help in the shift of cropping pattern towards high-value crops which can boost India's agricultural exports.

Mechanism for Agricultural Credit in India

Post-independence government has realized the importance of agricultural credit and has taken many steps like the establishment of the National Credit Council, bank nationalisation, etc as of now, the following are major mechanisms available for agricultural credit in India.

- **Banking and Regulatory Reforms** Nationalisation of scheduled commercial banks that increased the bank branches in rural areas, emergence of Regional Rural Banks in 1976, launch of Lead banks scheme, regulatory reforms like 1:3 bank branch expansion, etc improved the agricultural credit in India.
  - As per Priority Sector Lending targets banks are required to achieve an agriculture target of 18% and a sub-target of 8% of Adjusted Net Bank Credit (ANBC) for small and marginal farmers.
- **Interest Subvention Scheme (ISS)** was launched for short term crop loans in 2006-07. 2% interest subvention is given to farmers, which is reimbursed to banks (through RBI and NABARD). Additionally, a 3% prompt repayment incentive (PRI) is provided for good credit discipline.
  - Interest subvention is also available on loan against negotiable warehouse receipts issued on the produce stored in warehouses accredited with Warehousing Development Regulatory Authority (WDRA).
- **Kisan Credit Card (KCC) Scheme** introduced in 1998, aimed at providing adequate and timely credit with a flexible and simplified procedure for agriculture-related and also consumption requirements of farmer households. It got expanded in 2004 to meet the investment credit requirement of the farmers.
- **Self-Help Group-Bank Linkage Programme (SHG-BLP)** aimed at harnessing the flexibility of an informal system with the strength and affordability of a formal system. The SHG-BLP model accepted informal groups as clients of banks – both deposit and credit linkage and allowed collateral-free lending to groups.
- **Joint Liability Groups (JLG) Scheme** was initiated by **NABARD** in 2006 to enhance credit flow to sharecroppers/tenant farmers who do not have land rights.

Direct Agricultural Credit as Percentage of Agricultural GDP (at current prices)

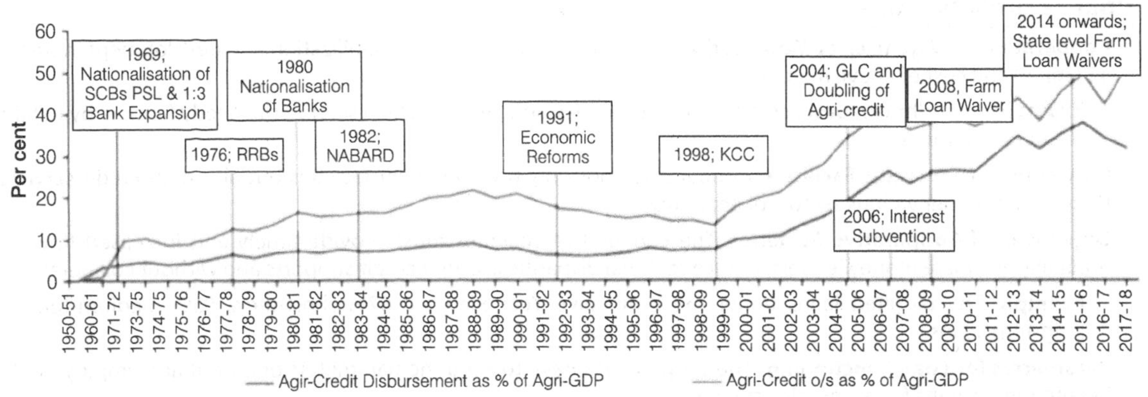

Agencies for Agricultural Credit in India

- The **Cooperative Credit Societies Act 1904** and a more comprehensive Cooperative Societies Act of 1912 were passed and provincial cooperative banks were established in almost all major provinces. During the period between 1935 and 1950, the Reserve Bank (having a separate agricultural credit department) was very active in continuing the attempt to reinvigorate the cooperative credit movement through a variety of initiatives. Besides providing financial accommodation to the cooperative movement, the RBI played a central role in the task of building the cooperative credit structure.
- The nationalisation of fourteen of India's largest scheduled commercial banks in 1969, radically changed the situation. The Banking Companies (Acquisition and Transfer of Undertakings) Act, 1969 which empowered nationalisation refers to commercial banks' 'larger social purpose' and the need to sub-serve national priorities and objectives such as rapid growth of agriculture. The RBI played a proactive role in expansion of bank branches to unbanked areas. In 1970, the RBI formulated its first 'socially coercive' licensing criterion requiring that for every new branch in the already banked area, each bank should open at least three in unbanked rural or semi-urban areas.
- In 1976, the Regional Rural Banks (RRBs) were created to develop the rural economy by providing 'credit and other facilities, particularly to small and marginal farmers, agricultural labourers, artisans and small entrepreneurs'. The RRBs were created especially to address the credit needs of weaker sections in rural areas which were often overlooked by cooperatives and commercial banks.

Conclusion

With the establishment of RRBs, there emerged three separate type of institutions viz. commercial banks, cooperatives and RRBs for providing rural credit, which is often described as 'multi-agency approach'. Post-economic reforms, microfinance has also witnessed a growth through the micro-finance institutions and SHG-Bank linkage model.

Role of Cooperative Society in Agricultural Credit

Q.14 "In the villages itself no form of credit organisation will be suitable except the cooperative society." – All Indian rural credit survey. Discuss this statement in the background of agriculture finance in India. What constraints and challenges do financial institutions supplying agricultural finances? How can technology be used to better reach and serve rural clients? **UPSC Mains PYQ 2014**

Ans. **Introduction** Agricultural finance is given priority since planning in 1950's and through nationalisation of banks along with priority sector lending. But the role played by the cooperative society in the villages as credit organisation is worthy.

Co-operative societies is the most suitable form of credit organisation among the agricultural finance organisations

- **Cooperatives as Agencies of Mobilisation** These stand as agencies of mobilization and development in rural areas in a planned and cost effective manner.
  - **Example** In Andhra Pradesh, credit cooperatives play an effective role in serving the needy farmers by fulfilling their credit requirements.
- **Provision of Non-credit Facilities** Cooperatives not only provide credit facilities but also non- credit services for all the activities under various sectors of economy.
- **Objectives of Cooperative Societies** The cooperative societies must provide timely and increased flow of credit, gradually eliminate money lenders, reduce regional disparities, longer credit supports and without collateral.
  - **Example** The targeted loans under the Ninth Five Year Plan are 67% short-term, 95% medium-term, 40-60% long-term loans.
- **Parameters for Loan Sanctioning** The cooperatives have to keep the parameters of output and employment growth in sanctioning loans for economic activities.
- **Credit Policy of Cooperatives** Credit flow to farm sector be increased by 30% every year, debt restructuring of loans over 5 years outstanding, new investment in agriculture at 2-3 projects/branch.

Issues with the Agricultural Credit

- **Inherent Risks Associated with the Agriculture** Agriculture has certain inherent risks like yield risk, market risk and nature risk. This is aggravated because of low irrigation coverage and inadequate insurance coverage of the farmers. This makes agriculture a risky business and therefore, commercial banks are generally reluctant to give loans to this sector despite priority sector lending requirements.
  - Climate change is further exacerbating the risks in Indian agriculture.
- According to the **National All India Rural Financial Inclusion Survey (NAFIS 2015)**, the share of non- institutional credit still persists at around 28%. Unavailability of credit for consumption purposes and to tenant farmers, sharecroppers and landless labourers, who are not able to offer collateral security, further pushes them towards non-institutional sources.
- **Skewed agency share in institutional credit** as dependency on scheduled commercial banks in agricultural and allied credit is still large (~78-80% of the credit). Though co-operative institutions (~15%) and Regional Rural Banks (~5%) play a significant role in extending agricultural credit, their share is highly skewed geographically.
- **Poor deployment of agricultural credit to allied sectors** (~6-7%) despite a share of 38-42% in the agricultural output indicates neglect of allied sectors by the banks. Though at the aggregate level banks have been able to achieve the overall PSL target of 40%, so far they have failed to achieve the agriculture target of 18% at a system-wide level.
- **Interest Subvention Scheme (ISS)** on short term loans have skewed distribution of agricultural credit in favour of production credit against crop-related investment credit, which is important for long- term sustainability of the agriculture sector. As per Agricultural Census 2015-16, only 45% of the farmers possess operative KCCs. Agricultural households are unable to get credit for their consumption requirements from and hence, they are compelled to go to money lenders. Existing 10% limit in the KCC scheme for consumption requirements is inadequate.
- **Overemphasis of Monetary Credit** The rural credit institutions have given overemphasis on the financial assistance to the cultivators. While the finance is very important factor but it should be complemented with the extension of services in form of guidance, expertise and counseling on agricultural issues.
- **Multiplicity of Institutions** Agricultural credit structure is based on multi agency credit system (Scheduled commercial banks, cooperative institutions, regional rural banks, etc) whereby there exist numerous organisations providing similar kind of financial services. There is a lack of coordination in the system and the commercial viability is adversely affected in this scenario.
- **Financial Exclusion** Despite of a large network of the institutional credit system, it has not been able to adequately penetrate the informal rural financial markets and the non-institutional sources continue to play a dominant role in purveying the credit needs of the people residing in rural areas.
- **High Interest Rates** The rate of interest charged by rural financial institutions (RFIs) from farmers continues to be considerably higher than those charged by financial institutions from urban consumers. The owners of small or marginal farms, which are non-viable or viable at the margin and self-employed in the informal sector, cannot afford to bear the level of interest charged by RFIs.

- **Procedural Delays** There is a problem of considerable delays in processing of loan applications and collaterals. Thus, farmers shy away from institutional financing and increase their dependency upon non-institutional sources.
- **Poor Recoveries** Banks are shying away from agricultural financing mainly because of poor recoveries which is inflicting the system. It is ironical that the recoveries position is adverse amongst rich farmers than amongst the small farmers. The political decisions of waiving off loans are further putting pressures on the financial system.
- Cooperatives still face various issues such as lack of autonomy, politicisation and inadequate resources. Thus, it has not been much successful in addressing the needs of rural credit.

Usage of Technology to better Reach and Serve Rural Clients In Agricultural Finance

- **Low Cost and Pervasive Connectivity** Technology can provide for the better reach of information regarding financial issues etc.
- **Accurate Evaluation** Farmer's field can be evaluated accurately by which financial services can be provided to them.
- **Risk management Tool** ICT can be used as a risk-management tool and promotes trust in food value chain.
- **Lowered Operation Costs** As ICT will be used for coordinated efforts, it will reduce the operation costs of getting loans from financial institutions.
- **Provides Wider Market Access** As farmers with integrated market access, it will provide for better financial services.

Futuristic Measures

The measures to address the challenges of agricultural credit can be dealt via taking steps under two major heads:

Improve the Reach of Institutional Credit

- Digitisation of Land Records
- Land Leasing Framework
- Federal Institution in Agriculture
- Technology driven solutions to reduce financial exclusion
- Collaboration of banks with agri-tech startups
- Awareness drives by State Government for land consolidation
- Separate targets for working capital and term loan towards allied activities

Inclusiveness and Innovation

- Revisiting of PSL guidelines for improving credit offtake and increased allocation of RIDF to in Central, Eastern and North-Eastern states
- Increased subtargets for small and marginal farmers
- Replace interest subvention scheme with DBT to targeted beneficiaries
- Reforms in KCC
- Financing Model by NABARD for FPOs especially women specific FPOs

Conclusion

Agriculture finance must be provided in an effective way by addressing the challenges such as lack of information, regional disparities etc. This provides for efficient development of agriculture which supports around 46% of employment.

Direct Income Support and Farm Loan Waivers

Q.15 To what extent, government interventions like farm loan waivers or direct income support to farmers can help in addressing agricultural indebtedness. Examine. (150 Words, 10 Marks)

Ans. **Introduction** With high levels of resource deprivation where farmers suffer low and unviable farming, regularly fighting volatile commodity prices, rising costs of inputs, fierce and uncertain impacts of weather and climatic changes, agrarian distress is seen in every corner of India.

To mitigate the issue of agricultural indebtedness, Central Government and State Government announces relief measure in the form of Loan waiver or Direct benefit transfer (PM KISAN by central Government, Odisha's KALIA, Telangana Rhythu Bandhu) etc.

About Farm Loan Waivers

- Farm loan waivers, though not a recent phenomenon, have seen an unprecedented increase since 2014-15 driven by State Governments. Around 10 State Governments have announced farm loan waivers since 2014-15.
- The first major programme on farm loan waiver, viz., Agriculture and Rural Debt Relief Scheme, 1990 (ARDRS), was undertaken in 1990 at the nationwide level, followed by another nationwide loan waiver in 2008, viz., Agricultural Debt Waiver and Debt Relief Scheme, 2008 (ADWDRS).

PM-KISAN

- It is a 100% Central sector scheme under which financial benefits of ₹ 6000 per year in three equal instalments, every four month is transferred into the bank accounts of farmers' families across the country through Direct Benefit Transfer (DBT) mode.

Rationale behind Farm Loan Waiver or Direct Income Support

- **Low Capita Income** Farmers in India are generally poorer than others in the economy. In 2015-16, India's per capita annual income was about ₹ 94,797 (NAS), while farmer's earns per capita average income of about ₹ 21,872, which was lower than a quarter of the national per capita income.
- **Small Land Holding** More than 86% of small and marginal farmers in India possess less than 1-2 hectares of holdings and lack basic inputs for farming.
- **Dependency on Monsoon** In India, the crop yield and production are highly dependent on monsoon as only 48% of the cultivated area is under irrigation coverage.
- **Need of Credit** In this context, the credit is a critical resource to farming households to purchase inputs for carrying out crop production.
- **Debt Trap** Farmers invest heavily in crops by taking loans. If the crop fails due to lack of rains or insufficient market demand, farmers will get trapped in debt. Due to this, there has been an increase in farmer suicides. (NCRB 2021 data says, farmers suicides comprise 7% of the suicides in the country).
- **Stability and Predictability** Direct Income Support can offer stability and predictability in income, ensuring a safety net during periods of agrarian distress. It can help in addressing the income volatility faced by farmers due to fluctuating crop prices, weather conditions and market uncertainties.
- **Income Diversification** It can allow farmers to diversify their income sources beyond agriculture, promoting entrepreneurship, off-farm employment and other non-agricultural activities. This diversification can reduce their dependency on a single income stream and make them more resilient to agrarian distress.
- **Targeted Support** It can be structured to target vulnerable farmers, ensuring that the benefits reach those most in need. By providing a steady income floor, it can assist small and marginalised farmers who may not have access to credit or face challenges in loan repayment.

Agriculture in India has been facing many issues i.e., fragmented land holding, depleting water table levels, deteriorating soil quality, rising input costs, low productivity. Output prices may not be remunerative. Farmers are often forced to borrow to manage expenses. Indebtedness is a key reason for the many farmer suicides in the country. Such interventions can provide some relief to farmers in such situations.

Farm Loan Waiver (FLW)/Direct income Support is not a long-term solution to Indian agrarian distress

- **Financial Sustainability** Implementing a minimum basic income/farm loan waiver for farmers on a large scale can pose significant financial challenges for the government.
  - This may result in reduced funding for other critical sectors such as education, healthcare and infrastructure development.
- **Lack of Targeting** Ensuring effective targeting of a minimum basic income scheme is crucial to prevent the misallocation of resources.
  - In practice, it can be challenging to accurately identify and exclude relatively well-off farmers who may not require additional income support. Even farm loan waivers benefits mainly those farmers who have taken loans from the formal sources which are mainly medium and large farmers.
  - As per RBI Report, only 40% of small and marginal farmers receives formal credit.

- **Promotes Corruption** Discrepancies were found in 22% of the loan waiver cases- Public Accounts Committee Report. Corruption, errors in inclusion and exclusion of beneficiaries, inadequate documentation, unused funds lying with lending institutions and ineffective monitoring are rampant.
  - As of March 2022, the poorest implementation of farm loan waiver schemes in terms of proportion of eligible farmers who had received the announced benefits, were in Telangana (5%), Madhya Pradesh (12%), Jharkhand (13%), Punjab (24%), Karnataka (38%) and Uttar Pradesh (52%).
- **Distorted Incentives** Critics argue that providing a guaranteed minimum income may undermine the motivation for farmers to strive for higher productivity and explore alternative income sources.
  - For instance, a study Published in the Journal of Development Economics found that cash transfers to farmers in Indonesia resulted in reduced labour supply in agriculture, as individuals allocated more time to leisure activities instead.
  - This raises concerns about the potential impact on agricultural productivity and overall economic growth.
- **Inadequate Debt Relief** While a minimum basic income provides stability and income security, it may not directly address the pressing issue of existing debt burdens faced by farmers.
  - In contrast, farm loan waivers offer immediate debt relief to farmers in distress.
  - However, it is important to note that farm loan waivers too do not address the root causes of indebtedness or provide long-term solutions.
- **FLW incentivises Wilful Defaulters** It disrupts credit discipline. Farmers turn into wilful defaulters due to the next loan waiver scheme, which is bad for economy.
- **Long-term Sustainability** Both minimum basic income and farm loan waivers can be seen as short-term measures that may not address the structural challenges in the agricultural sector.
- For example, improving access to credit, enhancing agricultural productivity through technology and innovation and creating a robust marketing infrastructure are essential for the long-term sustainability of the farming community.
- Neglecting these aspects in favor of income support measures may not result in a transformative change in the sector.

Conclusion

In conclusion, while minimum basic income and farm loan waivers may provide temporary relief to farmers in distress, there are valid concerns regarding financial sustainability, targeting efficiency, distorted incentives and the need for comprehensive long-term solutions.

A balanced approach that addresses the root causes of agrarian distress, such as market reforms, investment in infrastructure, agricultural diversification and access to credit, can complement income support measures and contribute to the sustainable development of the agricultural sector.

Crop Insurance

Q.16 Given the vulnerability of Indian agriculture to vagaries of nature, discuss the need for crop insurance and bring out the salient features of the Pradhan Mantri Fasal Bima Yojana (PMFBY). (150 Words, 10 Marks)

UPSC Mains PYQ 2016

Ans. **Introduction** Agriculture insurance is an important part of the safety net for farmers especially in the context of climate change, to deal with the impacts of extreme, uncertain and unseasonal weather patterns.

PMFBY is the flagship agriculture insurance scheme being implemented by the Union Government. It was launched in 2016 by the Ministry of Agriculture. The aim of the scheme is to provide comprehensive insurance cover to the farmers against failure of crops and help in stabilizing the income of farmers. The Scheme covers food crops, oilseed crops, commercial and horticulture crops.

PMFBY was more farmer-friendly provisions than its predecessors. It reduced the burden of premium on farmers significantly and expanded coverage. It also promoted use of advanced technologies to estimate losses accurately and accelerate payments to farmers.

Rationale of Crop Insurance

- **Rainfed Agriculture** Around 48% of the cultivated area is irrigated and thus, it makes Indian agriculture risky and prone to crop failure.
- **Technological Advancement** Farmers can go new technology adoption due to this insurance.
- **Climate Change and Crop Failures** Protects the crop yield especially in the wake of climate change.
- **Stability in Income** It protects the farmers against losses caused by crop failure. It acts like a tool that allows farmers to manage their yield and price risks. This can help in dealing with farmer's indebtedness.
  - Economic Survey (ES) 2018 estimated income losses of 15-18% (for irrigated farm) and 20-25% (for unirrigated farm) due to negative impacts of climate change (higher temperature, erratic rains).

Providing financial support to farmers suffering crop loss/damage arising out of unforeseen events
Stabilising the income of farmers to ensure their continuance in farming
Encouraging farmers to adopt innovative and modern agricultural practices
Ensuring credit worthiness of the farmers, crop diversification and enhancing growth and competitiveness of agriculture sector besides protecting the farmers from production risks.

- **Need of credit** from formal financial institutions.
- **Yield Protection** Crop Insurance protects farmers against production loss for crops. It also offers preventive planting and replant security.
- **Minimal Debts** Farmers are able to repay their loans even during the time of crop failure with the support of the right insurance partner.
- **Provides Awareness** Insurance companies provide awareness campaigns to help farmers understand the effect of natural calamities and also protect their farms.

Salient Features of Pradhan Mantri Fasal Bima Yojana (PMBFY)

- **Coverage of Farmers** The scheme covers loanee farmers (those who have taken a loan), non-loanee farmers (on a voluntary basis), tenant farmers and sharecroppers.
- **Coverage of Crops** Every state has notified crops (major crops) for the Rabi and Kharif seasons. The premium rates differ across seasons.
- **Premium Rates** The PMFBY fixes a uniform premium of 2% of the sum insured, to be paid by farmers for all Kharif crops, 1.5% of the sum insured for all Rabi crops and 5% of sum insured for annual commercial and horticultural crops.
- **Coverage of Risks** It aims to prevent sowing/planting risks, loss to standing crop, post-harvest losses and localised calamities.
- **Innovative Technology Use** It recommends the use of technology in agriculture. For example, using drones to reduce the use of Crop Cutting experiments (CCEs), which are traditionally used to estimate crop loss and using mobile phones to reduce delays in claim settlements by uploading crop-cutting data on apps/online.

Pradhan Mantri Fasal Bima Yojana (PMBFY) 2.0

- **Completely Voluntary** Enrolment 100% voluntary for all farmers from 2020 Kharif.
- **Limit to Central Subsidy** The Cabinet has decided to cap the Centre's premium subsidy under the scheme for premium rates up to 30% for unirrigated areas/crops and 25% for irrigated areas/crops.
- **More Flexibility to States** The government has given the flexibility to states/UTs to implement PMFBY and given them the option to select any number of additional risk covers/features.
- **Investing in ICE Activities** Insurance companies have to now spend 0.5% of the total premium collected on information, education and communication (IEC) activities.
- **Use of Technology under PMFBY** Crop Insurance App, use of latest technological tools such as satellite imagery, drones, machine learning and PMFBY portal for integration of land record. Example: Crop Insurance App: Provides for easy enrolment of farmers and facilitate easier reporting of crop loss within 72 hours of occurrence of any event. PMFBY Portal: For integration of land records.

Conclusion

However, there are some issues with regard to exclusion of sharecroppers and tenant farmers, delayed payments by insurance companies and building awareness among farmers which needs to be tackled to make PMFBY truly effective and protect farming in a warming world.

Analysis of Pradhan Mantri Fasal Bima Yojana (PMFBY)

Q.17 "Delay in the processing of claims and lack of co-ordination among stakeholders are becoming major hindrances for the implementation of Pradhan Mantri Fasal Bima Yojana (PMFBY)". Critically comment. Also, suggest measures for its effective implementation. (250 Words, 15 Marks)

Ans. Introduction Recently Andhra Pradesh has decided to rejoin the crop insurance scheme Pradhan Mantri Fasal Bima Yojana (PMFBY) from the ongoing kharif season. Andhra Pradesh was one of six states that have stopped implementation of the scheme over the last four years.

Positives of PMFBY

- It is the largest crop insurance scheme globally in terms of farmer participation and third largest in terms of the premium.
- The scheme covers over 5.5 crore farmer applications on average per year.
- Aadhaar seeding (linking Aadhaar through Internet banking portals) has helped in speedy claim settlement directly into the farmer accounts.
- One notable example is mid-season adversity claims of nearly ₹ 30 crore in Rajasthan during Rabi 2019-20 Locust attack.

Challenges in the Implementation of PMFBY

Data from the PMFBY dashboard show that since 2016, there has been a 62% decrease in farmers covered under crop insurance during kharif season to 15.1 million in 2021 and 46% decrease during rabi to 9.2 million in 2021. Area insured has also reduced 57% under kharif crops and 22% under rabi crops. This is mainly because of various issues at the level of states and insurance companies.

Issues from the Central and State Governments (Observations by Parliamentary Standing Committee)

- **Participation of States** The Committee noted that some revisions in the scheme guidelines may lead state governments to withdraw from it. Example: Centre limiting the subsidy upto 30% of the premium increased the fiscal burden on states and therefore, many stated withdraw from the scheme. Since the launch, 6 states have opted out of the scheme viz., Gujarat, Bihar, West Bengal andhra Pradesh (joining back), Telangana and Jharkhand while Punjab had never joined.
- **Technological Interventions** The Committee noted that yield-related disputes and delayed transmission of yield data are a major reason for delays in settlement of claims. It noted that this data is provided by State Governments based on crop cutting experiments which are highly time consuming and labour intensive.
- **Grievance Redressal** The Committee noted that only 15 States and Union Territories have notified Grievance Redressal Committees at both the state and district level, as mandated under the scheme.
- **Corporate Social Responsibility (CSR)** The Committee noted that the scheme does not mandate insurance companies to spend the share of their profits going towards CSR in the districts from where profits are earned.

Issue from the Insurance Companies

- **Delayed Pay-outs and Denial of Claims** Parliamentary Standing Committee recognised delays in settlement of insurance claims as one of the biggest challenges in implementation of the scheme. There are frequent disputes related to compensation. Farmers complain the compensation paid by insurance companies is less than the losses. There are long delays in payments, sometimes up to 18 months. Yield-related disputes, delayed transmission of yield data and delay in release of their share in premium subsidy by State Governments are the major reasons for delays in settlement of claims.
- **High Premiums** Insurance companies tend to charge high premiums in order to ensure that claims do not exceed premiums collected. This is more common in areas more prone to crop loss.
- **Awareness Activities** The Committee noted that farmers who have taken loans may opt out of the scheme by submitting a declaration form. However, due to lack of awareness, several farmers do not submit the requisite form and face mandatory deduction of premium from their bank accounts.

- **Local Offices** The Committee observed that insurance companies are required to have a functioning office in each tehsil. However, they are non-existent in several districts.
- **Opposition from Farm Leaders** Farm leaders claim insurance companies have made windfall gains at the behest of the public exchequer and farmers. Data from Maharashtra show that Insurance companies often earn more in premiums than paid in claims. However, for some years the trend is opposite.

Suggestions to Improve the Performance of PMFBY

- Union Government should consult with State Governments and explore the possibility of replicating the Beed Model in the PMFBY.
  - Beed Model was first experimented in Beed district of Maharashtra in 2020. Under this model, insurance companies provide cover to an extent of 110% of the premium collected. In case the claims exceed this amount, the State government will bridge the extra amount. In case the compensation amount is less than the premium collected, the company will refund 80% premium surplus (gross premium – surplus) to the State Government and keep 20% for its administrative expenses.

Working of the Beed Model

(Beed Model is also called 80-110 Model and balances the interest companies and the government)

Claims Exceed Premiums	Premiums Exceed Claims
• Premiums Collected INR 100 Claims INR 125	• Premiums Collected INR 100 Claims INR 60
• Claims Paid by Insurance Company INR 110	• Premium Surplus INR 40
• Amount Paid by the State Government INR 15 (Bridge Amount)	• Premium Surplus retained by Insurance Company 20%* INR 40 = INR 8
	• Premium Surplus returned to the Government INR 32 (Created by Formulas)

- **Rationalising Waivers and Service Delivery** Loan waiver schemes announced by state governments along with mandatory Aadhaar linkage should be rationalised to enable PMFBY of greater coverage.
- **Enable Timely Compensation** There has been reports of delayed compensation by some of the states.
- **Bringing Behavioural Change** A lot more needs to be done in bringing about a behavioural change regarding the cost of insurance being a necessary input and not a money-back investment.
- **Streamlining with Similar Schemes** PMFBY needs to be streamlined with state crop insurance schemes and schemes like Restructured Weather Based Crop Insurance Scheme to include more risk areas not covered under them.
- **Proper Implementation** Successful implementation of PMFBY is an essential benchmark in agricultural reform in India to make farmers self-sufficient in times of crisis and support the creation of an Aatmanirbhar Kisan.
- Farmers must be informed before deducting crop insurance premium. They must be given a proper insurance policy document, with all relevant details.
- Panchayati Raj Institutions and farmers need to be involved at different stages of implementation.
- Robust assessment of crop loss should be done through capacity building of State Governments, involvement of PRIs and farmers in loss assessment, auditing and multi-level checking to ensure credibility of data and testing incorporating technology such as remote sensing, drones and online transmission of data.
- Robust scheme monitoring and grievance redressal mechanism should be in place.
- Disputes related to yields should be addressed by enhancing quality of yield data and making it readily available. State Government should also be prompt in release of their share of premium subsidy

Conclusion

Farm insurance is critical to provide income security to the farmers. All the stakeholders including the Union and State Governments along with insurance companies must take appropriate steps to remove all the bottlenecks in the proper implementation of the scheme.

Agricultural Marketing and Storage (Problems in Agricultural Marketing)

Q.18 "Agricultural markets in India are characterized by poor competitiveness, deep segmentation and excessive crowding of the intermediaries." Examine the above statement in the context of impediments faced by farmers in price discovery. (250 Words, 15 Marks)

Ans. Introduction Agricultural marketing comprises all operations involved in the movement of farm produce from the producer to the ultimate consumer.

- It includes the operations such as collecting, grading, processing, preserving, transportation and financing.
- The actors in product marketing include farmers, traders, wholesalers, processors, importers, exporters, marketing cooperatives, regulated market committees and retailers.

Presently, India's agricultural markets are regulated by the states under the Agricultural Produce Marketing Committee (APMC) Act.

- Under the APMC Act, the states can establish agricultural markets, popularly known as mandis.
- The sale of agricultural commodities can occur only in the mandis through auction.
- The sales process in mandis is regulated through Commission Agents (CAs) who mediate between the farmers and traders.

The National Commission on Agriculture (1976), as well the National Commission for Farmers (2006), had emphasised that it is not sufficient to produce a crop or animal product; it must be marketed so as to return value to the produced.

Challenges of Agricultural Marketing

- **Limited Access of Agricultural Produce Markets** There is huge variation in the density of regulated markets across the country, varying from 118 sq km. in Punjab to 11,214 sq km in Meghalaya.
- **Market Fragmentation** Monopoly of APMCs in agriculture market reduces buyer competition in comparison to integrated markets, as it limits the geographical range of mandis, number of buyers and sector-specific buyers.
- **Cartelisation** It is quite often seen that agents in an APMC get together to form a cartel and deliberately restraint from higher bidding. Produce is procured at manipulatively discovered price and sold at higher price. Spoils are then shared by participants, leaving farmers in lurch.
- **Entry Barriers** License fee in these markets are highly prohibitive. In many markets farmers were not allowed to operate. Further, over and above license fee, rent/value for shops is quite high which keeps away competition. At most places only a group of village/urban elite operates in APMC.
- **Lack of Market Infrastructure in Agricultural Markets** Cold storage units exist in less than one-tenth of the markets and grading facilities in less than one-third of the markets.
- **High Incidence of Market Fees and Charges** In some states, this works out to total charges of about 15% of the sale produce which is excessive.
- **Large Number of Marketing Channels with Long Supply Chain** With large number of intermediaries between the producers and the consumers, adding up more of costs without adding significant value. All these middlemen and dalals claim a good amount of margin and thus reduce the returns of the cultivators.
- **Lack of Storage Facility** There is no proper storage or warehousing facilities for farmers in the villages where they can store their agriculture produce. Every year 15 to 30% of the agricultural produce are damaged either by rats or rains due to the absence of proper storage facilities.
- **Lack of Transportation** In the absence of proper road transportation facilities in the rural areas, Indian farmers cannot reach nearby mandis to sell their produce at a fair price. Thus, they prefer to sell their produce at the village markets itself.
- **High-post-harvest losses** which amounts to around ₹ 92,000 crore annually.
- **Distress Sale** Most of the Indian farmers are very poor and thus have no capacity to wait for better price of his produce in the absence of proper credit facilities and therefore, farmers go for distress sale.
- **Lack of Market Intelligence** There is absence of market intelligence or information system in India. Indian farmers are not aware of the ruling prices of their produce prevailing in big markets. Thus, they have to accept any un-remunerative price for their produce as offered by traders or middlemen.

- **Conflict of Interest** APMC play dual role of regulator and market. Consequently its role as regulator is undermined by vested interest in lucrative trade. They despite of inefficiency won't let go any control. Generally, Members and Chairman are nominated/elected out of the agents operating in that market.

Institutional Issues	Infrastructural Issues	Governance/Policy
• Highly fragmented markets --> Poor competitiveness • License requirements --> High corruption • Market Fees/Charges • Cartelisation • Asymmetry in Price information	• Inadequate marketing infrastructure --> Lack of cold storage facilities + Perishable Goods and long-distance ---> Distress sale • Lack of grading and standardisation • Huge wastage of fruits and vegetables	• Conflict of Interest • Monopoly of APMCs • Limited private investment in marketing infrastructure • Insufficient markets and huge regional variation

Reform Measures (Detailed given in Q.20)

- **Market Integration** Physical integration through multimodal connectivity and digital integration through e-NAM (National Agricultural Market) where entire country is a unified market. This will also boost inter-state trade.
- **Promoting Value Addition** Farmers can also realise maximum profits by selling the produce directly to food processing units. This would also create more employment in non-agricultural sectors.
- **Transport and Storage Infrastructure** This would help in better supply and availability of the produce.
- **Adopting a Facilitative Statutory Framework** This includes asking states to adopt Model Agricultural Produce and Livestock Marketing (Promotion and Facilitation) Act, 2017, reviewing essential Commodities Act to incentivise companies to invest in trading of agricultural commodities freely etc.
- **Encouraging Contract Farming** Through contract farming, buyers can provide farmers or Farmer Producer Organisation (FPO) access to modern technology, quality inputs and guaranteed price. It would provide better avenues at collective bargaining to small and marginal farmers. It would also act as a direct marketing channel to supply produce from surplus regions to high demand states.

Model Agricultural Produce and Livestock Marketing (Promotion and Facilitation) Act, 2017

- The new model law seeks to establish a regulated wholesale agri-market at a distance of every 80 km. To enable this, it has been proposed to issue licenses to new private players and traders who wish to set up a wholesale market. Even private market yards, warehouses and cold storages will be allowed to act as regulated markets.
- Unlike the current system, now only by paying unified single fees, farmer/trader will be able to transact in all such regulated agri-markets within the state. There will be no separate fees for individual markets.
- It caps market fee (including developmental and other charges) at not more than 1% for fruit and vegetables and 2% for food grain. It caps commission agents' fee at not more than 2% for non-perishables and 4% for perishables.
- Besides, it stipulates a single license for trading within the State and at the National level.
- All regulatory powers will lie with the office of the director of agricultural marketing in the state, who will also issue licenses to traders and new private players. As of now this power lies with the mandis managed by the Board of directors.
- It also has the provision for promoting online or spot (e-national agriculture market) agriculture market platforms.

Conclusion

The Central Government including NITI Aayog should work with states in undertaking marketing reforms. For better price discovery, agriculture has to go beyond farming and develop value chains comprising farming, wholesaling, warehousing, logistics, processing and retailing.

E-NAM: Gamechanger in Agricultural Marketing

Q.19 While E-NAM is a considered a gamechanger in reforming India's agricultural marketing, there is still a long way to go in achieving the goal of 'One Nation, One Market'. Critically examine. (250 Words, 15 Marks)

Ans. **Introduction** National Agriculture Market (NAM) is envisaged as a pan-India electronic trading portal which seeks to network the existing APMCs to create a unified national market (One Nation, One Market) for agricultural commodities. NAM will create a national network of physical mandis which can be accessed online.

It seeks to leverage the physical infrastructure of the mandis through an online trading portal, enabling buyers situated even outside the state to participate in trading at the local level.

The Central Government fully funds e-NAM, which is implemented by the Small Farmers Agribusiness Consortium (SFAC).

Need of E-NAM

Integration of agri-markets across the country through the e-platform is seen as an important measure for overcoming challenges posed by the present agri-marketing system namely fragmentation of state into multiple market areas each administered by separate APMC, multiple levy of mandi fees, requirement for multiple license for trading in different APMCs, licensing barriers leading to conditions of monopoly, poor quality of infrastructure and low use of technology, opaque process for price discovery, high level of market charges, movement controls, etc.

This led to the launch of e-NAM in 2016 to ensure online trading platform for agricultural commodities. This market is facilitating the farmers, traders and buyers with online trading of commodities and further helps in better price discovery.

Features and Significance of E-NAM

- **Online Trading (Digital Transformation and Efficiency)** e-NAM provides a digital platform for farmers, traders and purchasers to undertake agricultural commodity trading online. It does away with the need for consumers to be physically present in mandis (marketplaces) and allows them to trade from anywhere using a computer or mobile device.
  - This digitisation streamlines the entire value chain, resulting in speedier transactions, less paperwork and overall efficiency gains.
  - According to official data, e-NAM has cut transaction times from 8-10 hours to 30 minutes, resulting in speedier and more efficient trading.
  - The electronic weighing equipment at the e-NAM mandis has boosted the accuracy and transparency of produce weighing, decreasing conflicts and disagreements.
- **Single Market (Market Integration)** By connecting different agricultural mandis across the country, e-NAM aspires to create a unified national market. It gives farmers access to multiple markets and consumers outside of their area, giving them more market prospects.
- **Transparent Price Discovery** The platform enables transparent price discovery by giving real-time information on commodity prices and arrivals in various markets. This enables farmers to make informed sales decisions and assures fair market prices.
- **Reduction of Intermediaries** In the trading process, e-NAM also eliminates intermediaries and many layers of middlemen. Farmers benefit from lower transaction costs and higher prices for their produce as a result. According to official data, the average reduction in intermediaries in e-NAM mandis is around 2-3, resulting in a higher income for farmers.
- **Liberal Licensing of Traders/Buyers and Commission agents by State authorities** without any pre-condition of physical presence or possession of shop/premises in the market yard.
- **One license for a trader** valid across all markets in the state.
- **Quality Testing and Grading** The platform offers agricultural commodities quality testing and grading services. This ensures that purchasers obtain high-quality goods and motivates farmers to improve their product quality.
  - This emphasis on quality has resulted in increased market acceptance of Indian agricultural products, both domestically and globally.
  - As per official data, the platform has facilitated the issuance of over 8.47 lakh (847,000) electronic Negotiable Warehouse Receipts (eNWRs), providing assurance of quality and storage to buyers and enabling farmers to access credit against their stored produce.
- The National Agriculture Market (e-NAM) Platform of Platforms (POP) was launched in 2022. Farmers will be able to sell their produce outside of their state borders as a result of its implementation. This would improve farmers' digital access to a wider range of marketplaces, buyers and service providers, as well as boost transparency in commercial transactions.
- **Supportive Infrastructure** e-NAM wants to improve agricultural marketing infrastructure by constructing weighbridges, warehouses and cold storage facilities in mandis. This aids in the preservation and storage of agricultural produce. Warehouse based trading module was also launched in e-NAM to facilitate trade from warehouses based on e-NWR (electronic Negotiable Warehouse Receipt).

- **Mobile App** e-NAM has a mobile app that allows users to access the platform and trade while they are on the go. The app includes features such as bidding, price alerts and market information. During the COVID-19 epidemic, the e-NAM platform/mobile application was strengthened by the addition of an FPO (Farmer Producer Organisation) trading module in e-NAM, allowing FPOs to trade their products without taking them to the APMC.
- **Single point levy of market fees**, i.e., on the first wholesale purchase from the farmer.
- Harmonisation of quality standards of agricultural produce and provision for assaying (quality testing) infrastructure in
- Provision of Soil Testing Laboratories in/ or near the selected mandi to facilitate visiting farmers to access this facility in the mandi itself.
- **Data-Driven Decision-Making** Commodity prices, arrivals and trading patterns are all generated by e-NAM. This information can be analysed to learn about market trends, demand-supply dynamics and buyer preferences. Data-driven decision-making can assist farmers, traders and policymakers in making educated decisions about production planning, market strategy and policy interventions.

Achievements of E-NAM

- On the e-NAM platform, more than 1.75 crore farmers and 2.43 lakh traders have registered (as of 31st March, 2023). 2,575 FPOs have been added to the e-NAM platform.
- A trade value of 2.50 lakh crore has been recorded on the e-NAM platform. As of 16th March, 2023, 1361 mandis from 23 States and four UTs were integrated with the e-NAM platform.
- **Digital India Award 2022** The Ministry of Agriculture's Electronic National Agriculture Market (e-NAM) programme received the Platinum Award (1st) in the Digital Empowerment of Citizens Category.

Implementation Challenges

- According to the Ministry of Agriculture and Farmers Welfare, there are 6,946 regulated wholesale APMC mandis as of March 2018. According to data from the e-NAM website, 1,000 mandis (14%) are integrated across 18 States and three Union Territories. This excludes 5,946 mandis from the equation. 'One Nation, One Market' is still a long way off because of various challenges:
- **Infrastructure and Connectivity** One of the most difficult obstacles in adopting e-NAM is the lack of reliable internet connectivity, particularly in rural areas with agricultural markets.
- **Inadequate Digital Infrastructure** Many agricultural mandis lack the infrastructure necessary for flawless digital transactions, such as proper computer systems, internet access and electronic weighing devices.
- **Awareness and Training** Many farmers, particularly those in distant or less technologically sophisticated areas, may be unaware of the e-NAM platform and its benefits. Farmers' participation in online commerce can be hampered by a lack of understanding and sufficient training on how to use the digital platform.
- **Resistance to Change** India's traditional agriculture marketing system is heavily established in physical trading practices and face-to-face contacts. Some stakeholders, such as farmers, traders and commission agents, may be resistant to the shift to online trading because of worries about the digital platform, job security issues or opposition to changes in established practices.
- **Agricultural Produce Market Committee (APMC) Laws and Regulations** Agriculture is a state topic in India and each state has its own set of Agricultural Produce Market Committee (APMC) laws and regulations. It can be difficult to harmonise these disparate legislation and ensure uniform application throughout all states. Some states have been sluggish to adopt and implement the reforms required to integrate their mandis with the e-NAM platform.
- **Commodity Coverage is Limited** While e-NAM covers a large range of commodities, there are certain gaps in commodity coverage. Fruits and vegetables, for example, are high-value and perishable commodities that have not yet been fully integrated into the platform. Extending coverage to include more commodities can improve e-NAM's efficacy and reach.
- **Technical Issues and User Interface** The e-NAM platform has had technical issues as well as user interface and experience concerns. These obstacles can influence user uptake and happiness, particularly for farmers and dealers who may have minimal digital literacy or expertise.
- **Price Discovery and Transparency** Although e-NAM attempts to promote transparent price discovery, there have been cases of price manipulation and collusion among dealers. Ensuring appropriate monitoring methods and resolving any malpractices that undermine the intended benefits of e-NAM remains a challenge.

Conclusion

e-NAM platform promotes better marketing opportunities for farmers to sell their produce through online competitive and transparent price discovery system and online payment facility. So far e-NAM has helped in many ways especially by integrating mandi's across the states. In future NAM will not only become the big service provider to the farmers and traders but consumers will also benefit by produce price stability and availability.

Liberalisation of Agricultural Marketing

Q.20 To what extent liberalisation of Mandi system is the solution for the various ills of agricultural marketing in India? Comment. What are the alternate reform measures that can be taken to improve the marketing system? (250 Words, 15 Marks)

Ans. **Introduction** Presently, India's agricultural markets are regulated by the states under the Agricultural Produce Marketing Committee (APMC) Act.

- Under the APMC Act, the states can establish agricultural markets, popularly known as mandis.
- The sale of agricultural commodities can occur only in the mandis through auction.
- The sales process in mandis is regulated through commission agents (CAs) who mediate between the farmers and traders.

These agricultural markets are characterised by inefficient physical operations, excessive crowding of intermediaries and fragmented market chains. Due to this, farmers are deprived of a fair share of the price paid by final consumers.

Liberalisation of the Mandi System

The **liberalisation of the Mandi system** is often seen as a potential solution to address the various challenges faced in agricultural marketing:

- **Enhanced Market Competition** Liberalisation of the Mandi system can lead to increased competition among buyers, potentially resulting in better prices for farmers.
  - Removing barriers to entry, such as restrictive licensing requirements and multiple intermediaries, can enable more players to participate in agricultural markets, providing farmers with a wider range of buyers and better price discovery mechanisms.
- **Efficient Price Discovery** The liberalization of agricultural markets can facilitate more transparent price discovery mechanisms.
  - By allowing farmers to sell their produce outside the APMC mandis, they can access a broader market and potentially receive better prices based on supply and demand dynamics.
  - This can result in improved market efficiency and fairer remuneration for farmers.
- **Infrastructure and Value Chain Development** Liberalisation can encourage private investment in agricultural infrastructure and value chain development.
  - Opening up markets beyond the APMC mandis can attract private sector players to invest in logistics, cold storage facilities and post-harvest infrastructure.
  - This can help reduce post-harvest losses, improve storage capacities and enable farmers to access wider markets.
- **Farmer Empowerment and Choice** Liberalisation allows farmers to have more control over the selling process, giving them the freedom to choose where and how to sell their produce.
  - It promotes farmer empowerment by reducing the dependency on traditional intermediaries and enabling direct transactions with buyers.
  - This can potentially lead to better market access and improved bargaining power for farmers.

However solely relying on mandi liberalisation may not be a long-term solution to agriculture marketing reform as:

- **Large Proportion of Produce Sold Outside Mandi** Official data show that for paddy and wheat, respectively, only 29% and 44% of the harvest is sold in a mandi, while 49% and 36% is sold to either a local private trader or an input dealer.
  - In other words, de facto, a large proportion of Indian harvest is not directly sold in a mandi.

- **Inadequate Number of Mandis** The National Commission on Agriculture (NCA) had recommended that every Indian farmer should be able to reach a mandi in one hour by a cart. Thus, the average area served by a mandi was to be reduced to 80 sq km.
  - However, there were only 6,630 mandis in 2019 with an average area served of 463 sq km.
  - Therefore, India needs not less but more mandis.
- **Marginal Farmers Domination** In India, nearly 86% of landholding are owned by small and marginal farmers. These farmers, given their small marketable surplus, do not find it economical to bear the transport costs to take their harvests to mandis.
  - Thus, they end up selling their harvest to a village trader even if at a lower price.
  - Even if private markets replace mandis, small and marginal farmers will continue to sell to traders in the village itself.
- **Poor Private Investment In Liberalised Agricultural Markets** The freedom to sell outside mandis already exists in many states.
  - **Already, 18 States have allowed the establishment** of private markets outside the APMC and have allowed the direct purchase of agricultural produce from farmers.
  - **Despite such legislative changes,** no significant private investment has flowed in to establish private markets in these states.
  - The **reason for poor private investment in markets** is the presence of high transaction costs in product collection and aggregation. Moreover, due to a large number of small and marginal farmers, this cost will be higher.
  - This is why many retail chains prefer purchasing bulk quantities of fruits and vegetables from mandis rather than directly from farmers.
- **No Evidence of Higher Prices** In the existing private markets too, there is no evidence of farmers receiving higher prices than in the mandis.
  - In fact, if transaction costs exceed mandi taxes, the costs would be transferred to the farmers at a lower price.
  - This, then, would imply a stronger squeeze on the farmer than at present.
  - Further, if mandis weaken and private markets do not sufficiently replace them, there are fears that the void would be filled by unscrupulous and unregulated traders.

Alternate Reform Measures that can be Taken to Improve the Marketing System

- **Strengthening Infrastructure** Investment in rural infrastructure is crucial to improve the efficiency of agricultural marketing.
  - This includes developing storage facilities, cold chains, warehouses and transportation networks to reduce post-harvest losses, ensure quality preservation and enable smooth movement of agricultural produce from farms to markets.
- **Promoting Direct Farmer-market Linkages** Facilitating direct farmer-market linkages can help farmers access better prices and reduce dependency on intermediaries.
  - This can be achieved through the establishment of farmer-producer organisations, agricultural cooperatives and farmer's markets, where farmers can directly sell their produce to consumers or institutional buyers.
- **Encouraging Contract Farming Promoting** contract farming arrangements can provide farmers with assured markets, fair prices and access to technical know-how.
  - Robust contract farming regulations that protect the interests of both parties, ensure transparent agreements and provide mechanisms for dispute resolution can incentivise private investment in agriculture and improve market access for farmers.
- **Strengthening Agricultural Value Chains Supporting** the development of robust agricultural value chains can improve market integration and value addition.
  - This involves promoting forward and backward linkages between farmers, processors, aggregators, retailers and exporters.
  - It also includes encouraging investment in processing and agro-industries to add value to agricultural produce and expand market opportunities for farmers.
- **Improving Market Intelligence and Information Dissemination** Enhancing access to market information and intelligence is crucial for farmers to make informed decisions regarding crop selection, pricing and marketing strategies.

- Establishing market information systems, mobile applications and online platforms that provide real-time price information, weather updates and market trends can empower farmers and enable them to optimise their marketing decisions.

- **Enforcing Quality Standards and Certifications** Implementing and enforcing robust quality standards and certifications can enhance the competitiveness of Indian agricultural produce in domestic and international markets.
  - It instills confidence in buyers and consumers, reduces information asymmetry and improves price realisation for farmers.
  - This requires effective quality control mechanisms, certification processes and capacity building initiatives for farmers.
- **Facilitating Access to Credit and Insurance** Ensuring farmers have access to affordable credit and insurance products is vital to mitigate risks and improve their marketing capabilities.
  - Expanding institutional credit facilities, promoting crop insurance schemes and introducing innovative financial products tailored to the needs of farmers can enhance their resilience and encourage investment in agriculture.

Legislative and Institutional Measures	Infrastructural and Other Measures	Ashok Dalwai Committee Recommendations
• APMCs .... > Encourage Farmer's Organisations • APMC Act .... > States should implement APLM Act. • Number of Markets-More than 10000 mandis. • Density of Markets with a radius of 5 km (approx. 80 sq km). • Fruits and vegetables outside the purview of APMC Acts and exempted from market fees. • Promotion of alternate marketing channels such as Farmer's market, private market, contract farming.	• Cold-storage facilities, banking facility, digital connectivity and other facilities in these markets. • Investment in market yards. • Standardised scientific assaying and grading. • Warehouse-based trading system. • Roping of AgTech startups for price discovery mechanism.	• One India Market .... > Agricultural Marketing under Concurrent List. • Greater private sector participation • Implement Model APLM Act. • Reduce wastages by investment in Infrastructure for cold-chain integration. (Post-production agri-logistics infrastructure) • Minimum target of 7000 FPOs. • Country need around 1000 wholesale and nearly 20,000 rural retail markets. • Comprehensive guidelines to promote warehouse based post-harvest loans and eNWR based trading.

Conclusion

In conclusion, while the liberalisation of the Mandi system can be a potential solution to the challenges of agricultural marketing in India, it should be implemented carefully and accompanied by complementary reforms.

A balanced approach that addresses infrastructure development, market linkages and supportive policies is necessary to ensure a smooth transition, safeguard the interests of all stakeholders and maximise the benefits for farmers.

Contract Farming

Q.21 While explaining the working of contract farming, critically evaluate its pros and cons. Also, highlight the various provisions of NITI Aayog's Model Contract Farming Act, 2018. (150 Words, 10 Marks)

Contract Farming

- Contract farming signifies an agricultural production (including livestock and poultry) based on a pre-harvest agreement between buyers (such as food processing units and exporters) and producers (farmers or farmer organisations).

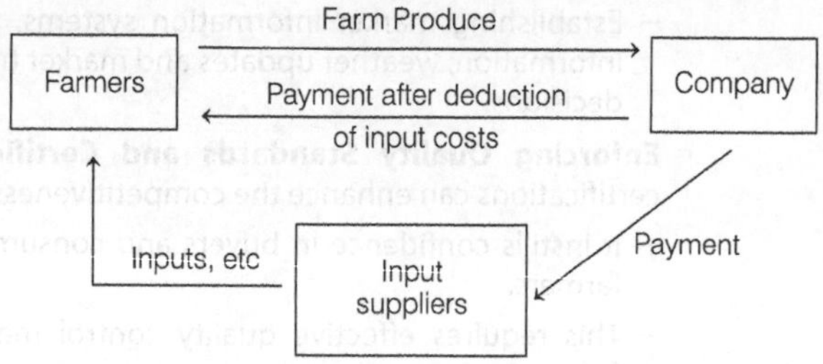

- Under contract farming, farmers can be given seeds, credit, fertilisers, machinery and technical advice so that their product is tailor-made for the requirements of the companies.
- There would be no middlemen involved and farmers would get a predetermined sale price from the companies.
- The farmer does not have to make trips to the mandis nor worry about getting seeds and credit for farming operations.
- In India, contract farming is regulated under the Indian Contract Act, 1872. In addition, the Model APMC (Agricultural Produce Market Committee) Act, 2003 provides specific provisions for contract farming, like compulsory registration of contract farming sponsors and dispute settlement. Since agriculture is a state list subject, therefore contract farming is not uniform.

Some Cases of Contract Farming in India

- The first widely acknowledged incident of contract farming in the Indian context was the entrance of Pepsi Foods Ltd. into Punjab in 1989. The company intended to specifically focus on exports of value-added processed foods. This led to the birth of Pepsico's backward linkage with farmers of Punjab. The PepsiCo model of contract farming opened up new options for farmers, led to productivity increase and introduced modern technology for the tomato crop.
- Following the Pepsico example, local firms such as Nijjar in Punjab and Bhilai Engineering in Madhya Pradesh also took up a tomato contract cultivation.
- **Rallis India Case** The company provides all inputs, technical support and finance to registered growers for a specific crop and facilitates the sale of produce at reasonable prices. The company follows a consortium approach. It has tied up with banks like ICICI and SBI and with buyers of produce like HLL, Picric and Cargill.

Pros and Cons of Contract Farming

Benefits (Pros)	Challenges (Cons)
Farmers	**Farmers**
• Reduced the fluctuating market price risk • Stable and consistent demand from bulk consumers • Improved access to markets • Technical assistance, management support and supply of quality inputs by the agri-business firms • Access to cheaper institutional credit • Improved competitiveness of small scale farming via assured quality inputs and certain market	• Biased towards large farmers and exclusion of small producers. • Exploitation of poor farmers; manipulative prices practiced by large buyers; highly technical contract terms and conditions • Contracting agreements are mostly informal or verbal. • Dis-empowerment of farmers such as unable to grow multiple crops in the land and forced to grown only one type of crop in the same land. • Other issues such as undue quality cuts, delayed deliveries at the factory, delayed payments, etc.
Buyers	**Buyers**
• Un-interrupted supply of raw materials. • Prevented from market price fluctuations • Diversified supply base and thus reduced risk involved with crop damage and loss. • Reduced cost of collection.	• Breach of contract by the farmers and thus reducing factory output. • Not able to generate required yield as per the contract terms.
Other	**Other**
• Addressing traditional ills of marketing • Reduced government burden of procurement • Enhances private investment in agriculture • Enables the food processing industries to invest in warehouses and cold storages in long-term.	• Promotes monoculture and thus puts a burden on the natural resources. • Enhancing the disparity between small and large farmers. • Negative Externalities such as decline in soil fertility, pollution, etc. as the firms are interested only in profits.

Experience of Contract Farming in India

The Punjab and Haryana Contract Farming experience has been far from satisfactory with studies revealing that contract growers faced many problems like the undue quality cut on produce by firms, delayed deliveries at the factory, delayed payments, low price and pest attack on the contract crop which raised the cost of production. The firms also manipulated provisions of the contracts in practice and also delayed payments up to 60 days.

Model Contract Farming Act, 2018

- **Farmer's Protection** The Act lays special emphasis on protecting the interests of the farmers, considering them as weaker of the two parties entering into a contract.
- **Contract Farming** Contract framing to be outside the ambit of APMC Act. In addition to contract farming, services contracts all along the value chain including pre-production, production and post-production have been included.
- 'Registering and Agreement Recording Committee' or an 'Officer' for the purpose at district/block/ taluka level for online registration of sponsor and recording of agreement is provided.
- **FPOs** Promotion of Farmer Producer Organisations (FPOs) / Farmer Producer Companies (FPCs) to mobilise small and marginal farmers has been provided
- **Protecting Farmland** No rights, title ownership or possession to be transferred or alienated or vested in the contract farming sponsor etc. No permanent structure can be developed on farmers' land/premises
- **Contract Farming Facilitation Group (CFFG)** for promoting contract farming and services at village/panchayat.
- **Accessible and simple dispute settlement mechanism** at the lowest level possible provided for quick disposal of disputes.

Conclusion

Contract farming is viable alternative farming model in India which provide assured and reliable input services to the farmers and desired farm produce to the contracting firms. Success of the contract farming depends on the profitable market, the physical and social environment and government support.

Issues related to Storage

Q.22 Availability of adequate storage infrastructure has a direct bearing on agricultural yield and farmer's income. Comment. In this context, discuss the measures that can be undertaken to enhance India's agriculture storage capacity. (250 Words, 15 Marks)

Ans. **Introduction** The total agriculture storage capacity in India is about 91 MMT with state agencies owning around 41% of the capacity. The remaining capacity is shared among private entrepreneurs, cooperative societies and farmers, among others.

Due to insufficiency of the covered storage capacity of food grains and progressively increasing government stocks, a considerable amount of food grains has to be stored under open Cover and Plinth (CAP) storage. This leads to massive wastage, leakages and pilferages. It is estimated that around 20-30% of the total food grain harvest is wasted due to inadequate storage capacity.

Recently, Union Cabinet has given its approval for the establishment of the 'world's largest grain storage plan in the cooperative sector'.

Impact of Storage Infrastructure on the Agricultural Yield and Consequently Farmer's Income

- **Reduction of Post-harvest Losses** It directly impacts farm yield and farmer income. According to the Ministry of Food Processing Industries, India experiences post-harvest losses of agricultural produce valued at approximately ₹ 92,651 crores annually. With improved storage infrastructure, these losses can be significantly reduced.
  - According to a study conducted by the National Institute of Agricultural Economics and Policy Research (NIAP), inadequate storage facilities contribute to post-harvest losses of perishable commodities, such as fruits and vegetables, leading to a decline in farm yield and farmer income.

- **Better Price Realisation** Adequate storage capacity enables farmers to store their produce and sell it during periods of high demand and better prices. It provides them with the flexibility to time their sales strategically, thereby maximising their income.
- The Economic Survey 2019-2020 highlighted the importance of storage facilities in ensuring remunerative prices for farmers. It emphasised that improved storage infrastructure empowers farmers to store their produce and sell it at opportune times, reducing distress sales and improving their income prospects.
- **More Power to Farmers** Having access to storage facilities can not only make villages self- reliant, but also allow farmers to leverage it in many other ways. Farmers can go in for staggered sale of the produce to multiple agencies such as mandis, co-operatives, local traders, etc. This, in turn, would also make the farmers more commercialised.
- **Facilitates Access to Credit and Loans** With proper storage infrastructure, farmers can store their produce as collateral and access credit or loans from financial institutions. This ensures investment in better inputs and farming practices, leading to increased farm yield and income.
  - Reserve Bank of India's (RBI) priority sector lending guidelines emphasise the importance of storage infrastructure for farmers' access to credit.
- **Enhances Value Addition and Marketability** Adequate storage capacity enables farmers to store their produce for longer durations, allowing them to explore value addition opportunities such as processing, grading and packaging. This enhances the marketability of their produce and increases their income potential.
- **Supports Crop Diversification and Higher-value Crops** This diversification can lead to increased farm yield and improved income prospects for farmers.
  - **National Bank for Agriculture and Rural Development (NABARD)** has highlighted the role of storage facilities can encourage farmers to shift from traditional crops to high-value crops like fruits, vegetables and spices, which have longer shelf lives and higher market demand.
- Also, it will help in achieving the objectives of food security, controlling inflation and mitigating the effects of climate change on agriculture.

Futuristic Measures

- **Infrastructure Investment** Increase government funding for the development of storage infrastructure, including construction of warehouses, cold storage facilities and silos. This should be accompanied by improved maintenance and regular upgradation of existing facilities to ensure their optimal functioning.
  - **Indian Government's Warehousing Development and Regulatory Authority (WDRA)** has supported the creation of storage infrastructure through its Warehouse Infrastructure Fund (WIF).
  - **Upgrading State Infrastructure** Most of the warehouses owned by state agencies are over 15- 20 years old and need upgradation to contain wastage levels. Further, the produce under open Cover and Plinth (CAP) storage needs to be converted into coverage storage.
- **Building Village Storage Capacity** There is a need to improve storage capacity at a micro level, such as at the Gram Panchayat level.
- **Public-Private Partnerships (PPPs)** Encourage PPPs in the construction and operation of storage facilities. This can leverage private sector expertise and resources while ensuring that the infrastructure benefits farmers and meets their specific needs.
  - **CWC**-Central Warehousing Corporation has collaborated with private companies like Container Corporation of india (CONCOR) to establish containerised warehouses for efficient storage and transportation.
- **Capacity Building and Training** Provide training and support to farmers, cooperatives and other stakeholders to enhance their knowledge and skills in modern storage practices, such as proper packaging, pest management and maintenance of quality standards.
  - National Institute of Agricultural Extension Management (MANAGE) has been conducting training programs for farmers and other stakeholders to enhance their knowledge of storage practices.
- **Technology Adoption** Promote the adoption of technology-driven solutions in storage, such as sensor-based monitoring systems, remote temperature control and automated inventory management.
- **Financial Incentives** Offer financial incentives, subsidies and low-interest loans to farmers and private entities for the establishment and expansion of storage facilities.

- Pradhan Mantri Kisan Sampada Yojana (PMKSY) launched by the Indian Government offers financial incentives and subsidies for the development of food processing and preservation infrastructure, including cold storage facilities.

- **Integrated Supply Chain Management** Develop integrated supply chain management systems that connect farmers, aggregators, processors and retailers. This ensures seamless movement of produce from farm to market, reducing wastage and increasing the efficiency of storage and distribution.
  - **Companies like ITC Limited and Big Basket** have established integrated supply chain systems that include storage facilities.
- **Promote Farmer Producer Organisations (FPOs)** Encourage the formation and strengthening of FPOs to enable collective bargaining power and shared access to storage facilities. FPOs can pool resources, negotiate better storage contracts and facilitate cost-effective storage solutions for small and marginal farmers.
  - Sahyadri Farms in Maharashtra is an example of a successful FPO that has set up its own storage and processing facilities.

Best Practices from Around the World

Netherlands

- **Agriport A7** Learn from the Dutch model of Agriport A7, a large agro-industrial park that integrates various components of the agricultural value chain, including state-of-the-art storage facilities, logistics and processing units. This holistic approach maximises efficiency, reduces wastage and promotes value addition.

China

- **Grain Reserves System** China's Grain Reserves System establishes a strategic grain reserve network across the country. It includes both government-owned and private storage facilities to ensure food security and stabilise prices. This approach combines centralised planning and decentralized implementation to effectively manage storage capacity.

Conclusion

In order to balance food grain production to consumption, a total peak storage capacity required works out to be around 70% of annual production. Recently, the government announced ₹ 1-lakh crore package to boost agricultural infrastructure. Of this, a total of ₹ 500 crore is earmarked for providing subsidies to build storage facilities for fruits and vegetables and bee-keeping. However, much more needs to be done in making farmers self-reliant in terms of storage capacity in the longer run.

Post-Harvest Losses

Q.23 How can an effective farmer market linkage lead to reduction of post-harvest losses and reduce volatility in food prices? Also, enumerate the steps taken by the government at several stages of the agriculture supply chain to reduce post-harvest losses in the country. (250 Words, 15 Marks)

Ans. **Introduction** Post-harvest losses in India pose a significant challenge to the agricultural sector, impacting food security, farmer livelihoods and the overall economy. The economic impact of post-harvest losses is substantial. The Indian Council of Agricultural Research (ICAR) estimates that the value of post-harvest losses in India amounts to around ₹ 92,000 crores (approximately USD 12.6 billion) annually. The post-harvest losses are estimated to be from 10 to 25% in durables, semi-perishables. For perishables and fruits and vegetables these losses are higher and reached from 30 to 40%.

Causes of Post-Harvest Losses

The post-harvest value chain has four critical phases: harvesting and primary processing; storage and crop protection; processing and market linkage. Each of these has inefficiencies which result in crop losses.

- **Value chains remain poorly developed**, in terms of storage facilities at the farm level, transportation and food processing units, especially in the case of the perishables.
  - **Committee on Doubling Farmers' Income (2019)** At the all-India level, farmers are unable to sell about 40% of the total fruits and vegetables produced in the market.

- **Lack of Cold Storage Infrastructure** While post-harvest losses vary depending on crops, agricultural practices, climate, etc storage is usually the primary reason in most cases. India's current cold storage capacity is barely sufficient for 10% of fruit and vegetables produced in the country. This is one of the major contributors to low farmers' income, distress sale by farmers and hence, seasonal food deficits at the household level.
- **Lack of Sufficient Transportation Infrastructure** Due to inadequate transportation infrastructure, commodities get damaged through bruising and bad roads, spillage due to repeated loading, unloading and contamination and heat and humidity in the absence of cold chain transportation.
- **Traditional Storage** Most of the harvested grains, fruits and vegetables are stored in traditional structures, made of grass, wood or mud, without any scientific design that cannot protect crops against pests and decay.
- **Lack of Private Investment** Corporates are wary of investing large sums in improving the supply chains of perishable produce incurring losses (like horticulture and meat) unless they see an opportunity to sell the products through organised retail.
  - In contrast, in the milk sector, the marketing is better organised; there are better corporate investments here. e.g., Amul. This has also resulted in lower losses despite their high perishability.
- **Improper handling of the produce** also causes damages and affects the quality of the produce, which can result in significant post-harvest losses.
- **Dominance of small/marginal farmers** leading to the absence of scale economies. Multiple intermediaries and lack of transparency and traceability lead to fragmented supply chains.
- **Delays in the APMC mandis** due to manual weighing and lack of modern grading and sorting processes result in large post-harvest losses to the tune of 4-6% in cereals and pulses, 7-12% in vegetables and 6-18% in fruits.

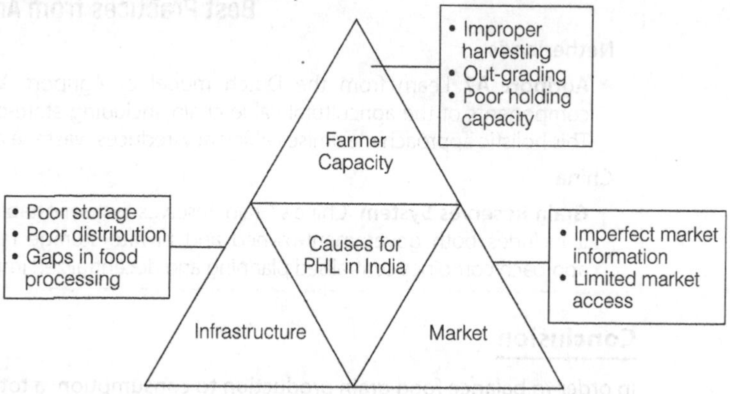

- **Lack of Food Processing Facilities** Only 2.2 % of the agricultural produce in India gets processed. In contrast, countries like the USA (65%) and China (23%) are far ahead of India in reducing the wastage and enhancing the value addition and shelf life of the farm products.

Efficient Market Linkages Brings Down Post-harvest Losses

- **Efficient Supply Chain** Strong market linkages reduce delays and storage issues, minimising post-harvest losses. Improved supply chain management can decrease post-harvest losses by up to 25% in fruits and vegetables.
- **Market Information Access** Farmer market linkages provide timely market information, helping farmers align production with demand. Access to market information can reduce post-harvest losses by 5-10% in grains and pulses.
- **Infrastructure Development** Market linkages involve developing cold storage facilities and transportation networks. Increased cold storage capacity in India can reduce post-harvest losses of fruits and vegetables by 10-15%.
- **Value Addition and Processing** Market linkages enable value addition near the farm gate. Value addition reduces perishability and increases the shelf life of agricultural products. Processed food products have lower post-harvest losses compared to raw produce. **Example** Fruit Processing like jam, juices, etc.
- **Price Stabilisation and Risk Mitigation** Diversifying customer base through market linkages mitigates price fluctuations. Farmer market linkages help stabilize prices and improve farmer incomes. **Example** TOP scheme for vegetable

Steps taken by the Government to address post-harvest losses

- **Infrastructure Development** Pradhan Mantri Kisan Sampada Yojana (PMKSY) focuses on creating modern infrastructure for food processing and preservation, including cold storage facilities, warehouses and silos.
  - **Scheme of Cold Chain, Value Addition and Preservation Infrastructure** A sub-scheme of PM Kisan SAMPADA, to provide integrated cold chain and preservation infrastructure facilities.

- **Transport initiatives such as Kisan Rail** to build a seamless national cold supply chain for perishables (milk, meat, fish, etc) and Krishi Udan to improve the value of agri-products.
- **Market Linkages** National Agricultural Market (e-NAM) facilitates online trading of agricultural produce, connecting farmers with buyers across different states and reducing post-harvest losses.
- **Value Addition and Processing** Pradhan Mantri Kisan Sampada Yojana promotes food processing activities near the farm gate, enabling value addition and reducing post-harvest losses.
- **Technology Interventions** Initiatives like AgriMarket app, e-NAM, use of mobile applications and online platforms to disseminate market information, provide weather forecasts and facilitate direct farmer-buyer interactions.
- **Training and Capacity Building Programmes** Capacity building initiatives for farmers, educates farmers on best practices in post-harvest management, including proper harvesting, sorting, grading and packaging techniques.
- **Financial Support** Rashtriya Krishi Vikas Yojana (RKVY), Pradhan Mantri Kisan Samman Nidhi (PM-KISAN) provides financial assistance to farmers for infrastructure development, procurement of equipment and adoption of advanced technologies.
- **Research and Development Efforts** Research institutes and agricultural universities invest in research and development activities to improve storage techniques, develop new packaging materials and enhance post-harvest handling practices. Example: PROJECT CHAMA.
- **Model Contract Farming Act** To reduce post-harvest losses and increase income of farmer due to price assurance and sale if produce.
- **One-Product One-District** for better marketing and export in the Horticulture sector. It will reduce uncertainties and delays.
- **Warehousing in Line with Warehouse Development and Regulatory Authority (WDRA) Norms** Viability Gap Funding for setting up such efficient warehouses at the block/taluk level.
- **Village Storage Scheme** to be run by the SHGs to provide farmers with a good holding capacity and reduce their logistics cost.

Futuristic Measures

- **Push to Contract Farming** Contract farming is found to be more profitable than independent production. As it includes agricultural production (including livestock and poultry) based on a pre-harvest agreement between buyers and farmers. Buyers also provide inputs (on credit), extension services or other technical assistance to assist farmers.
- **Integration with Commodity Markets** Commodity market is a market that trades in the primary economic sector rather than manufactured products, such as cocoa, fruit and sugar. Derivatives trading using spot prices, forwards, futures and options on futures can lead to increased transparency and Fair Price discovery.
- **ConFarm Model of Agricultural Market** This brings farmers and consumers on the same platform for their benefit.
  - **Example** Consumer-Farmer Compact in Telangana is ensuring food availability and access in COVID-19 times.
- **Effective Forward and Backward Linkages** Cold storage facility in India is highly skewed with nearly 70% of the country's total capacity limited to four states-Uttar Pradesh, West Bengal, Punjab and Gujarat. o Need for the creation of mega food parks, integrated cold chains, processing units through effective implementation of PM Kisan Sampada Yojana.
- **Reforming e-NAM** Only 8.42% of the total mandis are connected through the e-NAM platform. There are no scientific sorting/grading facilities or quality testing machines.
- **Increase Awareness** Among farmers on the need for delinking with the mandi system and benefits of FPOs.
- **Focus on Agri RandD** The Economic Survey (2021-22) explicitly highlighted the correlation between spending on agri-RandD and agricultural growth. But, expenditure on agri-RandD and education hovers around 0.6% of agri-GDP.

Conclusion

These steps and schemes implemented by the Indian Government aim to enhance the agriculture supply chain, reduce post-harvest losses and improve the income and livelihoods of farmers across the country.

Farmer Producer Organisations (FPOs)

Q.24 The aggregation of marginal, small and landless farmers by Farmer Producer Organisations (FPOs) can provide solutions to many of the problems in agriculture. Discuss. Also, highlight the measures taken by the government to promote FPOs. (250 Words, 15 Marks)

Ans. Introduction The concept of 'Farmer Producer Organisations, (FPO)' consists of collectivisation of producers especially small and marginal farmers so as to form an effective alliance to collectively address many challenges of agriculture such as improved access to investment, technology, inputs and markets. Department of Agriculture and Cooperation under Ministry of Agriculture, Government of India has identified 'Farmer Producer Organisations 'registered under the special provisions of the Companies Act, 1956 as the most appropriate Institutional form around which the mobilisation of farmers is to be made for building their capacity to collectively leverage their production and marketing strength.

Need for Farmer Producer Organisations (FPOs)

- **Structural Challenges in Agriculture** Such as poor market infrastructure, credit unavailability, access and knowledge about market, information asymmetry, lower bargaining power and holding capacity, higher input costs, lower yield due to fragmented buying and selling etc leading to low remunerative prices for farmers.
- **Failure of Cooperatives** Due to political interference, bureaucratic control and capturing of management by poor leadership and powerful elite, cooperatives have not been as effective as expected. As professionally-managed enterprises, FPOs enjoy better flexibility.
- **For better Price Realisation and Higher Income** FPOs enable member-farmers to reap benefits of economies of scale in purchasing of inputs, processing and marketing of their produce. FPOs ensure better income to the member-producers through aggregation and value addition.
- **Better Access to Government Services** FPOs can also work as a platform to facilitate liaison with the government leading to better access to government services, like PDS, MGNREGA, Scholarships and Pensions, etc.

FPOs providing solutions to various problems of Agriculture

Some core areas where FPOs can contribute to a great extent are summarised under following broad headings:

Areas	Problems	FPOs Providing Solutions
Promotion of Mechanisation in Agriculture	Level of farm mechanisation in India is 45-50% of which majority contribution (60-70%) is of rice and wheat harvesting, which is less compared to other developed countries (up to 95 %).	FPO can play important role in making available these machineries and equipments to the members collectively by charging nominal fee from the members through custom hiring centres. Small and marginal farmers can have access to machineries by collectively purchasing the machineries in FPOA good example of promotion of mechanisation through farmers' organisation is the Satmile Satish Club, an NGO from Cooch Behar district of West Bengal.
Post-Harvest Losses and Value Addition	As per estimates of Ministry of Food Processing industries (2016), post-harvest loss of India's major agricultural produce is estimated at ₹ 92,651 crore. Despite of second largest producer of fruits and vegetables, only 2.2% of fruits and vegetables are processed (Much lower than Brazil-70 %, USA-65 %) and in case of milk, 37.7% is processed.	Farmer Producer Organisations can mobilise investment opportunities for establishment of processing and storage infrastructures at grassroots level which will help in reducing post-harvest losses, enhancing shelf life and better price realisation for the farmers produce. In Maharashtra, MAHAGRAPES, a marketing partner to grape growers cooperative had established cold storage units at each cooperative society.

Areas	Problems	FPOs Providing Solutions
Extension and Research	Provision of extension has been sole responsibility of the states till 1990s. However, after training and visit system of extension, external source of fund reduced drastically, constraining the government ability to fund the national extension system. Considering vast diversity in agriculture, public extension system in country was not enough to fulfil the extension needs of the country.	Farmer Producers Organisations (FPOs) can complement and supplement the efforts of public, private and NGOs in providing extension services to the farmers. There are different FPOs which became successful in providing timely, relevant information and training services to farmers by establishing knowledge linkages. Maharashtra state grape grower's association provide extension services to its members by organising seminars at block level where experts from related field would guide and educate the farmers.
Market Related Problems	International Food Policy Research Institute (IFPRI), South Asia, observed that in India, market surplus is relatively low, producers share in consumer rupees is low, transaction cost is high, price volatility is more, cold storage facilities are less and inaccessible and there is greater price variability and volatility.	Many Farmer producer organisation in Maharashtra, by establishing direct marketing with the companies (Pepsico, Patanjali etc) are able to remove the middlemen in the market and give more and assured price to farmers produce. Collective marketing by FPO will help in reduction in transaction cost and more bargaining power to the farmers. By mobilising resources FPO can start their own cold storage, pre cooling and cooling units which can help in prevention of distress sale and managing price volatility in the market. By pooling out their resources, more economy of scale can be achieved by small and marginal farmers.
Input and Credit Facilities	It has been seen that during few years input prices in agriculture increases by 4-5 folds, but price of the output remained same. This leads to more cost of cultivation and less profit to the farmers.	Through the FPO, farmers can collectively purchase the inputs like fertilisers, pesticides etc directly from the company at wholesale rate and even can bargain for lower rate. By doing this, Sai Pravara Farmers Producers Company from Maharashtra could save about 25-30% input cost to the members than other farmers in the village. By associating themselves to the FPO, farmers can get the credit facility provided by the NABARD based on group approach.

Challenges Faced by FPOs

- **Cost of Institutional Funding** FPOs do not have assets of their own to serve as collaterals and often are not seen to be as viable business enterprises. Consequently, FPOs have to raise working capital at very high interest rates from NBFCs.
- **Inadequate Professional Management** Farmers' Organisations are required to be efficiently managed by experienced, trained and professionally qualified personnel. However, such trained manpower is presently not available in the rural areas.
- **Lack of Risk Mitigation Mechanism** Presently, while the risks related to production at farmers' level are partly covered under the existing crop, livestock and other insurance schemes, there is no provision to cover business risks of FPOs.
- **Inadequate Access to Infrastructure** The producers' collectives have inadequate access to basic infrastructure required for aggregation like transport facilities, storage, value addition (cleaning, grading, sorting, etc.) and processing, brand building and marketing. Further, in most of the commercial farming models, the primary producers are generally excluded from the value chain.

Measures Taken by the Government to Promote FPOs

- Formation and Promotion of Farmer Producer Organisations, 2020 Launched to promote 10,000 FPOs in the next five years.
- **Budgetary Support to Small Farmers Agri-business Consortium (SFAC)** for its Equity Grant and Credit Guarantee Fund Scheme for the Farmer Producer Company.
- **Credit Guarantee Funds (CGF)** to be setup by NABARD and NCDC (National Cooperative Development Corporation)
- **Agri-Market Infrastructure Fund** can be used for assisting FPO's in creating marketing and farm level value addition infrastructure.
- **Focus on Small Farmers** 10% limit on maximum shareholding by a single member to prevent capture of profits by rich farmers.

Conclusion

FPOs have the potential to transform subsistence farming of small and marginal farmers into commercial farming. Implementation of FPO scheme must be effective to realise this objective. **Usha Thorat Panel** recommended that partnership model between FPOs and Micro-finance institutions can help achieve true potential of FPOs.

Agricultural Exports (Potential and Issues of Agricultural Exports)

Q.25 Along with highlighting the potential of agricultural exports, describe the supply-side and demand-side issues that is hampering India's agricultural export competitiveness. (250 Words, 15 Marks)

Ans. **Introduction** India ranks within the world's five largest producers of over 80 percent of agricultural produce items, including many cash crops such as coffee and cotton. It is also one of the world's five largest producers of livestock and poultry meat, registering one of the fastest growth rates. However, its total agricultural export basket accounts for a little over 2.15% of the world agricultural trade. India has remained at the lower end of the global agri export value chain given that the majority of its exports are low value, raw or semi-processed and marketed in bulk. The share of India's high value and value added agri produce in its agri export basket is less than 15% compared to 25% in US and 49% in China.

Potential of Agricultural Exports

- **Abundance of natural resources**
  - **Arable Land** India has the largest arable land or land capable of being cultivated.
  - **Irrigation** India has the second largest area under irrigation after China with highest groundwater well irrigation
  - **High Cropping Intensity** The current intensity is 14% indicating the ability to crop multiple crops on a single land.
  - **Agro-Climate** India has 20 types of agro-climate zones that help cultivation of almost all varieties of food crops.
- **High Agricultural Production**
  - **Dairy** India is the largest milk producer in the world.
  - **Fisheries** India has the third largest fisheries production in the world.
  - **Horticulture** India is the world's second largest producer of fruits and vegetables after China.
  - **Spices and Condiments** India is the world's largest producer and exporter of spices in the world.
  - **Organic Farming** India has been ranked first in the number of organic farmers and ninth in terms of area under organic farming.
- **Huge Available Population**
- **Largest Employer** The share of Agriculture in employment is close to 54% as of 2016-17.
- **Traditional Knowledge** A large population of indigenous people, also bring traditional knowledge in making organic and unique varieties of food crops.
- **Demographic Dividend** India has a high population of young which can be leveraged to increase export based sectors.

- **Robust Infrastructure**
  - **Rail Network** A vast rail network connects India's farmlands to the ports and cities for export.
  - **Agri-Export Zones** The Central Government has sanctioned 60 AEZs throughout India comprising about 40 agricultural commodities.
  - **Special Economic Zones** India has 8 SEZ's that facilitate export processing and also aid in increasing exports.
  - **Long Coastline** A long coastline with numerous ports allow agri export from various corners of the country.
  - **High FDI** The continuous upsurge in FDI allowed across the industries and sectors, has proven that foreign investors have faith in the resilience of Indian markets.
  - **Data** 100% FDI is allowed under the automatic route for horticulture, animal husbandry, fisheries and agri services.
  - **Agri-Tech** India's agritech start-ups have been growing at 25% YoY, thus promising high returns in the sector in the future.

The incongruence between India's global ranking between production and exports may be categorised into supply side as well as demand side constraints.

Supply-side Issues

- **Productivity Issues** The Indian yield levels are lower than even some smaller ASEAN and African countries. According to the World Bank, India's rice yields are one-third of China's and about half of those in Vietnam and Indonesia. This is mainly because of small size of landholding, dependence upon monsoon, etc.
- **Poor Price Competitiveness due to Lack of Initial Aggregation** Since the average size of a land holding in India is small, the consequent marketable surpluses from individual farmers are small, which is insufficient to be pooled into exportable containers later on due to lack of uniform quality and variety of produce.
- **Poor Logistics Connectivity** Congestion at the ports due to high waiting periods of shipment, lack of proper road connectivity to the hinterland, volatile freight rates etc increases the cost and also becomes critical in case of perishable exports.
- **Absence of Market Information and Global Market Linkages** Poor market intelligence, in terms of consumer preference, dynamic monitoring of market share, qualitative feedback, etc. in the target export market are also a constraint.
- **Policy Issues** One of the reasons for these issues is inward looking policies of India which are largely aimed at food security and price stabilisation. Further, rural electrification is yet to focus on supplying uninterrupted power to village level post-harvest management uses.
- **Lack of Awareness in Farmers** Farmers also need to be made aware about Pre-Harvest Intervals (PHI) of various crops, judicious use of permitted and registered pesticides, certified packaging, etc to ensure that produce meets standards of importing countries.

Demand-side Issues

- **High Tariff Peaks** Indian agro-products bearing high export potential have been facing high import duties in some premier importing countries.
- **Import Quotas** Import quota limitation in markets like China (for wheat, corn, sugar etc) and Thailand (instant coffee, rice, pepper etc.) are examples of restrictions on Indian exports.
- **Tariff Escalation for Value Added Exports** Certain niche sectors in India's processed food industry, including milled products, confectionery etc face increased import duty due to high level processing. It ensures that most imports to such countries are raw produce or products.
- **Stringent Non-tariff Barriers** Compliance to non-tariff measures such as technical barriers to trade and sanitary and phytosanitary measures, requires meeting stated process benchmarks and certifications. This adds to cost, thus wearing out the competitive advantage due to low labour costs or enhanced market access acquired through tariff cuts during negotiations. A multi-dimensional strategy needs to be adopted to improve export competitiveness which includes steps like.

Productivity Challenge	• Lower than the world average. Yield rate of rice (2.4 t/ha) and wheat (3.15 t/ha) lower than China, South Africa and many developed countries. • Fragmented land-holdings. Small-scale farming. • Monsoon dependent and poor irrigation coverage. • Environmental Factors-Declining water table, soil degradation, overuse of fertilisers.
Government Policies	• Adhoc and unstable foreign trading policy regime. • Pro-consumer bias leads to export restrictions. Eg - Wheat exports ban. • Poor post-harvest infrastructure such as cold storages etc leading to higher wastages. • Inadequate implementation of Agricultural Export Policy such as low market diversification. • Inadequate trade support to the exporters.
International Trade	• India's exports are low-value, semi-processed items and the share of high-value and horiculture crops is lower than global average. • Sanitary and phyto-sanitary issues leads to the rejection of Indian agri-exports. • Disputes at the WTO • India's poor export competitiveness

Conclusion

Government has taken various initiatives like SAMPADA Yojana, dedicated Agriculture Export Policy 2018, Speedy Custom Clearance, One District One Product programme, etc to tackle the challenges to India's agricultural exports. The need of the hour lies in better implementation of these initiatives along with proper support of all states, especially coastal states in order to achieve larger objective of Doubling farmer's income as suggested by Ashok Dalwai Committee.

Agricultural Export Policy, 2018

Q.26 Promoting agricultural exports entails the integration of Indian farmers and agricultural products with global value chains. In this context, can the new agriculture export policy will create better market for agriculture exports? (250 Words, 15 Marks)

Ans. **Introduction** Agriculture Export Policy was launched in 2018 with an aim to utilise the export potential of Indian agriculture, by means of appropriate policy instruments and make India a global power in agriculture and raise farmer's income. The following are the objectives of policy:

- The 'National Agriculture Export Policy' is formulated in line with the vision to doubling the farmers' income by 2022.
- It is also towards the goal of increasing the share of agricultural exports from present about USD 30 billion to over USD 60 billion.
- Getting to one of the top 10 exporting countries of agricultural products is also one of the goals of this policy.

Promotion of Agri-exports and Integrating with Global Value Chain

- **Agricultural Export Challenges** The policy can resolve challenges to exporting agricultural products from India such as low farm productivity, poor infrastructure and global price volatility to market access.
- **India's Share in Agro Products** In 2016, India's share in global exports of agriculture products was just 2.2%. India has remained at the lower end of the global agriculture export value chain due to the fact th at most of its exports are low value, semi-processed and marketed in bulk.
- **Share of High-value Agro Products** The proportion of India's high value and value-added agriculture produce in its agri-export basket is less than 15% when compared to 25% in the US and 49% in China. Considering the globalisation of value chains, it is necessary that the country make proper efforts to boost exports of high margin, value-added and branded processed products.

- **Shortfalls** Exports even in these items are frequently interrupted by self-imposed and arbitrary trade curbs. State-level curbs on movement of produce add to already high costs from fragmented farms and poor logistics.
- High rejection rates on consignments due to poor quality, antibiotic and pesticide residues and other phytosanitary grounds are major concerns.
- **Policy** Domestic price and production volatility of certain agricultural commodities lead to using the existing policy for short-term goals. These include taming inflation, providing price support to farmers and protecting the domestic industry. These decisions may serve the immediate purpose of maintaining domestic price equilibrium. However, they end up distorting India's image in international trade as a long term and reliable supplier. It is thus imperative to frame a stable and predictable policy.
- **Low Horticultural Exports** India is unable to export its vast horticultural produce because of lack of uniformity in quality, standardisation and its inability to reduce losses across the value chain. It is imperative that the country make concerted efforts to boost exports of high margin, value-added and branded processed products.

Salient Features of Policy

- **Stable Trade Policy Measures** to ensure recommends providing an assurance that the processed agricultural products and all kinds of organic products will not be brought under the ambit of any kind of export restriction. The Model Agricultural Produce Market Committee (APMC) Act must be adopted by all states and E-NAM must be established.
- **Liberalising Land Leasing Norms** and adoption of the Model Contract Farming Act by State Governments in order to promote agricultural exports. Contract farming is expected to bring in large-scale private investments in agriculture thus leading to large-scale mechanisation. This will further produce surplus volumes of the standardised, exportable quality of agricultural products.
- **Infrastructure and Logistics Boost** by identifying ports for the export of agricultural products. Development in port infrastructure like dedicated perishable berths.
- **Whole Government approach** which will ensure all government department and ministries like Ministry of Agriculture, Ministry of Food Processing Industries, Ministry of Shipping and Transport, Ministry of Railways and Ministry of Consumer Affairs involved in agricultural production, processing, transportation and export should work together to address bottlenecks at every level.
- **State Government Involvement** As agriculture is a state subject it is necessary to bring on board the State governments for positive agricultural reforms. Each state has its own agricultural nuances, like one state may be experiencing a drought while another may be dealing with floods. Thus, it is necessary to align state agricultural policies with the nation's overarching goals.
- **Focus on Export Centric Clusters** for pre- and post-harvest management of the production as well as in upgrading the supply chain to attain much higher levels of export from those clusters.
- **Promoting Value Added Exports of Indigenous and tribal products** Through the National Programme on Organic Production (NPOP), organic food parks and by the uniform quality and packaging standards India can tap the potential for increasing organic exports. Promotion of Research and Development (RandD) activities, promoting 'produce in India' through the Constitution of separate funds dedicated to organic, value-added, ethnic, GI and branded products.
- **Post-Harvest Infrastructure** that can support the smooth logistical movement of agri-produce exports. This will have a direct co-relationship in increasing export volumes, assuring quality and ensuring better price realisation per unit.
- **Establishment of Strong Quality Regimen** with the focus on strong RandD, new varieties, state of the art lab and a lab networking process for effective accreditation and monitoring. An institutional mechanism should be provided that would pursue market access, tackle barriers and deal with sanitary and phytosanitary issues against India's agricultural exports that come up from time to time.
- **Research and Development** led by private industry along with higher infrastructure spend by the government will be the key to boosting agricultural exports. Along with this, innovations in packaging, improving the shelf life of products and greater R&D in developing products to suit the palates of importing countries should be a priority.

Challenges in Doubling the Farmer's Income

- **Unrealistic Goals** Relying on only export for improving the income potential is a steep task. Given the depressed international market for food grain, sugar, cooking oil as well as dairy and meat products. There will be an effort to dispose the excess in the international market, but the challenge is that prices in the international market are already lower than domestic prices.

- **MSP Regime** Unless the current MSP regime is rationalised realising the goals of doubling the income is a challenge. As MSP of food-grain is linked to politics not to world trade and political considerations drive MSPs, instead of world trade considerations.
- **Policy Uncertainties** By sticking to the same essential commodities like onions and potatoes under review means that farmers, exporters and importers will continue to operate under the current unpredictable regime. If the domestic exporter is unsure that the government will allow unhindered export of onions or potatoes, it will not develop the required infrastructure for storage and transport.
- **Land Holdings** with disaggregated farm holdings, there exists a great deal of heterogeneity in a single product produced by different farmers. This indicates the need for developing effective pre-harvest linkages to boost exports.

Suggestions

- **Niche Products** Some experts recommend that India should change its focus towards indigenous, unique products from food grain for the international market.
- **Awareness** The farmers must be made aware and they should know when to start sowing, as external factors like global price, impact the domestic situation.
- **Post-production Losses** It is essential that perishable produce be properly packed, stored and transported. This is where pack houses, ripening chambers, cold storage and refrigerated (reefer) vehicles come in. As NITI Aayog's strategy document shows, there exists a large gap in India's cold chain infrastructure. A majority of cold storages in India are single commodity storages, which leads to them remaining idle for up to six months. Cold chain infrastructure is unevenly distributed amongst states as well. However, significant progress has been made under schemes such as SAMPADA.
- **Branding** The government must set up 'Brand India' to promote exports and establish as strong quality regime for exports in which the states can also be extensively involved.
- **Value Chains** According to infrastructure status agriculture value chains will provide a much-needed fillip to this sector, enabling cheaper access to finance. Similarly, the government, working with the private sector, should endeavor to set up village-level procurement centres, reducing the cost of transporting produce for farmers. Private market yards should be encouraged.
- **Clusters** To implement the policy, dedicated clusters could be created for items such as mangoes, pomegranate, bananas, grapes, tea, coffee, turmeric and marine products, etc.
- **Research and Development** Agricultural research has the biggest impact on yield and profitability but it is weak in states where agriculture is relatively more important (Eastern and Northern states, except Punjab and Haryana).
- **FPO** The Agriculture Export Policy rightfully targets a cluster-based development approach. These clusters should be supported with farmer producer organisations (FPOs) or cooperatives. Not only will this enhance bargaining power of farmers, but will also ensure consistent quality of produce when combined with revamped extension services.

Conclusion

The share of India's high value and value-added agriculture produce in its agri-export basket is less than 15% compared to 25% in the US and 49% in China. India is unable to export its vast horticultural produce due to lack of uniformity in quality, standardisation and its inability to curtail losses across the value chain. Given the globalisation of value chains, it is imperative that the country make concerted efforts to boost exports of high margin, value-added and branded processed products.

The vision of doubling farmer's income by 2022 will require a series of interventions to improve production and productivity along with economising the cost of production. This would also require India to augment its exports to the global market. Hence, it is necessary to have an agriculture export policy in place.

Role of Technology in Agriculture (Importance and Challenges of Adoption of Technology)

Q.27 Discuss the significance of technology in the Indian agricultural sector along with highlighting various e-technology related interventions taken by the government. Also, state the challenges in realising its potential to improve agricultural efficiency and increase the income of the farmers. (250 Words, 15 Marks)

Ans. **Introduction** Agriculture is the primary source of livelihood for about 50% of India's population. But various reports highlight the issue of low productivity of Indian agriculture in comparison to the developed countries and low income of Indian farmers with many living below the poverty line.

Significance of Technology in Agriculture

In this context, existing as well as new technologies such as Machine Learning (ML), Internet of Things (IoT), Big Data Analytics (BDA) and Cloud Computing become significant to improve efficiency and income of farmers:

- **Improved Productivity from Mechanization of Agriculture** Agricultural mechanisation has the potential to directly and indirectly affect yields through reduction in post-harvest losses and increase harvest gains.
- **Climate/Weather Prediction Through Artificial Intelligence** Modern equipment and tools based on AI enable data gathering and assist in precision farming and informed decision-making using vital information on temperature, rainfall, soil, humidity, etc.
- **Resilient Crops Developed via Use of Biotechnology** Genetic engineering helps in increasing crop resistance to pests and the development of high-yielding varieties which makes improvements to livestock.
- **Agriculture Sensors** Sensors help farmers in determining soil composition and moisture content, nutrient detection, location for precision, airflow, etc. and thus allow farmers to maximise yields using minimal natural resources.
- **Supply Chain Management using Big Data** With the help of data analysis, farmers can receive information about the prevailing market prices of crops, demand and supply situation and platform to buy and sell their products quickly. This greatly reduces their inventory cost, post- harvest loss and transportation costs.
- **Improved Outreach** Not only small and medium farmers, but even backyard farmers also play a role in promoting agriculture. Use of e-technology will help in spreading ideas and innovations to all levels of farming sects.
- **Better Price Realisation** It has potential to connect each farmer to anywhere in the country helping farmers to cut the cost born to intermediaries and would help to realise better profits.
- **Livestock Monitoring** Use of chips and body sensors can help prevent disease outbreaks and are crucial in large-scale livestock management. Similarly, ultrasounds can be used to judge the quality of meat.

E-Technology Interventions in Boosting Farm Productivity

- **E-NAM** The launching of this platform has established direct linkage between producers and purchasers which has promoted contract farming. Companies link directly with farmers for pre-specified production of grains and in the process guide, direct and invest in the production through better technology and investment.
- **AGMARKNET** It facilitates the generation and transmission of prices, commodity arrival information from agricultural produce markets and web-based dissemination to producers, consumers, traders and policymakers transparently and quickly.
- **Digital Agriculture Mission (2021–2025)** It aims to support and accelerate projects based on new technologies, like AI, blockchain, remote sensing and GIS technology and the use of drones and robots.
- **Unified Farmer Service Platform (UFSP)** It is a combination of core infrastructure, data, applications and tools that enable seamless interoperability of various public and private IT systems in the agriculture ecosystem across the country
- **AgriStack** It will create a unified platform for farmers to provide them with end-to-end services across the agricultural food value chain.
- **ISRO's Village Resource Centres (VRC)** The VRCs are connected to Knowledge/Expert Centres like Agricultural Universities, Skill Development Institutes and Hospitals. Programmes are conducted by the VRCs in the areas of water resources, micro credit and finance etc.
- **Soil Health Card Scheme** It has led to scientific mapping of the soil in order to determine the required inputs like nutrients, water content etc which has directly improved soil productivity.
- **SENSAGRI** It is a research project aimed at developing indigenous prototype for drone based crop and soil health monitoring system using Hyperspectral Remote Sensing (HRS) sensors. Drone technology based UAVs are used to gather precise information from farm fields and transmitting the data on real time basis.

- **National Land Records Modernisation Programme** This e-governance project aims to develop a modern, comprehensive and transparent land records management system to implement a land-titling system with title guarantee. Digital record will be tamper proof and would promote formal mutation and titling and spur credit availability for agriculture.
- **GPS Mapping** It has promoted agro-climatic farming and better field documentation by providing inputs on farm yield, moisture, maps for field drainage, etc.
- **Agropedia** It is an initiative by ICAR to use social networking technology to spread agricultural information.

Challenges in Realising its Potential

However, following challenges in realising the potential of technology in agricultural sector need to be addressed:

- **Poor Communication of Science to Farmers** While agri-tech companies have good expertise of emerging technologies, they often lack the application-level domain expertise required for testing and validation for credibility among farmers and scaled field deployment. Moreover, low literacy levels of farmers makes it more difficult.
- **Subsidies Structure** The existing subsidy regime does not provide incentives and support for adopting agriculture technologies and innovations rather it prevents diversification, promotes excessive reliance on fertilisers and encourages usage of more water and electricity.
- **Small Landholdings** India has more than 650 start-ups that offer agri-tech innovations in partnership with industries and financial institutions, but lack scale due to the very high costs of serving small-holding farmers and building their own distribution system.
- **Issues in Adoption** Poor IT infrastructure, high deployment costs, lack of awareness and trust towards technology coupled with the fear of being replaced by it is increasing the technophobia in farmers.
- **Lack of Seamlessness** Limited expertise, existing gaps in agricultural research, poor data quality and lack of access to data and a lack of collaboration among different stakeholders affects the integration of different data under one roof.
- **Funding for Agri-Techs** Agri-techs have seen very good development in the last decade. However, they are still faced with limited funding and yet to be validated business models in Indian agriculture systems.

Conclusion

India has potential economic value of USD 50-65 billion through digital agriculture by 2025 translating to 23% addition to the current value of agricultural produce. Thus, there is an urgent need to work towards the success of Digital Agriculture.

Precision Farming

Q.28 What do you understand by 'Precision Farming'? Discuss the benefits and challenges in the adoption of precision farming. (150 Words, 10 Marks)

Ans. Introduction By 2050, India's agri-food production will face a formidable task of feeding close to 1.7 billion people using limited cultivable land, water and energy resources. Our net sown area has almost stagnated at around 140 million hectares and there is little scope to increase it.

Precision farming is one of the solutions for sustainable development of agriculture, which advocates applying right inputs in right amounts at right time and at right place using the right technologies or techniques.

About Precision Farming

- Precision farming is an approach where inputs are utilised in precise amounts to get increased average yields, compared to traditional cultivation techniques. It is the science of improving crop yields using high technology sensor and analysis tools.
- Precision Farming utilises multitude of advanced technologies and tools to monitor several parameters and collect information related to crop growth (like soil moisture, pH etc.). The information is used for targeted interventions.
- It is referred to as 'precision' because it is focused on performing the right intervention (e.g., providing water to crops), in the right place, at the right time, responding to the specific demands of individual crops and individual areas of land with superior levels of precision.

Technologies include a vast array of tools of hardware, software and equipment

- **Global Positioning System** GPS is used to identify the location of farm equipment in the field. It provides an accurate positioning system necessary for field implementation of variable rate technology in agricultural input management.
- **Grid Sampling** It is a technique for segmenting fields into small units (~0.5–5 hectares). Soil samples from those grids are used to calculate the proper application rates for crop inputs.
- **Variable-Rate Technology** Variable-rate Technology (VRT) consists of farm field equipment with the ability to precisely control the rate of application of crop inputs that can be varied in their application including fertilisers, irrigation, tillage, insect control etc.
- **Yield Monitors** Crop yield measuring tools fitted on harvesting machinery are called yield monitors. Alongwith the positioning data from the GPS device, the yield data from the monitor is recorded and saved. Utilising the yield data, GIS software creates yield maps. The data helps in decisions related to the requirement of targeted intervention.
- **Remote Sensors** Remote sensing (in agriculture terms) means viewing crops from overhead (from a satellite or low-flying aircraft/drone) without coming into contact, recording and displaying the image.
- **Proximate Sensors** Proximate sensors can be used to measure soil parameters (Nitrogen content, pH etc) and crop properties as the tractor passes over the field.
- **Computer Hardware and Software** Computer support is required to analyse the data gathered by other components of precision farming technology and to make it accessible in formats such as maps, graphs, charts or reports.

Benefits of Precision Farming

- **Increase Agriculture Productivity** Precise agriculture inputs (like fertilisers, water) determined scientifically through analysis of data captured by sensors enhances the agriculture output and promotes the yield.
- **Reduction of Chemical Application in Crop Production** Amount of input is determined based on requirement. fertilisers are supplied only where specific nutrients are missing. Similarly, weedicides are used at location of weeds. Drones can be used for targeted delivery of chemicals with desired precision. This reduces unnecessary usage and cuts down waste.
- **Prevents Soil Degradation** Since over-use of chemicals is avoided, prevents the leaching of undesired chemicals into soil, preventing their harmful impact on soil.
- **Efficient Use of Water Resources** Targeted delivery of water through techniques like fertigation reduces water usage. Fertigation is the process of directly applying fertiliser to a crop through the irrigation system.
- **Improvement in Farm Incomes** Increase in productivity, reduction in use of inputs and wastage improves farm incomes and helps in raising the socio-economic conditions of farmers.
- **Job Creation** Precision farming has potential to create a lot of employment opportunities e.g., operating drones is a specialised skillset. Youth in rural areas can be trained and employed as certified drone operators. According to one estimate, these new-age technologies have a potential to create 2.1 million jobs in rural areas.

Moreover, it leads to dissemination of modern farm practices which are more sustainable and climate-friendly.

Challenges of Precision Farming

Research suggests educational and economic challenges as the two most important in the application of precision agriculture. Among the variables that contribute to educational challenges, lack of local experts, funds, knowledgeable research and extension personnel have more of an impact compared to others. PA and initial costs have more of an impact among the economic challenges compared to the other issues.

- **High Cost** Precision farming is dependent on technologies like GPS, drones and sensors. All these technologies are capital intensive and require large investments in the beginning. Spending the requisite amounts is beyond the capacity of small and marginal farmers.
- **Lack of Technical Expertise Knowledge and Technology** Deploying and using the technologies, interpreting the captured data require high level of awareness and skills.

- **Not Viable for Small Land Holdings** Precision farming require high investments. Moreover, proximate sensors (say to capture information/samples of soils) are generally deployed on farm machinery like tractors. Thus, precision farming is more conducive with mechanised farming. High investments and mechanised farming are viable only in large holdings. Return in small landholding are too little (due to low absolute output even though yield may be high) to justify high investments required in precision farming.
- Furthermore, technology behind the practices is creating opportunities for extremists, terrorists and adversarial governments to attack farming machinery, with the aim of disrupting food production. For example, in 2021 a ransomware attack forced ~20% of the beef processing plants in the U.S. to shut down, with one company paying nearly USD 11 million to cybercriminals.

Policy Approach to Promote Precision Farming at Farm Level

- Identify the niche areas for the promotion of crop specific precision farming.
- Creation of multidisciplinary teams involving agricultural scientists in various fields, engineers, manufacturers and economists to study the overall scope of precision agriculture.
- Provide complete technical backup support to the farmers to develop pilots or models, which can be replicated on a
- Creating awareness among farmers about consequences of applying imbalanced doses of farm inputs like irrigation, fertilisers, insecticides and pesticides.
- Precision farming can be promoted for specific progressive farmers who have sufficient risk bearing capacity as this technology may require capital investment. The agriculture research institutes can provide technical back-up to farmers to develop the models. The learnings can then be utilized to replicate the models at a larger scale.

Conclusion

- In the wake of climate change, depletion of natural resources and an imminent food crisis, India must move beyond aggressive farming and towards precision farming.

Role of Biotechnology in Agriculture

Q.29 How can biotechnology improve the living standards of farmers. (250 Words, 15 Marks) **UPSC Mains PYQ 2019**

Ans. **Introduction** According to the United Nations Food and Agriculture Organisation–Feeding a world population of 9.1 billion in 2050 will require raising overall food production by 70% (nearly 100% in developing countries). In this context, biotechnology becomes important because it allows farmers to grow more food on less land using farming practices that are environmentally sustainable.

Biotechnology is the use of living organisms, cells and molecules to create products and technologies that can improve human health, agriculture and industry. Biotechnology can have a significant impact on the lives of farmers by improving their productivity, increasing their incomes and enhancing productivity, increasing their incomes and enhancing their food security.

Role of Biotechnology in Improving the Living Standards of Farmers

Some of the ways in which biotechnology can improve the living standards of farmers are:

- **Improved Crop Yields** Biotechnology can be used to develop crops that are resistant to pests and diseases, have improved nutritional value and can grow in adverse environmental conditions. This can lead to increased crop yields, which can improve the incomes and food security of farmers.
  - The yield of Bt cotton has increased from 300kg/ha in 2002 to over 500 kg/ha after introduction of Bt cotton in India.
- Genetic engineering can accelerate improvements in plants by increasing the diversity of the gene pool. It can also help in the production of plants that have a short maturing period, higher yield, potential to promote food production even in adverse conditions like drought, salinity.
- **Better Pest and Disease Management** Biotechnology can be used to develop pest and disease-resistant crops, reducing the need for chemical pesticides and herbicides. This can reduce the cost of farming and improve the health and safety of farmers.
  - GM Crops can reduce pesticide use in brinjals, known to be most pesticide-intensive vegetable.

- **Efficient Use of Resources** Biotechnology can be used to develop crops that require less water and fertiliser, reducing the cost of farming and improving the sustainability of agriculture.
  - This will reduce the input costs and Indian farmers being traditionally dependent on intensive subsistence agriculture will be benefitted.
- **Livestock Productivity** Biotechnology can be used to improve the health and productivity of livestock by developing vaccines and diagnostic tests for animal diseases. This can increase the incomes of farmers who rely on livestock for their livelihoods.
- **Climate-Resilient Crops** The technology can be used to cultivate crops making it resilient to the climate change which is impacting agriculture yield.
  - **Example** Water-resistant paddy can tackle incessant rains
- **Bioremediation** Biotechnology can be used to clean up contaminated soils and water bodies, which can improve the environmental conditions and livelihoods of farmers.
- **Post-Harvest Management** Biotechnology can be used to develop technologies that can improve the storage and preservation of crops, reducing post-harvest losses and increasing the incomes of farmers.
- **Addressing Hidden Hunger** Genetic engineering can help to improve nutritional content of crops and simultaneously enhance the nutrition intake by the farmers.
  - **Example** Golden rice can help fight Vitamin A deficiency; Costa Rica's pineapple has high levels of Carotenoids compounds.
- **Diversified Income** The health and productivity of livestock and poultry can be enhanced, giving the farmers the diversified income and reduced vulnerability to market fluctuations.
  - **Example** Transgenic cows produce milk with a more balanced protein, which can give higher income by selling such premium products to farmers.
- **Poverty Alleviation and Reduced Bank's Dependence** The increased outputs and the remunerative prices brought by using the biotechnology will help in generating a surplus income, alleviating poverty and thus reducing farmer's dependence on the banks.

However, there are concerns that genetically modified crops may transfer genetic material into natural, unmodified plants. For instance, a crop that is herbicide-resistant may transfer some of its traits to a weed, which would result in a herbicide-resistant weed. Genetically modified crops have a higher yield and the overproduction may lead to market instability, reduced export income, fewer product varieties etc.

Conclusion

The government needs to harness the potential of biotechnology through innovative initiatives like Biotech-Kisan. While continuing and increasing the share of funding in basic research, the government should encourage and incentivize the private sector to invest substantially in applied research.

Climate-Smart Agriculture

Q.30 In the light of climate change posing a threat to food and nutrition security, explain the concept and characteristics of 'Climate Smart Agriculture'. How is it crucial in mitigating the impact of climate change on Indian agriculture? (250 Words, 15 Marks)

Ans. **Introduction** Climate change and resultant increased frequency of extreme weather events such as droughts, floods and storms has put many developing countries at the risk of growing food insecurity. Yet the demand from agriculture farm is continuously increasing. Hence there is need to adopt climate-smart agriculture.

Impact of Climate Change on Indian Agriculture

The Economic Survey 2018 shows that climate change is taking a toll on India's agricultural productivity and farmers' incomes. It observed that the impact of temperature and rainfall on Agriculture is felt during extreme changes - when temperatures are much higher, rainfall significantly lower and the number of "dry days" greater than normal. The Economic Survey also noted that such impact is more adverse in unirrigated lands compared with irrigated areas.

It is affecting the agriculture in the following ways:

- **Extreme Heat** Crops need suitable soil, water, sunlight and heat to grow. However, extreme heat events and reductions in precipitation and water availability have hampered the crop productivity.
  - The World bank report warned that by 2040s, India would see a considerable reduction in crop yields due to extreme heat.
  - Heat waves threaten livestock by increasing their vulnerability to disease, reducing fertility and milk production.
  - Heat stress also considerably affect the commercial poultry.
- **Changing Rainfall Patterns** Rainfall patterns have already begun shifting across the country and such changes are expected to intensify over the coming years. This is likely to mean more intense periods of heavy rain and longer dry periods, even within the same regions.
- **Floods** Flooding in many agricultural regions of the country have been witnessed and these floods have devastated crops and livestock, accelerated soil erosion and have polluted water.
  - Rising sea level may result in loss of farmland by inundation and increasing salinity of groundwater in coastal areas.
- The survey says that the change in agricultural productivity patterns as a result of climate change could reduce annual agricultural incomes by between 15% and 18% on average and between 20% and 25% particularly for unirrigated areas. Since agriculture contributes 16% of India's GDP, climate change causes about 1.5% loss in GDP.
- Furthermore, the International Food Policy Research Institute discovered that 'rice production will decline by 14% by 2050 in South Asia; wheat by nearly 49% and maize, millets and sorghum by around 19% over the same period.'
- Such a deleterious effect on crop yields compounds the already serious challenge of food security in India. Its agricultural sector already suffers from low productivity as compared to the rest of the world. The Food and Agriculture Organisation estimates that India's cereal yield (2,993 kg per hectare), as of 2016, is drastically lower than in North America (7318 kg per ha), East Asia and the Pacific (5,976 kg per ha) and Europe (4,155 kg per ha).

Climate Smart Agriculture

Climate Smart Agriculture (CSA) may be defined as an approach for transforming and reorienting agricultural development under the new realities of climate change. The most commonly used definition is provided by the Food and Agricultural Organisation which defines CSA as "agriculture that sustainably increases productivity, enhances resilience, reduces/removes GHGs where possible and enhances achievement of national food security and development goals". In this definition, the principal goal of CSA is identified as food security and development while productivity, adaptation and mitigation are identified as the three interlinked pillars necessary for achieving this goal.

Climate-smart agriculture that broadly works on three parameters

- Sustainably increasing agricultural productivity and farmers' incomes
- Adapting to climate change and making farming more resilient
- Reducing greenhouse gas emissions (GHG)

Some interventions taken in this regard by the government - National Mission for sustainable agriculture, National initiative on Climate Resilient Agriculture (NICRA), National Adaptation Fund, state action plans on climate change, etc.

Techniques used in Climate Smart Agriculture

- Identifying and promoting sustainable agriculture practices and tools. e.g. organic farming; Agroforestry; Use of erosion control plants.
- Controlling soil moisture by farm ponds, bunds, trenching, mulching, drip irrigation etc.
- Using inputs more efficiently and effectively to grow more from less e.g. alternate wetting and drying of paddy by letting the fields drain periodically, methane emissions from flooded rice production can be cut to half.
- The practice save water and increase profit margin of farmers.
- Increasing the productivity of milk and meat production so that fewer animals are required to produce the same amount of milk or meat, which also reduces the emissions generated in producing that food.

Smart Agriculture can help India improve its farm productivity due to following benefits that it offers

- **Precision Agriculture** It makes the agricultural practices more precise and well-planned by including processes like real-time crop and soil condition monitoring, plant health tracking and weather prediction. The farmers can administer their fields based on the insights obtained by this system.
- **Soil Study** Sensors will collect soil data which can be analysed to generate actionable messages for farmers besides helping in precision agriculture.
- **Estimation of Water Requirements of Crops** Crop water requirements depend on various conditions: crop types, season, climate and growth stages of crops. ICT will help farmers make decisions on the amount of water their crops need in real time.
- **Disease Detection and Diagnosis** Many crops get ruined due to lack of proper pesticide control mechanism. It can help in timely discovery of diseases by capturing images of plant leaves and analysing them through AI or transmitting them to remote libraries for detection.
- **Fertiliser Optimisation** Applying fertiliser is an important farming activity with a potential to greatly affect farm productivity. It will help farmers taking decisions on which chemicals to apply and their crop-specific appropriate quantities.
- **Agricultural Drones** Since drones collect multispectral, thermal and visual imagery while flying, the data they gather provide farmers with insights into a whole array of metrics like canopy cover mapping, field water pond mapping, scouting reports, nitrogen content in wheat, drainage mapping, weed pressure mapping and so on.
- **Tackling Climate Change** Agriculture production is estimated to decrease by 10-20% by 2050 because of climate change. IoT based solutions can help cut GHG by precision farming and reducing agricultural wastage.

Conclusion

The geographical location of India makes it vulnerable regarding the climate change. The effect of climate change on agriculture and the state of soil and water with the increasing pollution poses a serious threat to Indian agriculture. Therefore, a need to focus on climate smart agriculture.

Agri-Tech Startups

Q.31 Concerted efforts should be made for the promotion of agri-startups as they are transforming the way agriculture is traditionally being done across all stages of the value chain. Analyse the above statement. (150 Words, 10 Marks)

Ans. **Introduction** India has become the third-largest start-up ecosystem hub. India is home to the highest number of unicorn startups after the US and China. Among them, Agri-startups are providing relevant and innovative solutions to a number of challenges faced all across the agricultural value chain.

- These Agri-startups have been connecting the missing link between the farmers, input dealers, wholesalers, retailers and consumers; connecting each of them and providing strong marketing linkages and quality products on time.
- Agri-startups are not only creating new employment avenues but are also leaving a ripple effect on the socio-economic fabric of the Indian demography in which they are operating.
- Currently, 3.8% or 600+ of the total recognised startups in the country are in the Agri-startup space as per the Economic Survey of 2019-20. Of these, 54% are classified as agri-tech while the rest are in the field of dairy farming, food processing and others.

Agri-startups are transforming the way agriculture is traditionally being done across all stages of the value chain

- **Innovation and Technology Adoption** Agri-startups bring innovation and technology to the agricultural sector, offering novel solutions to address various challenges.
  - These startups leverage advancements in areas such as precision agriculture, data analytics, remote sensing, IoT (Internet of Things) and artificial intelligence.
  - By introducing these technologies, they can enhance productivity, optimize resource utilisation, improve decision-making and streamline operations throughout the agricultural value chain.

- **Farmer Empowerment** Agri-startups empower farmers by providing them with access to knowledge, information and tools that can enhance their agricultural practices.
  - Through mobile applications, online platforms and advisory services, these startups enable farmers to make data-driven decisions, access market information, receive agronomic guidance and manage their operations more efficiently.
  - By bridging information gaps and providing tailored solutions, agri-startups empower farmers to improve their yields, reduce costs and enhance their income potential.
- **Market Linkages and Value Addition** Agri-startups play a crucial role in establishing market linkages for farmers.
- They create platforms that connect farmers directly with buyers, processors and retailers, eliminating unnecessary intermediaries and enabling fairer and more transparent trade.
  - These startups often support value addition activities by promoting the processing, packaging and branding of agricultural produce.
  - This allows farmers to capture higher value for their products and expand their market reach.
- **Sustainable and Efficient Practices** Agri-startups often focus on promoting sustainable agricultural practices.
  - They encourage the use of organic farming techniques, precision irrigation systems, eco-friendly pest management methods and resource-efficient technologies.
  - By promoting sustainable practices, these startups contribute to environmental conservation, resource optimization and the production of healthier and safer food.
- **Job Creation and Economic Growth** The growth of agri-startups has the potential to create employment opportunities, particularly in rural areas.
  - These startups require a skilled workforce in areas such as technology, data analysis, marketing, logistics and customer support.
  - By generating jobs, they contribute to local economic development and rural revitalisation.

Government Steps for Supporting the Agri-startups

- Government schemes like the setting up of the National Centre for Management and Agricultural Extension in Hyderabad (MANAGE) and the Department of Science and Technology have given a tremendous boost to Agri-startups. The focus area of the DST has been on accelerating agri-tech startups by providing mentoring, industry networking and investor pitching guidance.
- According to a NASSCOM report, the Indian Government specifically supports agri-tech startups through its Startup India Programme.
- **Startup India Seed Fund Scheme (SISFS)** The scheme aims to provide financial assistance to startups.
- Ministry of Agriculture and Farmers' Welfare is supporting the startups through initiatives like the Agriculture Grand Challenge which further validates Agri-startups.
- Department of Agriculture, Cooperation and Farmers Welfare (DACFW) has launched a new component called 'Innovation and Agri- Entrepreneurship Development'.
  - It has been launched under the Rashtriya Krishi Vikas Yojana (RKVY-RAFTAAR).

Conclusion

Agri-startups are playing a significant role in revolutionising traditional agriculture practices by leveraging technology, empowering farmers, establishing market linkages, promoting sustainability and driving economic growth.

- Their impact is visible across the entire agricultural value chain, from farm management and production to post-harvest handling, processing and marketing.
- Encouraging and supporting the growth of agri-startups can accelerate the transformation of the agricultural sector, improving productivity, profitability and sustainability while benefiting farmers, consumers and the overall economy.

Integrated Farming System (IFS)

Q.32 How far is the Integrated Farming System (IFS) helpful in sustaining agricultural production? (150 Words, 10 Marks) **UPSC Mains 2019**

Ans. **Introduction** The Integrated Farming System (IFS) is a combined approach aimed at efficient sustainable resource management for increased productivity in the cropping system. The IFS approach has multiple objectives of sustainability, food security, farmer's security and poverty reduction by involving livestock, vermi-composting, organic farming etc.

Integrated Farming System ensures Sustainable Agricultural Production through

- **Economic Activity** IFS provides an opportunity to increase economic yield per unit area by virtue of intensification of crop and allied enterprises especially for small and marginal farmers. Due to interaction of enterprises, IFS provides flow of money round the year amongst the farming community.
- **Reduced Use of Fertilisers** It has the capability to make the sector profitable by reducing the use of chemical fertilisers and recycling nutrients.
  - **Example** Cattle dung mixed with crop residues and farm waste can be converted into nutrient-rich vermi -composting.
- **Environmentally Sustainable** In IFS, subsystem of one by product works as an input for the other subsystem, making it environmentally sustainable. Moreover, IFS components are known to control the weed and regarded as an important element of integrated pest management and thus minimise the use of weed killers as well as pesticides and thereby protect the environment.
- **Recycling** Effective recycling of products, by-products and waste material in IFS is the cornerstone behind the sustainability of farming system under resource poor condition in rural areas.
- **Enhanced Profits** Produce/waste material of enterprise can be used for other enterprise at least for crop, thus reducing the cost of production and increasing profitability per rupee investment.
  - **Example** An extensive study in a district of Karnataka has revea19d that IFS has led to increase in net farm income by 25% to 150% depending on the local conditions.
- **Resource Management** IFS promote the efficient management of resources. This enhances the productivity of the farming. The IFS promotes for rejuvenation of systems productivity and to achieve agro-ecological equilibrium.
- **Suitability to Hilly Regions** Integrated Farming System is suitable particularly for hilly regions of the North-Eastern Region.
  - **Example** Some are as–Integrated Fish cum Pig farming, Integrated Fish cum Duck Farming, Integrated Fish Farming- Chicken, Integrated Fish farming-cum-Cattle farming. Sikkim being an organic state is a good example.
- **Availability of Fodder, Fuel and Timber** IFS utilises every part of land. Growing of fodder trees on border will not only provide fodder but also enrich the soil by fixing atmospheric nitrogen.
  - **Example** In multi-storeyed cropping including of fodder component like cowpea as second or third tier also meet the fodder crises.

Challenges in the Adoption of Integrated Farming System

While integrated farming system can help improve the income and nutritional security of farmers, however it is not free of challenges such as:

- **Affordability** For financial reasons small and marginal farmers cannot afford large cattle so we have to encourage small ruminants such as goats and sheep.
- **Acceptance** There is hesitation among the farmers in non coastal areas to adopt fisheries, poultry, duck rearing because of lack of role models and religious perceptions.
- **Not under MSP** Mushroom farming and beekeeping are not covered under the Minimum Support Price (MSP) system. Better integration with the food processing industries and hotel industries is therefore necessary.

Way Forward

- **Integrating Subsistence Agriculture** Indian farmers in many regions such as in North-Eastern part, practice subsistence agriculture. They also have a rich traditional base in water harvesting, soil management etc which could be efficiently utilised under IFS.
- **Encouraging Livestock Enterprises** Combining crop with livestock enterprises would increase the labour requirement significantly and would help in reducing the problems of underemployment and unemployment to a great extent. IFS provides enough scope to employ family labour round the year.
- **Building Farmer Capacities** All stakeholders should make continuous efforts to build farmer capacities for adoption of productive, remunerative, eco-friendly and self-sustaining integrated farming systems.

Conclusion

IFS provides multiple benefits that are sustainable and can pave the way for climate-smart agriculture. India needs to adopt a 'well designed' Integrated Farming System (IFS) to realise the vision of doubling farmers' income by 2022 and having sustainable agricultural practices.

Check Your Preparation

1. Discuss the importance of micro irrigation in enhancing water use efficiency in agriculture in India with special focus on dry land agriculture. (150 word, 10 marks)
2. "Farm Loan Waiver Schemes does not provide a long-term solution to the India's agrarian crisis". Do you agree with this statement? Give logical arguments to justify your opinion. (150 words, 10 marks)
3. Do you agree with the view that PM KISAN holds the key to transform India's agricultural support ecosystem and tackle rural distress? Justify your opinion. (150 words, 10 marks)
4. 'Farmer Producer Organisations (FPOs) have the potential to give better bargaining power to farmers and lead to more transparent agri-markets.' Examine. (150 words, 10 marks)
5. Digital tools in agriculture helps farmers to produce with less resources and make data-driven decisions in real-time. Justify the statement. (150 words, 10 marks)
6. The idea of Evergreen Revolution needs to be explored if India wishes to achieve food security, raise farmer income and develop sustainable agriculture. Discuss. (150 words, 10 marks)

UNIT 5

Issues Related to Direct & Indirect Farm Subsidies & MSP; PDS; Issues of Buffer Stocks & Food Security; Technology Missions; Economics of Animal-Rearing

Issues Related to Subsidies (Types of Agricultural Subsidies)

Q.1 What are the different types of agriculture subsidies given to farmers at the national and state levels? Critically analyse the agriculture subsidy regime with the reference to the distortions created by it.
(200 Words, 12.5 Marks) **UPSC Mains PYQ 2013**

Ans. **Introduction** An agricultural subsidy is a governmental financial support paid to farmers and agri-businesses to supplement their income, manage the supply of agricultural commodities and influence the cost and supply of such commodities. According to Economic Survey 2021 India spends about 2% of GDP on Farm subsidies.

Agricultural Subsidies

- **Credit Subsidy** Government provides credit subsidy in the form of Interest Subvention scheme or farm loan waivers.
- **Electricity Subsidy** States throughout India provide free of cost electricity to farmers.
- **Fertiliser Subsidy** In the current fiscal year 2023-2024, fertiliser subsidy is estimated to be 1.75 lakh crore.
- **Agriculture Equipment Subsidy** Subsidies are provided to farmers through State Governments under various schemes such as the Sub-Mission on Agricultural Mechanisation (SMAM), Rashtriya Krishi Vikas Yojana (RKVY) for the purchase of various agricultural equipment and machines.
- **Income Support** Government also provides income support such as PM-KISAN scheme.
- **Minimum Support Price** Government procures the crops from the farmers at MSP prices for food security and provides to the beneficiaries under National Food Security Act, thus bearing huge subsidy burden.
- **Other Subsidies** Seed subsidy, Irrigation subsidy under PM-Krishi Sinchayee Yojana. etc.

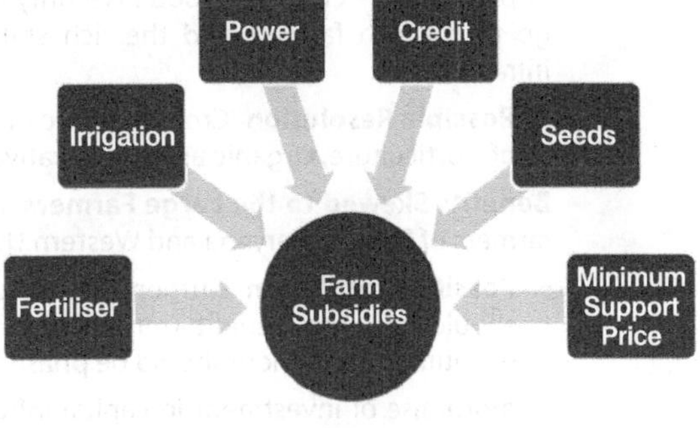

Benefits of Agricultural Subsidies

- **Support Farm Income** Farm subsidies provide assured income and increase the purchasing power of farmers. As per Ministry of Agriculture and Farmer's welfare, farm subsidies constitute around 21% of farmer's income.
- **Higher Growth to Fulfill Food Security and Obtaining Desirable Structure** The economic rationale of subsidies lies in incentivising the producers to increase production leading to high growth in national income and achieving desirable structure of production. Example: Recent push is being given for the production of millets, oilseeds and pulses and achieving the goal of nutritional security.
  - The farm subsidies assure adequate food supply and reduce the chances of food shortage and food inflation. Production went up from 50 million tonnes of food grains in the 1950s to more than 300 million tonnes presently.
- **Improvement in Productivity of Land** such as through fertiliser subsidies by greater adoption of fertilisers.
- **Improvement in HDI** Improved farm incomes and food security aids in addressing issues like malnutrition, improving overall living standard.
- **Crop Diversification** Incentivising 'less focussed' crops where subsidies on the crops having nutritional and environmental benefits are promoted. For example, boost to millet production.
- **Bridge the Income Divide** According to FAO, 70% of Indian rural households rely mostly on agriculture for a living. Income support for small and marginal farmers bridges the income gap.
- **Technology Adoption** Subsidy is necessary to accelerate new inventions, which are socially desirable but whose adoption needs huge capital and producers believe it to be risky investment. For example, Green Revolution provided support to adopt new HYV seeds and chemical fertilisers. Increased usage of technology and better infrastructure in agricultural activities lead to increased efficiency, increased profitability and reduce distress migration.
- **Achievement of National Goals** Farm subsidies are crucial levers in the achievement of goals such as achieving the USD 5 trillion economy status, Sustainable Development Goals (SDG). For example, KUSUM programme (subsidy for solar pumps).
- **Boost to Agricultural Exports** Subsidy to domestic producers may enable them to offer competitive price in global market and can lead to import substitution of such goods or it may even increase export.
- **Creation of capital assets through infrastructure subsidy**, for example cold storage to reduce post-harvest losses of perishable agricultural produce.
- **Addressing Inequalities and Imbalances** They help in reducing inter-personal income inequalities and inter-regional development imbalances.
  - To support farmers as majority of farmers have small/marginal landholdings and are dependent upon agriculture for subsistence.

Distortions Created by the Agricultural Subsidies

- **Cereal Centric, Regionally Biased and Input Intensive** Price subsidies has affected Indian agriculture negatively. This has made Indian agriculture cereal centric and neglectful towards pulses, oil seeds and coarse cereals. This has led to import of these crops and food insecurity in lower strata which depend upon coarse cereals. Also, most of the subsidies go to the rich farmers and the rich states which are able to grow marketable surplus and have well developed infrastructure.
  - **Possible Resolution** Crop diversification by including more crops under MSP, Mission on Integrated Development of Horticulture, Organic and Cooperative farming, food processing, mixed farming, Direct Benefit Transfer.
- **Benefits Skewed to the Large Farmers** Fertiliser subsidies are generally cornered by the manufacturers and the rich farmers of Punjab, Haryana and Western Uttar Pradesh.
  - **Possible Resolution** Nutrient based subsidy and Neem-Coated Urea has been introduced by government. There should be Direct Benefit Transfer of fertiliser subsidy through Aadhaar authentication, organic farming should be encouraged and there should be phased increase in the price of urea.
- Compromise of investment in capital infrastructure in agriculture. From 1976 to 2003-subsidies increased but public investment in agriculture declined.
  - **Possible Resolution** Kelkar Committee recommended the phased elimination of subsidies and convert them to capital investments. There is a need to invest more in agriculture R and D, build better infrastructure to create efficient value chains bringing Farmer Producer Organisations (FPO).

- **Excessive Use of Natural Resources** The policy design and implementation is such that it is skewed towards the excessive use of subsidised resources. For instance, power subsidy has led to overuse of ground water which has further resulted into dramatic fall in ground water levels. Electricity consumption in Indian agriculture is far greater than in any comparable large country.
  - **Possible Resolution** Separate agriculture feeder network (under Deen Dayal Upadhayay Gram Jyoti Yojana). This separate agriculture feeder will supply electricity only for a few hours a day. The process has shown positive results in arresting decline of ground water levels in Gujarat.
- **Environmental Effects and Decline in Soil Fertility** The Parliamentary Standing Committee on Agriculture observed that there is an imbalance in fertiliser use in terms of NPK as it is evidenced by their wider consumption ratio of (6.7) : (2.4) : 1 in the country as against their desirable ratio of 4:2:1. The situation is more grim in agriculturally important states like Punjab and Haryana where NPK use ratio is as high as (31.4) : 8 : 1 and (27.7) : (6.1) : 1, respectively. This harms the soil fertility, biodiversity and also leads to eutrophication (increased nutrients in water bodies, eventually leading to decreased oxygen concentration in them) and bio-accumulation/bio-magnification.
  - **Possible Resolution** Creating awareness among farmers, increasing penetration of soil Student Notes: health card scheme, promoting organic farming and innovative products like neem-coated urea will go a long way to check the issue.
- **Indiscriminate Use of Price Subsidies** Although price subsidies are better targeted, they tend to create inefficiencies since they embed incentives for fraud, diversion and waste. Such subsidies eventually become entrenched, accumulate and may ultimately pose a threat to the sustainability of subsidies itself.
  - **Possible Resolution** Alternatives to price interventions that have similar advantages of targeting beneficiaries must be explored and tried. For instance, Price deficiency payments are a substantial improvement on procurement-based price supports.
  - **Better Use of Credit or Interest Subsidies** There is no strong rationale backing credit and interest subsidies. This is because formal sector interest rates have not been the constraint to increasing access to formal sector institutions.
  - **Possible Resolution** These subsidies would be better spent in strengthening the credit infrastructure and rural banking.
- **Heavy Fiscal Burden** In 2017-18, the annual Central Government subsidies to farmers was of the order of ₹ 120,500 crores. In the same period, the annual State Government subsidies are almost of an equal amount of ₹ 115,500 crores. This significantly increased during the Covid-19 pandemic.
  - **Possible Resolution** A better targeting of subsidies with the usage of JAM (Jan Dhan – AADHAAR- Mobile Number) trinity can reduce the fiscal burden.
  - **WTO Concerns** India's farm subsidies are questioned by the developed nations at the WTO. MSP is considered trade distortionary and breaches the Aggregate Measures of Support (AMS) level limited by the WTO norms.

Conclusion

Farm subsidies have proven to be vital in supporting agriculture and providing income security to farmers. The government should take steps to rationalise farm subsidies and invest more on capital formation, R andD in agriculture as Kelkar Committee have recommended. This will improve agriculture productivity and make agriculture more remunerative.

Subsidies vs Cropping Pattern

Q.2 To what extent, agricultural subsidies were responsible for severe water stress in various regions of the country? What role subsidies can play to encourage crop diversity and changing cropping pattern according to the demands of people? (250 Words, 15 Marks)

Ans. **Introduction** An agricultural subsidy is a governmental financial support paid to farmers and agribusinesses to supplement their income, manage the supply of agricultural commodities and influence the cost and supply of such commodities. According to Economic survey 2021 India spends about 2% of GDP on Farm subsidies.

Impact of Agricultural Subsidies on Water Stress

- **Increased Water-intensive Crop Cultivation** Agricultural subsidies in India have historically incentivised the cultivation of water-intensive crops such as rice and sugarcane. These crops require substantial amounts of water for irrigation, leading to increased water stress in regions where water resources are limited.
  - In states like Punjab and Haryana, subsidies on rice cultivation have contributed to the overexploitation of groundwater and declining water tables.
- **Over-extraction of Groundwater** Subsidies on electricity or diesel for pumping groundwater have led to the over-extraction of groundwater in various regions.
  - In states like Maharashtra and Rajasthan, subsidies provided for agricultural electricity have resulted in excessive groundwater pumping, exacerbating water stress and depleting aquifers.
- **Monocropping and Reduced Crop Diversity** Subsidies often focus on specific crops like assured procurement leading to monocropping practices and a lack of crop diversity. This can strain water resources and increase vulnerability to water stress.
  - In states like Gujarat and parts of Telangana, subsidies for cotton cultivation have contributed to the expansion of cotton monoculture, which requires substantial irrigation water.
- **Inefficient Irrigation Practices** Subsidies that promote inefficient irrigation practices, such as flood irrigation, can intensify water stress. Flood irrigation methods, prevalent in many regions, lead to high water losses through evaporation and runoff.
- **Groundwater Contamination** Subsidies on chemical fertilisers and pesticides can contribute to water pollution and degradation, impacting water availability and quality.

Other Factors Responsible for Water Stress

- **Inadequate Rainfall and Uneven Distribution** Regions with low and erratic rainfall face water stress due to inadequate water availability for agriculture, domestic use and other purposes.
  - Arid and semi-arid regions like Rajasthan and parts of Gujarat experience water stress due to limited rainfall and high evaporation rates.
- **Inefficient Water Management and Irrigation Practices** Poor water management practices, including inefficient irrigation techniques, contribute to water stress. Inefficient methods like flood irrigation and lack of water conservation measures result in high water losses.
  - Regions like Bihar and Eastern Uttar Pradesh face water stress due to inadequate water management practices.
- **Population Growth and Urbanisation** Rapid population growth and urbanisation strain water resources, particularly in urban areas. Increased demand for water from expanding cities and growing industries leads to water stress.
  - Cities like Chennai and Bengaluru experience water stress due to rising population and urban development.
- **Climate Change and Variability** Climate change impacts precipitation patterns, exacerbating water stress in some regions. Erratic monsoons, increased frequency of droughts and changing rainfall patterns affect water availability.
- **Inter-state Water Disputes and Governance Challenges** Water stress can also arise from inter-state water disputes and inadequate governance mechanisms. Conflicts over water sharing, as seen in disputes between states like Karnataka and Tamil Nadu over river water, can lead to water stress and strained relations between regions.

Role of subsidies in encouraging crop diversity and changing cropping pattern according to the demands of people

- **Financial Incentives for Diversification** Subsidies can provide financial incentives for farmers to diversify their crops by offering support or preferential treatment for cultivating a wider range of crops.
  - For instance, the Government of India's National Horticulture Mission provides subsidies for the cultivation of fruits, vegetables and other high-value crops, promoting crop diversification.
- **Support for Market-driven Crop Choices** Subsidies can be tailored to support crops that are in high demand or have greater market value, aligning cropping patterns with consumer preferences.
  - An example is the subsidy support provided by the government for the cultivation of pulses and oilseeds in response to increasing domestic demand and reducing import dependence.

- **Research and Development Subsidies** Subsidies can be directed towards research and development initiatives that promote crop diversification and the adoption of new cropping patterns.
  - For instance, subsidies for research in alternative crops or agroforestry systems can incentivize farmers to explore and adopt more diversified cropping practices.
- **Infrastructure Development Subsidies** Subsidies can be allocated for the development of infrastructure that supports crop diversification, such as storage facilities, processing units and market linkages.
  - For example, subsidies for cold storage facilities can facilitate the cultivation and marketing of perishable horticultural crops.
- **Risk Mitigation Subsidies** Subsidies that help mitigate the risks associated with crop diversification can encourage farmers to experiment with new crops and cropping patterns.
  - This can include subsidies for crop insurance, weather-based insurance or income support during the transition period.
- **Collaboration with Private Sector and NGOs** Subsidies can be utilised to encourage collaboration between the public sector, private sector and non-governmental organisations (NGOs) to promote crop diversification.
  - Subsidies can support public-private partnerships or engagement with NGOs working on promoting sustainable agriculture and crop diversification. These partnerships can provide technical expertise, market access and knowledge sharing opportunities.

Way Forward

- It is important to note that the impact of subsidies on water stress varies across regions, as it depends on factors such as existing water availability, cropping patterns and the specific design and implementation of subsidies.
- By aligning subsidies with sustainable water management practices and regional needs, they can play a positive role in mitigating water stress and promoting more sustainable agricultural practices.
- It is important to note that subsidies should be carefully designed and targeted to ensure they effectively promote crop diversity and align with sustainable agricultural practices.

Conclusion

In summary, agricultural subsidies can contribute to water stress when they incentivise water-intensive crops or unsustainable irrigation practices. However, subsidies can also be used as a tool to encourage crop diversity and adapt cropping patterns to meet market demands.

Subsidies vs Investment Debate

Q.3 Which of the two-Investment through higher government spending or Subsidies will facilitate higher agricultural growth? Critically comment. What measures have been taken by the government to improve capital formation in agriculture? (250 Words, 15 Marks)

Ans. **Introduction** The share of public sector investment in total agricultural investment was as high as 33.6% during the 1960s but has come down to 15% during 2010-17 (average ₹ 40,100 crore per annum). Corporate investment is only 3% of the total. Private investment, predominantly by farm households is 82% and it holds the major share of total investment in agriculture and allied activities.

Almost 80% of the public expenditure going to agriculture is in the form of input subsidies (fertilisers, power, irrigation) and only 20% as investments in agriculture.

Both investment through higher government spending and subsidies can play a role in facilitating higher agricultural growth but each approach has its own advantages and potential drawbacks.

Critical Analysis of impact of investment and subsidies on agricultural growth

Impact of Investments

Positive Impact

- **Infrastructure Development** Increased investment can be used to improve rural infrastructure such as irrigation systems, roads and storage facilities. This can enhance productivity, reduce post-harvest losses and improve market access for farmers.
- **Crop Diversification** Improved access to infrastructure in rural areas can encourage the cultivation of perishable products, thereby exerting favourable influence on crop diversification.
- **Research and Development** Government funding can support agricultural research and development, leading to the adoption of new technologies, improved seeds and better farming practices. This can enhance productivity and overall agricultural growth.
- **Capacity Building** Investments in farmer training programs, extension services, and education can help enhance the knowledge and skills of farmers. This can lead to improved agricultural practices and increased yields.
- **Higher Returns** Research clearly shows that marginal returns on agri-investments are 5 to 10 times higher than from agri-input subsidies. Every ₹ 10 lakh invested on farm research potentially pulled 328 people out of poverty. Likewise, every ₹ 1 spent on agricultural research and development increased farm GDP by ₹ 11.2.
- **Poverty Reduction** The period from the mid 1970s to the end of the 1980s when poverty showed a marked reduction was also a decade when investment in agriculture rose phenomenally and agriculture sector growth was highest.

Impact of Subsidies

Positive Impact

- **Input Subsidies** Subsidies on fertilisers, seeds and other agricultural inputs can reduce production costs for farmers, making agriculture more economically viable. This can encourage increased production and investment in the sector.
- **Price Support** Subsidies that maintain stable and remunerative prices for agricultural products can provide income security for farmers. This stability can incentivise farmers to increase production and invest in their farms.
- **Support Farm Income** Farm subsidies provide assured income and increase the purchasing power of farmers. As per Ministry of Agriculture and Farmer's welfare, farm subsidies constitute around 21% of farmer's income.
- **Technology Adoption** Subsidy is necessary to accelerate new inventions, which are socially desirable but whose adoption needs huge capital and producers believe it to be risky investment. For example: Green Revolution provided support to adopt new HYV seeds and chemical fertilisers.

Potential Concerns

- **Distorted Market Signals** Subsidies can artificially inflate production and distort market signals. Over-reliance on subsidies may result in overproduction, leading to price fluctuations and market imbalances.
- **Fiscal Burden** Farm subsidies form about 2% of India's GDP. Subsidies can strain the government's finances and potentially crowd out other essential sectors.
- **Inequitable Distribution** Subsidies may not always reach small-scale farmers or marginalised communities, exacerbating income inequalities. The Shanta Kumar Committee, report in 2015, stated that only 6% of the MSP could be received by the farmers.

Government Steps to Improve Capital Formation

- **Infrastructure Development** Governments invest in the development of rural infrastructure, such as irrigation systems, roads and storage facilities.
  - **Example** PM Krishi Sinchayee Yojana.
- **Setting up an Agri-tech Infrastructure Fund, Rural Infrastructure Development Fund (RIDF) and creating a Long-Term Irrigation Fund and Micro Irrigation Fund.**
  - Under the Agriculture Infrastructure Fund, entities such as farmers, start-ups, government agencies and local bodies benefit from setting up eligible infrastructure projects.
  - Under the Rashtriya Krishi Vikas Yojana (RKVY) Scheme, grants-in-aid are given to State Governments on the basis of the projects approved in the State Level Sanctioning Committee Meeting (SLSC).
- **Subsidised Loans and Interest Rate Subsidies** Governments offer subsidised loans or provide interest rate subsidies to farmers to encourage investments in agricultural activities.
  - **Example** Access to institutional credit is being provided through Kisan Credit Card and other channels.

- **Research and Development Support** Governments allocate funds for agricultural research and development to improve farming techniques, crop varieties and livestock breeds.
  - **Example** GM crops like BT MUSTARD
- **Incentives for Agribusiness Investments** These measures attract capital from domestic and foreign investors leading to improved agricultural value chains, processing facilities and marketing infrastructure.
- **Public-Private Partnerships** Governments foster collaborations between public and private sectors to mobilise capital for agriculture. Public-private partnerships can leverage the strengths of both sectors to enhance investment, technology transfer and market linkages in the agricultural sector.
- **Farmer Training and Capacity Building** Governments invest in training programmes, workshops and extension services to enhance farmers skills and knowledge.
  - **Example** Krishi Vigyan Kendras (KVKs)
- **Agricultural Credit and Financing Schemes** Governments often establish specialised financial institutions or modify existing banking systems to provide agricultural credit at affordable interest rates.
  - **Example** NABARD, Agriculture Infrastructure Fund (AIF), Income support is provided to farmers through PM KISAN Scheme

Way Forward

- Public investment in agriculture and irrigation must increase at 14% per annum as proposed by the Ashok Dalwai Committee. In addition, the capital use efficiency of the existing major-medium irrigation projects must improve.
- Each state must prioritise public expenditure, keeping in view the type of investment and the subsidy that will enable higher productivity gains.
  - Research shows that the low per capita income states, largely lagging in agricultural growth and having dominance of small holders, will get higher payoffs from additional public investment in irrigation and in power and irrigation subsidies.
- **R and D** in agriculture and allied sectors has largely been in the public domain. The government must increase the outlay of agriculture R andD, but it also must encourage private R andD to inject adequate capital.
  - Private capital can also be encouraged in certain rural projects such as in solar power, weather stations, digital information on rainfall, soil moisture and irrigation requirements, etc.
  - India spends barely 0.5% of national income on R andD in agriculture, which is very low compared to about 3% in the developed countries.

Conclusion

Both investment through higher government spending and subsidies can facilitate higher agricultural growth. While farm subsidies are essential for farmers to meet their input requirements in the short run, investment in the sector is needed to spur growth in the long run.

A balanced approach is crucial, taking into account fiscal sustainability, efficient resource allocation and equitable distribution of benefits.

Direct Benefit Transfer (DBT)

Q.4 Reforming the government delivery system through the Direct Benefit Transfer Scheme is a progressive step, but it has its limitations too. Comment. (150 Words, 10 Marks) **UPSC Mains PYQ 2022**

Ans. **Introduction** The Direct Benefit Transfer Scheme (DBT) is a government initiative in India that aims to reform the delivery system for various social welfare schemes and benefits by transferring them directly to the bank accounts of the beneficiaries.

- It aims to eliminate intermediaries and reduce leakages and corruption in the delivery of benefits, thereby improving the efficiency and effectiveness of the government's welfare programmes.

Funds Transferred via DBT in FY23 (Government data for FY22-23)

Scheme	Total Direct Benefit Transfer (In ₹ crore)	Scheme	Total Direct Benefit Transfer (In ₹ crore)
PAHAL	3.89719	PMAYG	28.94777
MGNREGS	24.736.5	PDS	100406.0
NSAP	1.54876	Fertiliser	72.961.97
Scholarship Scheme	1.692.21	Others	63.911.16
		Grand Total	**198.101.62**

- DBT was introduced on 1st January 2013 with the main aim of improving the government's delivery system and redesigning the current procedure in welfare schemes by making the flow of funds and information faster, secure and reduce the number of frauds.
- According to Economic Survey 2023, DBT has helped transfer more than ₹ 26.5 lakh crore till date for central schemes.
  - Union Government had managed to save about Rs 2.2 lakh crore as of March 2021 by removing the names of 9.4 crore beneficiaries across databases.
  - Within the span of the past decade, the DBT has already expanded from 24 schemes in 43 districts, to 200 central schemes and over 2,000 state government schemes pan India.

Direct benefit transfer is reforming government delivery system in the following ways

- **Good Governance** It has brought transparency and reduced instances of pilferage from the distribution of Central Government-sponsored funds.
- **Expanded the Coverage of Services** In a mission-mode approach, it endeavoured to open bank accounts for all households, expanded Aadhaar to all and scaled up the coverage of banking and telecom services.
- **Instant and Easy Money Transfer** It provided for time-bound transfers of benefits, which has helped recipients avoid delays in the transfer of money.
- **Targeted Distribution** it ensures precise targeting of beneficiaries.
  - DBT assists in the distribution of grants to worthy candidates who are living in poverty. It makes it easier for the government to communicate with the target recipients.
- **Financial Inclusion** DBT encourages people, especially from rural and underprivileged backgrounds, to open bank accounts, thus promoting financial inclusion.
- **Real-time Tracking** DBT allows for real-time tracking of fund disbursement, helping identify bottlenecks and areas of improvement.
- **Empowerment** It enable beneficiaries to have greater control over their funds, enhancing their decision-making power and overall empowerment.
- **Financial Assistance** In rural Bharat, DBT has allowed the government to provide financial assistance effectively and transparently to farmers with lower transaction costs – be it for fertilisers or any of the other schemes.
- **Transfer of Funds and Social Security** In urban India, the PM Awas Yojana and LPG Pahal scheme successfully use DBT to transfer funds to eligible beneficiaries. Various scholarship schemes and the National Social Assistance Programme use the DBT architecture to provide social security.

Limitations of DBT Schemes

- **Exclusion Errors** Cumbersome documentation requirements and opaque/delayed application processing often result in exclusion of eligible beneficiaries.
- **Payment Failures** Spelling errors in Aadhaar details, incorrect seeding of citizen's Aadhaar and bank account, pending KYC and frozen/blocked bank accounts, network failures, biometric authentication failures, point-of-sale (PoS) device malfunctioning are some of the most prominent reasons for payment failures in DBT.

- **Misuse of Money** Provision of cash might result in its misuse by the beneficiaries and may not serve the intended purpose.
- **Market Vulnerabilities** Replacement of welfare subsidies by DBT cash payments might subject the beneficiary to market vulnerabilities. e.g., DBT of LPG subsidy under PAHAL is not compensating the increase in gas prices in the market.
- **Inadequate Rural Banking** There are just 14.6 bank branches per 1 lakh adults in India. It is sparser in rural India.
  - Accessing banks in rural areas leads to loss of one wage day for the worker. Also, people have to spend money on transportation to access the bank to withdraw their payments/subsidies.
- **Dependence on Technology** The DBT scheme relies heavily on technology and requires beneficiaries to have access to a bank account and a mobile phone. This may exclude certain segments of the population, such as elderly people or those living in remote or rural areas, who may not have access to these technologies.
- **Administrative Challenges** The DBT scheme involves a complex process of linking beneficiaries' bank accounts and mobile numbers to their entitlements and requires coordination between various government agencies and banks. This can lead to administrative challenges and delays in the delivery of benefits.

Futuristic Measures to Improve the DBT Ecosystem

- **Systemising Innovation** Empowering innovation system are some of the aspects that would require continued focus.
  - This would play a vital role for India in meeting the diverse needs of its population and ensuring balanced, equitable and inclusive growth.
- **Availability** There is an urgent need to increase the accessibility of enrolment points for citizens across schemes, specifically in rural and peri-urban areas.
  - **A Common Body for All** A common grievance redress cell for all DBT schemes across tiers state, district and block to help the benficiers to resolve their issues.
- **Leasing** It can help both tenant and reverse-tenant farmers operate consolidated holdings, while allowing owners to take up non-agricultural employment without risking loss of their lands.

Conclusion

India's Direct Benefit Transfer scheme has revolutionised the delivery of social welfare benefits, ensuring efficient and direct access for beneficiaries while reducing corruption and wastage. The future plans for DBT in India promise to build upon its successes, further streamlining the process of benefit delivery and enhancing its impact. Indeed, the DBT paradigm is one of India's most significant contributions to the global welfare discourse.

Minimum Support Price and Crops Procurement (Statutory backing of MSP)

Q.5 Tracing the evolution of Minimum Support Price (MSP) regime in India, discuss how statutory backing to MSP can help in dealing with the agrarian stress in the country? Comment. (250 Words, 15 Marks)

Ans. **Introduction** The MSP is the price at which the government guarantees to purchase agricultural commodities from farmers to ensure a minimum income and provide price stability. The MSP was fixed by the government based on recommendations from the Commission for Agricultural Costs and Prices (CACP), which considers factors like cost of production, demand-supply dynamics and price trends. The mandated crops include 14 crops of the kharif season, 6 rabi crops, 2 other commercial crops and FRP for sugarcane.

Evolution of MSP Policy

The government continues to review and adjust MSPs based on changing circumstances to ensure adequate support to farmers and promote agricultural growth in the country.

- **Green Revolution Era (1960s-1970s)** The MSP regime was introduced in the 1960s as part of the Green Revolution to boost agricultural production. Initially, MSP was focused on wheat and paddy, the main staple crops, to incentivise farmers to adopt modern farming techniques and increase production.

- **Expansion of MSP Coverage (1970s-1990s)** Over time, the MSP regime expanded to include more crops such as coarse grains, pulses, oilseeds and cotton, addressing the needs of a diverse agricultural sector. The government aimed to support farmers in various regions and promote crop diversification.
- **Liberalisation and Reforms (1990s-2000s)** With economic liberalisation in the 1990s, the government gradually reduced its intervention in agriculture, including the procurement and distribution of food grains. However, the MSP system remained in place to provide a safety net for farmers and stabilise prices during periods of market volatility.
- **National Policy for Farmers (2007)** It emphasised the need to enhance and stabilise farm incomes and called for a comprehensive approach to MSPs and procurement. The policy aimed to ensure remunerative prices to farmers, adequate market infrastructure and efficient procurement and distribution systems.

State of Agrarian Stress in the Country

- **Farmer Suicides** India has witnessed a distressing number of farmer suicides over the years.
  - According to the National Crime Records Bureau (NCRB), in 2019, there were 10,281 farmer suicides in India, accounting for 7.4% of total suicides in the country.
- **Climate Change Impact** Climate change has severely affected Indian agriculture. Erratic rainfall patterns, prolonged droughts and extreme weather events have led to crop failures and reduced agricultural productivity.
  - According to the Indian Council of Agricultural Research (ICAR), India's agricultural GDP is projected to decline by 2.8-3.2% by 2050 due to climate change.
- **Water Scarcity** Water scarcity is a significant challenge for Indian agriculture. Groundwater depletion, inadequate irrigation infrastructure and inefficient water management practices contribute to water stress.
  - As per the Composite Water Management Index (CWMI) report by NITI Aayog, around 54% of India's agricultural areas face high to extremely high-water stress.
- **Land Degradation** Land degradation, including soil erosion and fertility loss, poses a threat to agricultural productivity.
  - According to the Indian Space Research Organisation (ISRO), about 30% of India's total geographical area is affected by land degradation, leading to decreased crop yields and economic losses.
- **Economic Challenges** Indian farmers often face economic challenges such as low farm incomes, rising input costs, lack of access to credit and market volatility. The Minimum Support Price (MSP) mechanism, intended to provide price support to farmers, often falls short in reaching all farmers effectively.
- **Crop Losses** Crop losses due to pests, diseases and inadequate pest management practices also contribute to agricultural stress. Insect infestations, such as locust attacks, can cause significant damage to crops and result in financial losses for farmers.

Reasons Behind the Statutory Backing to the Minimum Support Price (MSP)

- **Price Stability and Income Security** Statutory backing of MSP ensures a guaranteed minimum price for agricultural commodities, offering income security to farmers. It enables farmers to plan their cultivation, investment and expenditure with more confidence.
- **Hight Input Costs but Lesser Prices than MSP** Largest fertiliser seller IFFCO announced an up to 58% hike in the prices of (the decontrolled) non-urea fertilisers. In most crops grown across much of India, the prices received by farmers, especially during harvest time, are well below the officially-declared MSPs.
- **Reduced Market Exploitation** With a legally mandated MSP, farmers have the assurance of fair prices for their produce. It reduces the risk of exploitation and ensures that farmers receive reasonable remuneration for their hard work.
- **Incentive for Crop Diversification** A robust MSP regime, supported by legislation, can provide incentives for farmers to diversify their crop choices.
  - MSP distorted the nature of crop diversity and created a binary of wheat and rice systems. Only 10% of pulses and oilseeds are getting procured under MSP system.
- **Risk Mitigation** Statutory backing of MSP acts as a risk mitigation measure for farmers. Even in adverse situations, such as crop failures or market downturns, farmers are assured of a minimum price for their produce.

- **Farmer Empowerment and Negotiating Power** Statutory backing of MSP empowers farmers by giving them a stronger negotiating position in the market. They can demand better prices from traders and buyers.
- **Calculation of MSP based on A2+FL Cost** The criticism of A2+FL is that it doesn't cover all costs and that a more representative measure, C2, needs to be used. For example, in the 2017-18 rabi season, CACP data shows that C2 for wheat was 54% higher than A2+FL. The Swaminathan Commission had also stated that the MSP should be based on the comprehensive cost of production, which is the C2 method.
- **Agricultural Growth and Food Security** It will incentivize farmers to increase productivity, adopt modern farming practices and invest in agricultural activities. Adequate MSPs also ensure the availability of food grains and contribute to national food security.

Challenges Associated with Statutory Backing to MSP

- **Distortion of Market Forces** The statutory backing of MSPs can distort market forces by creating price floors for certain crops. This can lead to a supply-demand mismatch and affect price discovery based on supply and demand dynamics.
- **Costly and Inefficient Procurement** Procurement operations require substantial financial resources, including storage, transportation and distribution infrastructure, which can be inefficiently utilised.
  - Government spend 6,02,156 crore in paddy procurement during last 5 years (2016-17 to 2020-21)
- **Unsustainable Fiscal Burden on the Government** Implementing large-scale procurement operations can impose a significant fiscal burden on the government.
- **Market Distortions and Trade Issues** When MSPs are set above market prices, it can discourage private buyers and exporters from participating in the market. This can restrict trade and limit market access for farmers.
- **India and WTO Dispute on Agreement on Agriculture** India's price support measures have been continuously opposed by the developed countries at the WTO. India had invoked the Bali Peace Clause in 2020 because India had exceeded the ceiling on support it can offer farmers for rice in the year 2018-19. With a legally guaranteed higher MSP, India will face stiffer opposition at the WTO.
- **Lack of Targeting and Inefficiency** Small and marginal farmers who often cultivate non-MSP crops or have limited access to markets, may not receive the same benefits.
  - The Shanta Kumar Committee, in its report in 2015, stated that only 6% of the MSP could be received by the farmers.
- **Dependency and Overproduction** It would discourage farmers from exploring alternative crops or diversifying their agricultural activities. This can lead to overproduction of MSP crops, which may result in surplus stocks, storage challenges and wastage of resources.
  - 38% of Net sown area are under binary of rice and wheat foodgrains.

Conclusion

Addressing these negative aspects requires careful policy considerations and reforms that strike a balance between price stability for farmers and the efficient functioning of agricultural markets. A comprehensive approach should focus on strengthening market mechanisms, improving farm-level productivity, promoting value addition and encouraging diversification, alongwith appropriate price support measures.

Critical Analysis of MSP

Q.6 Examine how MSP procurement regime is neither economically nor agro-ecologically sustainable. Also, evaluate the alternative approaches that can be adopted to improve the existing MSP regime. (150 Words, 10 Marks)

Ans. **Introduction** Minimum Support Price (MSP) is a form of market intervention by the central government that insulates farmers against the unwarranted fluctuations in prices; creates an incentive structure in order to direct the allocation of resources towards desired crops and; insulates consumers against sharp price rise.

Existing Procurement Regime is Neither Economically Nor Agro-ecologically Sustainable

Economically Unsustainable

- **High Fiscal Burden** The economic cost of procured rice and wheat is much higher for the FCI than the market price of the same. Due to this, the FCI's economic burden eventually will have to be borne by the Union Government and may subsequently lead to divergence of funds from being invested in agriculture infrastructure.
  - In the 2021-22 rabi season, the government procured 146.4 million tonnes of wheat and rice at MSP, which was 86% of the total procurement target. This was the highest-ever procurement of wheat and rice at MSP in a single season. The government also paid a total of ₹ 1.95 lakh crore to farmers as MSP.
- **Wastage of Agricultural Produce** It has also led to procurement of twice the buffer stock creating storage issues which results in huge wastage of agricultural produce.
- **Procurement Related Problems** Almost two-third of the cereal produce is taken through the MSP route leaving very little for the open market. This creates an overreliance of farmers on the MSP system and distorts the open market.
- **Reduced Agricultural Exports** Hikes in MSP also adversely affect the exports by making Indian farm goods un-competitive especially when international market prices are lower.
- **India and WTO dispute on Agreement on Agriculture** India's price support measures have been continuously opposed by the developed countries at the WTO. India had invoked the Bali Peace Clause in 2020 because India had exceeded the ceiling on support it can offer farmers for rice in the year 2018-19. With a legally guaranteed higher MSP, India will face stiffer opposition at the WTO.
- **Lack of Targeting and Inefficiency** Small and marginal farmers who often cultivate non-MSP crops or have limited access to markets, may not receive the same benefits.
  - The Shanta Kumar Committee, in its report in 2015, stated that only 6% of the MSP could be received by the farmers.
- **No MSP for Allied Sector** There is no minimum support price (MSP) for products of animal husbandry or fisheries and no procurement by the government. Allied sector has the potential to raise farmer's income and the target of doubling of farmers income.

Agro-ecologically Unsustainable

- **Skewed Policy** The benefits of MSP have accrued to farmers of a few crops and regions. It has mostly been confined to four crops i.e. sugarcane, paddy/rice, wheat and cotton. MSP coverage accounts for nearly three-fourths of the country's sugarcane production, roughly 50% for paddy/rice, 40% for wheat and 25% for cotton.
  - The area under cultivation of rice and wheat from the time of the Green Revolution till recently increased from 30 million hectares to 44 million hectares (~50% increase) and 9 million hectares to 31 million hectares (~250% increase), respectively, while that of coarse cereals plunged from 37 million hectares to 25 million hectares (~33% increase).
- **Facilitates Water Intensive Agriculture** In addition to the four crops accounting for just over 22% of India's agricultural output by value, all four are water-guzzling. Almost 100% of sugarcane and wheat area in India is under irrigation. The same goes for paddy/rice grown in Punjab, Haryana, Telangana andhra Pradesh and Tamil Nadu.
- **Environmental Problems** Higher MSPs on such crops leads to groundwater depletion, soil degradation and increased water pollution.
- **Incentivises Production Beyond Requirements** MSP does not hold much value today when India has become surplus in cereals and sugar. Furthermore, data from successive National Sample Survey rounds points to declining or stagnant per capita household consumption of both cereals and sugar.

Alternative approaches to improve the existing MSP regime

- **MSP Model Covering All Crops** Making MSP legally enforceable on all crops can potentially address the aforesaid distortions. Farmers can be assured of getting MSPs for at least the 23 officially notified crops. It should further be possible to fix MSPs in such a way to ensure higher returns on crops consuming less water. However, extending to more crops would have serious implications for the exchequer if it is backed by open-ended procurement.

- **Price Deficiency Payment** To solve the problem of MSP, Both NITI and Economic Survey recommend Price Deficiency Payment (PDP) in which the government pays the farmers the difference between modal rate (the average prices in major mandis) and the MSPs. Some states like Madhya Pradesh (Bhavantar Bhugtan Yojana), Haryana Government (Bhavantar Bharapai Yojana) have launched price deficit financing schemes.
- **Direct Income Support** It would benefit farmers in the times of agrarian distress, that too without distorting markets. They have also been found to be more inclusive and promote more equity across farm sizes.
- **Area Planning** Currently, farmers make plans according to their own needs, their limited knowledge of land and technology, labour and capital available. However, area planning by the government would enable production objectives to be set by demand, social or political imperatives and the existing situation in the country. This is a time taking process but would help in overcoming over-supply and falling price problems.
- In its 'Strategy for New India@75' document, the NITI Aayog suggested many reform like:
  - **Unified National Market** Raising MSP or prices can only be a partial solution to the problem of assuring remunerative returns to farmers, a long-term solution lies in the creation of a competitive, stable and unified national market to enable better price discovery and a long-term trade regime favourable to exports.
  - **Modernisation** Modernising the agriculture sector through improving irrigation facilities, marketing reforms, post harvesting management and better crop insurance products.
  - **Contract Farming and Future Trade** The report also advocated contract farming. Emphasis was laid on the need to encourage futures trade and removal of entry barriers to increase market depth.
- **Learning Best Practices** To encourage crop diversification and thereby reduce the consumption of water, some State Governments are taking measures to incentivise farmers to shift away from paddy and wheat.
  - Haryana has launched a scheme in 2020 to provide Rs 7,000 per acre to those farmers who will use more than 50% of their paddy area (as per the area sown in 2019-20) for other crops.
  - The farmers can grow maize, bajra, pulses or cotton in such diversified area.
  - Crop produce grown in such diversified area under the scheme will be procured by the State Government at MSP.

Conclusion

The procurement policy of the government needs reforms that are easier to implement. Efforts must be made to balance market price and farmers' support. Cash transfer gives better choices to farmers than imposing subsidies.

PM-AASHA Scheme

Q.7 The PM-AASHA scheme is aimed at improving procurement mechanism as well as ensuring remunerative prices for farmers. In this context, highlight the various components of the scheme and discuss the concerns associated with it. (150 Words, 10 Marks)

Ans. Introduction Pradhan Mantri Annadata Aay Sanrakshan Abhiyan (PM-AASHA) is an umbrella scheme aimed at ensuring remunerative prices to the farmers for their produce. It guarantees Minimum Support Price (MSP) to the farmers.

Various Components of PM-AASHA

- **Price Support Scheme (PSS)** In Price Support Scheme (PSS), physical procurement of pulses, oilseeds and copra will be done by Central Nodal Agencies with proactive role of State Governments.
  - The procurement expenditure and losses due to procurement will be borne by Central Government as per norms.
- **Price Deficiency Payment Scheme (PDPS)** Under it, direct payment of the difference between the MSP and the selling price will be made to pre-registered farmers selling their produce in the notified market yard and thus it does not involve any physical procurement.
  - **Aim** To provide compensation to farmers for agriculture products whenever its price falls below the announced Minimum Support Price (MSP) and thereby protecting them from losses suffered on account of distress sale.
- **Pilot of Private Procurement and Stockist Scheme (PPPS)** Under this scheme, participation of private sector in procurement operations will be piloted.
  - States have the option to roll out the scheme on pilot basis in selected districts/APMCs involving private stockists.

Significance of PM-AASHA for Indian Farmers

- It is an innovative, MSP-plus approach to the problem of non-remunerative prices.
- The different components would cover the gaps in the procurement and compensation mechanism for crops.
- It would ensure better coverage of MSP and provision of crop-wise procurement is expected to benefit both farmers and states.
- It will benefit the farmers by providing options to the state governments to compensate farmers when the market prices fall below MSP.
- It is expected to help revive the rural economy by assuring better income to farmers and thus address farmers' distress.

However, there are different concerns associated with the scheme, which need to be dealt with like

- **Undue Benefit to Traders (Traders Cartel)** The experience of Madhya Pradesh which implemented the PDPS under the Bhavantar Bhugtan Yojana revealed that
  - Traders plotted with each other and depressed the prices at mandis.
  - They forced farmers to sell at lower prices and pocketed the compensation from the government.
  - Many small and marginal farmers are unable to sell their produce under the Bhavantar scheme.
  - **Lack of Funding** The funding and financial condition of NAFED is a major concern over successful implementation of Price support scheme. If all states apply to NAFED/FCI for procurement of oilseeds or pulses, the agencies will fall short of funds.
- **Poor Procurement by Private Players** Previously, FCI and state agencies have engaged private companies for procurement of wheat and paddy from farmers at MSP. However, the process has not been smooth and the companies have taken years to get their expenses reimbursed by the government.
- **Lack of Efficient Distribution System** NAFED has a stock of 4 million tonnes of pulses and oil seeds because of previous 2 years' procurement. However, their distribution policy is still non-existent.
- **Limited Reach of Procurement** Status of procurement linked to MSP has not been even either in terms of crops covered or geographic spread. For example, in the case of wheat, of the average 33% of marketed surplus procured, 90 percent procurement is accounted only from Punjab, Haryana and Madhya Pradesh.
- **Payment Delays** It have negative effects on the farmers and needs to be corrected to ensure timely payments.
- **Logistics and Storage Issues** The procurement of commodities, other than wheat and paddy, has not been very encouraging.
  - Procurement has largely benefited wheat and paddy growers where almost 33% of the marketed surplus crop is procured.
  - However, PM-AASHA have not focused on improving the procurement infrastructure.

Steps Need to be Taken for Improving Efficient Functioning of PM-AASHAA

- Efficient Market System: Though marketing in general and agriculture marketing in particular cannot be perfect or even near perfect in the classical sense, efficient market system has an important role in transferring remunerative prices (that are more than the MSP) to the farmers.
  - Thus, market architecture and marketing system must be improved, to enable farmers to capture the more optimal share of the market value of their produce.
  - Over time, MSP should be the second choice for any farmer, with markets being the preferred method of monetising their produce.
- **Learning Best Practices** The Haryana Government has launched the Meri Fasal-Mera Byora e-procurement portal. Due to this portal, Haryana has become the first state in India where as many as 14 crops are procured at the Minimum Support Price (MSP).
- The scheme should target small and marginal farmers so as to improve their economic condition.
- The government should effectively check price manipulation by traders, by widening the competition by inter-linking mandis.
- The government should ensure hassle-free and easy registration of farmers.

- **Promoting Digital Mandis** It will enable farmers to directly negotiate with wholesale traders and other local traders, putting an end to the middlemen involved in the process who hamper their movement and freedom of choosing crop type, variety and price point.

Conclusion

Therefore, to ensure the success of this scheme, the government should implement the recommendation of NITI Aayog on making a robust procurement system including strengthening infrastructure such as godowns, drying yards etc. This will go a long way in ensuring the success of any farmer's oriented welfare scheme in the country.

Issues of Buffer Stock and Food Security (Meaning of Food Security)

Q.8 Along with highlighting the components of food security, examine how monoculture and climate change are the two major threats in ensuring food security and sustainability of Indian agriculture. Suggest measures to be taken to ensure long-term food security. (250 Words, 15 Marks)

Ans. **Introduction** According to Food and Agriculture Organisation (FAO), 'food security exists when all people, at all times, have physical and economic access to sufficient, safe and nutritious food to meet their dietary needs and food preferences for an active and healthy life.'

Components of Food Security in India

- **Availability of food means** food production within the country, food imports and the previous years stock stored in government granaries.
- **Accessibility means the food** is within reach of every person.
- **Affordability implies that an individual** has enough money to buy sufficient, safe and nutritious food to meet one's dietary needs.

However, India's performance on food security has been deteriorating as can be seen from Global Hunger Index, where India's ranked 107th out of 121 nations in the Global Hunger Index 2022 (down from the index of 101 in 2021), indicating 'serious' hunger level and Food Security issues.

Current Framework of Food Security in India

- **Constitutional Provision** Though the Indian Constitution does not have any explicit provision regarding right to food, the fundamental right to life enshrined in Article 21 of the Constitution can be interpreted to include the right to live with human dignity, which may include the right to food and other basic necessities.
- **Buffer Stock** Food Corporation of India (FCI) has the prime responsibility of procuring the food grains at Minimum Support Price (MSP) and stored in its warehouses at different locations and from there it is supplied to the State Governments in terms of requirement.
- **Public Distribution System** Over the years, Public Distribution System has become an important part of government's policy for management of the food economy in the country. PDS is supplemental in nature and is not intended to make available the entire requirement of any of the commodity. Under the PDS, presently the commodities namely wheat, rice, sugar and kerosene are being allocated to the States/UTs for distribution. Some States/UTs also distribute additional items of mass consumption through the PDS outlets such as pulses, edible oils, iodized salt, spices, etc.
- **National Food Security Act, 2013 (NFSA)** It marks a paradigm shift in the approach to food security from welfare to rights based approach. NFSA covers 75% of the rural population and 50% of the urban population.

Monaculture and climate change are the two major threats in ensuring food security in India and sustainability of Indian Agriculture

- **Monoculture** It is the agricultural practice of growing a single crop, plant, or livestock species, variety or breed in a field or farming system at a time. According to Food and Agriculture Organisation (FAO), just nine plant species form two-thirds of total crop production. Monoculture is affecting Food Security by:
- **Impact Nutritional Security** Monoculture distorts food consumption patterns, replacing nutritious millets with polished rice and wheat and negatively affected our nutritional security.

- **Reduced Soil Fertility** Wheat and paddy, unlike pulses and legumes, cannot fix nitrogen from the atmosphere. Their continuous cultivation without any crop rotation leads to depletion of soil nutrients and growing dependence on chemical fertilisers and pesticides.
  - It is estimated that about 33% of the world's farmland will be lacking the essential nutrients for crop production.
- **Reduced Climate resilience** Rice-wheat cropping system in Punjab constitutes about 84.6% of total area and has been profitable to the farmers. But these crops are sown compromising on pulses, maize, bajra and oilseeds and cotton, which are known to be climate resistant.
- **Irrigation Demand Increases** Due to Monoculture, topsoil loses elements that could help it retain moisture.
  - In India, a little over 50% of India's net sown area is under rainfed farming and a large part of the irrigated area depends on groundwater extraction through borewells, which needs to be recharged with the groundwater.
- **Increase in Pest Attack** Monocultures are shown to be increasing the spread of new pathogens, which led to reduce agricultural yield.

Climate Change The monsoon accounts for around 70% of India's annual rainfall and irrigates 60% of its net sown area.

- Changing precipitation patterns and growing frequency and intensity of extreme weather events such as heatwaves, floods are already reducing agricultural productivity in India, posing a serious threat to food security.
- Current agricultural practices is creating a vicious cycle, as the agriculture sector is the second-largest greenhouse gas emitter, which is happening due to unsustainable agricultural practices—increasing use of pesticides and insecticides causing soil disturbance.

Measures to be Taken to Ensure Long-term Food Security

- **Promoting Sustainable agriculture Practices** It is the practice of cultivating and maintaining food fibre and other agricultural products in a way that preserves and improves ecosystem health and productivity while promoting social and economic well-being.
  - For ensuring Food Security in India, improvement in productivity through greater use of biotechnology, intensifying watershed management, use of nano-urea and access to micro-irrigation facilities and bridging crop yield gaps across states through collective approach should be at priority.
- **Promoting agricultural production system to match the agro-ecological resources** is critical for sustainability.
  - For example, promotion of dry land agriculture rather than input-intensive farming in arid and semi-arid areas and promoting less water-intensive crops like pulses and millets. Similarly, crops like rice needing large amount of water can be shifted to other regions that are relatively more endowed with water.
- **Poly-cultures and Crop Rotation** Moving farmers from mono-cultures to poly-cropping and the rotation of crops can lead to reductions in the need to apply fertilisers and pesticides.
  - Such diverse systems are likely to be more productive, labour intensive and provide enhanced ecosystem services and, therefore, much more sustainable.
- **Emphasis on Nurturing the Soil** Greater emphasis on nurturing the soils rather than plants will provide higher benefits on sustaining yields, improving ecosystem health and sequestering carbon.
- **Promotion of Zero Budget Natural Farming** Initiatives such as Zero Budget Natural Farming, with low external input and production costs, could help restore ecosystem health and diversified livelihoods of smallholder farmers.
- **Reducing Food Waste and Promoting Sustainable Consumption Patterns** To reduce food wastage, greater investments are needed in improving post-production infrastructure, including storage space in rural areas and improved harvesting techniques and transportation.

Conclusion

With growing population, depleting resources and the increasing threat of climate change, it will be impossible to fulfil the needs of the future unless we transition to sustainable food and agricultural systems that would ensure food security, provide economic and social opportunities and protect the ecosystem services on which our future depends.

Best Practices

- Efforts should be undertaken to shift cultural and behavioural preferences to encourage uptake and create market demand for the new crops.
- The 'Millet Mission' in India is an example. The revival of the hardy, drought-resistant crop, which is a better fit for increasingly water-stressed regions, was promoted among farmers, encouraging a shift away from water-intensive paddy and maize, across states in India.
- This was accompanied by inclusion of millet in the Public Distribution System (PDS) and awareness drives to change consumer dietary patterns through millet recipe books in local languages and supporting local centres to create millet-based products.

Grain Storage Plan in the Cooperative Sector

Q.9 The dichotomy of overflowing food grains in warehouses and poor ranking on Global Hunger Index (GHI) can be attributed to poor management of buffer stock maintained by government. Examine. Also, what are the expected benefits from the recently approved grain storage plan in the cooperative sector? (250 Words, 15 Marks)

Ans. Introduction The GHI 2022 report has placed India at 107th out of 121 nations, much behind Bangladesh, Pakistan and Nepal. The situation is grim and the country is battling widespread hunger. This poor ranking is despite the fact that India recorded a record food production in 2022-23.

According to the third advance estimates released by the agriculture ministry, India's food grain production in 2022-23 is estimated to be 330.53 million tonnes, with record output of rice, wheat, maize, soybean, rapeseed, mustard and sugarcane.

Food Buffer Norms in India

- **Food Buffer** is the minimal amount of food grains that the central government must keep on hand at the start of every quarter to ensure adequate supplies for the public distribution system and other government distribution programmes.

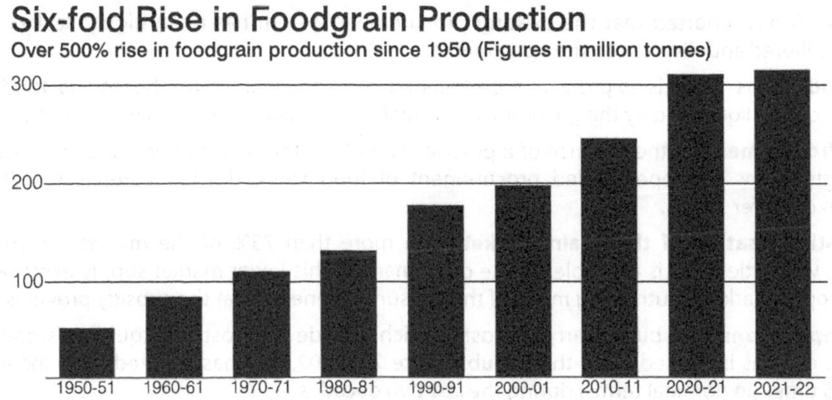

- **Surplus Food Buffers** About 159 lakh tonnes of wheat and 104 lakh tonnes of rice was be available as on 1st January, 2023 as against the respective buffer norms requirement of 138 lakh tonnes of wheat and 76 lakh tonnes of rice as on 1st January.
- Under the PMGKAY, the Centre provides five kilogrammes of foodgrains per month free of cost to around 80 crore people covered under the NFSA.

About Buffer Stock

The concept of buffer stock was first introduced during the Fourth Five Year Plan (1969-74). The Food Corporation of India was set up in 1964 under the Food Corporation Act 1964 to achieve the aims of the Food Policy.

- Buffer stock of food grains in the Central Pool is maintained by the Government of India (GOI) / Central Government for:
- Meeting the prescribed minimum buffer stock norms for food security,
- Monthly release of food grains for supply through Targeted Public Distribution System (TPDS) and Other Welfare Schemes (OWS),
- Meeting emergency situations arising out of unexpected crop failure, natural disasters, etc. and
- Price stabilisation or market intervention to augment supply so as to help moderate the open market prices.

Relationship Between Food Security and Buffer Stocks

- **Source of Food Grains for Welfare Programmes** The food stock procurement helps the government-run its social welfare schemes like the Targeted Public distribution System (TPDS) and Other Welfare Schemes (OWS) like mid-day meals scheme for school-going children, distribution of food grains to people displaced due to natural calamities, etc.
- **Availability of Food Grains** The quantity of food grains that the government purchases and stores in order to maintain price stability and guarantee food security.
  - In times of natural disaster like drought, buffer stocks can be put on the market to make sure that the population has enough food to eat.
- **Price Stability** Food security is dependent on buffer stocks' ability to maintain price stability. Food prices can be stabilized and food remains affordable and accessible to all by maintaining buffer stocks.

Issues in the Buffer Stock Management

Inspite of having surplus food buffer, India's poor ranking in GHI is due to challenges associated with buffer stock utilisation:

- **Lack of Storage Infrastructure** In India, a significant portion of the population is dying from hunger and inadequate storage practices are also contributing to the depletion of enormous food stocks. After the purchase, warehousing issues include a lack of storage space and other infrastructure.
- **Leakage** ICRIER has reported that the existing procurement system has been highly 'leaky', with large amounts of grains being pilfered and diverted to the open market.
- **Residual Food Grains** There is no pro-active, pre-defined, sustainable policy for the residual food grains. In general, such 'excess stock' can be liquidated by the government through export, open market sales or additional allocation to states.
- **Open-End Procurement** In the absence of a precise estimate of the total buffer stock required to run the PDS and in emergency situations, the open-ended procurement of food stocks further complicates the proper storage and consumption of buffer stocks.
- **De-facto Nationalisation of the Grain Market** With more than 75% of the marketable surplus procured by the government, very little grain is available for the open market. This lower market supply exerts an upward pressure on prices in the open market, neutralising much of the consumer benefits that the subsidy provides.
- **Financial Implications** The buffer-carrying costs, which include the cost of acquiring, storing, warehousing, stock maintenance etc. has increased more than double since 2001- 02. This has resulted in an increase of food subsidy to more than 25 times (in nominal terms) during the last two decades.
- **Issues with Transportation** During transportation, lot of food is wasted due to spills and deterioration, contributing to an increase in losses.
- **Abuse and Robbery** Ghost recipients, alcoholic beverage manufacturing facilities and illicit markets may occasionally receive the buffer stockpiles. A significant portion of the population suffers from hunger as a result, while others benefit from buffer stocks of food grains in place of the target population.
- **Unfair Trade Practices** The government's purchase of food grains and maintenance of buffer stocks are seen as trade-distorting by many Western industrialised nations.
- **Problem of Marginal Farmers** Though we have surplus food, most small and marginal farming households do not produce enough food grains for their year-round consumption.

World's Largest Grain Storage Plan in Cooperative Sector

The Union Cabinet has given its approval for the establishment of the 'world's largest grain storage plan in the cooperative sector' with an outlay of around ₹ 1 lakh crore.

The plan focuses on the creation of godowns and other agricultural infrastructure at the level of Primary Agricultural Credit Societies (PACS) to strengthen food security, reduce wastage and empower farmers.

- **Addressing Infrastructure Shortage** The plan aims to establish godowns at the level of PACS to alleviate the shortage of agricultural storage infrastructure in the country.
- **Diversification of PACS Activities** PACS will be empowered to undertake various activities, including functioning as procurement centres for state agencies or the Food Corporation of India (FCI), serving as fair price shops and setting up custom hiring centres and common processing units. This diversification will enhance the incomes of farmer members.
- **Reduction of Food Grain Wastage** By creating decentralised storage capacity at the local level, the plan aims to reduce grain wastage, contributing to improved food security.
- **Preventing Distress Sale** The plan provides farmers with various options, preventing distress sale of crops and enabling them to realise better prices for their produce.
- **Cost Reduction** The establishment of storage facilities at the PACS level will significantly reduce transportation costs of food grains to procurement centres and fair price shops.

Futuristic Reform Measures

- **Enlarging the Scope of Food Security Schemes** Universalising the access to the Public Distribution System and One Nation One Ration Card scheme (ONORC), at least during the pandemic.
  - The PDS should be strengthened and the food basket can be enlarged to include millets, pulses and oil.
  - This may certainly help in addressing the issue of hidden hunger.
- **Regular Monitoring of Food Security** The sharp increase in food insecurity points to an urgent need for the government to establish systems for regular monitoring of the food security situation in the country.
- There is an urgent need to implement Shanta Kumar committee recommendations to improve operational effectiveness in the purchase, storage and distribution of food grains.
  - **Clear and Open Buffer Stock Liquidation Procedures Food Corporation of India (FCI)** should be given more freedom to conduct business; when needed, it should sell surplus goods on the open market or export.
  - Permit the private sector to buy and store grains of food.
  - **Grain Outsourcing** Implementation of a Negotiable Warehouse Receipt (NWR) system. Farmers can deposit their produce in these authorised warehouses under the new arrangement and the bank will advance them 80% of the MSP value of their produce.
  - Only in states with weak procurement capabilities could FCI engage in full-fledged grain procurement.
  - States should handle procurement in the cases of conditions that are performing well, such as Haryana, Punjab andhra Pradesh, Chhattisgarh, Madhya Pradesh and Odisha.

Conclusion

To achieve the SDG (2) of zero hunger, India should consider a strategic initiative aimed at eliminating food insecurity by ensuring adequate-affordable-accessible-nutritionally diverse food, with a special and immediate focus on reforming administrative and implementing agencies involved in procuring and providing food.

National Food Security Act, 2013

Q.10 The National Food Security Act (NFSA), 2013 is a far-reaching public policy intervention to protect people against food insecurity, hunger and malnutrition. Critically examine its performance in the last 10 years. Also, discuss why various countries at WTO raise objections against India's NFSA? (250 Words, 15 Marks)

Ans. **Introduction** The National Food Security Act (NFSA) enacted in 2013 guarantees subsidised food grains to a large section i.e., two-third of total population, making it the largest food security programme in the world. With the intention of providing food security to approximately 800 million people, the NFSA plays a crucial role in ensuring access to essential nutrition and combating hunger across the country.

Features of NFSA

The Act has several key features that contribute to its far-reaching impact. Some of the key features of the NFSA are:

- **Entitlements** The NFSA guarantees certain entitlements to eligible individuals and households, including subsidised food grains, under the Targeted Public Distribution System (TPDS).
- **Subsidised Food Grains** The eligible persons will be entitled to receive 5 Kgs of foodgrains per person per month at subsidised prices of ₹ 3/2/1 per Kg for rice/wheat/coarse grains. The existing Antyodaya Anna Yojana (AAY) households, which constitute the poorest of the poor, will continue to receive 35 Kgs of foodgrains per household per month.
- **Coverage and Identification of Beneficiaries** The act aims to cover a large section of the population (75% rural and 50% urban population) by categorising priority households and general households. Priority households are entitled to receive a higher quantity of food grains at a subsidised rate.
  - Identification of households to be done by States/UTs, which are required to frame their own criteria.
- **Diversifying the Food Basket** Inclusion of other nutritious cereals (such as bajra, jowar, ragi and maize) as part of the food security basket finds a place in the Act.
- **Nutritional Support** The act places a special emphasis on providing nutritional support to pregnant women, lactating mothers and children through the provision of nutritious meals and take-home rations.
- **Maternity Benefit** The NFSA includes the provision of maternity benefits, ensuring proper nutrition and support to pregnant and lactating women during their pregnancy and six months after childbirth.
- **Women Empowerment** Eldest woman (18 years or above) to be the head of the household for the purpose of issuing of ration cards.
- **Grievance Redressal Mechanism** The Act establishes a robust grievance redressal mechanism to address any complaints or issues related to the distribution of food grains and benefits under the NFSA.
- **Transparency and Accountability** The NFSA promotes transparency and accountability in the implementation of food security programmes. It requires the use of technology, such as Aadhaar-based identification, to ensure the proper targeting and delivery of benefits.

Achievements of the National Food Security Act (NFSA) in the Last 10 Years

- **Increased Food Coverage** The NFSA has significantly expanded the coverage of food security programmes in India. As of 2021, around 80 million people are intended beneficiaries under the Act, ensuring access to subsidised food grains.
- **Reduction in Hunger** The Act has contributed to a decline in hunger and improved food security indicators. According to the Global Hunger Index, India's hunger score improved from 38.9 in 2010 to 27.2 in 2022, indicating progress but still we have a long way to go.
- **Nutritional Support for Women and Children** The NFSA has made notable strides in providing nutritional support to women and children through ICDS and Midday Meal.
- **Strengthened Public Distribution System** The Act has focused on strengthening the Public Distribution System (PDS) to ensure efficient and transparent delivery of subsidised food grains. Digitisation, Aadhaar-based identification and reforms in storage and distribution mechanisms have helped in reducing leakages and improving targeting.
  - **Example** Chhattisgarh PDS.
- **Increased Awareness and Citizen Participation** The NFSA has raised awareness about food security rights among the population and encouraged citizen participation in monitoring the implementation of the Act. Social audits and grievance redressal mechanisms have empowered beneficiaries to hold authorities accountable.
- **Addressing Vulnerabilities During Pandemic** The NFSA played a crucial role during the COVID-19 pandemic by providing additional food grains and expanding coverage to support vulnerable populations affected by the lockdowns and economic disruptions. Example: PM Garib Kalyan Yojana.

Challenges Faced by the National Food Security Act (NFSA)

- **Implementation Bottlenecks** The implementation of the NFSA has faced challenges related to inadequate infrastructure, weak monitoring systems and inefficient targeting, leading to issues such as leakages and exclusion errors.
- **Quality of Food Grains** Ensuring the quality of food grains distributed through the PDS remains a challenge. Complaints of substandard grains, infestations and spoilage have been reported in some regions, affecting the nutritional value and acceptability of the provided food.
- **Identification and Exclusion Errors** The process of identifying eligible beneficiaries under the NFSA has faced challenges, resulting in exclusion errors where deserving individuals are left out, while some ineligible individuals receive benefits.
- **Pricing and Subsidy Burden** The subsidy burden on the government to provide affordable food grains has been a challenge. Balancing the cost of procurement, storage and distribution with the subsidies provided to beneficiaries poses financial constraints.
- **Targeting Vulnerable Groups** Despite the progress made, effectively targeting and reaching vulnerable groups, such as migrant workers, homeless populations and remote rural communities, remains a challenge. Inclusion of these groups in the food security programmes requires concerted efforts and improved mechanisms.

Countries at WTO Raise Objections Against India's NFSA

The key areas of contention are

- **Price Distortion** The NFSA involves providing subsidised food grains to a large section of the population. This can lead to lower prices for domestically produced agricultural products, creating a price distortion in the market. Other countries argue that this could affect their ability to export agricultural commodities to India at competitive prices.
- **Market Access** Some countries argue that the procurement and distribution mechanisms under the NFSA, such as the Minimum Support Price (MSP) and the Public Distribution System (PDS), may create barriers to market access for foreign agricultural products.
- **Subsidy Limits** Currently, India's de minimis level is set at 10% of the value of agricultural production. Countries at the WTO raise concerns about the level of subsidies provided under the programme and they exceed the limits set by WTO rules.
- **Trade Distorting Effects** The provision of subsidised food grains to low-income households can lead to trade-distorting effects, as it may result in excessive production of certain crops and overstocking of food grains. This can impact global markets by influencing supply and demand dynamics, potentially affecting prices and trade flows.
- **Transparency and Notification Requirements** Countries expect transparency and timely notification of measures that may affect international trade. Some objections may stem from concerns about India's compliance with the WTO's notification requirements, particularly regarding the details and updates related to the NFSA's implementation and its impact on agricultural trade.
- **Export Subsidies** Some countries raise concerns about India's potential use of export subsidies for agricultural products, which could give Indian exporters an advantage in global markets, thereby affecting the competitiveness of their own agricultural sectors. For example, India provides incentives to sugar mills for exports, which can impact global sugar prices.

Conclusion

India has advocated for higher de minimis levels to accommodate its food security programmes currently, India's de minimis level is set at 10% of the value of agricultural production. During the WTO's Eleventh Ministerial Conference in 2017, India proposed an increase in the de minimis level to 20%.

India has engaged in negotiations and discussions at the WTO to address these concerns and find mutually acceptable solutions that support both its food security goals and international trade obligations.

Public Distribution System (PDS: Challenges and Reform Measures)

Q.11 What are the major challenges of Public Distribution System (PDS) in India? How can it be made effective and transparent? (150 Words, 10 Marks)

UPSC Mains PYQ 2022

Public Distribution System (PDS)

- It is an Indian Food Security System established under the Ministry of Consumer Affairs, Food and Public Distribution. PDS evolved as a system of management of scarcity through distribution of food grains at affordable prices. PDS is operated under the joint responsibility of the Central and the State Governments.
- Under the PDS, presently the commodities namely wheat, rice, sugar and kerosene are being allocated to the States/UTs for distribution. Some States/UTs also distribute additional items of mass consumption through the PDS outlets such as pulses, edible oils, iodised salt, spices, etc.

Evolution of PDS System

- PDS was introduced around World War II as a war-time rationing measure.
- By the 1970s, PDS had evolved into a universal scheme for the distribution of subsidised food.
- Subsequently, in 1997, the government launched the Targeted Public Distribution System (TPDS), with a focus on the poor. TPDS aims to provide subsidised food and fuel to the poor through a network of ration shops.
- **Antyodaya Anna Yojana (AAY)** was launched in 2000 as a step in the direction of making TPDS aim at reducing hunger among the poorest segments of the BPL population.
- In September 2013, Parliament enacted the National Food Security Act, 2013. The Act relies largely on the existing TPDS to deliver food grains as legal entitlements to poor households. This marks a shift by making the right to food a justiciable right.

Management of Food Grains under the PDS System

The Central and State Governments share responsibilities in order to provide food grains to the identified beneficiaries. The Centre procures food grains from farmers at a Minimum Support Price (MSP) and sells it to states at Central Issue Prices. It is responsible for transporting the grains to godowns in each state. States bear the responsibility of transporting food grains from these godowns to each fair price shop (ration shop), where the beneficiary buys the food grains at the lower central issue price. Many states further subsidise the price of food grains before selling it to beneficiaries.

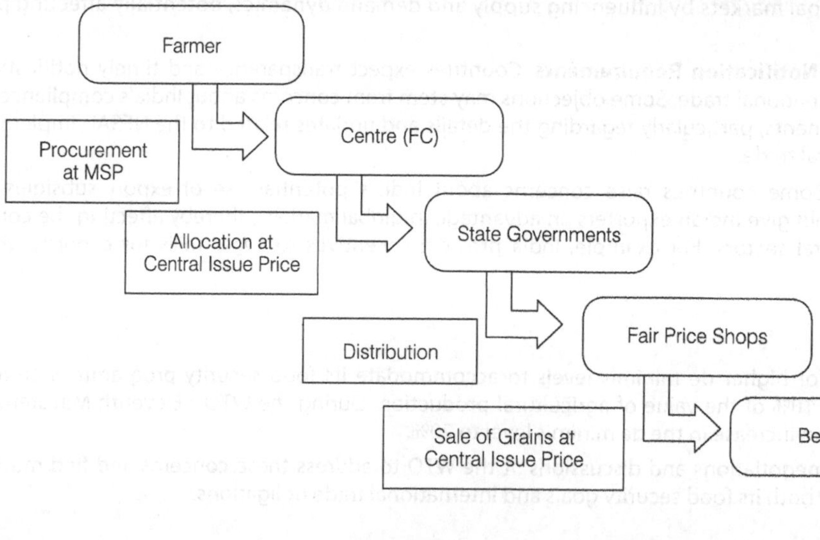

Issues Associated with PDS System

- **Identification of Beneficiaries** Studies have shown that targeting mechanisms such as TPDS are prone to large inclusion and exclusion errors. This implies that entitled beneficiaries are not getting food grains while those that are ineligible are getting undue benefits. According to the estimation of an expert group set up in 2009, PDS suffers from nearly 61% error of exclusion and 25% inclusion of beneficiaries, i.e. the misclassification of the poor as non-poor and vice versa.
- **Leakage of Food Grains** TPDS suffers from large leakages of food grains during transportation to and from ration shops into the open market. In an evaluation of TPDS, the erstwhile Planning Commission found 36% leakage of PDS rice and wheat at the all-India level.
- **Rising Food Subsidy** The food subsidy has increased over the years, having more than quadrupled from ₹ 21,200 crore in 2002-03 to ₹ 1.97 lakh crore in 2023-24.
- **Issue with Procurement** Open-ended Procurement i.e., all incoming grains accepted even if buffer stock is filled, creates a shortage in the open market.
- **Inadequate Storage** A performance audit by the CAG has revealed a serious shortfall in the government's storage capacity.
- **Environmental Issues** The over-emphasis on attaining self-sufficiency and a surplus in food grains, which are water-intensive, has been found to be environmentally unsustainable. Procuring states such as Punjab and Haryana are under environmental stress, including rapid groundwater depletion, deteriorating soil and water conditions from overuse of fertilisers.
- **FCI Inefficiency** FCI operational inefficiencies due to poor technology, over-bureaucratisation, lack of coordination with state governments lead to wastage of food grains.
- **Low Purchase-Entitlement Ratio** Lack of demand by households due to poor quality; irregularity of FPS operations in most rural areas are cited as key reasons
- **Migrant Workers** These workers are unable to access FPS as their stay is not fixed. Due to failure of PDS in this regard also make them to feel discouraged to register for BPL/AAY cards leading to more exclusion errors
- **High Operational Costs** Besides so high levels of corruption and inefficiencies, the running cost of such a massive subsidy programme due to high transportation and storing costs leads to significant financial burden on the exchequer. The expected expenditure on Food subsidy through PDS is about 1% of GDP and is rising as the evaluation of data reveals that growth of subsidy is higher the growth of national income

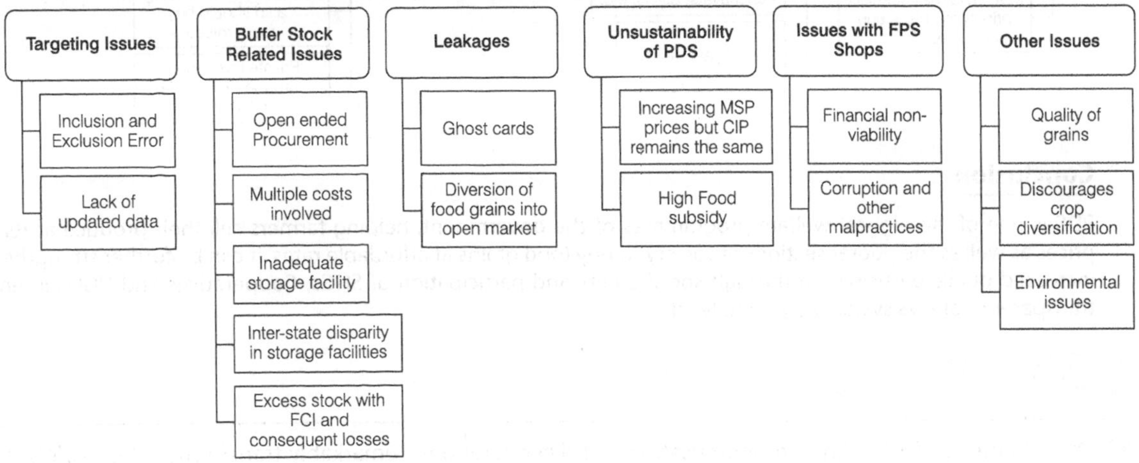

Reform Measures to be Undertaken

- **Aadhaar Linked and Digitised Ration Cards** This allows online entry and verification of beneficiary data. It also enables online tracking of monthly entitlements and off-take of food-grains by beneficiaries.
- **Technology Based Reforms** Wadhwa Committee, appointed by the Supreme Court, found that certain states had implemented computerisation and other technology-based reforms to TPDS. Technology-based reforms helped plug leakages of food grains during TPDS.

- **Computerised Fair Price Shops** FPS automated by installing 'Point of Sale' device to swap the ration card. It authenticates the beneficiaries and records the quantity of subsidised grains given to a family.
- **Adoption of Direct Benefit Transfer** Under the Direct Benefit Transfer scheme, cash is transferred to the beneficiaries' account in lieu of food-grains subsidy component. They will be free to buy food grains from anywhere in the market. For taking up this model, pre-requisites for the States/UTs would be to complete digitisation of beneficiary data and seed Aadhaar and bank account details of beneficiaries. It is estimated that cash transfers alone could save the exchequer ₹ 30,000 crore every year.
- **Use of Web-based Citizens Portal** Public Grievance Redressal Machineries, such as a toll-free number for call centres to register complaints or suggestions.
- **Recommendations Made by Shanta Kumar Committee** Reduce the number of beneficiaries under the Food Security Act—from the current 67% to 40%. Allow private players to procure and store food grains.
- **Stop Bonuses on Minimum Support Price (MSP) paid by states to farmers** and adopt cash transfer system so that MSP and food subsidy amounts can be directly transferred to the accounts of farmers and food security beneficiaries.
- **FCI should involve itself in full-fledged grains procurement only in those states which are poor in procurement** In the case of those states which are performing well, like Haryana, Punjab andhra Pradesh, Chhattisgarh, Madhya Pradesh and Odisha, the states should do the procurement.

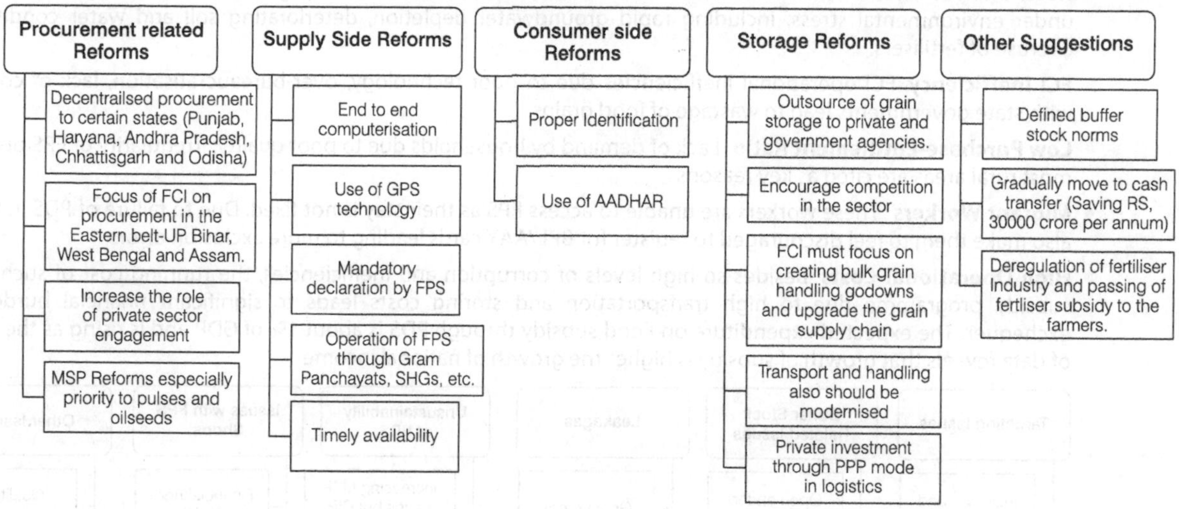

Conclusion

PDS is one of the biggest welfare programmes of the government, helping farmers sell their produce at remunerative prices as well as the poorer sections of society to buy food grains at affordable rates. It can be further strengthened by the increased public participation through social audits and participation of SHGs, Cooperatives and NGOs in ensuring the transparency of PDS system at ground level.

Technological Solutions of PDS

Q.12 The scheme on 'End-to-End Computerisation of TPDS operations' remarkably transformed the world's largest foodgrain distribution network but still there are several challenges in the existing IT system of PDS. Comment. (250 Words, 15 Marks)

Ans. **Introduction** The scheme on 'End-to-End Computerisation of Targeted Public Distribution System (TPDS) Operations' is an initiative by the Government of India to leverage technology for efficient management and delivery of food grains under the TPDS. The TPDS is a government programme that aims to provide subsidised food grains to eligible households.

Features of the Scheme

- **Digitisation of Beneficiary Database** Under the scheme, the beneficiary data is digitised and maintained in a centralised database.
- **Electronic Point of Sale (ePoS) Devices** Electronic Point of Sale devices are provided to Fair Price Shops (FPS) to automate the process of ration distribution. These devices enable real-time authentication of beneficiaries using Aadhaar or other identification methods, ensuring that subsidised food grains reach the intended beneficiaries.
- **Online Procurement and Supply Chain Management** The scheme aims to computerise the procurement and supply chain management processes, from the allocation of food grains to states to their distribution at the FPS level.
- **Aadhaar Integration** Aadhaar, a unique biometric identification number, is integrated into the TPDS system to authenticate beneficiaries and eliminate duplication or impersonation. This ensures that subsidised food grains are provided to genuine beneficiaries.
- **Management Information System (MIS)** The scheme establishes a robust Management Information System to capture and analyse data related to TPDS operations. This helps in monitoring the performance, identifying gaps and making data-driven decisions for effective implementation of the programme.
- Setting up **grievance redressal systems** through implementation of toll-free helplines (1967/1800-series), online grievance registration facility.

Type of Reforms	Benefits of Reform	States Implementing Reforms
Digitisation of ration cards	• Allows for online entry and verification of beneficiary data • Online storing of monthly entitlement of beneficiaries, number of dependants, offtake of food grains by beneficiaries from FPS, etc	Andhra Pradesh, Chhattisgarh, Tamil Nadu, Madhya Pradesh, Gujarat,
Computerised allocation to FPF	• Computerises FPS allocation, declaration of stock balance, web-based truck challans, etc.	Chhattisgarh, Delhi, Madhya Pradesh, Tamil Nadu. etc.
Issue of smart cards in place of ration cards	• Secure electronic devices used to store beneficiary data such as name, address, biometrics. • Prevents counterfeiting	Haryana, Andhra Pradesh Orissa, etc.
Use of GPS technology	• Use of Global Positioning System (GPS) technology to track movement of trucks carrying food grains from state depots to FPS	Chhattisgarh, Tamil Nadu
SMS based monitoring	• Allows monitoring by citizens so they can register their mobile numbers and send/receive SMS alerts during dispatch and arrival of TPDS commodities	Chhattisgarh, Uttar Pradesh, Tamil Nadu
Use of web-based citizens portal	• Publicises grievance redressal machinery, such as toll free number for call centres to register complaints or suggestions.	Chhattisgarh

Transformation of PDS

- **Transparent and Targeted Distribution** The computerisation of beneficiary data and the implementation of electronic Point of Sale (ePoS) devices have helped in ensuring transparent and targeted distribution of food grains.
  - As a key indicator, presently almost about 65%-70% of monthly allocated foodgrains by the Government of India to States/UTs are being distributed to beneficiaries through biometrically/Aadhaar authenticated ePoS transactions, thus systematically reducing the ghost lifting of highly subsidised foodgrains and at the same time are progressively increasing the rightful targeting of genuine beneficiaries.
- **Reduction in Leakages** The scheme has significantly reduced leakages in the TPDS by eliminating ghost beneficiaries and reducing the scope for corruption and pilferage.
  - **Example** As an outcome of digitisation beneficiary records, de-duplication due to Aadhaar seeding, a total of ₹ 2.75 crore ration cards have been deleted/cancelled in 29 States/UTs.

- **Efficient Supply Chain Management** The computerisation of TPDS operations has improved the efficiency of supply chain management. It has facilitated the timely allocation of food grains to states, better tracking of stock movements and improved coordination between various stakeholders involved in the distribution process.
  - SMSs are also being delivered to beneficiaries in some States/UTs, informing about quantity and expected time of arrival of foodgrains at their FPSs to plan their visit.
- **Accurate Targeting of Beneficiaries** The digitisation of beneficiary data and the integration of Aadhaar have helped in accurate targeting of beneficiaries.
- **Real-time Monitoring and Data Analysis** The scheme has established a Management Information System (MIS) to capture and analyze data related to TPDS operations. This real-time monitoring and data analysis have provided valuable insights into the functioning of the TPDS.
- **Proper Financial Accounting** These devices have also enabled proper accounting of monthly closing balances of foodgrains in each FPS which flows back into the online allocation and supply chain management system for accurate allocation to all FPSs for the subsequent months.
- **Pilferage of food grains** has also been addressed as now with use of technology the vehicles are tracked.

Current IT Challenges in TPDS System

- Fragmented systems across states and lack of integration with other ministries.
- **Limited Use of Data Analytics and Other Cutting-edge Technologies** As a lot of soft data is being generated every day, it is expected to bring continuous improvements in beneficiary servicing through mainstreaming of Data Analytics, etc. allowing us to generate critical data of TPDS beneficiaries, their food security needs, patterns of migration etc.
- **Lack of Proper Infrastructure** There are major hindrances in ICT adoption due to inadequate telecommunication systems, improper device design, poor network strength and lack of information technology personnel. In this context, wide inter-State variations exist in both seeding and use of e-POS devices at Fair Price Shops.
- **Technical Expertise** The successful implementation of computerisation requires technical expertise in terms of software development, system integration and data management. Training and capacity building of staff involved in the TPDS operations is crucial to ensure efficient use of the computerised system.
- **Identification Failures** Due to arbitrary identification failures because of poor quality of fingerprints and poor internet connectivity, beneficiaries tend to lose their entitlements. Also, real-time verification, if disrupted, leaves the possibility of grain diversion.
- **Digital Divide** Direct use of e-governance technology by citizens in India is hindered by lack of training and education as well as the existing digital divide. For instance, North-Eastern states show their incapability in this regard due to persisting network connectivity issues.
- **Financial Incapacity of Fair Price Shops** These shops lack the financial capacity needed to make e-PoS purchases, install them and train necessary personnel to work on them.
- **Data Accuracy and Integration** Integrating data from various levels, including beneficiary databases, supply chain information and transaction records, can be complex.
- **Cybersecurity and Data Protection** With computerisation comes the need to address cybersecurity risks and protect sensitive data.
- **Resistance to Change** Transitioning from traditional manual processes to a computerised system may face resistance from stakeholders who are accustomed to the old methods.
- **Monitoring and Evaluation** Implementing a computerised system requires effective monitoring and evaluation mechanisms to assess its performance, identify bottlenecks and make necessary improvements.

Conclusion

The technology-driven reforms in Targeted Public Distribution System (TPDS) are envisioned to continuously foster the introduction of new beneficiary-centric initiatives, even beyond the institutionalisation of ONORC system to empower all NFSA beneficiaries/ households. Further, it is targeted to achieve near 100% Aadhaar seeding of all NFSA beneficiaries and complete automation of all ₹ 5.4 lakh Fair Price Shops in the country, as some are remaining in a few States/UTs while institutionalising the ONORC throughout the country. These reforms are expected to be further strengthened by continuously upgrading the technology used, introducing the use of new technologies and practices, such as Artificial Intelligence, predictive analysis, etc. to enable the State/UT Governments to deliver maximum allocated food-grains to the right beneficiaries, anywhere in the country with maximum flexibility.

One Nation, One Ration (ONOR)

Q.13 The 'One Nation, One Ration Card' (ONORC) scheme is a huge step forward in empowering the poor and disadvantaged, yet it faces obstacles in terms of design and implementation. Discuss. (150 Words, 10 Marks)

About One Nation, One Ration Card (ONORC)

- One Nation One Ration card (ONORC) is a central scheme under the National Food Security Act, 2013 that allows nation-wide portability of ration cards under National Food Security Act (NFSA) with biometric authentication.
- This system allows all NFSA beneficiaries, particularly migrant beneficiaries, to claim either full or part foodgrains from any Fair Price Shop (FPS) in the country through existing ration card with biometric/Aadhaar authentication in a seamless manner.
- The system also allows their family members back home, if any, to claim the balance foodgrains on same the ration card.
- Under this plan, the distribution of highly subsidised food grains is enabled through nation-wide portability of ration cards through the implementation of IT-driven system by the installation of ePoS devices at FPSs, seeding of Aadhaar number of beneficiaries with their ration cards and operationalisation of biometrically authenticated ePoS transactions in the State/UTs.
- Beneficiaries can quote either their ration card number or the Aadhaar number to any Fair Price Shop's dealer across the country. Anyone in the family, who have seeded Aadhaar in the ration card can undergo authentication and lift the ration.
- There is no need to share or carry the ration card or Aadhaar card with ration dealer to avail the benefit. Beneficiaries can undergo Aadhaar authentication by using their finger prints or iris-based identification.

ONORC is a Step Towards Empowerment of the Poor

- **Removing Inter-state Barriers** It removes inter-state barriers by allowing all NFSA beneficiaries to claim their ration at place wherever they are. Thus, ONORC envisages removing the geographical hindrance to social justice and enabling the right to food.
  - Previously, ration cardholders can avail their entitlement of subsidised food grains under the National Food Security Act, only from the designated Fair Price Shop (FPS) within the concerned state.
- **Supporting One-third of Population** Nearly, 37% of the population is that of migrant labourers as per Census 2011. The scheme is therefore important for anyone who is going to move from one place to the other

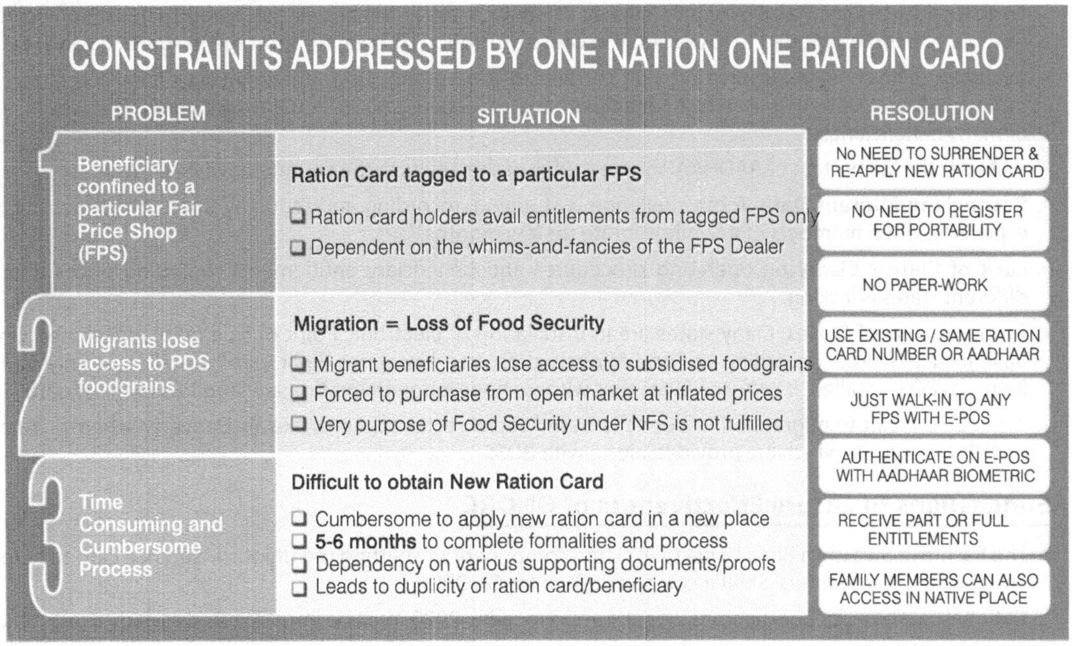

- **Flexibility** It allows individuals to choose their FPS according to their convenience. For migrant labourers, it allows individual's family members back home to claim the balance food grains on same ration card, thereby ensuring food security of the entire family.
- It will curtail corruption and increases PDS system efficiency by reducing dependence on a single FPS. Beneficiaries can avail services from the dealer of their choice.
- **Reducing Social Discrimination** ONORC will be particularly beneficial for women and other disadvantaged groups, given how social identity (caste, class and gender) and other contextual factors (including power relations) provide a strong backdrop in accessing PDS (Public Distribution System).

Obstacles in ONORC

Though ONORC is a visionary scheme, it has following obstacles in terms of design and implementation:

- **Does Not Account for the Interstate variation in PDS** Due to historical, political and varying consumption habits, PDS across the country varies with respect to the items supplied through fair price shops to the below-poverty-line (BPL) card-holders. Even the quantity and the price of items supplied varies from state to state.
  - **Product difference** Maharashtra supplies only wheat to the BPL families, while Andhra Pradesh provides only rice. BPL households in a few states like Himachal Pradesh and Chhattisgarh are also given pulses.
  - **Quantity difference** In Tamil Nadu, a BPL family gets 20 kg of rice, while in Karnataka a BPL household receives 5 kg of rice per member.
  - **Cost difference** In Tamil Nadu, 20 kg rice is given free of cost while in Uttar Pradesh and Bihar, it is provided at ₹ 3 per kg.
- **State-Specific Issues**
  - Low Aadhaar seeding in Assam (only 36-38% against all India average of 92%) due to concern related to National Citizens register.
  - Centre-State tussle has been delaying the scheme in states such as Bengal. Delhi wants to implement its own door-to-door ration delivery system.
  - Chhattisgarh has its own digitised system of PDS which creates issue of compatibility with ONORC system
- **Operational Challenges** Internet penetration is still less in India for the smooth functioning of ONORC.
  - Changes in Fingerprints have also been reported both due to genetics and due to constant wear and work-related wear and tear especially in case of labourers.
- **Logistical Bottleneck and Demand-supply Mismatch** An FPS receives the monthly quota in accordance with the number of people assigned to it. ONORC can cause disruption by creating shortage in some FPS and wastage in others.
- **Exclusion** The scheme seeks to provide subsidised food grains, to Aadhaar linked, digitalised ration cards. 100% of ration cards are yet to be linked to Aadhaar with many sections still lacking Aadhaar cards. This would lead to exclusion of many beneficiaries.
  - As per the '2019 state of AADHAAR Survey', 95% of the adults in the country have AADHAAR.
- **Reconciling Migrant Data** A big challenge is studying, recording and regularly updating labour migration patterns, especially, when members of a family migrate for few months.
- **Lack of Clarity** Clarity on operating procedures and beneficiary entitlements regarding prices and food habits in different states is lacking.
- **Preparedness of States** Many states are in installation of electronic Point of Sale (ePoS) machines. Only 77% of FPSs have installed ePoS. According to Food Ministry data, two key states Bihar (ePoS installed at only 62 FPSs) and West Bengal (ePOS installed at only 366 FPSs) that witness huge labor emigration are laggards in this regard.
- It will be difficult to migrate other domicile-based social sector schemes like anti-poverty schemes, rural employment, mid-day meals, etc which are provided along with PDS.

Suggestions to Ensure Effectiveness of ONORC

- The Rashtriya Swasthya Bima Yojna (RSBY) had component of splitting the unique insurance card to help both migrants and their family members. Similar can be adopted for ONORC.
- National database for unorganised workers announced in 2020 must be implemented as early as possible.
- A dedicated e-commerce platform for ONORC can be established to resolve logistics challenges.

- Impetus to BharatNet and deeper internet penetration should be promoted.
- **Eliminating Exclusion Errors** Constant monitoring and empowerment of Village Panchayats at least in the initial phase. Social Auditing may weed out any inclusion error and help in reducing exclusion error by recommending the names.

Conclusion

ONORC is a step towards achieving SDG 2 i.e., zero hunger. As observed by Supreme Court, all states must implement ONORC scheme. States must be pushed for technological readiness for ePOS at FPS. In longer run, PDS system can be replaced by food coupons or DBT for poor, so that they can buy food grain from any store.

Technology Missions and Animal Rearing (Agricultural Diversification vs Issues of Agriculture)

Q.14 The diversified and accelerated agricultural growth would enhance the food security by improving the income of the poor in the perplexing situation of shrinkage in agricultural holdings, declining new investments in agriculture and increasing degradation of natural resources. Elaborate. (250 Words, 15 Marks)

Ans. **Introduction** Agriculture contributes about 16.5% to the country's overall GDP and employs nearly 45.9% of the country's workforce (PLFS 2021-22) and therefore, it holds a seminal importance in Indian economy for ensuring inclusive growth and sustainable development.

But the agriculture sector in India is facing many hurdles related to low land holding size of just 1.08 hectares (Agriculture Census 2015/16), low farmer income, poor price realization and vagaries of climate change and land degradation situation of Indian Agriculture.

Need for Agricultural Diversification (Issues of Indian Agriculture)

Shrinkage of Agri-Land Holding

- **Decline in Average Land Holdings** According to the Agriculture Census 2015-16, the average size of operational holdings reduced from 2.28 hectares in 1970-71 to 1.08 hectares in 2015-16. It disproportionately affects small and marginal farmers (86%). They face challenges in achieving economies of scale, accessing credit, adoption of modern farming techniques
  - According to NSS 70th Round, only 13.3% of small and marginal farmers use tractors, highlighting the challenges in accessing mechanisation.
- **Loss of Agricultural Productivity** Small farms typically have lower yields per hectare as compared to larger farms due to limited resources, inadequate access to technology and fragmented land parcels.
- **Challenges in Crop Diversification** Shrinkage in land holdings makes it challenging for farmers to diversify their crop patterns.
- **Socio-economic Implications** The shrinking land holdings have socio-economic implications, such as rural poverty and increased migration from rural to urban areas.
- **Implications for Food Security** The limited land availability affects food production. The FAO estimates that India will need to produce 355 million tonnes of food grains by 2030 to meet the growing demand. The declining average land holdings pose challenges to meet this demand.

Declining New Investment

- **Decline in Public Investment** Public investment in agriculture as a percentage of GDP has been declining. It decreased from 2.3% in 2014-15 to 1.6% in 2021-22, as reported in the Economic Survey 2022-23. This downward trend signifies a reduced allocation of funds for agricultural development and infrastructure.
- **Declining Private Sector Participation** Private sector investment in agriculture has also witnessed a decline. According to the NSS data, the private sector's share in agricultural investment decreased from 33.4% in 2012-13 to 31.8% in 2017-18.
- **Insufficient Infrastructure Development** The decline in new investments has hindered the development of agricultural infrastructure. Inadequate investments in irrigation facilities, storage and processing units, rural roads and market linkages limit the potential for agricultural growth and value addition.

- **Limited Research and Development Funding** Insufficient funds allocated to R andD curtail innovation and technological advancements in farming practices, crop improvement and sustainable agriculture, which are crucial for boosting productivity and enhancing farmers' incomes.
- **Impact on Farm Mechanisation and Technology Adoption** Insufficient investment affects the adoption of farm mechanisation and modern agricultural technologies. Limited funds constrain farmers' ability to purchase machinery and equipment, hindering their access to advanced tools that can improve efficiency, productivity and income.

Degradation of Natural Resources

- **Soil Degradation** Around 120 million hectares of land in India are affected by soil degradation (Soil erosion, nutrient depletion and chemical contamination) according to the Indian Council of Agricultural Research (ICAR).
- **Pressure on Livelihoods** The increased pressure on resources is evident in the declining availability of water for agriculture. The Central Ground Water Board reported that 61% of groundwater wells in India have experienced a decline in water levels.
- **Water Scarcity** More than 54% of India's total land area faces high to extremely high-water stress, as reported by the Composite Water Management Index (CWMI) 2018.
- **Deforestation and Biodiversity Loss** India has experienced significant deforestation, with an annual deforestation rate of 0.59% between 2010 and 2020, according to the Global Forest Resources Assessment 2020.
- **Chemical Pollution** Excessive and improper use of chemical fertilisers and pesticides in Indian agriculture has resulted in chemical pollution of soil, water bodies and ecosystems. A study conducted by the Central Pollution Control Board revealed that more than half of India's groundwater samples tested were contaminated with excessive nitrate levels, mainly due to agricultural practices.

Agricultural Diversification is a solution to above issues of Indian Agriculture

- **Risk Mitigation** Crop diversification helps mitigate risks associated with mono-cropping, such as pest outbreaks and weather-related disasters.
  - **Example** The adoption of mixed cropping systems, where multiple crops are grown together, has shown promising results in risk reduction. For instance, intercropping of legumes with cereals improves soil fertility, enhances pest control and provides income diversification for farmers.
- **Increased Income Opportunities** Crop diversification enables farmers to tap into new markets, increase their income and reduce dependence on a single crop.
  - **Example** One District One Product (ODOP) scheme aims to convert each district of the country into an Export Hub by identifying products with export potential in the district.
- **Soil Health Improvement** Diversifying crops promotes better soil health by reducing the risk of nutrient depletion and erosion. Example: The adoption of crop rotation practices, such as alternating between legumes and cereals, enhances soil fertility and reduces the need for synthetic fertilisers. Farmers in Punjab have successfully implemented crop rotation by incorporating legumes like pulses in their rice-wheat cropping system.
- **Efficient Resource Utilisation** Crop diversification optimises resource utilization by matching crops with specific soil and climatic conditions, resulting in improved water and nutrient management. Example: The cultivation of drought-tolerant crops like millets in arid regions of Rajasthan and Karnataka has enabled farmers to maximise water efficiency and adapt to water scarcity conditions.
- **Enhanced Nutritional Security** Diversifying crops promotes a balanced diet by increasing the availability of diverse and nutrient-rich food options.
  - **Example** The Millets Mission in India focuses on the cultivation and promotion of millets, which are rich in protein, fiber and micronutrients, addressing nutritional deficiencies.
- **Climate Resilience** Crop diversification contributes to climate resilience by reducing vulnerability to climate change impacts, such as erratic rainfall and temperature fluctuations. Example: In the flood-prone areas of Assam, farmers have successfully diversified their crops by incorporating flood-tolerant varieties of rice and vegetables, ensuring food security even during periods of flooding.
- **Market Diversification** Diversifying crops allows farmers to access diverse markets, catering to varied consumer preferences and reducing market risks.
  - **Example** The cultivation of specialty crops like aromatic rice, exotic vegetables, or organic produce enables farmers to tap into niche markets, local markets, or export markets, generating higher returns.

- **Sustainable Farming Practices** Crop diversification promotes the adoption of sustainable farming practices, reducing the reliance on synthetic inputs and enhancing agroecosystem resilience. Example: Integrated farming systems incorporating crop diversification, livestock rearing and agroforestry, have shown promising results in sustainable agricultural practices. For instance, the System of Rice Intensification (SRI) integrates crop diversification, reduced water usage and organic practices, resulting in higher yields and reduced input costs.

Conclusion

Crop diversification and accelerated growth offer a path towards a more resilient, profitable and sustainable agricultural system in India. By embracing diversified cropping systems and implementing good agricultural practices, farmers can improve their incomes, enhance resource utilisation, ensure food and nutritional security and adapt to changing climatic conditions.

Oilseeds Sector

Q.15 Examine the significance of 'National Mission on Edible Oil-Oil Palm (NMEO-OP)' in fulfilling India's aim of reducing import dependency in the edible oil sector. How can NMEO-OP overcome the various challenges in the production of palm oil in India? (250 Words, 15 Marks)

Ans. Introduction India's imports of edible oils increased to ₹ 140.3 lakh tonne in 2021-22 from ₹ 131.3 lakh tonne in the previous year. In value terms, imports of edible oils rose 34% to about ₹ 1.57 lakh crore in 2021-22 from ₹ 1.17 lakh crore in 2020-21. National Mission on Edible Oil-Oil Palm (NMEO-OP) is a crucial initiative undertaken by the Indian Government to reduce the country's dependence on imported edible oil.

Information about Edible Oil Sector

- India is the world's second-largest consumer and number one importer of vegetable oil.
- The present rate of edible oil consumption in India surpasses the domestic production rate. At present, India meets nearly 55% to 60% of its edible oil demand through imports. Therefore, India needs to be independent in oil production to meet the domestic consumption demand.
- Palm oil (Crude + Refined) constitutes roughly around 62% of the total edible oils imported and are imported mainly from Indonesia and Malaysia, while Soyabean oil (22%) is imported from Argentina and Brazil and Sunflower oil (15%) is imported mainly from Ukraine and Russia.
- The Government of India launched National Mission on Edible Oils-Oil Palm as a Centrally-sponsored scheme, being implemented jointly by the Central and State Governments with a special focus in the North-East region and the Andaman and Nicobar Islands. It is proposed to have an additional 6.5 lakh hectares for palm oil by 2025-26.
- In order to improve and systemise the data management system in the vegetable oil sector, the Directorate of Sugar and Vegetable Oils under Department of Food and Public Distribution has developed a web-based platform (evegoils.nic.in) for online submission of inputs by vegetable oil producers on monthly basis. The portal also provides window for online registration and submission of monthly production returns.

Reasons for Import Dependency

India has traditionally been heavily dependent on imports to meet its domestic demand for edible oils. The import dependence arises due to several factors:

- **Insufficient Domestic Production** India's domestic production of edible oils, primarily from oilseeds like soybean, mustard, groundnut and sunflower, has not been able to keep pace with the rising demand. Limited availability of arable land, low productivity and unfavourable agro-climatic conditions contribute to the shortfall in domestic production.
- **Growing Demand** India is one of the largest consumers of edible oils globally, driven by factors such as population growth, urbanisation and changing dietary patterns.
- **Price Competitiveness** Imported edible oils, particularly palm oil and soybean oil, often prove to be more price competitive compared to domestically produced oils.

- **Non-availability of Certain Oils** India's demand for edible oils includes specific types such as palm oil, which is not produced domestically in significant quantities. Therefore, imports are necessary to meet the demand for these specific oils.
- **Trade Agreements** India's participation in various regional and bilateral trade agreements has facilitated the import of edible oils.

Challenges in the Production of Palm Oil in India

- **Climate Limitations** Palm oil cultivation requires tropical or sub-tropical climates with high temperatures and abundant rainfall. The country's diverse agro-climatic zones limit the suitable regions for palm oil cultivation, restricting its production potential.
- **Land Constraints** Palm oil cultivation requires significant land availability for large-scale plantations. However, the availability of suitable land in India is limited due to competing land uses for food crops, forests and other agricultural activities.
- **Low Productivity** Palm oil yields in India are relatively low compared to other major palm oil-producing countries like Indonesia and Malaysia. This can be attributed to various factors, including suboptimal agronomic practices, limited adoption of modern technology and best practices and inadequate access to quality planting materials and inputs.
- **Pests and Diseases** The palm oil crop is susceptible to various pests and diseases, which can significantly affect productivity.
- **Infrastructure and Processing Capacity** Insufficient processing capacity and outdated processing technologies also pose challenges, impacting the value addition and competitiveness of domestically produced palm oil.
- **Environmental Concerns** Palm oil cultivation has faced criticism globally for its impact on deforestation, biodiversity loss and greenhouse gas emissions. Balancing the need for increased palm oil production with sustainable land use and environmental conservation is a significant challenge.
- **Water Footprint** Oil palm requires a large quantity of water for its normal growth thus increasing the water footprint.
- **Consumption Pattern** India has a diversified consumption pattern i.e., edible oil consumption is region-specific. E.g Cotton Seed oil in West India, Mustard Oil in North India, etc.
- **Long Gestation Periods** Oil palm needs around 3-4 years of gestation period to start bearing results.

Significance of NMEO-OP in Fulfilling India's aim of Reducing Import Dependency in the Edible Oil Sector

- **Enhancing Domestic Production** NMEO-OP focuses on increasing the production of oilseeds and oil palm within the country. This is achieved through various interventions such as promoting high-yielding varieties, providing technical support to farmers and expanding area coverage. For instance, under the NMEO-OP, the production of oilseeds increased from 27.51 million tonnes in 2014-15 to 37.31 million tonnes in 2019-20, showcasing a growth of nearly 36% over five years.
  - Under NMEO-OP aims to increase the domestic production of Crude Palm Oil (CPO) to 11.20 lakh tonnes by 2025-26 and up to 28 lakh tonnes by 2029-30.
- **Improving Productivity** One of the key objectives of NMEO-OP is to improve the productivity of oilseeds and oil palm crops. This is achieved by implementing advanced agricultural practices, promoting efficient irrigation techniques and adopting modern technologies.
  - The major focus of the scheme is to substantially increase the assistance of inputs/interventions. A substantial increase has been made for planting material for oil palm and this has increased from ₹ 12,000 per hectare to ₹ 29000 per hectare.
- **Special Focus** The special emphasis of the scheme will be in India's North-Eastern (NE) states and the Andaman and Nicobar Island in which special provisions are being made for half-moon terrace cultivation, bio fencing and land clearance along with integrated farming.
  - As per assessment by the Indian Institute of Oil Palm Research (IIOPR), India has a potential of ₹ 28 lakh hectare for palm oil production, out of which more than 9 lakh hectares in the North-Eastern region
- **Strengthening Value Chain Linkages** NMOOP focuses on strengthening the entire value chain of oilseeds and oil palm, including production, processing and marketing. The mission encourages the establishment of modern processing units, facilitates market linkages and promotes value addition through product diversification.

- **Price Assurance** For the first time, the Government of India will give a price assurance to the oil palm farmers for the FFBs. This will be known as the Viability Price (VP). This will protect the farmers from the fluctuations of the international CPO prices and protect him from the volatility.

Conclusion

NEOM-OP will provide necessary condition to give a fillip to Atmanirbharta in edible oils. But the sufficient condition would be revisiting the existing incentive structure that unduly favours rice, wheat and sugarcane through heavy subsidisation of power, fertilisers and open-ended procurement. The need is to devise a crop-neutral incentive structure where cropping patterns are aligned with demand patterns and the crops are produced in a globally competitive manner.

Horticulture Sector

Q.16 Assess the role of National Horticulture Mission (NHM) in boosting the production, productivity and income of horticulture farms. How far has it succeeded in increasing the income of farmers? (250 Words, 15 Marks)

UPSC Mains PYQ 2018

Ans. Introduction National Horticulture Mission, a sub-scheme of Mission for Integrated Development of Horticulture (MIDH), is a centrally sponsored scheme launched in 2005-06 to enhance horticulture production and income support to farm households through area-based differentiated strategies.

- The horticulture production has been estimated at more than 340 million tonnes in 2021-22 in an area of 28.08 million hectares. It has surpassed the food grain production of around 330 million tonnes in 2022-23.
- Apart from ensuring nutritional security of the nation, it provides alternate rural employment opportunities, diversification in farm activities and enhanced income to farmers.
- Increase in demand for horticultural produce due to greater health awareness, rising income, export demands and increasing population poses the challenge for further increasing the production and productivity of horticultural crops.

Role of National Horticulture Mission (NHM) in Boosting the Productivity and Income

- **Modernising Production** NHM focuses on modernising production through adoption of improved technologies for ensuring the quality of all horticultural crops. NHM provides support for rejuvenating senile plantations at 50% of the cost subject to a maximum ceiling of ₹ 15,000 per hectare limited to 2 hectare per beneficiary.
  - Productivity of horticultural crops has increased by about 38% between 2004-05 and 2019-20 and is much higher compared to productivity of food grains (12.49 tonnes/hectare against 2.23 tonnes/hectare).
- **Provision of Critical Inputs** Under production and distribution of planting material, nurseries for producing planting material are established through central assistance.
  - **Example** Public sector nursery established by agriculture university at Pali, Punjab.
- **Creation of Water Sources** Under NHM, grant will be provided for creating water sources through the construction of community tanks and farm ponds with plastic lining.
  - **Example** Establishment of farm ponds at Morasar village, Rajasthan.
- **Nutrient Management** Developing facilities like disease forecasting units, biocontrol labs, plant health clinics and tissue labs will enhance the productivity of horticulture crops.
  - **Example** Banana tissue culture unit established at Hamalpur, Madhya Pradesh.
- **Increased Efficiency** NHM provides holistic growth through an area based differentiated strategies and automation in harvesting which will increase the efficiency of the produce.
  - **Example** Kinnow Cultivation in Amritsar district, Punjab.
- **Creating Integrated Boards** Specific boards created under NHM streamlined the rules for thereby promoting production and sale of the horticulture crops.
  - **Example** Coffee boards, Cashew boards etc.
- **Increase in Cultivated Area** NHM has played a significant role in increasing the area under horticulture crops. Area and production from 2014-15 to 2019-20 has increased by 9% and 14% respectively.

- **Training of the Farmers** The NHM provides training to farmers to adopt modern method of planting, protecting and harvesting which help in increasing the productivity of crops.
  - **Example** Farmers were trained in Grape Cultivation in Karnataka under NHM.

Successes of NHM in Increasing Income of Horticulture Farms and Farmers

- **Enhanced Incomes** An impact evaluation study by Department of Agriculture revealed that nearly 4% of the beneficiaries reported remarkable income addition (of over 50% to their base level earnings) while 65% reported substantial increase due to adoption of NHM.
- **Income Stability** The prices of crops under NHM are fixed by the board. This will ensure that farmers are not entirely dependent on the conventional crops for their subsistence.
- **Easy Access to Credits** The boards under NHM handle marketing and take care of needs of its members by providing credit facility and storage for their members.
- **Technological Advancements** Technology for enhancing the water and nutrient efficiency through micro-irrigation and fertigation has been developed for a number of horticultural crops.
- **Alternative Source of Income** The mission promoted the growth of the horticulture sector covering vegetables, fruits, root and tuber crops, spices, mushroom, flowers, aromatic plants, cashew which provides alternative source of income to farmers
- **Decrease in Costs** The adoption of technology under NHM reduces the costs for farmers from planting to harvesting of crops which results in higher profits.
  - **Example** Use of harvester machines for sorting out coffee beans.
- **Reduced Vulnerability** Farmers from the regions experiencing low rainfall and droughts are less exposed to natural. losses due to adoption of NHM.
  - **Example** Farmers in Bagepalli, a drought prone area in Karnataka-Andhra Pradesh border benefitting from NHM and the region emerged as horticulture hotspot.

Limitations of National Horticulture Mission

- **Infrastructure Deficit** Under NHM, there is lack of focus on cold-storage development and transport networks which increases post-harvest losses and reduce the incomes of farmers.
- **Higher Input Costs** Higher input costs than food grains make it a difficult set up, especially when there is no support from the local governments to the smaller farmers.
- **Market Support** Limited availability of market intelligence under National Horticulture Mission makes it a tougher option to choose especially for exports.
- **No Assured Return** Horticulture does not enjoy a safety net like the Minimum Support Price (MSP) for food grains.

Challenges in the Horticulture Sector

- Horticulture does not enjoy a safety net like the Minimum Support Price (MSP) for foodgrains.
- Lack of good cold chain storage and transport networks to extend the life of perishable products.
- Very less or limited input by machinery and equipment so it is tough to minimise the time restraints.
- Higher input costs than foodgrains make it a difficult set up, especially when there is no support from the Local Governments to the smaller farmers.
- It gets challenging for marginal farmers to cope with the high price fluctuations.
- Limited availability of market intelligence, mainly for exports makes it a tougher option to choose.

Way Forward

- **Improved Planning** Achievement against the set targets can be logical and effective, only when the annual action plans are scientifically based on the strengths and weaknesses of the area, duly visualising the opportunities and threats.
- **Identification of Thrust Areas** Thrust areas such as 'Greenhouse Cultivation' should be identified for the implementation in the future.

- **Capacity Building** Strengthening of human resources both supporting and technical is the need of the hour, to augment the implementation of the scheme.
- **Awareness Generation** Creation of awareness among farmers by extending more practical, on farm training programmes and interaction with research organisations will be helpful for horticultural development.

Conclusion

With NHM the overall share of horticulture in the agriculture GDP has grown to 30%, even though it accounts for just 17% of the farm land. The scheme needs to be further strengthened through increased funding to cater to the country's estimated demand of 650 million tonnes of fruits and vegetables by the year 2050.

Livestock Sector and Inclusive Growth

Q.17 Livestock rearing has a big potential for providing non-farm employment and income in rural areas. Discuss suggesting suitable measures to promote this sector in India. (150 Words, 10 Marks) **UPSC Mains PYQ 2015**

Ans. **Introduction** Livestock sector plays an important role in Indian economy. The total Livestock population is 535.78 million in the country showing an increase of 4.6% over Livestock Census-2012. In 20th Livestock Census, 35.94%-Cattle (2nd), 27.80%-Goat (2nd), 20.45%-Buffaloes (1st), 13.87%-Sheep (3rd), 1.69%-Pigs. *(In bracket, ranking are given at the world level).

Its contribution to total agriculture GVA (at constant prices) has increased from 24.3% in 2014-15 to 30.1% in 2020-21. Rapid growth of this sector can lead to more egalitarian and inclusive growth. This is because those engaged in it are mostly small landholders and the landless farmers.

Role of Livestock in Economy

- **Income** Livestock is a source of subsidiary income for many families in India especially the resource poor who maintain few heads of animals. Cows and buffaloes provide regular income to the livestock farmers through sale of milk. Animals like sheep and goat serve as sources of income during emergencies to meet exigencies like marriages, treatment of sick persons, children education, repair of houses etc. The animals also serve as moving banks and assets which provide economic security to the owners.
- **Employment** A large number of people in India being less literate and unskilled depend upon agriculture for their livelihoods. It provides employment to about 8.8 % of the population in India. The landless and less land people depend upon livestock for utilising their labour during lean agricultural season.
- **Food** The livestock products such as milk, meat and eggs are an important source of animal protein to the members of the livestock owners. The per capita availability of milk is around 375 g/day and eggs is 74/annum during 2017-18.
- **Social Security** The animals offer social security to the owners in terms of their status in the society. The families, especially the landless which own animals are better placed than those who do not. Gifting of animals during marriages is a very common phenomenon in different parts of the country.
- **Gender Equity** Animal husbandry promotes gender equality. More than three/fourth of the labour demand in livestock production is met by women. The share of women employment in the livestock sector is around 90% in Punjab and Haryana where dairying is a prominent activity and animals are stall-fed.
- **Protection Against Disasters** Livestock are the best insurance against the drought, famine and other natural calamities. Majority of the livestock population is concentrated in the marginal and small size of holdings. Further, agricultural productions get valuable organic manure provided by the livestock.

Important Initiatives by the Government

- **Animal Husbandry Infrastructure Development Fund (AHIDF)** Under this scheme, the Central Government provides a 3% interest subvention to the borrower and credit guarantee up to 25% of total borrowing.
- **Rashtriya Gokul Mission** It aims to develop and conserve indigenous breeds of bovine population. This is important to enhance milk production and to make it more remunerative to the farmers.

- **National Livestock Mission** Its objective is to ensure quantitative and qualitative improvement in livestock production systems and capacity building of all stakeholders.
- **National Artificial Insemination Programme** To suggest novel methods of bringing about impregnation in female breeds. Also, to prevent the spread of certain diseases which are genital in nature, thereby enhancing the efficiency of the breed.
- **National Animal Disease Control Programme (NADCP)** It is being implemented to control Foot and Mouth Disease and Brucellosis by completely vaccinating cattle, buffalo, sheep, goat and pig populations against Foot and Mouth Disease and bovine female calves of 4-8 months of age against brucellosis.
- **National Cattle and Buffalo Breeding Project** To genetically upgrade important indigenous breeds on priority basis with a focus on development and conservation.
- **Animal Husbandry Startup Grand Challenge** To appreciate innovations coming from the villages to expand the dairy sector in India.

Suitable Measures to Promote Livestock Sector in India

- **Towards One-Health Approach** There is a need to recognise One Health Approach and understand the interconnection between people, animals, plants and their shared environment.
- **Sufficient Resources** Providing sufficient fodder and drinking water is the need of hour to increase productivity of livestock rearing in India, in the rain-shadow region.
- **Marketing** Trade Policies like marketing have to be more effective for promotion of various livestock products like egg, fish, milk etc and providing sufficient price to farmers by reducing influence of middlemen.
- **Promoting Indigenous Breeds** Our indigenous breed of cattle shall be promoted, because most foreign breed cattle are not suitable to our climate and even provide low quality. There are some exceptions like Jersey cows, but overall introduction of foreign breeds has not been very successful.
- **Training** Necessary training and subsidies shall be provided to farmers to adopt livestock rearing as an alternate source of income.
- **Research and Development** Government shall also focus on Research and Development in livestock sector to increase per livestock productivity to provide more benefits to small and marginal farmers.

Conclusion

There is a need to encourage livestock husbandry to reap its full potential. If implied with utmost priority, these advice can boost the production. Thus would further attract the landless and small farmers to take advantage of this sector for sustaining their livelihood and make India competent in the global market.

Animal Husbandry

Q.18 While animal husbandry plays a significant role in food security, supplementing family incomes and generating gainful employment in the rural sector, it is beset with a number of challenges. Examine. (150 Words, 10 Marks)

Ans. **Introduction** Animal husbandry refers to the practice of breeding and rearing animals for benefits such as subsistence needs including meat, fibre, milk, eggs etc and income generation. According to NSSO 68th Round Survey, about 16.44 million workers are engaged in the activities related to rearing animals, mixed farming, fishing and aquaculture etc.

Importance of Animal Husbandry

- **Additional Source of Income** Farmers and landless labourers can earn extra income from animal husbandry. In the arid and semi-arid regions, livestock sector is the main source of family income. These animals serves as moving banks and assets, which provide economic security to the owners.
  - They contributed about 16% to their income, more so in states like Gujarat (24.4%), Haryana (24.2%), Punjab (20.2%) and Bihar (18.7%).

- **Employment Generation** In regions where agriculture does not create adequate livelihood opportunities, animal husbandry can provide a subsidiary occupation especially to marginal and landless farmers. For instance, by products of animals such as skin, fat, wool etc could be used to make leather products, woollen clothes etc.
  - Livestock employed 8.8% of the agricultural work force albeit it varied widely from 3% in North-Eastern states to 40-48% in Punjab and Haryana.
- **Food and Nutritional Security** In areas characterised by low cultivation of food crops such as hills and deserts, animal products such as milk, eggs, meat etc provide essential protein and nutrients and also reduces rural poverty by preventing additional expenditure for food by households.
- **Risk Aversion** Agriculture is a major source of employment in the rural areas, however, excessive dependence on monsoon, exposes farmers to vulnerabilities such as lack of adequate rainfall and consequent crop failure. Simultaneous practice of animal husbandry helps offset the risks and sustain livelihood.
- **Equitable Distribution** The rural poor have limited opportunities in crop production. In comparison, livestock wealth is more equitably distributed and the expanding demand for animal food products generates significant opportunities for the poor to escape poverty through diversifying and intensifying livestock production.
- **Social Security** The animals offer social security to the owners in terms of their status in the society, which also acts as a guard against getting driven into poverty.
- **Resilience to Climate Change** As livestock is less prone to global warming and climate change, it can be considered more reliable than rain-fed agriculture. Livestock production and marketing can help stabilise the food supplies and provide individuals and communities with a buffer against economic shocks and natural disasters.
- **Provides Agricultural Input** They provide draught power (bulls/oxen), dung, urine etc., that are used as biofertilisers. Further, animals are also used as means of transportation in rural areas.
- **Animal Husbandry Promotes Gender Equity** More than three-fourth of the labour demand in livestock production is met by women. The share of women employment in livestock sector is around 90% in Punjab and Haryana where dairying is a prominent activity.
- **Incidence of rural poverty is less** in states like Punjab, Haryana, Jammu and Kashmir, Himachal Pradesh, Kerala, Gujarat and Rajasthan where livestock accounts for a sizeable share of agricultural income as well as employment. Empirical evidence from India as well as from many other developing countries suggests that livestock development has been an important route for the poor households to escape poverty.

Challenges of Animal Husbandry

- **Degradation and encroachment of grazing land** is taking place due to fast paced industrialisation, urbanisation, agricultural expansion etc.
- **Limited artificial insemination services** owing to a deficiency in quality germplasm, infrastructure and technical manpower coupled with poor conception rate following artificial insemination.
- **Markets for livestock product are unorganised and underdeveloped** Most of these markets are irregular, uncertain and non-transparent. This restricts access to markets and disincentivises adoption of improved technologies and quality inputs. Further, the markets are often dominated by informal intermediaries who exploit the producers.
- **There is inadequate veterinary care** due to insufficient budgetary allocation to the sector. Further, there is lack of drugs and vaccines quality control, insufficient facility for disease diagnosis, reporting, epidemiology, surveillance and forecasting. This is compounded by frequent outbreaks of diseases such as foot and mouth disease, black quarter infection, influenza etc.
- **Inadequate Extension Services is an Important Challenge** The extension format, methodology and set-up established for agriculture have failed to cater to the needs of the livestock sector. Consequently, only about 5.1% of the farm households were able to access any information on animal husbandry against 40.4% for crop farming.
- **There is a Lack of Testing Facilities** for milk products and quality parameters at the collection centres are almost non-existent. Microbial contamination, antibiotic residues, adulteration and lack of proper anaerobic waste treatment are additional concerns.

- **The sector also Faces Export Constraints** There is lack of adherence to international processing standards which hinders the export of meat and meat-based products. Further, schemes on modernisation of slaughterhouses and by-product utilisation have not been effectively implemented.

Challenges	Government Initiatives
• Degradation and encroachment of grazing land • **Outbreak of Diseases** Food and Mouth Disease, Black Quarter Infections, etc. • **Yield and Productivity issues** Largest producer of milk but yield is only but 50% of the global cattle average. • **Emission of GHGs** Contributes 58% of agricultural emissions. • **Lack to Technology Advancements** Limited artificial inseminations, deficiency in quality germplasm, lack of technical manpower. • **Funding Issues** Only 12% of the total expenditure on agriculture and allied resulting in inadequate veterinary care, • **Poor extension Services** Only 5.1% of farm households • Poor Insurance coverage • Underdeveloped and unorganised markets for livestock • High presence of informal sector • Lack of testing facilities for quality checking and standardisation of animal products • **Export Constraints** Ad-hoc export policy	• Dairy Processing and Infrastructural Development Fund • Animal Husbandry Infrastructure Development Fund • National Livestock Mission • National Animal Disease Control Programme (NADCP) • National Artificial Insemination Programme • National Programme for Dairy Development • Rashtriya Gokul Mission • E-Pashu Haat Portal • Pashu - Aadhar • Gobar-Dhan • E-Gopala App • Dairy Entrepreneurship Development Scheme • Geotagging of animals

Conclusion

Realising the potential of this sector, the government has brought schemes such as Rashtriya Gokul Mission, E-Pashu Haat etc to promote sustainable animal rearing practices, create organised markets and channelise sufficient funds towards expansion of animal husbandry.

Dairy Sector

Q.19 The current situation demands a sustainable development of the dairy sector which should be in line with the environmental, nutritional and socio-economic demands of the country. Elaborate. (150 Words, 10 Marks)

Ans. Introduction The dairy sector in India plays a pivotal role in the country's agricultural GDP and employment landscape, making it a vital component of the national economy. With a population of over 1.3 billion people, India is the world's largest milk producer with 200 million MT production in 2022 accounting for approximately 23% of global milk production, providing employment to 70 million people.

- The sector's current situation reflects its immense potential for growth and its ability to drive economic development and livelihood improvement across the country.

Significance of the Dairy Sector in India

- **Tackling Agricultural Uncertainties** Farmers keep 2-5 milk animals for livelihood. They provide great support to them, especially during drought and flood. Further, dairying is not a seasonal occupation in nature, like agriculture.
- **Nutritional Support** The milk and associated products have immensely helped India in reducing the malnutrition and undernourishment levels in the country. Thus, the dairy sector is indispensable for meeting the nutritional requirement of the country's rising population.
- **Employment Generation** It is a significant contributor to farmers' income as approximately 70 million farmers are directly involved in dairying.
- **Reduces Import Bill** Operation Flood (also called as White Revolution) converted India from a milk importer to the world's largest producer. The programme launched in 1970 and adopted a multi-pronged approach. This included tax incentives, food quality standards, subsidies on inputs, infrastructure provisions such as cold chain and electrification. All this helped in reducing import bills and made India an exporter. The country exported dairy products worth USD187 million in 2019-20.

- **Women Empowerment** Female population comprises around 69% of the sector's workforce. They are dependent on the sector for their livelihood. Therefore, the dairy sector's development automatically augments women's empowerment.

Current Situation of Dairy Sector

- **Rising Milk Production** The dairy sector in India has been experiencing a steady growth in milk production. India produced around 207 million metric tonnes of milk, making it the world's largest milk producer. (Source: Ministry of Agriculture and Farmers Welfare).
- **Growing Dairy Cooperative Movement** Dairy cooperatives such as Amul, Mother Dairy and Sudha Dairy NANDINI, have emerged as successful examples of farmer-owned organisations. These cooperatives ensure fair prices for farmers, facilitate milk collection and provide support in terms of infrastructure and marketing.
- **Increasing Demand for Value-Added Dairy Products** There is a rising demand for value-added dairy products in India, including processed milk, yogurt, cheese and ice cream.
- **Technological Advancements** The dairy sector in India is adopting advanced technologies to improve milk production, processing and distribution. For example, the use of automatic milking machines, IoT-enabled sensors for monitoring cattle health and cold chain infrastructure
- **Government Initiatives and Support** The Indian Government has introduced various initiatives to support the dairy sector. Schemes like the Rashtriya Gokul Mission, Dairy Processing and Infrastructure Development Fund (DIDF), KCC for Animal Husbandry, etc provide financial support for dairy infrastructure development.

With a series of measures being taken by the government as well as the growing role of the private sector in dairy development, India is expected to sustain its growth in milk production and milk processing in the coming decades but it needs to be aligned with environmental, nutritional and socio-economic demands of the country.

Environmental Concern

- **Greenhouse Gas Emissions** The dairy sector is a significant contributor to greenhouse gas emissions globally. According to the FAO enteric fermentation and manure management in livestock, including dairy cattle, account for around 14.5% of global greenhouse gas emissions (GHGS).
- **Water Footprint** Dairy production requires substantial water resources. According to a study published in the journal Science, it takes approx 628 liters of water to produce one liter of milk.
- **Efficient Water Management Practices**, such as improved irrigation techniques and water recycling, can help reduce the sector's water footprint.
- **Land Use and Deforestation** The expansion of dairy farming often leads to deforestation and land degradation. A report by the United Nations Environment Programme (UNEP) estimates that livestock production, including dairy, is responsible for approximately 80% of deforestation in the North-East.
- **Sustainable Land Management Practices** and promoting agroforestry can help mitigate these environmental impacts.
- **Waste Management** Dairy production generates substantial amounts of organic waste, including manure and processing by-products. Proper waste management systems, such as anaerobic digestion or composting, can help convert these wastes into valuable resources while minimising their environmental impact. Example Godhan Nyay Yojana of Chattisgarh.
- **Biodiversity Conservation** Intensive dairy farming practices can negatively affect biodiversity, including soil health, pollinators and native species. Promoting sustainable grazing systems, preserving natural habitats and avoiding the use of harmful agrochemicals can contribute to biodiversity conservation in the dairy sector.

Nutritional Aspect

- **Protein and Essential Nutrients** Dairy products are rich in high-quality protein and calcium, vitamin D and B vitamins. According to the National Family Health Survey (NFHS-5), dairy consumption contributes significantly to meeting protein and micronutrient requirements in India.
- **Childhood Nutrition** Comprehensive National Nutrition Survey (CNNS) highlights the importance of dairy in providing essential nutrients for growth and development in children, particularly in rural areas where malnutrition rates are higher.
- **Nutritional Security** Encouraging dairy consumption, particularly in vulnerable populations, can help combat nutritional deficiencies and improve overall health outcomes. Example POSHAN is linked to milk distribution.
- **Sustainable Food Systems** The National Nutrition Strategy of India emphasises the importance of promoting sustainable and diversified diets that include dairy products for improved nutrition and food security.

Socio-Economic Aspect

- **Employment Generation** According to the National Dairy Development Board (NDDB), the dairy industry in India generates direct and indirect employment for over 100 million people, including small-scale farmers, milk vendors and dairy workers.
- **Livelihood Improvement** Dairy farming offers an avenue for improving livelihoods, especially for small and marginal farmers. Small-scale dairy cooperatives, like Amul, have empowered farmers by providing access to fair markets, better prices for their milk and improved income stability.
- **Boost to Rural Economy** The growth of the dairy sector contributes significantly to the rural economy, as it stimulates demand for various goods and services. Increased dairy production and processing activities create market linkages, supporting local businesses and contributing to rural development.
- **Women Empowerment** Dairy farming plays a vital role in empowering women in rural areas. The Self-Help Group Dairy Programme initiated by the National Rural Livelihoods Mission (NRLM) promotes women's participation in dairy cooperatives, providing them with training, access to credit and market opportunities.
- **Income Diversification** Engaging in dairy farming allows farmers to diversify their income sources, reducing their dependence on seasonal crops and mitigating agricultural risks.
- **Poverty Alleviation** According to the International Livestock Research Institute (ILRI), dairy production can be a pathway out of poverty for smallholder farmers, enabling them to escape the cycle of poverty and achieve economic independence.
- **Social Inclusion** Dairy farming can promote social inclusion by offering opportunities for marginalised communities, including scheduled castes, tribes and landless farmers.

Conclusion

Embracing sustainable development in the dairy sector is not only an environmental imperative but also a means to ensure nutritional security, empower communities and foster a prosperous future for both the industry and the nation as a whole. By implementing eco-friendly practices, prioritising nutrition and promoting inclusive socio-economic growth, we can pave the way for a sustainable and thriving dairy sector.

National Mission on Sustainable Agriculture (NMSA)

Q.20 Examine the importance of sustainable agriculture in India for the country to become more resilient to food security challenges. Discuss in the background of National Mission for Sustainable Agriculture (NMSA). (250 Words, 15 Marks)

Ans. **Introduction** Food security challenges refer to the obstacles and issues that hinder the availability, accessibility and affordability of nutritious and safe food for individuals and communities. In the context of being the most populous country, limited natural resources and threat of climate change, food security in India faces several challenges.

Food Security Challenges

- **Low Productivity** The yield per hectare of rice, one of India's principal crops, is 2177 kgs lagging behind countries such as China and Brazil that have yield rates of 4263 kg/hectare and 3265 kg/hectare respectively.
- **Market Volatility and Price Fluctuations** Market fluctuations, price volatility and speculation can lead to unpredictable food prices, making it challenging for vulnerable populations to afford a nutritious diet.
- **Climate Change** Climate change is causing extreme weather events which poses significant challenges to agricultural productivity and food production. Example Punjab had a record wheat production of 17 million tonnes in 2021. But in 2022, it came down to 13.9 million tonnes due to the heat wave.
- **Environmental Degradation** Natural resources like land, water is being severely degraded due to unsustainable economic practices which can reduce agricultural productivity in the future.
  - According to the CGWB, with 230 billion metre cubes of groundwater drawn out each year for irrigating agriculture lands in India, many parts of the country are experiencing rapid depletion of groundwater.
- **Limited Access to Resources** Limited access to land, water, credit and modern agricultural technologies hampers agricultural productivity and efficiency, particularly for small-scale farmers and marginalised communities.

- **Food Waste** India faces significant challenges in terms of food wastage and post-harvest losses which increases cost of food products.
- **Import Dependence** India is dependent on import particularly for oilseeds and pulses thus reliable supply of such food products cannot be ensured.
- **Challenges in PDS** Inadequate distribution of food (exclusion errors, corruption and poor service at PDS shops etc) through PDS is also a reason for growing food insecurity in the country.
- **Overpopulation** Overpopulation is linked to competition for food and can lead to malnutrition amongst children, especially in rural areas where access to food is limited.
- **Lack of Inter-sectoral Coordination** Lack of coherent food and nutrition policies along with the absence of inter-sectoral coordination between various ministries of government such as Ministry of Women and Child Health, Ministry of Health and Family Welfare, Ministry of Agriculture, Ministry of Finance etc have added to the problem.

Importance of Sustainable Agriculture for Ensuring Food Security

- **Conservation of Natural Resources** Sustainable agriculture promotes the conservation of natural resources. By preserving these resources, sustainable agriculture ensures their availability for future generations, enabling long-term food security. **Example** NMSA through Rained area development promotes effective management of available water resources and enhancing water use efficiency through application of technologies.
- **Climate Change Resilience** Sustainable agriculture focuses on climate-smart practices that build resilience against these challenges. **Example** NMSA popularises resource conservation technologies (both on-farm and off-farm) and introducing practices that will support mitigation efforts in times of extreme climatic events or disasters like prolonged dry spells, floods etc.
- **Increased Productivity** Sustainable agricultural practices aim to enhance productivity in a manner that preserves the natural resources and the environment.
  - NMSA promotes integrated farming system covering crops, livestock and fishery, plantation and pasture based composite farming for enhancing livelihood opportunities, ensuring food security and minimising risks from crop failure through supplementary/ residual production systems.
- **Reduced Food Waste** Sustainable agriculture emphasises efficient post-harvest management practices, including proper storage, processing and transportation techniques. By minimising post-harvest losses, more food can reach consumers, reducing the overall demand-supply gap and improving food security.
- **Enhancing Rural Livelihoods** By promoting sustainable agricultural practices, farmers can achieve higher incomes and better livelihood opportunities. Sustainable agriculture emphasises diversification, value addition and market linkages, enabling farmers to earn more from their produce and improve their overall standard of living.
- **Soil Enhancement** Use of bio-fertilisers, limiting the use of pesticides or fertilisers and integrated pest management helps to conserve the health of soil and retain its fertility for crop growth.
- **Profitability to Farmers** Sustainable agriculture techniques enable higher resource efficiency – they help produce greater agricultural output while using lesser land, water and energy.
- **Biodiversity** Several SAPSs like agroforestry, Integrated Farming Systems (IFS), permaculture, natural farming, organic farming, conservation agriculture and crop diversification strategies (rotation, intercropping, mixed) tend to increase the spatial, vertical and temporal diversity of species at a farm (and landscape) level.

National Mission for Sustainable Agriculture

The National Mission for Sustainable Agriculture (NMSA) is a government initiative in India aimed at promoting sustainable agriculture practices and addressing the challenges faced by farmers in adapting to climate change.

Key Initiatives under NMSA

- Promotion of organic farming and certification schemes.
- Introduction of climate-resilient crop varieties and technologies.
- Strengthening weather forecasting and agro-advisory services.
- Establishment of climate-smart villages to showcase best practices in sustainable agriculture.
- Implementation of watershed development projects and rainwater harvesting structures.
- Encouraging Farmer Producer Organisations (FPOs) and cooperative farming.

Focus Areas

- Soil health management, including soil testing, nutrient management and organic farming practices.
- Water resource management, including water conservation, efficient irrigation techniques and watershed development.
- Crop diversification and integrated farming systems to improve farm income and reduce risks.
- Livestock development and promotion of dairy, poultry and fisheries for enhanced livelihood opportunities.
- Capacity building of farmers and extension workers through training and knowledge dissemination.

Status of Sustainable Agriculture in India

- **Not Mainstreamed** Sustainable agriculture is far from mainstream in India, with only 5 (crop rotation; agroforestry; rainwater harvesting; mulching and precision) SAPSs scaling beyond 5% of the net sown area.
- **Low Adoption** Most SAPSs are being adopted by less than five million (or 4 %) of all Indian farmers. Many are practised by less than1%.
- **Status of Crop Rotation** Crop rotation is the most popular SAPS in India, covering around 30 million hectares (Mha) of land and approximately 15 million farmers.
- **Agroforestry Popular Among Large** Cultivators Agroforestry, mainly popular among large cultivators and rainwater harvesting have relatively high coverage - 25 Mha and 20- 27 Mha respectively.
- Organic farming currently covers only 2.8 Mha — or 2% of India's net sown area of 140 Mha.
- **Increase in Natural Farming and Integrated Pest Management** Natural farming is the fastest growing sustainable agricultural practice in India and has been adopted by around 800,000 farmers. Integrated Pest Management (IPM) has achieved a coverage area of 5 Mha after decades of sustained promotion.
- **Low Budget Outlay** The budget outlay for the National Mission for Sustainable Agriculture (NMSA) is only 0. 8% of the Ministry of Agriculture and Farmers' Welfare's total budget ₹ 142,000 crore (excluding ₹ 71,309 crore spent annually on fertiliser subsidies by the Centre)
- **Concentration of Civil Society in Some Pockets** Most Civil Society Organisations (CSOs) involved in SAPSs were active in Maharashtra, Rajasthan and Madhya Pradesh. Organic farming, natural farming and vermin composting get the most interest from CSOs.

Conclusion

A shift to sustainable architecture and practices will help address the carbon debt humans have created for the soil by delivering more from less. While states like Andhra Pradesh are leading the way on sustainable agriculture in India, the adoption remains on the margins at a country-wide level. In this regards suggestion of Madhav Chitale Committee of maintaining a record/portal of good agricultural practices and rewarding them can boast environment sustainability in agriculture.

Check Your Preparation

1. How do subsidies affect the cropping pattern, crop diversity and economy of the farmers? Explain briefly different crop subsidy schemes provided by the government? (150 words, 10 marks)
2. How will the 'One Nation, One Ration Card' scheme bring perceptible changes in the lives of vulnerable migrant workers in India? Can 'Direct Benefit Transfer (DBT)' be more effective in ensuring food security of the migrant population? Comment. (250 words, 15 marks)
3. Digitisation of PDS Scheme by Linking Ration Card with Aadhaar to curb leakages should not lead to "Digital exclusion" of marginalised section. In light of the above statement examine the challenges in digitisation of social welfare schemes. (150 words, 10 marks)
4. Improved efficiency of livestock, with its various commodities and service products, is crucial to achieving sustainable agricultural development and food security, particularly in low-income, food-deficit countries. Discuss. (250 words, 15 marks)
5. Diversification of small farms is often suggested as a means for rapid rural development in India. In this context discuss the need for small farms agricultural diversification. How are the present policies in the agricultural sector contrary to small farms diversification and farmers well-being? (250 words, 15 marks)

UNIT 6

Food Processing and Related Industries in India-Scope and Significance, Location, Upstream and Downstream Requirements, Supply Chain Management

Food Processing Sector (From Farm Labour to Non- Farm Labour)

Q.1 Examine the reasons behind the shifting of labour force from the farm sector to non-farm sector. How can the development of food processing sector facilitate this transition? (150 Words, 10 Marks)

Ans. **Introduction** The NSSO's latest annual Periodic Labour Force Survey (PLFS) report for 2021-22 (July-June) shows the farm sector's share in the country's employed labour force at 45.5% from 46.5% in 2020-21.

Reasons behind the Shifting of Labour Force from the Farm Sector to Non-farm Sector

- **Economic Diversification** The growth of the non-farm sectors like manufacturing, construction, services, and information technology reflects the need for economic diversification which requires a larger labor force to meet the growing demand for goods and services.
- **Higher Income Opportunities** With high income, non-farm sector looks attractive. As per PLFS, average income in farm sector is ₹ 4650 while in non-farm sector its ₹ 12000 for similar work.
  - Reducing the dependence of rural masses on agriculture as a source of income will help improve the overall income of the rural population.
- **Technological Advancements in Agriculture** Technological advancements and mechanisation in agriculture have led to increased productivity, resulting in reduced labor demand in the sector. The number of agricultural workers in India decreased from around 263 million in 2001 to approximately 200 million in 2015 as per Agriculture Census, 2015-2016.
- **Urbanisation and Rural-Urban Migration** The process of urbanisation and rural-urban migration has contributed to the shift of labor from the farm sector to the non-farm sector. Better employment prospects, lack of infrastructure in rural is promoting such migration. The urban population in India increased from around 290 million in 2001 to over 460 million in 2019.
- **Government Policies and Initiatives** The Indian government has implemented various policies and initiatives like Make in India, Skill India, Mudra to promote industrialisation and job creation in the non-farm sectors.
- **Changing Consumer Preferences** Rising incomes and changing consumer preferences have resulted in an increased demand for non-agricultural products and services. This has driven the growth of sectors such as retail, hospitality, tourism, and entertainment, creating employment opportunities outside the farm sector.

- **Skill Development and Education** Skill development initiatives and improvements in education have equipped workers with the necessary qualifications and abilities to work in non-farm sectors, expanding their employment options. As of September 2022, over 11 million individuals have been trained and certified under the Skill India Mission
- **Income Stability and Social Security** Non-farm sectors often provide more stable and regular income opportunities compared to the seasonal nature of agricultural employment with social security benefit. The implementation of social security schemes such as the Employees' Provident Fund (EPF) and Employees' State Insurance (ESI) Act aims to provide workers with social security benefits.

Development of Food Processing Sector in Facilitating the Transition

- **Increased Value Addition** Food processing adds value to agricultural produce, creating opportunities for non-farm employment. For instance, processing fruits and vegetables into packaged juices and snacks increases their value and generates jobs in processing units.
- **Demand for Processed Food** The rising demand for processed and convenience food products drives the growth of the food processing sector, leading to job creation. The Indian packaged food market is projected to reach USD 270 billion by 2027, indicating significant opportunities for employment as per IBEF
- **Infrastructure Development** Investments in food processing infrastructure, such as cold storage, warehouses, and processing units, create employment opportunities. Pradhan Mantri Kisan SAMPADA Yojana aims to enhance infrastructure in the food processing sector with a budget of INR 6,000 crore.
- **Skill Development and Training** Skill development initiatives in food processing equip individuals with industry-relevant skills, enabling them to find employment in the non-farm sector. NSDC has collaborated with the food processing industry to provide skill training to thousands of individuals.
- **Agri-entrepreneurship Opportunities** Food processing promotes agri-entrepreneurship, encouraging farmers to engage in value-added activities and create non-farm enterprises. Examples include farmers setting up small-scale units for processing dairy products, spices, or grains like Mother Dairy, AMUL etc
- **Export Potential** Development in food processing enables the export of processed food products, leading to increased employment and revenue generation. India's food processing exports reached USD 44.25 billion in 2020-21, highlighting the export potential in this sector.
- **Rural Development** Food processing units in rural areas create job opportunities, reduce rural-urban migration, and contribute to overall rural development. Establishing food processing clusters in rural regions, such as Mega Food Parks, encourages employment generation locally.

Conclusion

It is important to note that the non-farm rural sector should not be seen as a replacement for employment in agriculture but rather as a complementary approach. Agricultural development remains crucial and should be pursued as a fundamental requirement for inclusive development.

Potential and Challenges of Food Processing Sector

Q.2 With growing population and unrestricted use of natural resources, demand for developing an efficient and sustainable food value chain will increase. In this regard, critically analyze the potential of food processing industries in India and the challenges associated with establishing a cost-effective supply chain management. (250 Words, 15 Marks)

Ans. **Introduction** In India, the growing population and unchecked use of natural resources pose significant challenges to the food value chain. To address this, an efficient and sustainable approach is crucial.

Need for Developing an Efficient and Sustainable Food Value Chain

- **Growing Population and Urbanisation** Demographic shift puts increased pressure on food production, processing, and distribution systems.
  - Developing an efficient food value chain becomes crucial to ensure a continuous and reliable supply of food to meet the demands of a growing population.

- **Demand for Safe and Nutritious Food** There is a growing demand for food products that are free from contaminants, produced sustainably and provide adequate nutrition.
  - 'An efficient food value chain ensures traceability, quality control, and facilitates the delivery of safe and nutritious food to consumers.
- **Environmental Sustainability** Developing a sustainable food value chain involves reducing the environmental footprint of food production, minimizing waste throughout the supply chain, and adopting environmentally friendly practices such as organic farming, efficient irrigation, and renewable energy use.
- **Food Loss and Waste Reduction** Food loss and waste occur at various stages of the food value chain, from production to consumption.
  - Developing an efficient value chain involves implementing measures to reduce post-harvest losses, improve storage and transportation systems, and promote responsible consumption to minimize food waste.
- **Resilience to Climate Change** An efficient and sustainable food value chain incorporates climate-smart practices such as crop diversification, water-efficient irrigation, and adaptation strategies to build resilience and ensure the continuity of food production in the face of climate-related disruptions.

Potential of Food Processing Industry

- **Contribution to GDP and Employment** The food processing industry in India contributes significantly to the country's GDP, accounting for around 8.8% of the total GDP in 2022. It is a major source of employment, providing livelihood opportunities for millions of people, particularly in rural areas.
  - Food Processing Sector gives employment to 11.36 % of the workforce and is expected to generate 9 million jobs by 2024.
- **Market size and growth** The market size of the industry was estimated at USD 258 billion in 2020 and is projected to reach USD 482 billion by 2025, growing at a CAGR of 11%.
- **Increase in Consumption Level** By 2030, Indian annual household consumption is expected to triple, making India the fifth-largest consumer in the world.
- **Value Addition** Food processing adds value to agricultural produce, thereby increasing farmer income and reducing post-harvest losses, improving nutrient content and shelf life.
  - Currently, India is processing less than 10% of its agricultural output, thus, presenting immense opportunities for increasing these processing levels and leading to investments in this sector.
- **Employment Generation** It employs over 12 million people directly and has the potential to generate additional jobs in allied sectors inculcating both skilled and non-skilled jobs.
- **Export Potential** It is one of the largest exporters of rice, spices, buffalo meat, and processed fruits and vegetables. The export of processed food products reached USD 33 billion in 2022, accounting for nearly 13% of India's total merchandise exports.
- **Government Support and Initiatives** The Indian government has launched various initiatives and policies to promote the food processing industry, such as the Pradhan Mantri Kisan Sampada Yojana (PMKSY). These initiatives aim to create modern infrastructure, provide financial assistance, and support research and development in the sector.
- **Growing Urbanisation and Changing Consumer Preferences** There is a growing market for packaged foods, ready-to-eat meals, and healthy snacks, creating opportunities for food processing industries due to changing consumer preferences.

Challenges in Establishing a Cost-effective Supply Chain Management in the Food Processing Industry in India

- **Infrastructure Limitations** The lack of proper storage facilities leads to approximately 10% wastage of perishable produce. Only about 10% of India's perishable produce goes through cold storage facilities, highlighting the infrastructure gap.
- **Fragmented Supply Chain** The food processing industry in India is characterized by a fragmented supply chain, with multiple intermediaries involved in the distribution process. It is estimated that farmers in India receive only about 30-35% of the final retail price, with the rest being captured by intermediaries.

- **Inefficient Logistics** According to a report by the Indian Council for Research on International Economic Relations, logistics costs in India account for approximately 14% of the GDP, compared to around 8-10% in developed countries.
  - Indian national highways account for only 2% of the total road network but carry 40% of all cargo.
  - Port capacity may be increasing, lack of connectivity to these ports leads to cost escalations and delays in the goods transferred.
  - Lack of last-mile connectivity from rail transporters.
- **Land Fragmentation** The small size of farms and decrease in land holdings inhibits large scale production. There is lack of common policy on contract farming on pan India basis.
- **Informalisation and Disadvantaged Smaller Processing units** More than 50% of the industries in the food processing sector is concentrated in informal sector and are small scale industries. FPI especially the SMEs have lack of finances but large proportion of FPI exists as SMEs only. According to the standing committee, Mega Food Park scheme require a minimum area of 50 acres and thus, it does not promote smaller or individual food processing and preservation units.
- **Quality and Safety Standards** Ensuring compliance with quality and safety standards throughout the supply chain poses a challenge. India ranks 77th out of 140 countries on the Food Safety Index, highlighting the need for improvements in food safety practices and regulatory frameworks.
- **Seasonality and Perishability** The seasonality and perishability of agricultural produce in India pose challenges for supply chain management. Approximately 30-40% of fruits and vegetables are wasted due to inadequate storage and handling facilities,
- **Pricing and Market Volatility** Fluctuating prices of raw materials, coupled with market volatility, make it challenging to maintain cost-effective supply chain management. Price volatility can affect profitability and planning for both manufacturers and farmers.
- **Limited Access to Finance** Only about 10-15% of Indian farmers have access to institutional credit, creating barriers to adopting modern supply chain practices.
- **Skill Gaps and Technology Adoption** Limited technical skills and awareness among stakeholders hinder the adoption of efficient supply chain practices. The adoption of technology, such as digital platforms for supply chain visibility and data analytics, is still relatively low in the food processing industry.
- **Inefficient Packaging** Qualitative packaging is not available for majority of the products. High cost of packaging increases the final prices of the product, e. g. packaging of fruit juice costs almost 19% of the total production cost.
- **Fragmented Market** There is a lack of organised wholesale and retail market for the processed food products. Indian retail sector is still dominated by small traders and Kirana shops.

Government Measures

- **Mega Food Parks Scheme** The government has established 18 mega food parks and 134 cold chain projects to develop the food processing supply chain.
- **PM-FME Scheme** Ministry of Food Processing Industries (MoFPI), in partnership with the State/ UT Governments, has launched an all India Centrally Sponsored PM Formalisation of Micro food processing Enterprises Scheme (PM FME Scheme) for providing financial, technical and business support for upgradation of existing micro food processing enterprises.
- **One District One Product** The scheme adopts the One District One Product (ODOP) approach to reap the benefit of scale in terms of procurement of inputs, availing common services and marketing of products. ODOP for the scheme will provide the framework for value chain development and alignment of support infrastructure.
- **Pradhan Mantri Kisan SAMPADA Yojana** Pradhan Mantri Kisan SAMPADA Yojana (Scheme for Agro-Marine Processing and Development of Agro-Processing Clusters) is a comprehensive package which will result in creation of modern infrastructure with efficient supply chain management from farm gate to retail outlet.

Way Forward

- **Infrastructure development** Increase investments in storage and cold chain infrastructure, particularly in rural areas, to reduce post-harvest losses and maintain product quality.
  - **Example** The Indian government's Pradhan Mantri Kisan SAMPADA Yojana provides financial assistance for the development of infrastructure, including cold chains, in the food processing sector.

- **Supply Chain Integration** Encourage vertical integration and the establishment of direct farmer-consumer linkages to reduce the number of intermediaries in the supply chain and increase farmers' share of the retail price.
  - **Example** Farmer Producer Organizations (FPOs) in India, such as Amul and Mahindra Agri Solutions, facilitate direct procurement from farmers and help in establishing efficient supply chains.
- **Technology Adoption** Promote the adoption of digital platforms for supply chain visibility, data analytics, and real-time monitoring of inventory and demand. Example: Companies like Ninjacart and AgNext are utilizing technology solutions like mobile applications and AI-powered quality assessment devices to optimize supply chain processes and ensure traceability.
- **Capacity Building and Training** Provide training programs to enhance technical skills Example: The Food Safety and Standards Authority of India (FSSAI) conducts training and capacity-building programs to improve food safety practices and compliance with quality standards.
- **Public Private Partnerships** Foster collaborations between government agencies, private sector players, and research institutions to address supply chain challenges collectively.

Conclusion

By focusing on infrastructure development, supply chain integration, technology adoption, capacity building, and public-private partnerships, the food processing industry in India can enhance supply chain efficiency, reduce costs, minimize wastage, and ensure the timely delivery of safe and high-quality products to consumers.

Small Food Processing Units

Q.3 What are the reasons for poor acceptance of cost-effective small processing unit? How the food processing unit will be helpful to uplift the socio-economic status of poor farmers? (150 Words, 10 Marks)

UPSC Mains PYQ 2017

Ans. Introduction Food processing is defined as a process of value addition to the agricultural or horticultural produce by various methods like grading, sorting and packaging. It is considered as a sun-rise industry with large growth potential because of availability of raw materials and changing lifestyles of people.

Reasons for Poor Acceptance of Cost-effective Small Processing Units

- **Infrastructure** Small processing units are debarred from the facilities of packaging, cold storage and logistics.
- **Quality of food** Use of harmful fertilizer impact the quality of food which makes these units unable to pass through quality checks, sanitary and phytosanitary measures. Also, small units do not follow the internationally recommended standards of packaging and labelling.
- **Less trained manpower** Poor skill levels and lack of manpower such as production managers, microbiologists etc. hampering the competitiveness of small processing unit.
- **Inefficiencies** Around 75% of food processing industries are small and concentrated in unorganized sector, causing inefficiencies leading to poor acceptance.
- **Technology** The small processing units lack basic technologies for food processing such as sampling, weighing and assorting. Most of the processing is manual and there is only limited use of technology like pre- cooling and irradiation facilities.
- **Low value addition** Due to fragmentation of small processing units, unorganized nature and primitive techniques also leads to poor acceptance.
- **Certification** The small processing units do not go for certification of food products by bodies like FSSAI which leads to poor acceptance of their products and make them uncompetitive in national and international markets.
- **Poor marketing** The individual small units are unable to invest in marketing and branding impacting performance of the sector.
- **Competition** The highly value-added products of large processing unit from different countries like China also act as hindrance for development of small processing units and make them economically unviable.

Significance of Food Processing in uplifting socio-economic aspects of farmers

Economic Aspects

- **Increasing Farmer's Income** With value addition and processing, the income of the poor farmers can be increased which will help in achieving the goal of doubling farmer income.
- **Crop Diversification** Food processing will require different inputs, thus creating an incentive for poor farmers to grow and diversify crops which will have economic benefits.
- **Employment Generation** It can absorb a major share of workers from the agriculture sector who face disguised unemployment leading to increased incomes for poor farmers.
- **Great export Potential** Food processing provides increased exposure of poor farmers to international markets.
- **Increased Opportunities** If FPIs are allowed to engage, such as contract farming, market intermediaries could be eliminated thereby resulting in better remuneration of farmers and control on food inflation.
- **Value Addition** With value addition and processing, the income of the poor farmers can be increased which help in achieving the goal of doubling famer's income by 2022.

Social Aspects

- **Reduce Malnutrition** Processed foods when fortified with vitamins and minerals can reduce the nutritional gap in the poor farmers.
- **Reduce Wastage of Perishables** It links poor farmers to the agricultural market in reducing post-harvest wastage of horticultural products.
- **Curbing Migration** Food processing being a labour-intensive industry will provide localized employment opportunities for poor farmers and thus reduce rural to urban migration.
- **Gender Empowerment** Food processing industry is closely related to animal husbandry where a large number of poor women farmers are employed.

Conclusion

Food processing have the potential to solve the key challenges faced by India such as promoting exports, increasing farmer's income, rural industrialization, and reduce rural urban migration. Considering its importance government launched various schemes such as Sampada Yojana, Mega food park scheme etc. It is the need for us to take advantage of this sector.

Role of Supermarkets

Q.4 Examine the role of supermarkets in supply chain management of fruits, vegetables and food items. How do they eliminate number of intermediaries? (150 Words, 10 Marks) **UPSC Mains PYQ 2018**

Ans. **Introduction** Supply chain management is the management of the flow of goods and services and includes all processes, from acquiring raw materials and production through distribution to the final customer, in the most streamlined and cost-effective way possible. Most of the marketing problems fruits, vegetables etc can be traced to its perishability which in turn is also responsible for high marketing costs, price fluctuations, market gluts etc.

Role of Supermarket in the Supply Chain Management of Food

- **Reduce Post-Harvest Wastage** About 30 % fruits and vegetables are rendered unfit for consumption due to spoilage after harvesting. Supermarkets with efficient backward linkages well equipped to reduce the wastages.
- **Efficient Transportation** in comparison to conventional methods, supermarket chains move their merchandise in a quick manner, maintaining the freshness of fruits, vegetables and other perishable foods
- **Enhances Farmers' Realization** As per International Food Policy Research Institute (IFFRI) and World Bank, share of farmers cultivating fruits and vegetable is less than 20% in consumer price. Organized retailers like supermarket help eliminating middleman and in turn benefits farmers.
- **Reduced Consumer Price** The bulk purchase made by the supermarket retailers will help them to sell the food at lesser price.

- **Demand will be Known with Certainty** When retailing becomes organized, the demand can be forecasted on the basis of the experience, hence the procurement can be well planned.
- **Integration of Small and Marginal Farmers** According to the Agriculture Census 2015-16, 86.21% of India's cultivated farmland is held by small and marginal farmers with less than 2 hectares of land. Supermarket provides opportunity for integration of farmers and in turn strengthen the bargaining capacity of farmers.
- **Financial/Technological Support** Supermarket retailers make small scale farming competitive through increased access to technology, credit, marketing channels and information.
- **Contract Farming** Through contract farming, the producer can reduce the risk of fluctuating market price and demand and the buyer can reduce the risk of non-availability of quality produce.
- **Enhances Export Opportunities** Once the products are part of the organized retail chain like Walmart, they can be easily exported by leveraging their existing retail outlets worldwide.
- **Guidance and Support**
  - Supermarkets helps farmers by providing technical guidance, market information on prices, perfect weights and spot payments etc.
  - They also educate the farmers in selecting the correct inputs and in postharvest handling like cleaning, food safety, drying, sorting, and packaging at the farm gate.

How Supermarket eliminate Intermediaries?

In the following illustration bracket indicates the usual intermediaries involved in the supply chain.

Farmers → Local Buyer → Wholesaler → Stockist → Wholesaler → Retailer → Consumer

Supermarket seeks to eliminate intermediaries in following ways:

- **Good Linkage with Farmers** Supermarkets engage in direct business with producers/farmers. Farmers no longer have to rely on middlemen to buy their produce and they can directly supply to the chains and get remunerative prices for their produce.
- **Farmer-Supermarket Direct Purchase Model** This strategy is adopted to eliminate intermediaries and establish long term relationship between supermarket and farmers.
- **Monitor and Control** Supermarkets aim to replace decentralized and fragmented networks of small farmers, brokers, and traders with new sourcing and distribution systems that help in eliminating a variety of inefficient practices.
- **New Infrastructure and Technology** Supermarkets also develop new infrastructure and technology which facilitates efficient management of warehouses and deliveries.
- **Sources of Finance Capital** Provides financial support to suppliers and in turn reduces the dependence on financial intermediaries.

Conclusion

The supermarkets have been a boon for most of the sections of producers by eliminating intermediaries and reducing post-harvest losses, benefitting both the farmers and customers from its existence. Therefore, supermarkets, if regulated properly will prove to be a tool in achieving the SDG-12 which advocates for reduction in food wastage and losses in supply chain.

Mega Food Park Scheme: Critical Analysis

Q.5 India's ambitious attempt to develop large food processing hubs under the Mega Food Park Scheme across the country has not yielded the desired results. Do you agree with this view? Critically comment.
(250 Words, 15 Marks)

Ans. **Introduction** India's food processing sector is one of the largest in the world and its output is expected to reach USD 535 billion by 2025-26.

Food Park Scheme

- The Mega Food Park Scheme in India is a government initiative aimed at developing large-scale food processing hubs across the country.
- It was launched in 2008-09 to give a major boost to the food processing sector by adding value and reducing food wastage at each stage of the supply chain with a particular focus on perishables.
- Under the scheme, the Centre provides 50 per cent of the project cost, up to Rs 50 crore.
- The Scheme is based on the "Cluster" approach and envisages creation of state of art support infrastructure in a well-defined agri/horticultural zone for setting up of modern food processing units in the industrial plots provided in the park with a well-established supply chain.
- A Mega food Park typically consists of supply chain infrastructure including collection centers (cc), primary processing centers (ppc) central processing centers (cpc), cold chain and around 25-30 fully developed plots for entrepreneurs to set up food processing units.

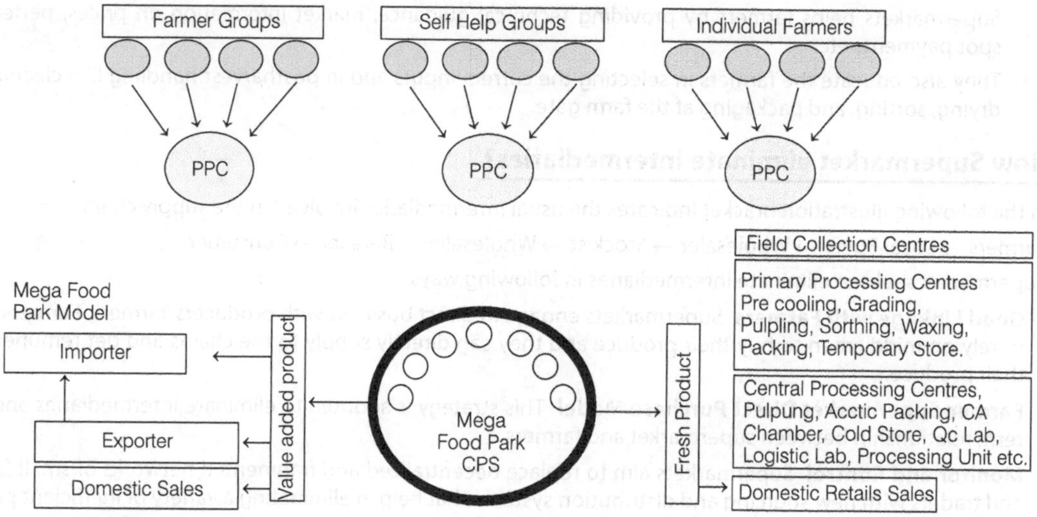

Positive Outcomes of the Scheme

- **Promote Investment in the food Processing Sector** The scheme aims to attract private investment in food processing infrastructure by providing a conducive environment for businesses to set up their operations.
  - Between 2014 and 2020, the government approved 69 Mega Food Park projects across various states in India, with an estimated investment of over ₹ 8,000 crores.
  - The FDI equity inflow in the Food Processing Sector for the period of April 2021- March 2022 was US$ 709.72 Million
- **Reduce Post-harvest Losses and Wastage** One of the key goals of the Mega Food Park Scheme is to address the significant post-harvest losses and food wastage that occur in India.
  - According to the Ministry of Food Processing Industries, India loses approximately 30-40% of agricultural produce due to inadequate storage and post-harvest management.
- **Create Employment Opportunities** The scheme is expected to generate employment opportunities, both direct and indirect, in rural and semi-urban areas.
  - As of 2020, the sector employed around 13.9 million people in various roles, including processing, packaging, and distribution.
  - The development of food processing parks under the Mega Food Park Scheme is expected to further contribute to job creation, especially in rural and semi-urban areas.
- **Enhance Value Addition and Product Diversification** The Mega Food Park Scheme seeks to promote value addition and diversification of agricultural produce.

- The key sub-segments of the Food Processing industry in India are Fruits and Vegetables, Poultry and Meat processing, Fisheries, dairy industry, etc.

- **Improve Infrastructure and Technology Support** The scheme focuses on developing state-of-the-art infrastructure and providing technology support to food processing units.
  - Under Pradhan Mantri Kisan Sampada Yojana (PMKSY), 41 Mega Food Parks, 376 Cold Chain projects, 79 Agro-Processing Clusters, 489 proposals under Creation/Expansion of Food Processing and Preservation Capacities (CEFPPC), 61 Creation of Backward and Forward Linkages Projects, 52 Operation Green projects, 183 Food Testing Laboratories projects have been approved across the country.
- **Facilitate Market Linkages** It aims to bridge the gap between farmers and the market by facilitating direct linkages between farmers, processors, and retailers. It seeks to create an integrated supply chain network, enabling farmers to access a wider market and ensuring a fair price realisation for their produce.

Challenges in Mega Food Park Scheme

- **Land Acquisition and Clearances** Acquiring land for setting up food processing parks has been a significant challenge. The process often involves multiple stakeholders, including farmers, government agencies, and private entities, leading to delays and complexities. Presently only 22 Mega Food Parks are operational.
  - According to the reports from the Ministry of Food Processing Industries, only about a quarter of Mega food parks are working with full capacity.
- **Infrastructure and Supply Chain Gaps** Insufficient transportation facilities and the absence of well-developed logistics networks have led to challenges in timely and cost-effective movement of agricultural produce to processing units.
- **The Gap between Demand and Availability in the Cold Chain Infrastructure has not reduced.**
  - According to the Dalwai Committee report, there was a staggering gap of 80-90 per cent between the availability and requirement of cold chain infrastructure.
- **Coordination and Market Linkages** Fragmented landholdings and a lack of coordinated efforts between farmers and food processors have hindered the seamless integration of the supply chain.
  - Limited awareness and demand for processed food products, particularly in rural areas, have affected the market potential of these parks.
- **Access to Finance and Investments** Lack of adequate financial support and limited availability of credit facilities have hampered investment and expansion plans. The estimated investment requirement for setting up a Mega Food Park is substantial, making it crucial to attract both domestic and foreign investments.
- **Policy and Regulatory Complexities** The food processing sector in India is subject to various regulations, licences, and quality standards. Navigating through these regulatory complexities, obtaining necessary approvals, and ensuring compliance have posed challenges for businesses operating within the food parks.

Conclusion

While the Mega Food Park Scheme in India has faced challenges and has not fully realised its objectives, it is important to consider the complexities involved in establishing large-scale food processing hubs. The scheme requires continuous evaluation, monitoring, and corrective measures to address the bottlenecks in land acquisition, infrastructure development, supply chain management, and market linkages.

With sustained efforts and targeted interventions, the scheme has the potential to contribute significantly to the growth of the food processing industry in India.

One District, One Product Scheme (ODOP)

Q.6 One district one product scheme may give a big boost in reviving India's traditional food products. Explain the challenges associated with the scheme and give suitable suggestions to make this scheme a big success. (150 Words, 10 Marks)

Ans. **Introduction** One District, One Product (ODOP) is initiated in all States/UTs of the country, as a transformational step towards realizing the true potential of a district, fueling economic growth, generating employment and rural entrepreneurship, taking to the goal of Aatmanirbhar Bharat.

- The ODOP Initiative is aimed at fostering balanced regional development across the country, enabling holistic socio-economic growth across all regions.
- The objective is to focus on District of the country as unit for converting into a manufacturing and export hub by identifying products with export potential in the district.

ODOP Giving Boost to Traditional Food Products

- **Quality Assurance and Standardization** By implementing proper quality control measures and certification, it ensures that the products meet hygiene, safety, and authenticity requirements. This helps in building consumer trust and expanding market reach, both domestically and internationally.
- **Market Expansion and Branding** The ODOP scheme can provide platforms and opportunities for traditional food producers to showcase their products at regional, national and international levels. It can facilitate market linkages, support market research, and enable branding and marketing initiatives.
  - **For example** ODOP products are showcased in various international forums such as World Economic Forum, DAVOS at International Yoga Day (IYD) in New York, US.
- **Economic Upliftment** By encouraging the production and marketing of traditional food products, the scheme can create employment opportunities and boost the income of local communities involved in food processing, farming, packaging, and distribution.
- **Entrepreneurship and Skill Development** It can encourage aspiring entrepreneurs to establish small-scale food businesses based on traditional recipes and ingredients. Training programs and financial assistance can be provided to individuals interested in starting food enterprises, helping them develop necessary skills and knowledge to run successful ventures.
- **Linking with Tourism Promotion** Diverse traditional food can be linked in a symbiotic relation with tourism under ODOP scheme.

Challenges Facing the ODOP Scheme

- **Lack of Market access and Distribution Networks** Traditional products may struggle to find suitable market access and distribution networks beyond local markets.
- **Limited Value Addition and Product Diversification** Some traditional products may lack value addition and may not have undergone product diversification to cater to evolving consumer preferences. For instance, a district known for its traditional pickles may need to explore new flavors, packaging options, or organic variants to attract a wider customer base.
- **Quality Control and Standardization Issues** Maintaining consistent quality standards across traditional products can be challenging.
- **Financial Constraints and Lack of access to Credit** Small-scale producers of traditional products may face difficulties in accessing affordable credit for scaling up production, upgrading equipment, or expanding marketing efforts. Limited financial resources can impede the growth and sustainability of traditional product industries within districts.
- **Resistance to Change and limited Innovation** Traditional industries may face resistance to change and innovation, which can hinder their competitiveness in the market.

Suggestions based on Some Global Successes

- **Comprehensive Market Research and Demand Assessment** This will help in understanding consumer preferences, market trends, and potential target segments. A demand-driven approach will enable producers to align their product offerings with market requirements.
  - **Case Study** Thailand's "One Tambon, One Product" (OTOP) scheme has been successful in identifying market demand. The scheme conducted surveys and market research to identify products with high market potential, leading to focused development and marketing efforts.
- **Strengthening Value Chains and Infrastructure** This includes improving infrastructure such as transportation, storage facilities, and processing units. Strengthening the value chain will enhance efficiency, reduce post-harvest losses, and improve product quality.

- **Case Study** The "One Village, One Product" (OVOP) movement in Japan emphasizes building efficient value chains. Through this movement, rural communities in Japan improved infrastructure, established quality control systems, and developed effective marketing networks, leading to successful product branding and market access.

- **Skill Development and Capacity Building** Provide training programs to artisans, farmers, and entrepreneurs involved in traditional product manufacturing. Training should focus on improving production techniques, quality control, packaging, and marketing strategies. Capacity building initiatives will enhance the skills of the workforce and empower them to adapt to changing market dynamics.
- **Access to Finance and Credit Facilities** This will support infrastructure development, technology adoption, and working capital requirements. Financial inclusion and easy access to credit will enable producers to invest in their businesses and expand operations.
- **Collaboration and Networking** Foster collaboration between stakeholders and encourage the formation of cooperatives, producer groups, and networks to facilitate knowledge sharing, resource pooling, and collective marketing efforts.
  - **Case Study** The "Creative Economy Agency" (Bekraf) in Indonesia has established partnerships between artisans, designers, and government agencies. This collaboration has resulted in product innovation, market expansion, and increased international recognition for traditional crafts.

Conclusion

The successful implementation of the ODOP scheme requires comprehensive planning, policy support, and collaborative efforts from the government, industry stakeholders, and local communities. Addressing these challenges can help unlock the full potential of traditional products, leading to their revival and sustainable growth.

Check Your Preparation

1. In order to make agriculture sustainable for the farmers, food processing must be developed as one of the principal industries of India in future. (150 words, 10 marks)
2. Development of food processing industry will help in achieving the twin goals of inclusive growth and food security. Discuss. Also, account for the competitive advantages enjoyed by India in the food processing sector. (250 words, 15 marks)
3. Highlighting the potential of micro and small enterprises in the food processing sector, enumerate the challenges that they face. In this regard, discuss the importance of the Scheme for Formalisation of Micro Food Processing Enterprises (FME). (250 words, 15 marks)

UNIT 7

Land Reforms in India

Land Reform Measures (British Land Revenue Policy)

Q.1 To what extent, the land tenure system adopted during British rule facilitated the commercialization of Indian agriculture? (150 Words, 10 Marks)

Ans. Introduction The commercialisation of Indian agriculture started post 1813 when the industrial revolution in England gained pace. Between 1893-94 to 1945-46, the production of commercial crops increased by 85 percent and that of food crops fell by 7 percent. There are number of factors especially the land tenure system that facilitated the commercialisation of Indian agriculture.

Different Land Tenure System Introduced during British Rule

- **Permanent Settlement** The Permanent Settlement was implemented in Bengal, Bihar, and Orissa, whereby revenue rates were fixed permanently and Zamindars became hereditary landowners along with having the responsibility of collecting revenue from the peasants. This system aimed to provide revenue stability but resulted in number of intermediaries between the British administration and tillers, oppressive rent collection, leaving peasants vulnerable to exploitation and impoverishment.
- **Ryotwari System** The Ryotwari system was implemented in some parts of South India, where individual peasants were recognized as direct cultivators and paid revenue directly to the British administration. This system aimed to establish direct control but often led to high revenue demands, causing distress and indebtedness among peasants.
- **Mahalwari System** The Mahalwari system was implemented in parts of North India, where villages or Mahals were recognized as revenue units. Revenue was collected collectively from the entire village community, with joint responsibility among villagers. This system aimed to maintain collective ownership and shared responsibility.

Land Revenue System Facilitating the Commercialisation of Indian Agriculture

- **Revenue Demands and Cash Crops** The British land revenue system imposed high exploitative revenue demands on farmers and that too in cash, compelling them to focus on cash crops for generating income. Farmers had to cultivate commercial crops, such as indigo, cotton, tea, and jute, to meet the revenue obligations imposed by the British administration.
- **Shift from Subsistence to Market-Oriented Farming** The revenue system created an economic imperative for farmers to produce surplus for sale in markets.

- **Britain's Industrial Revolution** The British administration actively encouraged the cultivation of cash crops for export to meet the demands of the British industrial revolution. Many commercial crops like, cotton, jute, tea, tobacco were introduced to meet the demand in Britain.
- **Zamindari System and Commercial Intermediaries** The Zamindars, motivated by profits, often played a crucial role in encouraging farmers to engage in commercial agriculture to maximise their own revenue collections.

Other Reasons for Commercialisation Apart from British Land Revenue System

- **Infrastructure Development** infrastructure development, such as railways, canals, and roads, which facilitated the transportation and marketing of agricultural produce enabled farmers to engage in commercial agricultural practices.
- **Introduction of Commercial Crops** The British encouraged the cultivation of commercial crops, such as indigo, tea, cotton, jute, and opium, for export to meet the demands of the British industrial revolution and global markets.
- **Market Integration** The establishment of a centralised market system by the British facilitated the integration of Indian agriculture into global markets.
- **Legal and Property Rights Framework** The British introduced legal frameworks that recognized individual property rights and facilitated the transfer of land. This provided security to landowners, encouraging investment in agriculture and the pursuit of commercial farming.
- **Shift in Consumption Patterns** The increasing demand for agricultural products, both domestically and internationally, fueled by industrialisation and population growth, led to the commercialisation of Indian agriculture.
- The **political unity established by the British** and the resultant rise of the unified national market was another important factor.
- **Spread of money economy** replaced the barter and agricultural goods became market items.
- The enlargement and expansion of international trade and the entry of British finance capital also belted commercialisation of agriculture.
- The **American Civil War** also indirectly encouraged commercialisation of agriculture in India: the British cotton demand was diverted to India. The demand of cotton was maintained even after the civil war ceased because of the rise of cotton textile industries in India.

Conclusion

While land revenue system were the driving factors behind the commercialization of Indian agriculture, there were other colonial and international factors which facilitated the commercialization of Indian agriculture.

Critical Analysis of Land Reforms

Q.2 Establish the relationship between land reforms, agriculture productivity and elimination of poverty in Indian economy. Discuss the difficulty in designing and implementation of the agriculture friendly land reforms in India. **UPSC Mains PYQ 2013**

Ans. Introduction Land ownership was highly unequal at the time of Independence as around 70% of the lands were owned by big landlords by 1940s and on the other hand, over 60 per cent of rural households either owned no land or were semi-proletarian (having marginal holdings of land).

There was a parasitic class of intermediaries (interested in only rent-seeking activities) who played no role in production. On the other hand, the vast majority of actual cultivators were either tenants or sub-tenants, without any security of tenure. This led to regressive agrarian structure which has impacted the agricultural productivity reaching to even zero and there was a decline in per capital agricultural production by 14 per cent between 1901 and 1941.

After Independence, it became necessary to undertake some land reforms measures for removing the feudal character of the agrarian economy and paving the way for rapid agricultural growth with social justice.

Objectives of Land Reforms

India's land reform policy had the following specific goals

- The first is to remove any impediments to increasing agricultural production that arises from the agrarian structure that has been passed down from generation to generation.

- The second goal, which is closely related to the first, is to eliminate all elements of exploitation and social injustice from the agrarian system.
- To provide security to the soil tiller, and to ensure equality of status and opportunity to all sections of the rural population.

Components of Land Reforms

- Land Reforms is a planned and institutional reorganisation of the relation between the man and the land i.e. changes introduced into the system of land tenure and the farming structure. Post-independence, it consisted of four main reforms i.e., tenancy reform, abolition of intermediaries, land ceiling and land consolidation.

Abolition of Zamindari System	• Ownership and land revenue related rights of the Zamindars were abolished. • Land transferred to the superior tenants. • Compensation to Zamindars and the lands for 'Personal Cultivation' exempted form the Act. • First such legislation was enacted by Madras in 1948. Orissa Estates Abolition Act, 1951.
Tenancy Reforms	• Regulation of Rent-Fair and reasonable rent. Maximum of 20 to 25 percent although varies state to state. • Security of Tenure-Increase in productivity and promotion of social justice. Tenants not evicted without any reason. Exception of 'Personal Cultivation' for the landlord. • Ownership Rights- State laws permit the tenants to acquire the land by paying fair compensation to the owners.
Land Ceilings	• Fixing the maximum amount of land that an individual or family can possess and second is distribution among the small farmers and the landless people. • Reduction of existing disparities in the pattern of land-ownership. • Upto 1972- Landowner was treated as the unit of application and After 1972 - Family was treated as the basis of land holding.
Land Consolidations	• Bringing together the various small plots of land of a farmer scattered all over the village as one compact block, either through purchase or exchange of land with others. • Subdivision and fragmentation of holdings results in several issues such as wastage of land, difficulties in land management and in the adoption of new technology, disputes over boundaries, low productivity etc. • As much as 120 lakh hectare had been consolidated by the end of the Fourth Plan, while 440 lakh hectare of land was consolidated by the end of the Fifth Plan.

There were other land reforms which were movement based and taken by the people rather than by the government such as Bhoodan and Gramdan Movement

- The movements were about urging the landed classes to voluntarily surrender a part of their land to the landless giving it the name- Bhoodan Movement. It began in 1951.
- Later, the Bhoodan gave way to the Gramdan movement which began in 1952. The objective of the Gramdan movement was to persuade landowners and leaseholders in each village to renounce their land rights and all the lands would become the property of a village association for an egalitarian redistribution and joint cultivation.
- The movement was the first post-independence movement that sought to bring social transformation through a movement and not through government legislation. It created a moral ambience that put pressure on the big landlords.
- Also, it was successful in collecting around 4 million acres of land by 1956.

Relationship between Land Reforms, Agricultural Productivity and Elimination of Poverty

Land reforms are visualised as an instrument of social justice as they seek to do away with exploitative relationships characterised by sharp inequalities between rich landowners and impoverished peasants with no security of tenure. In addition to bringing equity in land distribution, also improved efficiency of the land because of the following reasons:

- **Owner-cultivated plots of land tend to be more productive** than those under sharecropping tenancy as owners are willing to invest more in their farm. Tenancy reforms brought more land under ownership cultivation instead of share-cropping.
- **Abolition of intermediaries** strengthens the position of the actual landholders and cultivators that help them to enhance their social and economic stature. This also increased the profit margin because of direct procurement by the government.
- **Increased access to land for the poor landless masses** by the redistribution of land ensures them an income guarantee.
- **Optimum land size** Both, very large and very small size farm, are less productive. Land ceiling tend to raise productivity by breaking less productive excessively large farms into several more productive small farms.
- **Land Consolidation** Consolidating plots makes the task of irrigation management, land improvement and personal supervision of different plots efficient and easier, thereby improving productivity. This also raised the prospects of capitalist farming.
- **Land reformation** is required for mechanization of farming by utilizing latest technological tools like tractors, thrashers etc and deploying high cost & water efficient micro-irrigation technology which is not feasible for small and marginal farms.
- **Easier access to agricultural credit** due to land ownership or land tenancy agreements which has a direct impact on agricultural productivity.
- **Modernisation of Agriculture** Technology has touched the agricultural practice in India and has brought manifold advantages which are evident since the Green revolution. Land being its basis has to stay in tandem with technological changes for maximum benefits. For example: Green revolution was mainly successful in those states where land reforms were implemented.
- **Tenancy reform** can redress the issue by regulating aspects of the tenancy relationship, such as the crop share and the duration of the contract (security of tenure). Tenancy reform increases the bargaining power of tenants vis-a-vis landowners.
- **Increased agricultural growth and productivity** and thus enhanced farmers' income due to land reforms is directly related to rural poverty reduction.
  - Because the majority of India's population depends upon land for their livelihood, poverty issues are also closely associated with the land policy.
- However, **overall empirical analysis reveals that land reforms had a limited effect on agricultural productivity in India**. The broad reason for this seems to be inadequate implementation as well as indirect and unintended negative consequences of the policies. There are also considerable variations of this impact across types of land reform, as well as variations across the states. Further, fragmentation of landholdings due to increasing population pressure has negatively impacted productivity.

Challenges of Land Reform Policies

Given the complex nature of agriculture, variety of land and land holding pattern in different states, the designing and implementation of agriculture friendly land reforms policies is difficult because of the following reasons:

Issues with respect to designing of policies

- The report of the Task Force on Agrarian Relations of the Planning Commission of India (1973) had the following overall assessment of land reforms in India: "The programmes of land reform adopted since Independence have failed to bring about the required changes in the agrarian structure." The report directly blames the political will of the state governments for this failure.
- **Land is a state subject** This makes it difficult to design the land reform measures at the national level and thus there exists a variation in land reform policies among various states. There exists a lack of uniformity across state, which makes it discriminatory and slow.
- **Poor Land records** Lack of digitalization and incomplete land records make the determining of ownership difficult leading to obstacles in land reforms.
- **Legal definitions of the terms** have left room for different kinds of interpretation affecting the process of realising the goals of the programmes.

- **Loophole of 'Personal Cultivation'** The term "Personal cultivation' is quite loose. One could resume land for personal cultivation under the definition even while sitting at a distance of 200 miles. The Zamindars have been permitted to possess substantial areas of land for cultivation.
- **Optional nature of laws** Most of the laws granting ownership rights to tenants are not mandatory. They are rather optional. The tenants have to move the government for grant of ownership rights. They will not get them automatically.
- **Lack of an integrated approach** The absence of an integrated approach, such as the elimination of intermediary tenures, tenancy reforms, holdings ceilings, etc., was another factor in India's failed land reforms.
- **Emergence of new agriculture technology** The new seed-cum-fertilizer technology, for its successful adoption, needs ample resources and dynamic entrepreneurship. Only large farmers can fulfill these conditions. Therefore, many economists have come out in favour of the abolition of ceiling on land holdings.

Issues with respect to the implementation of policies

- **Lack of strong political will and Bureaucratic Apathy** Tenants, small and marginal farmers are often ignorant or lack the resources to approach the government for effective implementation of land reforms. There is also a lack of political will, and bureaucratic-political nexus preventing effective implementation of land reforms.
- **High number of litigation against land reforms** Land reform measures that aimed to bring social justice contradicts the constitutional requirement Right to Property which was once a fundamental right leading to increased litigation in the court. This delayed the implementation of land reforms.
- **Lack of Financial Support** Another obstacle standing in the way of implementing land reform is a lack of financial backing. The Five Year Plans did not provide any funding specifically for financing land reform. Many states refused to include even the cost of such necessary items as the creation of surveys and records in their budgetary plans.
- **Undue Advance Publicity and delay in Enacting Land Laws** This has enabled the landowners to make necessary adjustments so as to be able to evade various provisions of land reform legislation.
- **Bureaucratic Corruption** Land reforms provide a golden opportunity to the Patwari and other functionaries of the Revenue Department to make money. Again in many cases the highly placed officials are themselves landlords.
- **Malafide transfer of land** To escape the laws relating to land ceilings, the Zamindars have induljed in large scale transfer of land to their family members or kinsmen. Such Malafide transactions do not make any change in the operational aspect of agriculture.
- Only 4% of the land got transferred under the land ceiling laws and most of the surplus land is fallow and uncultivable.

Conclusion

On one hand, consolidation of holdings brings agricultural efficiency through economies of scale and mechanized farming. On the other hand, social equity might be compromised as it brings separation between the landed and landless. Hence, what is required is an efficient combination of land ceiling and consolidation so that both agricultural efficiency and social equity can be realized. This might be achieved through cooperative farming. A recent scheme called Paramparagat Krishi Vikas Yojana which promotes organic farming in clusters of 50 acres is a progressive model.

10th Agricultural Census

Q.3 Identify the problems faced by Indian Agriculture as a consequence of changing land holding pattern as witnessed in the findings of 10th Agriculture census, 2015-16. In light of these problems, suggest suitable ways to resolve such structural issues in agriculture. (250 Words, 15 Marks)

Ans. **Introduction** Agriculture Census in India is conducted at an interval of five years to collect information on structure of operational holdings in the country and monitor changes that take place over time. So far, ten Agriculture Censuses have been completed and Agriculture Census 2015-16 is the latest in the series. 11th Agricultural Census (2020-21) has been recently initiated after delay due to Covid-19 pandemic.

Findings of 10th Agriculture Census 2015-16

The Agriculture Census 2015-2016 gives an account of the change in nature of agricultural landholding. It indicates a 1.53 per cent decline in total operated area at 157.14 million hectare as compared to 2010-11 data, but a rise in both operational holdings and female participation, thus indicating further fragmentation of land holdings. Following are the findings of the census vis-a-vis land holdings in India:

- **Rise in the percentage of female landholding farmers** Not only is there the rise in the female tillers but the percentage of female operational landholders increased from 12.79% in 2010-11 to 13.87% in 2015-2016.
- **Increase in the number of operational holdings** which has gone up by 5.33 per cent to 146 million in 2015-16 from 138 million in 2010-11.
- **Decline in the average size of operational agricultural holdings** It has declined to 1.08 hectares (ha) in 2015-16 from 1.15 ha in 2010-11.
- **Increase in the number of smaller and medium level landholdings** Out of the total land holdings as much as 86.21% of India's cultivated farmland is held by small and marginal farmers with less than two hectares of land, while those with 10 hectares and more account for just 0.57%. The share of small and marginal farmers in total operational area — both cultivated and uncultivated were 47.34%, up from 44.31% five years earlier.

Problems Faced by Agriculture Associated with Prevalent Nature of Land Holdings

- **Less profitable agriculture** More profitable crops, like fruit crops, require larger plot areas, so if farmers possess small and fragmented plots they may be forced to grow less profitable crops and could not shift to high value crops.
- **Difficulty in the modernisation practices** The growing sub-division and fragmentation of agricultural holding make the adoption of modernized method in agricultural operation quite difficult. Application of new technology, use of fertilizer and making provision for irrigation facilities will be difficult in uneconomic holding.
- **Issues with mechanisation of agriculture and sustainable agricultural practices** Mechanization makes agriculture profitable, but requires larger areas for operation. Even environmentally friendly farm practices such as organic farming have extremely low yield in the small holdings.
- **Difficulty in the access to formal credit** is a prominent drawback related to small farm holdings. Only 14% of marginal and 27% of small holdings were able to get credit from institutional sources.
- **Land wastage** Land fragmentation involves a complicated boundary network among parcels which cause land wastage because a part of a holding remains uncultivated at the margins. This is important given limited availability of land for agriculture considering the structural changes going in an Indian economy. Example: In Punjab about 6 per cent of the land is wasted due to this reason.
- **Reduction in land productivity** Farmers employ various treatments and farming methods on small landholdings, which further degrades the quality and fertility of soil, impacting the productivity.
- **Problems in land management** Fragmentation of agricultural holding creates difficulties to the farmers to manage the agricultural operation smoothly. A considerable wastage of time and resources is resulting from transporting agricultural inputs to different fragmented lands.
- **Litigation** Small and fragmented farms indulged into frequent boundary disputes. All these quarrels over boundaries result in increasing volume of litigation in the rural areas.
- **Disguised Unemployment** Smaller size of holdings cannot provide full time job to all the members of farmer's family. Thus, in the absence of alternative occupations, disguised unemployment started to occur in the rural areas.

Measures to Overcome the Prevalent Issues

- **Encourage Land Consolidation** Consolidated holdings would make it easy for the government or private enterprises to acquire land, and for public agencies to lay the road, pipeline or electric supply.
- **Co-operative farming** A more participative practice can bring in better results. With the growing feminization of agriculture, a greater number of women cooperatives are likely to yield fruitful results.
- **Contract Farming and Collaborative Farming** initiatives can be a tool for farmers to collaborate for joint cultivation. For example, farmers could plough their pooled farm lands with tractors as most of the contracts are designed for raising a specific variety of the same crop. This would help the farmers also to reduce input costs and, ipso facto, have better price realization.
- **Corporate Farming** can be explored wherein they can substantially incentivised to specially invest in arid zones where large tracts of land may be available irrigation facilities are not present.
- **Proper access to institutionalised credit markets** to be able to provide suitable inputs to the small landholdings or to buy more land.
- **Skilling and educating the farmers** and providing high yielding variety seeds to enhance productivity.

- **Adoption of Model Leasing laws by the states** It should be adopted on a large scale to enable landholders with unviable holdings to lease out land for investment, thereby enabling greater income and employment generation in rural areas.
- **Encouraging Farmer Producer Organisations (FPOs)** FPOs are effective mechanisms where farmers can 'crowd in' and act as an aggregator to produce and then sale through e-trading as one or multiple lot depending on requirement. Due to the aggregator principle from input to output, it can potentially enhance the economy of scale and bargaining power of the member farmers. To facilitate this process, the Small Farmers' Agribusiness Consortium (SFAC) was mandated by Agriculture Ministry to support the state governments in forming FPOs.

Conclusion

Growing population, further fragmentation of land and land conversion will lead to lower productivity, shortage of labour and dwindling natural resources. Thus, rationalisation of land holding is of paramount importance in ensuring higher agricultural yield.

Small-Holder Agriculture

Q.4 Bringing resource efficiency in small-holder agriculture is significant for not only enhancing agriculture productivity but also for tackling poverty in the country. Justify the statement. (150 Words, 10 Marks)

Ans. **Introduction** Indian has a large number of small and marginal farmers, close to 126 million. The small and marginal holdings taken together (0 -2 ha) constituted 86.08% of the total holdings in 2015-16 against 85.01% in 2010-11 while their share in the operated area stood at 46.94% against 44.58% in 2010-11. Between 2010-11 and 2015-16, the number of small and marginal farms rose by about 9 million, the survey showed. According to 2019 report of Ministry of Statistics and Programme Implementation, most small and marginal agricultural households now depend on wage work and have essentially become wage earners.

Problems with Small-Holder Agriculture

- **Land Fragmentation** The average size of holdings in agriculture has shown a continuous decline and has reduced to 1.08 hectares. The small and medium farmers together owned about 74.4 million hectares of land, or an average holding of just 0.6 hectares each. This decreases their scale and adversely impacts higher productivity.
- **Land and Tenancy Security** Small and marginal farmers own and cultivate some land land on tenure but it is a limiting factor for getting resources. Land relations are extremely complicated and this complexity has contributed significantly to the problems facing actual cultivators. Unregistered cultivators, tenants, and tribal cultivators all face difficulties in accessing institutional credit and other facilities available to farmers with land titles.
- **Low level of formal education and skills** Education and skills are important for improving farming practices, investment and productivity. Literacy and mean years of education are lower for small holding farmers (44%) compared to medium and large farmers (55%). The low level of farmers' education limits public dissemination of knowledge.
- **Credit and Indebtedness** Overall indebtedness is not higher for small and marginal farmers compared to large farmers. However, the indebtedness for the small and marginal farmers from formal institutional sources is lower than large farmers and they have large dependency on informal sources like moneylenders. The share of formal source increases with the size of land and it varies from 22.6% to 58% for small and marginal farmers.
- **Globalisation Challenges** Increasing globalization has added to the problems faced by the small holding agriculture. The policies of huge subsidies and protection policies by developed countries have negative effects on small holding farmers in developing countries.
- **Impact of Climate Change** Climate change is expected to have adverse impact on the living conditions of farmers, fishers and forest-dependent people who are already vulnerable and food insecure. Adverse impact will be more on small holding farmers–they are facing an immediate and ever-growing risk of increased crop failure, loss of livestock etc.
- **Water Problems** Small holding agriculture depend more on ground water compared to large farmers who has more access on canal water. Ground water is depleting in many areas of India. Marginal and small farmers are going to face more problems regarding water in future.

- **Diversification** There has been diversification of Indian diets away from foodgrains to high value products like milk, meat products, vegetables and fruits. There is growing demand for non-foodgrain items in India. Small and marginal farmers can get higher incomes with diversification. But, there are risks in shifting to diversification as the support systems are more for food grains.
- **Risk and Vulnerability** There is enough evidence to suggest that poor and poorest of the poor households are vulnerable to a range of risks affecting their livelihoods and well- being; health shocks, labour market risk, harvest risks, social risk and special risks for vulnerable groups, community risks such as droughts, floods, cyclones, structural adjustment policies etc. Small and marginal farmers are vulnerable to all these risks.
- **No technology Adoption** Small landholdings disincentivise to use technology in small farms, the majority of small farmers follow traditional farming which is highly labour intensive and it is the family members who have been mainly involved in farming as labour.
- **Feminisation of Agriculture** There is a 'feminization in the agriculture sector' with the women in multiple roles as a cultivator, processor and entrepreneur. Profit maximization has never been the objective of the small farmers and thus the economic benefits received by them are very less and therefore there is a migration of small farmers from farming sectors to others and there is more involvement of household women in farming.

Measure to Increase Resource-Use Efficiency

- **Technology upgradation** Recently launched Nano Urea by IFFCO saves upto 50% in costs as well as Excessive Urea usage. Such technologies should be promoted.
- **Increasing Irrigation Water Productivity (IWP) in Agriculture** The focus in agriculture should shift from 'land productivity' to 'irrigation water productivity-Adopting improved methods of irrigation (suiting local agro-climatic conditions) and irrigation technologies (micro-irrigation, drip irrigation etc), re-calibrating the cropping patterns.
  - **Degrading Groundwater** In India almost 89 % of groundwater extracted is for irrigation. By 2050, India will be in the global hot spot for 'water insecurity' and agriculture is dependent highly on water.
  - **Skewed Cropping Pattern** The incentive structures like MSP, heavily subsidized electricity, water and fertilizers have played a significant role in the misalignment of crop patterns in the country.
- **Economising the Use of Fertilisers and Pesticides** For the small and marginal farmers, the costs of fertilizers are key determinants of profitability of farming. There is a need to increase farmers' knowledge regarding the right product, dosage, time and method of application.
  - **Declining Fertiliser Response Ratio** There is a decline in fertiliser response ratio from few years - indicating declining responsiveness of soil fertility to fertiliser application.
- **Increasing Sustainability in Agriculture - Turning to Organic and Natural Farming** There is a need to increase focus on Natural Farming, Vedic Farming, Cow Farming, Homa Farming, Zero Budget Natural Farming etc. National Mission for Sustainable Agriculture (NMSA) has its main objective is to make agriculture more productive, sustainable, remunerative and climate resilient. Government has been promoting organic farming in the country through Paramparagat Krishi Vikas Yojana and Rashtriya Krishi Vikas Yojana.
- **Adopting Appropriate Technologies for Smallholder Farms** There is need to promote use of environment friendly automated farm machinery tools suited to small scale operations like Custom Hiring Centers (CHCs). ICT applications are needed to facilitate communication and reduce transaction costs
  - **Economic Feasibility** The use of technology, investment in costly farm machinery, or scaling up the existing technology may not be economically feasible for small and marginal farmers.
- **Improving Infrastructure and Access to Markets** A combination of enhancing rural infrastructure to improve connectivity, ICT to provide timely information about prices, aggregation and storage facilities can help small and marginal farmers in overcoming the marketing bottlenecks.
  - **Prominence of Local Dealers** The informal actors like local traders and input dealers are more prominent in the marketing channels of the smallholder farmers.
- **Increase in Extension Services** There is an increasing need to share knowledge and skills in order to provide locally relevant services that meet the information needs of small and marginal farmers – through increased reach of Krishi Vigyan Kendras.

- **Agriculture Credit** There is a need to increase penetration of formal credit for small farmers – subsidized loans, Krishi Credit Cards etc. are in right direction but there is a need to promote financial inclusion among small and medium farmers mainly in eastern, north-eastern and central region.
  - **Committee Recommendations** UC Sarangi Committee has suggested targeted lending to small and medium farmers
- **Allied Sectors-Animal Husbandry, Dairying and Fisheries** As per the 70th round of NSSO, livestock rearing was the principal source of income to about 3.7 % of the agricultural households. Sectors like Dairy Farming and Fisheries have a huge potential to increase income of small and medium farmers.

Conclusion

In the coming decades, world agriculture will need to undergo major changes to meet the future food demands of a growing and increasingly rich and urbanised population. Smallholders in developing countries play a key role worldwide in this food security equation. They need continued public support in these challenging times to fully fill their role as food producers.

Dynamic Issues of Land Reforms (Conclusive Land Titles)

Q.5 There is a need to create a workable and conclusive system of land titling which will allow poor to access formalized credit structure, reduce judicial burden and boost the development in the country. Examine the statement in the context of Model Bill on Conclusive Land Titling prepared by NITI Aayog. (250 Words, 15 Marks)

Ans. **Introduction** At present in India, ownership of land is determined by registered sale deeds, property tax receipts, and survey documents. In this system, the buyer is responsible for proving ownership of the land. Recently the NITI Aayog proposed to change this system by implementation of Conclusive Land Titling system. NITI Aayog also framed a Model Bill on Conclusive Land Titling for this purpose. But the states are reluctant to implement it.

From Presumptive Land Titling to Conclusive Land Titling

- Under conclusive land titling method, the State (the government) will provide a guarantee on land titles. The government will also include provisions for compensation in case of any dispute of land title between two parties. It is a type of land titling method followed in countries such as Australia, England, Canada, etc.

There are following differences between presumptive land titling and conclusive land titling

Presumptive Land Titling	Conclusive Land Titling
In the current system, ownership is granted based on a record of the property transaction between the buyer and the seller (registered sales deed). The buyer is not entitled to the previous ownership records of the property. Hence, this system is called a presumptive one	In a conclusive titling system, the government provides guaranteed titles. These land records designate actual ownership.
It means the registration of land is actually a registration of transactions, such as sale deeds, records of inheritance, mortgage, and lease. So, anyone can dispute the transactions with the titleholder.	The title is granted by the government. So, if there is a dispute, then the claimant has to settle disputes with the government, not the titleholder.
If the disputed claimant proves the land as his property, then he will be the new titleholder and the previous titleholder will lose his/her ownership.	Further, according to agricultural economist T. Haque, the government may provide compensation to claimants in case of disputes. But the titleholder is not in any danger of losing ownership
These are not the government-guaranteed title to the property. These are only a record of the transfer of property.	These are the guaranteed title to the property.

Need of Conclusive Land Titling

In a conclusive titling system, the government provides guaranteed titles, and compensation in case of any ownership disputes. Achieving this will require shifting to a system of registered property titles (as opposed to sale deeds) as the primary evidence of ownership, and having clear and updated land records.

- **Access of Formal Credit** The need of such system is more acute in rural areas as access to agricultural credit is dependent on the ability to use land as collateral.
  - Without being able to prove their ownership of land and access formal credit from banks, small and marginal farmers are often left at the mercy of unscrupulous moneylenders, entrenching themselves in a mountain of debt.
- **Reduction of Judicial Burden** The conclusive system will drastically lower litigation related to land.
  - According to a 2007 World Bank study on 'Land Policies for growth and poverty reduction', land-related disputes accounted for two-thirds of all pending court cases in India.
  - A NITI Aayog study on strengthening arbitration estimated that disputes on land or real estate take an average time of 20 years in the courts to be resolved.
- **Boost the Development** In conclusive titling, the businesses will be guaranteed and investments will be secured. This can avoid large delays and create hurdles for investment in many sectors of the economy.
  - Land disputes and unclear titling also create hurdles for infrastructure development and housing construction, leading to costly delays and inefficiency.
  - Ambiguity in ownership also results in a black market for land transactions, which deprives the government of taxes. In cities, urban local bodies depend on property taxes that can be levied properly only if there is clear ownership data available.

NITI Aayog Model Bill on Conclusive Land Titling

- **Power to State Governments** It will provide state governments power to order for establishment, administration and management of a system of title registration of immovable properties.
- **Land Authorities** Land Authorities to be set up by each State government, which will appoint a Title Registration Officer (TRO) to prepare and publish a draft list of land titles based on existing records and documents. This will be considered a valid notice to all potential claimants interested in the property, who will have to file their claims or objections within a set period of time. If disputing claims are received, the TRO will verify all the relevant documents and refer the case to a Land Dispute Resolution Officer (LDRO) for resolution. However, disputes which are already pending in courts cannot be resolved in this way. Having considered and resolved all the disputed claims, the Land Authority will publish a Record of Titles.
- **Land Titling Appellate Tribunals** Over a three-year period, these titles and the decisions of the TRO and the LDRO can be challenged before Land Titling Appellate Tribunals, which will be set up under the law. After a three-year period, entries in the Record of Titles will be considered conclusive proof of ownership.
- **Special Bench of High Court** A special bench of High Court shall be designated to deal with appeals against the orders passed by the Land Titling Appellate Tribunal.

Difficulties in Conclusive Land Titling System

The introduction of a Conclusive Land Titling system can be feasible with proper land records. But, there are many challenges associated with the land records in India.

- **Land is a State Subject in India** The individual States are responsible for the proper implementation of land records. In the absence of a uniform system, existing land records are maintained in different scripts and languages in different States.
- **Land Records are not Updated for Decades,** especially in rural and semi-urban areas. Conclusive land titles can create more problems if the land records are not updated.
- In India, the majority of the land records are in the name of the **grandparents of the current owner, with no proof of inheritance**.
- Apart from that, **forgery, cases of fraud and misconduct surrounding land ownership** are also there in India. This increases the ownership disputes reaching courts and overburden the judicial mechanism.

- High cost of registration along with not mandatory registration registration: While registering a property transaction, the buyer has to pay a registration fee along with stamp duty which is very high as compared to the other countries. This raises the cost of property transactions, leading to people avoiding registering them. Further, under the Registration Act, 1908, registration of property is not mandatory for all transactions.

Futuristic Measures

India needs to move towards proper land records, then only we can shift towards a Conclusive Land Titling system. The government can follow suggestions like:

- **Implementing the recommendation of the Committee on State Agrarian Relation in 2007** The committee recommended:
  - A comprehensive village-level survey with community involvement is required to solve the land-related problems.
  - Providing adequate skill training to the local government employees.
  - Further, it suggested that the government should use technologies such as GIS, GPS, and satellite imagery to update land records.
- Further, the government needs to integrate the cadastral maps (Comprehensive land maps) with textual data of land. This can be performed during the sale, inheritance, purchase, gift, mortgage, and tenancy of a property. This will ensure complete information with relation to land is available and updated.
- Moving to conclusive titling would require amending the various central and state laws, and creating a unified legal framework that provides for government-guaranteed land ownership.

Conclusion

Other states should also take an initiative like Rajasthan which became the first state to pass Rajasthan Urban Land (Certification of Titles) Act, 2016 that provides statutory backing to land records, effectively guaranteeing land and property ownership.

Digitisation of Land Records

Q.6 How Digital India Land Records Modernisation Programme (DILRMP) is transforming land administration in India? Also, do you agree with the view that mere adoption of technology is a one-stop solution to address the land governance in India? Comment. (250 Words, 15 Marks)

Ans. **Introduction** Digitisation of land records was introduced to computerise all land records to improve transparency in the land records maintenance system, digitise maps and surveys, update all settlement records and minimise the scope of land disputes.

In a year-end review by the Department of Land Resources, computerization of Land Records completed in over 6.20 lakh villages out of 6.56 lakh villages in India covering over 94% areas in 29 States/UTs. More than 1.17 crore Cadastral Maps (Bhu Naksha) digitized out of total over 1.66 crore in the country.

About Digital India Land Records Modernisation Programme (DILRMP)

The National Land Record Modernisation Programme (NLRMP) was a centrally sponsored scheme that was launched by the Government of India in 2008 with the aim to modernise the land records system in the country and implement the conclusive land-titling system with title guarantee. The NLRMP was later revamped and renamed as the Digital India Land Records Modernisation Programme (DILRMP) in 2016 as a central sector scheme with 100% funding by the Centre.

Salient Features of DILRMP

- A Unique Land Parcel Identification Number (ULPIN) or Bhu-Aadhaar number has been assigned for a land parcel, which is a 14-digit alphanumeric unique ID based on geo-coordinates which will serve as a pan-India number for obtaining ownership details of a plot along with its size and geolocation.
- A uniform system called National Generic Document Registration System (NGDRS) has been developed for addressing the diversity prevailing across states with regards to registration of deeds/documents.

- The Records of Rights have been transliterated in all the 22 scheduled languages mentioned in the Constitution to address the problem of linguistic barriers in land governance in the country.
- The DILRMP scheme will also facilitate various services such as providing caste, income and domicile certificates, and online information on crop profile, crop insurance and e-linkages to credit facilities/banks.

How DILRMP transform land administration in India?

- **Improve the Quality and Accessibility of Land Records** The DILRMP aims to digitize and update the textual and spatial records of land ownership and transactions, such as sale deeds, inheritance records, mortgage and lease documents, cadastral maps, etc. These records are made available online to the public and are updated regularly. This helps to reduce errors, inconsistencies, and gaps in land data, and make them more reliable and transparent.
- Free accessibility to the records will reduce interface between the citizen and the government functionaries, thereby reducing rent seeking and harassment.
- **Reduce Litigation and Frauds** The DILRMP aims to implement the conclusive land-titling system with title guarantee, which means that the land records provide a conclusive proof of ownership of land and are backed by the government. The title holder is protected from any challenge or dispute by other claimants and is indemnified by the government in case of any loss arising from any defect in the title. This helps to reduce the scope and frequency of land-related disputes and frauds, which account for a large proportion of pending court cases in India.
  - As per study by the World Bank, nearly 66% of litigations pending in Indian courts are related with land disputes and subsequent crimes.
  - A NITI Aayog paper suggests that land disputes on an average take about 20 years to be resolved. Land disputes add to the burden of the courts, tie up land in litigation, and further impact sectors and projects that are dependent on these disputed land titles.
- **Promote Development and Growth** The DILRMP aims to create a conducive environment for land markets and transactions by reducing transaction costs, risks, and uncertainties. It also enables landowners to access credit, insurance, and markets by using their land titles as collateral. This helps to attract investment, promote industrialization, and boost growth in various sectors such as agriculture, infrastructure, etc.
- **Urbanisation and Housing shortage** Under new schemes for urban development (Smart Cities Mission, AMRUT), cities are trying to raise their own revenue through property taxes and land-based financing. This further necessitates the importance of providing a system of clear land titles in urban areas.
- **Ensure Equity and Empowerment** The DILRMP aims to support the implementation of land reforms that aim to redistribute land among the landless and marginalized sections of society. It also empowers women and other vulnerable groups by recognising their land rights and enhancing their access to land-related services. This helps to improve their livelihoods, dignity, and social status.

Challenges Associated with the Digitisation of Land Records

- **Issues with respect to the adoption of Technology as a Solution to address land Governance in India** The concerns relating to technology in land governance are less about its efficiency and more about the architecture behind such technology.
  - Issues like the selection of technology, the usage of such data and its access, concerns on privacy, the methodology behind such data collection and interpretation are primary concerns. There are concerns like the lack of gender inclusivity, persisting land conflicts and non-uniformity across the states among various things.
  - The accuracy of land digitization is dependent on the reconciliation of three data sets- textual records, spatial records and satellite map data and how a mismatch in any of these data sets could potentially invite further legal dispute.
- **Lack of Conclusive land Titling System** In India, we have a system of registered sale deeds and not land titles. The Transfer of Property Act, 1882, provides that the right to an immovable property (or land) can be transferred or sold only by a registered document. These documents are registered under the Registration Act, 1908. Therefore, the transaction gets registered, and not the land title.
- **Lack of Coordination and Cooperation among States** Land is a state subject and the implementation of DILRMP depends on the willingness and cooperation of the State Governments. However, some states are reluctant or slow to adopt the DILRMP due to various reasons such as political, administrative, legal, or technical constraints. There is also a lack of coordination and standardisation among states in terms of land laws, policies, procedures and systems.

- **Inadequate Resources and Capacity** The DILRMP require adequate financial, human, and technical resources and capacity to carry out the massive task of modernizing the land records system in the country. However, there is a shortage of funds, staff, equipment, and infrastructure at various levels of implementation. There is also a need for training and capacity building of the concerned officials and functionaries on the use of modern technology and tools for land record management.
- **Lack of Awareness and Participation among Stakeholders** The DILRMP requires the active involvement and participation of various stakeholders such as landowners, buyers, sellers, tenants, intermediaries, etc., who are directly affected by the changes in the land records system. However, there is a lack of awareness and sensitization among them about the benefits and procedures of DILRMP.

Other Government steps for digitization of land records

- **Bhoomi Project (Karnataka), 2000** It was the first project in India started by Karnataka government to digitize land records. The necessary documents like the record of crops, rights and tenancy have been made available with the help of kiosks. o This project was soon followed by Andhra Pradesh and Tamil Nadu in 2001.
- **Dhatitree** It is the first web-based land records management system in India implemented in the state of Assam.
- **National Generic Document Registration System (NGDRS)** NGDRS is an in-house advanced software application for the registration of land and is a big step towards national integration and leap towards 'One Nation One Software'.
- **Integrated Land Management Information System (ILMIS)** Under this land-related information is available in a single window. It aims to integrate the land records database with the banks, financial institutions, circle rates, Registration Offices and other sectors to provide effective and efficient service deliveries by the respective offices.

Conclusion

Thus, digitisation of land records is an essential step towards improving overall governance and the government has rightly taken many steps in this direction.

Swamitva Scheme

Q.7 Digitisation of land records has a major role to play in the financial resilience of Gram Panchayats. Examine the statement in the context of Swamitva Scheme. What are the challenges in the successful implementation of this scheme? (150 Words, 10 Marks)

Ans. **Introduction** The PM Swamitva Scheme (Survey of Villages and Mapping with Improvised Technology in Village Areas) is a government initiative launched in April 2020 in India. The primary objective of the scheme is to provide rural property owners with legal documents, including a record of rights, which establishes their ownership of residential properties in rural areas.

Objectives of Swamitva Scheme

- **Establishing Property Rights** The PM Swamitva Scheme aims to establish and recognise property rights for rural landowners.The scheme seeks to bring clarity and certainty to land ownership in rural areas.
- **Preventing Land Disputes** The scheme intends to reduce land-related disputes and conflicts by providing an official record of rights to property owners.
  - Land disputes account for the largest set of cases in Indian courts – 25 per cent of all cases decided by the Supreme Court involved land disputes, of which 30 per cent were related to acquisition.
  - Reports suggest that 66 per cent of all civil cases in India are related to land or property disputes.
- **Facilitating Access to Credit and Financial Services** The issuance of property cards through the PM Swamitva Scheme enables rural property owners to use their land as collateral for accessing credit and financial services.
- **Promoting rural Development and Planning** Accurate information of land can be utilised for effective planning of infrastructure development, implementation of government schemes, and overall rural development initiatives.

- **Encouraging Economic Growth and Investment** By establishing clear property rights, the PM Swamitva Scheme aims to encourage economic growth and investment in rural areas
  - An estimated 7.7 million people in India are affected by conflict over 2.5 million hectares of land, threatening investments worth more than Rs 14 lakh crore.
- **Digitisation and Mapping of Rural land Records** The scheme utilises modern technology, such as drones and other geospatial tools,and aims to create a comprehensive and accurate database of rural landholdings, enhancing efficiency and transparency in land administration.

Role of PM Svamitva Scheme in Enhancing the Financial Resilience of Gram Panchayats in India

- **Facilitating Revenue Generation** Accurate and digitized land records enable Gram Panchayats to effectively assess and collect property taxes and other forms of revenue.
- **Enhancing Transparency and Accountability** Digitization of land records brings transparency to land administration processes. It reduces the scope for corrupt practices and unauthorized alterations to land records.
- **Enabling Land-based Economic Activities** Access to digitized land records allows Gram Panchayats to identify land parcels suitable for various economic activities such as agriculture, horticulture, livestock rearing, or setting up small-scale industries.
- **Streamlining Land-related Transactions** Digitized land records simplify and expedite land-related transactions, such as sale, purchase, or lease of land within the Gram Panchayat jurisdiction. Such streamlined transactions can attract investment and generate revenue for the Gram Panchayat.
- **Supporting Implementation of Government Schemes** Accurate and up-to-date digitized land records help Gram Panchayats in identifying eligible beneficiaries for various government schemes and subsidies.

Challenges in the Successful Implementation of Scheme

- **Land Ownership Disputes** Inaccurate or conflicting land records, multiple claims, and complex inheritance patterns can complicate the process of determining clear property rights.
- **Lack of Awareness and Participation** Limited awareness and understanding of the scheme can result in low participation and reluctance to undergo the necessary procedures to obtain property cards.
- **Technical and Infrastructure Limitations** The digitization of land records requires adequate technical infrastructure, and the absence of these essential resources can hamper the smooth implementation of the Swamitva Scheme and the issuance of property cards.
- **Capacity Building and Training** Training and capacity building of local authorities, such as revenue officials and Gram Panchayat members, are vital for effective implementation. Ensuring proper training and capacity building at all levels is essential to overcome implementation challenges.
- **Integration with Existing land Records Systems** The data collected through the scheme needs to be effectively synchronized and integrated with the broader land administration systems to maintain consistency and avoid duplication or conflicts in land records.
- **Financial Constraints** Adequate funding is crucial for the successful implementation of the Swamitva Scheme. Provision of funds for conducting surveys, digitization of records, capacity building, and creating necessary infrastructure requires significant financial resources.
- **Policy and Coordination Challenges** The implementation of the Swamitva Scheme involves coordination between various stakeholders, including central and state government agencies, revenue departments, Gram Panchayats, and local communities. Ensuring effective coordination and alignment of policies, rules, and procedures among these entities can be challenging.

Conclusion

Addressing these challenges requires concerted efforts from the government, local authorities, and other stakeholders involved. Timely resolutions and appropriate measures to overcome these obstacles can help in the successful implementation of PM Swamitva Scheme and ensure its intended benefits reach rural property owners.

Land Leasing

Q.8 Legalisation and liberalisation of land leasing would help in promoting agricultural efficiency, equity, occupational diversification and rapid rural transformation. Examine the statement in the context of NITI Aayog's Model Land Leasing Act, 2016. (250 Words, 15 Marks)

Ans. **Introduction** It has been noted that an estimated 36% of India's tenant farmers were completely landless, around 86% owned less than two hectare and 56% owned less than one hectare of land. In this background, Model Land Leasing Act, 2016 seeks to permit and facilitate leasing of agricultural land to improve access to land by the landless and marginal farmers. It also provides for recognition of farmers cultivating on leased land to enable them to access loans through institutional credit.

State Government's Leasing Restrictions

At the time of independence, India inherited a feudal agrarian structure in which land rights were concentrated in the hands of a few landlords/zamindars, while actual cultivators/ tenants did not have any right or security of tenure. Most state governments have either legally banned or imposed restrictions on agricultural land leasing. Restrictive land leasing laws have forced tenancy to be informal, insecure and inefficient. Informal tenants are most insecure and inefficient, as they do not have legal sanctity and access to institutional credit, insurance and other support services. In addition, restrictions on land leasing have reduced the occupational mobility of many landowners who have interest and ability to take up employment outside agriculture and yet are forced to stay in agriculture due to fear of losing land if they lease out and migrate.

Some of the leasing laws adopted by various State Governments are as follows:

- States such as Kerala, Jammu and Kashmir and Manipur that have legally prohibited leasing out agricultural land without any exception.
- States such as Bihar, Karnataka, Madhya Pradesh, Chhattisgarh, Uttar Pradesh, Uttarakhand, Himachal Pradesh, Tripura, Telengana and Odisha that allow leasing out only by certain categories of land owners, such as those suffering from physical or mental disability, widows, unmarried, separated or divorced women, members of armed forces etc.
- In Andhra Pradesh, Tamil Nadu, Rajasthan and West Bengal, there is no legal ban on leasing. But there are several restrictive clauses. In West Bengal, only sharecropping is allowed and not leasing on fixed rent or fixed produce basis.

Rationale behind the Land Leasing

There are certain concerns from restrictive land leasing laws:

Agricultural Efficiency

- **Legal ban or restrictions on land leasing have led to concealed tenancy** in almost all parts of the country. Informal tenants are most insecure, as they either have short duration oral leases or get rotated from plot to plot each year which acts as a disincentive to tenant farmers to make any investment in land improvement for productivity enhancement.
  - **Legalisation of land leasing** would ensure security of land ownership right for the land owners, which in turn would provide security of tenure to the tenants. This will incentivise tenant cultivators to invest and conserve agricultural land resources.
  - Land leasing can also **attract private investments in agriculture.**
- **Informal tenants do not have access to institutional credit, insurance and other support services**, which affect productivity of land cultivated by them.
  - Legalisation/formalisation of land leasing would help improve tenant farmers' access to credit, insurance and input use and consequently productivity of leased in land.
- Due to legal restrictions, **many land owners prefer to keep their lands fallow** due to the fear of losing land right if they lease out. Keeping the land fallow results in underutilization of land and loss of agricultural output.
  - The lifting of ban or restrictions on leasing in such cases will result in better utilization of the available land and labour and increased farm output.

Equity and Poverty Alleviation

- **Ban or restrictions have only reduced the extent of land available in the lease market** and have reduced the welfare of poor tenants by forcing them to enter into informal arrangements, in contravention of the rules.
  - Liberalisation of land leasing would result in the maximisation of poor's family income by way of farming on lease, along with access to other farm, off-farm and non-farm employment opportunities.
  - Improved access to land on lease by the poor would help reduce their poverty and enhance economic and social status.

Occupational Diversification and Rural Transformation

- **Legalisation of land leasing would encourage large land owners to lease out land** without fear of losing their land ownership rights and invest in non-farm enterprises (with appropriate capital and technology support), which is vital f or occupational diversification and rapid rural transformation. This will reduce the pressure of population on agriculture and enable small farmers to augment their size of operational holdings by leasing in land.
- Many marginal and small farmers would be better off leasing out their land to more viable farmers for rent, while **seeking paid employment within or outside agriculture**. This would help them to maximise incomes by way of rentals as well as wage incomes

In the past few decades, even socialist countries such as the Peoples Republic of China and Vietnam have liberalized agricultural land leasing with significant positive impact on economic growth as well as equity.

NITI Aayog Model Land Leasing Act, 2016

- **Land Lease Agreement** The lease agreement between the land owner and cultivator will include information pertaining to: (i) the location and area of leased out land, (ii) the duration of lease, (iii) the lease amount and the due date by which it has to be paid, and (iv) terms and conditions for the renewal or extension of lease. The lease period and lease amount will be based on a mutual agreement between the land owner and cultivator. Additionally, the lease agreement will not confer any protected tenancy right on a cultivator.
- **Enforcement of Lease Agreement** The tahsildar or a revenue officer of equal rank will be responsible for, (i) enforcement of terms of lease, and (ii) facilitating return of the leased out agricultural land to the owner on expiry of the lease period.
- **Rights and Responsibilities of Land Owner** The landowner is entitled to automatic possession of the land on the expiry of the agreed lease period. He can put the leased out land for use such as sale, gift, mortgage, etc. However, this should not affect the cultivator's right to cultivate the land till the end of the lease period.
- **Rights and Responsibilities of Cultivator** The cultivator, to whom the land has been leased out, will be entitled to an undisturbed possession and use of this land. He can use the land only for agriculture and allied activities. Further, he cannot sub-lease or mortgage the land. He will be eligible to raise loans from banks and other financial institutions without mortgaging the leased in land.
- **Termination of Lease** The lease agreement may be terminated on grounds including: (i) failure of cultivator to pay the lease amount after a grace period of three months, (ii) use of land for purposes other than those specified in the agreement, (iii) sub-leasing of land or damage caused to it by the cultivator.
- **Dispute Resolution** The cultivator and the owner can settle disputes between them using third party mediation, or gram panchayat, or gram sabha.
- **Special Land Tribunal** State Governments will constitute a special Land Tribunal, which will be the final authority to adjudicate disputes under the Model Act.

Concerns Associated with the Model Land Leasing Act, 2016

- **Absence of Tamper-proof Land Records** The biggest challenge to the Model Land Leasing Act is the lack of tamper-proof land records with the revenue department. This is one of the reasons why landowners fear leasing out their farms.
- **Diversion of Land from Crop Cultivation to Commercial Use** Model Land Leasing agreement Act (2016) may encourage the diversion of agricultural land from crop cultivation to commercial use because it allows leasing of agricultural land for activities like animal husbandry, plantation crops etc.in addition to crop cultivation.
- **Absentee Landlordism** Model land leasing act will prevent redistribution of land through transfer ownership as people living outside the area will prefer leasing instead of selling. Otherwise, land distribution through selling was an important means of redistribution and consolidation of land. Land leasing will promote absentee landlords.

- **Lack of Uniformity** Since agriculture is a state subject, the disparity and abundance of laws create confusion, and lack of uniformity, which may prevent the formation of a healthy leasing ecosystem. The act is also silent on whether a land already under lease agreement can be mortgaged or not, keeping in view that the lessee might be interested in availing crop loans or term loans in case of allied activities.
- **Exploitation of Small and Marginal Farmers** The model Land Leasing Act doesn't specify the rent on leased land and the period of lease and has rightly left it to the concerned parties in the land lease market which could lead to exploitation of small and marginal farmers.
- **Food Security** Leasing out land to activities other than agriculture might endanger the food security of the country in the long run.

Conclusion

A land reforms agenda, particularly the land leasing legislations and updated land records, should receive the highest priority to increase incomes of smallholders, tenant farmers and sharecroppers.

Check Your Preparation

1. In the background of declining size of operational land holdings, explain the linkage between the size of land holdings and farmer's income. (150 words, 10 marks)
2. Tenancy reform laws enacted by most State Governments immediately following the independence has led to several problems. Elucidate. Give your opinion on legalising the land leasing and its liberalisation in India. (250 words, 15 marks)
3. Lack of conclusive land titles alienates the poor from accessing the formalised credit structures and therefore, several measures should be undertaken to adopt a conclusive system of titling. Examine. (150 words, 10 marks)

UNIT 8

Effects of Liberalisation on the Economy, Changes in Industrial Policy and their Effects on Industrial Growth

Manufacturing and MSME Sector (State of Manufacturing Sector)

Q.1 Despite a focused approach on manufacturing sector through initiatives such as Make in India, the share of manufacturing sector in the Gross Domestic Product (GDP) has stayed stagnant. In this context, bring out the reasons for subpar performance of manufacturing sector. Also, suggest reforms that can enable the sector to meet the targets of National Manufacturing Policy 2011. (250 Words, 15 Marks)

Ans. **Introduction** Make in India initiative was announced to encourage manufacturing in India and galvanize the economy with investments in manufacturing and services. Similarly, initiatives like stand-up India, start-up India etc. were launched, but over last 30 years the share of manufacturing sector in the GDP remained stagnant at around 16- 17%.

Reasons for the Sub-par Performance of Manufacturing Sector

- **High Compliance Cost Leading to "Dwarfism"** Economic Survey in the past talked about the "regulatory cholesterol" in the country. It breeds informal, sub-scale and uncompetitive enterprises.
- **Inverted Duty Structure** It leads to the situation, where it is better to import finished goods rather than intermediate goods and raw materials for manufacturing the goods.
- **Free Trade Agreements (FTAs)** Though, FTAs tend to increase trade, but many of India's recent FTAs have benefited the other partners more. For example, India-ASEAN trade agreement led to the increase in India's trade deficit with ASEAN.
- **Global Competition** India's manufacturing sector faced a stiff competition from other developing countries like Bangladesh and Vietnam in the case of apparels, Vietnam and Indonesia in the case of leather and footwear and Bangladesh, Pakistan and Sri Lanka in case of textile.
- **Infrastructural Bottlenecks** The current logistics cost of India is around 14% of GDP, which is very high in comparison to U.S. and Europe, where it ranges between 8-10%.
- **Human Resource with Poor Skill Set** It is estimated that only 5% of India's workforce is formally skilled (South Korea 96%). It affects the quality of workers.

- **Land Acquisition and Environmental Clearances** Land acquisition act, made acquiring of land very difficult. Repeated PILs and courts' interventions also affect the growth of and setting up of manufacturing facilities.
- **Poor expenditure on Research and Development** India's expenditure on R&D has remained stagnant at around 0.6-0.7% of GDP (Economic Survey). Israel & China spends 4.3% & 2.1% respectively.
- **Intellectual Property Protection and Enforcement** Poor patent protection and enforcement affect investment and innovation climate in the country.
- **Growing Protectionism** There is a rise in protectionist tendencies in western economies. The export market which helped in the growth of Asian tigers, is no more supportive.
- **Restrictive Labor Laws** It discourages employers from hiring workers on a regular basis. It has probably also led to entrepreneurs choosing to stay away from labor intensive sectors.
- **Absence of Incentives for Raising Efficiency** Focusing attention on internal liberalization without adequate emphasis on trade policy reforms resulted in 'consumption-led growth' rather than 'investment' or 'export- led growth'.
- **Slow Technology Adoption has led to low Productivity** and higher costs adding to the disadvantage of Indian products in international markets.
  - Productivity as measured by value added per worker and average wages in manufacturing in India are only one-third of that in China.

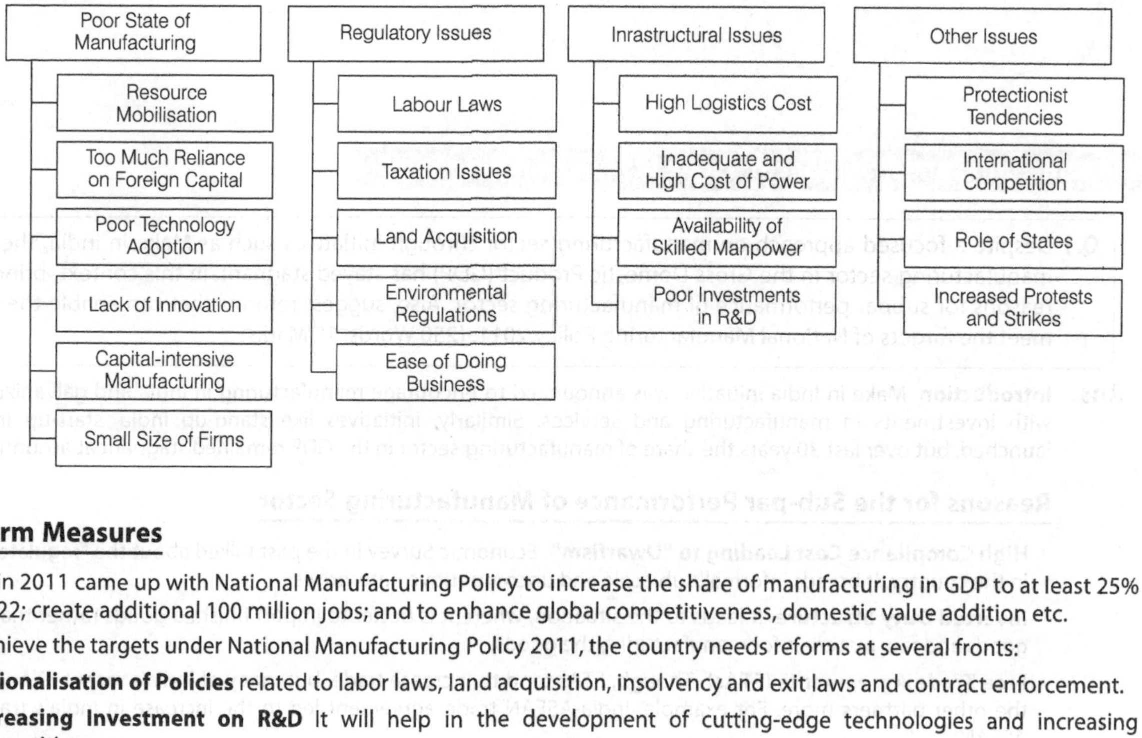

Reform Measures

India in 2011 came up with National Manufacturing Policy to increase the share of manufacturing in GDP to at least 25% by 2022; create additional 100 million jobs; and to enhance global competitiveness, domestic value addition etc.

To achieve the targets under National Manufacturing Policy 2011, the country needs reforms at several fronts:

- **Rationalisation of Policies** related to labor laws, land acquisition, insolvency and exit laws and contract enforcement.
- **Increasing Investment on R&D** It will help in the development of cutting-edge technologies and increasing competitiveness.
- **Improving the Infrastructure** Implementation of National Infrastructure pipeline can help speed up infrastructure delivery.
- **Promote the growth of Labor-intensive Industries** Economic Survey also supported the idea of supporting textile (especially technical textiles), leather industries etc. due to India's competitive advantage and their labor-intensive nature.
- **Promote MSMEs** MSMEs account for 8% of GDP, 45% of manufacturing output and 40% of exports. There is a need to increase the credit accessibility, and larger support for their growth and expansion.
- Filling the skill gap among the demographic dividend.

- **Bank Recapitalisation** Rising number of non-Performing assets hamper banks' lending ability, which in turn affects the growth of Indian industries.
- **Improving the Availability of Power** to the sector which is the 2nd most important obstacle for manufacturing firms as per World Bank.

Conclusion

India's manufacturing sector needs a definite upgradation, not only to enhance economic growth, but also to make it more inclusive. Focus should not be on import substitution, but on increasing the competitiveness of Indian products through reforms in factor markets. Few steps taken by government under Atmanirbhar Bharat Abhiyan will go a long way in creating sustainable manufacturing growth environment.

Labour-intensive vs Capital-intensive Manufacturing

Q.2 Account for the failure of manufacturing sector in achieving the goal of labour-intensive exports rather than capital-intensive exports. Suggest measures for more labour intensive rather than capital-intensive exports. (150 Words, 10 Marks) **UPSC Mains PYQ 2017**

Ans. **Introduction** As per data from Ministry of Commerce, India's labour-intensive exports grew by 2.1% in 2021 to $5.2 billion, which is far less when compared to capital intensive exports. According to Arvind Subramaniam, India is exporting about $60bn- $140bn less of labour-intensive items than it should be despite having very high low skilled workforce.

Reasons for Less Labour-Intensive Exports

- **Credit crunch of MSMEs** MSMEs account for more than 45% of all exports and they are majorly responsible for labour intensive exports. However, poor credit availability for MSMEs hindered the growth of labour-intensive exports.
- **Issues of Scale** Labour intensive industries is composed mostly of small and local shops and hence scaling up them for exports becomes difficult.
- **Emphasis on Capital-intensive Industries** Since second five-year plan, India has given more emphasis on heavy capital-intensive industries such as steel, coal which require large capital and face competition from industrialized countries.
- **Poor Technical Infrastructure** India's labour-intensive industries are based on obsolete technology which hampers its production efficiency and increase costs which make the exports uncompetitive.
- **Low Production Capacity** Most labor-intensive industries lack the proper efficiency and streamlined production leading to poor production and exports.
- **Red Tapism** There are multiple procedures and delayed setting up of labor-intensive industries which discourages investors and thereby the exports.
- **Sector Specific Problems** Industries like footwear, leather, apparel was not given enough exposure to capital and technology.
- **Protectionist Measures** The increasing protectionist measures by countries like United States, China also hamper the export potential of Indian labour-intensive industries.
- **International Competition** Increasing competition and cheap products from various countries like China, Vietnam and Bangladesh. Indian exports are losing out to low wage rates in countries like Vietnam and China.

Measures for More Labour-intensive Exports

- **Liberalise Imports on low Skilled Product Inputs** Long standing tariff on man-made yarn need to be liberated from the import duties as man-made fiber-based exports are labour intensive and most dynamic segment of world export.
- **Encourage Labour Intensive Sectors** Government must encourage the labor-intensive industries like garments, leather, gems and jewellery which has huge potential for exports.
- **Easing Labour Laws** The labour law regulations need simplification and should suit emergent conditions and provide more flexibility to employers.
- **Skill Development** To fill the gap in exports, skilling the workers is quintessential.

- **Separate Industrial Corridors** The government must create separate industrial corridors for improving the export potential of labor-intensive industries.
- **Finalize Pending FTAs** FTA with Europe is crucial as it impose heavy duty on India's clothing exports of close to 10% which disadvantages India when compared to Bangladesh which enjoy preferential treatment.
- **Tax Benefits** More tax benefits could be provided to labour intensive industries for a set of period to enable them to increase their exports.
- **Promotion of Indian Exports in Apparel Sector**
  - Easing barriers: Ease barriers to imported inputs such as man-made (synthetic) fabrics since the global market for synthetic clothing is much larger than for cotton clothing.
  - Improving logistics: Improve export logistics through coastal employment zones.
  - Market access: Enhance market access through the completion of trade agreements and a general lowering of tariffs
- **Promotion of Indian Exports in Gems and Jewellery Sector**
  - **Reducing Custom Duty** Facilitate the import of rough diamonds and enhance access to finance for diamond processing firms.
  - **Facilitate Exchange** Facilitate exchanges with industry experts and association in other top exporters
  - **Skilling** Using RPL to recognize the prior learning of artisans will help provide them with suitable opportunities and help in overall growth and exports in this sector.

Sectors for Labour-intensive Exports

There are two groups of industries that hold the greatest potential for export growth and job creation.

First, there exists a significant unexploited export potential in India's traditional unskilled labour-intensive industries such as textiles, clothing, footwear and toys.

- **Labour-intensive** The data picked up from Economic Survey 2016-17 shows that the apparel sector is the most labor-intensive, followed by footwear. Apparels are 80-fold more labor-intensive than autos and 240-fold more jobs than steel. Leather goods are 33-fold more labor-intensive than autos and 100-fold more jobs than steel.
- **Women-centric Sectors** Apparels and Leather sectors offer tremendous opportunities for creation of jobs, especially for women. The opportunity created for women implies that these sectors could be vehicles for social transformation. In Bangladesh, female education, total fertility rates, and women's labour force participation moved positively due to the expansion of the apparel sector.

Second, India has huge potential to emerge as a major hub for final assembly in a range of products, referred to as "network products".

- The GVCs in these industries are controlled by leading MNEs such as Apple, Samsung, Sony etc. o In general, these products are not produced from start to finish within a given country; instead, countries specialize in particular tasks or stages of the good's production sequence.
- Labour abundant countries, like China, specialize in low skilled labour-intensive stages of production such as assembly while the richer countries specialise in capital and skill-intensive stages such as R&D.
- The Economic Survey 2019-20 advised that by integrating "Assemble in India for the world" into Make in India, India can raise its export market share to about 3.5 per cent by 2025 and 6 per cent by 2030, which is highly feasible.

Conclusion

Thus, resisting the misleading allure of domestic market, India should zealously boost labour intensive exports performance and deploy all means to achieve the goal. A favourable policy and private sector focus on labour intensive industry would help improve labour intensive exports.

Critical Analysis of MSME Sector

Q.3 What could be the possible reasons for MSMEs insignificant contribution to output and employment in the manufacturing sector as compared to the large firms? Suggest some measures to enable MSMEs in contributing to job creation and productivity in an economy. (250 Words, 15 Marks)

Ans. **Introduction** Economic Survey 2018-19 observed that contribution of small firms to output and employment in the manufacturing sector is insignificant though they account for close to 85 per cent of all firms. MSMEs account for only 23 per cent of the total employment in organized manufacturing and its share in Net Value Added (NVA) from organized manufacturing was only 11.5 per cent.

The above findings dispel the common notion that small firms generate the most employment. Small firms may generate a higher number of new jobs. However, they destroy as many jobs as well. Thus, higher levels of job creation in small firms co-exist with job destruction, thereby leading to lower levels of net job creation.

Challenges of MSME sector

- **Creation of Dwarfs** Government policies in India fostered dwarfs which accounted for more than 50% of all firms in organised manufacturing but contributes only 14% in employment and 7.6% in Net Value Added. Thus, the growth of these firms hampers the productivity in an economy.
- **Labour Regulations** Various labour legislations such as Industrial Disputes Act (IDA), 1947 mandates companies with more than 100 employees to get permission from the Government before retrenchment of employees. Thus, a large majority of firms would prefer to be below the threshold of 100 employees.
- **Policy of Small-scale Reservation** The Small Scale Industries (SSI) reservation policy was introduced in 1967 to promote employment growth and income re-distribution. Various schemes such as Priority Sector Lending (PSL), Credit Guarantee Fund Scheme, Marketing Assistance Scheme etc, creates perverse incentives for the firms to remain small and thus affecting the productivity.
- **Competition from Multinational Companies** In present era of globalisation, the MSME's are facing threat from the international manufacturing companies who are proving quality goods at cheapest price. Therefore, it is very difficult to compete with the multinational companies.
- **Infrastructure Bottlenecks and Competition** The MSME clusters, particularly the micro enterprises, are inadequately equipped with necessary support systems which not only impede their day-to-day business operations but also their future growth prospects. With poor infrastructure, their production capacity is very low while production cost is very high.
- **Lack of Advanced Technology** The owners of MSME's are not aware of advanced technologies of production. Their methodology of production is outdated. The owners are using older method in the field of fabricated metal and textile.
- **Lack of Expertise** Lack of expertise in product development, designing, packaging and marketing strategy due to their small size add up to the pressure of adapting to the changing environment around them.
- **Attitude Difference** MSMEs in India are not in habit of forward expansions and depend heavily on government support. The strategy for MSMEs should be to gradually expand in size and reduce the dependence on the incentive structure provided by the Government.
- **Access to Credit** Credit plays a vital role in development of MSME sector as funds at a reasonable cost can increase their competitiveness. Credit disbursal to this sector has, however, remained sluggish in recent periods. There are issues of collateral, underwriting because of their informal nature of working. Due to their small-scale operations, MSMEs are not able to raise risk capital.
- **Informalisation** Because of being an informal sector, MSMEs are unable to take advantage of most of the Government schemes which are mostly based on digital infrastructure and require beneficiaries to have some form of digital identify and presence.

- **Delayed Payments** A large number of MSMEs are ancillary units catering to the needs of large industries, both in the public and private sector. They often face the problem of delayed payments, affecting their cash flow and working capital availability. A primary survey conducted by Reserve Bank in December 2019 showed that 44 per cent of MSMEs engaged in manufacturing activities faced delay in payments.
- **Procurement of Raw Materials** Due to financial constraints, most of the small industries are bound to procure the low-quality raw material from the local region.
- **Lack of Marketing** MSMEs have not adopted the innovative channels of distribution and marketing, resulting in poor brand building and weak sales.
- **Absence of Standardised Policies** In India, just a few policies are in place to support small and medium-sized businesses. As a result, MSME growth and entrepreneurship development programs lack coherence.
- **Poor Access to the Potential Market** MSMEs are finding it difficult to get access to potential markets due to inadequate capital and unavailability of the marketing tools. Therefore; it creates obstacles for MSMEs to sell out their offering to government-based agencies. Also, this could narrow their reach in the market and let their counterpart to take advantage.

Government Efforts

- **Zero Defect and Zero Effect** Government has inculcated an amicable solution for quality production in MSMEs by launching an initiative "Zero Defect and Zero Effect" (ZED) in association with ministry of MSME and Quality Council of India. The primary objective of this initiative is to develop an ecosystem of Zero-Defect Manufacturing among the existing MSMEs.
- **Atmanirbahar Bharat Package** To help MSMEs during COVID:
  - ₹ 3 lakh crore collateral-free automatic loans for MSMEs to buy raw material, meet operational liabilities and restart businesses
  - Revision of MSME definition to extend maximum benefits to the sector
  - Disallowing global tenders in procurements upto INR 200 crs to create attractive opportunities for domestic players
  - Clearing of MSME dues by the Government and Public Sector Units (PSUs) within 45days
- **Raw Material Assistance Scheme** Indian Government in association with National Small Industries Corporation (NSIC) has launched "Raw Material Assistance Scheme". Under this scheme, distressed MSMEs can avail financial credit from the designated sources for the purchase of raw material (both import and indigenous).
- **Establishing Common Facility Centers (CFCs)** The Ministry of MSME has opted for collective approach for improving productivity as well as capacity building of MSEs. The scheme aims at establishing Common Facility Centers (CFCs) for testing, raw material depot, training, and effluent treatment, etc. The primary objective of this scheme is to support the growth and sustainability of Medium and Small enterprises by undermining key problems as improvement of technology, market access, skill and quality, etc.
- **Skill Mapping** Indian Government in collaboration with ministry of MSMEs has introduced an initiative namely "Skill Mapping" for the identification of skilled individuals.
- **Marketing Promotion Schemes** This scheme aims to educate and promote the existing MSMEs by organizing awareness programs/ Trade fair about Government e-Marketplace portal, and online services.

Futuristic Measures

- **Incentivizing 'infant' firms rather than 'small' firms** With the appropriate grandfathering of existing incentives, they need to be shifted away from dwarfs to infants based on the age criterion.
- **Sunset Clause for Incentives** Every incentive for fostering growth should have a 'sunset' clause of five to seven years after which the firm should be able to sustain itself. The policy focus would thereby remain on infant firms.
- **Focus on High Employment Elastic Sectors** To step up the impact of economy growth on employment, the focus has to be on such high employment elastic sectors such as the manufacture of rubber and plastic products, electronic and optical products, transport equipment, machinery, basic metals and fabricated metal products, chemicals and chemical products, textiles and leather & leather products.
- **Easy Access to Finance and Credit** Institutional finance/credit from banks and other financing institutions should be promptly available without long and cumbersome procedures.

- **Stepping up Infrastructural and Support Facilities** Deficiencies in basic infrastructural facilities like water, power supply, road/rail and telephone connectivity, etc. should be addressed on priority basis. Use of solar or renewable energy as an alternative source should be encouraged in rural areas on subsidized basis.
- **Access to Modern Tools and Technology** MSMEs today need to adopt and adhere to quality parameters of international standards in the context of a globalized market. Technological obsolescence should be replaced by the adoption of modern and latest tools and technology for increased productivity and quality product for competitive advantage.

Conclusion

As the MSME sector holds immense potential, the need is to have a right set of policies and enabling framework which guide and support MSMEs to effectively handle their existing problems and venture into new areas. While both the Government and the RBI have introduced a plethora of measures for improving access to finance and to promote growth of the sector, the small size of individual units and informal nature of the sector continue to pose challenges.

Problem Areas	Government Initiatives
• Issues in MSME Sector with respect to the problem area	
Access of Credit	Government Initiatives: 59 minute portal, 2% interest subvention for GST registered MSMEs, TReDS, Udyami Mitra Portal , MSME Samadhaan, MUDRA Scheme
• Informal Loans: 90% of MSMEs are dependent on informal sources • Procedural Challenge: Lack of sufficient collateral and high working capital needs. Delay in loan processing • Delayed payments from ancillary clients and large buyers.	
Access of Market	E-Commerce companies, ONDC, GeM portal, compulsory procurement from MSMEs by PSUs, MSME Sambandh,SFURTI
• Low outreach and non-availability of new markets. Ineffective advertisement and poor marketing channels. • Lack of skilled manpower and therefore, no innovation in the production and distribution of goods and services. • Difficult for MSMEs to sell products to government agencies • Competition from MNCs and other big industries in the era of globalisation. (Issue of Economies of Scale)	
Technology Access	Financial assistance for Lean Manufacturing Competitive Scheme (LMCS); Digital MSME Scheme; Credit Linked Capital Subsidy Scheme; MSME Innovative Scheme
• Limited human resources and weak financial standing • Lower adaptability of new technology such as digital presence, automation in production, etc.	
Quality and Export Issues	Zero Effect, Zero Defect Scheme; Product certification licenses
• Low quality products and low productivity (due to poor infrastructure) impact exports competitiveness • Inadequate access of raw materials.	
Ease of Doing Business	Labour Reforms, improved regulatory compliances, Udyog Aadhar Memorandum (UAM), CHAMPIONS Portal
• Regulatory Cholesterol: Cumbersome government procedures and rules for establishing new units. Increasing the compliance cost. • Red-Tapism: Bureaucratic delays in getting clearances. • Poor insolvency and poor litigation system in the country	

Production-Linked Incentive (PLI) Scheme

Q.4 'Production-Linked Incentive (PLI) schemes, which are aimed at making India a global manufacturing hub, is struggling across the most sectors.' In this context, analyze the various challenges being faced by the scheme and suggest some measures for improving their performance. (150 Words, 10 Marks)

About PLI Scheme

The PLI scheme is a financial initiative launched by the Indian government to boost domestic manufacturing and make it globally competitive. It began in March 2020, covering mobile manufacturing and IT hardware initially, and has since expanded to include 14 sectors such as pharmaceuticals, telecom, food products, automobiles, textiles, and drones.

Under the PLI scheme, eligible companies receive financial incentives or subsidies based on their incremental production or sales. The objective of the scheme is to boost the competitiveness of Indian manufacturers, attract investment, create employment opportunities, and enhance exports in targeted sectors.

The scheme aims to encourage both domestic and foreign companies to set up or expand their manufacturing operations in India, thereby strengthening the country's manufacturing ecosystem and reducing reliance on imports.

Achievements of PLI Scheme so far

- **Increased Export Growth** Under the PLI scheme, sectors such as electronics, automobiles, pharmaceuticals, white goods, and textiles have witnessed significant growth in exports. For example, exports of electronic goods increased by 57.36 percent during March 2023 at USD 2.86 Billion as compared to USD 1.82 Billion in March 2022.
- **Attracting Investments** The PLI scheme has successfully attracted both domestic and foreign investments in various sectors. Companies have shown interest in setting up manufacturing facilities in India to leverage the incentives provided by the scheme. For instance, 20 automobile companies have proposed a total investment of around Rs. 45,000 crores (US$ 5.95 billion).
- **Job Creation** The PLI scheme has played a crucial role in generating employment opportunities across sectors. For example, the drone manufacturing sector alone is expected to create more than 10,000 direct jobs, while the textile sector is estimated to create over 7.5 lakh additional jobs.
- **Incremental Production and Investments** The PLI scheme have stimulated incremental production and investments in targeted sectors. It is expected to bring in incremental investment of INR 7,920 crore and incremental production worth INR 1,68,000 crore
- **Improving India's "Global Manufacturing Rankings"** India's efforts towards manufacturing growth, including the PLI scheme, have been recognized globally. India secured second position after China in the Global Manufacturing Risk Index 2021, reflecting the progress made in the manufacturing sector.
- **Contribution to GDP** The PLI scheme is expected to have a positive impact on India's GDP. It is estimated to add 1.7% to the country's GDP by 2027, generating significant economic growth and contributing to overall prosperity.

Challenges to the PLI Scheme

However, the scheme is not performing to its potential and many companies are failing to achieve the targets. Some of the reasons behind it are:

- **Regulatory hurdles** Despite efforts to simplify the regulatory environment, Indian businesses often grapple with red-tapism, bureaucratic hold-ups, and complex regulatory requirements that can slow down or complicate the implementation of the PLI scheme. Achieving consistency and transparency in policy regulations across states and sectors is a challenge.
- **No Common Framework** There is no standard framework to calculate and compare value addition by companies. Different ministries use different parameters to calculate the concerned PLI. Further, there is no common database to understand and compare different parameters like jobs created, or exports rise.
- **Steep Targets** Many times, the targets fixed for companies are too steep to achieve.
- **Financial Cap on Incentives** The financial cap prevents the over performing companies from reaping benefits of achievements.
- **Lack of Advanced Technology** India does not have enough technology and inadequate attention to R & D has led to a brain drain which affects the scheme. The cost and complexity associated with technology adoption can pose challenges for companies looking to benefit from the PLI scheme.
- **Lack of Scale** The small, fragmented companies that make up some value chains cannot operate productively, let alone at peak efficiency; cannot innovate quickly enough to keep up with competitors; and cannot command price premium because they lack strong brands.
- **Administrative Efficiency** Efficient administration and implementation of the PLI scheme is essential. This involves the timely disbursal of incentives and the monitoring of compliance by beneficiary companies.
- **Sector-Specific Challenges** Different sectors within the manufacturing industry have unique challenges that need to be considered during the implementation of the PLI scheme. These challenges could include technological barriers, supply chain complexities, skill gaps, or global market dynamics.
- **Structural Issues in the Economy** Structural issues, such as small-scale operations, regulatory constraints, and fragmented supply chains, can hinder the effectiveness of incentive schemes like the PLI.
- **Higher Cost of Manufacturing** A study by Ernst and Young showed that despite the PLI scheme, India would not be a top investment destination because of higher effective manufacturing cost.

- **Dependence on Subsidies** There's a concern that the PLI scheme may create industries that are dependent on government subsidies for their survival. This could potentially lead to long-term problems, as these industries may not be competitive without ongoing government support.
- **Low Return on Capital for Indian Companies** Unfortunately, most companies in Indian manufacturing struggle to earn a return more than their cost of capital. According to McKinsey, over the past four years, from 2016 to 2020, sectors that saw healthier return saw an increase in invested capital; but out of the top 1,000 manufacturing companies, 700 earned a return that was less than their cost of capital in 2018.

Measures Needed to Improve the Performance of the Scheme

- **Reduction in Effective Cost of Manufacturing** Co-location of units and subunits will help lowering the cost of manufacturing and will improve the functioning of the scheme.
- **Inclusion of Service Industry** Service industry which contributes the most to Indian GDP has not been included. Its inclusion will aid the growth as has been seen in China.
- **Enhancing Competitive Federalism** Encouraging states to be competitive and not restoring to populist measures like job reservation would help the situation.
- **Infrastructure Development** Adequate and modern infrastructure, including transportation networks, power supply, logistics, and connectivity, is essential for the smooth functioning of manufacturing activities.
- **Boost skills and innovation** Encourage and invest in technical and vocational education and training to build a skilled workforce. In addition, promoting research and development can foster innovation, which can drive productivity growth in the manufacturing sector.
- **Improve "Ease of Doing Business"** Reducing bureaucratic red tape, simplifying regulations, and providing a clear and stable policy environment can make it easier for businesses to operate, invest, and expand their manufacturing capabilities.
- **Promote digital transformation** Leveraging Industry 4.0 technologies such as AI, IoT, and automation can improve efficiency, reduce costs, and boost the competitiveness of the manufacturing sector.

Conclusion

PLI Scheme has the potential to add 4% of GDP if the existing bottlenecks are removed. It would help India achieve self-dependence and help our economy become a 5 trillion economy which would have a multiplier effect across all segments.

Effects of Liberalisation (Impact on Employment Pattern)

Q.5 How globalisation has led to the reduction of employment in the formal sector of the Indian economy? Is increased informalisation detrimental to the development of the country? (150 Words, 10 Marks)

UPSC Main PYQ 2016

Ans. Introduction With the 1991 economic reforms India opened its door for the world and embraced globalisation that allowed Indian economy to engage with others. It enabled the global integration of production and markets across nations. It is said that globalisation has led to the informalization of the economy and reduced formal employment. Although informalisation has provided livelihood to many, it has not raised the living standard as was expected.

Despite witnessing rapid economic growth over the last two decades (propelled India's GDP growth rate to nearly 7-8% from the prevalent 2-3%), over 90% of workers in India have remained informally employed, producing about half of Gross Domestic Product (GDP).

Impact of Globalisation on the Formal Sector Employment

- **Decline in Public Sector Employment** The most stable source of formal employment has been the public sector. Because a major focus of liberalisation is a reduction in size of the public sector. The proportion of formally employed workers fall as governments cut their work force unless.
- **Restrictive Labour Laws** which promote contract hiring in order to circumvent rigid hiring and firing provisions. They also act as an impediment to industrial development and employment creation.

- **Predominance of Service-sector led growth** which requires skilled labour that was available with a miniscule section of the population.
- **Absence of thrust on Manufacturing** which can lead to creation of formal employment for millions looking to move away from agriculture. Inadequate growth of infrastructure and low investments in the manufacturing sector, hence restricting the employment potential of the secondary sector.
- **Market-mechanisms and Competition** led to closure of obsolete industries such as textile mills, reducing formal jobs. The newer industries were capital intensive rather than labour intensive, thus absorbing lesser workforce than what they laid to retrenchment of.
- **Need of Cheap Flexible Labour** During globalisation, big companies look for cheap labor due to competitive market, so they go for contract labour. This also provided them flexibility to hire more in time of good demand and layoff the workforce in times of slow growth rate. Thus, ensuring the profitability and sustainability of companies.
- **Lack of an exit mechanism such as Insolvency and Bankruptcy Laws** has led to firms remaining small, barely breaking even, and not scaling up. Such small firms can circumvent formal sector laws such as mandatory registrations with the EPFO etc. rendering them informal.
- The **advent of the Fourth Industrial Revolution and Automation** poses even more dangers to present formal sector jobs since workers with current skills will be rendered obsolete unless they undergo skill reorientation.
- **India, with increasing Integration into Global Economy**, also suffered during various global crises such as the Southeast Asian crisis, Global Financial Crisis in 2008 and the Eurozone crisis in 2011. This shelved corporate expansion plans and led to closure of several industries, reducing formal sector employment.
- **Decline of Small Scale and Cottage Industries** Independent India's preference to large scale industry and new industrial policy of 1990's along with globalisation resulted in decline of small-scale industries.

Increasing Informalisation is Detrimental to Economic Development

- **Hurdle to Inclusive Growth** Informal jobs often have low productivity and of low general quality. Informal workers lack proper wages and their wages are also less. Lower wages lead to increasing inequality, which is detrimental to inclusive growth.
- **Lack of Adequate Wages** Informal workers lack proper wages. Lower wages lead to increasing inequality, which is detrimental to development. Low wages lead to a low savings rate, which is detrimental for the credit cycle and further lending, hampering development.
- **Non-Applicability of Social Security Measures** There are many times when a worker cannot be economically active. For instance, due to biological circumstances such as sickness or old age, on account of personal calamities such as an accident or unemployment. There are no social security measures to provide risks coverage and ensure maintenance of basic living standards at times of crises such as unemployment or health issues.
- **Reduced Productivity** Contract labour has no affinity or loyalty towards the company, thus hampering productivity and economic development. Productivity of the economy decreases as a whole since companies lose the incentive to skill the employees, so that they can better reorient themselves to the demands of the economy.
- **Lacks of Financial Literacy** Informal sector workers usually lack financial literacy, depriving them of access to institutional credit, thus reducing domestic consumption and harming development.
- **Cash-based Sector** Informal sector is predominantly cash-based. This is a major source of generation of black money and tax evasion. Size of Indian black economy is estimated at nearly 24% of GDP. This deprives the State of legitimate taxes, hampering development.
- **Low Tax Base** A low tax base due to low formal sector leads to low tax revenue which results in increased government borrowing (for counter-cyclical purposes). These measure higher fiscal deficit affects the low-wage informal workers the most, thus perpetuating a vicious cycle and hampering development. High FD and high inflation also lead to credit downgrades and lead to outflow of foreign investments due to macroeconomic instability. This is catastrophic for a capital-starved country like India.
- **Poverty and Indebtedness** Workers in the unorganised sector had a much higher incidence of poverty than their counterparts in the organised sector. Due to low level of income and uncertain employment in the unorganised sector make the workers unable to meet their basic necessities and other social and other cultural responsibilities.
- **Lack of Control and Surveillance** The informal sector remains unmonitored by the government. Further, no official statistics are available representing the true state of the economy, which makes it difficult for the government to make policies regarding the informal sector in particular and whole economy in general.

- **Low-quality Products and less value-addition per Employee** Although the informal sector employs more than 75% of the Indian population, the value-addition per employee is very low. This means that a major portion of our human resource is under-utilized.
- **Gender Disparity** Women are more exposed to informality and are often in more vulnerable situations than their male counterparts

Conclusion

Informal employment although provides badly needed jobs for the poor, but it harms workers' protection, earning predictability and social benefits. Government initiatives like Make in India, Skill India, labour reforms, Insolvency code etc. all have to work in tandem to ensure that this workforce is formalized and the fruits of development accrue equitable to all workers within the country.

Impact of LPG Reforms on Industrial Growth

Q.6 "Industrial growth rate has lagged behind in the overall growth of Gross-Domestic-Product (GDP) in the post-reform period" Give reasons. (150 Words, 10 Marks)

Ans. **Introduction** Barring few years, industrial growth rate remained stagnantly low throughout the years post reform period. The share of industry is around 29.34% of GDP in 2020-21 which is very low when compared to service sector which contributes 53.89% of GDP in 2020-21. The overall value addition, product innovation and technology adoption remain dismal and they exist only on the back of existence of government support.

Reasons for slow Industrial Growth Rate during Post Reform Period

- **Infrastructure Bottlenecks** Physical infrastructure in India suffers from substantial deficit in terms of capacities as well as efficiencies. Rapid growth of the economy has put further stress on infrastructure. Lack of quality industrial infrastructure has resulted in high logistics cost (14% of GDP) and has in turn affected cost competitiveness of Indian goods in global markets.
- **No labour-intensive Manufacturing** Post reforms failure to raise labour-intensive manufacturing in India has also been a reason for India's low industrial growth. In the post reform period, the share of manufacturing in total employment remained virtually stagnant at 11-12%. In 2010, India accounted for 1.4% of the world manufacturing exports against China's share of 15%.
- **Poor Research and Development** Only 0.5% of GDP is spent on research and developmental activities in India which is very low as compared to other emerging economies.
- **Slow Technology Adoption** Inefficient technologies lead to low productivity and higher costs reducing the competitiveness of Indian products in global markets.
- **Lack of focus on Skill Development** During post reforms period there has been very sluggish progress in education and skill levels of workers. Not taking advantage of demographic dividend is one of the failures; young population is an asset only if it is educated, skilled and finds productive employment. Overall, 10% of the workforce in the age group of 15-59 years received some form of vocational training. Vast majority of workers have non- formal vocational training.
- **Restrictive Labour Laws** The rigid labour regulations have been other major region in the slow industrial growth in India. They have acted as a deterrent to employment generation. As per the World Bank, India's labour laws are among the most restrictive in the world. These laws have over riding provisions and facilitate inspector raj of the worst kind.
  - This has also reduced the labour productivity.
- **Inefficient Business Environment** The post reform period was the period of multiple taxes and permit raj. Industries were facing difficulties not only in getting permits but cascading effects of taxes, making business unprofitable and unattractive in India. High compliance costs adversely affect competitiveness of Indian industries.
- **Low Agricultural Growth** Low growth in agriculture has also been one of the reasons for low industrial growth. Agriculture provides not only raw materials but also generates demand for the goods produced by the industrial sector.

- **Poor Performance of the Public Sector** In-spite of attaining a substantial expansion during the planning period, the performance of public sector enterprises remained all along very poor. Large number of PSUs are incurring huge losses, due to faulty pricing policy and mismanagement. The public sector investment failed to generate required surpluses necessary for further investment in industrial sector of the country.
- **Industrial Sickness** In a regime of protection from international competition, industries had tended to get established at sub-optimal capacities, leading to a high-cost industrial structure. Adequate attention was not given to improvements in technology and quality of products. There was no focus on research and development to bring out any kind of innovation in India's industrial space.
- **Governance Failure** Reforms were expected to improve governance at various levels. However, there are new problems in governance–red-tapism, inspector raj, permit raj etc. and persistence of old problems including corruption.
- **Erosion of Competitive Advantage of Indian Exports** Due to substandard quality Indian products were not openly welcomed in the international export market and this has adversely impacted the industrial growth.

Conclusion

Reforms since 1991 have not been comprehensive enough to remove the bias towards capital and skill-intensive industries. The input markets such as land and labour are riddled with distortions. There is a need to enhance the productivity of SMEs and unorganised sector manufacturing. Reforms with their right implementation will fulfill the objectives of India's growth path.

Critical Analysis of Economic Reforms

Q.7 The 1991 economic reforms provided a leap forward and lifted millions out of poverty; however, comprehensive structural reforms remain incomplete resulting in sectoral imbalances and heightened inequalities. Elaborate. Also, highlight the key areas which should be the focus of reform 2.0 (250 Words, 15 Marks)

Ans. **Introduction** The 1991 economic reforms transformed Indian economy by shedding the socialist principles of state's economic intervention and license raj. A World Bank study revealed that poverty declined by 1.36% per annum after 1991.

Though economic growth led to significant development, comprehensive structural reforms remain incomplete and has resulted in sectoral imbalances and increased inequalities.

Impact of Economic Reforms

- **Increased Economic Growth** LPG reforms helped in increasing the rate of economic growth in India. From 1991 to 2020, India's GDP grew at an average rate of 6.7% compared to an average rate of 3.5% in the previous three decades.
- **Higher Foreign Investment** LPG reforms opened up several sectors of the Indian economy to foreign investment leading to an increase in foreign direct investment. According to Ministry of Commerce & Industry, FDI inflows into India increased from $98 million in 1990-91 to $81.72 billion in 2020-21.
- **Improvement in Industrial Productivity** According to a study by the Reserve Bank of India, the productivity of the Indian manufacturing sector increased by 6.8% annually between 1991 and 2006.
- **Expansion of the Service Sector** LPG Reforms led to the growth of the services sector in India, which became a major contributor to the country's GDP. Its contribution to India's GDP increased from 37.2% in 1990-91 to 54.3% in 2020-21.
- **Increase in Consumerism** LPG Reforms led to an increase in consumerism in India as people had access to a wider range of goods and services. According to NSSO, the average monthly per capita expenditure of Indian households increased from Rs. 206 in 1987-88 to Rs. 2,446 in 2017-18.
- **Impact on Exports** India's trade openness increased from a meagre 13 per cent in 1990-91 to 42 per cent in 2020. The exports, driven by the devaluation of the rupee in 1991 and further depreciation in later years, have increased from $17.96 billion in 1990 to $324.43 billion in 2019.
- **Impact on Forex Reserves** There has been a significant improvement in forex reserves, which are now sufficient to cover more than 12 months of imports as per the Economic Survey 2022-23.
- **Impact on Social Indicators** There have also been improvements in literacy rates, gross enrolments ratio and life expectancy, among others. Overall, human development has improved in India.

- **Faster Rate of Poverty Eradication** In the post-reform period, poverty declined faster in the 2000s than in the 1990s Poverty declined by 1.36 percentage points per annum after 1991, compared to that of 0.44 percentage points per annum prior to 1991.
  - Around 415 million people in India climbed out of poverty between 2005-06 and 2019-21, with the incidence of poverty falling from 55 per cent to just over 16 per cent over this period, according to the Global Multi-dimensional Poverty Index 2022.

Economic Reforms resulting in sectoral imbalances and inequalities

Sectoral imbalances are in the form of growth inequities in various sectors. The growth has been concentrated only in some areas in the services sector such as telecommunication, IT, finance, entertainment, travel and hospitality, trade etc., whereas vital sectors such as agriculture and manufacturing industry continue to struggle.

- Post-reforms, economic growth was disproportionately led by service sector. The share of services in GDP has risen from 28% in 1950s, 44% in 1990s to 54% in 2000s.
- Reforms did not lead to sustained growth of the manufacturing sector. After an acceleration in the mid- 1990s, growth slowed in the decade's second half. Contribution of manufacturing sector in GDP has remained almost stagnant.
- The share of agriculture in GDP declined after economic reforms. Data shows that agricultural share in GDP have declined by 7.3% since 1991 reforms.

Further, the evidence shows that inequalities have increased post-economic period as discussed below:

- According to World Inequality Database, the top 1% of India's population held 22% of the country's wealth in 1991 which increased to 42.5% in 2018 while the wealth of bottom 50% of the population decreased from 14% in 1991 to only 3% in 2022.
- Another report, by Council of Social Development, reported six-fold increase in India's wealth inequality between 2000 and 2017.
- The Gini coefficient measured in terms of consumption for rural areas increased from 0.29 in 1993-94 to 0.31 in 2011-12 and from 0.34 to 0.39 in urban areas. The India Human Development survey revealed that the Gini coefficient in income (rural + urban) was 0.52 in 2004-05 and increased to 0.55 in 2011-12.
- Economy witnessed a period of jobless growth: India experienced job growth of 3% per annum in the 70s at a time when India's economy grew at 3-3.5% per annum but over the last 3 decades India's economy grew at over 5-8% per annum but job growth has been close to 1% p.a.

Key areas of Reform 2.0

- **Macro-Economic Reforms** It should include controlling current account deficit, balancing growth and inflation, increasing tax revenues by broadening the tax base, and managing debt by setting up a separate Debt Management Office.
- **Social Sector Reforms** Should focus on reducing wealth and income inequality by raising the minimum wage, reducing gender pay gap, raise female labor force participation rate (FLFPR) and focus on health, education and skilling.
- **Market Reforms** Should include - infrastructure development, factor markets reforms including land, labor and energy reforms, industrial and bureaucratic reforms (PSUs, PSBs), easing regulations toward ease of doing business and encouraging new-generation entrepreneurs and start-ups by creating opportunities.
- **Strong push to manufacturing** India's manufacturing sector has not kept pace with other major economies and is stagnant at around 16% of the GDP. Reforms should focus on improving the competitiveness of domestic manufacturing and promote labor-intensive manufacturing.
- **Agricultural Reforms** Should focus on integration of the agricultural market, rationalization of supply chain, encouraging the formation of cooperatives and boosting agricultural exports.
- **Environment and Climate Change** Should focus on- pursuing mitigation priorities in environment targets (NDCs), designing better disaster management systems, improving legal framework for environment regulation and forest management.
- **Improvement of Infrastructure especially physical and Logistics Infrastructure** which reduces the cost of production and thus, making Indian goods competitive in the international market. Digital transformation is also required as it can drive innovation, increase efficiency and create new business opportunities.

- **Skill Development of Youth Population** focusing on new emerging technologies such as AI, Machine Learning, etc. in the background of Fourth Industrial Revolution.
- **Ease of Doing Business** aimed to attract foreign investment and boosting the overall productivity of an economy.

Conclusion

India's economic reforms led to transformation of Indian economy and lives of millions. With India facing a similar situation of economic crisis during pandemic, it is an opportunity to initiate economic reforms 2.0. Focus of these reforms should be on inclusive growth and reducing inequalities.

Need for a New Industrial Policy

Q.8 It has been argued that the Industrial Policy of 1991 did not achieve the desired results due to multiple reasons. Examine. Also, highlight the need for a new industrial policy especially in the background of Fourth Industrial Revolution. (250 Words, 15 Marks)

Ans. Introduction The Industrial Policy of 1991 marked a significant turning point in India's economic trajectory. In response to a looming balance of payments crisis and the need for structural reforms, the policy introduced a series of measures aimed at liberalizing and opening up the Indian economy but it didn't get the desired results in few sectors. In the advancements of the Fourth Industrial Revolution, there is a pressing need for a new industrial policy that can effectively address the challenges and leverage the opportunities presented by rapid technological advancements.

Reason for not getting desired results under Industrial Policy, 1991

- **Slow Industrial Growth** Despite the liberalization efforts, the industrial growth rate in India remained sluggish following the implementation of the 1991 Industrial Policy.
  - According to the Annual Survey of Industries (ASI), the average annual growth rate of industrial production between 1991 and 2000 was around 6.7%, which was lower than the growth rate of 8.6% between 1981 and 1990.
- **Unequal Distribution of Benefits** The benefits of the Industrial Policy were concentrated in certain sectors and regions, leading to an unequal distribution of growth.
  - The Confederation of Indian Industry (CII) reported that sectors such as software services and telecommunications witnessed significant growth, while traditional industries like textiles and small-scale manufacturing faced challenges and job losses.
- **Jobless Growth** Despite the policy's aim of promoting industrialization and creating employment opportunities, the actual impact on job creation was limited.
  - A report by the National Sample Survey Organization (NSSO) highlighted that employment growth in the organized manufacturing sector declined from 5.8% during 1983-1994 to just 0.8% during 1994-2000.
- **Persistent Informal Sector** The Industrial Policy did not adequately address the issue of the informal sector, which continues to dominate India's economy.
  - According to the National Commission for Enterprises in the Unorganized Sector, the informal sector accounted for about 92% of total employment in 2018, indicating that the policy did not effectively promote formalization.
- **Regional Disparities** The Industrial Policy failed to address regional disparities and promote balanced industrial development across the country.
  - Reports from the Reserve Bank of India (RBI) indicate that industrial growth was concentrated in certain states like Maharashtra, Gujarat, and Tamil Nadu, while other regions, particularly in the eastern and northeastern parts of India, lagged behind.
- **Inadequate Infrastructure** The existing infrastructure remains deficient and is utilized sub-optimally, resulting in high logistics cost, adversely impacting the global competitiveness of Indian industrial exports.
  - According to the World Bank's Logistics Performance Index, India's overall logistics performance ranked 38th out of 139 countries in 2023, indicating the need for substantial improvements in transportation, ports, and logistics infrastructure.
- **Incomplete Reforms** Despite the initial liberalization measures, certain key sectors remained highly regulated, hindering competition and efficiency.

- For instance, the agriculture and retail sectors faced restrictions, preventing the full potential of the Industrial Policy from being realized. The World Bank's Ease of Doing Business Index ranked India 63rd out of 190 economies in 2020, indicating the need for further reforms.

- **Outdated technology** Insufficient public investments in the Research & Development sector continue to pose a serious challenge in acquisition of advanced technology for production.

Need of new industrial policy

- **Jobless Growth in Manufacturing** Increased mechanisation has led to jobless growth in the industrial sector. Employment in the manufacturing sector has fallen from 12.8% to 11.5% over 2012 to 2016. Also, there has been overall stagnancy in the sector, whereas the share of the service sector, that is not a labour-intensive sector, has increased at the expense of the primary sector.
- **Job Creation and Workforce Development** While the Fourth Industrial Revolution presents risks of job displacement due to automation, it also offers potential for new job creation. An effective industrial policy should prioritize re-skilling and upskilling programs to ensure the workforce can adapt to changing skill requirements.
- **Ensure Coordination** There is a need to prevent coordination failures and avoid competing investments as seen in aviation and telecom sectors. This results in price wars affecting firms' profits, investments, and their sustainability.
- **Global Comparison with Like-Economies** While the share of manufacturing in GDP has remained stagnant at 16%, east Asian economies such as China, Malaysia, and Thailand have tripled their share during the same period.
- **Economic Competitiveness and Productivity** The Fourth Industrial Revolution is reshaping global value chains and redefining competitiveness. Countries that establish favorable policies to support the adoption of advanced technologies, encourage research and development and academia can enhance their economic competitiveness.
- **Missing Middle Phenomenon** India either has very large or very small industries. Successive industrial policies did not give due attention to small firms.
- **Adaptation to Technological Disruptions** The Fourth Industrial Revolution is disrupting traditional industries and business models at an unprecedented pace. To remain competitive, countries need a proactive industrial policy that fosters innovation encourages the adoption of emerging technologies, and supports the development of new industries.
- **Addressing Ethical and Societal Challenges** The Fourth Industrial Revolution raises complex ethical and societal issues. Issues such as data privacy, cybersecurity, algorithmic biases, and job displacement require careful consideration and regulation.
- **Sustainability and Environmental Concerns** The Fourth Industrial Revolution offer opportunities to address pressing environmental challenges. Industrial policies can encourage the adoption of green technologies, promote sustainable manufacturing practices, and incentivize clean energy solutions.
- **Negative effects of Open-economy Policies** Reduction in import tariffs and signing of FTAs, inverted duty structures (IDS) have resulted in rise in import of capital, intermediate and consumer goods in India from economies like China.
- **International cooperation and coordination** The Fourth Industrial Revolution is a global phenomenon that transcends national boundaries. To fully leverage its potential, countries need to foster international cooperation and coordination.

Conclusion

India is in an urgent need of a new industrial policy that targets both the formal and informal sectors, with an aim to create "frontier" firms in highly productive sectors, with a potential for employment generation and sustainable industrialisation.

Global Value Chains of Electronics Products

Q.9 Despite having all the essential elements in place, India lags far behind China and Vietnam in the Global Value Chain of Electronic Products. What could be the reason for this? Do you think recent steps undertaken by the government are sufficient to overcome these constraints? Give your opinion. (250 Words, 15 Marks)

Ans. **Introduction** Global value chain (GVC) refers to the people, roles, and activities involved in the production of goods and services and their supply, distribution, and post-sales activities when those activities must be coordinated across geographies.

Nearly 70 percent of GVCs of several electronics products are located in China and in 2020, China's and Vietnam's electronics exports were respectively 70 and 11 times that of India. India is currently a very small participant, with its GVC exports accounting for only about 1.5% of global GVC exports.

Recently (MeitY) has released vision document on 'Electronics Manufacturing' which highlights the sheer scale of opportunity and suggests a policy prescription for India to grow from the current about USD 75 billion in 2020-21 to USD 300 billion by 2025-26.

India is having essential elements in place

- **Strategic Opportunity** The pandemic had led to a colossal shift within the manufacturing and supply chain sector globally and the situation has paved the way for India to potentially become a global manufacturing hub.
- **The country has three key assets to capitalise on this unique opportunity** a significant domestic demand potential, the government's drive to encourage manufacturing, and a distinct demographic edge with a large working-age population.
- These factors will position India well for a larger role in global value chains (GVCs). World Economic Forum (WEF) observed that India can play a significant role in reshaping supply chains and could contribute more than $500 billion annually to the global economy by 2030.

But, in 2018, India accounted for approximately 0.53 percent of the total value created by electronics GVCs substantially lower than China (25.18 percent), Taiwan (9.55 percent), the US (2.01 percent), and Vietnam (2.68 percent). There are many reasons which are given below:

Reasons of India lagging behind in the global value chain of electronics products

- The lower local base for a local component supplier of electronic goods forces the industry to depend on importing material.
- Though under **WTO IT agreement of 1995**, the tariff on import has been made zero but due to customs duty on the product led to high expensive for domestic manufacturers and in turn, they are unable to compete in the global market at cheap price.
- **Limited Indigenous Capability in Upstream Industries** The value addition at the final stages of production is very low, especially in electronics because the more complicated processes, involving greater value addition, occur prior to assembly, in 'upstream' industries.
- The **Foreign Direct Investment (FDI) in electronics is less than 1% of the total FDI inflow** because of onerous labor laws, delays in land acquisition, and the uncertain tax regime that have kept investors at bay.
- **Regulatory and monitoring lacunas** The numerous forms, fees, inspections, and the associated time discourage domestic producers from exporting and keep them out of the international supply chain.
- **Competition from other countries like China, Vietnam, Korea**, Thailand which provide low cost and better products as compared to Indian products.

Steps undertaken by the Government

- **Production Linked Incentive Scheme (PLI) for Large-scale Electronics Manufacturing** The scheme proposes a financial incentive to boost domestic manufacturing and attract large investments in the electronics value chain including electronic components and semiconductor packaging.
- **Scheme for Promotion of Manufacturing of Electronic Components and Semiconductors (SPECS)** Under the scheme, a financial incentive of 25% of capital expenditure has been approved by the Union Cabinet for the manufacturing of goods that constitute the supply chain of an electronic product.
- **Modified Electronics Manufacturing Clusters (EMC2.0) Scheme** Electronic manufacturing clusters are to be set up under the scheme. North east part has been kept in focus. The EMC 2.0 scheme will provide financial assistance up to 50% of the project cost for the setting up of Electronics Manufacturing Cluster projects.

- **Modified Special Incentive Package Scheme (M-SIPS)** The scheme tries to solve the problem of capital requirement by providing a subsidy of 25-30% on the capital investment in the ESDM (Electronic System Design and Manufacturing) industry.
- The government has listed the **electronics industry as a priority sector under its Make in India campaign**.
- The government already have a comprehensive **'National Policy on Electronics 2012** that aims to make India a global hub of electronic system design and manufacturing (ESDM).
- Schemes promoting the semiconductor manufacturing such as Semicon India programme, PLI scheme, Design linked incentive scheme, etc.
- Due to these initiatives, the domestic production of electronic goods has increased substantially from USD 25 billion in 2014-15 to USD 74.7 billion in 2020-21 growing at a Compound Annual Growth Rate (CAGR) of 25%.
- The Electronics sector has become India's fastest-growing export for the 11-month period from April 2022 to February 2023 and crossed the $20 billion mark. (Government's target is to reach exports of $120 billion by 2025-26)
- India's share of global exports has increased to approximately 1.8% in the current year from 1.2% last year. Among states, Karnataka led the electronics exports followed by Uttar Pradesh.

Policy Interventions

To catapult the integration into electronics GVCs, India must 'broaden' as well as 'deepen' its electronics supply chains.

- To **broaden the supply chains**, efforts are already underway to widen the scope of electronics products manufactured in India. For instance, the PLI schemes for large-scale electronics manufacturing and IT hardware incentivize the domestic manufacturing of mobile phones, electronic components, laptops, tablets, all-in-one personal computers and servers.
- Further, the government **intends to deepen the supply chains by building an electronics ecosystem.** The objective is to facilitate the manufacturing of final electronics goods and to enable the domestic viability of components and assemblies manufacturing; distribution, testing, and packaging; and designing activities.

Recommendations of the Vision document

- **Firstly**, the report focuses on a five-part strategy that is based on an "all of the government" approach. The strategy includes:
  - Building competitiveness and scale by attracting global electronics manufacturers/brands;
  - Shifting and developing sub-assemblies and component ecosystems;
  - Building a design ecosystem;
  - Nurturing Indian champions and;
  - Steadily removing cost disabilities faced by India.
- **Secondly**, the report makes a strong recommendation on the need to focus on aggregate domestic value addition in the electronics sector, as India transforms from its current state to one that is gearing to compete with the likes of China and Vietnam.
- **Thirdly**, the report seeks a competitive tariff structure on electronic components and the removal of all regulatory uncertainty.
- **Fourthly**, it recommends a "winner takes all" strategy backed by economies of scale and global competitiveness, new and revised incentive schemes for some sectors and the need to address issues of sustainability and ease of doing business.

Conclusion

Electronics manufacturing is a highly dynamic and rapidly emerging sector. It has the potential to add huge value to economic growth as well as employment generation, the industry has the potential to provide millions of jobs, directly and indirectly. Threats of Artificial Intelligence-based manufacturing are already looming over the world and opportunities presented by China's rising labor cost. By harnessing the opportunities India's electronics sector has the potential to become one of the top exports of the country.

Sectoral Analysis of Industries (Electric Vehicle Industry)

Q.10 India's approach in giving a boost to the electric vehicle industry need to transform from incentive driven approach to an infrastructure driven approach. In this context, identify the enablers and barriers in making india a hub for the production of electric vehicles (EVs). (250 Words, 15 Marks)

Ans. Introduction India has set an ambitious goal to become a leader in the electric vehicle market by 2030 with the government laying out a comprehensive roadmap to achieve this goal, which includes several initiatives and policies to accelerate the adoption of electric vehicles in the country.

Enablers of Electric Vehicle Industry in India

- **Reduced oil imports** EVs contribute to energy diversity by reducing dependence on oil imports. This reduces vulnerability to fluctuations in oil prices and enhances energy security by reducing reliance on fossil fuel imports.
- **Reduced Greenhouse Gas (GHGs) Emissions** In India, transport sector is the second largest contributor to CO2 emissions after the industrial sector and in that road transport accounts for around 90% of the total emissions in the transport sector. Unlike fossil fuel engine vehicles, EVs produce zero tailpipe emissions.
- **Reduced Environment Pollution** Electric vehicles help reduce harmful pollutants such as nitrogen oxides (NOx), particulate matter (PM), and volatile organic compounds (VOCs). This has a direct positive impact on public health, as cleaner air reduces the risk of respiratory and cardiovascular diseases.
- **Sustainable Urban Mobility** Increasing vehicle ownership has led to increased demand for the fossil fuels. Given the large import dependence of the country for petroleum products, it is imperative that there be a shift of focus to alternative fuels to support our mobility in a sustainable manner.
- **Skilled Human Resources** High availability of skilled manpower and technology in manufacturing and IT software.
- **Shared mobility** in India with the coming up of Taxi aggregators such as Ola and Uber increasing exponentially. This has increased a) Vehicle utilisation, which plays to the economic advantages of EVs, and b) Natural and large-scale purchases of EVs.
- **Achieving the climate commitments (net-zero emission target made in CoP26)** coupled with the increasing awareness of the consumers on environmental aspects are likely to enhance the share of electric vehicles in the future demand of automobile sector.
- **Long-Term Cost Savings** Electric vehicles have lower operating costs, as electricity is generally cheaper than gasoline or diesel.

According to NITI Aayog, if India reaches an optimum EV sales penetration by 2030, a saving of 846 million tons of net CO2 emissions and oil savings of 474 MTOE can be achieved. It also provides an opportunity to grow India as a manufacturing hub for EVs (Detroit of EVs), provided policies are supportive.

Challenges facing the electric vehicle industry in India

Infrastructural Challenges

- **Lack of Associated Infrastructural Support** Policy uncertainty is affecting the development of associated infrastructural support for the industry, for example, the charging infrastructure. The lack of clarity over AC versus DC charging stations, grid stability and range anxiety (fear that battery will soon run out of power) are other factors that hinder the growth of EV industry. This comes in the backdrop of already debilitated existing infrastructure like roads, bridges etc.
- **Charging Infrastructure** The market share of EVs increases with increasing availability of charging infrastructure. This is primarily due to the limited driving range of batteries in the EVs. In India, the limited availability of charging infrastructure seems to be a major impediment to increased adoption of EVs.
- **Lack of Standardisation** The lack of standardisation in charging infrastructure and lack of uniformity in regulations across states and union territories is a challenge.
- **Technological Challenges** India is technologically deficient in the production of electronics that form the backbone of EV industry, such as batteries, semiconductors, controllers, etc.

- **Lack of Availability of Materials for Domestic Production** Battery is the single most important component of EVs. India does not have any known reserve of lithium and cobalt which are required for battery production. India is dependent on countries like Japan and China for the import of lithium-ion batteries.
- **Battery Technology** Since the battery is the heart of any EV, development of appropriate battery technologies that can function efficiently in the high temperature conditions in India need to be given utmost importance. The current battery technology still has some limitations, such as limited driving range and long charging time.
- **Power Grid Infrastructure** India's power grid infrastructure is not fully developed and is not capable of handling the high-power demand of EV charging stations.
- **Funding** Assuming a moderate level of adoption, India needs about \$6 billion for charging infrastructure, \$4 billion in incentives and a further \$7 billion to build battery capacity, according to estimates by Goldman Sachs Group Inc.

Other Challenges

- **Lack of Awareness** There is still a lack of awareness about the benefits of EVs among the general public in India.
- **High Initial Cost** Even if the charging issue was adequately addressed, EVs are currently priced nearly double the cost of comparable range diesel/petrol cars. Currently, Indian market share of electric cars is a meagre 0.06% when compared to 2% in China and 39% in Norway.
- **Lack of a stable policy for EV production** Profit determination becomes uncertain considering the high capital costs and the uncertainty in policies related to EV production. This discourages investment in the industry. For example, the launch of Faster Adoption and Manufacturing of (Hybrid) and Electric Vehicles (FAME) framework has been extended repeatedly.
- **Multiple Agencies** Currently, EV makers, have to deal with the Ministry of Heavy Industries and Ministry of Road Transport for guidelines, the Ministry of Power on charging infrastructure, as well as the Ministry of Finance and GST Council over taxation issues.

According to Economic Survey 2018-2019, charging infrastructure is a more important factor for electric vehicle adoption than incentives. The Survey identified that apart from lack of proper charging infrastructure, the time taken to charge electric vehicles is also a major hindrance for EV uptake in India.

Government Initiatives to Promote EV Adoption

- The **Faster Adoption and Manufacturing of Electric Vehicles (FAME) scheme II**, which provides incentives for the purchase of EV and installation of charging infrastructure. These incentives include subsidies, tax rebates, preferential financing, and exemptions from road tax and registration fees.
- The **National Electric Mobility Mission Plan (NEMMP)**, which sets out the target to achieve 6-7 million sales of hybrid and electric vehicles year on year from 2020 onwards by providing fiscal incentives. It aims to have at least 30% of vehicles on Indian roads be electric by 2030.
- The **National Mission on Transformative Mobility and Battery Storage**, which seeks to create a comprehensive ecosystem for the adoption of EVs and support the establishment of giga-scale battery manufacturing plants in India.
- The **Production Linked Incentive (PLI) scheme**, which provides incentives for the manufacturing of electric vehicles and components.
- **The Go Electric campaign** aims to create awareness on the benefits of EVs and EV charging infrastructure.
- India is among a handful of countries that support the **global EV30@30 campaign**, which aims for at least 30% new vehicle sales to be electric by 2030.
- **Tax benefits** The Government has announced plans to provide an additional income tax deduction of INR 1.5 Lakh on the interest paid on loans taken to purchase electric vehicles.
- The Ministry of Power, in its **revised guidelines on charging infrastructure (MoP Guidelines)**, has prescribed that at least one charging station should be present in a grid of 3 km and at every 25 kms on both sides of the highways.
- **Public transport: The Government has also announced plans to promote the use of electric vehicles in the public** transportation sector, by providing financial assistance to states for the purchase of electric buses. .Eg., E-buses in Delhi

Measures to re-invigorate EV industry

- **Private Investment** India needs to encourage private investment in battery manufacturing plants along with an emphasis on the development of low-cost production technology.
  - Reduce the charging time of EVs by developing fast-charging and battery-swapping technologies and standards.
- **Policy Issues** Stabilizing policy environment by working on tax incentives, non-fiscal incentives can address the uncertainty of demand which can, in turn, help the industry to achieve economies of scale (maximum utilization of resources on the conditions of maximum efficiency which will reduce the per unit cost).
- Expand the **EV charging infrastructure by creating a network of public and private charging stations** across the country with adequate quality and accessibility.
- **Rare Earths Elements** Signing of Memorandum of Understanding (MoU) with countries rich in materials like Lithium, rare earth materials etc. to deal with lack of availability of these materials.
- **Promoting co-ordination** Establishing the right coordination among three pillars of EV industry i.e. urban planning, transportation and power sectors will assist in systematic adoption of EVs.
- **Technical Concerns** such as AC versus DC charging stations, handling of peak demand, grid stability, etc. should be addressed promptly.
- **Renewable Energy Sources** should also increase with the increase in EV demand as high dependence on thermal sources would negate the EV's environmental benefits.
- **Financial Concerns** can be addressed by providing a waiver of road tax and registration fees, GST refunds and free parking spaces for EVs.
- Creating a **Phased Manufacturing Program (PMP)** to localize production across the entire electric vehicle value chain

Conclusion

In an attempt to leverage the potential of e-vehicles, the Indian Government needs to provide more incentives and subsidies for the purchase of EVs, invest in charging infrastructure and battery technology, and promote domestic manufacturing capabilities for electric vehicles and their components.

Semiconductor Manufacturing

Q.11 Analyse the reasons for the crisis in semiconductors-"the tiniest yet most exacting product ever manufactured on a global scale". Also, assess the potential and roadblocks of India's Semiconductor Mission in catalysing India's rapidly expanding electronics manufacturing and innovation ecosystem. (250 Words, 15 Marks)

Ans. **Introduction** Recently, Vedanta group and the Foxconn of Taiwan have come together to build the first semiconductor manufacturing unit in Dholera of Gujarat as India currently imports all chips and the market is estimated to touch $100 billion by 2025 from $24 billion now.

The semiconductor industry is not evenly distributed and is dominated by a few countries, mainly U.S., Taiwan, South Korea, Japan, China, and Europe. Companies across the semiconductor value chain operate in different processes and technologies (like design, fabrication, and assembly) in pursuit of economic efficiency. However, no region has achieved strategic autonomy in the industry. The US companies rely on foundries in Taiwan to manufacture the chips.

Reasons for Semiconductor Crisis

The industry is facing a shortage crisis which due to its wide application and has a cascading effect on other industries. The reasons for the crisis in semi-conductor chips:

- **Pandemic led surge in Sales** The lockdown led to an unprecedented sale in electronics like phones, tablets, laptops due to various requirements of work, education and entertainment. But the chips take a long time to manufacture therefore resulted in supply crunch.
- **Russia-Ukraine Conflict** Russia Ukraine conflict disturbed the exports of essential commodities for chip making. Russia is a supplier of rare materials like palladium while Ukraine provides rare gases to make semiconductors.
- **Stockpiling** Many smartphone makers like Huawei started stockpiling chips during early warning periods of an expected supply crunch.

- **High Lead Time for Production** Manufacturing advanced logic chips requires extraordinary precision, along with huge long-term bets in a field subject to rapid change. Plants cost billions of dollars to build and equip, and they have to run flat-out 24x7 to recoup the investment.
- **Shift to 5G Technology** Semiconductor companies have been gearing up to ramp up capacity for manufacturing advanced chips required by 5G Technology. They were already cutting down on the production of older chip systems. The pandemic and supply chain disruption exacerbated this shortage.
- **Complex Manufacturing Systems** Each segment of semiconductor manufacturing involves roughly 25 countries in the direct supply chain, and 23 countries in allied functions, according to a joint study by Global Semiconductor Alliance and Accenture. Due to this, the industry was unable to produce sufficient chips when the pandemic hit the world.

Potential for India

India is now the world's biggest smartphone manufacturer after China. And in its next step to make the country a global hub for electronics production, the government has approved a $10 billion incentive package to semiconductor and display manufacturers. The global crisis can help India if it takes the lead as India can emerge as the global hub as:

- **Huge Market** The demand for semiconductors is growing astronomically globally and India's semiconductor component market will rise manifold and reach a total revenue worth $300 billion during 2021-2026. Therefore, investing in it will catalyse electronics and innovation sector,
- **Local Sourcing** Currently, only 9% of India's semiconductor requirement is met locally. The share of local sourcing is expected to grow to over 17% by 2026. This will mean a six-fold rise in potential locally-sourced semiconductor revenues.
- **Human Resources** India has exceptional semiconductor design talent pool, accounting for up to 20% of the world's semiconductor design engineers.
- **Increase in Manufacturing** Semiconductors are the heart and brain of all modern electronics and ICT products and is the lifeblood of the modern information age. They play an integral role in automobiles, essential medical devices (like ECG machines) and household gadgets like refrigerators. Therefore, investment in semiconductors would increase manufacturing.
- **Supporting Innovation** It is said that before the end of this decade, there will be nothing that will not be touched by electronics. Be it fighting carbon emissions, renewable energy, food safety or healthcare, the semiconductor chip will be all-pervasive. Thus, investment will foster innovation too.
- **Leader in Industry 4.0** India is taking initiatives to emerge as a leader of fourth industrial revolution by investment in emerging technologies such as Artificial Intelligence, Internet of Things (IoT), 5G or the automotive sector.
- **Diversification of Supply Chain** The current decade presents a unique opportunity to India. Companies are looking to diversify their supply chain and for alternatives to their bases in China.

India's Semi-conductor Mission (ISM)

- The vision of ISM is to build a vibrant semiconductor and display design and innovation ecosystem to enable India's emergence as a global hub for electronics manufacturing and design.
- It will formulate a comprehensive long-term strategy for developing semiconductors & display manufacturing facilities and semiconductor design ecosystem in the country in consultation with Government ministries/departments/agencies, industry, and academia.
- It will facilitate the adoption of trusted electronics through secure semiconductors and display supply chain, including raw materials, specialty chemicals, gases, and manufacturing equipment.
- It will enable a multi-fold growth of Indian semiconductor design industry by providing requisite support in the form of Electronic Design Automation (EDA) tools, foundry services and other suitable mechanisms for early-stage startups.
- It will also promote and facilitate indigenous Intellectual Property (IP) generation and encourage, enable and incentivize Transfer of Technologies (ToT).
- ISM will also enable collaborations and partnership programs with national and international agencies, industries and institutions for catalyzing collaborative research, commercialization and skill development.

Government Efforts

- **Semicon India programme** It provides \$10 bn fiscal support and other non-fiscal measures. The Semicon India Program aims to provide attractive incentive support to companies/consortia that are engaged in Silicon Semiconductor Fabs, Display Fabs, Compound Semiconductors / Silicon Photonics / Sensors (including MEMS) Fabs, Semiconductor Packaging (ATMP / OSAT) and Semiconductor Design.
- **Production-linked Incentive Scheme (PLI)scheme** Under the scheme, the Centre will offer financial support to companies that want to manufacture a range of semiconductor goods in India.
- India has also launched the Scheme for **Promotion of Manufacturing of Electronic Components and Semiconductors (SPECS) for** manufacturing of electronics components and semiconductors.
- In **2021, the MeitY also launched the Design Linked Incentive (DLI) Scheme** to nurture at least 20 domestic companies involved in semiconductor design and facilitate them to achieve a turnover of more than Rs.1500 Crore in the next 5 years.

Roadblocks in the India's Semi-conductor Industry

- **Huge Investment Required** Semiconductors and display manufacturing is a very complex and technology-intensive sector involving huge capital investments, high risk, long gestation and payback periods, and rapid changes in technology, which require significant and sustained investments.
- **Resource Inefficient Sector** Chip fabs are also very thirsty units requiring millions of litres of clean water, an extremely stable power supply, a lot of land and a highly skilled workforce.
- **Logistics Issue** Inadequate logistics and absence of proper waste disposal have further exacerbated the poor state of its production.
- **Inadequate Support from Government** The level of fiscal support currently envisioned is very less when the scale of investment required is considered.
- **Insufficient Grants under PLI Scheme** The financial support given by the government under PLI scheme is not sufficient to increase semiconductor manufacturing.
- **Lack of Fab Capacities** Although India has two fabs — SITAR, a unit of the Defence Research and Development Organisation (DRDO) in Bengaluru and a semiconductor laboratory in Chandigarh. These build silicon chips for strategic purposes like defence and space and not for commercial use.
- **Russia-Ukraine conflict** The Russia-Ukraine conflict and its implications for raw material supplies for the semiconductor value chain has also poised chipmakers to invest in strengthening the semicon supply chain.

Conclusion

India has the potential to cater to the global demand of semi-conductors but that would require improving the existing capabilities. It is also required for the industry and the government to work together. The Indian government has taken an important step in this direction and has approved a "Semicon India" programme for the development of the semiconductor industry.

Pharmaceutical Sector

Q.12 India's pharmaceutical industry, renowned as the largest manufacturer of generic medicines globally, is facing significant challenges related to product quality and drug safety among many others. Examine. What measures should be taken by the government to address these challenges? (150 Words, 10 Marks)

Ans. Introduction India is the largest manufacturer of generic medicines globally. It supplies over 50% of global demand for various vaccines, 40% of generic demand in the US and 25% of all medicine in the UK. The Indian pharmaceutical market is estimated at USD 40 billion and pharma companies export another USD 20 billion.

Its pharmaceutical industry plays a crucial role in global healthcare, providing affordable generic medicines that impact the lives of the global poor. But, recent incidents of contaminated medicines and substandard drugs have raised concerns about the regulatory framework and the industry's commitment to ensuring high-quality pharmaceutical products.

Recent incidents highlighting quality control failures

- **Anaesthetic Drugs** Latest of the reports is the deaths of two patients in Sri Lanka who were administered Indian-made anaesthetic drugs.
- **Eye Drops** Recently, eye drops manufactured in India had caused eye infection in about 30 patients and blindness in 10 in Sri Lanka.
  - While anaesthetic drugs made in India causing deaths are a first in the recent past, eye drops causing infections, blindness and even deaths were reported a few months ago in the United States, with the Atlanta-based Centers for Disease Control and Prevention (CDC) finding a highly drug-resistant bacteria in them.
- **Cough Syrups**
  - The series of adverse reports against drugs produced in India began last year when the World Health Organization (WHO) linked the deaths of at least 70 children in Gambia from acute kidney injury to cough syrups.
  - The culprit ingredient in the syrups was diethylene glycol and ethylene glycol — deadly chemicals used as a cheaper substitute for propylene glycol — that should never have been found in any medicine.
  - Soon after the deaths in Gambia, cough syrups made in India and containing the two deadly chemicals killed 18 children in Uzbekistan in December 2022.
  - Indian-made cough syrup was again in the news when WHO flagged the contaminated drugs found in the Marshall Islands and Micronesia; the contamination was identified by the Australian regulator.

Challenges of India's Pharmaceutical Sector

- **Safety of Drugs** Except for some customary inspections, the Indian drug regulator has so far failed to institute measures to make sure drugs produced in India for export and domestic use are safe.
- **Failing the Quality Tests** According to a Central Drugs Standard Control Organization (CDSCO) survey in 2014-2016, about five per cent of Indian drugs, several of them manufactured by large pharma companies, failed the quality test.
  - The country's pharma industry has largely been in denial over quality-related concerns expressed by national and international observers.
- **Quality Compliance Inquiry** India has undergone the highest number of Food and Drug Administration (FDA) inspections since 2009; therefore, continuous investment for upgrading quality standards will distract the capital away from other areas of development and growth is reduced.
- **Lack of Stable Pricing and Policy Environment** The challenge created by unexpected and frequent domestic pricing policy changes in India. It has created a vague environment for investments and innovations.
- **Violation of IPR Rules** Indian pharmaceutical companies have faced allegations of violating Intellectual Property Rights (IPR) laws, resulting in legal disputes with multinational pharmaceutical companies.
  - One such case involved Swiss pharmaceutical company Roche and Indian drug manufacturer Cipla in 2014.
- **Unethical practices by the pharma companies** by providing freebies and gifts to doctors to promote their drugs.
- **Import of Active Pharmaceutical ingredients (APIs) from China** The import of bulk drugs or APIs and drug intermediates (materials produced during API synthesis) from China was over 66 per cent of India's total imports of medical products.
  - India's import dependence on China remains alarmingly high - as much as 90-100 per cent for some critical raw materials that go into manufacturing high-selling drugs such as paracetamol, penicillin, ibuprofen and vitamin B12, among others.
- **High costs of Production** The cost of production in India is 50 percent less than in developed nations, but it is still around 18 percent higher than China. This is attributable to raw materials being 25-30 percent costlier, electricity being 20 percent more expensive, and other costs such as financing, logistics, transportation, etc., being 30 percent more expensive.
- **Low public Expenditure on R&D** which is less than 1% of GDP lower than China and even Brazil.
- **Fragmented Regulation** Lack of coordination between central and state drug control organisations.
- **Regulatory Lacunae** Many states have an inadequate number of drug inspectors–sometimes even as high as 53% vacancies like in Karnataka. The CDSCO itself suffers from insufficient personnel with 22% vacancies.

Measures to be taken by the Government

- **Legislative Changes and Centralised Database:**
  - Drugs and Cosmetics Act (1940) needs to be amended and the establishment of a centralised drugs database can enhance surveillance and ensure effective regulation across all manufacturers.
  - India has 36 regional drug regulators; consolidating them into a single entity can reduce the risk of regulatory capture and influence networks.
  - Also, implementing common quality standards across all states is necessary to ensure consistent product quality.
- **Encouraging Certification:**
- Encouraging more pharmaceutical manufacturing units to obtain WHO's Good Manufacturing Practice certification can elevate industry-wide quality standards.
- **Transparency, Credibility, and Accountability:**
  - The regulator and the industry must collaborate to enhance India's drug regulatory regime, making it transparent, credible, and aligned with global standards.
  - Public disclosure of drug application reviews and inspection records, violation history can ensure accountability.
  - The cancellation of manufacturing licences for 18 pharma companies by the Drugs Controller General of India (DGCI) is a positive step. However, more comprehensive measures are required to address the root causes of quality issues.
- **Focus on Sustainable Manufacturing Practices:**
  - Emphasising sustainable manufacturing practices, including green chemistry, waste reduction, and energy efficiency, can enhance the sector's environmental sustainability while reducing costs.
  - Adopting environmentally friendly practices can also contribute to a positive brand image and attract environmentally conscious consumers.
- **R&D boost** India will need to make exponential investments in R&D, manufacturing and digital transformations to become a global pharmaceutical innovation hub. The government needs to urgently explore mechanisms to incentivize investment in R&D and evaluate various funding mechanisms that can help co-research.
- **Focus on API** This is also an opportunity to bring a much larger proportion of manufacturing of APIs back into India, so that the country is not dependent on imports of critical inputs.

Conclusion

India can continue to be the pharmacy of the global south only if the regulator begins to behave like a watchdog to ensure drug safety, and not as a facilitator for the pharma industry.

Renewed efforts are being made by the government to strengthen regulatory mechanisms for drug manufacturers. Recently, the government said it had prepared an action plan for nationwide inspection of manufacturing units which are identified to be at the risk of manufacturing Not of Standard Quality (NSQ)/adulterated/spurious drugs.

Textile Sector

Q.13 Textile sector is the 2nd largest job creator in India, yet this labor-intensive sector faces a number of constraints to be competitive at the global level. Examine along while highlighting the significance of National Technical Textiles Mission. (150 Words, 10 Marks)

Ans. **Introduction** India's textile industry contributes about 14 per cent to industrial production; 4 per cent to the country's gross domestic product (GDP); 17 per cent to its export earnings; and is a source of direct employment for over 51 million people and indirectly 61 million people, which makes it the second-largest provider of employment after agriculture. Recently, it has lost ground to Bangladesh and Vietnam in the global market as the preferred supplier for readymade garments.

Constraints faced by textile sector at the global level

- **Outdated Technology** The Indian textile industry has its limitations of access to the latest technology (especially in small-scale industries) and failures to meet global standards in the highly competitive market.
  - In terms of technology adoption in the weaving sector, India has only a 2% share in global shuttle-less looms installed capacity. Bangladesh has envisioned the year 2041 for technological advancement, especially in ICT.
- **Lack of Scale** While India's spinning capacity is of a global scale, the same cannot be said about weaving and apparel making. In fact, apparel units in the country have an average size of 100 machines as compared to Bangladesh which has on an average of at least 500 machines per factory.
- **Highly Fragmented** Indian textile industry is highly fragmented and is being dominated by the unorganized sector and small and medium industries along with a bias towards cotton. Approximately 95% of the weaving sector in India is unorganized in nature.
- **Lack of Economies of Scale** Economic Survey 2015-16 observed the mushrooming for 1 person apparel establishments.
- **Stagnant Exports due to less Diversification** The export from the sector has been stagnating and remained at the $40-billion level for the last six years.
- **Supply chain bottleneck** An Indian manufacturer takes 90-120 days to ship an order of 20,000-30,000 pieces while in Bangladesh and Vietnam, where the supply chain is more clustered, it takes 14-21 days.
- **Lack of efficiency due to Manual Work** Unlike in developed countries, textile factories in India are not fully automated and remain labor-intensive. It has led to lower efficiency and thus output overall does not meet the required demand and the overall cost of production remains compared to other countries.
- **Lack of Trade Agreements** The Indian textile Sector is losing to competition because of the lack of FTAs (Free Trade Agreements) with the EU and the USA, which, otherwise, levy 12- 14 per cent import duty on imports from India. It will help Indian players counter Bangladesh, Vietnam which, as a 'least developed nation', gets duty-free access along with FTAs.
- **Lack of Foreign Investment** Despite allowing 100 percent FDI in textiles sector through automatic route it has not been able to attract the foreign investment it requires because of the aforementioned challenges. Though the sector has witnessed a spurt in investment during the last five years, yet the industry (including dyed and printed) attracted Foreign Direct Investment (FDI) of only US$ 3.75 billion from April 2000 to March 2021.
- **Uneven Regional Development** The country's textile industry is concentrated in a few pockets of Gujarat and Maharashtra in the west and Tamil Nadu and Karnataka in the south. A large proportion of workers employed by these units comes from Bihar, Uttar Pradesh, and West Bengal.
- **Pressure to meet stringent social and environmental norms** Failing to comply with environmental regulations can put supply chain in jeopardy, as pressure mounts for the apparel industry to improve environmental compliance efforts.

National Technical Textiles Mission

Technical textiles are textiles materials and products manufactured primarily for technical performance and functional properties rather than aesthetic characteristics.

- **Research, Innovation and Development** The mission will focus on promoting both fundamental research at fibre level and application-based research in geo-textiles, agro-textiles, medical textiles etc.
- **Promotion and Market Development** The penetration level of technical textiles is low in India varying between 5-10% against the level of 30-70% in developed countries. The mission aims at an average growth rate of 15-20% per annum through market development, market promotion, international technical collaborations, investment promotions and 'Make in India' initiatives.
- **Export Promotion** It aims at export promotion of technical textiles enhancing. An Export Promotion Council for Technical Textiles will be set up for effective coordination and promotion activities in the segment.
- **Education, Training, Skill Development** The Mission will promote technical education at higher levels. Skill development will be promoted and adequate pool of highly skilled manpower resources will be created.

- **Inclusive Growth** The Mission will focus on usage of technical textiles in various flagship programmes including strategic sectors. The use of technical textiles in agriculture, dairy and in programmes like Jal Jeevan Mission, Swachh Bharat Mission and Ayushman Bharat will bring an overall improvement in economy, better agricultural productivity and higher income to farmers.
- **Infrastructure** The use of geo-textiles in highways, railways and ports will result in robust infrastructure, reduced maintenance cost and higher life cycle of the infrastructure assets.
- **Waste Disposal** It will also develop suitable equipment for environmentally sustainable disposal of used technical textiles, with emphasis on safe disposal of medical and hygiene wastes.
- **Indigenous Manufacturing** There is another important component in the research activity aiming at development of indigenous machineries and process equipment for technical textiles, in order to promote 'Make in India' and enable competitiveness of the industry by way of reduced capital costs.

Futuristic Measures

- **Technology Upgradation and Expanding Weaving Capacity** To ensure rapid transformation of the textile sector in India, there is a dire need of technology upgradation.
- **Reskilling and Upskilling** Reskilling and upskilling of the labour force should also be a priority for India to stay aloft in the market. Workforce should be trained in order to meet modern requirements this move will also make workers less resistant to accepting technology.
- **Signing Trade Agreements** Bangladesh and Vietnam enjoy the benefit of zero duty, FTAs and PTAs. India also needs to find a favorable FTAs with countries like Australia, EU, Canada and USA which will help improve our exports in these countries.
- **Promotion of Domestic Brands** There is a need for the promotion of Indian brands instead of selling products of international brands in the Indian market.
- **Capital Subsidy** The weaving sector is getting a subsidy at 10% subject to a cap of 20 crores under ATUFS, whereas for garments and technical textiles, subsidy is provided at 15% subject to a cap of 30 crores. The Government of India may consider providing some enhanced subsidy under ATUFS, for select players, purely on an outcome basis.
- **Meeting World's Demand** There is huge demand for fabric, man-made textile and technical textile and thus, we need to explore and try to boost exports in every way.
- **Research and Development** Research and development are one of the most important components of growth in any industry. Government funds for this purpose can produce wonders if used properly.

Government Measures

- **Production Linked Incentive (PLI) Scheme for Textile Sector** Government approved PLI Scheme for Textiles products, namely MMF Apparel, MMF Fabrics and Products of Technical Textiles, for enhancing India's manufacturing capabilities and enhancing exports.
- **PM MITRA Park Scheme** The seven Mega Integrated Textile Region and Apparel (PM MITRA) parks will be set up at Greenfield or Brownfield sites located in different states. It is in line with the vision of 'Atma Nirbhar Bharat' and to position India strongly on the Global textiles map.
- **National Technical Textile Mission** It aims to position the country as a global leader in technical textiles and increase the use of technical textiles in the domestic market. It aims to take the domestic market size from USD 40 billion to USD 50 billion by 2024.
- **Scheme for Integrated Textile Parks (SITP)** To assist small and medium entrepreneurs in the textile industry to cluster investments in textile parks by providing financial support for world-class infrastructure in the parks. 59 textile parks were sanctioned under it, out of which, 22 have been completed.
- Amended Technology Upgradation Fund Scheme (ATUFS) In 2015, the government approved the "Amended Technology Upgradation Fund Scheme (ATUFS)" for technology upgradation of the textiles industry.
- **SAMARTH (Scheme for Capacity Building in Textile Sector)** To address the shortage of skilled workers, the government launched the Scheme for Capacity Building in Textile Sector (SCBTS) and named it SAMARTH Scheme.

- **Silk Samagra Scheme** It focuses on improving the quality and productivity of domestic silk thereby reducing the country's dependence on imported silk.
- **Power-Tax India** It comprises new research and development in power loom textiles, new markets, branding, subsidies and welfare schemes for the workers.
- The New Textiles Policy 2020 for overall development of the sector was released by the Ministry of Textiles.
- Government has allowed **100% FDI in the sector** under the automatic route.

Conclusion

In order to make a giant leap in exports and domestic sales, the industry has to also be price competitive right from the raw material stage and gear up to meet the sustainability and traceability demands of international buyers. India can take a cue from countries such as Turkey where integrated textile parks are highly efficient.

IT Sector

Q.14 What were the factors that helped India to become a major player in the Information Technology (IT) sector at the global level? Assess the strengths of this sector and challenges confronting it. (150 Words, 10 Marks)

Ans. **Introduction** Information technology became one of the premier segments of the services sector of Indian economy from the 1990s. It not only helped to generate millions of jobs but was able to garner a sizeable share of global exports and place India on the global map for its tech prowess.

India's strength in IT and ITeS sector

- India's performance in the IT and IT-enabled services has grown from strength to strength over the years. According to a NASSCOM, the industry's apex body, the software services and products sector generated US$105 billion revenue over a decade from 2009 to 2019, created 2 million jobs and added 10,000 companies including start-ups.
- In addition to being one of the largest job provider and creator in the organized industry segment, this sector also plays a key role in enabling higher levels of indirect employment in other verticals such as transportation, real estate and hospitality, security services, and housekeeping.
- A notable feature is that the IT/ITeS workforce is becoming increasingly diverse in terms of socio-economic, linguistic, multinational and regional backgrounds.
- Out of total of 3.968 million employees in the sector in 2017-18, women employees constituted 34 per cent which is significant.

India's strategic advantages that helped to become a major player

India had several strategic advantages which helped her to secure a premier position in the global IT industry. The following factors helped India to forge ahead in the sector.

- **Early entrant** India was an early entrant in this domain and has continued to maintain its first mover advantage and retained its leadership position in the global sourcing arena with a share of 55 per cent.
- **Skills and Start-ups** India developed and honed the IT skills and formed many start-ups, which with their technical expertise, innovative, and entrepreneurial capabilities have captured much of the overseas business. These companies steadily grew into large enterprises and earned global fame for their impeccable performance and excellence in service delivery.
- **Proficiency in English** India's skilled, English-speaking technical personnel, and relatively low-cost operations, helped to attract much of the outsourced business from abroad.
- **Technology competence** India also showed prowess in technology development and innovation as a result of which some of the major MNCs set up not only their offices in India, but even R&D centres in Bengaluru, Hyderabad, etc,

- **Telecom Expansion** The opening up of the telecom sector, following reforms of 1990s, led to phenomenal expansion of the telecom facilities. The introduction of broadband and rapid growth in mobile services gave fillip to the IT sector. This also coincided with the rapid development of the software industry, IT-based automation in various industries, development of supercomputer technology, etc.
- **Sourcing Destination** India was the leading sourcing destination across the world, accounting for approximately 55 per cent market share of the US$ 185 190 billion global services sourcing business in 2017-18. Indian IT & ITeS companies have set up over 1,000 global delivery centres in about 80 countries across the world.
- **Potential Market** India also remains a high potential market worldwide, offering multiple opportunities. With the world's second largest population, 1189 million mobile subscribers, 494 million Internet users, a US$ 38.5 billion e-Commerce market, India offers a large, burgeoning end-user market which will further propel the IT industry.
- **Digital India Scheme** The Digital India programme launched by the government, which is designed to transform India into a knowledge-based economy and a digitally empowered society, will give further boost to this sector. The National Optical Fibre Network (NOFN) under BharatNet is envisaged as an information super-highway which will provide broadband connectivity and digital access to 2.5 lakh Gram Panchayats. Over 3 lakh km. optical fibre cable has been laid by 2019-20 connecting 1.21 lakh Gram Panchayats.

Challenges faced by IT sector

- **Offshoring issue** The transfer of work and jobs to India and other countries, causing loss of job opportunities to the citizens in the US and Europe has been a major issue. The major threat is from the US which provides sizeable chunk of the outsourced business to Indian IT companies. Consequently, many of the major Indian IT firms have set up offices in the US and Europe to undertake the jobs onshore and, to the extent possible, employing locals.
- **Competition** India is also facing competition from other emerging countries like China, Philippines, Vietnam, countries of the Commonwealth of Independent States (CIS), South Korea, etc. who are also trying to grab the global IT business. Many of those countries which were not proficient in English have taken steps to overcome this deficiency. India would have to plan strategies for retaining competitive advantage in Terms of pricing, skills, and efficiency in service delivery.
- **Insourcing** After nearly two decades of outsourcing back-office operations and software projects to Indian IT firms, some of the transnational companies have been shifting the work – software development, programming, maintenance, etc. – back to their own offices to get the jobs done in-house. This will mean more productive use of their personnel.
- **Global Slowdown** Amidst the current global economic slowdown, hiring companies are also forced to cut their IT spending. The increasing competition among IT companies will put pressure on prices and margins. This is bound to impact the profit margins of Indian IT companies. Automation and digitisation in IT sector could help to bring down operating costs.

Outlook for future

- **Dispersal of IT units** Until recently, India's IT industry was mostly concentrated in the large Metros, viz. Bengaluru, Hyderabad, Chennai, New Delhi, and Mumbai which are almost saturated.
  - As these cities are bursting at the seams, with consequent problems of land availability, overcrowding, transportation bottlenecks, housing shortages, and rising costs both for the employers and employees, the IT companies have been moving towards Tier-II and Tier-III cities and towns which could mitigate some of these problems.
  - This is a healthy trend as it will provide greater opportunities to potential job seekers in the smaller towns and help upgrade their skills. It will also give fillip to development of these towns and their hinterland areas supported by the Digital India programme.
- **Digital transformation** A key trend witnessed now is the prominence of digital technologies and systems. There is continued focus on digital revenues, which is growing at a steady pace. Indian enterprises have spent over US$ 2 billion domestically to accelerate digital transformation.

- **Skills Programme** Investment in digital skills continues to rise with organisations building their capabilities and aligning business models to digital practices.
  - Nasscom has launched a Future Skills platform that seeks to initially upskill 40 lakh IT employees and prospective job seekers in eight emerging technologies that could drive IT jobs in the future.
  - These technologies include Artificial Intelligence (AI), virtual reality, robotics, process automation, Internet of Things (IoT), big data analytics, 3D printing, cloud computing. Nasscom has also identified 55 job roles that are going to be in high demand globally.
  - Nasscom and Ministry of Electronics & IT will work together to enable "skill development and continuous learning" not only for IT employees but also for those in the other sectors.

Conclusion

The IT industry remains a key catalyst for the country's overall growth, with increasing focus on the digital transformation of businesses and expansion of digital-driven services to enterprises the world over.

To keep pace with the advances in technology, the industry is embracing disruptive technologies such as artificial intelligence (AI), machine learning (ML), cloud computing and big data analytics leading to substantial increase in digital revenue.

Vehicle Scrappage Policy

Q.15 How does India's vehicle scrappage policy aims to achieve its twin objectives of boosting automobile industry and reducing environmental emissions? Highlight the concerns associated in the implementation of policy. (250 Words, 15 Marks)

Ans. **Introduction** The vehicle scrappage policy is a government-funded programme to replace old vehicles from Indian roads. The policy is expected to reduce pollution, create job opportunities and boost demand for new vehicles. Several countries including the US, Germany, Canada and China have introduced vehicle scrappage policies to boost their respective automotive industries and check vehicular pollution.

For instance, the US has implemented the Car Allowance Rebate System (CARS), also called Cash for Clunkers programme, which offers credit incentives on scrapping older vehicles and replacing them with new and more fuel-efficient vehicles.

About India's Vehicle Scrappage Policy

- **Aim** The Vehicle Scrapping Policy is aimed at creating an eco-system for phasing out unfit and polluting vehicles in an environment friendly and safe manner.
- **Infrastructure** The policy intends to create scrapping infrastructure in the form of Automated Testing Stations and Registered Vehicle Scrapping Facilities across the country.
- **Fitness Test** Old vehicles will have to pass a fitness test before re-registration and as per the policy government commercial vehicles more than 15 years old and private vehicles which are over 20 years old will be scrapped.
  - Old and unfit vehicles whose life cycle is complete shall be scrapped. This will be a voluntary process but defined by rules.
- **Road Tax Rebate** The state governments may be advised to offer a road-tax rebate of up to 25% for personal vehicles and up to 15% for commercial vehicles to provide incentive to owners of old vehicles to scrap old and unfit vehicles.

- **Vehicle Discount** Vehicle manufacturers will also give a discount of 5% to people who will produce the 'Scrapping Certificate' and registration fees will be waived off on the purchase of a new vehicle.
- **Coverage** The policy would cover an estimated 51 lakh light motor vehicles (LMVs) that are above 20 years of age and another 34 lakh LMVs above 15 years of age.

Boosting Automobile Industry

- **Stimulating Demand** The policy provides incentives such as tax rebates and discounts on new vehicle purchases, which stimulate demand for automobiles. This leads to increased sales and production in the automobile sector.
  - More than 51 lakh light motor vehicles (private and commercial) are more than 20 years old.
- **Market Expansion** The scrappage policy encourages vehicle owners to replace their old vehicles, expanding the potential market for automobile manufacturers. This provides an opportunity for manufacturers to introduce new models and attract a broader customer base.
  - Vehicle Manufacturers are advised to provide a 5% discount on the purchase of a new vehicle against the scrapping certificate.
  - State governments were advised to offer a road tax rebate of up to 25% for personal vehicles and up to 15% for commercial vehicles.
- **Job Creation** The increased demand for vehicles resulting from the scrappage policy leads to higher production levels, which, in turn, creates job opportunities in the automobile manufacturing sector and related industries.
  - In the new fitness centers, 35 thousand people will get employment and an investment of Rs 10,000 crores will be pumped in.

- **Economic Growth** The growth of the automobile industry, fueled by the scrappage policy, has positive implications for economic growth. It contributes to the country's Gross Domestic Product (GDP), attracts investments, and generates revenue for both the government and industry players.
- Policy boosts sales of heavy and medium commercial vehicles. The government treasury is expected to get around Rs 30,000 to 40,000 crores of money through Goods and Services Tax (GST) from this policy.
- **Fleet Modernization** By encouraging the scrapping of old vehicles, the policy promotes the replacement of outdated and less fuel-efficient vehicles with newer models. This drives the demand for newer vehicles, thereby boosting the automobile industry.
- **Technology Adoption** The scrappage policy incentivizes the purchase of new vehicles equipped with advanced technologies, such as electric and hybrid vehicles. This fosters technological innovation and investment in the automobile industry.
- **Supply Chain Development** The growth in automobile production due to the policy drives the development of a robust supply chain, including component manufacturers, spare parts suppliers, and logistics providers. This strengthens the overall automotive ecosystem in the country.

Reducing Environmental Emissions

- **Removal of Old and Polluting Vehicles** The policy encourages the scrapping of old vehicles, particularly those that do not comply with current emission norms. By removing these vehicles from the road, the policy helps reduce the overall emissions of pollutants such as particulate matter (PM), nitrogen oxides (NOx), and hydrocarbons.
  - Older vehicles pollute the environment 10 to 12 times more, and estimated that 17 lakh medium and heavy commercial vehicles are more than 15 years old.
- **Promotion of Fuel-Efficient Vehicles** The policy incentivizes the replacement of old vehicles with new, more fuel-efficient models. Modern vehicles equipped with advanced emission control technologies produce fewer emissions per kilometer traveled, contributing to a reduction in environmental pollution.
- **Adoption of Electric Vehicles (EVs)** The scrappage policy provides additional incentives for the purchase of electric vehicles. EVs produce zero tailpipe emissions, leading to a significant reduction in air pollution and greenhouse gas emissions.
- **Improved Air Quality** By removing older vehicles with higher emission levels, the policy helps improve air quality, particularly in densely populated areas and cities where vehicular pollution is a significant contributor to pollution-related health issues.
- **Enhanced Emission Standards** The policy aims to promote the adoption of vehicles that adhere to the latest emission standards. This encourages automobile manufacturers to produce vehicles with lower emissions and invest in research and development of cleaner technologies.
  - A green cess of 10 to 15% over and above the road tax shall be applicable for such older vehicles.
- **Encouraging Vehicle Manufacturers to Adopt Sustainable Practices** The scrappage policy incentivizes vehicle manufacturers to adopt sustainable practices, including eco-friendly manufacturing processes and the development of greener vehicles. This contributes to a reduced carbon footprint across the entire vehicle lifecycle.
- **Reduction of Greenhouse Gas Emissions** The replacement of old vehicles with newer, more fuel-efficient models helps reduce greenhouse gas emissions, particularly carbon dioxide (CO_2), which is a major contributor to climate change.
- **Support for Green Technologies** The policy provides financial incentives and support for the development and adoption of green technologies in the automotive sector. This includes promoting hybrid vehicles, hydrogen fuel cells, and other alternative fuel options that offer lower emissions and contribute to a greener transportation ecosystem.

Challenges in the successful implementation of policy

- **Entire onus on State Governments** The proposed policy puts the entire onus of incentivizing fleet renewal on the state governments. They have been advised to waive off a big chunk of road tax and registration fees on replacement vehicles.
- **Infrastructure** Due to the lack of a supporting infrastructure, implementation of the scrappage policy will be challenging. Currently, India has just seven automated fitness test centres and two authorised scrappage centres, which is inadequate to cater to the market.
- **Cost and Economic Impact** One of the primary concerns is the financial burden it places on vehicle owners. This can be expensive, especially for low-income individuals. It can also have broader economic implications, such as impacting the automotive industry and potentially leading to job losses.

- **Equity and Social Impact** Scrappage policies can exacerbate existing social and economic inequalities. Low-income individuals who cannot afford to replace their vehicles may be disproportionately affected, as they rely heavily on older, less fuel-efficient vehicles.
- **Environmental Impact** While scrappage policies aim to reduce emissions and improve air quality, the environmental impact of the policy implementation itself should be considered. The manufacturing and disposal processes for new vehicles can generate significant carbon emissions and waste.
- **Administrative Challenges** Implementing and managing a scrappage policy requires robust administrative systems and infrastructure. It involves identifying eligible vehicles, verifying their age and condition, managing the scrapping process, and tracking the replacement vehicles.
- **Market Distortions** Scrappage policies can disrupt the natural vehicle market dynamics. The sudden increase in demand for new vehicles due to the policy can lead to price increases. This can affect consumers' choices and may lead to unintended consequences such as increased demand for imports or changes in the vehicle manufacturing landscape.
- **Enforcement and Compliance** Ensuring compliance with the scrappage policy and preventing fraudulent activities can be challenging. Inadequate enforcement can undermine the effectiveness of the policy and create a sense of unfairness among compliant vehicle owners.
- **De-registering vehicles** Further, the process to deregister vehicles also needs to be simplified. At present, deregistering vehicles is a dreadful experience for most owners who want to sell or scrap their old vehicles, thereby discouraging many interested in discarding old vehicles.

Way Forward

- **Financial Support and Incentives** Provide financial assistance and incentives to low-income individuals to help them afford newer, more environmentally friendly vehicles. This could include subsidies, low-interest loans, or tax credits targeted towards those who are most affected by the financial burden of the policy.
- **Equity and Social Considerations** Implement measures to ensure that the scrappage policy does not disproportionately impact vulnerable populations. This could involve providing alternative transportation options, improving public transportation infrastructure, or offering targeted support programs for low-income individuals who are unable to replace their vehicles.
- **Comprehensive Environmental Analysis** Conduct a thorough life cycle analysis to assess the overall environmental impact of the scrappage policy, including the carbon emissions and waste generated during the manufacturing and disposal of new vehicles.
- **Efficient Administrative Systems** Develop streamlined and efficient administrative systems to manage the scrappage policy effectively. This could involve implementing digital platforms for vehicle registration and verification, utilizing data analytics to identify eligible vehicles, and ensuring proper tracking and documentation throughout the process.
- **Market Stability Measures** Implement measures to mitigate market distortions caused by the scrappage policy. This could involve working closely with the automotive industry to ensure an adequate supply of new vehicles, regulating pricing practices, and promoting competition among manufacturers to avoid excessive price increases or shortages.
- **Enforcement and Compliance Mechanisms** Establish robust enforcement mechanisms to ensure compliance with the scrappage policy. This could include increased monitoring, strict penalties for non-compliance or fraudulent activities, and public awareness campaigns to educate vehicle owners about their responsibilities and the benefits of compliance.

Conclusion

By implementing these measures, policymakers can address the concerns associated with scrappage policies, promote fairness, protect the environment, and ensure effective implementation and enforcement. Continuous evaluation and adjustments based on feedback and data will be essential to optimize the outcomes of the policy.

Industrial Clusters (SEZ: Potential and Challenges)

Q.16 There is a clear acknowledgement that Special Economic Zones (SEZs) are a tool of industrial development, manufacturing and exports. Recognizing this potential, the whole instrumentality of SEZs requires augmentation. Discuss the issues plaguing the success of SEZs with respect to taxation, governing laws and administration. (200 Words, 12.5 Marks)

UPSC Mains PYQ 2015

Ans. Introduction A Special Economic Zone (SEZ) is a specially delineated duty-free enclave and shall be deemed to be foreign territory for the purpose of trade operations and duties & tariffs. Goods and services going to the SEZ area from domestic tariff area (DTA) shall be treated as exports and goods & services coming from the SEZ area to DTA shall be treated as imports. With a view to overcome the shortcomings experienced on account of the multiplicity of controls and clearances; absence of world-class infrastructure and an unstable fiscal regime and with a view to attract larger foreign investments in India, the Special Economic Zones (SEZs) Policy was announced in 2000 followed by SEZ Act 2005.

Importance of SEZs

Tool of industrial development and manufacturing growth

- SEZ aims to provide facilities world class infrastructure for industrial growth such as customized support infrastructure, adequate warehousing and cold storage etc.
- SEZs can be particularly helpful for small and mid-sized entities that cannot afford to set up captive infrastructure facilities.
- By offering privileged terms, SEZs attract investment and foreign exchange, spur employment and boost the development of improved technologies and infrastructure.
- Investment of Rs. 4,035.51 Crore in 2005-06 has increased to Rs. 6,17,499 Crore (cumulative basis) by 2020-21, which would further help in diversifying the export basket.
- Better infrastructure facilities in SEZs have enabled hassle- free manufacturing, as evident from an increase in exports.

Tool of Exports

- Tax exemption given on export income for SEZ zone units and exemption from various domestic taxes promote exports.
- Duty free import or procurement of goods for development and operations of SEZ units further aids the objective of export promotion.
- Exports of Rs. 22,840 Crore in 2005-06 has increased to Rs. 7,59,524 Crore in 2020-21.
- Today, there are approximately 3,000 SEZs operating in 120 countries, which account for over US$ 600 billion in exports and about 50 million jobs.

Issues in the functioning of SEZ's

- **Withdrawal of taxation benefits** Taxation issue that cropped up was the introduction of the sunset date for termination of Direct Taxation benefits for SEZ developers in the year 2017 and SEZ units in the year 2020. Also, the income tax benefits were neutralised by the introduction of minimum alternate tax.
- **Lack of sectoral diversity** 57% of SEZs were in the IT (information technology) and ITES (information technology-enabled services) sector, and only 9.6% were for multi-product manufacturing sectors.
- **Small size of SEZ** The size of a Shenzen SEZ is 327 sq. km as compared to an Indian SEZ which averages around 1 sq. km. This is mainly because of the problem of acquiring large swathes of land.
- **Unutilized Land** The fall in demand for SEZs has led to unutilized land and/or unoccupied built-up premises within SEZs and there is a lack of flexibility to utilize land in SEZs for different sectors. A Comptroller and Auditor General (CAG) audit found that 52% of the land allotted has remained idle, even though permissions were given as far back as 2006.
- **Lack of Support Infrastructure** The absence of complementary infrastructure outside the SEZs, like port connectivity, proved to be a hindrance for manufacturing investment.
- **Duty issues** Export incentives like Focus Product and Focus Market Schemes were not extended to SEZs, making them less attractive.
- **Competition from ASEAN Countries** Because of fewer incentives in India, companies in SEZs have shifted to other Asian countries like Indonesia, Vietnam etc. SEZs in Indonesia and Costa Rica enjoy Income Tax exemption for 12 years
- **Emerging FTA's** The proliferation of Free Trade Agreements between 2005-15 robbed SEZs of their advantages, as importers outside SEZs benefited from zero-rated imports without being subject to Domestic Tariff Area (DTA) related restrictions.
- **Interstate Disparity** Analysis of the distribution of SEZ highlights the fact that more than a two-thirds of the notified SEZs are located in 5 States — Andhra Pradesh, Tamil Nadu, Maharashtra, Telangana and Karnataka, which account for more than 90 per cent of the investment made and 83 per cent of the employment generated.

- **State Apathy** The lack of support from the state government when it comes to developing effective single- window system for clearances.
- **Underutilization of Capacity** SEZs have not been allowed to do jobs for domestic tariff area units.
- **Existence of Multiple Models** There are multiple models of economic zones such as SEZ, coastal economic zone, Delhi-Mumbai Industrial Corridor, National Investment and Manufacturing Zone, food park and textile park which pose challenges in integrating the various models.

Because of the given above issues, while 378 SEZs have received final approval, only 268 of them are operational.

Futuristic Measures

- **Recommendations of the Baba Kalyani Committee (2018):**
  - Rename SEZs in India as 3Es- Employment and Economic Enclave.
  - Framework shift from export growth to broad-based employment and economic growth.
  - Separate rules and procedures for manufacturing and service SEZs.
  - Ease of Doing Business (EoDB) in 3Es such as one integrated online portal for new investments.
  - Extension of Sunset Clause and retaining tax or duty benefits.
  - Dispute resolution through arbitration and commercial courts.
- **Budget 2022-23** The Budget says that the SEZ Act will be replaced by a new legislation that will enable large existing and new industrial enclaves to optimally utilise available infrastructure and enhance competitiveness of exports. It will enable the States to become partners in development of enterprise and service hubs.
  - Development of Enterprise and Service Hubs (DESH) Bill is underway and not passed till now.
- **Infrastructure status to SEZs** to improve access to finance and to enable long-term borrowing.
- **Procedural Relaxations** for developers and tenants to improve operational and exit issues.
- **Administrative Efficiency** Setting up of an SEZ Rules Interpretation Committee. The five-member committee would include officers from commerce and finance ministries. This measure will help in ease of operations.
- **Size of SEZ** Size plays a key role for example Shenzhen, the most important SEZ, covers 32,000 hectares. In India, there are just three privately developed SEZ, exceeding 1,000 hectares. Most of the others approved are less than 100 hectares.

Conclusion

The recent proposal of DESH bill is a welcome step in reinvigorating the SEZs. Through this, the government is seeking to go beyond export-oriented manufacturing and focus on broad-based parameters such as boosting additional economic activity, generating employment, and integrating various industrial hubs.

Industrial Corridors

Q.17 'Industrial corridors are, undoubtedly, the pathways to a more uniformly distributed economic development and greater industrial competitiveness.' Elaborate along with highlighting the various initiatives undertaken by the government with special reference to NIMZ. (250 Words, 15 Marks)

Ans. **Introduction** An industrial corridor is basically a corridor comprising of multi-modal transport services that would pass through the states as main artery. Industrial corridors constitute world-class infrastructure, such as: High-speed transportation network-rail and road; Ports with state-of-the-art cargo handling equipment; Modern airports; Special economic regions/industrial areas; Logistic parks/tran-shipment hubs; Knowledge parks focused on catering to industrial needs; Complementary infrastructure such as townships/real estate and other urban infrastructure along with enabling policy framework. Industrial corridors have emerged as key drivers of economic development, promoting regional growth and enhancing industrial competitiveness. They serve as pathways for attracting investments, fostering innovation, and facilitating infrastructure development. The establishment of industrial corridors helps in achieving a more evenly distributed economic growth by attracting industries to less-developed regions and reducing regional disparities.

Industrial Corridors in India

- **Delhi-Mumbai Industrial Corridor (DMIC)** covers Uttar Pradesh, Haryana, Rajasthan, Madhya Pradesh, Gujarat and Maharashtra. t is being developed with the help of Japan. DMIC Project aims to create futuristic Industrial Cities by leveraging the "High Speed–High Capacity" connectivity backbone provided by the Western Dedicated Freight Corridor (DFC)
- **Chennai-Bengaluru Industrial Corridor (CBIC)** covers Tamil Nadu, Andhra Pradesh and Karnataka. It is being funded by the Japan International Cooperation Agency (JICA).
- **Bengaluru-Mumbai Economic Corridor (BMEC)** covers Maharashtra and Karnataka. It is being developed with the help of Britain (UK).
- **Amritsar-Kolkata Industrial Corridor (AKIC)** covers Punjab, Haryana, Uttarakhand, Uttar Pradesh, Bihar, Jharkhand and West Bengal. The Project extends from Amritsar (Punjab) to Dankuni (West Bengal) for a length of 1839 kms. The Eastern Dedicated Freight Corridor is the backbone of this economic corridor.
- **East Coast Economic Corridor (ECEC)** covers West Bengal, Odisha, Andhra Pradesh and Tamil Nadu. Vizag to Chennai segment of this Corridor has been taken as phase-1. Vizag-Chennai Industrial Corridor (VCIC) is the first coastal economic corridor in the country. It covers more than 800 km of Andhra Pradesh's coastline and is aligned with the Golden Quadrilateral. It also plays a critical role in the "Act East Policy" of India.

Importance of Industrial Corridors

- **Avenues for Exports** The Industrial Corridors are likely to lower the cost of logistics thereby increasing the efficiency of industrial production structure. Such an efficiency lowers the cost of production which makes the Indian made products more competitive in international markets. The production of export surplus would generate employment opportunities and raise per capita incomes.
- **Regional Development** Industrial corridors facilitate the equitable distribution of economic development across regions.
  - The Delhi-Mumbai Industrial Corridor (DMIC) aims to develop 24 industrial regions across six states, covering a length of 1,500 km. This project intends to create a more balanced regional development by attracting industries and generating employment opportunities in areas along the corridor.
- **Employment Generation** Industrial corridors have the potential to generate substantial employment opportunities.
  - The DMIC, as an example, is expected to create around 25 million jobs across various sectors by 2040. This demonstrates the significant employment potential of well-planned industrial corridors.
- **Enhanced Industrial Competitiveness** By creating clusters of industries, industrial corridors promote synergies and collaboration among businesses, leading to enhanced industrial competitiveness.
  - The development of dedicated zones for specific sectors within industrial corridors fosters specialization and innovation.
  - This enables industries to benefit from economies of scale, shared resources, and efficient supply chains.
- **Infrastructure Development** Industrial corridors require robust infrastructure, including transportation networks, logistics facilities, and utilities. The development of infrastructure along these corridors not only supports industrial activities but also contributes to overall economic growth.
  - The Eastern Dedicated Freight Corridor (EDFC) in India aims to enhance freight transportation capacity, thereby reducing logistics costs and improving industrial competitiveness.
- **Foreign Direct Investment (FDI) Attraction** Industrial corridors serve as attractive destinations for foreign direct investment. The presence of well-planned infrastructure, favorable policies, and industry-specific zones along these corridors creates a conducive environment for foreign companies to invest.
  - The Chennai-Bengaluru Industrial Corridor (CBIC) in India has been successful in attracting significant foreign investments in sectors such as automobiles, electronics, and textiles.
- **Agglomeration Effects** Industrial corridors encourage the agglomeration of industries, suppliers, and support services, leading to economies of scale and knowledge spill-overs. This fosters innovation, research and development, and technological advancements, contributing to industrial competitiveness.

- **Social significance** The establishment of NMIZ in a scattered manner along the industrial corridor across the length of the state would prevent distress migration and provide people with job opportunities close to their dwelling place.
  – The spread effects of industrial corridors in socio-economic terms are many such as setting up of industrial townships, educational institutions, roads, railways, airports, hospitals that will generate employment and raise standard of living.
- **Environmental significance** It will prevent concentration of industries in one particular location which exploited the environment beyond its carrying capacity and caused environmental degradation.

Initiatives of National investment Manufacturing Zones (NIMZs)

NIMZs are large integrated industrial townships with state-of-the-art infrastructure, designed to promote manufacturing and industrial activities. They aim to create a conducive environment for industries by providing land, connectivity, utilities, and supportive policies.

- **National Manufacturing Policy** The National Manufacturing Policy was launched in 2011 to promote the growth of the manufacturing sector and establish NIMZs as world-class manufacturing hubs. It provides various incentives, infrastructure support, and streamlined regulatory frameworks to attract investments.
- **Development of NIMZs** The government has identified specific areas across the country for the development of NIMZs, such as Nagpur in Maharashtra, Tumkur in Karnataka, Prakasam in Andhra Pradesh, and Medak in Telangana. These zones offer a favorable business environment with developed infrastructure, connectivity, and necessary amenities.
- **Infrastructure Development** The government focuses on developing robust physical infrastructure within NIMZs, including roads, railways, power supply, water resources, and waste management systems. This ensures smooth operations and encourages investment.
- **Single Window Clearance** The government has implemented a single-window clearance mechanism for obtaining necessary approvals, licenses, and permits to set up industries within NIMZs. This simplifies the bureaucratic process and expedites project implementation.
- **Financial Incentives** To attract investments, the government provides financial incentives such as tax benefits, subsidies, and grants to industries operating in NIMZs. These incentives help reduce costs and enhance the competitiveness of manufacturing units.
- **Skill Development** Skill development initiatives are implemented to create a skilled workforce that meets the requirements of industries within NIMZs. This includes setting up training centers, vocational programs, and collaboration with educational institutions to bridge the skill gap.
- **Foreign Direct Investment (FDI) Promotion** The government actively promotes foreign direct investment in NIMZs by easing regulations, allowing higher FDI limits, and providing a favorable investment climate. This facilitates technology transfer, employment generation, and overall economic growth.
- **Make in India Initiative** The Make in India campaign, launched by the government, aims to transform India into a global manufacturing hub. The initiative provides impetus to the development of industrial corridors and NIMZs.

Conclusion

The development of industrial corridors, including the NIMZs, plays a vital role in achieving more uniform economic growth and enhancing industrial competitiveness. These initiatives foster investment, create employment opportunities, and facilitate the growth of manufacturing and industrial sectors. They contribute to the overall socio-economic development of the regions and the country as a whole.

Check Your Preparation

1. Economic Survey stated that one of the Indian cities can emerge as the 'Detroit of Electric Vehicles' in future. In this context, discuss the potentials and challenges for the development of the Electronic Vehicle industry in India. (250 words, 15 marks)
2. There have been indications of sluggish growth in labour intensive industries in India in recent times. Analyse the reasons behind this trend. What can be done to reverse the trend? (150 words, 10 marks)
3. Special Economic Zones (SEZs) in India have not been as successful as their counterparts in many other countries. Analyse. Also, discuss the measures being taken for reviving SEZs in India. (250 words, 15 marks)

UNIT 9

Infrastructure : Energy, Ports, Roads, Airports, Railways etc

Overview of Infrastructure (Infrastructure and Economic Growth)

Q.1 Investment in infrastructure is essential for a more rapid and inclusive economic growth. Discuss in the light of India's experience. (250 Words, 15 Marks) **UPSC Mains PYQ 2021**

Ans. **Introduction** As per Economic survey, India requires around $4.5 trillion worth of investments till 2040 to develop infrastructure. However, the current trend shows India can only meet around $3.9 trillion infrastructure investment

Investment in Infrastructure is Essential for More Rapid and Inclusive Growth

Rapid Growth

- **Stimulates Growth** Investment in infrastructure leads to industrial development, thereby stimulating the growth in the economy.
  - **World Bank Study** The 1% increase in investment in the stock of infrastructure leads to a corresponding 1% increase in the GDP of a nation.
  - PM Gati Shakti which subsumes National Infrastructure Pipeline projects of more than 110 lakh crore will give a huge boost to the economy
- **Increased Efficiency** Investment in the infrastructure lowers production and transportation costs through improved logistics.
  - **NITI Aayog** A 10% decrease in indirect logistics cost has the potential to increase exports by 5-8%.
  - **Example** Bharatmala scheme
- **Improves Market Competition Mechanism** To achieve the optimal allocation of resources, investment in infrastructure is quintessential for rapid economic growth.
- **Rippling Effect** Increasing investment in infrastructure has wide implications on various sectors of the economy.
  - **Example** Power shortages lead to dependence on expensive captive power, which in turn impels high costs and lack of competitiveness for the economy.
- **Forward-induced Effects** It will produce demand of factors of production, thereby increasing the investment of factor markets and consumer market.

- **FDI Inflows** Investment in infrastructure leads to improved ease of doing business, thereby increasing the foreign capital inflows into the country.
  - In FY21, infrastructure operations accounted for 13% of overall FDI inflows of US$ 81.72 billion
- **Reduction in Bottlenecks** Adequate transport infrastructure leads to less bottlenecks in supply of raw materials and movement of finished goods to the marketplace.
- **Growth of Digital Infrastructure** Digital economy is expected to be $1 trillion economy by 2025-26 and thus, initiatives like JAM Trinity, Digital India programme, application of emerging technologies such as Artificial Intelligence, Quantum computing, etc. will give a strong push to the economic growth.

Inclusive Growth

- **Provides Employment** The infrastructure sector has immense potential to generate jobs especially for the unskilled sections and thereby increases the demand to boost the growth.
  - **Example** Bharatmala Pariyojana is expected to create 14.2 crores man-days of jobs.
- **Poverty Reduction** Economic growth is a pre-condition for inclusive growth and the economic growth is dependent hugely on the investments in infrastructure.
  - **Example** Investments under Gramin Bhandaran Yojana for cold storage development is expected to give almost 5 to 10 times more returns as against subsidies.
- **Reduced Income Disparities** By providing job opportunities for unskilled sections of the society, infrastructure investments reduce the income disparities.
  - **Example** Pradhan Mantri Gram Sadak Yojana (PMGSY) provide rural connectivity to North eastern and Himalayan States, increasing the employment opportunities for rural population.
- **Agriculture Development** Infrastructure expansion, such as irrigation, rural electrification, highways, and road transport, would encourage agricultural growth and the establishment of agro-processing enterprises.
  - **Example** For effective price realization by farmers for his produce, good connectivity is needed, which in turn helps in increased rural incomes and resultant boost in the growth.
- **Addresses Regional Imbalances** Infrastructure not only contributes towards the development of backward regions but also acts as an instrument of social change.
  - Integration of rural areas, tribal areas, LWE affected regions, J&K and North-east.
- **Improving Social Indicators** Investment in infrastructure is crucial for improving access to key facilities such as health, education, and other basic services.
  - **Investments under SBN-Grameen** improved the sanitation and 35 states declared open defecation free (ODF).
  - **Example** Poshan Abhiyan 2.0, PM Ujjwala Scheme, etc.
- **Promotion of MSMEs** MSME production and growth require access to quality and dependable infrastructure services in order to compete efficiently with large-scale enterprises.
  - **Example** With the emergence of AI, Data Analytics, Robotics and related technologies investments in infrastructure is a necessity for organized large-scale manufacturing.

Challenges of Infrastructure Development

- **Physical Infrastructure**
  - **Land Acquisition** One of the biggest challenges in building physical infrastructure is acquiring land, as it often involves resettlement of people and compensation issues.
  - **Funding** Funding large-scale infrastructure projects is also a major challenge, as the government may not have sufficient resources and private investment may be limited due to economic and regulatory hurdles.
  - **Lack of Technology** India faces challenges in terms of the availability of technology and expertise necessary for complex infrastructure projects.
- **Social Infrastructure**
  - **Inadequate Human Resources** The shortage of skilled workers, engineers, and managers can be a hindrance to the development of social infrastructure projects.
  - **Lack of Public Support** Social infrastructure projects, such as healthcare and education, require public support and buy-in, which can be difficult to secure in a complex political environment.

– **Inadequate Planning and Implementation** Poor planning and implementation can result in substandard facilities and a lack of sustainability, ultimately reducing the impact of the infrastructure push.

- **Digital Infrastructure**
  – **Digital Divide** There is a digital divide in India, with limited access to technology and the internet in rural areas, which can hinder the development of digital infrastructure.
  – **Cybersecurity Concerns** The increasing use of technology also raises concerns about cybersecurity and privacy, making it necessary to have strong regulations and infrastructure in place.
  – **Lack of Standardisation** The lack of standardisation and coordination among different players in the digital infrastructure sector can create problems for users and limit the potential for growth and innovation.

Conclusion

Infrastructure plays a key role in shaping and scripting India's growth story. Consequently, the momentum of investments in infrastructure needs to accelerate substantially, and the government efforts to promote world class infrastructure – NIP, PM Gati Shakti Master Plan are the steps in right direction.

PM Gati Shakti Critical Analysis

Q.2 'PM Gati Shakti, with a multi-modal approach, is designed to fill the gaps in physical infrastructure and to integrate existing and proposed infrastructure development initiatives of different agencies.' Examine the statement. (150 Words, 10 Marks)

Ans. **Introduction** PM Gati Shakti is a National Master Plan for multi-modal connectivity which includes a digital platform under which 16 ministries will be brought together for integrated planning, coordination, and implementation of all the infrastructure projects. It subsumes National infrastructure pipeline which aims to invest 110 lakh crores in infrastructure.

How Gati Shakti fill gaps in physical infrastructure?

- **Addressing Lack of Coordination** Lack of coordination among departments is major roadblock in the creation of infrastructure which Gati Shakti programme aims to reduce by integrating 16 ministries, including railways and roadways, with a view to ensuring holistic planning and execution of infrastructure projects.
- **Increasing Pace of Infrastructure** It plans to construct more roadways, providing better connectivity to the hinterland, where a large majority of businesses operate. The government also plans to tackle the issue of logistics by creating a unified logistics interface platform (ULIP) that will help in the efficient transportation of goods.

- **Bridging the Infrastructure Gap** Poor infrastructure such as lack of proper roadways, seaports, and airports makes connectivity between various business stakeholders more difficult, time-consuming, and costly which increases the cost of goods.
- **Reduction in the cost of Infrastructure Creation** Coordinated planning, execution and monitoring of infrastructure projects will result in cost and time saving. It will improve the sentiments of banks towards infrastructure lending.
- **Improving the Quality and reach of Multimodal Connectivity** PM Gati shakti plans to integrate various agencies and development initiatives that will incorporate the infrastructure schemes of various Ministries and State Governments like Bharatmala, Sagarmala, inland waterways, dry/land ports, UDAN etc. Hence, it will facilitate the last mile connectivity of infrastructure and also reduce travel time and logistics cost.
- **Real time Monitoring and Resolution of Issues** The portal will allow various government departments to track, in real time and at one centralized place, the progress of various projects. which will also enable fast resolution of issues.

PM Gati Shakti envisages integrating existing and proposed infrastructure development initiatives through following six pillars

- **Comprehensiveness** It will include all the existing and planned initiatives of various Ministries and Departments with one centralized portal. Each and every Department will now have visibility of each other's activities providing critical data while planning & execution of projects in a comprehensive manner.
- **Prioritization** Through this, different Departments will be able to prioritize their projects through cross-sectoral interactions.
- **Optimization** The National Master Plan will assist different ministries in planning for projects after identification of critical gaps. For the transportation of the goods from one place to another, the plan will help in selecting the most optimum route in terms of time and cost.
- **Removing silo-based Working** Individual Ministries and Departments often work in silos. There is lack of coordination in planning and implementation of the project resulting in delays. Gati Shakti will help in synchronizing the activities of each department, as well as of different layers of governance, in a holistic manner by ensuring coordination of work between them.
  - NMP will rely on creation of various data layers including geographical features, land records, etc., to facilitate coordinated and integrated planning, project preparations and implementations, optimization of logistics arrangements and efficient transportation systems.
- **Analytical** The plan will provide the entire data at one place with GIS based spatial planning and analytical tools having 200+ layers, enabling better visibility to the executing agency.
- **Dynamic** All Ministries and Departments will now be able to visualize, review and monitor the progress of cross-sectoral projects, through the GIS platform, as the satellite imagery will give on-ground progress periodically and progress of the projects will be updated on a regular basis on the portal. It will help in identifying the vital interventions for enhancing and updating the master plan.

Challenges that need to be addressed

- **Infrastructure Financing**
  - **Insufficient Funding** One of the key challenges is the availability of adequate financial resources to support the ambitious infrastructure projects under the PM Gati Shakti scheme.
  - **Delayed Disbursement** Timely disbursement of funds is crucial for project execution, but bureaucratic processes and administrative delays can hinder the efficient utilization of allocated funds.
- **Public-Private Partnership (PPP)**
  - **Encouraging Private Sector Participation** Attracting private investments in infrastructure projects requires a conducive policy environment, streamlined approval processes, and risk-sharing mechanisms. Creating an investor-friendly ecosystem can be challenging.
- **Land Acquisition Delays** Acquiring land for infrastructure projects often involves complex legal and procedural hurdles, leading to significant delays and cost overruns.
- **Project Implementation and Monitoring**
  - **Coordination and Integration** The PM Gati Shakti scheme involves multiple sectors and agencies, requiring effective coordination and integration of efforts. Lack of coordination can lead to delays and inefficiencies.
  - **Monitoring and Evaluation** Ensuring effective monitoring and evaluation mechanisms to track project progress and identify bottlenecks is crucial. However, establishing robust monitoring systems can be challenging.
- **Technology and Innovation**
  - **Adoption of new Technologies** Embracing innovative technologies and practices can enhance project efficiency and reduce costs. However, there can be resistance to change and a lack of awareness about the potential benefits.
  - **Digital Infrastructure** The development of digital infrastructure and connectivity is crucial for the effective implementation of the PM Gati Shakti scheme. However, there can be challenges in providing seamless digital connectivity across the country.
  - **Environmental Concerns** Infrastructure projects can have significant environmental implications, and conducting comprehensive impact assessments and implementing mitigation measures is crucial. However, this can lead to delays and added costs.

Conclusion

Apart from government departments, the private sector plays an important role in the creation of infrastructure. In this regard, Kelkar committee recommendations could be implemented to overcome the challenges which will be helpful in implementation of Gati Shakti.

Logistics Sector (Multi-Modal Logistics)

Q.3 How can multimodal logistics play a prominent role in bringing down the overall logistics cost of the nation? Also, discuss the efforts taken by the government with special reference to Multi-Modal Logistics Parks (MMLP). (250 Words, 15 Marks)

Ans. **Introduction** India improved its rank in the World Bank Logistics Performance Index from 44 in 2018 to 37 in 2022 but still India's logistics sector is highly fragmented with logistics costs of around 14% of the GDP of our country which is higher than the other country. Due to this, the movement of goods from source to destination is a major problem in India.

Reasons behind High Logistic Costs

- **Skewed Multimodal Mix** In India, a predominant mode of freight cargo transportation is via road. Nearly 60% cargo is moved by road, while the share of railways is ~32%. Waterways have a meagre share of ~5%. The global average is 25% for roads and 60% for railways. Share of railways is lower because of over-saturated rail networks and high rail tariffs.
  - Road is an inefficient way of transportation because of poor infrastructure, slower speed of movement, multiple check-points etc. The skewed modal mix raises costs of logistics. The higher logistics costs are reducing the competitiveness of India's exports.
- **Port Sector Issues** The turnaround times for ships is high (~62 hours in 2020-21, ~8 hours in Japan). This is because of overcrowded berths and delay in cargo evacuation due to poor infrastructure. In addition, time consuming custom clearances add to delay. Coastal shipping in India gets hampered due to the weak land side and port facilities. Insufficient depth at ports discourage large vessels, thus curbing the large scale use of it for freight movements.
- **Tax Structure** The complicated tax regime places several hardships on logistics companies in India. Multiple State and Centre taxes lead to considerable loss of time in transit on roads.
- **Warehousing Issues** The poor state of warehousing and their restricting locations are one of the major concerns of logistics sector. Storage facilities are quite fragmented for low margin products thereby resulting in a disincentive to create a large integrated warehousing space.
- **Fragmented Sector** Unorganized players control 90% of the logistics market. Most Indian logistics companies are very small, and have limited fleet of trucks/vehicles. This prevents scale and cost economies. Fragmentation leads to low margins which prevents investments to scale-up operations or adoption of new efficient digital technologies. It also makes it hard to streamline supply chains. So the road transportation sector remains inefficient overall.
- **Infrastructure** It is one of the biggest hurdles that has cramped growth of the logistics sector. It gets reflected in inadequate and low-quality modal and terminal transport infrastructure, suboptimal modal mix, inefficient and ill-designed storage facilities for cargo and containers and inefficient operational and maintenance protocols, and poor adoption/adaptation of technology. This leads to high and inconsistent cargo transit time, inefficient use of resources and poor fleet management.
- **Skill Development** Lack of skilled manpower is the result of inadequate training and proper leadership and support. Also, due to the unorganized nature of the sector, which is characterized by poor working conditions and low pay scale, it is not a preferred choice among skilled personnel.
- **Information Technology** Slow adoption of new technologies has been another big constraint. Awareness about the economic benefits of using digital technology is low and collaboration among stakeholders far from satisfactory.
- **Regulatory Hurdles** Obstacles in land acquisition and consolidation, and change in land use still continue to be major impediments. Lack of transparency in compliances further adds to the woes of the sector.
- **Fuel Costs** The high fuel costs continues to be a detriment to the sector. Higher fuel prices increase the transportation costs. Rising fuel prices are increasing the surcharges to the freight tariffs. This reduces profitability of the logistics sector.

Multi-modal logistics bringing down cost of logistics

Multimodal Logistics can be viewed as "the chain that interconnects different links or modes of transport–air, sea, and land into one complete process that ensures an efficient and cost-effective door-to door movement of goods under the responsibility of a single transport operator, known as a Multimodal Transport Operator (MTO), on one transport document".

- Multimodal logistics serves to **interconnect different modes of transport** - road, rail, air, water – and therefore improve efficiency and speed of goods movement. It is designed to cut transit times, decongest congested modes and reduce logistics cost. Estimates indicate that Multimodal logistics can potentially reduce transit times by 40-50%.
- **Minimises Time loss at Transhipment points** Multi-modal transport, which is planned and coordinated as a single operation, minimises the loss of time and the risk of loss, pilferage and damage to cargo at trans-shipment points. The multimodal transport operator maintains his own communication links and coordinates interchange and onward carriage smoothly at trans-shipment points.
- **Provides Faster Transit of Goods** The faster transit of goods made possible under multimodal transport reduces the disadvantages of distance from markets and tying-up of capital. In an era of Globalization, the distance between origin or source of materials and consumer is increasing thanks to the development of multimodal transport.
- **Reduces Burden of Documentation and Formalities** The burden of issuing multiple documentation and other formalities connected with each segmented of the transport chain is reduced to a minimum.
- **Saves Cost** The savings in costs resulting from these advantages are usually reflected in the through freight rates charged by the multimodal transport operator and also in the cost of cargo insurance. As savings are passed onto the consumer, demand increases.
- **Single Window Operation** The consignor has to deal with only the multimodal transport operator in all matters relating to the transportation of his goods, including the settlement of claims for loss of goods, or damage to them or delays in delivery at destination.
- **Reduced Cost of Exports** The inherent advantages of multimodal transport system will help to reduce the cost of exports and improve their competitive position in the international market.

Government Initiatives

- Logistics sector finds a place in the **Harmonized Master List of Infrastructure Subsector**. This inclusion is set to benefit the logistics industry as it will now have an access to cheaper and long-term credit. Such a move will also lead to simplification of the approval process for the construction of multimodal logistics parks.
- **Multi-Modal Logistics Parks (MMLP)** The Cabinet Committee on Economic Affairs (CCEA) authorized the Ministry of Road Transport and Highways (MoRTH) to develop 35 Multi-Modal Logistics Parks under the Bharatmala Pariyojana. The MMLPs are to be developed under Public Private Partnership (PPP) on Design, Build, Finance, Operate and Transfer (DBFOT) mode.
- **National Logistics Policy (NLP)** It aims to achieve 'quick last-mile delivery' and end transport-related challenges. The policy focuses on key areas such as process re-engineering, digitisation, and multi-modal transport with an aim to reduce the cost of logistics from 14-18% of GDP to global best practices of 8%
- **Bharatmala Pariyojana** It focuses on optimizing the efficiency of freight and passenger movement across the country by bridging critical infrastructure gaps. Example: India's first International Multi-Modal Logistics Park (MMLP) in Jogighopa, Assam, Multi Modal Logistics Park is likely to boost connectivity in the Northeast. The park is being developed under the ambitious Bharatmala Pariyojana of the Government.
- **PM Gati Shakti** Besides cutting logistics costs, the scheme is also aimed at increasing cargo handling capacity and reducing the turnaround time at ports to boost trade.
- Government initiatives like the Sagarmala program, Inland Waterways program and coastal shipping will provide the much-needed fillip to infrastructure development in the country.

Benefits of Multi Modal Logistic Parks (MMLP)

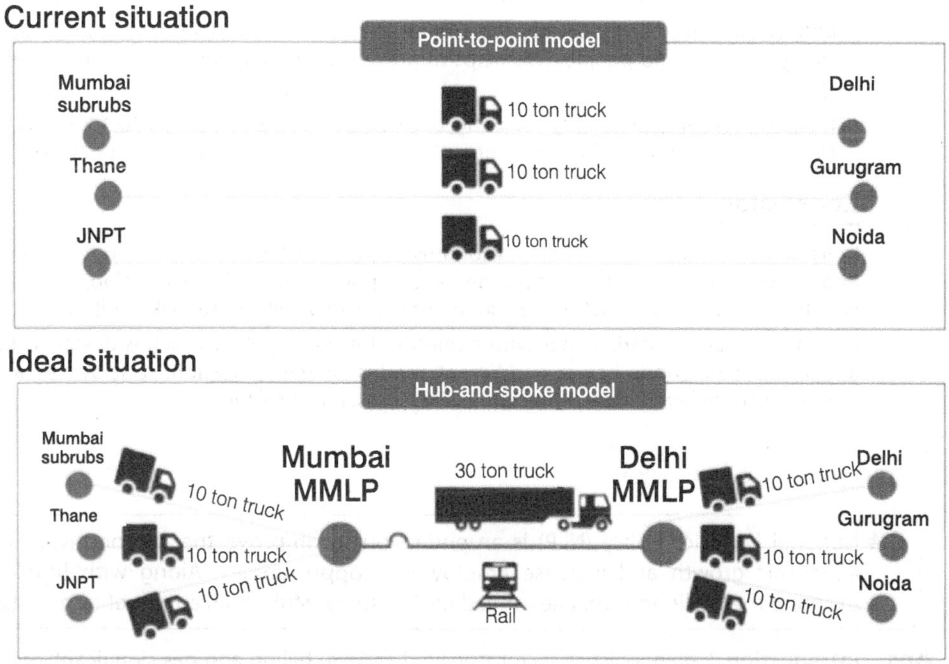

Multi-modal logistics parks are large land parcels with rail and road connectivity, where goods coming in get seamlessly transferred to trains and other modes of transport in a hub-and-spoke model.

They form a key policy initiative of the Government of India, which are aimed at improving the freight logistics sector by lowering overall freight costs and time, cutting warehousing costs, reducing vehicular pollution and congestion, and improving the tracking and traceability of consignments through infrastructural, procedural and technological interventions. Logistics parks drive reduction in overall freight cost by enabling freight transportation on higher-sized trucks and rail.

The benefits of MMLPs will include

- **Efficient Cargo Movement** Multi-modal logistics parks facilitate the smooth transfer of cargo between different modes of transport, such as trucks, trains, ships and airplanes. They provide the infrastructure and facilities necessary to handle and transfer goods, reducing delays, cargo handling costs and overall transit times.
- **Inter-modal Connectivity** By bringing together multiple modes of transport in one location, multimodal logistics parks can enhance connectivity and improve the efficiency of cargo movement.
- **International Trade Facilitation and Supply Chain Efficiency** Multimodal logistics parks play a vital role in facilitating international trade. They provide customs clearance facilities and streamlined processes, enabling efficient border crossings and regulatory compliance. This helps to expedite the movement of goods across borders, reducing trade barriers and improving supply chain efficiency.
- **Reduction in the Transportation Cost** This is estimated to achieve at least a 10 per cent reduction in transportation cost. MMLPs enable small trucks to transfer load to larger trucks, which have 60 percent lower freight cost on a per tonne per kilometre basis when compared to smaller-sized trucks. They will provide value-added services such as customs clearance, labelling, repackaging, and packaging.
  - All these features will ultimately bring down the overall logistics cost from the current about 14% of GDP to less than 10% of GDP.
- **Reduction in Carbon Emissions** Freight movement by rail has 65 percent lower CO_2 emissions compared to road freight on a per tonne per kilometre basis. With India targeting 45 per cent reduction in carbon intensity by 2030, MMLPs will go a long way in reducing freight pollution.
- **Reduced Congestion** Increased freight movement on higher-sized trucks and rail will lead to a 20 per cent reduction in freight vehicles catering to the demands. Further, with the shifting of warehouses and wholesale markets, currently which are based in urban areas, space in cities will be freed up, thus reducing congestion.
- **Improved Warehousing** The MMLPs will increase the warehouse capacity of the country. Additionally, modern and mechanised storage solutions provided by logistics parks will enable reduction in storage and handling losses improving the efficiency of freight movement and reduction of freight transportation cost.

- These parks will ensure improved train services, use of modern equipment, and electronic data interchange. So, the time taken for the entire process of moving goods from the production centre to ports will be reduced.
- **Enhanced Safety and Security** MMLPs often have advanced security systems and protocols in place to ensure the safety of goods and people. This helps to prevent theft, damage, and other security issues that can impact the supply chain.
- **Environmental Benefits** By reducing the number of trips required to transport goods, MMLPs can help to reduce carbon emissions and other environmental impacts associated with transportation.

Conclusion

India aims to become US$ 5 trillion economy in the near term and a developed economy by 2047. For this, connectivity and robust infrastructure will become crucial points. As logistics develop, manufacturing and other industries like warehousing and infrastructure development will also develop and make India a manufacturing hub.

Multimodal Logistic Park comes with a solution for the problem which is designed to facilitate the efficient movement and transfer of goods between different modes of transportation. It serves as a central hub where cargo can be seamlessly transferred between trucks, trains, ships, and airplanes.

National Logistics Policy, 2022

Q.4 National Logistics Policy (NLP) is an endeavour to improve the competitiveness of Indian goods, enhance economic growth and increase employment opportunities. Along with highlighting the goals of policy, examine the challenges that lies ahead for the successful achievement of targets. (250 Words, 15 Marks)

Ans. **Introduction** Indian logistics sector is valued at $250 billion and has significant potential to grow but it is fragmented and unorganized in nature. Therefore, National Logistics Policy (NLP) is envisaged to bring efficiency in logistics services through streamlining processes and adoption of suitable technologies.

Goals of National Logistics Policy, 2022

Since 2014, the government has put significant emphasis on improving both, Ease of Doing Business and Ease of Living. National Logistics Policy, a comprehensive effort to address issues of high cost and inefficiency by laying down an overarching interdisciplinary, cross-sectoral and multi-jurisdictional framework for the development of the entire logistics ecosystem, is yet another step in this direction.

The Policy sets targets and includes a detailed action plan to achieve them. The targets are:

- **Reduction in the Cost of Logistics** Policy aims to reduce cost of logistics to be near global benchmarks of 8% from 14% by 2030 by integrating the unorganized and fragmented logistics sector. Example: Unified Logistics Interface Platform (ULIP) is a digital platform which aims to provide end-to-end logistics solutions by integrating all stakeholders thus helping in resolving all logistics-related issues.
- **Improving the rank in Logistics Performance Index Ranking** Policy aims to make India among the top 25 countries in the World Bank's LPI by 2030. India's latest policy of Comprehensive Logistics Action Plan (CLAP) will be critical if India has to achieve its target.
- Creating **data-driven Decision Support Systems (DSS)** to enable an efficient logistics ecosystem.
- **Harnessing Technology** Use of technologies such as robotics as a service, artificial intelligence, cloud automation, blockchain, and big data can help in bringing efficiency and reduce redundancies. Example: Under Integration of Digital System (IDS) there will be digital integration of different systems of seven various departments (like road transport, railways, aviation, commerce ministries and foreign trade)

Possible impact from National Logistics Policy

- **First, the policy paves way for reduction in logistics cost in the country** Focus will be on enabling adequate development of warehouses with optimal spatial planning. Establishing multi-modal logistics parks (MMLPs) in crucial markets will improve firs-and last-mile connectivity. This will enable better inventory management making the supply chains more efficient bringing down the costs.

- **Second, promotion of standards, measures to facilitate seamless coordination** between different stakeholders, speedy issue resolution, and streamlined EXIM processes will reduce unnecessary delays.
- **Third, measures to improve digitization, automation across the logistics value chain** and better track and trace mechanisms will enable faster movement of goods and reduce wastage in transit.
- **Fourth, the government will also offer management courses around Logistics and Supply Chain** This will lead to human resource development to create an employable pool of skilled manpower, for the sector's growth.
- **Fifth,** this policy supports enhancing competitiveness of Micro, Small and Medium Enterprises, and other sectors such as agriculture and allied sectors, fast moving consumer goods and electronics. With greater predictability, transparency and reliability, wastages in supply chain and need for huge inventory will reduce.

Proper implementation of the policy will result in increasing competitiveness of Indian goods, greater integration of global value chains and higher share in global trade besides facilitating accelerated economic growth in the country. This will lead to generation of employment and thus will be able to reap demographic dividend.

Challenges in the Achievement of Targets

- **Lack of Multimodal Transportation System** Nearly 65 percent of India's cargo movement is by road, where fuel costs are very high. Moving cargo away from the roads to alternative forms like railways of transport will be vital to bringing down logistics costs.
- **Requirement of huge Investment** Infrastructural development is capital intensive thus mobilization of financial resources is an uphill task.
- **Coordination between Stakeholders** Logistics policy implementation between different stakeholders like central, state governments and private players is crucial for successful implementation of policy.
- **Single-window Clearance** Creation of a unified logistics interface platform and the adoption of digital infrastructure in the logistics space is another big challenge. The integration of various e-platforms will be a challenge. There are many e-platforms and all of them need to be integrated seamlessly into one platform which will be a huge task.
- **Warehouse/storage Facilities** The lack of proper logistics infrastructure like warehousing and cold chains is a major challenge.
- **Specific Sectoral Issues** Every sector has its own peculiar issues related to regulatory issues, taxation, poor state of infrastructure etc. For example, ports have high turnaround time due to overcrowded berths, time consuming custom clearances etc.
- **Fragmented Nature of Sector** Unorganized players control the logistics market. Most Indian logistics companies are very small, and have limited fleet of trucks/vehicles. This prevents scale and cost economies.

Futuristic Reform Measures

- **Allocation of adequate Financial Resources** will be needed for implementation of policy.
- **Multimodal Transport Infrastructure** is needed for bringing efficiency and reducing cost in logistics.
- **Public-private Partnership** Coordination is needed between government and private players for seamless implementation of policy and reducing the fragmentation in industry.
- **Centre-State Coordination** Spirit of cooperative federalism is needed to successfully meet the challenges in implementation of policy.
- **Inland Waterways have remained Underdeveloped** They provide a cost-efficient and environment-friendly way to move goods. Inland port development must become a priority for the Government.
- **A Technology-driven Documentation Approach** would highly impact the logistic sector by avoiding transit delays and untimely deliveries caused due to improper documentation.
- The focus has to be on the implementation of the policy. There should be periodic review to check for the outcomes and course-correction.

Conclusion

National Logistic Policy is a timely intervention for making the Indian manufacturing sector cost competitive which will enable higher economic growth and help in harnessing export potential provided challenges related to its implementation are tackled in an inclusive manner involving all relevant stakeholders.

Transportation Sector (Road Safety)

Q.5 Despite high number of accidents, road safety has remained low policy priority for the Government. In this context, explain the reasons behind high number of road accidents and fatalities in India. Keeping different stakeholders in mind, suggest some measures which can be adopted for reducing road accidents in India. (150 Words, 10 Marks)

Ans. Introduction According to latest National Crimes Records Bureau (NCRB) report on Accidental Deaths in India (2021), over 1.55 lakh lives were lost in road crashes across India in 2021 or 18 deaths every single hour.

- States of Tamil Nadu (57,000), Madhya Pradesh (49,500), Uttar Pradesh (36,500), Kerala (33,000) and Maharashtra (30,000) reported high number of accidents.

According to World Bank, India accounts for 11% of the global death in road accidents despite having just 1% of the world's vehicles.

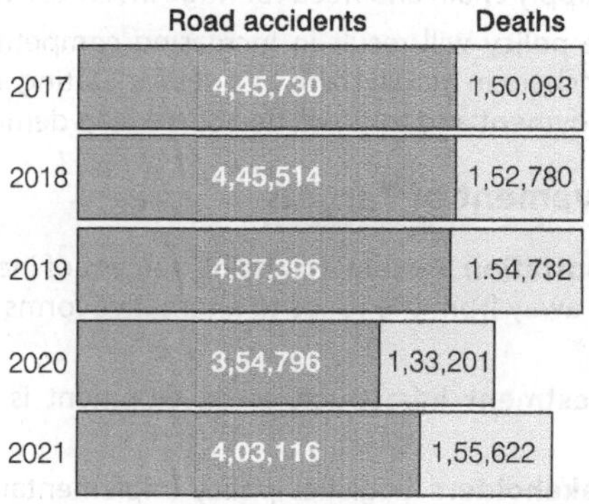

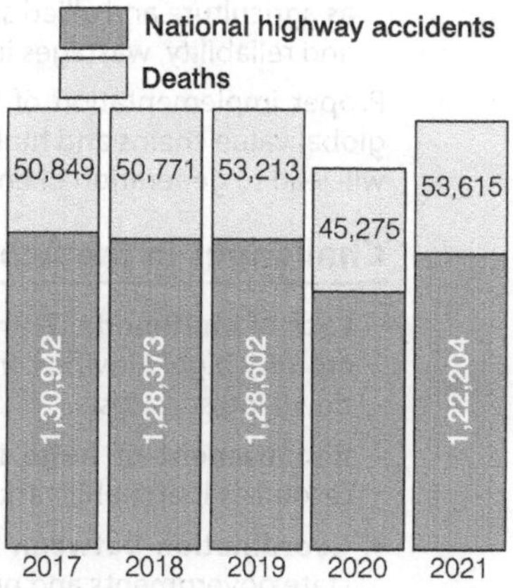

- **Financial Implication** Road accidents costs INR 6 lakh crore or 3.14% of Gross Domestic Product (GDP).
- **Socio-Economic Disparity** There is a distinct correlation between socio-economic status and road use patterns in low- and middle-income countries like India and 'poor people are more likely to be involved in a road traffic crash'.

Reasons Behind High Number of Road Accidents and Fatalities in India

- **Human Factors** According to the NCRB report, most of the accidents and fatalities are attributable to human factors.
  - Over-speeding.
  - Careless driving like jumping a red light, driving or overtaking on the wrong side of the road, talking on the mobile phone while driving etc.
  - Neglecting safety measures like not wearing helmets or seat belts.
  - Driving under influence of alcohol or drugs.
- **Poor Quality of Vehicular design** Vehicles in India lack safety features of global standards e.g., most low end cars don't have airbags e.g.
  - In 2014, the Global New Car Assessment Programme (NCAP) revealed that some of India's top-selling car models have failed the frontal impact crash test.
- **Road Design** Many roads are not designed from the perspective of safety and accident prevention.
  - **National Highway More Susceptible to Accidents** According to an IIT Delhi report, while the national highways constitute only 2% of the total length of roads in India, they account for ~35% of the fatalities.
  - **Many roads have multiple black spots** Black spots are road locations that have a high number of crashes e.g., sharp corners in a straight road, a hidden junction on the fast road, etc. A survey found out that, these black spots are the prime location for 90% of the road accidents.
- **Lack of Infrastructure** The absence of over bridges, underpasses and alternative roads for village traffic means that speeding vehicles compete with slow-moving farm and rural traffic.
- **Lack of Long-term Master Plans** Most cities do not have long-term master plans for transport and traffic. Ad hoc and non-uniform solutions to local road situations are common.
- **Lack of Knowledge of Road Safety Rules** There is a basic lack of knowledge of road safety rules among users. Driving tests in India never examine the actual driving skills on regular roads.

Post-accident factors Absence of quick response (like immediate information to medical authorities) and lack of emergency medical facilities increase the number of fatalities. In addition, possibility of harassment by law-enforcement agencies (like accident related investigations) deter by-passers to respond.

Futuristic Measures which can be Adopted for Reducing Road Accidents in India

- **Role of Government** Government can implement the important recommendations of the KS Radhakrishnan panel on Road Safety. The important recommendations were:
  - **State Governments to perform a compulsory Audit** on road safety to ensure adequate safety standards in the design, construction, and maintenance of roads;
  - **Creating awareness among people** on road safety rules, insurance policies, etc.;
  - **Providing enough compensation** to victims on time.
- **Role of Regulatory Authorities**
  - **Periodic fitness certification** Periodic fitness certification for all motorised vehicles, universalisation of road signs and enforcement of law and safety regulations are crucial.
  - **Zero tolerance towards underage drivers** We should have zero tolerance for underage drivers. India needs to consider severe penalties for violations; cumulative penalties for recurrent infringements should result in temporary withdrawal of licences or a permanent ban on driving.
  - There is a need to review standards pertaining to safety in the design of rural and urban roads and bring them into consonance with international best practices, keeping in view traffic conditions in India. There can be separate lanes for 2-wheelers and heavy vehicles.
- **Role of Vehicle Manufacturer** Vehicles in India must conform to global best standards e.g., The European Union's General Safety Regulation requires new vehicles to incorporate advanced emergency braking technology that launches automatically when a collision is imminent and intelligent speed assistance to reduce speed.
- **Role of Citizen** General public must conform to the rules regarding road safety.
  - Rash driving, lack of respect for traffic rules, low awareness about safety measures (like wearing seat belts) are symptomatic of casual attitude of Indians towards safety (self as well as of the others).

Conclusion

- **Road accidents have remained a silent killer** in India. Despite high number of accidents, road safety has remained low policy priority for the Governments.
- The approach to road safety has to be proactive, rather than reactive. A concerted and focused effort can help bring down road accidents and help save precious lives. SDG target 3.6 calls to halve the number of global deaths and injuries from road traffic crashes.
- **SDG target 11.2 calls for improving road safety and access to public transport** The Government must take all possible steps to meet the targets.

Railways Reform Measures and Private Participation in Railways

Q.6 Along with highlighting the various reforms undertaken for the modernisation of Indian railways, critically examine the entry of private sector in the operation of passenger trains. (150 Words, 10 Marks)

Ans. **Introduction** Indian railways is 4th largest and most complex railway networks in the world, carrying over 23 million passengers and 3 million tonnes of freight every day. It is also a vital lifeline for the country's economy, social development and national integration.

Reform Measures taken for the Modernisation of Railways

Indian Government has initiated several measures for the modernisation of Indian railways. Some of these measures are:

- **Electrification of Railway tracks** With the aim to provide an eco-friendly and energy efficient mode of transportation, a lot of emphasis has been given to railway electrification. India plans to have the largest green railway network in the world. According to the Ministry of Railways, 14 states and union territories have already achieved 100% electrification of rail networks as of 31st March, 2023.

- **Dedicated Freight Corridors (DFCs)** These are high-speed and high-capacity railway corridors exclusively for freight movement, which will reduce congestion and improve the efficiency of the existing network. Example: Eastern and Western Dedicated Freight Corridors.
- **High-Speed Rail (HSR)** This is a project to introduce bullet trains in India, which will run at speeds of over 300 kmph and reduce travel time between major cities. The first HSR corridor is being developed between Mumbai and Ahmedabad, with assistance from Japan.
- **Station Redevelopment** This is a scheme to redevelop railway stations into modern, world-class facilities with amenities such as shopping malls, hotels, restaurants, parking lots, etc. The government has identified 400 stations for redevelopment under the public-private partnership (PPP) mode.
- **Introduction of semi-High Speed Trains** These are self-propelled trains with faster acceleration and deceleration, which will improve the punctuality and comfort of passengers.
  - The government has introduced indigenous trainset named Vande Bharat Express. The government plans to manufacture more trainsets in India and replace conventional trains on various routes.
  - **Gatiman Express which is operational between Delhi and Jhansi** is also known as India's first semi high-speed train. The train can run upto a maximum speed of 160 km per hour and also features new Linke-Hofmann-Busch coaches
- **Digitalisation** To leverage information technology and data analytics to improve operational efficiency, passenger convenience and safety of railways.
  - The government has launched several digital platforms such as the IRCTC website and app for online ticket booking and catering services, the UTS app for unreserved ticketing system, the Rail MADAD app for grievance redressal, the Rail SAARTHI app for integrated services, etc.
  - The government has also installed CCTV cameras, Wi-Fi hotspots, GPS devices and RFID tags on various trains and stations.
- **Safety and Security Reform**
  - **LHB Design Coaches** Lighter and safer coaches for Mail/Express trains.?These coaches are based on German technology and have better anti-climbing features, fire retardant materials, higher speed potential and longer service life than conventional ICF design coaches.
  - **Automatic signalling systems at railway stations** The automatic signalling system has been installed with the purpose of increasing line capacity and safety measures on tracks
  - **GPS based Fog Pass Device** A device to help loco pilots navigate in foggy conditions. It is a GPS enabled hand-held device that displays the exact distance of the approaching landmarks such as signals, level crossing gates, etc.?It also alerts the loco pilot with a loud buzzer when the train approaches a signal or a level crossing gate.
  - **Modern Track Structure** Stronger and more durable tracks and bridges.?This includes using Prestressed Concrete Sleeper (PSC), higher Ultimate Tensile Strength (UTS) rails, fan shaped layout turnout on PSC sleepers, Steel Channel Sleepers on girder bridges, etc.
  - **Ultrasonic Flaw Detection (USFD)** A technique to detect and remove faulty rails. It is a non-destructive testing method that uses high frequency sound waves to inspect the rails for cracks, defects or flaws that may cause derailments or accidents. The defective rails are then removed and replaced with new ones.
- **Outcome-oriented Action** The Railways has taken several measures to improve its operational efficiency and customer satisfaction by way of increasing speed, safety, punctuality and comfort. For example, the speed of freight trains has doubled in 2020-21 to 46 kmph from 23 kmph in earlier years.
- **Expanding Railway Network** The Modi government has expanded the railway network by laying new rail tracks in various states of the country. For example, providing rail connectivity to North East India has been the topmost priority of the Government of India
- **PPP Model** In July 2020, the Railway Ministry invited RFA (Request for Qualifications) from private players for operating passenger train services.
  - It is expected to result in an influx of about Rs. 30,000 crore of private sector investment.
  - Overall, the private sector can bid only for 5% of the total train operations and for 35 years, not a lifetime.

Advantages of the Entry of Private Sector in the Operation of Passenger Trains

- **Improved Infrastructure** It will lead to better infrastructure which in turn would lead to improved amenities for travellers.

- NITI Aayog's strategy for New India @75 envisages many targets in railway infrastructure such as increasing the speed of infrastructure creation, 100% electrification of broad gauge track by 2022-23.

- **Quality of Service: It would foster competition** and hence lead to overall betterment in the quality of services.
  - The **Privatization of Indian Railways will remove some long lasting problem** like Poor sanitation; pick pocketing, insecurity around stations, unruly behaviour of railway employees, sanitation problem, food poisoning, inconvenience to passengers etc.
- **Lesser Accidents: It could result in better maintenance**, reduce the number of accidents, thus resulting in safe travel and higher monetary savings in the long run.
- **Better technology: Increased competition** will incentivise private players to innovate new things which will result in better convenience and better performance of Indian Railways
- **Monetisation of Assets: Railways owns large tracts of land along its tracks**, in various parts of the country and this can be optimally monetised by inviting private players to invest, build and manage properties that may be developed on these lands.
  - Selling state-owned assets to the private sector raised significant sums for the UK government in the 1980s.

Reduced burden on the public exchequer.

- **Less political interference**: With the presence of private investors in Indian Railways, there would be less political In the current scenario, the majority of public-sector enterprises in India are working under political pressure.

Disadvantages of Entry of Private Sector in the Operation of Passenger Trains

- **Profit vs Welfare** The Indian Railway is meant for the welfare of citizens till it is in the control of the government. The privatization could make Railway profit based which will slowly be out of reach of poor Indian Citizens.
- **Connectivity Disparity** Private players will run more trains on high revenue- generating paths rather than in remote areas. This will severely affect the connectivity of the country. The metro cities will shine at the expense of the outlying regions. The remote areas will be more isolated.
- **Cost of Travel** The privatization of Indian Railway could give a hike in fares because as it is obvious that the privatized Railway will focus only on profits.
- **Lack of Transparency** Private companies are unpredictable in their dealings and do not share their governance secrets with the world at large. In such a scenario it would be difficult to pin the accountability on a particular entity, should there be a discrepancy.
- **Monopoly** Privatisation creates private monopolies and thus, it needs regulations to prevent abuse of monopoly power.
  - Private players may seek to increase short term profits and avoid investing in long term projects.
  - For example, the UK is suffering from a lack of investment in new energy sources; the privatised companies are trying to make use of existing plants rather than invest in new ones.

Measures For Sustainable Growth of Indian Railways

- **Modernization of Railways** There is a need to implement the recommendations of the Bibek Debroy committee, such as expansion of Indian Railways manufacturing company, Corporatization of core functions of railways, etc.
- **Sustainable Pricing** There is a need to revisit Indian Railways pricing model to make the passenger and freight segments sustainable. The tariffs should be competitive with the cost of road transportation.
- **Independent Regulator** Setting up an independent regulator will be critical for creating a level playing field for private players.
- **Price regulatory mechanism** Government should declare a maximum price beyond which fares should not be increased so that passengers can have travelling at affordable prices.
  - There must be layered prices, according to the type of the coach.
  - Fare prices for commodities like agriculture and other life sustaining commodities can be regularised
- **Global best practises** Privatisation of railways in Japan is a success story. Government can privatise railways on the lines of Japanese model with appropriate modifications according to the local needs

Conclusion

With the success story of privatisation in the aviation industry to refer to, it may be wise to focus more on robustness of privatization in the world's 4th largest rail network in the world by size to avoid pitfalls of other countries privatisation measures and instead ensure a world class transportation network for citizens of India.

Railways Safety

Q.7 Recent Balasore train tragedy again brings up the issue of railway safety which was once considered a thing of the past. In this background, examine the primary reasons behind railway accidents. To what extent, 'Kavach' initiative will be helpful in improving the railway safety? (250 Words, 15 Marks)

Ans. Introduction The rail accident in Balasore in Odisha, involving the collision of three trains, is a tragic reminder of the challenges of Railway safety in India.

According to the National Crime Records Bureau, an average 23,000 people died every year between 2010 and 2021 in railway accidents. Despite such fatality, railway safety was considered a thing of past due to decline in:

- In the year 2001-02, there were 415 train accidents, which has significantly decreased to 34 incidents by the year 2021-22.
- **Pandemic Impact** The number of accidents further decreased to 59 in 2018-19 and 21 in 2020-21 due to the COVID-19 pandemic
- **Rare Collisions Accidents** On average, train collisions have accounted for approximately 4.7% of all train accidents in the past two decades.
- **Decline in Fatality** With 315 passengers losing their lives and 627 sustaining injuries in the year 2005-06, only 16 passengers were killed, and 86 were injured in train accidents in 2018-19.

Reasons behind Railway Accidents

- **Infrastructure Defects** The railway infrastructure, which includes tracks, bridges, overhead wires, and rolling stock, is often defective due to poor maintenance, ageing, vandalism, sabotage, or natural disasters.
  - **Derailments** Much of the infrastructure was built in the 19th and 20th centuries and has not been upgraded to meet the growing demand and modern standards. The railway system also suffers from a lack of funds, corruption, and inefficiency, which hamper its development and maintenance.
  - **For example, the derailment of the Puri-Haridwar Utkal Express in 2017**, which claimed 23 lives and injured many, was attributed to negligence in track maintenance.
  - Moreover, many routes are operating at over 100% capacity, which increases the risk of accidents due to congestion and overloading.
- **Human Errors** The railway staff, who are responsible for operating, maintaining, and managing the trains and tracks, are prone to human errors due to fatigue, negligence, corruption, or disregard for safety rules and procedures.
  - Human errors can result in wrong signalling, miscommunication, over speeding, or overlooking defects or hazards.
  - The railway staff also lack adequate training and communication skills, which affect their performance and coordination.
- **Signalling Failures** The signalling system, which controls the movement and direction of trains on the tracks, can fail due to technical glitches, power outages, or human errors.
  - Signalling failures can lead to trains running on the wrong track, colliding with other trains or stationary objects, or overshooting stations. For example, the recent train accident in Odisha was reportedly caused by a change in electronic interlocking that was not communicated properly to the drivers.
  - One such incident was the collision between the Gorakhdham Express and a halted goods train in Uttar Pradesh, in 2014, resulting in a high number of casualties and injuries.
- **Unmanned Level Crossings (UMLCs)** UMLCs are places where railway tracks crossroads without any barriers or signals to regulate traffic.

- UMLCs pose a high risk of accidents as vehicles or pedestrians may not notice the approaching train or may try to cross the track when the train is near. In 2018-19, UMLCs accounted for 16% of all train accidents in India.
- For instance, in 2011, 38 people have been killed and 17 others injured in a train-bus collision in the Kanshiramnagar district of Uttar Pradesh.

CAG's 2022 Report on Safety in Indian Railways also Highlighted several Shortcomings in the Safety of India's Railways that include:

- **Shortfalls in Inspections** The report found that there were significant deficiencies in inspections conducted by Track Recording Cars, which are responsible for assessing the geometrical and structural conditions of railway tracks. The inspections were found to have shortfalls ranging from 30% to 100%.
- **Failures to Submit or Accept Inquiry Reports** The report pointed out that there were failures to submit or accept inquiry reports after accidents. This hampers the process of learning from past mistakes and preventing recurrences of incidents.
- **Inadequate use of Dedicated Railway Fund** The report found that the dedicated railway fund, which is meant for priority tasks, was not effectively utilized. It highlighted failures to use the fund for essential safety-related activities.
- **Decline in Funding Track Renewal** The CAG report revealed a decline in funding for track renewal, which is crucial for maintaining the safety and integrity of railway tracks. Insufficient funding in this area can lead to track deterioration and increase the risk of derailments.
- **Inadequate Staffing in Safety Operations** The report identified inadequate staffing in safety operations as a serious concern. Insufficient manpower can affect the timely execution of safety-related tasks and compromise the overall safety of the railway system.
- **Costs of Derailments** The report estimated the costs of derailments to be around Rs 32.96 crore. This includes the financial impact of accidents across 16 railway zones and the associated damages and losses.
- **Non-operational Track Management System (TMS)** The TMS, a web-based application for online monitoring of track maintenance activities, was found to be non-operational. The in-built monitoring mechanism of the TMS portal was not functioning, and information related to closure of inspection notes was not filled in the portal.
- **Link between Derailments and Track Renewals** The report stated that out of the 1,127 derailments that occurred during 2017-2021, around 289 derailments (26%) were linked to track renewals.

Measures taken to reduce Railway Accidents

- **Rashtriya Rail Sanraksha Kosh (RRSK)** A safety fund for critical assets. It was established in 2017-18 with a corpus of ₹ 1 lakh crore over a period of five years for critical safety related works such as track renewals, signalling projects, bridge rehabilitation, etc.
- **Technological Upgradation** Improved design and features of coaches and wagons. This includes introducing Modified Centre Buffer Couplers, Bogie Mounted Air Brake System (BMBS), improved suspension design and provision of Automatic fire & smoke detection system in coaches. It also includes installing KAVACH - an indigenously developed Automatic Train Protection (ATP).
- **GPS based Fog Pass Device** A device to help loco pilots navigate in foggy conditions. It is a GPS enabled hand-held device that displays the exact distance of the approaching landmarks such as signals, level crossing gates, etc.
- **Modern Track Structure** Stronger and more durable tracks and bridges.?This includes using Prestressed Concrete Sleeper (PSC), higher Ultimate Tensile Strength (UTS) rails, fan shaped layout turnout on PSC sleepers, Steel Channel Sleepers on girder bridges, etc.
- **Ultrasonic Flaw Detection (USFD)** A technique to detect and remove faulty rails. It is a non-destructive testing method that uses high frequency sound waves to inspect the rails for cracks, defects or flaws that may cause derailments or accidents.?The defective rails are then removed and replaced with new ones.
- **Interlocking System** A system to control points and signals centrally. It is a system that uses electrical or electronic devices to operate the points and signals from a central location. It eliminates the need for manual operation of points and signals by staff on the ground.?It also reduces the chances of human failure and enhances safety.
- **Elimination of Unmanned Level Crossings (UMLCs)** UMLCs are being eliminated progressively by closing, merging, manning, or providing subways/road under bridges/road over bridges.

KAVACH and Railway Safety

- **KAVACH is an indigenously developed Automatic Train Protection (ATP) system** developed to enhance safety in Indian Railways.
- Developed in collaboration with three Indian vendors by the Research Designs and Standards Organisation (RDSO), Kavach has been adopted as the National ATP System for Indian Railways.
- It is designed to prevent accidents and ensure the smooth operation of trains.
- It is a Safety Integrity Level 4 (SIL-4) certified technology with the probability of error being one in 10,000 years.

In this context, Kavach' initiative will be helpful in improving the railway safety by:

- **Prevention of Signal Passing at Danger (SPAD) KAVACH** helps to prevent trains from crossing red signals and ensures adherence to signal instructions.
- **Real-Time Update** The system provides real-time updates on movement authority, displaying signal aspects in the Driver Machine Interface (DMI) or Loco Pilot Operation cum Indication Panel (LPOCIP).

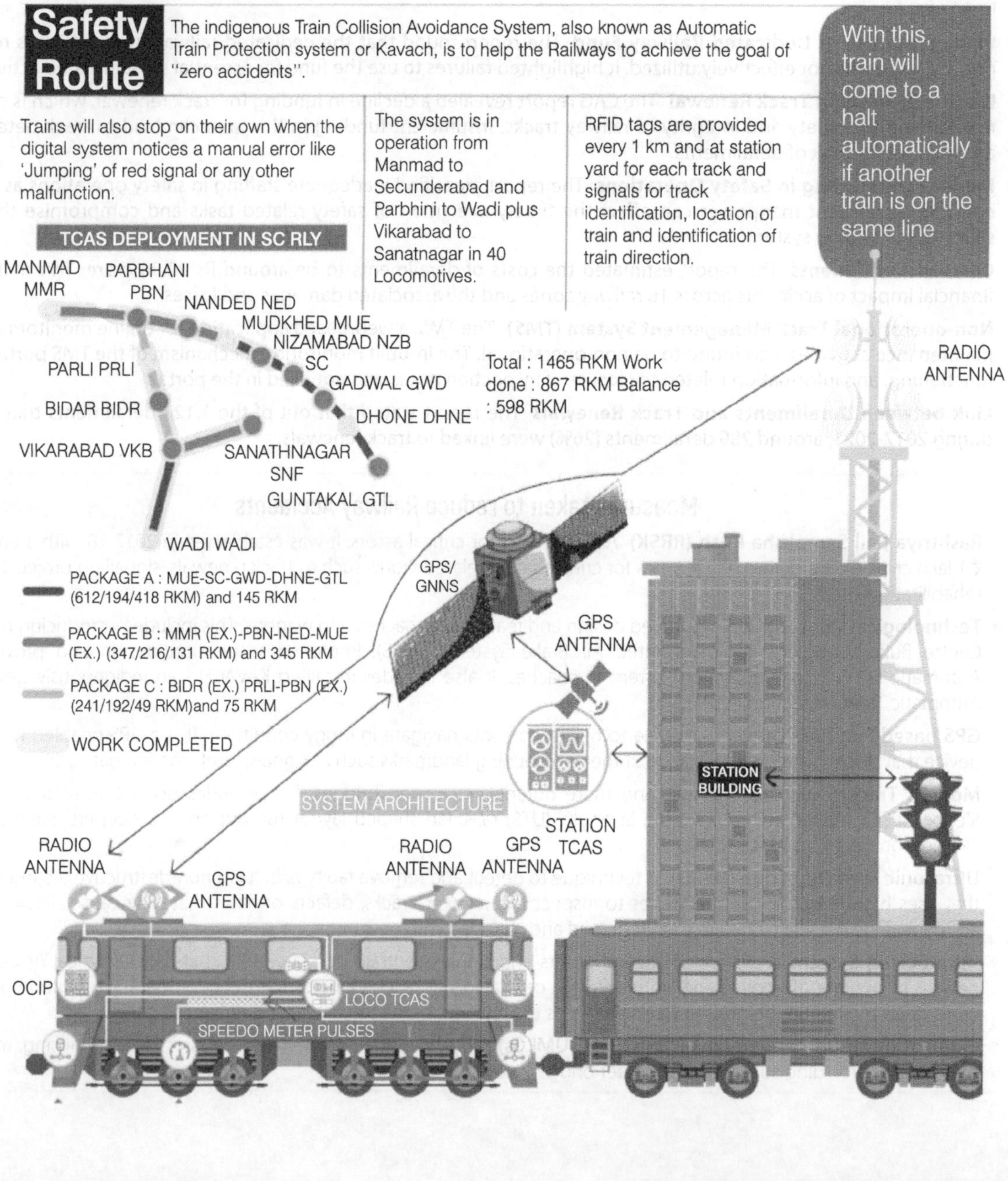

- **Automatic Braking KAVACH automatically initiates** the braking system if the train exceeds the prescribed speed limits, preventing accidents caused by over-speeding.
- **Prevention of Collision** KAVACH helps prevent collisions between two locomotives equipped with the system, adding an extra layer of safety. If two trains are approaching each other on the same track, SOS signals are sent to both trains and Kavach automatically stops the trains at least 300 metres from each other.
- **Live Monitoring** The system allows for centralized live monitoring of train movements through a Network Monitor System, providing real-time information on train positions and ensuring effective management.

KAVACH could have potentially prevented the Odisha accident, however it was not implemented on that particular route at the time. More importantly, Kavach system is only active along 2% of India's rail network.

Futuristic Measures to Improve Railway Safety

Anil Kakodkar Committee (2012) to review the safety of the Indian Railways had recommended certain improvements like:

- **Creation of a Railway Safety Authority** Establishment of a statutory Railway Safety Authority with sufficient powers to oversee and regulate safety on the railways, independent of the Railway Board. This was even recommended by Vinod Rai Committee (2015).
- **Restructuring of RDSO: The Research Design and Standards Organization (RDSO)** should be restructured for greater empowerment, enabling it to embrace emerging technologies effectively.
- **Adoption of Advanced Signalling System** The entire trunk route length of 19,000 km should be equipped with an Advanced Signalling System, similar to the European Train Control System, within five years.
- **Elimination of Level Crossings** All Level Crossings, both manned and unmanned, should be eliminated.
- **Switch to LHB Design Coaches** The Committee recommends switching from the ICF design coaches to the safer LHB design coaches.
- **Safety Infrastructure Maintenance** The Committee suggests investing approximately Rs 20,000 crore in the maintenance of safety-related infrastructure.
- **Financial Investment** A total financial investment of Rs 1,00,000 crore over a five-year period to address the current safety and infrastructure challenges.

Other Steps which can be taken for improving railway safety are

- **Strengthen Maintenance** Focus on regular inspection and maintenance of tracks, coaches, and infrastructure, addressing backlogs and improving overall conditions.
- **Embrace Technology** Invest in advanced sensors, GPS-based systems, and automatic fire detection to enhance safety features in coaches and wagons.
- **Ensure Safety Oversight** Establish an independent regulatory body to monitor and enforce safety standards, ensuring accountability and adherence to protocols.
- **Allocate Adequate Funds** Prioritize safety expenditure, effectively utilize funds like the Rashtriya Rail Sanraksha Kosh, and regularly review funding to meet evolving safety requirements.
- **Learn from International best Practices** Collaborate with experts and organizations to gain insights and expertise from countries with exemplary railway safety records.
- **Promote a Safety Culture** Foster a safety-first mindset through awareness campaigns, training programs, and public outreach initiatives.
- **Train Employees to Minimize Human Errors** Provide regular and comprehensive training to the railway staff on the latest technologies, equipment, systems, safety rules and procedures.
- **Introduce Performance-Linked Incentives** Reward the railway staff based on their performance and compliance with the safety rules and procedures. (Vinod Rai Committee Recommendations in 2015)

Conclusion

Indian Railways has been the lifeline of India. There has been a lot of progress in many fields but safety should come first. Indian Railways needs an infrastructure revamp focused on improving safety, speed, and punctuality so that Indian railways can reclaim its role as the lifeline of India.

Best Practices

- **United Kingdom** The UK has one of the lowest rates of train accidents in Europe. The UK has implemented various safety measures, such as: **The Train Protection and Warning System (TPWS)**, which automatically stops trains that pass signals at danger or exceed speed limits; **The European Train Control System (ETCS)**, which provides continuous communication between trains and signalling centres and The **Rail Accident Investigation Branch (RAIB)**, which conducts independent and impartial investigations of railway accidents and incidents.
- **Japan** Japan is known for its high-speed trains, such as the Shinkansen or Bullet trains, which operate at speeds of up to 320 km/h has achieved a remarkable record of safety, with zero passenger fatalities since the Shinkansen started operating in 1964. Japan has adopted various safety measures, such as: The **Automatic Train Control (ATC)** system, which monitors and controls the speed and braking of trains; The Comprehensive Automatic Train Inspection System (CATIS), which detects defects and faults in trains using sensors and cameras.

Inland Waterways

Q.8 Inland Water Transport (IWT) provides supplementary mode of transport which has many advantages over other modes of transport but requires urgent resolution of problems plaguing it. Critically comment.
(150 Words, 10 Marks)

Ans. **Introduction** India has 7500 km long coastline with approximately 14,500 kms of navigable waterways but only a small percentage of trade is currently carried out through inland waterways and coastlines as it accounts for only about 0.4% of trade (China - 8.7%; USA - 8.3% and Europe - 7%). This offers a huge potential for developing a cheaper and greener mode of transport.

Benefits of Inland Water Transport (IWT)

- **Low cost** Inland waterways need less capital for development and less maintenance costs. A World Bank study has found that water transportation is about 30% cheaper than railways and 60% less expensive than roadways.
- **Energy efficient** Inland water transport is considered to be the most cost-effective mode of transport from the point of view of fuel efficiency.
  - For example, the Integrated National Waterways Transportation Grid Study states that one litre of fuel will move 24 tons through one kilometre on road, 85 on rail and 105 km on inland water transport. Further, 1 HP can 150 kg on road, 500 kg on rail and 4000 kg on water.
- **Environment friendly** CO_2 emissions from container vessels are much lesser than road transport vehicles. Capacity: It has an enormous capacity to carry bulk cargo, goods etc.
- **Navigable** In India, around 14,500 km of river channels are navigable. But only 2000 km is used.
- **Growth** The development of waterways will stimulate industrial growth and tourism. It will also promote export and import as it reduces logistics cost of moving cargo between ports and hinterland. Fewer accidents and less congestion compared to roads.
- **Accessibility** It can provide access to remote areas. For instance, North-eastern states now receive coal, food grains through inland water transport.

Challenges in the IWT

- **Inadequate depth** To be viable for a navigable inland waterway, river needs enough depth throughout the year However, in their natural state; many Indian rivers simply do not have that level of water which will necessitate extensive dredging.
- **Problem of siltation** Indian rivers (especially rivers in the northern plains) face severe problems of siltation round the year.
- **No Navigability throughout the Year** Some rivers are seasonal and do not offer navigability through the year. Around 20 out of the 111 identified national waterways have reportedly been found unviable.
- **Social Impact** All the identified waterways require intensive capital and maintenance dredging, which could be resisted by the local community on environmental grounds, including displacement fears, thereby posing implementation challenges.

- **Environmental Impact** Dredging operations will damage river bed, and can lead to change in habitats for various aquatic flora and fauna. Dredging may also impact aquifers along the river, damaging the ability of water to percolate underground.
- **Other Uses of Water** Water also has important competing uses, viz. need for living as well as for irrigation, power generation etc. It would not be possible for the local government/others to overlook these needs.
- **Exclusive Jurisdiction of the Central Government** The exclusive jurisdiction of the Central Government is only in regard to shipping and navigation on inland waterways declared to be 'national waterways' by an act of Parliament. Utilisation/sailing of vessels, in other waterways, is within the ambit of the concurrent list or is in the jurisdiction of the respective state governments.
- **Shortage of IWT Vessels** Vessel building is highly capital intensive and faces difficulties in obtaining project finance from banks and financial institutions.
- **Inadequate Industries** Inadequate number of Industrial units on the riverside, especially not along the Brahmaputra is a major discouragement hindering development of inland waterways.

NITI Aayog Recommendations

- **Streamline the Governance of Inland Waterways** NITI Aayog recommends streamlining the regulatory structure and bringing an overarching body to oversee Inland Water Transport such as the IWAI to more consistency in the rules and strategy of the sector.
- **Develop Measures for Year-round Navigation** Efforts should be made to develop deeper stretches of the river, i.e., at least 2.5 m to 3 m to achieve year-around navigation adequate maintenance of rivers, including continuous dredging to maintain adequate water depth for servicing shipping lines should be ensured
- **Ease Restrictions on River-sea Movement** Utilizing a single vessel for both inland and coastal waters, lowers transport costs and minimizes handling. Thus, by 2020, state authorities should draw up coordinates for inland vessel limits under the Inland Vessel Act for their coastal waters
- **Develop Inland Waterways transport to facilitate movement of goods to neighbouring countries and the Northeast** State governments should commence work on dredging and channel stabilization to create about 20 new ports in the Brahmaputra and Barak rivers. The protocol for Inland Waterways between Bangladesh and India should be extended for at least 10 years to reduce uncertainty.
- **International Best Practice** China has an inland waterway system of more than 5600 navigable rivers and 2000 inland ports. IWT development is concentrated on 5 specific areas (Yangtze River, Pearl River, Beijing-Hangzhou Grand Canal, Yangtze River Delta and the Pearl River Delta).

Government Initiatives to Promote Inland Waterways

- **The Inland Waterways Authority of India Act, 1985** The Act establishes an Authority for the management and development of inland waterways for the purposes of shipping and navigation, as well as things relating to it. The Inland Waterways Authority of India was established in 1986.
- **Jal Marg Vikas Project (JMVP)** It aims at capacity augmentation of navigation on National Waterway-1 (NW-1), along the river Ganga. It is being implemented with the technical assistance and investment support of the World Bank.
- **Project Arth Ganga** With the local community's help and an emphasis on economic activities in and along the Ganga River, Project Arth Ganga aims to re-engineer the JMVP. As part of the "Project Arth Ganga" to revitalise economic activity in Uttar Pradesh, Bihar, Jharkhand, and West Bengal, small jetties along the Ganga will be constructed to enhance local economic activities.
- **The National Waterways Act of 2016** The National (inland) Waterways Act designated 111 rivers or river sections, creeks, and estuaries as National (inland) Waterways. It permits the Central Government to regulate the growth of these waterways in terms of shipping, navigation, and transport via mechanically propelled vessels.
- **Sagarmala Project** In addition to developing coast trade routes, the Sagarmala project aims to expand inland waterways to drive industrial development.

Conclusion

National waterways provide a cost-effective, logistically efficient and environment-friendly mode of transport, whose development as a supplementary mode would enable diversion of traffic from over-congested roads and railways. Government intends to increase the share of Inland Water Transport (IWT) to 5% as per Maritime India Vision (MIV)-2030.

Ports Sector

Q.9 Recently, the government has asked all ports to prepare a master plan in order to become 'mega ports' by 2047. In this background, examine the challenges faced by ports and suggest remedial measures.
(150 Words, 10 Marks)

Ans. Introduction A mega port can be called 'mega' because of three factors: the cargo volume it handles, the economic value it represents, or the land and water surface utilized, or any combination of them. Having mega ports helps develop the 'blue economy', which according to the World Bank refers to sustainable use of ocean resources for economic growth, improved livelihood and jobs, and ocean ecosystem health. To achieve this, the government is working to make all ports as mega ports by 2047.

Major Hurdles Faced by the Port Sector in India

- **Low Capacity** Despite handling 90% of cargo by volume and 70% by value, the traffic handled at ports is far less than their capacity. For example, the capacity of 13 major ports is more than 1500 million tonnes per annum (MTPA) in 2021, but traffic handled at these ports was to the tune of around 670 MT during 2020-21.
- **Physical Infrastructure** Indian ports are plugged with issues like low productivity, high turnover and pre-berthing time, and high freight costs.
  - **High Turnaround times** Ports in India suffer from high turnaround times for ships. Although the turnaround time has improved it is still poor compared to global standards e.g., Japan (8.16 hours), Taiwan (10.56 hours), Hong Kong (12.48 hours) have much better turnaround times than Indian ports (62.16 hours).
  - **Port Congestion** Port congestion due to container volume, shortage of handling equipment and inefficient operations is a major concern. **Example: In Nhava Sheva port**
- **Digital Infrastructure** There is absence of a common online portal with end-to-end stakeholder coverage. The IT solutions work in isolation and do not interact with each other in the absence of a common integrated platform for information exchange.
- **Logistical Bottlenecks** The lack of expressway connectivity between major ports as well as industrial clusters, and high fuel cost make hinterland transportation inefficient and slow.
- **Labour Issues** The low productivity of ports is attributable to local labour being hired, which is often unskilled and operates inefficiently, thereby affecting the overall productivity and cargo traffic volumes handled.
- **Lack of Competitiveness** Due to high taxation and high compliance burden, the operational costs of Indian vessels are high.
- **Investment Issues** Despite 100% FDI and 10-year tax holiday to enterprises engaged in maintenance and operation of ports, a cumulative FDI of only US$ 1.63 billion was received from April 2000 to March 2021.
- **Regulatory Issues** The port operations in India are marred by complex custom procedures, regulations, and lengthy documentation process. The major problem with regulation is that major and non-major ports fall under different jurisdictions. Further, the regulatory framework is rigid.

In order to address these Challenges, the following measures can be adopted

- Ministry should develop an **efficient system which can support seamless movement of cargo across all modes**. The Ministry should emphasize all the Major and Minor Ports to enhance the productivity and infrastructure to the level of best Ports in the world which will enable them to compete globally.
- The government needs to open up the **dredging sector** to attract more players, particularly international players, to increase and **maintain draft depth** at ports to attract large vessels and enable them to become hub ports.
- There is a need to expedite the **completion of various projects under** the **Sagarmala programme**, especially those aimed at improving port connectivity, setting up coastal economic zones (CEZs), and establishing new ports.

- A comprehensive programme **to reduce the cost of movement of goods behind the borders** from hinterland to ports needs to be undertaken.
- There is a need for a **common digital platform**, which brings all stakeholders on a single platform proposed as the **'National Portal for Cargo Facilitation (NPCF)**.
- The government and other stakeholders should enhance the use of technology like big data, Artificial Intelligence etc. in ports and, wherever feasible, draw lessons from successful global ports such as Rotterdam, Felixstowe, and Singapore to improve efficiency.
- Ministry of Ports should also work in close coordination with the Ministry of Road Transport and Highways, NHAI, and Ministry of Environment to address the delays in projects due to land acquisition and environmental clearances.
- **Vijay Kelkar Committee on PPP** With regards to ports, the committee recommended review of role and need of Tariff Authority for Major Ports (TAMP), review of MCA, quicker clearances, rationalized leases and stamp duties

Conclusion

The Government has set a target to make India a developed nation by 2047. This will require rapid economic growth supported by domestic demand, investments and robust exports. Maritime trade and port infrastructure will play a vital role in achieving a robust growth in exports. Thus, the government has to support the development of world-class port infrastructure in India to make Indian ports and exports globally competitive.

Aviation Sector

Q.10 Despite being touted as the 'fastest growing aviation sector' in the world, airlines in the India have struggled to survive in the highly competitive and unforgiving aviation industry. What are the challenges being faced by the airlines? Also, suggest measures that can be taken to address these challenges. (250 Words, 15 Marks)

Ans. **Introduction** India is the world's third-largest domestic air passenger market. The domestic aviation market in India is predicted to reach US$ 30 billion by 2024, making it the third-largest industry globally.

- The number of domestic passengers increased by more than doubled, from 120 million to nearly 275 million, over the course of the six years between FY14 and FY20, at a CAGR of 14.5%.
- Indian airlines are predicted to increase capacity by at least 25%, making India the fastest-expanding aviation market with 7% annual growth by 2040.

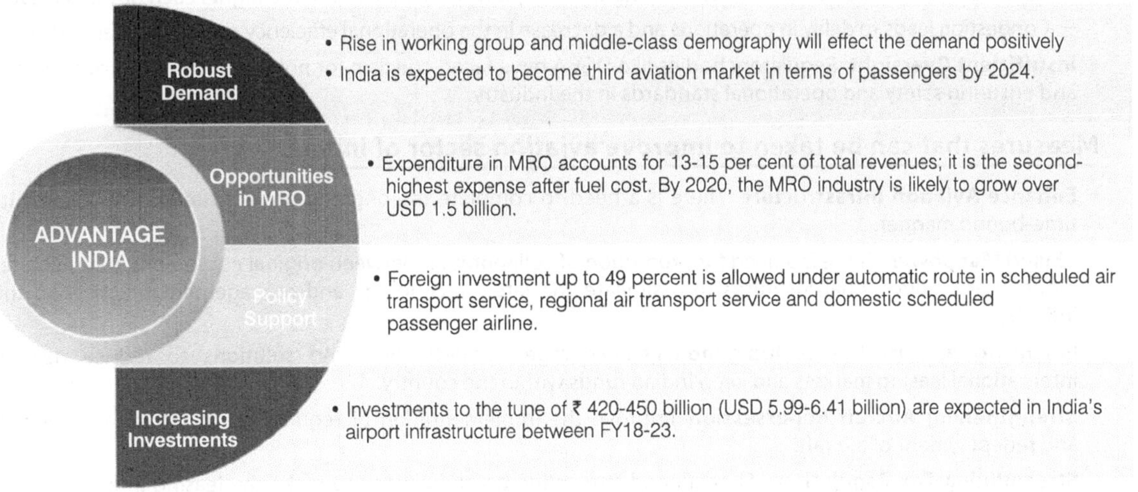

However, private airlines in India have struggled to survive, with many failing over the past decade.

- Recently, budget airline Go First filed for insolvency. It is the third airline to go bankrupt in the past decade after Kingfisher and Jet Airways.

Challenges faced by the Airlines in India

- **High Service charge and Low-ticket Price** Airlines have to pay for using airport facilities like runways and terminals and low-ticket prices for the competitive edge in business works against the economic viability.
  - Privatization of airports has raised concerns about fee increases.
- **Financial Challenges** Indian airlines are projected to record a consolidated loss of $1.6 to 1.8 billion in FY24, with full-service carriers incurring up to $1.2 billion in losses.
  - **Financial Difficulties** Seventeen airlines, both domestic and regional, have gone out of business due to financial difficulties.
  - **Pandemic Incurred Losses** Indian airlines and airports incurred financial losses worth Rs 22,400 crore in the last financial year amid the coronavirus pandemic.
  - In 2019-20, IndiGo was the only airline to make a profit, while all other players posted losses led by then state-run Air India at ?4,600 crore.
  - **Rupee Depreciation** Any deterioration of the exchange rate of rupees to the US dollar also causes adverse impacts on the profits of the airlines.
- **Uneven Market Share** The consolidation of four carriers including Air India and Vistara by the Tatas.
  - **Consolidated Air India and Indigo will** capture 75-80% of the market, leaving just about 20% for players like SpiceJet, and the newest entrant Akasa.
- **High Fuel Costs** Fuel cost as a percentage of operating charges amounts to 45% in India as compared to the global average of 30 per cent.
- **Inadequate Human Resource Capabilities** Shortage and gaps in the availability of industry-recognised skills – from airline pilots and crew to maintenance and ground handling personnel – constrains the growth of different segments of the sector.
  - **High Training Cost of Crew** Training airline crew is expensive and there is a shortage of pilots due to a lack of Flight Training Organizations.
- **Weak Maintenance, Repair, And Operations (MRO) Sector** 90% of the Indian MRO work is outsourced to countries like Singapore, Dubai, UAE, Sri Lanka and others.
- **Procedural Complexities** Taxes and approvals by both Central and States governments increases the transaction costs of the aviation sector
- **Airports Congestion** India's major airports suffer from congestion of passengers and limited runways.
  - For instance, Mumbai Airport, which is a single runway airport handles over 900 flights each day on an average.
  - Congestion leads to delay in operations and a decrease in the operational efficiency of both airlines and airports.
- **Insufficient Oversight** Regulatory bodies like DGCA have faced criticism for not conducting thorough financial audits and ensuring safety and operational standards in the industry.

Measures that can be taken to improve aviation sector of India

- **Enhance Aviation Infrastructure** There is a need to complete the ongoing projects under the UDAN initiative in a time-bound manner.
- **Skilled Manpower** There is a need for promotion of collaboration between original equipment manufacturers (OEMs), industry and educational institutes to assimilate the latest technology and management practices in the aviation industry.
- **Financing Aircraft Leases Indigenously** Encourage domestic financing solutions to reduce dependency on international leasing markets and keep Indian funds within the country.
- **Strengthening Aircraft Repossession** Improve the implementation of regulations to facilitate faster repossession and redeployment of aircraft.
- **Streamlining Tax Regulations** Simplify and streamline tax regulations to make the leasing industry more attractive and competitive.
- **Promoting Maintenance, Repair, and Operations (MRO) Ecosystem in India** Develop an ecosystem that caters to the leasing industry's maintenance and operation needs, creating a self-sufficient and robust industry within India.

- **Making India a Trans-shipment Hub** India can reap multiple benefits by establishing itself as a trans-shipment hub in the region. This will augment India's trading capacity as a service provider, emerging as a foreign exchange earner and enabler for better connectivity in the region.

Conclusion

By addressing these challenges and implementing the suggested reforms, India can pave the way for a thriving aircraft leasing industry, making the country a global leasing hub and bolstering the aviation sector.

Energy Sector (Energy Linkage with SDGs)

Q.11 Access to affordable, reliable, sustainable and modern energy is the sine qua non to achieve Sustainable Development Goals (SDGs). Comment on the progress made in India in this regard. (150 Words, 10 Marks)

UPSC Mains PYQ 2018

Ans. **Introduction** Affordable and reliable energy is one of the fundamental necessities for development. Public health burden, loss of productivity and efficiency can be improved with access to modern energy. India is home to the maximum population with lack of electricity & clean cooking energy. In such cases access to affordable energy is of prime importance for achieving the Sustainable Development Goals (SDGs) 7 i.e. Access to affordable, reliable, sustainable and modern energy.

SDG 7 is the sine qua non to achieve Sustainable Development Goals (SDGs)

- **Access to Affordable Energy** it aims to increase supply of energy to all the inaccessible areas and ensure that there is no deprivation in consumption of energy due to economic and other constraints. The SDGs promoted by it are:
  - **SDG 4 (Target 4.1)** Ensure equitable and quality primary and secondary education leading to effective learning outcomes.
  - **SDG 8** Access to affordable energy promotes inclusive growth and helps realize the full productive employment of people.
  - **SDG 10 (Target 10.3)** Ensure equal opportunity and reduce inequalities of outcome.
- **Access to Reliable Energy** It aims at meeting the energy requirements of rising population and establishes nexus between need and ecosystem. The SDGs promoted by it are:
  - **SDG 6 (Target 6.1)** Achieve universal and equitable access to safe drinking water for all.
  - **SDG 9 (Target 9.1)** Developing quality, reliable and resilient infrastructure to support economic development and human being.
- **Access to Sustainable Energy** Its objective is to establish balance between present and future generations. The SDGs promoted by it are:
  - **SDG 11 (Target 11.3)** Enhances inclusive and sustainable urbanization and capacity for sustainable human settlement planning.
  - **SDG 12 (Target 12.2)** Achieving the sustainable management and efficient use of natural resources by 2030.
- **Access to Modern Energy** It aims for production of energy which is not much polluting and clean energy which has lesser environmental implications
- **SDG 13 (Target 13.2)** Integrating climate change measures into national policies, strategies and planning.

Progress made by India in this regard

- **Promotion of Renewable Energy: At COP-21 in Paris in 2015,** India committed to a 40% share of power generation from non-fossil fuel sources. This target has been achieved a decade ahead of the 2030 timeline. Now it has been extended to meet 50% of energy requirements from renewable energy by 2030
- **PM Ujjwala Yojana** It aims to provide 8 crore LPG connections to the deprived households by 2020. It reduces their drudgery of firewood collection and protects them from negative health effects of smoke. As on 1st March 2023 there are 9.59 crore PMUY beneficiaries.

- **PAHAL Scheme** All LPG Subsidy beneficiaries to be linked to Aadhar payment system. This increased availability of subsidized cylinder and encourage poor families to switch from firewood and kerosene stoves.
- **UJALA (Unnat Jyoti by Affordable LEDs for All)** It provides subsidized LED bulbs to households. This encourages families to switch from kerosene lanterns to electricity-based lighting.
- The **Chiller Star Labelling Program** has been launched by the Bureau of Energy Efficiency (BEE) to encourage the deployment of Energy Efficient chiller systems. The program envisages providing star rating in terms of its energy performance.
- **Deen Dayal Upadhyaya Gram Jyoti Yojana (DDUGJY)** It aims for 24x7 electricity to rural areas through separation of feeder lines for rural households and agricultural activities.
- **Saubhagaya Scheme** To provide last mile electricity connections to all remaining un-electrified households in rural and urban areas. There has been 100% household electrification achieved under this scheme.

Futuristic Measures

- **Better targeting** Mapping of areas deficient in energy and monitor the capability to harness energy by each local area
- **Waste to Energy plants** Development of adequate infrastructure in the cities to convert the municipal wastes into -useful resource for generation of electricity.
- **Increase in R&D** The government should promote through adequate funding domestic R&D laboratories to harness energy especially the green and renewable sources of energy.
- **Focus on 3G's** Enhanced focus on green technologies, green infrastructure and green funding.

Conclusion

India has a crucial role to play in shaping the SDGs and has done a commendable job in providing clean and efficient energy to the people. However, the road is a long one and it needs to put renewed focus for ensuring universal access to affordable energy by 2030.

Energy Security

Q.12 India's energy mix has to create a balance between meeting energy demand from 1.4 billion population and the desire to generate clean & sustainable form of energy. Discuss. (150 Words, 10 Marks)

Ans. **Introduction** With a population of 1.4 billion, India has a massive demand for energy to fuel its rapidly growing economy. From a power deficit nation at the time of Independence; today, we are a power surplus nation with a total installed electricity capacity of over 4 lakh MW.

Rapid economic growth, urbanization, a rising population and fast industrial development have contributed to an increased need for energy. Commercial primary energy consumption in India has grown by about 700% in the last four decades.

So keeping in mind the sustainable development goals, India's power generation mix is rapidly shifting towards a more significant share of renewable energy. Today, India is the world's third largest producer of renewable energy, with 40% of its installed electricity capacity coming from non-fossil fuel sources.

India's existing Energy Mix

Installed Generation Capacity (Fuelwise)

Catagory	Installed Generation Capacity (MW)	% of Share in Total
	Fossil Fuel	
Coal	204.435	49.7%
Lignite	6.620	1.6%
Gas	24.824	6.1%
Diesel	589	0.1%

Total Fossil Fuel	**2,36,469**	**57.4%**
RES (Incl. Hydro)	168.963	41.0%
Hydro	46.850	11.4%
Wind, Solar and other RE	122.113	29.6%
Wind	42.015	10.2%
Solar	64,381	15.6%
BM Power/Cogen	10,218	2.5%
Waste to Energy	523	0.1%
Small Hydro Power	4,943	1.2%
Nuclear	6.780	1.6%
Total Non-Fossil Fuel	**175.743**	**42.6%**
Total Installed Capacity	**4,12,212**	**100%**

India's Growing Energy Demand

- India is the world's third-largest energy consuming country, because of rising incomes and improving standards of living.
- Energy use has doubled since 2000, with 80% of demand still being met by coal, oil and solid biomass. On a per capita basis, India's energy use and emissions are less than half the world average, as are other key indicators such as vehicle ownership, steel and cement output.
- An expanding economy, population, urbanization and industrialisation mean that India sees the largest increase in energy demand of any country, across all of our scenarios to 2040.
- India's electricity demand is set to increase much more rapidly than its overall energy demand.
- According to the Ministry of Power, as of October 2021, the country achieved 100% household electrification under the Saubhagya scheme, which aimed to provide electricity connections to all rural and urban households.

Renewable Energy Push

- **At COP-21 in Paris in 2015**, India committed to a 40% share of power generation from non-fossil fuel sources. This target has been achieved a decade ahead of the 2030 timeline.
- **Adoption of Panchamrit principles at COP-26 in Glasgow summit, 2022**
  - Increasing non-fossil energy capacity to 500 GW by 2030;
  - Meeting 50% of energy requirements from renewables by 2030;
  - Reducing cumulative emissions by one billion tonnes by 2030;
  - Reducing emissions intensity of India's gross domestic product (GDP) by 45% by 2030.
  - Net-zero emissions target by 2070.
- **Promoting Solar Energy** Development of solar parks and ultra-mega solar power projects
  - Under the solar park scheme, 57 Solar Parks with a cumulative capacity of 39.28 GW in 13 states were approved.
  - India has spearheaded the International Solar Alliance (ISA) which is an action-oriented, member-driven, collaborative platform for increased deployment of solar energy technologies.
- **National Green Hydrogen Mission** The intent of the mission is to incentivise the commercial production of green hydrogen and make India a net exporter of the fuel.
  - The Mission aims to increase the export of green hydrogen and simultaneously reduce fossil fuel imports of over Rs 1 lakh crore.
- Natural gas is being promoted as a cleaner alternative to coal and petroleum-based fuels. Prime Minister Narendra Modi wants to raise the share of gas in India's energy mix to 15% by 2030 from 6.2%, helping it progress towards meeting a 2070 net zero carbon-emission goal.

Challenges with clean and sustainable form of energy in ensuring Energy Security

- **Impact on Environment** While RE generation is zero-carbon (barring some biofuels), there are emissions at other points of its lifecycle, such as during raw material extraction and equipment manufacturing. There are also RE's detrimental impacts on biodiversity and ecology.
- **Intermittency and Reliability** One of the main challenges with renewable energy sources like solar and wind is their intermittent nature. They depend on weather conditions and are not available consistently throughout the day or year.
- **Installation Cost Issue** The high initial cost of installation is one of the major hurdles in the development of renewable energy. Although the development of a coal plant requires high investment, it is known that wind and solar power plants also require huge investment. In addition to this, storage systems of the generated energy are expensive and represent a real challenge in terms of megawatt production.
- **E-Waste from Renewable Technologies** The manufacturing, installation, and maintenance of renewable energy technologies, such as solar panels and wind turbines, can generate electronic waste (e-waste). The improper disposal of batteries can lead to environmental contamination due to the release of toxic chemicals.

Still continuation of traditional sources

- **Transition Challenges** The transition from traditional energy sources to renewables involves economic, social, and technical challenges. A sudden and abrupt shift could lead to disruptions and economic hardships. A gradual and well-planned transition allows for a smoother integration of renewable energy while minimizing adverse impacts.
- **Energy Access and Affordability** In many parts of India, access to reliable electricity is still a challenge. Traditional energy sources, such as coal-fired power plants, have been instrumental in providing electricity to remote areas and expanding energy access. These sources can be established quickly and at a relatively lower cost compared to renewable energy installations.
- **Role of Coal-Fired Power Plants** Coal has been the dominant source of electricity generation in India. It provides a significant share of the country's baseload power and has played a crucial role in expanding energy access to remote areas. Coal-fired power plants have been established quickly and have traditionally been cost-competitive compared to renewable energy installations.

Conclusion

It is important to note that while traditional energy sources continue to be utilized, efforts should be made to reduce their environmental impact by adopting cleaner technologies, improving efficiency, and implementing emission control measures. Additionally, research and development should continue to advance renewable energy technologies, energy storage solutions, and grid integration techniques to overcome the challenges associated with their widespread adoption.

Coal Sector Reforms

Q.13 Give an account of the reforms being undertaken in the liberalization of coal sector from a highly regulated resource in India. What challenges still remain in the coal industry inspite of various reform measures? (250 Words, 10 Marks)

Ans. **Introduction** Coal remains the primary source of fuel in India, at least for the next few decades, contributing to around 50% of the power generation. At present, despite being the world's second-largest producer (it produced 893 million tonnes in 2022-23 and the target for FY 2023-24 is 1012 MT), it is also the one of the largest importers of the coal (estimated imports of around 237 million tonnes in FY 23).

From a highly regulated sector to completely liberalised sector

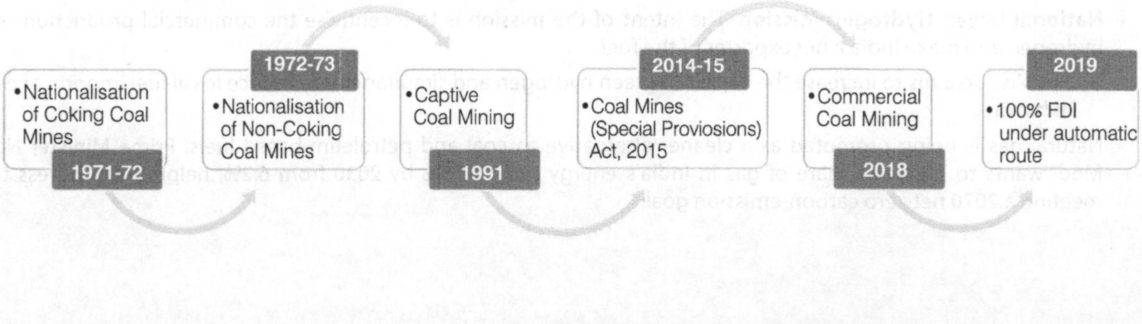

- **The Coal-Bearing Areas (Acquisition and Development) Act, 1957** Unlike the Land Acquisition Act which grants general power to the Government to acquire land, the Coal Bearing Areas Act specifically grants power to the Government of India to acquire coal bearing land and vest in any Government Company rights in or over the land. The process under the Coal Bearing Areas Act is not available to private companies and therefore puts them at a competitive disadvantage.
- **Nationalization of coal** The nationalisation of coal in 1972 and 1973 for coking coal and non-coking coal mines meant that domestic coal could be mined only by public sector companies.
- **LPG Reforms, 1991** To meet the increasing energy demands, the government decided to allocate coal mines to various players for captive consumption (in captive mining coal is taken out by a company for its own use and it won't be able to sell it in the market).
  - Despite private sector participation in a restricted manner, state run Coal India Ltd continued to dominate the market. During the high growth years of 2000s the increasing demand of Coal could not be fulfilled by the state run Coal India Ltd., leading to higher demand-supply gap.
  - **Monopoly of Coal India** As per Annual Report & Accounts 2014-15 of Coal India Limited (CIL) accounts for approximately 80-82% of the production. As State-owned enterprise(s) receiving benefits and preferential treatment not available to other firms which appear to have the effect of limiting competition in the relevant market.
- **Increased Imports** Demand Supply gap, procedural delays, environmental clearances led to increase in imports – the CAGR of coal import from 2009-10 to 2013-14 was 23%.
- **Data Availability to Private Players** Most of the exploration i.e. prospecting activity is done by the government agencies and companies and the private players will have to purchase this information otherwise available and easily accessible to the government companies.
- **Coal Mines (Special Provisions) Act, 2015** The CAG report followed by the Supreme Court verdict in 2014 resulted into cancellation of allocation near all coal mines allocated after 1993. Thereby, this act was passed to enable the allocation of coal mines through transparent auctions.
  - Supreme Court cancelled the allocation of 204 coal blocks out of 218 coal blocks allocated since 1993.
- **Commercial Mining** In 2018, Cabinet Committee on Economic Affairs permitted entry of private firms in commercial coal mining in the country
- **Removal of End-use Restrictions** Earlier, there were restrictions on who could bid for coal mines only those in power, iron and steel and coal washer business could bid for mines and the bidders needed prior experience of mining in India and thus effectively limited the potential bidders to a select circle of players. This restriction has been done away with.
- **Shakti (Coal-Linkage Policy)** The Cabinet Committee on Economic Affairs (CCEA) has approved a new coal linkage policy to ensure adequate supply of the fuel to power plants through reverse auction. The new policy will help in ensuring fuel supplies to the power plants in an organised manner.
- **In April 2018, Ministry of Coal has launched UTTAM** (Unlocking Transparency by Third Party Assessment of Mined Coal) Application for coal quality monitoring. The app aims to ensure transparency and efficiency in coal quality monitoring process and bring coal governance closer to people.
- **Open for Foreign Players** The law earlier excluded companies without mining operations in India from participating in the auctions. This bar has been done away with, paving the way for local and foreign mining majors and non-mining ones, too, to participate in the domestic coal sector.
- **Revenue Sharing Reforms** The government has introduced a more equitable system of sharing revenues, moving away from fixed rates to an ad-valorem system. So when the prices go up, the miner shares more with the government and if they decrease, they share less.
- **Single Window Clearance** The Union government has launched Single Window Clearance portal on 11.01.2021 for the coal sector to speed up the operationalisation of coal mines. It is an unified platform that facilitates grant of clearances and approvals required for starting a coal mine in India.

Concerns in the Coal Industry

- **Poor quality of domestic coal** Around 87% of India's proven coal reserves of nearly 150 billion tonnes is non- coking coal. That means India has to turn to imports to meet four-fifths of its coking coal requirements. NITI Aayog estimates that it would be 180 million tonnes (MT) by 2030.
- **Monopoly of Coal India Limited** Union government owned Coal India, the world's largest coal miner, still accounted for around 80% of India's coal production.

— The current commercial coal mining regime will find it difficult to compete with Coal India. As the major consumer of coal in India (thermal power plants and steel sector) are in long term purchase agreements with Coal India.

- **Delays in receiving approval and clearances** Environment and forest clearance are extremely cumbersome, involving numerous layers of bureaucracy. The process of seeking clearances is a long drawn process involving central and state ministries, and sometimes also lack clarity. This causes significant delays in production from the allotted blocks.
- **High Import bills** Around a fifth of our thermal coal requirement is still imported despite of various reforms undertaken by the government.
- **Poor quality of captive blocks offered to private players** The blocks offered to private players for captive mining are of poor quality and are generally not good. The blocks are often located in remote and undeveloped areas, which have challenging geographies.
- In the era of intense competition from renewables, the rising NPAs of thermal power plants (TPPs) and a massive global withdrawal from fossil fuel for climate and environmental reasons poses a challenge of viability for commercialising coal.
- **Transport Costs** Most coal lies in inaccessible areas of the country. Hence, transporting it to the location of its use posed additional challenges. Though trains are the most economical way of transporting coal, a large number of mines are not connected to a rail network. Additionally, there was shortage of rakes on account of competing demand from sectors like food and steel.

Conclusion

With government's efforts to push renewable energy due to international conventions on climate change, increase in carbon cess and other initiatives for lesser use of coal, there is a need for 'Vision 2030 for the coal sector', which takes into account the environmental factors such as reduction of carbon footprint, abatement of global warming.

Issues in India's Power Sector

Q.14 Although there has been a significant increase in the power generation capacity, India still faces challenges to meet the growing demand for power as reliable supply remains low in the country. In this context, critically analyse the issues in India's power sector. What measures are taken by the government to address constraints in power sector? (250 Words, 15 Marks)

Ans. **Introduction** The power sector in India plays a crucial role in supporting the country's economic growth and meeting the energy requirements of its vast population. With a rapidly growing economy and increasing urbanization, the demand for energy has been rising steadily.

Despite significant progress, India still faces challenges in meeting the growing need for energy due to infrastructure constraints, distribution inefficiencies, and environmental concerns. Meeting this energy demand sustainably is a critical priority for the country's development.

Power Generation Capacity of India

- India is the third largest producer and the third largest consumer of electricity in the world.
- It also has the fifth largest installed capacity in the world.
- India's power sector has made significant inroads over the last decade, growing its installed capacity from 200 GW in FY12 to 412 GW in FY23.
- Although there has been a significant increase in the power generation capacity, India still faces challenges to meet the growing demand for power as reliable supply remains low in the country. The plant load factor (PLF) has declined significantly from 78% in FY10 to 56% in FY20.
- In terms of fuel mix, 58%% of the total installed capacity indicates India's dependence on conventional fuel sources. Coal-fired (including lignite) thermal power plants account for more than 50% of the total installed capacity.
- In terms of ownership mix, the private sector contributes around 50% of India's installed capacity. This proportion has increased from 27.2% in FY12 owing to continued strong growth in demand and initiatives of the government to encourage private sector participation in power generation.

Installed Generation Capacity (Sectorwise) As on 28-02-2023		
Sector	**MW**	**% of Total**
Central Sector	99,455	24.2%
State Sector	1,04,925	25.4%
Private Sector	2,07.832	50.4%
Total	**4,12,212**	—

Installed Generation Capacity (Fuelwise) As on 28-02-2023		
Catagory	**Installed Generation Capacity (MW)**	**% of Share in Total**
Fossil Fuel		
Coal	204.435	49.7%
Lignite	6,620	1.6%
Gas	24,824	6.1%
Diesel	589	0.1%
Total Fossil Fuel	**2,36,469**	**57.4%**
Non-Fossil Fuel		

Challenges in Power Sector

- **Insufficient Power Supply** Despite the increase in power generation capacity, India still faces a significant gap between supply and demand. According to the Central Electricity Authority, the peak power deficit stood at 0.5% in 2020-21, indicating an inadequate supply to meet the growing demand.
- **High Aggregate Technical and Commercial (AT&C) Losses** AT&C losses remain a major issue in India's power sector. As of 2020-21, the national average AT&C losses were around 21.4%. States like Bihar and Jharkhand reported even higher losses, exceeding 30%. These losses impact the financial viability of DISCOMs and hinder the provision of reliable power supply.
- **Financial Distress of DISCOMs** Many DISCOMs in India face financial distress, leading to inefficiencies in power distribution. Outstanding dues owed by DISCOMs to power generators and transmission companies reached around INR 1.35 trillion (USD 18.2 billion) in November 2020, indicating financial challenges within the sector.
- **Obsolete Transmission Infrastructure** India's transmission infrastructure often lags behind the growth in power generation capacity. According to the Ministry of Power, transmission losses stood at around 2.57% in 2020-21, indicating inefficiencies in power evacuation and transmission.
- **Dependency on Fossil Fuels** India heavily relies on fossil fuels, particularly coal, for electricity generation. As of 2020-21, coal-based power plants accounted for around 70% of India's total installed capacity. This dependency poses challenges in terms of fuel availability, price volatility, and environmental concerns.
- **Fuel Security Concerns** Thermal capacity addition is plagued by the growing fuel availability concerns faced by the industry. Coal supply is restricted, leading to increased dependence on imported coal with the cascading result of high-power generation costs.
  - A significant natural gas-based capacity of more than 20,000 MW is idle due to non-availability of natural gas.
- **Inefficient Power Subsidies** Subsidies provided to certain consumer categories contribute to the financial burden on DISCOMs. In some cases, subsidies are not adequately targeted or properly accounted for, leading to a strain on the financial health of DISCOMs.
- **Challenges in Renewable Energy Integration** While India has made significant progress in renewable energy capacity addition, integrating intermittent renewable energy sources into the grid remains a challenge. Issues such as grid stability, forecasting, and balancing the variability of renewable energy pose operational challenges.
- **Inadequate Demand-Side Management** Demand-side management practices, including energy conservation and efficiency programs, need further attention. Energy efficiency measures are not fully optimized, resulting in higher overall electricity demand and increased stress on the power system.
- **Environmental Concerns** The power sector, particularly thermal power plants, contributes to environmental issues such as air pollution and carbon emissions, necessitating the adoption of cleaner and sustainable energy sources.

- **Coordination Issues** Multiple ministries and agencies are currently involved in managing energy-related issues, presenting challenges of coordination and optimal resource utilisation, hence undermining efforts to increase energy security, as reported by the Kelkar Committee in 2013.

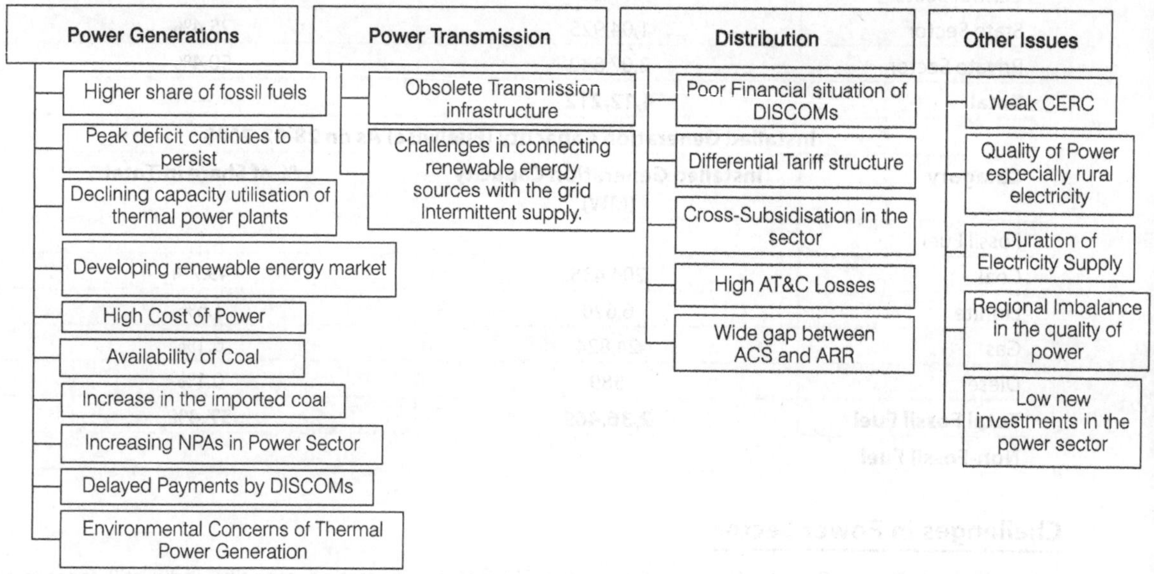

Government Measures

- **UDAY (Ujwal DISCOM Assurance Yojana)** Launched in 2015, UDAY aimed to improve the financial health of DISCOMs by reducing their debt burden, improving operational efficiency, and implementing financial discipline. It included measures such as debt restructuring, tariff revisions, and operational improvements.
- **Integrated Power Development Scheme (IPDS)** IPDS aimed to upgrade urban power distribution infrastructure, including measures such as installation of smart meters, feeder segregation, system strengthening, and IT enablement of DISCOMs. It focused on improving the reliability and quality of power supply in urban areas.
- **Renewable Energy Initiatives** The government has implemented various measures to promote renewable energy, including setting up large-scale solar and wind power projects, providing incentives and subsidies for renewable energy generation, and implementing renewable purchase obligations for DISCOMs.
- **National Tariff Policy** The National Tariff Policy provides guidelines for determining electricity tariffs, ensuring transparency, and promoting cost efficiency. It aims to bring about rationalization and consistency in tariff structures across the country.
- **Green Energy Corridors** The government has established Green Energy Corridors to facilitate the integration of renewable energy into the grid. These corridors involve the development of transmission infrastructure to transmit renewable energy from resource-rich regions to demand centers.
- **Power Sector Financial Restructuring** The government has undertaken financial restructuring measures to address the financial stress faced by DISCOMs, including the issuance of bonds, debt restructuring, and providing financial assistance to DISCOMs.
- **The Revamped Distribution Sector Scheme (RDSS)** The scheme aims to address challenges faced by DISCOMs and foster a more efficient and sustainable power distribution ecosystem in the country.

Conclusion

While these measures have shown some positive outcomes, continued efforts are required to address the challenges in India's power sector and ensure a reliable, sustainable, and affordable power supply for the country's growing energy needs.

New DISCOM Reform Scheme

Q.15 In the context of reviving DISCOMs, explain how Revamped Distribution Sector Scheme (RDSS) is different from the previous schemes such as UDAY? What are the expected outcomes from this scheme?
(150 Words, 10 Marks)

Ans. Status of DISCOMs DISCOMs have faced various challenges such as financial distress (high losses), high Aggregate Technical and Commercial (AT&C) losses and poor infrastructure because of which power quality is poor. According to a report by the Ministry of Power, the overall AT&C losses in DISCOMs were around 21.4% in 2019-20. Additionally, the outstanding dues of DISCOMs to power generators and transmission companies stood at around INR 1.35 trillion (USD 18.2 billion) as of November 2020. The government has been implementing various schemes and initiatives to address these issues and improve the performance of DISCOMs. The two most prominent ones are:

- **Revamped Distribution Sector Scheme (RDSS)** is a government initiative in India aimed at revitalizing and strengthening the power distribution sector, specifically the state-owned power distribution companies (DISCOMs). RDSS takes a comprehensive approach by promoting sectoral reforms, encouraging technology adoption, and linking performance outcomes to financial support. The scheme aims to address challenges faced by DISCOMs and foster a more efficient and sustainable power distribution ecosystem in the country.
  - **Broad Objectives of the Scheme are** Strengthening institutional capabilities for modernization of DISCOMs; Lowering of AT&C losses to 12-15% by 2024-25 nationally and lowering of the Average Cost of Supply (ACS) - Average Revenue Realised (ARR) gap to zero by 2024-25.
  - Its budgetary outlay is INR 3 lakh crore spread over five years, of which 32 per cent will be centrally funded.
- **The UDAY (Ujwal DISCOM Assurance Yojana)** scheme was a government initiative in India aimed at improving the financial health and operational efficiency of state-owned power distribution companies (DISCOMs). Launched in 2015, UDAY focused on debt restructuring, reducing aggregate technical and commercial (AT&C) losses, and promoting financial discipline among DISCOMs.

How RDSS is different from the UDAY scheme?

- **Focus on holistic sustainability** While UDAY primarily focused on improving the financial health of DISCOMs, RDSS takes a more comprehensive approach by addressing both financial and operational sustainability. It aims to strengthen the entire power distribution ecosystem, including infrastructure, technology, governance, and institutional capacity.
- **Outcome-Based Approach** RDSS adopts an outcome-based approach, shifting the focus from input-based targets to measurable outcomes. It sets specific performance targets for DISCOMs and incentivizes them based on achieving those targets. This approach encourages DISCOMs to improve their operational efficiency, reduce losses, and enhance service quality.
- **Technology Adoption** RDSS emphasizes the adoption of advanced technologies to modernize the power distribution sector. It encourages the implementation of smart meters, meter data management systems, distribution management systems, and other digital solutions to improve billing, metering, and customer services.
  - The scheme mandates the installation of 25 crore smart prepaid meters over the next four years to the current installed base of 0.27 crore.
- **Conditional Financial Support** While UDAY provided financial assistance in the form of debt restructuring and state government guarantees, RDSS offers financial support through grants and incentives linked to the achievement of performance targets. This incentivizes DISCOMs to improve their financial viability and operational efficiency.
- **Multi-Stakeholder Engagement** RDSS promotes multi-stakeholder engagement and partnerships to drive sectoral reforms. It encourages DISCOMs to collaborate with state governments, regulators, power generators, consumers, and other stakeholders to identify and implement necessary reforms.

Expected outcomes from the Revamped Distribution System Scheme (RDSS)

- **Reduction in Aggregate Technical and Commercial (AT&C) Losses** AT&C losses refer to the combined losses from technical inefficiencies and commercial issues such as theft and billing inefficiencies. RDSS aims to reduce these losses, which in turn improves the financial health and operational efficiency of DISCOMs. For instance, under the UDAY scheme, there was an observed reduction in AT&C losses from 20.7% in 2015-16 to 18.4% in 2018-19.

- **Improvement in Billing and Revenue Collection** The scheme aims to enhance billing and revenue collection efficiency through the adoption of smart meters, digital payment systems, and improved consumer grievance redressal mechanisms. This will increase revenue realization for DISCOMs and reduce revenue leakages.
- **Improvement in Financial Viability** RDSS seeks to improve the financial viability of DISCOMs by reducing their losses and enhancing revenue collection. This is crucial to address the financial distress experienced by many DISCOMs. For example, through UDAY, DISCOM losses reduced by about INR 22,000 crore (USD 3.25 billion) between 2015-16 and 2018-19.
- **Enhanced Operational Efficiency** The scheme aims to enhance the operational efficiency of DISCOMs through measures such as technology adoption, better infrastructure, and improved management practices. This leads to better power distribution and supply reliability.
- **Enhanced Customer Services** RDSS focuses on improving customer services through digital solutions and effective grievance redressal mechanisms. It aims to provide consumers with reliable power supply, accurate billing, and prompt customer support.
- **Financial Viability of DISCOMs** The scheme aims to improve the financial viability of DISCOMs by reducing their losses and enhancing their revenue generation capacity. This will help DISCOMs meet their payment obligations to power generators and ensure a sustainable power ecosystem.
- **Sectoral Reforms and Modernization** RDSS encourages DISCOMs to undertake sectoral reforms and adopt modern technologies for efficient power distribution. This will facilitate the integration of renewable energy sources, improve grid stability, and promote sustainable and reliable power supply.

Suggestions to make RDSS work

- **First, Address States' concerns about Insufficient Resources** States are required to shoulder two-thirds of the expenses needed (more than INR 2 lakh crore) to carry out activities prescribed under the RDS scheme. The status quo on financial position will not change unless the Centre provides them with transitional support in the form of low-cost conditional loans.
- **Second, Handhold States during Scheme Implementation** In a bid to secure a higher share of central funding, discoms often announce ambitious targets without putting together effective plans to achieve them. It is critical for central and state-level committees and agencies, including regulators, to work together to scrutinise the feasibility of discoms' action plans and project reports.
- **Third, Adopt a Systemic Deployment Strategy for Smart metering Infrastructure** Several think tanks have pointed out the need for a standardized methodology to validate claims of efficiency gains from smart meters and track benefits. They should build internal capacity and overhaul their billing and IT systems. A comprehensive consumer engagement and grievance redressal strategy will also be critical to build.

Conclusion

Overall, the Revamped Distribution Sector Scheme (RDSS) represents a comprehensive and outcome-based approach to revive DISCOMs in India. It aims to strengthen financial viability, operational efficiency, and service quality in the power distribution sector, ultimately benefiting both DISCOMs and consumers.

Alternative Energy Sources (Status of Renewable Energy)

Q.16 Do you think India will meet 50 percent of its energy needs from renewable energy by 2030? Justify your answer. How will the shift of subsidies from fossil fuels to renewables help achieve the above objective? Explain. (250 Words, 15 Marks)

UPSC Mains PYQ 2022

Ans. **Introduction** The Government of India at UNFCCC COP-26 announced enhanced climate commitments in form of Five Nectar Elements (Panchamrit), which include among others, the commitment to meet 50 percent of its energy needs from renewable energy sources. However, various experts have questioned the feasibility of this target.

Prospects for India to meet half of its Energy needs from Renewable Energy

- **Installed Renewable Energy Capacity** It is the fourth largest in the world. A total of 156.60 GW of Renewable Energy capacity (including large hydro) has been installed in the country as on 31st March, 2022.
- **Electricity Generation from Renewables** Presently, around 39% of India's installed electricity generation capacity is from renewable sources. The MoN&RE is also working towards achieving 500 GW of installed electricity capacity from non-fossil sources by 2030.
- **Wind Energy Capacity** The total installed wind power capacity is 40.35 GW, the 4th largest installed wind power capacity in the world.
- **Active private sector participation** Most of renewable energy projects in the country are being set up by private sector developers selected through transparent bidding. The Government has issued standard bidding guidelines to enable distribution licensees to procure power at competitive rates in a cost-effective manner.

Challenges for India to meet the Target

- **Funding** Renewable energy requires setting up large projects to harness the economies of scale. This requires a large initial investment from the government and private sector.
- **Slowdown in Renewable Energy Tendering Process** India's RE growth was at the slowest pace in the past four years.
- **Dependence on Imports** Little Manufacturing base for systems and solar component and heavy dependence on import for solar cell and modules.
- **Non-reliability** Solar and wind energy generation are dependent on seasons and weather.
- **Availability of Land** Difficulty in finding proper land that is non-agriculture and which is suitable for setting up of wind and solar energy plants.
- **Liquidity Crisis** Public sector banks are hesitant to grant loans to Renewable energy projects. The interest rate of existing loans to RE companies has also witnessed a rise in recent years.
- **Topographic Barriers** Most renewable energy plants occupy large areas of space. This brings in the issue of the cost of the vast land area and other issues related to land acquisition.
- **Effect of Covid-19** Projected addition of solar capacity in a COVID-19 affected future could fall short of stated goals.
- **Others** Enabling the penetration of renewable energy sources into hard-to-decarbonize sectors and integrating a larger share of renewables with the grid.

Government Subsidies to Renewable Sector

- **Modified Special Incentive Package Scheme (M-SIPS) Scheme of Ministry of Electronics & Information Technology** It provides subsidy for capital expenditure – 20% for investments in Special Economic Zones (SEZs) and 25% in non-SEZs. It covers solar PV cells, solar PV modules, EVA, backsheet and solar glass.
- **Waiver of Inter State Transmission System (ISTS) charges** For inter-state sale of solar and wind power for projects to be commissioned by 30th June 2025.
- **Renewable Purchase obligation** Declaration of trajectory for Renewable Purchase Obligation (RPO) up to the year 2022.
- **Renewable Energy Research and Technology Development Programme** It encourages research and technology development proposals and provides up to 100% financial support to Government/non-profit research organizations and up to 50-70% to Industry, Start-ups, Private Institutes, Entrepreneurs and Manufacturing units.
- The Government has provided a 10-year tax exemption for solar energy projects;
- The Ministry of New and Renewable Energy provides 30% subsidy to most solar powered items such as solar lamps and solar heating systems. It has further extended its subsidy scheme to solar-powered cold storages;
- The Government has allowed 100% Foreign Direct Investment (FDI) in the renewable energy under the automatic route.

Role of Shifting Subsidies from Fossil Fuels to Renewables in achieving Desired Target

- **More fiscal space** Fiscal savings can be allocated to boost domestic manufacturing capabilities in renewable sector.
- **Taxing fossil fuels** Government can tax fossil fuels which will reduce emission and motivate people to shift towards renewable energy sources.

- **Reduction of barriers** The technical and economic barriers for setting up of renewable projects can be eliminated and companies are incentivized for set up of renewable industries.
- **Cluster approach** It creates SEZs that focus on manufacturing of renewable equipment and technologies. ? Enhance storage capacity: The subsidies encourage renewable energy storage technology and thus enable India to meet renewable energy targets.
- **Facilitate private sector investments** Currently a miniscule amount of private sector participation in renewable energy sector, which will be increased with shifting of subsidies.

Way forward

- **International leadership** As we did in ISA, we can do the same in other sources of renewable energy.
- **Bilateral agreements** This can help with technology revolution in renewable energy field. Example: Indo-US climate and clean energy agenda 2030 partnership.

Conclusion

India is at the cusp of a renewable energy revolution. Apart from subsidies, multi-pronged approach involving synchronised efforts of all the stakeholders viz Government, private players, international communities are needed to achieve target of meeting half of energy needs from renewable energy by 2030.

Solar Manufacturing Sector

Q.17 India's ambitious targets of solar energy were missed in 2022 due to various challenges being faced in scaling up the sector. Examine the concerns with special reference to poor solar manufacturing in India. (150 Words, 10 Marks)

Ans. **Introduction** In 2014, the Government had set an ambitious target of 175 GW of installed capacity of renewable energy. The target for Solar Energy was set to be 100 GW by 2022. The installed capacity is around 60 GW at the end of 2022 which indicates h a remarkable growth from just 2.6 GW of solar energy capacity in 2014 but the targets were missed as it was only 60% of the 100 GW target.

At COP26 in Glasgow (2021) India updated its Nationally Determined Contributions (NDCs). India set a target of 500 GW of non-fossil electricity capacity and half of energy from renewables. Of this, ~300 GW is expected to be contributed by Solar Energy. This calls for 30 GW of solar capacity every year until 2030 which is a daunting task and requires measures to be taken for addressing the challenges of solar sector especially domestic manufacturing.

Potential of Solar Energy

- India is endowed with vast solar energy potential. India receives nearly 3000 hours of sunshine every year. About 5,000 trillion kWh per year energy is incident over India's land area with most parts receiving 4-7 kWh per sq. m per day. Solar photovoltaics power can effectively be harnessed providing huge scalability in India.
- National Institute of Solar Energy has assessed India's solar potential to be about 750 GW assuming 3% of the waste land area to be covered by Solar PV modules.
- Gujarat and Rajasthan have the highest solar energy potential.
- The top States in terms of installed solar energy capacity (March 2021) include: Karnataka (7.35 GW), Rajasthan (5.73 GW), Tamil Nadu (4.47 GW), Gujarat (4.43 GW) and Andhra Pradesh (4.2 GW).

Challenges of Solar Industry in India

- **Higher per-unit Production Costs** Solar power costs have come down considerably but the costs of small solar power projects is higher than other sources. The Union Government is facilitating establishment of large solar parks.
- **Basic Challenges** Large Solar Parks face hurdles in acquiring large tracts of land. Other challenges include high transmission and distribution losses, grid integration etc. Grid integration is a challenge due to intermittent nature of solar energy and the problem of load balancing (e.g., high load during night but non-availability of solar power at night).

- **Environmental Issues** Establishment of large solar parks has led to conflict with the local communities and issues in bio-diversity protection e.g., in Rajasthan and Gujarat, some projects have been halted because the transmission lines encroach upon the habitat of the critically endangered Great Indian Bustard.
- **Slow Pace of Growth** Despite significant growth in the installed solar capacity, the contribution of solar energy to the country's power generation has not grown at the same pace. The capacity expansion of rooftop solar projects has particularly low (< 20% of target by October 2022).
- **Financial Constraints** Residential consumers and Small and Medium Enterprises (SMEs) who want to install solar rooftop projects face financial constraints as initial investments are generally high. A critical issue is an absence of innovative financing options offering higher sums at lower interest and longer durations.
- **Waste Management** India's solar waste is estimated to grow to 1.8 million tonnes by 2050. However, India's e-waste rules do not mandate solar cell manufacturers to recycle or dispose of waste from this sector.
- **Poor Domestic Manufacturing** India's current solar module manufacturing capacity is limited to around 15 GW per year and rest is met through imports. An estimated 85 per cent of this import need is met by three countries China, alongside Vietnam and Malaysia. There are multiple reasons for this:
  - **Investment Crunch** Major part of investment is raised within the country and there is less investment from foreign direct investment (FDI).
  - Solar cell technology sees upgrades every 8-10 months making manufacturing inefficient for new entrants.
  - **Technology and R&D** Solar cell manufacturing is a complicated process that is technology intensive. Establishing state-of-the-art manufacturing facilities needs access to technology. India in comparison to China does not bring latest (next generation) technology at a competitive price, which hampers development of solar manufacturing in India.
  - **Uncompetitive Cost** Indian solar cells are, on average, 20-30% more expensive than cells manufactured in China. Hence, manufacturers tend to choose affordable equipment through import from China.
  - Solar panel Manufacturing suffers from a huge raw material supply crunch. Silicon wafer, the most expensive raw material in the panel, is not manufactured in India.
  - **Quality Control Issues** Some companies have voiced their concerns about the quality of Indian made cells and reported some manufacturers falsely label their 380 Wp (capacity of a solar in watt peak) cells as 400 Wp because there are no government entities to ensure the quality of these cells.
  - **WTO Constraints** India's Domestic Content Requirement (DCR) clause has faced legal challenges at the World Trade Organisation (WTO). DCR mandates the use of both solar cells and modules manufactured domestically as per specifications and testing requirements fixed by the Ministry of New and Renewable Energy (MNRE).

Government Measures Undertaken To Promote Solar Sector

- The Union Government established a ₹ 19,500-crore production linked incentive (PLI) scheme on 'national programme on high efficiency solar PV modules', seeking to attract Rs 94,000-crore investment in the sector.
- To address the shortages on the raw material side with respect to silicon wafers, the Centre has decided to provide uniform fiscal support of 50 per cent of the project cost for setting up of semiconductor fabrication plants.
- **Modified Special Incentive** Package Scheme (M-SIPS) of Ministry of Electronics & Information Technology offers a 20-25 per cent subsidy for investments in capital expenditure for setting up a manufacturing facility.
- The government has mandated that a solar power producer should compulsorily source a certain percentage of solar cells and modules from local manufacturers, in order to be able to benefit from the government guarantee to purchase the energy produced.
- **Solar Park Scheme** The Solar Park Scheme plans to build a number of solar parks, each with a capacity of nearly 500 MW, across several states.
- **Atal Jyoti Yojana (AJAY)** The AJAY scheme was launched in September 2016 for the installation of solar street lighting (SSL) systems in states with less than 50% of households covered with grid power (as per Census 2011).
- **National Solar Mission** It is a major initiative of the Government of India and State Governments to promote ecologically sustainable growth while addressing India's energy security challenge.
- **SRISTI Scheme** Sustainable rooftop implementation of Solar transfiguration of India (SRISTI) scheme to promote rooftop solar power projects in India.

Conclusion

Although the solar energy target set for 2022 have been missed, the Union and State Governments have done well in facilitating the capacity expansion of solar energy. The Governments should continue to undertake policy reforms and provide financial and other incentives to the industry, so that India can enhance its climate action and fasten the pace towards Net Zero commitments.

Unconventional Hydrocarbons

Q.18 India has an untapped potential of unconventional hydrocarbons but there are immense challenges in the exploitation of these hydrocarbons. Examine. (150 Words, 10 Marks)

Ans. **Introduction** Unconventional hydrocarbons are sources of oil and gas which require methods for extraction which are not normally necessary in the conventional extraction of hydrocarbons such as Coal bed Methane, shale gas/oil, tight gas and gas hydrates.

Potential of Unconventional Hydrocarbons

- **Coal Bed Methane** India has the fifth largest proven coal reserves in the world. The CBM resources in the country are about 92 TCF (2600 BCM) in 12 states of India.
- **Shale Gas** It is a natural gas formed from being trapped within shale rocks. ONGC estimates 187.5 Trillion Cubic Feet (TCF) of shale gas in Cambay, KG, Cauvery, Ganga and Assam basins in India.
- **Gas Hydrate** A naturally occurring, ice-like combination of natural gas and water found in the world's oceans and Polar Regions. US Geological Survey states that India has the second largest gas hydrates in World. The Krishna Godavari, Cauvery and Kerala basins alone contributing 100-130 trillion cubic feet of estimated reserves.
- **Tight Gas** Tight gas refers to natural gas reservoirs locked in extraordinarily impermeable, hard rock, making the underground formation extremely "tight." India's Cambay field holds 413bn cubic feet of economically recoverable tight gas.

Challenges In The Exploitation Of These Hydrocarbons

Shale Gas exploitation

- **Use of Water** (Fracking technique) uses around 5-7 million litres of water per well.
- The massive amount of water used in the fracking process has led to water shortages in some drilling areas.
- **Environmental Concerns** Fracking has led to extensive deforestation and flooding of the nearby area.
- **Groundwater Contamination** Environmentalists say potentially carcinogenic chemicals are used in shale gas exploration which will contaminate groundwater.
- **Earthquakes** Fracking process can cause small earth tremors in the region.

Coal Bed Methane Exploitation

- Simultaneous operations of Coal Bed Methane and coal mining by multiple owners results in management issues.
- Despite the huge reserves, a mismatch exists between estimated resources and gas in-place.
- There is a possibility of damage of gas wells resulting in explosive atmosphere in coal mines during simultaneous extraction of coal and CBM.
- Multiple ownership for simultaneous exploitation may not be desirable for the life, health and safety of the workers employed in such mines.
- Safe Operating Procedures (SOP) for simultaneous exploration are not effectively implemented.

Gas Hydrates

- The natural gas from gas hydrate can be produced via Depressurization and Thermal stimulation. However, no country in the world has so far developed the technology to produce gas hydrates commercially and economically.
- Gas hydrates are also important for seafloor stability studies, because "melting" gas hydrate may cause seafloor "landslides".
- Methane released from gas hydrate may therefore play a significant role in climate change.

Apart from economic viability and ecological issues some of the other uses are complicated technology involved such as fracking and its viability. India's move for exploiting shale gas resources in the country has been red-flagged by The Energy and Research Institute (TERI) because India is a water-stressed country. India is already a water-stressed country and is fast approaching the scarcity benchmark of 1,000 m3 per capita with unabated growth in the irrigation sector.

Way Forward

Policy Framework for Unconventional Hydrocarbons The centre has approved the policy (Hydrocarbon Exploration Licensing Policy (HELP)) that permit exploration and exploitation of unconventional hydrocarbons such as shale oil/gas, Coal Bed Methane (CBM) etc. There is a single licence for exploration and production of all forms of ydrocarbons. It will be carried out under the existing Production Sharing Contracts (PSCs), CBM contracts and Nomination fields to encourage the existing Contractors in the licensed/leased area to unlock the potential of unconventional hydrocarbons in the existing acreages. Possible impact from the policy:

- Will lead to induction of new, innovative and cutting-edge technology and forging new technological collaboration to exploit unconventional hydrocarbons.
- Will enable the realization of prospective hydrocarbon reserves in the existing contract areas which otherwise would remain unexplored and unexploited.
- To promote ease of doing business in the oil and gas sector in India to attract higher foreign investments.
- Exploration and exploitation of additional hydrocarbon will spur new investment, impetus to economic activities, additional employment generation.

- NITI AAYOG Recommendations: There should be a Shale Oil and Gas Authority should be setup to exploit the shale oil and gas reserves in Assam and Arunachal Pradesh. It bats for liberalising trade of all petroleum products transparently in order to expand the coverage of un-served regions of the country through the participation of private players.

Conclusion

Unconventional energy sources are significant for India's energy security, but there should be a balance between exploiting energy sources and managing environment.

Digital Economy (Importance of Digital Infrastructure)

Q.19 Digital infrastructure has emerged as an equally or arguably a more significant infrastructure necessity, as compared to the traditional infrastructure necessities such as power, water, and roads. Elaborate. Also, explain how India can secure its interests in a digital ecosystem? (150 Words, 10 Marks)

Ans. **Introduction** Digital infrastructure refers to the underlying technological components, systems, and networks that enable the functioning of digital services and the flow of data. It includes elements such as internet connectivity, data centres, communication networks, cloud computing, and software platforms. Digital infrastructure provides the foundation for digital transformation, enabling activities like online communication, e-commerce, data storage, and access to digital services across various sectors.

Digital infrastructure has indeed become increasingly vital in today's interconnected world vis a vis traditional infrastructure. The COVID-19 pandemic further highlighted the importance of digital infrastructure as remote work, online education, and telemedicine became essential.

Digital Infrastructure as a Necessity

- **Economic Impact in terms of Contribution of GDP** According to a report by the World Bank, a 10% increase in broadband penetration can lead to a 1.38% increase in GDP growth in developing countries. The report also highlights that digital technologies have the potential to add $13 trillion to the global economy by 2030.
- **Facilitates Connectivity and Inclusion** The International Telecommunication Union (ITU) estimates that around 51% of the world's population now has access to the internet. Increased connectivity helps bridge the digital divide, enabling marginalized communities to access education, healthcare, financial services, and employment opportunities.

- **Job Opportunities** A study by the McKinsey Global Institute suggests that by 2030, digital technologies could create up to 85 million new jobs in emerging economies. The growth of e-commerce, digital services, and technology-driven industries contribute to employment generation.
- **Fosters Innovation and Entrepreneurship** The Global Innovation Index 2021 ranks countries based on their innovation capacity, and digital infrastructure is a crucial factor. Countries like the United States, Singapore, and Sweden, known for their robust digital ecosystems, consistently rank high in terms of innovation.
- **Healthcare and Telemedicine** Digital infrastructure enhances healthcare delivery. The COVID-19 pandemic accelerated the adoption of telemedicine, enabling remote consultations and healthcare access. According to a report by Research and Markets, the global telemedicine market is expected to reach $191.7 billion by 2025, indicating the increasing reliance on digital infrastructure in the healthcare sector.
- **Improved E-governance and public service delivery** Countries like Estonia and South Korea have implemented comprehensive digital government initiatives, leading to streamlined services, reduced bureaucracy, and improved citizen participation. Digital platforms enable online voting, digital identification, and efficient service delivery.
- **Environmental Sustainability** The International Energy Agency (IEA) estimates that digital technologies and smart systems can help reduce global CO_2 emissions by up to 15% by 2030.Smart grids, energy management systems, and IoT-enabled solutions optimize energy consumption, transportation, and resource allocation.
- **Resilience and Flexibility** The COVID-19 pandemic highlighted the importance of digital infrastructure in maintaining business continuity. The World Bank emphasizes the need for digital infrastructure investments to enhance resilience and preparedness for future shocks.

To secure its interests in the Digital Ecosystem, India can focus on the following Strategies

- **Internet Connectivity** Enhancing access to affordable and reliable internet connectivity across the country is crucial. This can be achieved through policies that promote infrastructure development, such as laying fiber optic cables and expanding mobile networks to rural areas. Initiatives like BharatNet aim to connect all gram panchayats (village-level local self-government institutions) with high-speed broadband.
- **Digital Literacy** The government has launched programs to enhance digital literacy and digital skills among citizens, particularly in rural areas. Initiatives like Pradhan Mantri Gramin Digital Saksharta Abhiyan (PMGDISHA) aim to empower individuals with digital knowledge and enable them to access digital services.
- **Aadhaar** The Aadhaar program is a biometric identification system that assigns a unique identification number to each Indian resident. It has been instrumental in facilitating digital identification and authentication, enabling citizens to access various government services online securely.
- **Digital Payments** The government has actively promoted digital payments through initiatives like Unified Payments Interface (UPI), which facilitates easy and secure transactions. The demonetization move in 2016 further accelerated the adoption of digital payments in India.
- **Data Localization** To protect data privacy and national security, the government has introduced regulations mandating the localization of sensitive data within the country's borders. This ensures that critical data remains under regulatory oversight and reduces the risk of unauthorized access.
- **Cybersecurity Initiatives** The government has established cybersecurity initiatives and agencies such as the Indian Computer Emergency Response Team (CERT-In) to enhance the country's cybersecurity capabilities. These efforts aim to safeguard critical infrastructure, digital assets, and protect against cyber threats.
- **Digital Skills and Education** Investing in digital skills training and education is essential to build a digitally literate workforce. India should prioritize programs that provide technical training, promote digital literacy, and nurture entrepreneurship in the digital space.
- **Innovation and Startups** Fostering an environment conducive to digital innovation and startups can drive economic growth and technological advancements. India can support startups through incubators, funding mechanisms, and regulatory frameworks that encourage entrepreneurship, research, and development.
- **International Cooperation** Engaging in international forums and partnerships can help India protect its interests in the digital ecosystem. Collaborative efforts can address global issues like cross-border data flows, cybersecurity, and standardization, while also providing India with a platform to influence global digital governance.

Conclusion

While traditional infrastructure necessities like power, water, and roads remain essential, digital infrastructure has indeed become equally important in today's interconnected world. India can secure its interests in the digital ecosystem by focusing on internet connectivity, data localization, cybersecurity, digital skills, innovation, and international cooperation. By adopting a comprehensive approach, India can harness the potential of the digital age for the benefit of its citizens and the overall development of the country.

Digital Payments

Q.20 Reshaping India's payment landscape requires to address deep rooted challenges that are hindering digital payments ecosystem. Critically examine. Suggest measures that can enhance the greater acceptability of digital transactions. (250 Words, 15 Marks)

Ans. **Introduction** A digital payment sometimes called an electronic payment, is the transfer of value from one payment account to another using a digital device such as a mobile phone, POS (Point of Sales) or computer.

- According to government data, India with 89.5 million digital transactions (46% of the global real-time payments) in the year 2022 has topped the list of 5 countries (followed by Brazil, China, Thailand and S. Korea) in digital payments.
- During last five years, various easy and convenient modes of digital payments, including Bharat Interface for Money-Unified Payments Interface (BHIM-UPI), Immediate Payment Service (IMPS), and National Electronic Toll Collection (NETC) have registered substantial growth and have transformed digital payment ecosystem by increasing person-to-person (P2P) as well as person-to-merchant (P2M) payments.
- **BHIM UPI has emerged as the preferred payment mode of the citizens** and has recorded 803.6 crore digital payment transactions with the value of ? 12.98 lakh crore in January 2023.

Benefits of Digital Payments

- **Convenience and Efficiency** Quick and hassle-free digital transactions through smartphones.
- **Financial Inclusion** Access to digital payments for individuals.
- **Reduced Cash Dependency** Minimizing risks and combating illicit transactions.
- **Enhanced Transparency** Tracking and monitoring financial activities.
- **Boost to Digital Economy** Promoting digital entrepreneurship and innovation.

However, there are certain Challenges that are hindering Digital Payments Ecosystem

- **Connectivity Issues** Regardless of the wide internet and mobile penetration across India, not everyone is able to get seamless and uninterrupted connectivity.
  - There is also a network connectivity problem in remote locations and not all telecoms work in all locations.
- **Digital Divide** Around 70% of the total population resides in rural India. Unfortunately, issues like digital illiteracy, underdevelopment, lack of infrastructure, etc. pose huge challenges.
  - Digital empowerment of rural areas is essential to bridge the digital gap.
- **Lack of awareness among small merchants** Lack of awareness about how digital payments work is common among small merchants.
  - The language barrier is also one of the important points that need to be considered as most of the time payment confirmation, invoices, and charge slips are in the English language.
- **High Cash Transaction** India has a high cash penetration in almost all of its transactions that happen as B2C transactions. Total cash flow in the market accounts for 12.04% of the GDP, which is among the highest in developing countries.
- **Infrastructure Challenges for Banks** Banks face difficulties in keeping up with the surge in UPI payments, leading to transaction failures.

- **Other Infrastructure Problems** In the current scenario, digital payment systems are heavily reliant on smart phones that are enabled with data connections, NFC, Bluetooth etc. Out of India's 800Mn mobile phone users, only 200Mn use smart phones. Of these phones, only 6Mn are NFC-enabled. An even smaller percentage of users have access to QR code mechanisms. This translates to approximately 85% Indians who do not have access to the infrastructure required to adopt the current digital payment systems that are heavily reliant on smart phones.
- **Cyber Fraud** According to a report, around 52% of people don't know how to protect themselves from cyber fraud and crime. With the lack of public awareness and inadequate investments into security technology, people fell for cybercrimes, thus it reduces their trust in digital payments.
- **Need for Data localisation** Majority of payment system like Visa and Master card and digital payments like Google pay, Paypal store the data in their parent countries where there is no guarantee for data security.

Measures that can enhance the Greater Acceptability of Digital Transactions

Many of the recommendations of Nandan Nilekani and Ratan Watal Committee have been implemented to boost digital payments. There are some more measures that can be taken:

- The **RBI's Payments Vision 2025 document** It highlights 5Is - integrity, inclusion, innovation, institutionalisation and internationalisation - for digital payment landscape.
- **Digital Education** To make citizens aware of fraudulent practices that they can come across while making digital payments.
- **Use of Technology** Developing a framework for an internet of things (IoT)-based payments systems that would enable customers to pay via connected devices apart from users' phones and tablets.
- **Blockchain Integration** Explore the integration of blockchain technology into the UPI infrastructure to enhance transparency, security, and scalability.
- **Reviewing Legal-institutional Infrastructure** The RBI should undertake a comprehensive review of the Payment and Settlement Systems (PSS) Act 2007, to bring it in line with India's digital payment landscape.
- **Innovation and Robust Regulatory Framework** Like the new Digital Personal Data Protection Bill, Digital India Bill to drive growth and cutting-edge innovation for digital payments, not just in the country but globally.

Conclusion

The success of UPI has been truly inspirational. To augment the impact of this success and carry it forward to other industry spaces, the government of India, in association with industry bodies, has launched several new initiatives.

Some of these initiatives include the account aggregator model based on the consent architecture, OCEN (Open Credit Enablement Network) to democratize lending and ONDC (Open Network for Digital Commerce) to drive decentralization of eCommerce. This potent combination of collaborative innovation and robust regulatory steer in India will continue to drive growth and cutting-edge innovation for digital payments, not just in the country but globally.

Open Network for Digital Commerce (ONDC)

Q.21 Open Network for Digital Commerce (ONDC), billed to be UPI of India's E-commerce, has the potential to curb digital monopolies of large companies and creates a level playing field for small and medium enterprises. Critically analyse. (150 Words, 10 Marks)

Ans. **Introduction** Recently, the government has launched the pilot phase of Open Network for Digital Commerce (ONDC) with an aim to "democratize" the country's fast growing digital e-commerce space that is currently dominated by the two U.S.-headquartered firms — Amazon and Walmart.

HOW INDIA'S OPEN e-commerce network model plans to disrupt platform power

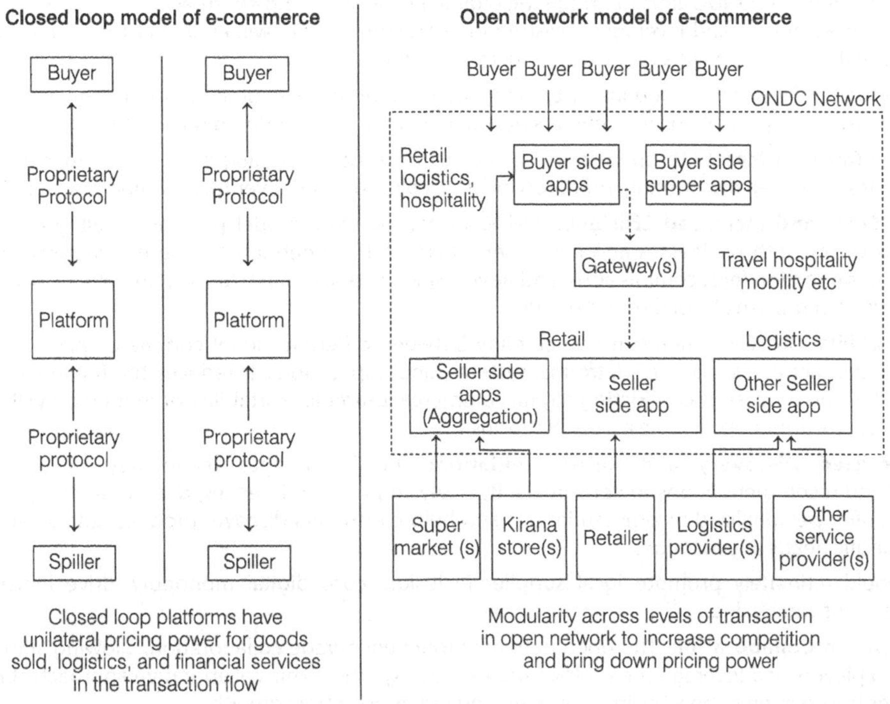

About Open Network for Digital Commerce (ONDC)

- ONDC is a freely accessible government-backed platform that aims to democratize e-commerce by moving it from a platform-centric model to an open network for buying and selling of goods and services. It is a community-led network that aims to create an open, inclusive and competitive marketplace.
- Under ONDC, it is envisaged that a buyer registered on one participating e-commerce site (for example, Amazon) may purchase goods from a seller on another participating e-commerce site (for example, Flipkart).
  - Presently, buyers and sellers have to be on the same app for a transaction which happens through the same platform. For example, a buyer needs to go to Amazon, to buy a product from a seller on Amazon.
  - Currently, in the platform-centric model, marketplaces have end-to-end control, right from seller on-boarding, customer acquisition, order fulfilment, complaint redressal and managing payments.
- The ONDC aims at promoting open networks developed on open-sourced methodology, using open specifications and open network protocols, independent on any specific platform.
- Implementation of ONDC, which is expected to be on the lines of Unified Payments Interface (UPI) could bring various operational aspects put in place by e-commerce platforms to the same level.

Opportunities from ONDC

- **Democratization of digital commerce** One of the primary goals of ONDC is to democratize e-commerce access by enabling small and medium-sized enterprises (SMEs) to participate in online trade. ONDC's open network will provide a level playing field, allowing even the smallest businesses to showcase their products and reach a wider customer base.
  - ONDC will develop the e-commerce ecosystem from an operator-driven platform-centric model to a facilitator-driven interoperable decentralised network. Everyone will have equal opportunities.
  - ONDC fosters a competitive environment by providing a level playing field for businesses of all sizes. It reduces barriers to entry and allows small and medium enterprises (SMEs) to compete with larger players, encouraging innovation and driving market efficiency.

- **Increased Market Reach** ONDC can expand the market reach for businesses by connecting them to a broader network of platforms and users. This can lead to increased visibility, customer base, and opportunities for growth.
- **Strengthening Rural e-commerce which is a game changer for Indian Economy** By leveraging the vast reach of India's postal network, ONDC aims to bridge the digital divide and empower rural entrepreneurs. Through partnerships with local entrepreneurs and leveraging existing infrastructure, ONDC will enable last-mile delivery and provide rural consumers with access to a wide range of products and services.
- **Standardisation** By standardizing inventory management, order management and fulfilment, and other operations, ONDC can further help small business owners by reducing their costs of doing business online.
- **Restrict Unfair Practices** With open-source protocols for product cataloguing, vendor match, and price discovery, ONDC can restrain deep discounting, predatory pricing, collusion, and inventory-owning practices in e-commerce.
- **Reduced Costs and Increased Efficiency** ONDC's open network model promote healthy competition, leading to reduced costs for both businesses and consumers. Increased competition among e-commerce service providers will drive down transaction fees, commissions, and advertising costs. Example: Networking effects over time tend to create virtuous cycles of growth like in the case of UPI.
- **Interoperability** ONDC promotes interoperability between different digital commerce platforms, allowing users to seamlessly transact across various platforms, systems, and applications. It reduces the friction of compatibility issues and simplifies the process of conducting digital commerce. Example: Portability of reputation will encourage sellers to deliver better customer experience across platforms.
- **Hyper-localized Discovery and Recommendations** ONDC leverages technology to provide hyper-localized discovery and recommendations to consumers. By analyzing user preferences, demographics, and geographical data, ONDC will offer personalized recommendations and help consumers discover products and services that are relevant to their specific needs and locations.
  - This would ultimately promote local supplier inclusion, curb digital monopoly, drive logistic efficiencies, and enhance consumer value.
- **Innovation and Collaboration** The open network model encourage collaboration, allowing startups to partner with established players and leverage their infrastructure and expertise. This collaborative approach stimulates innovation, encourages the creation of new business models, and drives economic growth.
- **Sellers Stand to Benefit Greatly** The network-centric approach of ONDC reduces the skewed bargaining power in favor of the platforms, which often results in higher entry barriers and lower margins for sellers.
- **Improved user Experience** ONDC aims to provide a seamless and user-friendly experience for consumers. It streamlines the process of discovering products, making purchases, and completing transactions, making it convenient and efficient for users.

Challenges in the Implementation of ONDC

While Open Network Digital Commerce (ONDC) offers numerous benefits, there are also challenges associated with its implementation. Here are some common challenges:

- **Technical Integration** Implementing ONDC requires integrating various digital commerce platforms, systems, and stakeholders. It can be challenging to ensure seamless interoperability and data exchange between different systems with diverse technologies, protocols, and standards.
- **Data privacy and Security** As ONDC involves the exchange of sensitive user data and financial transactions, ensuring robust data privacy and security measures is crucial.
- **Stakeholder Cooperation** Successful implementation of ONDC requires collaboration and cooperation among various stakeholders thus aligning different interests, resolving conflicts, and fostering a spirit of cooperation can be challenging.
- **Standardization and Governance** Establishing common standards and protocols for ONDC implementation is essential for seamless integration and interoperability. However, developing and agreeing upon these standards, as well as establishing effective governance mechanisms to ensure their adoption and enforcement, can be a complex task involving multiple stakeholders.
- **User Adoption and Trust** The success of ONDC relies on user adoption and trust. Convincing users to embrace the new framework, ensuring a smooth user experience, and addressing their concerns can be significant challenges.

- **Scalability and Infrastructure** Ensuring sufficient infrastructure capacity, reliability, and performance can be a challenge, particularly in regions with limited technological resources can be a challenge.
- **Cost Considerations** Implementing ONDC may involve significant upfront and ongoing costs. Managing these costs and ensuring a viable business model for all parties involved can be a challenge.

Conclusion

The Open Network for Digital Commerce (ONDC) is poised to revolutionize the Indian e-commerce landscape by democratizing access, promoting interoperability, reducing costs, and enhancing efficiency. Through data empowerment, privacy protection, hyper-localized discovery, and strengthened rural e-commerce, ONDC addresses the diverse needs of Indian consumers and businesses.

As ONDC gains momentum, it will undoubtedly reshape the Indian e-commerce industry, creating new opportunities, empowering businesses, and enriching the digital commerce experience for millions of Indians.

India Stack – Digital Public Infrastructure (DPI)

Q.22 Development of 'India Stack' made India the first country to develop all three foundational Digital Public Infrastructure (DPIs). In this context, explain about the India Stack and highlight certain concerns that needs to addressed to maximize its potential. (250 Words, 15 Marks)

Ans. About Digital Public Infrastructure (DPI)

- India's digital public infrastructure (DPI) refers to blocks or platforms such as digital identification, payment infrastructure and data exchange solutions that help countries deliver essential services to their people, empowering citizens and improving lives by enabling digital inclusion.
- **DPIs mediate the flow of people, money and information.**
  - First, the flow of people through a digital ID System.
  - Second, the flow of money through a real-time fast payment system. And
  - Third, the flow of personal information through a consent-based data sharing system to actualize the benefits of DPIs and to empower the citizen with a real ability to control data.
- These three sets become the foundation for developing an effective DPI ecosystem. Each DPI layer fills a clear need and generates considerable value across sectors.
- **India, through India Stack, became the first country to develop all three foundational DPIs,** Digital identity (Aadhar), Real-time fast payment (UPI) and Account Aggregator built on the Data Empowerment Protection Architecture (DEPA).

India Stack

- India Stack is a set of APIs (Application programming interface) that allows governments, businesses, startups and developers to utilize a unique digital Infrastructure to solve India's hard problems towards presence-less, paperless, and cashless service delivery.
- This project was conceptualized and first implemented in India, where its rapid adoption by billions of individuals and businesses has helped promote financial and social inclusion and positioned the country for the Internet Age.

The four major layers of India Stack include

- **Identity Layer (Using identity as a utility; an enabler)** This allows one to authenticate oneself from any location as it serves as both a tool for identification and a facilitator of authentication, controlled by the Unique Identification Authority of India (UIDAI).
- **Paperless Layer (Store & Retrieve Data digitally)** Managed by the Ministry of Electronics & Information Technology (MeitY), it offers a paperless ecosystem that stores information and documentation digitally, verify them, and authenticates them anytime and on any device. It provides the ability to store & retrieve data digitally in the following ways: Aadhar based e-KYC; e-sign and Digilocker.
- **Payments Layer (Increasing transparency and ease)** Digital payments are now accessible to everyone with the National Payments Corporation of India (NPCI) as the administrator. It seeks to transition everything in the digital era, making payments and financial transactions cashless in order to enable transparency and usability.

– This is an electronic interoperable payment network and includes IAEPS (Aadhar enabled Payment Systems), APB (Aadhar Payment Bridge) and UPI (Unified Payment Interface) and is owned by the National Payments Corporation of India (NPCI).

- **Data Layer** (Data Empowerment and Protection Architecture: Enabling easy data flow) This enables safe data transfer facilitated by MeITY and the Reserve Bank of India and authenticated by the data owners. Data Empowerment & Protection Architecture (DEPA), an electronic consent architecture, securely democratises the market for data while allowing user-controlled data sharing, flow, and retention. This regulation has given rise to the concept of "data access fiduciaries," which are organizations designed to enable the management of individual consent such as Account aggregators.

Foundations of the India Stack

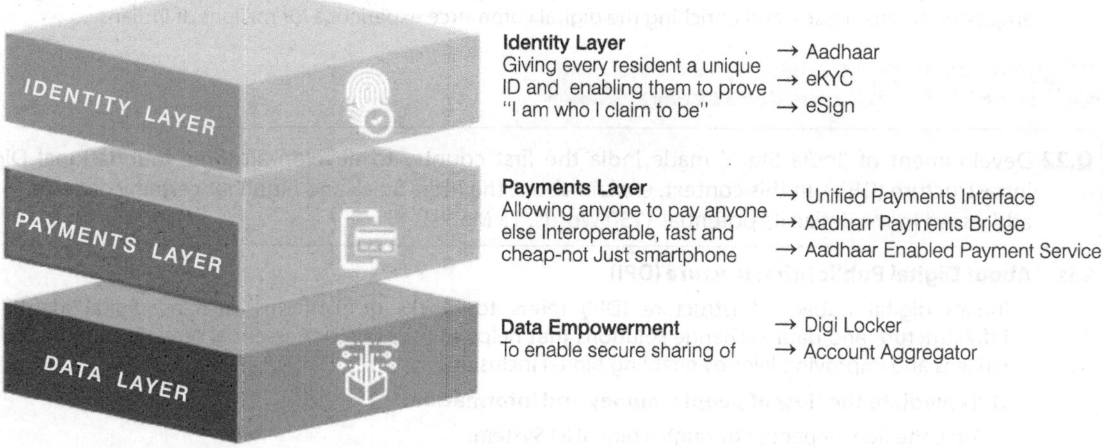

Importance of Digital Public Infrastructure (DPI)

- **Improve Efficiency** Digital Public Infrastructure can streamline and automate processes, reducing the time and effort required to access services. For example, the use of online portals for government services like passport application and income tax filing can reduce the need for physical visits to government offices.
- **Increase Access** Digital Public Infrastructure can improve access to services for people living in remote areas. For example, the use of digital learning platforms can provide students in rural areas with access to quality education.
- **Better Service Quality** Digital Public Infrastructure can help deliver services of higher quality by enabling real-time monitoring and feedback mechanisms. For instance, the use of digital health records can help healthcare providers deliver personalized and efficient care.
- **Increase Transparency** Digital Public Infrastructure can improve transparency in service delivery by providing citizens with access to information and data. For instance, the use of online portals for government services can provide citizens with information on the status of their applications and transactions.
- **Digital Financial Inclusion** Digital Public Infrastructure can help expand financial access to underbanked and unbanked populations in India. For example, the use of mobile wallets and digital payment platforms can enable easy and secure transactions for people who do not have access to traditional banking services.
- **Secure Online Transactions** Digital Public Infrastructure can provide secure and trusted platforms for online transactions. For instance, the use of digital signatures and secure communication channels can prevent fraud and ensure the confidentiality and integrity of sensitive data.

Concerns in Digital Public Infrastructure (DPI)

- **Digital Divide** There is a significant digital divide in India, with many people lacking access to digital infrastructure such as smartphones and internet connectivity. For instance, people living in rural areas may not have access to reliable internet connectivity, which can limit their access to digital services.

- **Cybersecurity** Digital Public Infrastructure is vulnerable to cyber-attacks and data breaches, which can compromise sensitive data and transactions. For example, online payment gateways and digital wallets can be targeted by hackers, leading to financial losses.
- **Interoperability** There is a lack of interoperability among different digital platforms and systems in India, making it difficult for users to access services seamlessly. For instance, different government departments may use different platforms for service delivery, which can create confusion and inefficiencies.
- **Data Privacy** Digital Public Infrastructure raises concerns around data privacy, as personal and sensitive data may be collected and shared by various entities. For example, the collection of biometric data for digital identity verification may raise privacy concerns among citizens.
- **Digital Literacy** There is a need to improve digital literacy among citizens in India to enable them to fully utilize digital services and platforms. For instance, many people may not be aware of the benefits of digital platforms or may lack the necessary skills to access and use digital services.
- **Funding Challenges** The creation and maintenance of a robust digital public infrastructure require significant investment, and governments may face budget constraints in funding these projects. Additionally, financing models that support the long-term sustainability of the infrastructure may be difficult to establish.
- **Legal Challenges** The creation of digital public infrastructure may require changes to existing legal frameworks to enable the sharing of data and the provision of digital services. Governments must navigate complex legal issues such as data protection, intellectual property rights, and liability for data breaches.

Futuristic Measures

- **Strengthen Cybersecurity** This includes developing robust security protocols and implementing regular audits to identify vulnerabilities. It can be strengthened by building a comprehensive legal and regulatory framework to combat cyber threats, including laws on data protection, cybercrime, and information security.
- **Expand Digital Infrastructure** This includes improving internet connectivity, building data centres, and providing digital access points. Investing in emerging technologies, such as 5G, artificial intelligence,?the Internet of Things (IoT) and, Blockchain Technology can be very much helpful for expanding digital infrastructure.
- **Increase Access to Digital Services** Expanding internet connectivity to rural and remote areas using innovative technologies such as satellite broadband, Gigamesh networks. Creating user-friendly digital interfaces and supporting the creation of local language applications and content will increase the accessibility of digital services to non-English speaking populations. Establishing community centres and digital literacy programs to educate and train people on how to use digital services.
- **Promote Data Protection** This includes establishing clear guidelines on data usage, storage, and sharing. Implementation of Data protection bill to regulate the collection, storage, processing, and sharing of personal data of individuals can be very much helpful in data protection.
- **Encourage Digital Skills** The government must promote digital literacy and provide training and upskilling opportunities to create a skilled workforce.
- **Improve Interoperability** The government must ensure that digital systems are interoperable with each other, enabling seamless integration between different digital platforms.
- **Foster Public-Private Partnerships** The government must collaborate with the private sector to drive innovation, investment, and knowledge-sharing, to develop more effective and sustainable digital public infrastructure.

Conclusion

It has been recognized recently by IMF that India has built a world-class digital public infrastructure that has lessons for many countries.

In the last 7 years, India has launched many digital transformational projects, including Aadhaar, Unified Payment Interface, Digilocker, UMANG, Aarogya Setu, CoWIN Vaccination Platform, Government e-Market Place (GeM), DIKSHA, Ayushman Bharat Digital Health Mission, etc. But the most successful story of India Stack has been the inclusion of the underbanked population in the financial services sector through UPI and payments.

Urban Infrastructure (Municipal Bonds)

Q.23 In the background of urban local body finances, critically examine the importance of municipal bonds in fulfilling the massive investment requirement in the urban infrastructure sector. (250 Words, 15 Marks)

Ans. Trends of Urban Local Bodies (ULBs) finances

- The ULBs' key revenue sources are taxes, fees, fines and charges, and transfers from Central and State governments, which are known as intergovernmental transfers (IGTs).
- The share of own revenue (including revenue from taxes on property and advertisements, and non-tax revenue from user charges and fees from building permissions and trade licensing) to total revenue is an important indicator of ULBs' fiscal health and autonomy.
- ULBs' own sources of revenue were less than half of their total revenue, with large untapped potential. The ULBs' own revenue was 47% of their total revenue. Of this, tax revenue was the largest component - 29% of the total.
- **ULBs still lacked revenue buoyancy** as their share in GDP of own revenue was only 0.5% for the five-year period.
- **Property tax, the single largest contributor to ULBs' own revenue, accounted for only about 0.15% of the GDP**. The corresponding figures for developing and developed countries were significantly higher (about 0.6% and 1%, respectively) indicating that this is not being harnessed to potential in India.
- **Many ULBs were highly dependent on IGTs.** Transfers from the Central government are as stipulated by the Central Finance Commissions and through grants towards specific reforms. Whereas, the State government transfers are stipulated as grants-in-aid and devolution of State's collection of local taxes. Most ULBs were highly dependent on external grants. IGTs accounted for about 40% of the ULBs' total revenue.
- **Stable and predictable IGTs are particularly important since ULBs' own revenue collection is inadequate.** While dependence on IGTs dipped over the years due to modest increase in own revenue, the scale of IGTs in India remained at around 0.5% of GDP, which is far lower than the international average of 2% to 5% of GDP.

Urban Infrastructure Requirements

- **Investment Required** World Bank estimates that India will need to invest USD 840 billion over the next 15 years into urban infrastructure if it is to effectively meet the needs of its fast-growing urban population.
- **People Living in Urban Cities** By 2036, 600 million people will be living in urban cities in India, representing 40% of the population.
  - This is likely to put additional pressure on the already stretched urban infrastructure and services of Indian cities with more demand for clean drinking water, reliable power supply, efficient and safe road transport amongst others.
  - Currently, the central and state governments finance over 75% of city infrastructure, while Urban Local Bodies (ULB) finance 15% through their own surplus revenues.
  - Only 5% of the infrastructure needs of Indian cities are currently being financed through private sources.
- **Slow Implementation of Centre's Flagship Urban Missions** There has also been slow implementation performance by states and Urban Local Bodies (ULBs) on several of the Centre's flagship Urban Missions - such as the Smart Cities Mission (SCM) and the Pradhan Mantri Awas Yojana (PMAY) for instance - due to constraints on implementation capacity at the city level.
  - ULBs across India have so far executed only about one-fifth of the cumulative cost or outlay of approved projects under SCM and (Atal Mission for Rejuvenation and Urban Transformation (AMRUT) over the last six financial years.
  - Urban rejuvenation missions like Smart cities Mission, AMRUT, Swachh Bharat Mission etc. are also requiring substantial funding.
- **PPP transactions for Urban Infrastructure** Public Private Partnership (PPP) transactions for urban infrastructure in India registered a marked decline in the last decade both in monetary value and transaction volume.

In this background, financial empowerment of ULBs is the need of the hour and issuing of municipal bonds (as government own revenue is less) by some municipal corporations of Surat, Chennai, Pune, Ahmedabad, Indore is the step towards strengthening capacities of ULBs.

Municipal Bonds in India

- A municipal bond is a debt security issued by a state, municipality or county to finance its capital expenditures, including the construction of highways, bridges or schools. Municipal bonds are mostly exempt from federal taxes and from most state and local taxes, making them especially attractive to people in high income tax brackets.
- In India, municipal bonds are in existence since 1997. Previously, cities like Ahmedabad, Bengaluru, Nasik and Madurai have issued municipal bonds. However, since 2010, there have been no new issues. Municipal bond issues are yet to gain pace in India.
- The Government of India allowed ULBs to issue tax-free municipal bonds in 1999-2000 and has amended the Income Tax Act, 1961 vide the Finance Act 2000.
- Ahmedabad Municipal Corporation (AMC) was the first ULBs in India (2002) to issue tax-free municipal bonds for water and sewerage projects.
- In order to give regulatory clarity, SEBI came up detailed guidelines in 2015.

Prospects of Municipal Bonds as a Source of financing Urban Infrastructure

- **Own Revenue Augmentation** Municipal bonds help municipal corporations to directly raise funds without depending upon the support extended by government agencies and World Bank.
- **Attractive for Institutional Investors** Large institutional investors like pension funds and insurance companies are looking forward to invest in less risky avenues to invest. Municipal bonds provide avenues to tap these investments.
- **Alternative to Traditional Savings** The municipal bonds can increase the quality of life in cities. They can act as a better alternative for investors beyond fixed deposits and small saving schemes.
- **Emergence of GST Regime** Many municipal corporations raised huge revenue from octroi. With the advent of GST, octroi would go away. Municipalities have to look forward towards other avenues for augmenting their finance base.
- **Long term Financing Options** Municipal bonds can also simultaneously deepen the long-term infrastructure financing market in India as well as redirect retail investments into liquid securities away from real estate and gold.
- **Building Culture of Ownership among Citizens** By creating opportunities for citizens to invest in tangible public causes in their cities, these bonds can also build strong bonds of trust between municipalities and citizens, bonds of trust that can galvanise citizen participation in cities at historic scale and to mutual financial benefit.

Challenges of Municipal Bond Market in India

- **Lack of Marketability Options** Lack of a secondary market to trade municipal bonds enable buyers to hold them till they reach maturity, which prevents marketability.
- **Unattractive to Investors** Conservative approach followed by insurance and pension firms to invest in municipal bonds. This is coupled by lack of incentives to municipal bodies to make use of debt market.
- **Poor Accounting Standards** Non-transparent accounting techniques followed by Municipalities is a major constraint.
- **Doubtful Credit Worthiness of Cities** Credit worthiness of cities is a major constraint. This can be highlighted by ratings of 94 cities, which are part of Smart City Mission and AMRUT were detailed by the ministry of housing and urban affairs. Of these, 55 cities got investment grade rating (BBB- and above), while other 39 were rated below BBB.
- **Bonds and Credibility** Non-application of Bankruptcy norms don't lend credibility to such bonds. There are several international examples such as Detroit wherein lack of proper bankruptcy mechanisms for municipal bonds led to a complete collapse of municipal structures
- **Reduced Investor Trust and Confidence** Weak financial position and poor governance and management of city agencies have limited their ability to issue bonds, and reduced investor trust and confidence.
- **No authentic Financial Data available** Investors have doubt over local bodies as there is no authentic financial data available.

Futuristic Reform Measures

- **World Banks's Suggestions** The solutions suggested include improving the fiscal base and creditworthiness of the Indian cities. Cities must institute a buoyant revenue base and be able to recover the cost of providing its services. In simpler terms, it means increasing property taxes, user fees and service charges to name a few.

- **Development of a Healthy Municipal Bond Market** depends on the presence of a strong legal foundation and authority to Municipalities; Urban Development Authorities, Waste and Sewage Boards etc to incur and repay debt; adopt economic pricing approach aimed at cost recovery from users of services; carry out comprehensive reforms of accounting practices; professionalisation of municipal management for critical appraisal of projects; suitable fiscal incentives to encourage investors, transparency of regulatory mechanism and an improved market image of the urban infrastructure sector to instil confidence in investors.

Urban Transport

Q.24 Despite many modes of public transport systems available in Indian cities, switching between them is not seamless. An integrated multi-modal transportation system is the need of the hour. Elaborate.
(150 Words, 10 Marks)

Ans. **Introduction** Public transport is the primary mode of road transport for most of the Indian citizens, and India's public transport systems are among the most heavily used in the world.

Despite it being the lifeline of urban Indian economy, our public transportation systems are increasingly coming under strain due to faster pace of urbanisation, lack of efficient traffic management systems and seamless integration of urban transport systems.

Realizing this, governments over the time introduced various modes of mobility ranging from city buses, metro trains both underground and surface. Plans are afoot to develop a massive network of inland waterways. Apart from this, there are also non- formal transportation systems like auto-rickshaws, private buses, taxis, etc.

Issues with India's Public Transport

- **Infrastructure Gaps** In many Indian cities, there are infrastructure gaps that hinder the integration and connectivity of different modes of transport.
- **Limited Interoperability** The lack of interoperability between different transport systems is a significant barrier to seamless switching.
- **Inconsistent Timings** The lack of synchronization in the timings of different modes of transport can create difficulties for commuters. If the timing of one mode does not align with another, it can lead to delays, missed connections, and longer waiting times. For instance, if a bus or metro arrives late, a commuter may miss a connecting train or bus, disrupting the overall journey.
- **Poor Last-Mile Connectivity** Last-mile connectivity, which refers to the connectivity between transport hubs and final destinations, is often inadequate in Indian cities.
  - For example, in Delhi, both DMRC feeder buses and Delhi government buses ply on the same route and compete against each other. The consequence of this is the lack of bus services in mainly last mile connectivity in most of the routes.
- **Policy and Governance Challenges** Coordinating and integrating multiple transport agencies, each with their own administrative structures, can pose governance and policy challenges.
  - There is a lack of horizontal and vertical coordination among central, state and local levels, making accountability very difficult. There is an absence of any effective coordinating agency where urban transport and land use plans can be formulated and integrated keeping an overall goal in mind.
- Another issue in urban transportation problems is while most of the cities are growing in the periphery, the focus of providing connectivity is limited to core cities. Delhi-NCR is the best example of this phenomenon.

Need for Integrated Multi-modal Transportation

Integrated Multi-Modal Transport System (IMMTS) comprises one trip that involves two or more than two different modes of transportation like bus, metro, car, tram, etc. either government or privately operated; where in-between passengers have to transfer into another mode. For example, Urban bus systems serving train and subway stations and often extending to even local airports.

To minimize the use of private transport facilities, major Indian cities have been moving towards a multi-modal urban transport network. Such networks could help integrate different public transport options and provide end to end transportation facilities for the people.

- Many studies have found that one of the major reasons for use of private transportation systems and app-based taxis in urban India is due to lack of seamless and end to end connectivity.
- **Multimodal Transport System (MMTS)** explores the use of multiple modes of transport for safe, convenient and efficient movement of passengers. Generally, MMTS has been characterized by increased capacity, efficient access and better location of both interchange and integration nodes.
- A major goal of integrated multi-modal transport systems is to reduce dependence on the automobile as a major mode of ground transportation and increase the use of public transport. This aspect is particularly crucial in vastly urbanising countries like India, where we can see heavy traffic congestion due to a large number of private vehicles.
- **An efficient and properly managed MMTS**, can reduce travelling times effectively, and increase the productivity of the economy. For example, Delhi and NCR lose nearly 42 crore man-hours every month while commuting between home and office through public transport, due to the traffic congestion.
- **Presence of MMTS** in the metro region enhances accessibility, economic growth, public health, environmental protection, security & safety, social cohesion, etc. In this connection, it is desirable to establish a single authority for planning, development, implementation and enforcement of the policies.
- MMTS helps in devising need-based traffic circulation plans to integrate various modes and improvement of major road stretches and intersections to facilitate smooth movements.

Way Forward

The idea of implementing a multi-modal system in India gained momentum after the government proposed a 'National Transport Card' to allow commuters to pay for rides across various multiple modes of transport. This was a welcome step to promote public transport, along the lines of Hong Kong's 'Octopus card' first issued in 1997. However, there are certain aspects that need to be kept in mind to develop efficient MMTS:

- Efficient development and maintenance of infrastructure on which the transportation systems run, like roads, metro bridges and tracks, parking facilities etc.
- Indian context it is very important to integrate all various modes of transport like bus, feeder services, bicycle, rickshaw, etc. with rapid transit systems. It is equally important to integrate non-motorized modes (pedestrian, cycles, rickshaws, etc.) to mass rapid transits.
- The transfer of commuters from one mode of transport to another must be seamless, and practical. Here walking time to shift between different systems, waiting for time and mode of transportation in light of traffic must be considered.

Check Your Preparation

1. Highlight the factors that constrain the growth of logistics sector in India. What can be done to remove these constraints? (150 words, 10 marks)
2. Identify the challenges faced by the railways in India. In this context, also discuss the ways in which the Railways can be transformed into an efficient public service provider as well as commercially viable entity. (250 words, 15 marks)
3. Inland waterways have largely been neglected as a viable means of transport for carrying goods and people. Discuss the challenges in the development of inland water ways in India. (150 words, 10 marks)
4. Civil aviation presents a contrasting mix of study in India. Despite extraordinary growth in traffic, most of the Indian airlines are in a precarious condition. Analyse the reason behind this situation. Discuss the policy support and potential growth prospects. (250 words, 15 marks)
5. 'Power is often identified with progress in modern civilisation and is a critical component of infrastructure that determines the economic development of a country.' Elaborate. While discussing the source of power generation capacity, examine the challenges faced by the power sector in India. (250 words, 15 marks)
6. India is going to face an increasing demand for energy as it grows. Evaluate the significance of renewable energy in achieving energy security with special emphasis on solar power. (150 words, 10 marks)

UNIT 10

Investment Models

Infrastructure Financing (Infrastructure Financing Sources and Challenges)

Q.1 Highlight the innovative sources of infrastructure financing that goes beyond the traditional finance options such as banks and government budgetary support. Along with discussing the challenges of infrastructure financing, suggest various reform measures. (250 Words, 15 Marks)

Ans. **Introduction** Infrastructure development is a prerequisite for economic growth, productive investment, job creation, and poverty reduction. Poor infrastructure remains the biggest hurdle to sustaining a fast pace of economic growth and job creation in the future. India's biggest challenge is the huge infrastructure financing gap, which is estimated to be more than 5% of GDP

Infrastructure involves huge investments, long gestation periods, procedural delays and delayed returns. This makes infrastructure financing complex. the past, government budgets, banks and international donors were the traditional funding sources. But, the infrastructure needs exceed sources of traditional funding. Therefore, there is a need to look beyond into novel and innovative financing mechanisms.

Innovative Sources of Infrastructure Financing

- **Asset Monetisation** The National Monetisation Pipeline (NMP) envisages an aggregate monetisation potential of 6-lakh crore through the leasing of core assets of the Central government in sectors such as roads, railways, power, oil and gas pipelines, telecom, civil aviation etc, over a four-year period (FY 2022-25).
- **Public-Private Partnership (PPP) Model** PPP is an arrangement between government and private sector for the provision of public assets and public services. It allows large-scale government projects, such as roads, bridges, or hospitals, to be completed with mix of public and private funding. This helps in improving transparency and efficiency. E.g.: **HAM, BOT, EPC, etc.**
- **Development Finance Institutions (DFIs)** They are government-owned or public institutions that provide funding for infrastructure and large-scale projects. The National Bank for Financing Infrastructure & Development (NaBFID) is making significant strides in infrastructure financing, with ambitious goals for loan disbursement and expansion.
- **Infrastructure Investment Trust (InvITs)** InvITs work like mutual funds. They pool small sums of money from a number of investors to invest in assets that give cash flow over a period of time. Part of this cash flow is distributed as a dividend back to investors. Example: National Highways Infra Trust, PowerGrid Infrastructure Investment Trust, etc.

- **Viability Gap Funding (VGF) Scheme** Viability Gap Finance means a grant to support projects that are economically justified but are not financially viable. A grant under VGF is provided as a capital subsidy in order to attract the private sector players to participate in PPP projects that are otherwise financially unviable.
  - The Department of Economic Affairs, Ministry of Finance introduced "the Scheme for Financial Support to PPPs in Infrastructure" (Viability Gap Funding Scheme) in 2006 with a view to support infrastructure projects undertaken through PPP mode that are economically justified but commercially unviable due to large capital investment requirements, long gestation periods and the inability to increase user charges to commercial levels
- **Foreign Direct Investment (FDI)** FDI is an ownership stake in a foreign company or project made by an investor, company, or government from another country. FDI upto 100% under automatic route is permitted in projects for construction and maintenance of roads, highways, vehicular bridges, toll roads, vehicular tunnels, ports and harbors. Further, FDI is permitted in other sectors through approval route.
- **India Infrastructure Finance Company Ltd (IIFCL)** IIFCL is a wholly-owned Government of India company set up in 2006 to provide long-term financial assistance to viable infrastructure projects through the Scheme for Financing Viable Infrastructure Projects through a Special Purpose Vehicle. IIFCL raises funds from domestic as well as external markets on the strength of government guarantees.
- **National Infrastructure Investment Fund** National Infrastructure Investment Fund (NIIF) with an initial corpus of Rs 40,000 crore was launched.

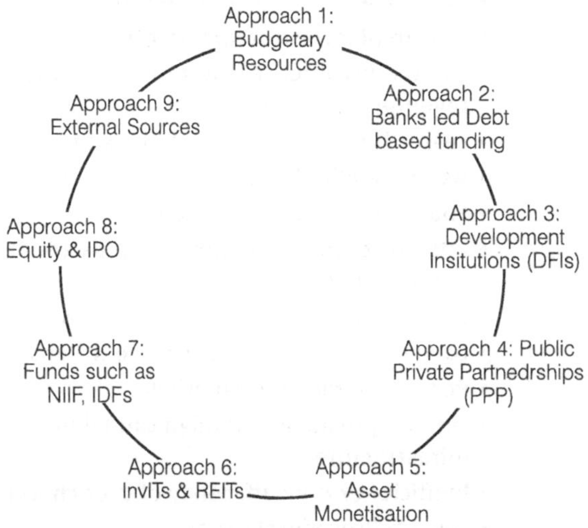

- **Infrastructure Debt Fund (IDF)** An IDF is a company or a trust formed for the purpose of investing in infrastructure debt instruments or public-private partnership projects. The funds of the various IDF plans are managed by the fund's Asset Management Company (AMC).
- **Easing norms for Retail Investors** Retail investors are now able to directly bid for government securities (G-Secs) in Reserve Bank of India auctions to help fund the government's massive borrowing plan for the next fiscal. The government is developing a new framework that will permit small investors to fund infrastructure projects.
- **Tapping the retail investor base through Infrastructure Bonds** To provide further impetus to infrastructure financing, Government of India has permitted IFCI, IDFC, LIC and infrastructure finance firms to issue long-term infrastructure bonds.
- **Government, Municipal, and other Sub-sovereign Bonds** Securities in this category include bonds issued by public entities in capital markets in order to finance the construction and operation of an infrastructure asset.
- **Green Bonds** Green bonds are corporate bonds, project bonds, and sub-sovereign bonds that finance investment in green infrastructure assets such as clean energy.

Challenges of Infrastructure Financing

- **Fiscal Burden** Almost half of the total investment in the infrastructure sector is done by the Government through budget allocations. But Government funds have competing demands, such as, education, health, employment generation, among others.
- **Asset-Liability Mismatch of Commercial Banks** Commercial banking sector's ability to extend long-term loans to the infrastructure sector is limited.
- **Subdued Investments in PPP Projects** Private sector investment is yet to revive in the backdrop of subdued interest from potential stakeholders. Legacy issues and weak balance sheets have led to limited participation from existing infrastructure players in India.
- **Investment Obligations of Insurance and Pension Funds** Insurance and pension funds are constrained by their obligation to invest a substantial portion of their funds in Government securities.
- **Need for an Efficient and Vibrant Corporate Bond Market** The corporate bond market is still a long way to go in providing adequate financing to the infrastructure sector in India.

- **Insufficiency of User Charges** A large part of the infrastructure sector in India especially irrigation, water supply, urban sanitation, and state road transport is not amenable to commercialisation for various reasons. Due to this, the Government is not in a position to levy sufficient user charges on these services.
- **Legal and Procedural Issues** Issues relating to land acquisition and environmental clearances add uncertainty which affects the risk appetite of investors as well as banks.

Issues

- **Nature of infrastructure assets**
- **Limited fiscal space. More tilted towards revenue expenditure.**
- **Lesser funds available with the states**
- **Asset-Liability Mismatch of Commercial Banks**
- **Four Balance Sheet Problem**
- **Infrastructure Development Funds are at nascent stage.**
- **Subdued Investment in PPP projects**
- **Lower penetration of Insurance & Pension funds**
- **Poor corporate bond market**
- **Limited private and foreign capital in infrastructure**
- **Inefficiency & insufficiency of user charges**
- **Legal & Procedural issues.**

Reforms Required

- **Revitalising the Bond and Credit Markets**
- **Tapping the long-term resources from the insurance & pension sector.**
- **Strengthening the municipal bond market in India: Financial discipline, revenue base and improving credit-worthiness.**
- **Successful implementation of National Monetisation Pipeline (NMP).**
- **Revitalising land monetisation (National Land Management Corporation)**
- **Push to InvITs and REITs**
- **Revival of PPP projects**
- **Encouraging green financing**
- **Institutional reforms needed in project financing**
- **Understanding the ESG parameters**
- **Enabling User charges to finance infrastructure**

Conclusion

According to a GOI report, every Re. 1 spent on infrastructure leads to a GDP stimulation of ₹ 3, therefore, it is of immense importance to improve financing through non-traditional sources. Building modern, sustainable, and reliable infrastructure is critical for meeting the rising aspirations of people.

Asset Monetisation vs PPP

Q.2 Compare and contrast between the Asset Monetisation and Public Private Partnership (PPP). What learnings can be drawn from the PPP experience in India for the successful implementation of National Monetisation Pipeline (NMP)? (250 Words, 15 Marks)

Ans. **Introduction** Asset monetisation is the process of creating new sources of revenue for the government by unlocking the economic value of unutilised or underutilised public assets.

- The strategic objective of Asset Monetisation programme is to unlock the value of investments in public sector assets by tapping private sector capital and efficiencies which can thereafter be leveraged for augmentation/ greenfield infrastructure creation.
- It presents an opportunity for public asset owners to avail new financial structures and vehicles for tapping capital from private sector investors (strategic, institutional, retail etc).
- In the process, it helps public sector authorities/entities in easing fiscal constraints and freeing up the balance sheets for taking up more greenfield infrastructure creation.

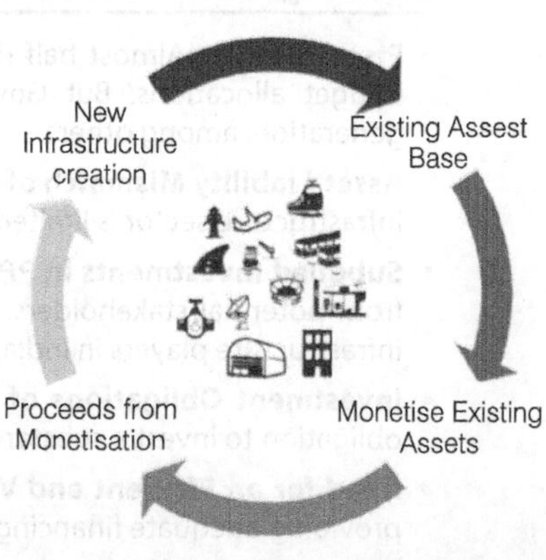

Public-Private Partnership (PPP) PPP is a contract between a private entity and the governmental body, with a goal of providing some public benefit, either a service or an asset. PPP typically are long-term and involve large corporations on the private side.

Asset Monetisation vs PPP

Basis	Asset Monetisation	PPP
Working	In asset monetisation, the government parts with its assets such as roads, coal mines for a specified period of time in exchange for a lump sum payment.	Involve collaboration between a government agency and a private-sector company that can be used to finance, build, and operate projects example-greenfield and brownfield.
Asset Creation	Asset created by leasing out the brown field project and subsequently earning by its management by private companies	Private sector partner under BOT has to bring the finance for the project and take the responsibility to construct and maintain it.
Allocation of risk	No risk is involved for private player.	Well defined allocations of risk between private and public sector.
Responsibility of management	Responsibility of management in private hand.	Full responsibility by government for providing services under models like HAM, EPC, BOT (Annuity), etc.
Transfer of ownership	In such an arrangement no transfer of ownership is involved.	PPP under BOT, the government gives a concession to a private entity to build a facility (and possibly design it as well), own the facility, lease the facility to the public sector and then at the end of the lease period transfer the ownership of the facility to the government.
Construction risk	The concessionaire need not to take any of the construction risk.	Private entity generally takes entire responsibility for the design, construction, finance, and operation of the project for the period of concession.
Experience Requirement	What will be required is operational experience in running a particular class of infrastructure assets and a strong understanding of the potential cash flows generated over the life of the concession.	Required a proven ability to navigate and manage the system.

National Monetisation Pipeline is a solution to address the Infrastructure Deficit

- **Resource Mobilisation** NMP is critical to attract the required quantum of capital into infrastructure sector because it has aggregate monetisation potential of ₹ 6-lakh crore
- **Better Utilisation of Existing Assets** A faster turnaround in the China-US route is attracting the shipping traffic, while Indian cargo is waiting at trans-shipment ports in Colombo, Singapore or Port Klang due to poor infrastructure.
- **Inclusion of capital generated through NMP in other sectors** The government is building $28 billion worth of highway infrastructure in the north-east and USD five billion is spent on rail infra.
- **Supporting Better Logistics in Hinterland** The Mumbai-Ahmedabad bullet train will cost nearly $13 billion, western and eastern DFCs (dedicated freight corridor) together will cost an estimated $11 billion; USD 10 billion is going to create expressways in Uttar Pradesh alone.
- **Regional Infrastructure Development** The entire hinterlands of Bihar, Madhya Pradesh, Chhattisgarh, Jharkhand, etc. need infrastructure.
- **Running Stalled Projects** The primary reason behind the failure was money. The government didn't have money, so they took an easy route, Build-Own-Operate-Transfer or BOOT, under the aegis of private-Public-Partnership (PPP).
- **Fiscal Prudence** The revenue occurred by leasing out these assets will help fund new capital expenditure without pressurising government finances.
- **Mobilising Private Capital** Resources and capital efficiency of private sector along with the ability to dynamically adapt to the evolving global and economic reality will foster value creation on infrastructure.
- **Generating Investment Avenues** Creates an enabling environment for participation of long- term institutional investors in infrastructure asset management.

- **Reducing Cost Overruns** In some cases, project completion time is exceeded, leading to elevated project cost so much so that either the project itself becomes unviable at the time of its launching.
- **Utilising Underutilised Public Assets** The NMP advocates unlocking idle capital from non- strategic underperforming government owned assets.

PPP Experience can be useful for National Monetisation Pipeline (NMP)

- **Success in Revenue Growth** The PPP project are usually successful in sectors with high revenue growth potentials. The NMP is focused on top 5 sectors such as Roads, Railways, Power, oil & gas pipelines and Telecom which can offer good revenue.
- **Applicability in Different Sectors** The PPP initiative in railways indicates government's willingness to open all sectors for private investment. The NMP includes railways as one of the core sector to be focused upon.
- **Capacity Utilisation** The NMP investment in natural gas and petroleum pipeline networks for expanding across the nation has huge potentials for economic development growth in India and neighbouring nations such as Nepal and Bhutan. This can be efficiently done with PPP.
- **Energy Sector** Power sector is witnessing increase in demand after the slow down due to covid pandemic. After the successful growth due to PPP projects, the NMP can be used to invest in green energy power projects such as solar power, wind energy and tidal energy.
- **Multi-stakeholders** The NMP will have investment from Union and State Government as well. Any assets like railways, airports in smaller cities, dedicated freight corridor assets, warehousing assets of state-run companies, etc. will have multiple stakeholders. A PPP model will better suit to these conditions.
- **Successfully Earlier Implementation** Since 2017, the NHAI has been successfully monetising its brownfield road assets through Toll Operate Transfer (TOT)-based PPP concessions.

Conclusion

Asset Monetisation needs to be viewed not just as a funding mechanism, but as an overall strategy for bringing about a paradigm shift in infrastructure operations, augmentation and maintenance. This is especially considering the potential for resource and capital efficiencies as also the ability to dynamically adapt to the evolving global and economic reality.

National Monetisation Pipeline

Q.3 Bring out the critical challenges in implementation of National monetisation pipeline. Also suggest ways to ensure optimum resource mobilisation through public asset monetisation. (150 Words, 10 Marks)

Ans. **Introduction** National Monetisation Pipeline is an initiative by the Government of India for resource mobilisation through monetisation of brownfield, but underutilised infrastructure assets. The Union Budget 2021-22, identifies monetisation of public assets as one of the three pillars for infrastructure financing in the country. ₹ 6 Lakh Crore worth of assets will be monetised under the NMP over a 4-year period from FY2022 to FY2025.

The top 5 sectors (by estimated value) capture ~83% of the aggregate pipeline value. These top five sectors include: Roads (27%) followed by Railways (25%), Power (15%), oil & gas pipelines (8%) and Telecom (6%).

Challenges in the implementation of National Monetisation Pipeline (NMP)

- **Attracting Private Players** Privatisation in government companies such as Air India and BPCL or the PPP initiative in railways did not attract enough private sector interest. Similar problems are likely to plague the NMP as well.
- **Providing a Balanced Risk Profile of Assets** Making correct projections of risks associated with long-term projects in diverse sectors will be difficult as well as crucial to attracting large-scale investors such as sovereign funds.
- **Lack of Identifiable Revenues Streams** Though investors may be interested in few projects, assets or sectors which are profitable, monetisation of assets in less profitable sectors might suffer due to immediate lack of revenue streams or poor investment sentiments for such sectors.

- **High valuation** High value of most assets under consideration is likely to limit the number of potential bidders to few Industrial or sectoral conglomerates. This can create issues of coordinated bidding, raise concerns of crony-capitalism and undermine the real value of assets.
- **Asset-specific Challenges** Issues such as low level of capacity utilization in gas and petroleum pipeline networks, regulated tariffs in power sector assets, low interest among investors in national highways below four lanes etc. will create specific challenges.
- **Effective Execution** In absence of effective implementation, NMP can go the route of many previous over- ambitious schemes.
- **Monopolisation** A significant criticism of the NMP is that the transfer would end up creating monopolies, leading to a rise in price. It is inevitable in the case of highways and railway lines.

The above challenges might undermine resource mobilization possible under the NMP Following measures can help in optimum resource mobilization

- **Development Finance Institution (DFI)** DFIs can help in domain-specific assessment of risks and benefits, and in overseeing effective utilization of mobilized resources in the projects.
- **Dispute Resolution Mechanism** Efficient and effective dispute resolution will help improve attractiveness of projects and assets, credit rating as well as investment sentiments through speedy resolutions and certainty of returns.
- **Transparent Bidding** Sustained flow of transparency and visibility about assets, bids and investments across sectors, promotes trust and helps create a level playing field which is crucial to bringing in competitive and competent bidders, efficient price discovery and best management practices.
- **Investor-friendly Taxation** There should be synergy between taxation and investment promotion measures in attracting foreign investments as well as in promotion of financial instruments such as Infrastructure investment trusts, Masala Bonds etc. Unpredictable policies such as retrospective taxation should be avoided.
- **Multi-stakeholder Approach** The success of the infrastructure expansion plan would depend on other stakeholders playing their due role, this includes State governments and their public sector enterprises and the private sector.
- **Dealing with Cronyism** The only way of ensuring that asset monetisation doesn't lead to cronyism is to make the bidding conditions such that the people eligible to bid are not a small, predetermined set.
  - However, the high capital intensity of the project itself makes it difficult for everyone to bid but ensuring sufficient participation on the government's part is important.

Conclusion

National Monetization Pipeline provides a critical diversification of options in mobilizing resources for infrastructure expansion in the country. Effective management of issues inherent to public-private partnerships, asset valuation, predictable government policies and execution will be crucial for success

Public Private Partnership Models (Importance of PPP in Infrastructure)

Q.4 Why is Public Private Partnership (PPP) required in infrastructural projects? Examine the role of PPP model in the redevelopment of Railway Stations in India. (150 Words, 10 Marks) **UPSC Mains PYQ 2022**

Ans. **Introduction** Public-private partnership (PPP) is a long-term contract between a private party and a government entity, for providing a public asset or service, in which the private party bears significant risk and management responsibility, and remuneration is linked to performance.

The most common forms of PPPs in infrastructural projects are build-operate-transfer (BOT), Design-build-operate-transfer (DBFO), operate-maintain-transfer (OMT), etc.

The broad-gauge railway-line between Gandhidham and Tuna-Tekra Port in Gujarat is India's first railway-line built with private sector participation

Need for PPP in Infrastructural Projects

- **Bridging gaps in infrastructure Financing** When governments are cash poor, PPP can offer access to private capital for infrastructure projects. Supplementing limited public sector capacities to meet the growing demand for infrastructure development
- **For Instance** The Hyderabad Metro Rail Ltd (HMRL), the largest Metro project in the world to be implemented in the public-private partnership (PPP)
- **Faster Completion of Projects** With the efficiency of private sector, there will be faster completion of projects and reduced delays. Incentivizing the private sector to deliver projects on time and within budget.
  - **Road Sector** PPP has helped NHAI clock 29.81 Km/day (in 2014-15, the rate was 16.61 km/day).
- **Improved Outcomes** PPP in redevelopment of railway stations increases the quality of infrastructure by mechanism of accountability and responsibility owing to presence of private players.
- **Reduces burden on Government** Since the private sector shares the costs with the government initially, the fiscal strain on the government is reduced.
- **Extracting long-term Value-for-money through appropriate risk transfer** to the private sector over the life of the project – from design/construction to operations/maintenance
- **Innovation** It is considered that involvement of private in the infrastructure sector, especially in redevelopment of railway stations help in bringing innovations and upgraded technologies.
- **Adequate Facilities** PPP model in redevelopment of railway stations ensures security and ample facilities for passengers and for cargo delivery.
- **Expertise and Professionalism** Long-term maintenance by private partners and suitable upgrades are brought into the infrastructure sector.
- **Reduced Corruption and Wastage** PPP reduces corruption and wastage in government projects. The PPP tender and award process based on open competitive bidding following international best practice procedures lead to transparency.
- **Introducing private sector technology and innovation in providing better public services** through improved operational efficiency.
- Using PPPs as a way of gradually exposing state owned enterprises and government to increasing levels of private sector participation (especially foreign) and structuring PPPs in a way so as to ensure transfer of skills leading to national champions that can run their own operations professionally and eventually export their competencies by bidding for projects/ joint ventures
- **Other Benefits** Cost-effectiveness through competitive selection, higher productivity by linking payments to performance and Demand centric delivery of projects.

Role of PPP model in the Redevelopment of Railway Stations in India

- **Redevelopment of 60 Railway Stations** Rail Land Development Authority (RLDA) is spearheading the redevelopment of 60 railway stations across India on a PPP Model. Two components: Mandatory station redevelopment and Station Estate (Commercial) development.
  - The mandatory station redevelopment will make travel smooth and hassle-free without diluting the historical significance of these stations whereas commercial development will enable developers to tap several revenue streams to ensure the viability of the entire project.
- **Better Facilities to Passengers** PPP can improve the condition of railway stations and it can bring state-of-the-art amenities such as segregation of arrival and departure, excellent road connectivity with multi-modal transport integration to enhance travel experience.
- **Optimum Utilization of Space** Most of the railway stations are in heart of the cities. Shopping complexes and commercial spaces can be constructed at unused space of railway stations.
- **More Revenue to Railways** It can help to generate more revenue for railways due to development of commercial spaces.
- **Adequate funding** PPP helps in bringing required funding and timely completion of the projects. Example: Rani Kamalapati railway station was India's first PPP based railway station which was successfully redeveloped.
- **Security** PPP can help to provide better security to passengers at railway stations. It can help to reduce incidents of pick pocketing and theft at railway stations.

- **Reduction in the Maintenance Costs** of railway stations for government.
- **Efficient Management** PPP help in providing smooth and efficient management when it comes to safety and cleanliness by linking payments to performance.
- **State of art Technologies** PPP Mode could bring advanced state-of-the-art technologies that are capital intensive like Video Management System (VMS).
- **Developing Railways not as a service, but as an Asset** Station redevelopment is planned by leveraging the real estate potential of separable land and air space in and around the stations, through private participation. These redeveloped hubs will be called "Railopolis."
- **Others** It will augment the tourism potential, boost real estate, encourage employment generation and lead to a cascading effect on the local economy.
  - Issues with PPP model in the redevelopment of Railway Stations in India
- **Losses in Employment** Private companies are more interested in acquiring profit with a limited number of employees, which results in job loss.
- **Increase in User Fee for the Customers** The government has opted for EPC contracts for station redevelopment of New Delhi instead of public-private partnerships in order to avoid putting the burden of user fee on passengers.
- **New players** The new players have little experience and are struggling with economics and logistics of providing connectivity from remote locations.
- **Apprehension of Corruption** Corruption and misallocation of funds based on private player's interests.
- **Less focus on Welfare** The private sector is more likely switch to profit making trajectory and in the meanwhile passenger's interests might be compromised.
- **Absence of independent Regulator** In the absence of independent regulator in railway sector, there are chances of litigation or other issues as cropped up in the road sector.
- **No past experience in the PPP model** for the implementation of projects for railways.
- **Accountability** Private companies are unpredictable in their dealings and do not share their governance secrets with the world at large.

Way Forward

- **Implementing Vijay Kelkar Committee recommendations** Formulation of PPP Law-A PPP law which gives an authoritative framework to implementing executives.
- **Infrastructure PPP Project Review Committee (IPRC)** Should be there for evaluating stressed PPP projects.
- **Swiss challenge Method** For awarding Contracts, to discourage unsolicited proposals.
- **Viability Gap Funds** Prudent utilisation of Viability Gap Funds (VGF) and Improved
- Fiscal Reporting Practices.
- **Institutionalised mechanism** Like National Facilitation Committee (NFC) to ensure time bound resolution of issues.

Conclusion

Over the years, Public-Private Partnership (PPP) has emerged as a resilient model to undertake infrastructural development. The redevelopment of railway stations is just an example of realizing the benefits of PPP to accelerate infrastructural development. Overall PPP projects help change our infrastructure model from Build-Neglect-Rebuild to Build-Nurture-Repair. (Rakesh Mohan committee)

Critical Analysis of PPP

Q.5 Public Private Partnership (PPP) model in India is facing financial issues and procedural challenges along with policy, regulatory and institutional gaps. Substantiate the statement along with some suggestions to strengthen the PPP ecosystem in India. (250 Words, 15 Marks)

Ans. **Introduction** Public-private partnerships involve collaboration between a government agency and a private-sector company that can be used to finance, build, and operate projects, such as public transportation networks, parks, and convention centres.

Challenges being faced by the PPP

India has emerged as one of the largest PPP market in the world but since some recent years, PPP model in India is facing various challenges. PPP is facing challenges in across three broad categories:

- Financing issues and Viability constraints;
- Capacity and Procedural Challenges; and
- Policy, Regulatory and Institutional gaps.

Financing issues and viability constraints	Capacity and procedural challenges	Policy, regulatory and institional gaps
Aggressive bidding and under pricing of projects	Lack of efficient project preparation activities	Strengthening of the regulatory regime through independent regulators
Huge dependency on commericial banks for PPP financing	Delay in land acquisition	Under development dispute resolution mechanism
Over leveraged balance sheet of developers	Delay in obtaining approvals and clearance	Absence of dedicated PPP policy or regulation at national level
Lack of equity in the market	Inadequate project monitoring activities	Multiplicity of institutions and overlap in roles
Inflation of the Total Project Cost (TPC) by bidders		

Financing Issues and Viability Constraints

- **Aggressive bidding and under-pricing of projects** have been a big challenge in the transport sector, particularly in roads and ports projects. This has become one of the major reasons for delays or cancellation of PPP projects as banks are becoming more and more cautionary in funding such projects.
- Project sponsors in PPP projects depend hugely on commercial banks for financing the debt portion of the project. These banks have reached their corresponding exposure limits for the sector and run with high level of non-performing assets (NPAs) in the sector.
- A variety of reasons including macroeconomic conditions, project delays and aggressive bidding have resulted in poor recovery from the projects, thereby making these companies over leveraged. This limits their capacity to raise funds from external sources and to take any more new projects.
  - Balance sheets of most prominent developers in the country are stressed and over leveraged. This fester twin balance sheet problem and results in inter-twined economic issues of over leveraged and distressed corporate and NPA encumbered banks.

Capacity and Procedural Challenges

- There is a lack of capacities at various levels of government to properly plan and prepare PPP projects. Lack of capacities at various levels of the governments are evident in project preparation activities in many projects, resulting in problems such as cancellation or delay of project, arising of disputes and undue advantages to the private partner.
- **Infrastructure projects require multiple clearances at the centre, state and local levels, resulting in serious delays.** Land acquisition and environmental clearance are the major contributing factors for project delays.
  - For example, more than two years were needed for the Gujarat Pipavav port project to receive the necessary clearances after achieving financial closure.
- Projects are generally not efficiently monitored on certain aspects like revenue safeguarding or fund management.
- **Inadequate Regulatory Framework and Inefficiency in the Approval Process** have been considered as serious disincentives for developers and contractors.

Policy, Regulatory and Institutional Gaps

Besides financial issues and capacity and procedural challenges, there are policy, regulatory and institutional gaps that need to be filled in order to strengthen the PPP ecosystem in the country.

- Due to the long-term nature of PPP contracts, uncertain market conditions, lack of capacity at both government and private player levels, etc. disputes are bound to arise during the life cycle of PPP projects. Absence of regulators results in many of these issues and disputes being unresolved, leading to litigations and cases.
- **Dispute resolution mechanisms are slow and not very well developed**, often derailing project timelines and freezing funds.
- A comprehensive National PPP act/policy which should clearly spell out the objectives, scope and implementing principles of the PPP program envisaged by the Government is required.
- Governments at all levels, including urban local bodies (ULBs), line departments, state agencies, are by and large unable to create a steady pipeline of projects due to institutional capacity constraints. The network of multiple agencies involved in project implementation and an overlap in the functions of these agencies is leading to inordinate project delays.

Recommendations to strengthen the PPP Ecosystem in the Country (Kelkar Committee)

- Clear-cut norms on resolving issues and clarifying norms on re-negotiation of contracts.
  - Infrastructure investments worth around Rs 12 Lakh Crore remained stuck at different stages as of end-December 2014 due to a variety of issues such as land acquisition, lack of clearances, unfavourable market conditions, and costly finances, according to Assocham study.
  - This puts stress on banks and the developers' balance sheet.
  - The Kelkar report has drawn up extensive guidelines regarding the re-negotiation of the terms of concession agreement, stipulating the reasons that form the basis for re-negotiation and those that should not be entertained as valid reasons.
  - Creation of Multi-Disciplinary Expert Institutions to address the problem of stalled PPP projects
- The report talks about setting up an Infrastructure PPP Project Review Committee (IPRC).
- It also recommended the creation of an Infrastructure PPP Adjudication Tribunal (IPAT).
- **Amend Prevention of Corruption Act, 1988**
  - The government should take early action to amend the Prevention of Corruption Act, 1988 which does not distinguish between genuine errors in decision-making and acts of corruption.
  - Measures may be taken immediately to make only malafide action by public servants punishable, and not errors, and to guard against witch hunt against government officers and bureaucrats for decisions taken with bonafide intention.
- **Moving away from the one-size-fits-all approach to PPP Model Concession Agreements (MCAs)**
  - The committee recommends that MCAs for each sector be reviewed independently to capture the interests of all participating stakeholders—users, project proponents, concessionaires, lenders and markets.
- **Creation of dedicated Institutions for PPP Projects**
  - The committee strongly endorses the 3P India (3PI), which can function as a centre of excellence, enable research, and review and roll out activities to build capacity.
  - Some countries have a legal framework for PPPs in the form of PPP Act/Law/Policy. MoF may develop and publish a national PPP Policy document.
  - Companies need access to long-term funds for infrastructure projects with long gestation periods. Globally, long-term capital is raised via capital markets where major investors are pension and insurance managers. There is an urgent need in India to tap such markets to fund its infrastructure requirements.

Conclusion

The success of public private partnership to a large extent depends on optimal risk allocation among stakeholders, the environment of trust and robust institutional capacity to timely implementation of PPP projects. To foster the successful implementation of a PPP project, a robust PPP enabling ecosystem and sound regulatory framework is essential.

Designing a Concession Agreement

Q.6 Explain the meaning of investment in an economy in terms of capital formation. Discuss the factors to be considered while designing a concession agreement between a public entity and a private entity.
(250 Words, 15 Marks) **UPSC Mains 2020**

Ans. Meaning of Investment Investment in an economy in terms of capital formation refers to increasing the capital stock of the country in a given year. It signifies that part of the national product which is not consumed, but used for increasing productive capacity of the country. It refers to addition of capital goods, such as equipment, tools, transportation assets, and electricity.

Example An investment which leads to capital formation in agriculture improves the stock of equipment, tools and productivity of natural resources making possible for farmers to optimize the use of their resources more productively, especially land and labour.

Factors to be considered for Designing a Concession Agreement

A concession agreement, which channelizes investment, is a contract that gives a company the right to use resources for a specified purpose and operate a particular business granted by a government with specified terms.

- **The scope of the project** The agreement should clearly define the scope of the project, including the nature of the infrastructure or service to be provided, the duration of the concession period, and the performance targets to be achieved.
- **Investment Requirements** The agreement should specify the investment requirements of the project, including the amount of capital to be invested, the source of funding, and the return on investment.
- **Risks and Rewards** The agreement should allocate risks and rewards between the public and private parties in a fair and transparent manner. This includes defining the mechanisms for sharing revenues, cost overruns, and other contingencies.
  - HAM model got initial success because it has better risk allocation between public and private sector.
- **Fair Competition** Tender design for award of concessions must ensure that competition for the market is vibrant and there are enough players who are able to participate.
- **Regulatory and Legal Framework** The agreement should be consistent with the regulatory and legal framework of the host country, including laws related to taxation, labor, and the environment.
- **Ownership and Management of the Assets** In various projects like road and ports, the final ownership lies with the Government where as often management is devolved whereas in various cases like in UDAN scheme the only viability gap funding is done by the government, the ownership is private.
- **Valuation of the Asset** For example, in the case of asset monetization correct evaluation of the revenue becomes important.
- **Monitoring Mechanism** There has to be a mechanism through which the enforcement of the terms and conditions of the contract is ensured, and the market standard is followed.
- **Funding Options** Like self-funding including build-operate-transfer (BOT) model and sources of financing such as budgetary allocation.
- **Service Delivery** Service delivery on time and effective targeted delivery system is another factor to be considered. Especially after completion of infrastructure development projects like roads, the timely maintenance is a very significant factor in deciding concession agreements.
- **Effective Resource Utilisation** Effective use of resources may reduce wastages in a very significant manner.
- **Time period of the partnership** There has to be intermediate time frames after which the partnership is allowed to be reassessed both from the perspective of the government and the private player.
- **Stakeholder Consultation** The agreement should provide for consultation with stakeholders such as local communities, civil society organisations, and other relevant parties to ensure that the project is socially and environmentally sustainable.

Conclusion

These agreements should be based on best international practices, and make certain that policies and regulatory frameworks would address the complexities and balance the diverse interests of all stakeholders in various sectors.

Issues in HAM

Q.7 Why has Hybrid Annuity Model (HAM), which was earlier proposed as a game-changer in Public Private Partnerships (PPP), received lukewarm response from private developers? What are the alternate PPP models that can be pursued for encouraging private investments? (150 Words, 10 Marks)

About Hybrid Annuity Model (HAM)

HAM is a type of PPP based on risk sharing where government contributes 40% of the project cost and 60% of cost is borne by the developer. Government agency collects the revenue from the project and pay annuity to the developer of the project. It is a mix of EPC and BOT model.

Some of the benefits of HAM

- **Risk-sharing in Terms of Funding** Government provides partial funding of the project. By adopting a middle path approach, it builds over BOT model (financial burden on private sector) and EPC model (financial burden on government).
- **Inflation Indexing** Inflation is incorporated in the project cost. Therefore, it provides a policy cushion for the private players against market vagaries.
- **Less Dependence on Traffic Volume** The annuity payment structure means that the developers aren't taking 'traffic risk'.
- **Timely Completion** Under the HAM model, there is a specified bonus amount for timely completion of the projects. Easy clearances: Under the HAM the government will bear the regulatory clearances risk, compensation risk etc., therefore, timely land acquisition, environmental clearances etc., are possible.
- **Increased Efficiency** Under the HAM model, the private players will be able to focus on activities like capital cost, quality, and expedient completion of the project, thus enhancing efficiency.
- **Better Credit Availability** HAM helps the developer cut the overall debt and improves project returns.

These HAM features have garnered a favourable response and mix of HAM awards has increased from 10% in FY16 to 48% in H1FY2021.

Reasons for Lukewarm Success of HAM

- **Structural Shocks** Several structural economic shocks like demonetization, hasty implementation of GST and consequent lockdown in the wake of Covid-19 further reduced the appetite of private players.
- **Bank issues and Cash Flows** Annuity payment to developers is linked to bank rates. Bank rate has come down but interest rate on loans have not (due to poor monetary policy transmission), resulting in reduced profit margins of private player. Banks are also sceptical about HAM due to low equity contribution from developers .
- **NBFC Crisis** Crisis in NBFC sector resulted in impaired ability of developer to raise finance for some HAM projects.
- **Issues related to Land Acquisition**: In FY19, the projects awarded through HAM slowed down to around 834 km of the overall 2,222 kms of projects awarded by NHAI. This was a result of problem related to land acquisition.
- Model doesn't take care of the cost and time overruns due to issues of administrative inefficiency.
- **Unsustainable** In the process of insulating the private players from commercial risk, HAM has unduly strained the government bodies.
  - **Example** It is estimated that the debt of NHAI may reach more than ₹ 3 lakh crores in FY 23.
- It does not address the issue of inefficient dispute redressal mechanisms plaguing the PPP.
- **Reducing Popularity** Logjams in project, incomplete closures, lack of funding etc., have considerably reduced the popularity of HAM.
  - **Example** 55% of highway projects were awarded through HAM in 2016-17, which reduced to just 28% in 2019-20.

Alternative Models of PPP

- **EPC** Under the EPC model, the project cost is completely borne by the government. The private
- sector's participation in this model is minimal as far as the cost is concerned and is limited to the providing technical and engineering expertise such as design and construction.
- **Build-Own-Operate (BOO)** is a type of old BOT but ownership of the newly built facility remains with private party. The Government largely agrees to 'purchase' the goods and services produced by the project on mutually agreed terms.
- **Lease-Develop-Operate (LDO)** Here, the government or the public sector entity retains ownership of the newly created infrastructure facility and receives payments in terms of a lease agreement with the private promoter. This approach is mostly followed in the development of airport facilities.
- **Management Contract** Here, the private promoter has the responsibility for a full range of investment, operation and maintenance functions. It has the authority to make daily management decisions under a profit-sharing or fixed-fee arrangement.
- **Service Contract** The private promoter performs a particular operational or maintenance function for a fee over a specified period of time.

Conclusion

- There is always a need to improve and improvise according to the needs of the present. No model would work indefinitely and we need to adopt and evolve them constantly.

Check Your Preparation

1. What are the issues faced in financing of infrastructure in India? Give an account of the steps taken by the government to resolve these in recent times. (150 words, 10 marks)
2. PPP mechanism is a major element of India's infrastructure creation effort as there is a huge level of investment required in the sector. Discuss the recent reform measures that have been attempted to enhance PPP effectiveness in India. (150 words, 10 marks)